COMPANY LAw
IN IRELAND

AUSTRALIA AND NEW ZEALAND
The Law Book Company Ltd.
Sydney : Melbourne : Perth

CANADA AND U.S.A
The Carswell Company Ltd.
Agincourt, Ontario

INDIA
N. M. Tripathi Private Ltd.
Bombay
and
Eastern Law House Private Ltd.
Calcutta and Delhi
M.P.P. House
Bangalore

ISRAEL
Steimatzky's Agency Ltd.
Jerusalem : Tel Aviv : Haifa

MALAYSIA : SINGAPORE : BRUNEI
Malayan Law Journal (Pte.) Ltd.
Singapore and Kuala Lumpar

COMPANY LAW IN IRELAND

by

Patrick Ussher, LL.M. (Cantab.), M.A. (Hons.) (Cantab.)
of the Inner Temple and Lincoln's Inn, Barrister
Senior Lecturer in Law, Trinity College, University of Dublin

LONDON
SWEET & MAXWELL
1986

Published in 1986 by
Sweet & Maxwell Limited
11 New Fetter Lane, London
Computerset by Promenade Graphics Ltd., Cheltenham
Printed in Great Britain by
Page Bros. (Norwich) Ltd.

Reprinted 1988

British Library Cataloguing in Publication Data

Ussher, Patrick
    Company law in Ireland.
    1. Corporation law—Ireland
    I. Title
    344.1506'66   KDK502

    ISBN 0–421–29750–6

To my mother

Preface

The bird which sings too early in the morning is brought in by the cat, says the Flemish proverb; indeed, the Early Christian was caught by lions. This book, being late, has avoided the perils of earliness, and has earned for me the patience of my publishers. I thank them too for the equanimity with which they accepted from me vastly amended galley proofs. Some, they had hopefully sent to me years before, and the law had not stood still. The last amended galley was completed at the end of August 1985. This book therefore has nothing to say about events after September 1, 1985, save that I have fully covered the 1985 Bill (implementing the EEC Fourth Directive) introduced in the Dáil in May 1985, and now set fair to become the Companies (Amendment) Act 1986.

This book talks about private enterprise in a corporate form, and about the participation of the public in such enterprise. It does not therefore deal with semi-State bodies, interesting though they be. Nor does it enter into the public regulation of economic activity. Thus, monopolies created by mergers, and competition law are excluded.

I have many people to thank. Mr. McVeigh, the Librarian of the Squire Law Library in Cambridge, welcomed me to it, and allowed me to use it freely. As well as a full collection of Irish reports, it boasts a collection of Irish unreported judgments not easily attained at home. Tony Kerr, my former pupil and now a lecturer at University College, Dublin, helped keep me up to date with current unreported judgments. My colleague at Trinity, Gerard Hogan, a repository of legal information, brought several interesting points to my attention; so did my colleagues Alex Schuster and Kieran Corrigan. Owen O'Connell of William Fry and Sons, Mr. Registrar Mongey, and John Cooke, S.C. each helped me track down an elusive unreported judgment. And, most importantly, I thank my wife Mary, whose support and knowledge of the sustained problems of legal authorship helped me bring this work at last to a conclusion.

After some of this book had gone to press, the British consolidated their companies legislation, something we might think of doing. The references I make to British legislation are therefore pre-consolidation.

Footnote references simply to a section or Schedule or Part of a statute are references to the Companies Act 1963, unless otherwise stated.

vii

The attractive abstractions of *Donoghue* v. *Stevenson* [1932] A.C. 562 are such that I must add a *caveat* disclaiming legal responsibility for the contents of this book. In that respect, readers must rely on their own judgments. Moral responsibility for its shortcomings is mine alone.

P.D.L.U.
The Day of Saint Thomas Aquinas, 1986

Contents

Table of Cases

Table of Statutes

Statutes applying to Ireland

Statutes not applying to Ireland

Table of Statutory Instruments

Irish

Table of EEC Instruments

Treaty of Rome

Council Directives

Proposed and Draft Council Directives

Chapter 1. Introduction

This book is concerned with the modern registered company, called registered because it is formed and corporate status attained by a simple process of registration, and called modern to distinguish it from an older form of association no longer with us, the deed of settlement company, superseded in 1844 and now so covered by the dust of history that the appellation modern for its successor verges on pedantry.

SOURCES OF COMPANY LAW

The modern registered company is a creature of statute, indeed statute upon statute, but the statutes are by no means a complete code of company law. They silently assume a considerable body of law manufactured through judicial decisions. The modern registered company in its one-and-a-half centuries of life has become encrusted with judicial doctrines affecting its internal workings and external relations. Statute often assumes their existence without stating them. Sometimes their first recognition by statute occurs when the legislature steps in to modify or destroy them. For example, section 8 of the Companies Act 1963 modifies wholly judge-made rules relating to a company's capacity,[1] and Part IV of the Companies (Amendment) Act 1983 destroys judicial rules on the distributability of profits.[2] No one who confines himself to a study of the legislation can become a company lawyer. Much of the case law hitherto followed in Ireland in company matters has been British, since much of the companies legislation, is, as we shall see, derived from Britain, as well as more general principles of law from which the affairs of companies are not immune. But if the courts are to follow foreign authorities, they may pick and choose among them. This

---

[1] See Chap. 4, *Objects.*
[2] See Chap. 10, *Capital and its Maintenance.*

1

book therefore cites some leading cases from those Commonwealth jurisdictions whose company law came from the same stable as our own. There is also a body of Irish case law on company matters, by no means confined to exclusively Irish aspects of the legislation, and this book gives preference in citation to them, hoping that doing so will establish a pattern in the courts. And company law, like any other Irish law, bows before the Constitution. This book will show that several aspects of companies legislation will have to be rethought if they are not to clash with the Constitution.

The principal legislation currently governing companies in Ireland consists of the Companies Act 1963, the European Communities (Companies) Regulations 1973,[3] the Companies (Amendment) Acts of 1977, 1982 and 1983,[4] and the European Communities (Stock Exchange) Regulations 1984.[5] All these are construed together as one Act.[6] Subsidiary legislation includes the Stock Transfer Act 1963, Rules of the Superior Courts relating to the winding up of companies,[7] and various statutory instruments concerning forms and fees.[8]

At the establishment of the State, Ireland inherited as its companies legislation, three statutes of the United Kingdom Parliament, the substantial Companies (Consolidation) Act 1908, and two minor pieces of legislation, the Companies Act 1913 and the Companies (Particulars as to Directors) Act 1917. Apart from legislation made necessary by the destruction of records in the burning of the Four Courts,[9] substantive companies legislation remained unchanged from the establishment of the State until 1959. In that year as a result of the deliberations of the Company Law Reform Committee[10] under the chairmanship of Mr. Arthur Cox, the slender Companies Act 1959 was passed, introducing into Irish law some of the developments which had occurred in the neighbouring island in

---

[3] S.I. 1973, No. 163.

[4] This Act was brought into force on October 13, 1983, the "appointed day" for the purposes of s.2(1) of the 1983 Act, by the Companies (Amendment) Act 1983 (Commencement) Order 1983 [S.I. 1983 No. 288] with the result that the re-registration period expired on January 12, 1985; the general transitional period expired on April 12, 1985; and the transitional period for share capital will expire on October 12, 1986.

[5] S.I. 1984 No. 282. They came into operation on January 1, 1985.

[6] *Ibid.* reg. 1(3); s.2(5) of the 1983 Act. The 1973 regulations are omitted from these interpretative provisions, but state that they are to be construed as one with the 1963 Act.

[7] S.I. 1966 No. 28, principally amending R.S.C., Ord. 74.

[8] Companies (Forms) Orders 1964 to 1983 [S.I. 1964 No. 45, 1982 No. 256, 1983 No. 289]; Companies (Fees) Orders 1964 to 1983 [S.I. 1964 No. 44, 1983 No. 259].

[9] Companies (Reconstruction of Records) Act 1924.

[10] 1958, Pr. 4523.

the preceding four decades. The Cox Committee had declared itself convinced that:

> " all company legislation in this country should be based primarily on a recognition of the fact that the great majority of companies in this state are small private companies and that elaborate legislation involving heavy and expensive professional and clerical work should not be introduced unless a strong case for its introduction is made. We have not heard any such case. . . . [11]"

That conviction was almost immediately confounded, and remains now only a distant aspiration. In 1962 the Jenkins Committee[12] reported in Britain, and Ireland hastened to follow many of its recommendations in the reforming and consolidating Companies Act 1963, still the principal Act, as well as introducing a few innovations of her own. The Jenkins Report has in fact had more legislative consequences in Ireland than in its country of origin. The Companies Act 1963 is broadly equivalent to the Companies Act 1948 [*U.K.*]. The similarities far outweigh the divergences; indeed, many sections are identical. The close association in 1963 between the stock markets in Dublin[12a] and London dictated that the Stock Transfer Act 1963 [*U.K.*] should be echoed at once by legislation in Ireland. Likewise, the fact that the Stock Exchanges of Britain and Ireland became unified in 1972 rendered it necessary that an Act uniform with the Stock Exchange (Completion of Bargains) Act 1976 [*U.K.*], dealing with the consequences of computerisation, be enacted in Ireland: this is the Act of 1977. Ireland has not sought to emulate the Companies Acts [*U.K.*] of 1967 and 1976. The Irish Act of 1982 is a short technical Act of domestic provenance.

Ireland's accession to the European Economic Community on January 1, 1973 has been, and will continue to be, grist to the legislative mill in company matters. One of the objects of the Treaty of Rome is "the abolition, as between member states, of obstacles to freedom of movement for persons, services and capital."[13] In attempting to attain this ideal, the Treaty seeks to abolish restrictions on what it calls "freedom of establishment,"[14] and as part of that process aims to create a certain uniformity in the laws governing business organisations, on the grounds, assumedly, that differences in these laws might make for difficulties in establishment and

---

[11] *Ibid.* para. 44.
[12] Report of the Company Law Committee 1962, Cmnd. 1749.
[12a] See An Act for the Better Regulation of Stockbrokers 1799, 39 Geo. III, c. 40 (*Ir.*).
[13] Art. 3, Treaty of Rome.
[14] *Ibid.* Arts. 52–58.

that the freedom of movement of persons, services and capital might be distorted if one jurisdiction provided more favourable laws than others. Specifically, Article 54(3)(g) of the Treaty requires the Council of Ministers, acting on proposals from the Commission, and after consulting the European Parliament and the Economic and Social Committee, to issue Directives to member states for the purpose of "co-ordinating to the necessary extent the *safeguards* which, for the *protection* of the interests of *members and others*, are required of member states of companies and firms[15] . . . with a view to making such safeguards equivalent throughout the Community."[16] This is not an invitation, but a duty. Since most company law is designed for the "protection" of one or more interest groups, members, potential investors, creditors actual and potential, employees, and so on, and since "safeguard" is a very wide word, the only significant limit to action under this Article is a failure to achieve consensus at the Council of Ministers.

Seven such Directives have so far been adopted. We do not look at their substance at this stage of the book, but only briefly at their subject-matter, and at what Ireland has done, and what she has still to do, by way of implementation. Irish company law already conformed to some of the First EEC. Companies Directive of March 9, 1968[17] covering the public disclosure of certain essentials concerning a company, the validity of its obligations, and the possibility of its nullity. The balance was purported to be implemented in Ireland by the EEC (Companies) Regulations 1973, made by the Minister for Industry and Commerce pursuant to section 3 of the European Communities Act 1972. The Second EEC Companies Directive of December 13, 1976[18] concerned the share capital of public limited companies, the plc, described below under *Types of Company*. Most of the Companies (Amendment) Act 1983[18a] was taken up with its implementation, though the opportunity was taken in that Act to introduce certain of its concepts, chiefly concerning the distributability of profits and the allotment of shares, to other companies as well. The 1983 Act is modelled quite closely on the Companies Act 1980 [18b][*U.K.*], but with small and significant departures, and omissions. The Third EEC Companies Directive of October 9, 1978[19] must be read with the Sixth EEC Companies Directive of December 17, 1982.[20] These concern amalgamations of plc's brought about by the

[15] As broadly defined by Art. 58.   [16] Italics supplied.
[17] 68/151/EEC.   [18] 77/91/EEC.
[18a] For a descriptive comment, see Forde, "The Companies (Amendment) Act 1983," (1983) *Irish Jurist (n.s.)*, 289.
[18b] Described by D.D. Prentice in *The Companies Act 1980* (London, 1980).
[19] 78/855/EEC.
[20] 82/891/EEC.

transfer of the assets and liabilities of one company to another together with the issue of shares by the latter to the shareholders of the former, and variants on that theme. Ireland has till January 1, 1986 to implement these two Directives. The Fourth EEC Companies Directive of July 25, 1978[21] covers the form, substance and disclosure of the accounts of limited companies. Ireland should have implemented it by August 1980, but introduced a Bill to do so only on May 29, 1985. This 1985 Bill is discussed in Chapter 11, *Accounts and Auditors*. Britain did so by the Companies Act 1981 [*U.K.*]. The consolidation of the accounts of groups of limited companies is the subject of the Seventh EEC Companies Directive of June 13, 1983.[22] Ireland must implement it by January 1, 1988. Still in the field of accounting, the Eighth EEC Companies Directive of April 10, 1984[23] governs the qualificiations, professional integrity and independence of company auditors. Ireland must bring its law into line with it by January 1, 1988.

There is not yet a Fifth EEC Companies Directive. As long ago as 1972, the Commission presented a proposal[24] for such a Directive affecting plc's only, and covering the structure, functions and duties of the board of directors, the functions and conduct of the general meeting of members, and the role of the company's auditors in relation to its accounts. The proposal foundered on resistance among member states to the notion that a two-tier board on the German pattern be forced upon them. The Commission has revised[25] the proposal to allow the option of a unitary board, such as we already have in our domestic law, but a politically charged element of contention remains: whether or not to have, as the proposal prescribes, worker participation on the board? This must be distinguished from another hotly contended proposal emanating from a different branch of the Commission, the draft Directive[26] on the information and consultation of employees, which introduces elements of rigid-

---

[21] 78/660/EEC.

[22] 83/349/EEC.

[23] 84/253/EEC.

[24] O.J. No. C 131; December 13, 1972.

[25] O.J. No. C 240/2; September 9, 1983.

[26] Often called the "Vredeling" proposal after the Commissioner who instigated its introduction (O.J. No. C 297, November 15, 1980). Its main thrust was aimed at multinationals operating in Europe through subsidiaries. The adverse response to it led the Commission to put forward a re-drafted proposal (O.J. No. C 217, August 12, 1983). During Ireland's last Presidency, this re-draft underwent the close scrutiny of an ad hoc working party of experts drawn from all member states under the chairmanship of Dr. Mary Redmond. Proposals made in her Presidency report on their deliberations (summarised in *European Industrial Relations Review*, February 1985, pp. 10–14) may result in a fundamental change in direction towards a social right for employees of all large commercial organisations.

ity, uniformity and compulsion, not yet acceptable to all member states.

Also at the proposal stage is the Tenth EEC Companies Directive concerning trans-national mergers of plc type companies[27]; a Ninth, seeking to regulate the conduct of groups of companies is in preparation; and so are several others on a variety of company law topics. There is no forseeable end to the process.

Closely related technically to the Companies Directives are those which draw their authority not only from Article 54(3)(g) of the Treaty, but also from Article 100, relating to the establishment and functioning of a common market throughout the Community. Three of these,[28] concerning the disclosures to be made by companies whose shares are, or are to be, quoted on the Stock Exchange were implemented in Ireland by the European Communities (Stock Exchange) Regulations 1984.[29]

As if all this piling of Pelion upon Ossa were not enough for practitioners and public to contend with, the Government has been casting round to heap on something more. There is in unofficial circulation according to the media a weighty document generally called the "domestic Companies Bill." The same sources indicate that it covers a variety of topics. Since there is no firm indication that it will ever become part of the Government's legislative programme, and since it has not been formally published, it would not be appropriate to comment on its reputed contents in this book, save in one respect. It has for some time been fashionable to suggest reform of the law relating to fraudulent trading, and the "Bill" seeks to do so. Since this was a topic in any event to be discussed in this book, the "Bill's" supposed proposals have been included, and weighed against others.[30]

This stream of legislation, drastically disproportionate to the rate of repeal, is disheartening to those who would wish to see a concise, practicable, readily intelligible code of company law, to those who see company law more as a means to facilitate and encourage the transaction of business than as an opportunity to throw obstacles in its path, and to those who would lessen rather than increase the non-productive, bureaucratic burden on enterprise. But all hope should

---

[27] O.J. No. C 23/11; January 25, 1985.

[28] Council Directive of March 5, 1979 (79/279/EEC): conditions for the admission of securities to Stock Exchange listing; Council Directive of March 17, 1980 (80/380/EEC): disclosure requirements in repect of securities to be listed; Council Directive of February 15, 1982 (82/121/EEC): publication of interim reports by publicly quoted companies.

[29] S.I. 1984 No. 282, which came into operation on January 1, 1985.

[30] See pp. 516, *et seq. infra.*

not be lost. Company law is littered with the relics of past expedients. Other countries have managed to clear them away.[31] Ireland too should attempt that task. From time to time, this book makes suggestions designed to assist.

TYPES OF COMPANY

The classification of registered companies is not altogether straightforward because the categories overlap. The subject must be approached with a subtlety to match that employed by the legislature. The legislation distinguishes between limited and unlimited, between the methods by which the liability of members is limited, between companies with and those without a share capital, between public and private companies, and between public and public limited companies (the plc), and between old public limited companies and plc's. Some of the distinctions are formed on unimportant differences, and could be scrapped. The distinctions of major practical importance are those between limited and unlimited, and the plc and the rest.

At the end of 1983,[32] there were 78,491 companies on the register in Ireland. Of these, all but 1,301 had a *share capital*. Very loosely, share capital may be defined as the contribution of the members of the company to its assets. Share capital will usually be divided into shares of fixed amount. In most companies, that amount constitutes the limit of the extent of the members' liability to contribute to its assets. This is the *company limited by shares*. Its two forms, the private company limited by shares and the plc limited by shares, are the main subject of this book.[33]

Others may be disposed of briefly here.

There are companies without a share capital called *guarantee companies* in which the liability of the members to contribute to its assets is limited in a different way. There were 981 on the register at the end of 1983.[34] Each member undertakes to pay a fixed, usually

---

[31] *e.g.* Canada and Australia (neither, admittedly members of the European Communities). See Sealy, *Company Law and Commercial Reality* (London 1984), *passim*.

[32] *Annual Report*, 1983, Department of Industry, Trade, Commerce and Tourism.

[33] For the limitation of liability, see Chaps. 2 and 10; and for shares, see Chap. 6. There is a third form, the *old* public company limited by shares which the 1983 Act envisages as having by now been phased out. See the transitional periods in n. 4, *supra*.

[34] See n. 32, *supra*. Probably more, since the separate item in the *Annual Reports*, "licence companies" (meaning companies dispensed by the Minister from the requirement to have "limited" or "teoranta" as part of their names: s.24, *infra*) are probably mostly guarantee companies.

token, amount to the company in the event of its being wound-up whilst he is a member, or within a year of his ceasing to be a member.[35] Winding up is the process leading to a company's dissolution and legal death. The company only looks to its guarantee fund at its own funeral. It cannot even use it as a security for a loan.[36] By contrast, share capital is available during the life of the company and may be used to finance the enterprise. A guarantee company is therefore generally considered an unsuitable medium through which to trade.[37] It is however a suitable form of association for professional bodies, trade associations, proprietary clubs, and people who wish, in the broadest sense, to do "good works." Its activities may be financed by donations or subscriptions. The chief inconvenience experienced by such people coming together for a common purpose are the arrangements for holding property, a difficulty circumvented by assuming a corporate form. It, the guarantee company, a separate person in the law which will survive changes in its membership and its office holders, will hold the property; and its constitution will in effect be theirs.[38] Being a limited company, a guarantee company must bear the words *limited* or *teoranta* in its title as a warning to the public that the members are not liable beyond a stated limit for its debts.[39] By section 24 of the Companies Act 1963, the Minister may dispense a limited company[40] from this requirement if he is satisfied that it has the purpose of:

"promoting commerce, art, science, religion, charity or any other useful object, and intends to apply its profits, if any, or other income, in promoting its objects, and to prohibit the payment of any dividend to its members . . . "

By the end of 1983, 290 guarantee companies had been granted this dispensation.

It is also possible to form a company limited by guarantee and

---

[35] s.6(3); s.207(1).

[36] *Re Mayfair Property Co.* [1898] 2 Ch. 28; *Re Irish Club* [1906] W.N. 127.

[37] The inadequacies of such a company are illustrated by *Re Industrial and Agricultural Fair Cork 1932* (1933) 67 I.L.T.R. 175, in which the allegation that the company "had exhibited to the world the cultural and industrial life of Ireland through a misconceived system of finance" came close to being substantiated. The tongue in cheek judgment of Johnston J. affords light amusement.

[38] Table C, Sched. 1 contains model form constitutional documents which may be adapted to circumstances.

[39] s.6(1)(a).

[40] But not in respect of a plc: 1983 Act, s.58.

having a share capital.[41] These hybrids are understood to be very rare. The published statistics do not show how many there are. The Jenkins Committee recommended that this form should be discontinued in Britain,[42] on the grounds that it was seldom used, and in Ireland since the 1983 Act[43] they may be formed only if they conform to the conditions for private company status, described below. A company limited by guarantee and having a share capital may afford a means of providing working capital to guarantee companies of the "good works" type described above. Those forming a company with a view to distributing its profits to themselves find that it offers no advantage over the simpler form of a company limited by shares. It has been argued that the guarantee fund in such a company, effectively untouchable during its life, could if both the guarantee and the guarantor were sufficiently substantial, provide a trading organisation in which its potential creditors might have confidence.[44] Doubtless, but few would be so altruistic unless compelled. Perhaps the idea might, suitably adapted, be used to compel a trader whose limited liability company has failed to the detriment of its creditors to put up a guarantee fund, preferably secured,[45] as a condition of starting a fresh enterprise. It would not have to be large, just sufficient to give pause for thought before fresh excesses.

Next we look at unlimited companies. Those without a share capital are rare beasts indeed. There were only 30 on the register at the

---

[41] Model form constitutional documents are given in Table D, Sched. 1. With effect from October 13, 1983 ["the appointed day"] s.7 of the 1983 Act prescribes that "no company shall be formed as, or become a public company limited by guarantee and having a share capital." Effectively, this means that such companies, other than those already public at that date, must be formed as private, or remain private companies. For private companies, see below. A model form of memorandum (one of a company's constitutional documents: see Chap. 3) to be adopted on becoming a plc by an exising public company limited by guarantee and having a share capital is given by the Sched. 2, 1983 Act. This document is remarkable not only for the rarity of its real life counterpart, but for the fact that it is the only model form in all the companies legislation that contains a woman as a subscriber. All the rest are men with interesting occupations and professions. The fictitious "Teresa O'Connor" is designated "Housewife." Had the legislature not by 1983 heard of women accountants, solicitors, farmers, travel agents and geologists?

[42] 1962, Cmnd. 1749, paras. 70, 78(d).

[43] See n. 41, *supra*.

[44] Rice, "Companies limited by guarantees," (1964) 28 Conv. (*N.S.*) 214. In fact, as the law stands, the guarantor could probably retire from membership in sufficient time before the commencement of the winding up to avoid liability: ss.6(3), 207(1)(a), (b), (e) and Sched. 1, Tables C and D; *Baird's Case* [1899] 2 Ch. 593 and *Premier Underwriting Association Ltd.* [1913] 2 Ch. 29.

[45] His dwelling-house, for example.

end of 1983.[46] More commonly an unlimited company will have a stated share capital, divided into shares of fixed amount. The statistics do not tell us how many of these there are; only that small but significant numbers are formed each year, *e.g.* in 1982, 135 were formed out of a total of 5,757 new registrations, and, in 1983, 101 out of a total of 6,334. If an unlimited company is wound-up, its members are liable to contribute to its assets:

> "an amount sufficient for the payment of its debts and liabilities, and the costs, charges, and expenses of the winding up . . . ."[47]

Past members may incur liability too.[48] Why then is such a company formed? There are two main reasons. It may purchase its own shares, or otherwise return its capital to its members. In a limited company, on the other hand, the share capital is viewed as a safeguard for its creditors taking the place of the full personal liability of the members, and is returnable only with the sanction of the court, and is not purchasable by the company.[49] This flexibility of an unlimited company can render it a useful vehicle for the holding of family assets. The other major advantage of an unlimited company will come to fruition when the Fourth EEC Companies Directive is implemented in Ireland. This conceives that the protection of creditors of a limited liability company requires that its annual accounts be published by being placed on public file in the Companies Registry, a premise questioned in Chapter 11. Unlimited companies will be exempt from this disclosure. In anticipation, section 52 gives a procedure under which limited companies may re-register as unlimited.

A further distinction in the classification of companies is that between *private* and *public* companies. The latter is the residual category, since a public company is defined as "any company which is not a private company."[50] The overwhelming majority of companies are private; at the end of 1983 the figure was 76,846 out of the total 78,941 companies on the register. The private company, introduced in 1907,[51] was and remains a half-hearted legislative attempt to create a corporate vehicle for enterprises in which public partici-

---

[46] Formed under ss.5(1), 5(2)(*c*). The Act contains no model form for its constitution.

[47] s.207(1); they must also contribute to the costs of adjusting their rights *inter se.*

[48] s.207(1)(*a*), (*b*), (*c*).

[49] s.72 and the 1983 Act, s.41.

[50] 1983 Act, s.2(1).

[51] Companies Act 1907 [*U.K.*].

pation was not anticipated. It might, and may still, be formed with fewer original participants than a public company, two instead of seven[52]; and the Acts provide minor adaptations for it of the model form regulations for the conduct of a company's affairs so as to render them marginally more suitable to an organisation with fewer participants than these regulations unadapted would envisage.[53] However, the main distinction between private and other companies was, and remains, that there should be no public market in their shares, an aim accomplished by restricting their transferability and limiting membership, and that they should be denied access to the capital market, a distinction upon which all other differences were built.[54] A private company is more precisely defined by section 33 of the Companies Act 1963 as being:

"a company which has a share capital and which by its articles[55]—(a) restricts the right to transfer its shares,[56] and (b) limits the number of its members to fifty, not including persons who are in the employment of the company and persons who, having been formerly in the employment of the company, were, while in that employment, and have continued after the determination of that employment to be, members of the company, and (c) prohibits any invitation to the public[57] to subscribe for any shares or debentures[58] of the company."

This prohibition against a private company raising capital from the public is now reinforced by section 21 of the Companies (Amendment) Act 1983 which makes any such offer, or arrangements made with a view to such an offer, a criminal offence.

Being barred from raising capital from the public, a private company was not required to observe certain safeguards designed to protect the investing public, chiefly the filing with the registrar of

---

[52] s.5(1).

[53] These regulations are the articles of association set out in Part II, Table A: Sched. 1. For the constitutional documents generally, see Chap. 3, *Internal Structure.*

[54] For a full list of the original distinctions between public and private companies, see Halsbury, *Laws of England* (1st ed., 1910), vol. 5, pp. 73 *et seq.*

[55] See n. 53, *supra.*

[56] Restrictions on transfer are discussed in Chap. 6, *Shares and Membership.*

[57] Invitations to the public to subscribe for shares and debentures are discussed in Chap. 12, *Promoters and Prospectuses.*

[58] A "debenture", more particularly defined at p. 457n, *post,* may be loosely defined as a written acknowledgement of a debt created by a loan to the company. A debt, unlike a share, involves the creation of an immediate debtor: creditor relationship. A company's debentures may commonly be called "loan stock." Debentures and the remedies of debenture holders are chiefly discussed in Chap. 14, *Floating Charges and Receivers* and Chap. 15, *The Charges Register and Other Disclosures.*

companies of a document called a statement in lieu of prospectus,[59] and publication in like manner of its annual accounts.[60]

A *prospectus* is a document actually soliciting subscriptions from the public, in which a high level of pertinent disclosure must be made, and which must be issued with any approach to the public.[61] A *statement in lieu of prospectus*, on the other hand, was designed to fill gaps in the public's knowledge of a public company's affairs at times when it was technically free to allot shares to anyone, but would not, if it were to do so, be acting on the basis of a current published prospectus. Before the Companies (Amendment) Act 1983 came into force a statement in lieu of prospectus was required to be filed on two rare occasions. They were when a private company became a public company by getting rid of the restrictions from its constitution,[62] or when a company was formed as a public company with a share capital but did not immediately invite subscriptions from the public, or, if it had done so, did not pursue the public offer further by actually allotting shares.[63] The statement in lieu of prospectus is now even rarer. It is now required only when the private company transforms itself into an *unlimited* public company,[64] or the public company is formed as an *unlimited* public company with a share capital.[65]

Whether or not a company need publish accounts will soon no longer be determined in accordance with the distinction between private and public companies. The criterion for immunity will not be the interests of the investing public, but the interests of creditors. Creditors may be prejudiced by the presence of limited liability. When the 1985 Bill giving effect to the Fourth EEC Companies Directive[66] has been enacted and brought into force, almost all limited liability companies of whatever nature will be obliged to publish accounts. The Bill, as did the Directive, gives options, to be discussed in Chapter 11 to allow differing levels of disclosure depending on balance sheet value, turnover and number of employees.

Effectively, old lines of distinction are being swept away, and with them, old privileges, and new lines are being drawn. Further new lines of distinction lie with the new burdens placed upon a new type of company known as the public limited company (plc), or *cuideachta phoiblí theoranta* (c.p.t.). These burdens involve a minimum paid up

[59] s.35 and Sched. 2, and s.54 and Sched. 4.
[60] s.128(4).
[61] ss.43 *et seq.*, Sched. 3. See Chap. 12, *Promoters and Prospectuses*.
[62] s.35.
[63] s.54.
[64] Para. 6, Sched. 1, 1983 Act. See also the ancillary s.115, as amended by para. 14, Sched. 1, 1983 Act.
[65] *Ibid.* para. 8.   [66] See n. 21, *supra*.

capital and capital maintenance, were dictated by the Second EEC Companies Directive,[67] and imposed by the 1983 Act. They are discussed in Chapter 10.

But what is a plc? It is not as one might at first think any company in which the liability of the members is limited, not being a private company. This is what the statutory definition of public company as being a company "which is not a private company"[68] might lead one to expect. Companies limited only by guarantee though public companies (for they have no share capital[69]) are not plc's. There are also barriers of registration and verification to be overcome before a company can be a plc. Formerly, an existing private company could attain the status of a public limited company simply by removing the necessary restrictions from its constitution.[70] A plc is defined by section 2(1) of the Companies (Amendment) Act 1983 as:

"a public company limited by shares or a public company limited by guarantee and having a share capital, being a company (*a*) the memorandum[71] of which states that the company is to be a public limited company; and (*b*) in relation to which the provisions of the Companies Acts as to the registration or re-registration of a company as a public limited company have been complied with on or after [October 13, 1983]."[72]

REGISTRATION AND RE-REGISTRATION

Registration of a private limited company is a simple operation, and provided all the formalities are meticulously observed should take about six weeks from start to finish. Those who want one quicker may acquire a "shelf" company from an agency, and make the necessary changes, if any, to its constitution[73] and name[74] after acquisition.

The first step in registration of a private limited company is to

---

[67] See n. 18, *supra.*   [68] See n. 4, *supra.*

[69] The share capital requirement that a company have a share capital in order to be private was introduced by the 1963 Act. Why? Before that a guarantee company which limited its membership to 50 could be private.

[70] s.35, now amended by para. 6, Sched. 1, 1983 Act.

[71] One of a company's constitutional documents. See Chap. 3, *Internal Structure.*

[72] See n. 4, *supra.*

[73] Chap. 3: *Internal Structure*, describes the alterability of the company's constitutional documents; also pp. 274 *et seq.*

[74] s.23: the consent of the Minister is required. He gave his approval to 1,889 applications in 1983 (*Annual Report*, Department of Industry, Trade, Commerce and Tourism). The change is complete only when the register has been altered, and a new certificate of incorporation issued: *Shackleford, Ford & Co.* v. *Dangerfield* (1868) L.R., 3 C.P. 407.

obtain the approval of the Companies Registry of the proposed company's name. Names which are identical or confusingly similar to names already on the register, names identical to well-known trade marks or to foreign companies, or names which could be regarded as deceptive or misleading will fail to win approval.[75]

Once conditional approval of the name has been obtained, the applicant will proceed to prepare the company's constitutional documents, its memorandum and articles of association.[76] They are required to be printed,[77] but typing by an electric typewriter will do, and usually does. The memorandum and articles must be signed by each subscriber of which there must be at least two, the signatures witnessed, and each must state in the memorandum the number of shares taken by him.[78] One each will suffice. It is advisable to write the number in words. Next, Form 9b containing a statement of the first directors, secretary and registered office must be completed.[79] Their names must be written out in full. Initials will not do. And *after* these steps, Form 41a certifying that all statutory requirements "in respect of registration and of matters precedent and incidental to have been complied with" must be sworn and executed either by the solicitor engaged in the formation of the company, or by one of the persons named as director or secretary in Form 9b.[80] It is advisable that Form 41a be executed and dated at least a day after the other preliminaries. Upon lodgment of the documents the prescribed fee must be paid, and the appropriate capital duty on the subscribed capital as declared on Form 25. In due course a certificate of incorporation is issued, certifying the beginning of the company's existence.[81]

Most plc's will be formed on the conversion of a private company, but before re-registration, the registrar will need to be shown in the prescribed manner that it satisfies the capital maintenance require-

---

[75] The actual power is to refuse any "undesirable" name, subject to an appeal to the court: s.21.

[76] There is a model in Table B, Sched. 1 to which memoranda are required by s.16 to conform. They are in practice so much longer that it must be doubted whether they do. See Chap. 4, *Objects*. Model form articles are given in Part II of Table A, 1st Sched.

[77] ss.7 and 14.

[78] ss.6, 7 and 14.

[79] ss.3 and 4 of the 1982 Act. A company must at all times have a registered office in the State to which all communications and notices may be addressed, and must notify changes in the situation of the registered office within 14 days; *ibid.* s.4. The office of the subscribers' accountant or solicitor is often chosen, particuarly if acting as the company's secretary.

[80] s.5(1), (5) of the 1983 Act.

[81] s.18.

ments in respect of a plc.[82] If a plc is formed on first registration, it is an offence for it to "do business or exercise any borrowing powers" until the registrar has been satisfied that its allotted share capital is not less than the authorised minimum, currently £IR30,000,[83] and has issued his trading certificate.[84] Transactions entered into by the plc before the issue of the certificate are not invalid, but the directors will be personally liable to the other party if the plc fails to perform its part.[85] A company which does not comply within a year is in danger of being struck off.[86]

All public companies in existence or in the course of formation on October 13, 1983, the commencement of the 1983 Act, and then being limited by shares or having a share capital and being limited by guarantee ("old public limited companies"), should by January 12, 1985 have applied for re-registration as a plc, or become another form of company.[87] Other forms available are the private company,[88] or the unlimited company.[89] If it chose to apply for re-registration as a plc, it has until October 12, 1986 to make its share capital conform.[90] A plc may be re-registered as a private company[91] and may be forced to do so if by court order its alloted share capital is reduced below the authorised minimum.[92]

An unlimited company may by re-registration become a limited company, including a plc.[93]

---

[82] 1983 Act, ss.9 and 10.
[83] *Ibid.* s.19.
[84] *Ibid.* s.6.
[85] *Ibid.* s.6(8).
[86] *Ibid.* s.8.
[87] *Ibid.* ss.12 and 13. For the relevant dates, see n. 4, *supra.*
[88] By altering its articles to conform to s.33, if it can comply with the restrictions.
[89] In accordance with 1983 Act, s.52.
[90] *Ibid.* s.12, and see n. 4, *supra.*
[91] The procedure is contained in 1983 Act, s.14.
[92] See 1983 Act, s.17. For reduction of capital by order of the court, see Chap. 10, *Capital and its Maintenance* and Chap. 9, *Minority Protection.*
[93] 1983 Act, ss. 11 and 54

Chapter 2. Incorporation and its Consequences

This book concerns modern registered companies, by which is meant companies registered under the Companies Acts 1963 to 1983 and their repealed predecessors.[1] It is a fundamental characteristic of the modern registered company, be it X.Y. Ltd or X.Y. plc or unlimited, that it is a corporation. A corporation is a distinct legal person, separate from its members. This commonplace of corporation law runs as a vital thread through all the branches of the subject. A legal person is capable of being the subject of legal rights and the object of legal duties. This quality of personality is now possessed by human individuals by virtue of their existence, but it may be helpful in understanding the personality of corporations to realise that legal systems have not always accorded a uniform legal personality even to human individuals. Roman law possessed many gradations in personality from the negligible attributes of the slave to the full *patria potestas* of the *pater familias;* in English law, the temporal status of monks and the civil death of outlaws, and in Ireland, the status of betaghs or villeins in Anglo-Norman feudal law, the non-recognition of the "mere Irish" in the courts of the Pale, the later disabilities of Roman Catholics under the penal laws, and the former status of married women are all examples from various epochs of variations in legal personality. Even today, individuals such as infants or the insane are accorded by Irish law a diminished capacity, and therefore a differing legal personality. Consequently, one is not required to find that the legal personality of a corporation accords exactly with that of the human, adult individual. It does not. We shall see in Chapter 4 that the capacity of a company is limited to the pursuit of its objects, and differs from company to company. We shall see in the present Chapter that there are doubts

---

[1] The principal repealed statutes are Companies Act 1862 [*U.K.*] and Companies Act 1908 [*U.K.*].

whether a corporation may be the subject of Constitutional rights,[2] and we shall see also the extent to which it is necessary for the law to flesh out the empty corporate shell with the attributes of human individuals behind it.[3] Legal personality is as much an invention of the law as the rights and duties which attach to it. Those unhappy about the according of separate personality to the mere abstraction which is a corporation should reflect upon *Mullick* v. *Mullick*[4] which shows that Hindu law recognises a stone idol as having sufficient legal personality to sue and be sued, and hold property.

In Ireland, as in the rest of the common law world, corporate status is viewed as a concession conferred by the State. This concession, or Italian[5] theory of corporations means in practice that corporations in Ireland can be created only by statutes, and of the statutes the Companies Acts are responsible for all save a few. Technically, another State source of incorporation, the former royal prerogative to create corporations by charter has probably been inherited by the Government, but its efficacy has not been tested since the establishment of the State,[6] and is not used. The concession theory remains intact under the 1937 Constitution, for Carroll J. has held in *Private Motorists Provident Society Ltd.* v. *Att.-Gen.*[6a] that the acquisition of corporate status is not to be regarded as a

---

[2] See pp. 53–56, *infra*.

[3] pp. 33 *et seq.*

[4] (1925) L.R. 52 Ind.App. 245 (P.C.). See Duff, "The Personality of an Idol", (1927) 3 C.L.J. 42.

[5] Its chief architect was Sinibald Fieschi who in 1243 became Pope Innocent IV. For a discussion of the theory and its reception into English, and thence Irish, law, see Maitland's introduction to his translation of Gierke, *Political Theories of the Middle Age*, (C.U.P., 1900).

[6] For succession to the prerogative, see Arts. 49. 1(2) and 28(2) of the Constitution, and *Byrne* v. *Ireland* [1972] I.R. 241. The case held that sovereign *immunities* from suit had not been transmitted, and is therefore not apposite to the survival of a *power*. s.377(4) of the Companies Act 1963 recognises the survival of the prerogative power by stating that s.377 which imposes certain requirements on unregistered companies including those created by charter "shall not . . . restrict the power of the Government to grant a charter in lieu of or supplementary to any such charter as aforesaid . . . ." However, amendments to charters are usually effected by private Acts of the Oireachtas, *e.g.* the Institution of Civil Engineers of Ireland (Charter Amendment) Act 1960 which interestingly recites in its preamble that "the amendments cannot be effected without the authority of the Oireachtas." The charter of the Institute of Chartered Accountants was otherwise amended by legislation in 1966. There were numerous corporations created by Royal Charter existing in Ireland at the establishment of the State. Trinity College, Dublin whose latest of many charters dates from 1911 (see *Gray and Cathcart* v. *Provost, Fellows and Scholars of Trinity College, Dublin* [1910] 1 I.R.370) is a prominent survivor; for a casualty, see *Re Commercial Buildings Company of Dublin* [1938] I.R. 477.

[6a] High Court, July 15, 1981, affirmed by the Supreme Court on other grounds, May 6, 1983, [1984] I.L.R.M. 88.

necessary concomitant of the right of free association given to citizens by Article 40, section 6. The chief consequence of the concession theory is that the courts are not free in the absence of a creating statute or charter to personify groups of persons, or in other words, to give them the attributes of corporations just because they act as if they were a single unit, whether economic or otherwise, and a unifying expression is used to describe them.[7] A good example is the partnership firm, X.Y. & Co. In the public eye, a partnership firm is viewed as a separate entity "the firm," but in law it is merely a collection of individuals bound together by a contract from which certain internal and external consequences flow. These consequences are almost entirely spelled out by the Partnership Act 1890. Internally, the partners owe each other fiduciary duties of good faith[8]; in a modern registered company, the equivalent duties are owed by the directors not to each other or to the members, but to the separate person, the company.[9] Externally, a contract made by a partner on behalf of the firm binds him and each of his partners individually down to his last penny[10]; a corporation is likewise liable to its last penny for its debts, but neither the agents who contracted those debts on its behalf nor its members are liable for them at all, not being parties to the contract. As Murnaghan J. said in *Revenue Commissioners* v. *Bank of Ireland*:

> "There is at common law no liability upon the members of a body corporate in respect of the debts and liabilities of the body corporate, and such liability in respect of the corporate acts must be created by statute."[11]

What then is limited liability? This is the duty owned by a member of a modern registered limited liability company to contribute a fixed, often token, sum to its assets.[12] In the much rarer type of modern registered company, the unlimited company, the members are liable to contribute to it an amount sufficient to pay off all its liabilities.[13] Although neither of these situations involves a direct liability by the members to the corporation's creditors, each is in a sense anomalous within the theory of corporations, and the presence

---

[7] For a tendency in this direction, see pp. 42 *et seq.*, *infra*.

[8] Partnership Act 1890, ss.28 *et seq.*

[9] See Chap. 7, *post.*

[10] Partnership Act 1890, s.5.

[11] [1925] 2 I.R. 90, 108.

[12] The actual mechanics of limited liability are to be found in s.5(2) and s.207(*d*), (*e*). The subject is further discussed in Chap. 10. *Capital and its Maintenance.*

[13] s.5(2)(*c*); s.207(1); unlimited companies are further discussed in Chap. 1 under *Types of Company.*

of statutory provisions imposing these liabilities requires some explanation. Corporate status came to the forerunner of the modern registered company as a means to combat a practical difficulty which was causing inconvenience in the business world in the first half of the nineteenth century. This forerunner was an unincorporated association known as the deed of settlement company, a means whereby owners of capital could participate in business enterprise without themselves being obliged to be involved in its management or to undertake a long term commitment. For this latter purpose, and to enhance their attractiveness as an investment, the deed of settlement would provide that the shares in these enterprises should be freely transferrable. The result, in the words of James L.J. in *Smith* v. *Anderson*[14] was an arrangement by which parties formed:

"a partnership which is constantly changing, a partnership today consisting of certain members, and tomorrow consisting of some only of these members along with others who have come in so that there will be a constant shifting of the partnership, a determination of the old and a creation of a new partnership, with the intention that so far as the partners can by agreement among themselves bring about such a result, the new partnership shall succeed to the assets and liabilities of the old partnership."

An agreement among the debtors themselves could not as a matter of law relieve the outgoing partner or member who had transfereed his shares from liability in respect of debts contracted whilst he was a member; for that, the concurrence of the creditor would be necessary. Who was the creditor to sue? The membership of the association might have altered from day to day and there might be no record of them available to the creditor; the managers of the association appointed by the deed of settlement would be prominent, but not necessarily worth suing or even members; and a member, if pursued to judgment, would have the same difficulties in obtaining contribution from his fellow members as the original creditor had suffered. All in all, this state of affairs was according to James L.J. "a public mischief to be repressed."[15] And repressed it was, by the Joint Stock Companies Act of 1844. The consequences of this Act are still with us. It forced large business associations of the deed of settlement type to assume corporate form, and provided a fairly simple procedure of registration with a registrar of companies by which they could obtain it. The 1844 prohibition against large unincorpor-

---

[14] (1880) 15 Ch.D.247 273–274.
[15] *Ibid.* p.273.

ated business associations survives relatively unchanged in section 376 of the Companies Act 1963 which says:

> "No company, association or partnership consisting of more than twenty persons shall be formed for the purpose of carrying on any business (other than the business of banking), that has for its object the acquisition of gain by the company, association or partnership, or by the individual members thereof, unless it is registered as a company under this Act or is formed in pursuance of some other statute."[16]

The object of the 1844 Act was that of providing a defendant, the separate person in the law who would own the assets and have a single continuity independent of the fluctuations in its membership, and whom, above all, the creditor could sue. This quality of continuity is known as perpetual succession. Coincidentally, the 1844 Act also ushered in the era of cheap incorporation, readily available as a matter of right: no longer was the acquisition of corporate status to be subject to the vagaries and expenses of acquiring a royal charter or promoting a private act of Parliament. Furthermore, there was no intention in 1844 of relieving the members of deed of settlement companies from the obligations which they had formally had as members of an unincorporated association. The preamble to the 1844 Act states the intention of investing deed of settlement companies[17] "with the qualities and incidents of corporations with some modifications," and these modifications consisted of an express provision imposing direct liability on the members for the debts of the corporation.[18] The Act contained ancillary provisions allowing judgments obtained against the corporation to be executed against the property and person of an individual member, and required for the first time a public register of members to be kept to aid the creditors in their pursuit. In a sense, the corporate status conferred by the 1844 Act was a gloss on the earlier partnership, and, indeed, vestiges of that partnership survive in the modern registered company in its present form.[19] This anomalous full liability of members was itself modified eleven years later by the Limited Liability Act 1855 to give us our present system, and to bring matters closer to the position

---

[16] See Calvert, "The Prohibition of Large Associations", (1962), 26 Conveyancer N.S. 253., s.376 has been relaxed by s.13 of the Companies (Amendment) Act 1982 to allow partnerships of more than 20 solicitors or qualified accountants respectively. In the case of banking, the limit is 10: s.372.

[17] Described there as "joint stock companies," but since this expression describes both the incorporated and unincorporated form, its use has been avoided in the text.

[18] s.25 of the 1844 Act.

[19] Particularly the definition of "the shareholder's contract" contained in s.25 of the 1963 Act discussed in Chap. 6. Shares and Membership.

which pertains in the absence of statutory modification, namely, as described by Murnaghan J. in *Revenue Commissioners* v. *Bank of Ireland, supra*, no liability on the members at all. Nowadays in fact, as we shall see,[20] the contribution from the total membership of a private company to its assets may lawfully be set as low as two pence, and therefore the liability of members may be regarded as illusory. In the case of a public limited company, the members together must have contributed at least £30,000.[21]; The position of members of unlimited companies remains similar to that of members in the 1844 Act, save that their debt of the amount needed to satisfy the creditors is no longer owed to them directly, but to the company.

There is no doubt that the system set up in 1844, as modified in 1855 and refined in 1856[22] and 1857[23], and eventually consolidated into the Companies Act 1862, was designed for a genuine business association betwen a number of participants, often many. Nonetheless the practice grew up of fewer participants in a business, commonly the only participant and sole proprietor, using the statutory machinery to create a corporation to carry on the business, with the benefit therefore for them of limited liability. Unfortunate Mr. Salomon was one of these; not only did his company's business fail, but he also suffered the further, perhaps greater, misfortune of being the subject of the test case of *Salomon* v. *Salomon & Co.*[24] Mr. Salomon had sold his leather business to a company incorporated for the purpose of acquiring it from him for the sum of £30,000, part of the purchase price being satisfied by the issue to him of 20,000 one pound shares in the company, the balance of £10,000 being left outstanding on a debenture secured by a floating charge over all the company's assets. There were six other initial members of the company, drawn from Mr. Salomon's family, but they held only one share each as nominee for him, and were there only because the statutory machinery then required at least seven members on formation.[25] Not only did Mr. Salomon have the overwhelming majority of shares, and therefore overwhelming voting power and control, in the corporation he had created, but he was also at its inception its principal creditor having priority, since his debt was secured, over all sub-

---

[20] See n. 12, *supra*.

[21] ss.5(2), 6(2), and 19 of the 1983 Act.

[22] Joint Stock Companies Act 1856.

[23] Joint Stock Companies Act 1857.

[24] [1897] A.C. 22. For a critical look at the decision, see O. Kahn-Freund "Some Reflections on Company Law Reform"(1944), 7 M.L.R. 54.

[25] The private company, allowing formation with only two initial members, was not introduced until 1907, and constitutes a legislative recognition of the situation in *Salomon's Case*.

sequent creditors. After the company fell upon bad times, a contest for the few available funds developed between the secured creditors holding Mr. Salomon's debentures (the bulk of which it must be added in fairness to him, he no longer held) and the unsecured creditors represented by the liquidator who would get nothing if the debentures prevailed. The liquidator alleged that the company was merely an agent for Mr. Salomon, his *alter ego*, his *alias*, and that therefore Mr. Salomon should like any other principal indemnify the company against its debts. Vaughan Williams J. at first instance[26] agreed with him; likewise the Court of Appeal where Lopes L.J. found that Mr. Salomon's arrangements were "merely devices to enable him to carry on business in the name of the company with limited liability, contrary to the true intent and meaning of the Companies Act 1862, and further, to enable him to obtain a preference over other creditors of the company by obtaining a first charge on the assets of the company by means of such debentures . . . "[27] The House of Lords would have none of this, and affirmed in judgments which are now the bedrock upon which many company formations are built that it does not matter that some of the persons forming a company are merely nominees for others,[28] or that the machinery of the Companies Acts might be used by an individual to carry on what in economic reality might be his business, but with the benefit of limited liability; and that the company thus formed was a separate person, capable of incurring a valid debt to its controller, and was not *per se* to be regarded as his agent or trustee. We shall be returning to the propositions that can be extracted from *Salomon's Case,* and qualifications to them, but for the moment it is appropriate to give briefly some further illustrations of the consequences of the separate personality of the modern registered company.

In *Lee* v. *Lee's Air Farming Ltd.,*[29] the Privy Council found nothing

---

[26] *Broderip* v. *Salomon* [1895] 2 Ch. 323.

[27] *Ibid.* p. 341. The judgments (see *per e.g.* Lindley L.J. at p. 338) tend towards finding a trusteeship rather than agency; in this context, a fine distinction.

[28] Indeed a company is not required to recognise beneficial interest in its shares: s.123. In *Irish Permanent Building Society* v. *Registrar of Building Societies* [1981] I.L.R.M. 242, the argument that the ten persons requisite to incorporate a building society under s.8 of the Building Societies Act 1976, should not be mere nominees "but ten individual wills converging on a particular course" (p.263) in order to avoid the formation of building societies which were the "creatures" or "subsidiaries" of large financial institutions" (p. 260) was firmly rejected by Barrington J. by express recourse to the House of Lords decision in *Salomon,* (pp. 262 – 264) but interestingly, he quoted from the judgment of Lopes L.J. in the Court of Appeal in that case as an illustration of the type of argument he was rejecting.

[29] [1961] A.C. 12; cited with approval by Kenny J. in *Re Diary Lee Ltd.* [1976] I.R. 314, 318, rep. *sub nom. Stakelum* v. *Canning.*

incongruous in Mr. Lee who was the beneficial owner of all the shares in his company and its governing director causing a valid contract to be made under which he would serve the company as a pilot. The cases show the separate personality of the company often operates to the disadvantage of its controller. In *Macaura* v. *Northern Assurance Co.*,[30] an appeal to the House of Lords from Northern Ireland, the appellant had sold all the timber on his estate in Co. Tyrone to a company in exchange for the issue by it to him of its whole share capital. Later, in February 1922, the appellant himself insured the timber against destruction by a policy taken out in his own name, a few weeks before the timber was destroyed by fire. The insurance company successfully contended that the appellant had no insurable interest in the timber which was wholly owned by the company. Lord Wrenbury, disposing of the matter, said that a member of the company "even if he holds all the shares is not the corporation and . . . neither he nor any creditor of the company has any property legal or equitable in the assets of the corporation."[31] One may steal from one's own company.[31a] In *Battle* v. *Irish Art Promotion Centre Ltd.*,[32] the defendant company was being sued for an alleged debt but had no assets to employ counsel to defend the action. The managing director of the company who was its major shareholder applied to the court for leave to conduct the defence on his behalf, stating that if judgment in default were given against the company, "it would be a reflection on [his] reputation and standing as a businessman".[33] O' Dáláigh, C.J. in giving the judgment of the Supreme Court refusing this request said:

"This is an infirmity of the company which derives from its own very nature. The creation of the company is the act of its subscribers; the subscribers, in discarding their own *personae* for the *persona* of the company, doubtless did so for the advantages which incorporation offers to traders. In seeking incorporation they thereby lose the right of audience which they would have as individuals; but the choice has been their own . . . [The applicant] cannot as major shareholder and managing director now substitute his *persona* for that of the company."[34]

[30] [1925] A.C. 619.
[31] *Ibid.* at p. 633. See also *General Accident Corporation* v. *Midland Bank Ltd.* [1940] 3 All E.R. 252, and the description of the nature of a share in Chap. 6: Shares and Membership.
[31a] *Pearlberg and O'Brien* [1982] Crim.L.R. 829; *Att.-Gen. Reference (No.2 of 1982)* [1984] 2 W.L.R. 447; and re Sullivan, [1984] Crim.L.R. 405.
[32] [1968] I.R. 252.
[33] At p. 253.
[34] At p. 254. See also *Abbey Films* v. *Att.-Gen.* [1981] I.R. 158, 172.

In *Tunstall* v. *Steigmann*[35] a landlord would have been able to recover possession of her premises from a tenant if she could have established that she intended to occupy them for the purposes "of a business to be carried on by her." Unfortunately, the business in question was carried on by her wholly owned company, and she failed.*

Not only the members, but also other persons dealing with modern registered companies, ignore its separate personality at their peril. In *Underwood (A.L.) Ltd.* v. *Bank of Liverpool*,[36] Mr Underwood was in the habit of indorsing cheques made payable to his eponymous company over to himself for payment into his private bank account. The bank, when successfully sued in conversion, evidently held the mistaken view that the inquiries which they normally would have made on finding a company's cheque indorsed over to an official of that company were inapplicable where the company concerned was of the "one man" type, and the indorser that one man.

The danger of confusing a company with its controllers goes far beyond the danger that the courts will later insist that rights and duties be located with their proper subject. In *Re David Ireland & Co*[36a] a director had so mixed up his personal affairs with those of his company that the liquidator was misled into starting proceedings against him for alleged breaches of duty to the company. Those proceedings failed, but the director was ordered to pay the costs of them for having caused the confusion in the first place. In *Johnston* v. *Langheld and others*[36b] litigation was occasioned by a testatrix' leaving her "farm" to a particular legatee whereas she herself had no farm but instead was the beneficial owner of all the shares in the company which owned the farm. In the particular circumstances of her will, the bequest succeeded, but at needless cost. Wills should be precisely drafted, and if necessary, subsequently revised, if relevant assets are, or become, vested in a corporation.

One may take *Salomon's Case* as a statement of normality. This normality has three aspects: first, that a modern registered company if properly formed is a legal person separate and distinct from its members; secondly, that such a company is not *per se* the agent of its

---

[35] [1962] 2 All E.R. 417 (C.A.); the case concerned the Landlord and Tenant Act 1954 [*U.K.*], *cf.* Landlord and Tenant (Amendment) Act 1980, p. 57, *post.*
[36] [1924] 1 K.B. 775.
[36a] [1905] 1 I.R. 133, 145; or such confusion may simply earn a judicial rebuke, *e.g.* *Re S. M. Barker Ltd.* [1950] I.R. 123, 127 where Gavan Duffy P. said: "The Company was a small affair, easily controlled by a single group of co-owners and the consequent disregard of its distinct corporate character goes some way towards explaining, though it does not excuse, the imbecility of the part which the Company was made to play in relation to the deal".
[36b] High Court, O'Hanlon J. November 18, 1982, unrep.

members; and, thirdly, that the motives of those who formed it are not material to its subsequent rights and liabilities.[37] These concrete propositions are not fully axiomatic, and the courts will in fact occasionally look at the characteristics of a company's members in order to augment its legal personality or to impose legal consequences upon it. Some commentators in expressing the normality of these propositions do so in the metaphorical language of "a veil of incorporation"[38] drawn between the company and its members; and correspondingly departures from these propositions are viewed as lifting, piercing or sweeping aside the veil, and in some sense as an abnormality. We shall see that the courts themselves in dealing with some such cases have shown a preference for imagery and metaphor over sober but more precise legal concepts and terminology.

Some classification of the circumstances in which the courts will "lift the veil" will now be attempted. Many of the cases, whilst abounding in metaphor, reveal themselves as solvable without resort to it.

Use of a company to circumvent an existing legal duty

It is salutary to begin with a case which did not involve a corporation at all. In *Smith* v. *Hancock*,[39] Mr. Hancock sold to the plaintiff his grocery shop and the business which he conducted there under the name of "T.P. Hancock," and as part of this transaction he entered into a valid covenant restraining himself from competing with the plaintiff purchaser. Later, Mr. Hancock's wife and nephew opened a new grocery shop a mere stone's throw away, and traded there under the style of "Mrs T.P. Hancock." In the subsequent action for breach of covenant, the courts were, as one might expect, concerned to see whether Mr. Hancock had in relation to the new business constituted his wife or his nephew his agents in carrying it on.[40] In the event, he was found innocent of participation but Lindley L.J. said: "If the evidence admitted of the conclusion that what was being done was a mere *cloak* or *sham*,[41] and that in truth the business was being carried on by the wife and [the nephew] for the Defendant, or by the Defendant through his wife or [the nephew], I certainly should not hesitate to draw the conclusion, and to grant the Plaintiff relief accordingly." One may ignore the italicised

---

[37] *Per* Lord Halsbury in *Salomon's Case*, at p. 30.
[38] *e.g.* Gower *Principles of Modern Company Law* (4th ed, London 1979) Ch. 6, "Lifting the Veil."
[39] [1894] 2 Ch. 377.
[40] *Ibid.* p. 385.
[41] Italics supplied.

imagery. The substantive decision turned on the fact that a recognised legal relationship, that of agency, did not exist between Mr. and Mrs Hancock. Had Mrs Hancock in fact been found to be her husband's agent, no one would suggest that her legal personality had in some way been tampered with or disregarded.[42] The value of this unremarkable case lies in contrasting it with the attitude of the courts to cases where the alleged agent is not of flesh and blood but a corporation, and the alleged principal is its controller accused of circumventing through it his pre-existing legal duty to the plaintiff. Here the courts concentrate more upon the defendant's motivation in forming the company and on satisfying themselves that he is truly in control of his creation. Searching for a substantive agency relationship between him and it would in most cases, but not all, be futile in view of the facility he has to create relationships other than substantive agency between himself and his own creature. However, as will appear,[43] there is nothing in *Salomon's Case* to prevent the courts finding that the arrangements which happen to have been made between a controller and his company render it substantively his agent in law. *Salomon's Case* says only that it is not his agent *per se*, that is to say, without more.

The attitude of the courts to the category under discussion is well put by Meredith M.R. in *Cummings* v. *Stewart*[44]:

> "In my opinion, the Companies (Consolidation) Act 1908 embodies a code framed . . . for the purpose of preserving and enforcing commercial morality, and it would be strange, indeed, if that code could be turned into an engine for the destruction of legal obligations, and the overthrow of legitimate and enforceable claims. The most casual reader of the speeches of the Law Lords in the case of *Salomon* v. *Salomon & Co.* cannot fail to observe that there is nothing in any of those speeches contrary to the view I have just expressed. In the present case all the ability and all the legal acumen and learning of [Counsel for the defendant] have failed to give any semblance of justification or reality to the trick by which the defendant endeavoured to evade his legal obligations."

These thunderous observations were not strictly necessary to the decision, which proceeded on the construction of the contract between the plaintiff and the defendant. Under that contract the defendant was obliged to pay to the plaintiff inventor heavy annual royalties for the right to use his patented invention. The contract

---

[42] Or even her veil lifted.
[43] See pp. 46 *et seq.*, *infra.*
[44] [1911] 1 I.R. 236, 240.

provided that the defendant might transfer the benefit and burden of it to any limited company he might form "to carry on his business or the business connected with and arising out of the said patents and this licence." The defendant transferred the agreement to a company with a capital of only two pounds which he had formed for the purpose of ridding himself of his liability under the agreement. Since there was no intention that the company should actually work the patents, the transfer to it was held not to be contemplated by the contract under which the defendant remained personally liable.

In *Gilford Motor Co. Ltd. v. Horne*,[45] Mr. Horne's contract of employment with the plaintiff had contained in it a valid covenant prohibiting him from competing with the plaintiff after he left its employment. Mr. Horne went into business on his own account in direct competition with the plaintiff, but after a little while he had qualms about this, and sent for and examined a copy of his former contract of employment. A week later he caused to be set up a company called J.M. Horne & Co. Ltd which then carried on the business in competition with the plaintiff. Mr. Horne was neither a director nor overtly a shareholder[46] in the new company; his wife held half of the shares and was a director; J.M.Horne was the name of his son; and yet, nevertheless everyone in the new company treated Mr. Horne as "the boss." The new company "was formed as a device, a stratagem in order to mask the effective carrying on of a business of Mr. Horne. The purpose of it was to try to enable him under what is a *cloak* or a *sham* to engage in business in respect of which he had a fear that the Plaintiffs might intervene and object."[47] The court was satisfied that the motive for forming the new company was that of avoiding a pre-existing duty, and the person under that legal duty was effectively in control of the company. An injunction restraining competition was granted not only against Mr. Horne but also against the new company, so that it cannot be said that its separate legal personality was wholly disregarded. In fact, the relationship between Mr. Horne and the company is described in loose language suggestive of agency, the latter being a "the *channel* through which the defendant Horne was carrying on his business."[48]

The blatant case of *Jones* v. *Lipman*[49] illustrates that the suspect motivation may be found in the acquisition of a company already in

[45] [1933] Ch. 935.
[46] The beneficial ownership of the shares was not investigated in the subsequent proceedings.
[47] *Per* Lord Hanworth M.R. at p. 956. Italics supplied.
[48] *Ibid.* p. 943. Italics supplied.
[49] [1962] 1 All E.R. 442.

existence. Mr. Lipman agreed to sell his house to Mr. Jones for £5,250. In the interval which inevitably elapses between contract and completion, Mr. Lipman regretted his bargain, asked to be released and was refused. He then took evasive action. Through his solicitors he acquired absolute control of a "ready-made" company incorporated for the purpose of acquiring land and property. He and his solicitors' clerk became the directors, and held all the shares beneficially for himself. Mr. Lipman then sold and conveyed his house to his new company for £3,000, half being borrowed by the company from a bank and the rest being left outstanding. Mr. Jones obtained direct orders for specific performance against the company and Mr. Lipman. Russell J. said "The defendant company is the creature of the first defendant, a *device* and a *sham*, a *mask* which he holds before his face in an attempt to avoid recognition by the eye of Equity."[50] This was doubtless a satisfying judgment to deliver, and it sounds well, but it avoids exploring three other more conventional methods which might have yielded the same result. First, there is the probability that under English land law the company was bound by the contract in any event as not having taken in good faith.[51] Certainly in Ireland the case could have been shortly disposed of on this ground as a simple instance of a purchaser taking with notice of the contract, a pre-existing equitable interest affecting the land, and therefore subject to it; no "veil lifting" exercise would have been necessary. Secondly, since Mr. Lipman was in a position to extricate his property from the company, an order for specific performance could effectively have been made against him alone; and, thirdly and more speculatively, the company might be said to have tortiously induced a breach of the original contract,[52] and thereby laid itself open to appropriate relief, including a mandatory injunction to restore the property. The use of emotive terms[53] masked the precise

---

[50] *Ibid.* p. 445.

[51] *Peffer* v. *Rigg* [1977] 1 W.L.R. 285, 295. This case concerned registered land (as did *Jones* v. *Lipman*) and therefore the construction of ss.20, 59 of the Land Registration Act 1925 [*U.K.*]. In the case of English unregistered land, a purchaser need *not* be in good faith to take free of a previous equitable burden on the land which has not been registered under the Land Charges Act 1925 [*U.K.*] and even a conveyance to a nominal purchaser with full knowledge of the burden and made solely for the purpose of avoiding it will be successful: *Midland Bank Trust Co. Ltd.* v. *Green* [1981] A.C. 513. The nominal purchaser there was an individual, but it is difficult to see how the result could have been different if a company had been chosen as purchaser.

[52] *Inter alia, Rookes* v. *Barnard* [1964] A.C. 1129.

[53] A little more of the attitude of Younger L.J. in *I.R.C.* v. *Sansom* [1921] 2 K.B. 492 where he deprecated "in connection with what are called one-man companies the too indiscriminate use of such words as simulacrum, sham or cloak" would not come amiss.

juridical ground of the decision; but whatever that may have been, the separate personality of the company was not disregarded or swept aside, since an order was made against it, and, doubtless, the bank still regarded it as its debtor.

The courts will not readily intervene if the company is formed not for the purpose of avoiding a pre-existing legal duty but with the motive of altering the controllers' legal relations with the world in some other way. In *Roundabout Ltd.* v. *Beirne*,[54] a company owned and ran a public house. In May 1958 all the staff joined a trade union. By November 1958, the controllers of the company had become tired of unionisation; they caused the company to close the public house and to dismiss all employees. Some union officials and some of the dismissed men began peacefully to picket the premises, and this picketing continued at all material times. There is no doubt that at this stage there was in existence a trade dispute within the meaning of the Trades Disputes Act 1906 and that accordingly the picketing was lawful.Three weeks later the public house re-opened for business, but a new company Roundabout Ltd. was now running the business as tenant of the old company, and forthwith sued the picketers for an unjunction to restrain them. Roundabout Ltd. had been formed to get around the problem of picketing. The controllers of the old company held the whip hand in the new company: they were permanant directors, and had a controlling interest in its share capital. True, there was in Roundabout Ltd., what the judge called some "new blood." Three barmen, naturally not union members, were additional directors of Roundabout Ltd., but under the articles they could be removed by the controllers at any time. Being directors, they were not as such employees,[55] and since Roundabout Ltd. had no employees, it could not be an employer with the consequence that there could not be in relation to it a trade dispute within the meaning of the 1906 Act. Dixon J. found the formation of the company to be a "successful subterfuge"[56] and granted the injunction accordingly. Relevant authorities such as *Gilford Motor Co. Ltd.* v. *Horne, supra,* were apparently not cited to the court, but even if they had been they would have been distinguishable on the ground that

---

[54] [1959] I.R. 423.

[55] On the status of a company's directors, see Chap. 3. Internal Structure.

[56] The judgment is somewhat confusing; the learned judge relied also on the fact that the new arrangements whilst containing "a considerable element of subterfuge" had the further purpose of bringing "new blood" into the business, namely the vulnerable barmen directors above mentioned. See also *Lescar Construction Co. Ltd.* v. *Wigman* [1969] 2 O.R. 846 (H.Ct. of Ontario).

they involved the attempted avoidance of a legal *duty*, whereas Roundabout Ltd. was formed to circumvent an *immunity* possessed by the picketers from being sued for nuisance. The victim of such an immunity is not obliged to continue to present himself as a target. When the *Roundabout* case was decided, there was nothing in Irish law which could be construed as imposing a duty upon a former employer to remain in possession of the place of employment or to continue to give employment there; now however, dismissed employees have the possibility of an order under the Unfair Dismissals Act 1977[57] that they be reinstated. Circumventions of the *Roundabout* type would certainly assume a different complexion if the circumstances of the employees' dismissal were such that the court would in its discretion order reinstatement.

In concluding this category, an obvious remark should be made in favour of Mr. Salomon. He was not in forming his company seeking to affect his existing legal relationships in any way.

Where the court is given a discretion

Courts frequently have a discretion whether or not to grant or withold a remedy. Where a court has such a discretion it is more inclined to investigate facts behind the corporate facade. Judicial discretions are usually conferred by statute but one important area is non-statutory in origin. These are the equitable remedies, chiefly specific performance and the injunction. Most of the cases in the last category concerned equitable remedies, and in one of them there was an assertion that the equitable nature of the remedy facilitated the relief granted.[58] Indeed, it would be possible to classify the former category of cases as falling within a traditional area of equitable intervention, namely, a statute being used as a cloak or engine of fraud.

---

[57] Unfair Dismissals Act 1977, s.7. The efficacy of a re-instatement order is questionable. See Redmond, *Dismissal Law in the Republic of Ireland*, Dublin, 1982, pp. 181 *et seq.*

[58] *Jones* v. *Lipman* [1962] 1 W.L.R. 832, 837 where Russell J. referring to *Gilford Motor Co. Ltd.* v. *Horne, supra*, says "the case cited illustrates that an equitable remedy is rightly be granted directly against the creature in such circumstances." And see also *Lescar Construction Co. Ltd.* v. *Wigman* [1969] 2 O.R. 846, 849 where an injunction against picketing was sought by an associated company of the original employer and Fraser J. said with reference to the wide powers in equity to grant or withhold injunctions that "where the Court is asked to exercise its *discretion* by granting an injunction it should have regard to the realities of the situation" particularly to a judicious change in the corporate garb.

Re *Bugle Press Ltd*[59] is an example of the use of a discretion given
by statute. Section 209(1) of the Companies Act 1948 [*U.K.*][60] provides that where *a company* has made a takeover bid for the shares of
another company, and has received 90 per cent. acceptances of its
offer, it may compulsorily acquire the remaining shares. The court,
however, has a discretion if it "thinks fit" to order otherwise upon
the application of the dissentient minority. Two shareholders in
Bugle Press Ltd. held 90 per cent. of the shares between them, and
wished to expropriate the third shareholder who held the remaining
10 per cent. They accordingly formed a new company which made a
bid for all the shares in Bugle Press Ltd. This bid was accepted with
alacrity by themselves, and, since the holders of 90 per cent. of the
shares had accepted the offer, the conditions of section 209(1) were
satisfied, and the bidder company proceeded to invoke the compulsory acquisition procedure against the third shareholder. Upon his
application to the court, Harman L.J. in a characteristically robust
judgment found the bidder company to be "nothing but a *little hut*
built around his two co-shareholders . . . a *hollow sham*. The applicant has nothing to knock down; he has only to shout and the walls
of this *Jericho* fall flat,"[61] and thus the court's discretion was exercised against this "bare-faced attempt to evade that fundamental
rule of company law which forbids the majority of shareholders,
unless the articles so provide, to expropriate the minority."

Another case, *Merchandise Transport Ltd.* v. *British Transport Commission*[62] concerned a statutory discretion given to an administrative
authority. This case arose out of British legislation, since repealed
and replaced, designed to protect the public haulier of goods from
unfair competition.[63] The public haulier was not to carry his own
goods, and businesses operating vehicles for their own private purposes were generally not to accept loads from outsiders. A manufacturing company had vehicles which it used to transport its own
goods, and it wished to transfer these to its subsidiary company
which ran a public haulage business; it was envisaged that the subsidiary company would use the transferred vehicles partly to carry
the holding company's goods, but spare capacity would be available
to carry the goods of outsiders. The licensing authority's decision,
pursuant to a wide discretion, to withhold public haulier's licenses

---

[59] [1961] Ch. 270.
[60] The similar but not identical Irish provision is s.204(1). See pp. 297–301 *post*.
[61] At p. 288. Italics supplied.
[62] [1962] 2 Q.B. 173.
[63] There was also similar legislation in Ireland.

from the subsidiary in respect of vehicles proposed to be transferred was upheld by the Court of Appeal, since to grant them would as a matter of economic fact put the holding company "in the position of the manufacturer who can carry his own goods to their destination and pick up return loads where he can get them,"[64] Devlin L.J. said:

> "The fact that two persons are separate in law does not mean that one may not be under the control of the other to such an extent that together they constitute one commercial unit. It may be the case of parent and subsidiary; or it may be the case in which one man, though nominally independent, is in truth the instrument of another; or it may be a case in which a man has simply put his vehicles in the name of his wife. Whenever a licensing authority is satisfied that that sort of relationship exists and the dominant party is using it to obtain contrary to the intent of the Act an advantage which he would not otherwise get, he is entitled if not bound to *exercise his discretion* so as to ensure that the scheme of the Act is complied with in the spirit as well as in the letter."[65]

There is nothing in these cases contrary to the *Salomon* principle, since in that case the courts were not given a discretion to exercise, and could only hold on the plain construction of the statute that Mr. Salomon's company was not as such the agent of its controller.

The courts will not always take the opportunities afforded to them by a discretion to investigate the facts behind the corporate facade. In *Pioneer Laundry & Dry Cleaners Ltd.* v. *Minister of National Revenue*[66] the Minister had a statutory discretion to allow reasonable amounts for depreciation for income tax purposes. The taxpayer company was incorporated to acquire all the assets of several existing companies controlled by the controllers of the taxpayer company. These assets had in the hands of the existing companies been accorded maximum depreciation. The taxpayer company sought to start the depreciation process afresh, and the Minister refused on the bald ground "that there was no actual change in the ownership of the assets purchased or taken over," which, of course, was not strictly true since the assets were now owned by a separate person in law. The Supreme Court of Canada held that the Minister in the exercise of his discretion could "look beyond the legal facade for the purpose of ascertaining the realities of ownership or the possibilities of

---

[64] *Per* Devlin L.J. at p. 196.
[65] *Ibid.* p. 202. Italics supplied.
[66] [1940] A.C. 127 (Privy Council, on appeal from the Supreme Court of Canada).

schemes to avoid taxation."[67] The Privy Council in reversing this decision was of the opinion that "the reason given for the decision was not a proper ground for the exercise of the Minister's discretion, and that he was not entitled, in the absence of fraud or improper conduct,[68] to disregard the separate legal existence of the appellant company and to inquire as to who its shareholders were and its relation to its predecessor." Had the Minister taken care to acknowledge the change in ownership and to base his decision on the close connection between the former and new owners of the assets, and the collusive nature of their transfer in order to gain a tax advantage, his decision might have been upheld.[69]

In conclusion, one should note the only Irish case in this category, with less prominence than it deserves since no full written record of the judgments in it survive. It is the 1977 Supreme Court case of *The State* v. *District Justice Donnelly*,[70] where the holders of a wine licence who had suffered two indorsements for breach of the Licensing Acts and were apparently about to suffer a fatal third, urgently created a new company Cynosure Ltd. to take a transfer of the licensed premises and, it was hoped, its licence. The licence holders were the only directors and shareholders of the new company. Their hopes were thwarted by the District Justice's refusal to grant a certificate of no objection to the transfer pursuant to section 15 of the Revenue Act 1862. Though there were strenuous objections by counsel to his having looked behind the corporate body to its controllers, he was held justified in doing so by the width of the jurisdiction conferred on him by the statute.

Where the law requires it

There are occasions when laws require the courts to determine whether a person has certain essentially human characteristics, such as, to take a few examples, a residence, an intention, or a good or other character. When that person is a corporation, a mere abstraction, the courts might in strict theory decline to find it capable of

---

[67] *Ibid.* p. 258.

[68] Which appears to beg the question.

[69] In *Comptroller of Income Tax* v. *Harrisons and Crosfield (Malaya) Ltd.* [1956] A.C. 459 the *Pioneer Laundry* case was treated as an instance of complete failure by the holder of a discretion to exercise it at all.

[70] *Irish Times,* November 5, 1977. See also *Garda Siochana Guide* 5th ed. Instances where by statute a discretion is given to make an order against *anyone* in respect of the fulfilment of another's obligation are really too obvious to come into this category. See for example s.27(2) of the Local Government (Planning and Development) Act 1976 and *Dublin County Council* v. *Elton Homes Ltd* [1984] I.L.R.M. 297.

bearing such attributes, and once indeed that was the position,[71] but nowadays the courts will readily impute human characteristics to a corporation, where necessary. That necessity occurs where laws, particularly statutes applicable to persons[72] are framed by reference to human characteristics. The fault, if any, lies with the Legislature which, by appropriate draftsmanship could take account of the fact that not all persons addressed by its laws are of flesh and blood.

Take residence, often a vital question for the purpose of liability to taxation. In *De Beers Consolidated Mines Ltd.* v. *Howe*,[73] Lord Loreburn said "In applying the conception of residence to a company, we ought, I think, to proceed as nearly as we can upon the analogy of an individual. A company cannot eat or sleep, but it can keep house and do business. We ought, therefore, to see where it really keeps house and does business . . . I regard that as the true rule, and the real business is carried on where the central management and control actually abides."[74] This does not mean that an Irish registered company trading here may escape being resident in Ireland by taking the precaution of securely keeping its controllers abroad. In *John Hood & Co. Ltd.* v. *Magee*,[75] Mr. Hood, the sole director of his eponymous Irish registered company, resided in New York, and directed its operations from there. These operations consisted of the manufacture of linen goods in Ireland, and the sale of them in America. Most of the shareholders of whom Mr. Hood had the largest but not a majority holding were likewise resident abroad. It was held that there was more to "central management and control" test than Mr. Hood's choice of his own residence, even if the

---

[71] *e.g.* Blackstone, *Commentaries*, 1, 476–477 and the remark attributed to Thurlow L.C. that since corporations have neither bodies to be punished nor souls to be condemned, they therefore do as they like (John Poynder, *Literary Extracts*, [1844], Vol. 1). The absence of soul was important to oust the jurisdiction of the Ecclesiastical Courts (10 Co.Rep. 32). Such questions have an immense history of discussion. A useful starting point is Maitland's Introduction to his translation of Gierke, *Political Theories of the Middle Age*, C.U.P., 1900. For a recent reverter to the early 19th century and beyond, see *M.C.B. (Galway) Ltd.* v. *Industrial Development Authority* [1981] I.L.R.M. 58 in which, fortunately *obiter*, O'Higgins C.J. he said he found it difficult to associate the words "personal qualifications" with a company, and Griffin J. reserved his opinion on the matter.

[72] Interpretation Act 1937, s.11(c) states that "the word 'person' shall, unless the contrary intention appears, be construed as importing a body corporate . . . and an unincorporated body of persons as well as an individual", and s.11(i) provides that references to "persons in relation to an offence . . . shall unless the contrary intention appears be construed as including references to a body corporate."

[73] [1906] A.C. 455.

[74] At p. 458.

[75] [1918] 2 I.R. 34.

company was "John Hood disguised in limited liability attire."[76] The judgments found the necessary measure of control in the general meetings of the company held in Ireland which might at any time supersede Mr. Hood by failing to re-elect him.[77] The test for determining residence is in fact most frequently used to find that a company registered abroad is nonetheless resident within the jurisdiction of the court exercising it. In the *De Beer's* case a South African company was found resident in England, and in *Unit Construction Ltd.* v. *Bullock*,[78] all the elaborate precautions taken by those responsible forming three Kenyan subsidiaries of an English company were in vain. Despite the fact that their constitution provided that all meetings of them were to be held in Kenya, the Kenyan boards were appointed by the parent company in London and danced to London's tune. Accordingly the subsidiaries were held resident in England.

The test for residence concentrates therefore upon the ascertainment of the ultimate control of a company's general operations. A similar test applies when a court has to ascertain whether a company possesses enemy status. In *Daimler Company Ltd.* v. *Continental Tyre & Rubber Co. (G.B.) Ltd.*,[79] a company which possessed British nationality through being registered in Britain was nonetheless infected with enemy status since its controllers were predominantly Germans resident in Germany.

But such matters as residence and enemy status are *general* attributes of a company. Occasionally, the quest for control will be limited to an investigation of a *particular* incident and the quest for control will be correspondingly more localised. If, for example, the courts have to find a company's "character" for the purpose of deciding whether it is a proper person to be granted a licence to sell intoxicating liquor at a public house, then the inquiry should be confined to those persons within the company concerned with the running of its public houses. In *The King (Cottingham)* v. *Justices of Co. Cork*,[80] Palles C.B. said:

"I cannot see why a public company cannot have a character. No doubt it has no soul[81] but it can act by others, and through

[76] *Per* Gibson J. at p. 43.
[77] See Gibson J. at p. 45; Madden J. at p. 49; and Kenny J. at p. 55. *Cf.* s.140 which shows the extent to which annual general meetings of Irish registered companies may be held outside the State.
[78] [1960] A.C. 351 (H.L.).
[79] [1916] 2 A.C. 307, discussed in *John Hood & Co. Ltd.* v. *Magee* [1918] 2 I.R. 34, particularly by Gibson J. at p. 46.
[80] [1906] 2 I.R. 415.
[81] See n. 71 *supra*.

others do acts which in the case of a natural person would affect conscience and be a foundation of that reputation which the law knows as 'character,' be it good or bad . . . Reputation is acquired by conduct. The conduct of the authorised agents of a company is its conduct. Why should not that conduct give rise to a reputation as to its character good, bad or indifferent?"[82]

But which agents' conduct is to be looked at? Johnson J. talked of the conduct of the agent or manager whom the company put in charge of a public house as being relevant to ascertain the company's character in relation to that house.[83] The choice of agents to be investigated in this more limited type of inquiry assumes most prominence in the decided cases where a mental element, usually involving culpability, is sought to be attributed to a company. Such cases mostly involve crime, but as will be seen, the Merchant Shipping Acts have given a few examples as have other civil causes[83a] where the company's mental state has been in issue. It should be strongly emphasised that such questions do not arise in determining a company's liability in tort for the acts for its servants and agents; there the issues are decided on the normal principles of vicarious liability without there being any necessity for a finding of mental or moral culpability or fault on the part of the company.[84]

Essentially the cases under discussion are resolved by determining whether the individuals who actually did or omitted to do the act or omission in question had the responsibility for it delegated to them within the company. In other words, were they to be the controllers of the situation, or merely controlled? The resolution of such questions involves in each case an analysis of the management structure of the company in question. In *Tesco Supermarkets Ltd.* v. *Nattrass*,[85] goods had been offered for sale in one of the defendant's supermarkets in circumstances which would amount to an offence under the Trade Descriptions Act 1968 [*U.K.*] unless the defendant could bring itself within a statutory defence by proving, *inter alia*, that it

---

[82] At pp. 422 *et seq.* This passage was cited with approval by Kenny J. in the Supreme Court decision of *The State (John Hennessy and Chariot Inns Ltd.)* v. *Commons* [1976] I.R. 238 and by Barrington J. in *McMahon* v. *Murtagh Properties Ltd.* (High Court, unreported October 20, 1981) which attempt to nail the fallacy that a company cannot itself directly hold a liquor licence but must hold through a nominee.

[83] At pp. 426 *et seq.* A particular company's character was not in issue in that case, and consequently the investigation was not pursued more closely and these remarks are technically *obiter*.

[83a] In *Re Hunting Lodges Ltd.*, [1985] I.L.R.M. 75 the guilty knowledge of a company's controllers caused fraud to be imputed to it. See also *Cook* v. *Deeks* [1916] 1 A.C. 554, 565.

[84] See pp. 159 *et seq.*, *infra*.

[85] [1972] A.C. 153 (H.L.).

had taken all reasonable precautions and exercised all due diligence to avoid the commission of the offence either by itself or by any person under its control.[86] The shop manager of the branch at which the offence had been committed was at fault. The sole question was whether his fault could be imputed to the company so as to deprive it of this statutory defence; in all other respects the company was guiltless, since at higher levels within the company systems had been devised to prevent the commission of such offences. It was held that the board of directors had not delegated or surrendered their powers of management in this area; instead they had retained control of it, and had caused directives on the subject to be issued down a lengthy chain of command.[87] The shop manager's fault was therefore not imputed to the company. In *The Lady Gwendolen,* [88] fault was imputed to the company, Arthur Guinness Son & Co. (Dublin) Ltd. This company was vicariously liable in tort for the negligence of one of its ship's captains who had caused a collision through failure to make proper use of radar in a fog. However, sections 502 and 503 of the Merchant Shipping Act 1894 allow shipowners to limit what would otherwise be their liability if the damage occurred "without their actual fault or privity." To determine whether such "actual fault" was present in the Guinness company the court examined every level of its management structure from the ship's captain upward, and found fault with each link in the management chain, the chief failure being to ensure that the captains of the company's ships were properly instructed in the use of radar in fog. Sufficient powers to control this situation had been delegated by the board to the Assistant Managing Director responsible for traffic, and his failure in responsibility was imputed to the company as its own "actual fault."

In the most celebrated Merchant Shipping Act case of this type, *Lennard's Carrying Co.* v. *Asiatic Petroleum Co. Ltd.,*[89] recourse was had to an "organic" theory of corporations in order to impute the necessary fault to the company. This organic theory is best illustrated by excerpts from the judgment of its chief architect, Lord Haldane L.C. He said:

"My Lords, a corporation is an abstraction. It has no mind of its own any more than it has a body of its own; its active and directing will must consequently be sought in the person of

---

[86] s.24(1) of the Trade Descriptions Act 1968 [*U.K.*]. The Irish equivalent is s.22 of the Consumer Information Act 1978.

[87] See in particular Lord Reid at pp. 132, 135.

[88] [1965] 2 W.L.R. 91. See Leigh, 28 M.L.R. 584.

[89] [1915] A.C. 705.

somebody who for some purposes may be called an agent, but who is *really the directing mind and will of the corporation, the very ego and centre of the personality of the corporation. . . .* Mr. Lennard took the active part in the management of this ship on behalf of the owners, and Mr. Lennard, . . . was registered as the person designated for this purpose in the ship's register. Mr Lennard was the natural person therefore to come on behalf of the owners and give full evidence not only about the events . . . which related to the seaworthiness of the ship, but about his own position and as to whether or not he was the *life and soul* of the company. For if Mr. Lennard was the *directing mind of the company*, then his action must, unless the corporation is not to be liable at all, have been an action which was the *action of the company itself* within the meaning of section (502 . . .* It could not have been successfully contended that section 502 is so worded as to exempt a corporation altogether which happens to be the owner of a ship, merely because it happens to be a corporation. It must be upon the true construction of that section in such a case as the present one that the fault or privity is the fault or privity of somebody who is not merely a servant or agent for whom the company is liable upon the footing of respondeat superior, but somebody for whom the company is liable *because his action is the very action of the company itself.*"[90]

This formulation, though new to English law[91] at the time, was not original. Its provenance was German, and Lord Haldane as well as being a statesman and lawyer, was one of the leading Germanic philosophers of his generation.[92] This German theory says that corporations, like other Group Units, have a Group Will manifested by its appropriate "organs" whose acts are those of the corporation itself.[93] Although in *Lennard's Case* in 1915 this theory provided a rational answer to the question whether a corporation could be guilty of fault at all, its utility as an analytical tool[94] now that that

---

[90] At pp. 713, 714. Lord Haldane also referred earlier to Mr Lennard as the "active spirit" of the company. Italics supplied.

[91] And hence Irish law, being a pre-1922 decision of the House of Lords.

[92] He confessed to having read Hegel's *Phänomenologie des Geistes* 19 times, a feat unlikely since to have been equalled. For this and an account of his philosophical development and works, see A. Seth Pringle – Pattison (1928) Proc. British Acad. 405.

[93] For the history of the German idea, see Maitland's edition of Gierke, *op. cit.* 71. The organic theory has been adopted in the Civil Code of Germany (BGb, 32), and thence into the language of the First EEC Companies Directive.

[94] It is interesting to see the extent to which each judge in the leading modern English case *Tesco Supermarkets Ltd.* v. *Nattrass supra*, n. 85 depends upon Lord Haldane's original formulation. Lord Dilhorne is the least metaphysical.

victory has been won may be questioned, chiefly because it displays an undesirable tendency towards anthropomorphism. To ask who is the very ego and centre of personality of the corporation with a view to attributing fault to it is no more than to ask in two stages rather than one who within the company was lawfully in control of that situation. Attempts to relate parts of an organisation to corresponding parts of the human body was a medieval pastime,[95] and Lord Denning is its chief modern exemplar. In *H.L. Bolton & Co. Ltd. v. T.J. Graham & Sons Ltd.*,[96] Denning L.J. was required to find whether the intention of directors meeting informally could be imputed to the company, and said:

> "A company may in many ways be likened to a human body. They have a brain and nerve centre which control what they do. They also have hands which hold the tools and act in accordance with directions from the centre. Some of the people in the company are mere servants and agents who are nothing more than hands to do the work and cannot be said to represent the mind or will. Others are directors and managers who represent the directing mind and will of the company, and control what they do. The state of mind of these managers is the state of mind of the company and is treated by the law as such."

Such anthropomorphic conceits may seem innocent, but there is an artificiality in seeking to force complex and varying corporate structures into a uniform human mould; in particular a search for Lord Haldane's very ego and centre of personality of the corporation may prove fruitless where power is diffused throughout a company. Irish company law recognises that the functions of the various "organs" may be interdependent and differ from company to company.[97]

And so to criminal liability of corporations. Here again, an act or mental state will be imputed to a corporation if, upon analysis of its structure, it is found that the servant or agent who did the act in question was so in control of the situation under the corporation's constitution as to be identified in respect of it with the corporation itself. There is not at common law any general principle of vicarious

---

[95] Gierke, *op. cit.*, p. 24 "John of Salisbury [1115 – 1180] made the first attempt to find some members of the natural body which would correspond to each portion of the State . . . The most elaborate comparison comes from Nicholas of Cues [1401 – 1464], who for this purpose brought into play all the medical knowledge of his time."

[96] [1957]. 1 Q.B. 159, 173.

[97] See the discussions in Chap. 3 on the role of the managing director at pp. 90 *et seq.*, *post* and on the relationship between the general meeting and the board, pp. 85 *et seq.*, *post*.

liability for crime.[98] If however, as happens, a particular statute *is* so phrased as to impose a vicarious criminal liability on the principal or employer in respect of acts done by servants or agents within the course of their employment the employer or principal may be convicted for the act of another, and the fact that it might be a corporation is irrelevant.

Where *mens rea* is an ingredient of the offence, or as Denning L.J. put it in the *H.L. Bolton & Co. Ltd.* case *"where the law requires* a guilty mind as a condition of a criminal offence,"[99] its imputation to a corporation is now commonplace. But it was not always so. The evolution from a corporation's immunity from liability for crimes involving a mental ingredient to the present position occurred mostly abroad, but a stage in that evolution is marked in Ireland by the contrast between two Irish cases reported in 1906. In the first, *The King* v. *The Chairman and Justices of Antrim*,[1-3] no *mens rea* was required for the offence[4] with which the company was charged. Nonetheless, in holding that the company was capable of being convicted of the offence, the learned judges were most careful to emphasise that no intent or other *mens rea* was involved.[5] The judgments certainly exhibit grave doubts about imputing an intent to a company; yet, only a few weeks later in the same court in *The King (Cottingham)* v. *The Justice of Co. Cork*[6] these doubts were beginning to be dispelled. In that case, Palles C.B. said of a corporation that "it can be guilty of fraud, of malice, and of various criminal offences, some of commission, others of omission; some punishable summarily, others by indictment,"[7] and Johnson J. said "it may be made criminally responsible for most offences which are not punishable solely by imprisonment or corporal punishment."[8] In this remark, Johnson J. had in mind the futility of proceeding against the company where no effective penalty can be exacted; he must not be taken as meaning that the company is incapable of the offence.

---

[98] *Tesco Supermarkets Ltd.* v. *Nattrass*, [1972] A.C. 153, 199 (*per* Lord Diplock).

[99] [1957] 1 Q.B. 159, 173. Italics supplied. He was referring to directors and managers "who represent the directing mind and will of the company and control what they do."

[1-3] [1906] 2 I.R. 298.

[4] s.80, Irish Fisheries Act 1842 "no person shall . . . cause to run . . . into any river . . . any deleterious matter."

[5] At pp. 323, 327.

[6] [1906] 2 I.R. 415.

[7] At p. 423.

[8] At p. 427. A fine will usually be the appropriate penalty. In proceedings against a company for contempt of court the appropriate measure is an order, or conditional order, of sequestration: *Re Hibernia National Review* [1976] I.R. 388, 392.

The evolution towards full criminal responsibility was consolidated by three English cases in 1944: *D.P.P.* v. *Kent & Sussex Contractors Ltd.*,[9] *R.* v. *I.C.R. Haulage Ltd.*,[10] and *Moore* v. *Bresler Ltd.*;[11] and culminated in *Tesco Supermarkets Ltd.* v. *Nattrass.*[12]

Finally, two minds are necessary for a conspiracy. The mind of a controller of a company cannot be imputed to it with a view to making it a conspirator with him,[13] but the owner of the mind may be convicted of aiding and abetting the offence which he has caused the company to commit.[14]

Artificial schemes for the avoidance of tax

The emphasis is on the word "artificial." Over the last few decades, the practice has grown up among tax consultants of selling to their clients a "package," or, in the words of Lord Wilberforce in *W.T. Ramsay Ltd.* v. *I.R.C.*,[15] "a preconceived and ready made plan," involving a series of transactions for the purpose usually of creating a loss to set off against what would otherwise be a taxable gain. Such schemes are regarded by the participants as in essence one transaction involving a number of individual steps. Unfortunately for them, the English Courts are now taking the same view. They decline to follow each individual step: the genuineness or otherwise of these is not disputed, or, indeed, relevant. The purported multiple transaction is treated as one whole, after which "the taxpayer's position is precisely as it was at the beginning, except that he has paid a fee, and certain expenses, to the promoter of the scheme."[16]

Occasionally, companies are used as steps in such schemes; occasionally, other legal institutions, such as settlements or trusts, depending on the statutory provisions of which advantage is to be

---

[9] [1944] 1 K.B. 146 (intent to deceive of transport manager of respondent company imputed to it).

[10] [1944] 1 K.B. 551 (dishonest mind of managing director imputed to company for the purpose of convicting it of conspiracy to defraud).

[11] [1944] 2 All E.R. 515. (the intent to deceive of two persons, the one a branch manager and the company secretary and the other a sales manager at the branch, was imputed to the company).

[12] n. 99, *supra.*

[13] *R.* v. *McDonell* [1966] 1 Q.B. 233.

[14] *McMahon* v. *Murtagh Properties Ltd.* (High Court, Barrington J., unreported October 20, 1980).

[15] [1981] 1 All E.R. 865, 870 (H.L.).

[16] *Ibid.* 870.

taken. To the extent that transactions with companies are involved, they are perforce disregarded.[17]

Other categories

One would contend that there should be none. However, some years ago Professor Gower felt that he had detected "evidence of a general tendency to ignore the separate legal entities of various companies within a group, and to look instead at the economic entity of the whole group."[18] Such is the influence of this giant among commentators on company law that his assertion was adopted without investigation by Lord Denning M.R. in *D.H.N. Food Distributors Ltd.* v. *London Borough of Tower Hamlets*,[19] and thence has crept into Irish law as the proposition, according to Costello J. in *Power Supermarkets Ltd.* v. *Crumlin Investments Ltd.*,[20] that it is "well established . . . that a Court may, if the justice of the case so requires treat two or more related companies as a single entity so that the business notionally carried on by one will be regarded as the business of the group, or another member of the group, if this conforms to the economic and commercial realities of the situation."[21]

Such statements lay an axe directly at the main trunk of *Salomon* v. *Salomon & Co.*,[22] since the only connection which they require to be shown between the companies thus rendered equivalent is the fact that one controls a majority shareholding in the other.[22a] In particular, they do not require the subsidiary company to be as a matter of substantive law the agent of the holding company. Such a finding of actual agency is in fact quite common, as will appear, and is not inconsistent with the *Salomon* principle. It is not too much to say that these statements strike at the very root of the theory of corporations in these islands, namely that corporate status is to be granted only

---

[17] *e.g. Floor* v. *Davis* [1980] A.C. 695 (C.A.). Eveleigh J.'s dissenting judgment in this case was subsequently approved by the House of Lords in *W.T. Ramsay Ltd.* v. *I.R.C., supra.*

[18] *Principles of Modern Company Law* (3rd ed., 1969) p. 216.

[19] [1976] 1 W.L.R. 852, 860.

[20] High Court, unreported, June 22, 1981; Hannigan, (1983) 5 D.U.L.J. (N.S.), 111.

[21] At p. 8 of the transcript.

[22] [1897] A.C. 22.

[22a] For the holding of shares as the usual key to control, see Chapter 3: Internal Structure. For present purposes, companies may be considered as forming a "group" if they are under common control. For the holding company/subsidiary company relationship, see s.155.

by statute or prerogative act, and that the law does not seek to personify other group units simply because they behave as if they were separate entities, whether economic or otherwise.[23]

Fortunately, there was only scant evidence for Professor Gower's original assertion which has, perhaps, been taken by the courts further than he intended; and the contrary evidence is far stronger. Secondly, both *D.H.N.* and *Power Supermarkets Ltd.* were expressly decided on other, more conventional grounds as well. Taking these first, the *D.H.N.* case arose out of a defect since corrected,[24] in the English law governing compensation in respect of a business disturbed by the compulsory acquisition of land. Under the statutory scheme in force at the material time, one was entitled to compensation in respect of a business disturbed on land compulsorily acquired only if one also had a proprietary interest in that land. In *D.H.N.* a holding company owned the business and its wholly owned subsidiary owned the land. In upholding the holding company's claim to compensation, the judges were prepared to view it as being sufficiently one entity with its subsidiary to accord it a proprietary interest in the land,[25] but each judge also found by other routes that the arrangements between the subsidiary company and the holding company were such that the former held the land upon trust for the latter, thereby giving it an equitable proprietary interest sufficient to found a claim for compensation.[26] In the *Power Supermarkets Ltd.* case, the first defendant company had as the landlord of a shopping centre covenanted with the plaintiff as lessee of one the units in that centre effectively not to allow any person other than the plaintiff to trade as a grocery supermarket in the shopping centre. The landlord company subsequently conveyed the fee simple of another unit in the shopping centre to the second defendant company which intended to conduct a supermarket grocery business in it. Here then was a case which could be satisfactorily and simply resolved by the well established principles governing the burden of restrictive covenants running with land, and, indeed, Costello J. did so as a second-

---

[23] See pp. 17–18, above.

[24] See now ss.37, 38 of the Land Compensation Act 1973 [*U.K.*] *D.H.N.* may be regarded as a classic example of hard cases making bad law: it is better to amend the law of compensation than to twist the law of corporations.

[25] Goff L.J. at p. 468 took care to say that he relied on the particular facts of the case, and "would not at this juncture accept that in every case where one has a group of companies one is entitled to pierce the veil."

[26] *Per* Lord Denning M.R. at p. 467 (irrevocable licence giving rise to equitable interest); *per* Goff L.J. at p. 471 (resulting trust); Shaw L.J. at p. 473 (resulting trust). An implied equitable interest has long been recognised as sufficient to found a claim for compensation: *Ex parte Cooper, Re North London Railway Co.* (1865) 2 Dr. & Sm. 312 (proprietary estoppel founded on expenditure).

ary ground of his decision. The primary ground arose out of the fact that both defendant companies were wholly controlled by a third company (via wholly owned subsidiaries). To this situation Costello J. applied the broader dicta of *D.H.N.* to treat the three companies as one, citing as well, without analysis, three other cases which involved respectively a court's express discretion,[27] the construction of a managing director's service contract,[28] and the finding of a substantive agency relationship,[29] none of which were alleged to be material to the facts in *Power Supermarkets*. Indeed, the only substantive ground relied upon by the learned judge as justifying the application of the dangerous generalisations of *D.H.N.* was that the "justice of the case" so required. It is difficult to see how that condition, albeit nebulous, was satisfied in a case where the law already provided a satisfactory, conventional remedy for the plaintiff.

It is patent from Professor Gower's own work that he was not seeking to assert a proposition as wide as that drawn by Costello J., but a brief examination of some of the authority he relied upon in support of his "tendency" and of the stronger contrary authorities[30] then current, would be salutary. Of *The Roberta*[31] Professor Gower said[32] "a parent company was held liable on a bill of lading signed on behalf of its wholly owned subsidiary, the court saying that the subsidiary was 'a separate entity . . . in name alone, and probably for the purposes of taxation.'"[33] In fact, in that case there was uncontradicted evidence that the actual arrangement between the parent and the subsidiary was that the profits of the latter were treated as belonging to the former, or, in other words, the relation of principal

---

[27] *Scottish Co-Operative Wholesale Society Ltd.* v. *Meyer* [1958] 3 All E.R. 66, 71; (a case involving the court's discretionary remedy for oppression under the former s.210, Companies Act 1948 [*U.K.*]: see Chap. 9 *post*, and the "discretion" cases, *supra*.

[28] *Holdsworth (Harold) & Co. (Wakefield) Ltd.* v. *Caddies* [1955] 1 W.L.R. 352 (a case involving a service contract which expressly provided that a managing director of a holding company could be required to confine his attention to subsidiaries of it). See p. 90, *post*.

[29] *Smith, Stone and Knight Ltd.* v. *Birmingham Corporation* [1939] 4 All E.R. 116 discussed *infra*.

[30] This brief exercise is conducted by reference to the 1969, (3rd ed.) of his work, *The Principles of Modern Company Law* since that was the edition cited with approval in *D.H.N.* and which started the judicial development in Ireland. It is not being suggested that a reader of his work would not have been exposed to the full impact of the "stronger contrary authorities" then available. The relevant chapter in the 1979 (4th ed.) has been entirely recast. The original statement is no longer asserted as a proposition; it is merely recorded as having been adopted in *D.H.N.*

[31] (1937) 58 Ll.L. Rep. 159.

[32] *Op.cit*, p. 213.

[33] At p. 169 of the report.

and agent subsisted between them in respect of the business; secondly, the nature of the relationship was conceded by counsel rather than found by judicial determination; and thirdly, that relationship appears to have been governed by Dutch law, the attitude of which to the topic is scarcely material. Professor Gower said of *Spittle* v. *Thames Grit & Aggregate Ltd.*[34] that "the court found no difficulty in treating a subsidiary as 'to all intents and purposes' the same as the parent company which held 90 per cent. of its shares."[35] This was in fact an *obiter* remark made in passing, which has no bearing on the decision in the case. In respect of *Cory (Wm.) & Son* v. *Dorman Long & Co.*[36] "in which after judgment had been given against the parent company by reason of the negligent navigation by the master of the ship owned by its subsidiary, the parent company was held not to be entitled to limit its liability under the Merchant Shipping Acts, since it was not the owner or charterer by demise,"[37] it is important to note that the earlier judgment imposing vicarious liability on the parent company for the negligence of the master was made on the basis of an invitation by it to the Court to assume that he was its servant rather than the servant of the subsidiary, without apparently recognising the importance that this concession would acquire in the later proceedings to limit liability.[38] In *Re London Housing Society's Trust Deeds*,[39] an industrial and provident society had converted itself into a limited liability company under the special procedure contained in section 54 of the Industrial and Provident Societies Act 1893. The question was whether the trusts declared under the society's pension fund in favour of its employees continued in favour of them as employees of it in its new form. It was held on the true construction of the statute that the society had not in fact been dissolved, but rather continued in new form. The case is not therefore an example of a judicial "lifting of the veil"; it is merely an example of the application of express provisions of a statute. Other instances where statute has taken a hand to alter or subvert what would otherwise be consequences of separate corporate status are given at the end of this chapter. Professor Gower also drew upon *Merchandise Transport Ltd.* v. *B.T.C.*[40] where, as has already been

---

[34] [1937] 4 All E.R. 101.
[35] *Op. cit.* p. 213.
[36] [1936] 2 All E.R. 386.
[37] *Op. cit.* p. 214.
[38] See Romer L.J. at p. 392 of the report.
[39] [1940] Ch. 777.
[40] [1962] 2 Q.B. 173.

observed[41] the court was given by law an express discretion as to the result.

The reports abound in robust assertions to the contrary of whatever "tendency" might be extracted from the foregoing authorities. Most of these assertions come from cases where the court has been investigating whether or not a subsidiary is the agent of its parent (or holding) company, the holding subsidiary relationship being one in which the former is in a position to control the affairs of the latter.[41a] It is not unusual to find a substantive agency relationship between a company and its corporate controller, and doing so does not subvert the *Salomon* principle which states only that the element of control alone is not sufficient to found agency. Cases where the parent subsidiary relationship has afforded an opportunity for a genuine agency relationship over and above that of control include *Smith, Stone and Knight Ltd.* v. *Birmingham Corporation*[42] and *Firestone Tyre and Rubber Co. Ltd.* v. *Lewellin.*[43] In *Smith, Stone and Knight Ltd.*, another compulsory acquisition case, the question was whose business had been disturbed, that of the parent company or that of the subsidiary company in apparent occupation of the acquired premises? Atkinson J. said:

> "It is well settled that the mere fact that a man owns all the shares in a company does not make the business carried on by that company his business, nor does it make the company his agents for the carrying on the business. That proposition is just as true if the shareholder is itself a limited company. It is also well settled that there may be such an arrangement between the shareholders and the company as will constitute the company the shareholders' agent for the purpose of carrying the business and make the business the business of the shareholders."[44]

The facts disclosed an extreme case: the arrangement between the two companies was such that the business and its profits belonged as a matter of law to the parent company, and the profits had been treated as the parent's without there being any need for the declaration of dividend in its favour by the subsidiary this being the

---

[41] At pp. 30 – 33, *supra.*

[41a] A more precise definition is found in s.155. See also the seventh E.E.C. Companies Directive (83/349/EEC), Arts. 1–3.

[42] [1939] 4 All E.R. 116.

[43] [1957] 1 W.L.R. 464 (H.L.).

[44] At p. 120 of the report. Also cited was a strong statement to similar effect by Cozens – Hardy M.R. in *Gramophone and Typewriter Ltd.* v. *Stanley* [1908] 2 K.B. 89 at pp. 95, 96.

method by which the profits of a company are distributed, if at all, to its members.[44a] This finding was determinative of the issue[45]; so much was the subsidiary in all respects the agent of its parent company that had the parent company wished to carry on the business in its own name it "had but to paint out the subsidiary company's name on the premises, change their business paper and form, and the thing would have been done."[46] In the *Firestone Tyre and Rubber Co. Ltd.* case, an American parent company was concerned to deny for reasons of taxation that its United Kingdom subsidiary was carrying on its trade as its agent. However, the actual arrangements between them pointed to agency as the only conclusion. The United Kingdom subsidiary was to place the goods it made at the disposal of the American company, and was to sell those goods on the parent company's behalf to customers approved of by it and on terms laid down by it, and was to account to it for the proceeds of sale less costs of production and a small commission.[47] In a sense, the parent subsidiary relationship was extraneous to the decision; it provided an explanation of the arrangement between those two persons but was not part of it. If there are no such arrangements one is thrust back upon the "ordinary rules of law [under which] a parent company and a subsidiary company, even a hundred per cent subsidiary company, are distinct legal entities, and in the absence of a contract of agency between the two companies one cannot be said to be the agent of the other," *per* Cohen, L.J. in *R. v. South Wales Traffic Licensing Authority, ex p. Ebbw Vale U.D.C..*[48] For the courts to investigate the substance of the relationship between two persons in order to find, perhaps against their will, that they are principal and agent is not unusual and by no means peculiar to the relationship between subsidiary and parent companies. For example, the courts undertake such investigations to find out whether a partnership, a species of agency,[49] exists between two or more persons, and in doing so, seek the substance of the relationship and are free to disregard the label which the parties have put upon it. As Lord Halsbury said in *Adam v. Newbigging*[50]:

[44a] See Chap. 10: Capital and its Maintenance.

[45] Atkinson J. in fact elaborated a six point test, but on analysis only the first proves pertinent: "Were the profits treated as the profits of the . . . parent company?" (p.121). See *The Queen v. Waverley Construction Ltd.* (1973) 30 D.L.R. 3d 224.

[46] At p. 121 of the report.

[47] Contrast *John Towle & Co. v. White* (1873) 29 L.T. 78 (H.L.) (affirming (1871) L.R. 6 Ch.App. 397), where on significantly differing facts no agency was found.

[48] [1951] 1 All E.R. 806, 808.

[49] *Cox v. Hickman* (1860) 8 H.L. Cas. 268, followed in Ireland in *Shaw v. Galt* (1864) 16 I.C.L.R. 357.

[50] (1888) 13 App.Cas. 308, 315.

"If a partnership in fact exists, a community of interest in the adventure being carried on in fact, no concealment of name, no verbal equivalent for the ordinary phrases of profit and loss, no indirect expedient for enforcing control over the adventure will prevent the substance and reality of the transactions being adjudged a partnership . . . and no "phrasing of it" by dexterous draftsmen . . . will avail to avert the legal consequences of the contract."

Another illustration from a different agency context is found in *Customs & Excise Commissioners* v. *Pools Finance Ltd.*[51] where the conditions of business under which a football pool company operated stated expressly that its collectors acted as agents for the bettors and not the company. It was nonetheless held that the true relationship was the contrary, *i.e.* that the collectors were the agents of the company.

Thus, attempts by the courts to go to the heart of the matter in ascertaining the relationship between parent and subsidiary cannot be claimed as being in anyway special to company law, or, indeed as a species of "veil lifting" since the separate personality of each person involved is at all times acknowledged. In concluding this topic, another failed attempt to disguise the true relationship between the parties, this time involving companies not apparently in the parent subsidiary relationship, should be mentioned. This is *Re F.G. (Films) Ltd.*[52] in which the sole question was whether a particular British company had within the meaning of the Cinematograph Films Act 1938 made a particular film, the maker of the film being defined by section 44 of that Act as "the person by whom the arrangements necessary for the making of the film are undertaken." An American company held the film rights of a story, made a film of it at a cost of £80,000, and it provided all the money and all the personnel. Before doing so, it had taken the precaution of agreeing with the British company, formed for the purpose by an officer of the American company, that it would make the film for the American company but that the American company would do everything necessary for the making of the film, including the provision of finance and personnel, for the British company as a service. The British company had only £100 capital, no place of business and no employees. It is scarcely surprising that the court cut through this circular arrangement to find that insofar as the British company acted at all, it did so as agent of the American company.

---

[51] [1952] 1 All E.R. 775.
[52] [1953] 1 All E.R. 617; also [1953] 1 W.L.R. 483. Both reports are sparse.

Returning to the parent subsidiary relationship, one should, at the risk of gilding the lily, add that the parent company is not *per se* vicariously liable for the torts of the servants of its wholly owned subsidiary. This point arose and was disposed of in *The Queen* v. *Waverley Construction Co. Ltd.*[53] where through procedural mismanagement the plaintiff had been debarred from joining the appropriate party as defendant. Nor, in the absence of other independent grounds, does a parent company have an insurable interest in the assets of its subsidiary or vice versa.[54]

This then was the state of authority at the time of the *D.H.N.* decision. Those who in the interests of certainty in legal relations would wish the courts to resist the temptation to equate a company with its controllers simply through the element of control and in the absence of some other connecting principle may feel encouraged by subsequent events. The departure of Lord Denning, too ready to see controlled companies as "puppets"[55] of their controllers, is encouraging. So too is the attitude to the *D.H.N.* case shown by the House of Lords in *Woolfson* v. *Strathclyde R.C.*[56] on appeal from Scotland, and not mentioned in *Power Supermarkets Ltd.*, which can scarcely be taken as supporting Costello, J.'s view that the general propositions in *D.H.N.* are "well established." This was a claim for compensation for disturbance of business by the holder of 999 out of the 1000 issued shares in the company whose business had been disturbed by the compulsory acquisition. The claimant owned the freehold of part of the acquired premises outright, and the remaining part was owned by another company controlled by himself and his wife. The disturbed company had paid rent for its occupation to the claimant and to this other controlled company as its landlords. The claimant first proceeded on the ground that the disturbed company conducted *his* business as his agent, and then abandoned this proposition as unsustainable, and asserted instead the bald ground that the court should "set aside the legalistic view" that each participant in the arrangements was "a separate legal *persona*, and concentrate

---

[53] (1973) 30 D.L.R. 3d 224. The profits entitlement test of *Smith, Stone and Knight Ltd.*, n. 34, *supra* was used with some reluctance.

[54] *General Accident Corporation Ltd.* v. *Midland Bank Ltd.* [1940] 3 All E.R. 252, 255 (English C.A.) and see p. 23, *supra*.

[55] *Wallersteiner* v. *Moir* [1974] 1 W.L.R. 991, 1013: " . . . they were just the puppets of Dr. Wallersteiner. He controlled their every movement. Each danced to his bidding. He pulled the strings. No one else got within reach of them. Transformed into legal language, they were his agents to do as he commanded. He was the principal behind them." Buckley L.J., at p. 1027, and Scarman L.J. at p. 1033, were not prepared to agree.

[56] 1978 S.C. 90.

attention upon the "realities" of the situation, to the effect of finding that [the claimant] was the occupier as well as the owner of the whole premises." Lord Keith of Kinkel in rejecting, *nem. diss.*, this argument based on the principle supposed in *D.H.N.* of a single economic entity founded on total control said:

> "I have some doubts whether in this respect the Court of Appeal[57] properly applied the principle that it is appropriate to pierce the corporate veil only where special circumstances exist indicating that it is a mere facade to conceal the true facts."[58]

This chapter has attempted to indicate what those "special circumstances" are; they were not found in *Woolfson* in which, *per* Lord Keith, there was "no basis consonant with principle upon which on the facts of this case the corporate veil can be pierced to the effect of holding [the claimant] to be the true owner of the [disturbed company's] business or of the assets of [the landlord company]. The remedy for such claimants was legislative intervention, which has in fact occurred in the United Kingdom.

Also ignored in *Power Supermarkets Ltd.* was the very pertinent authority of *Gresham Industries Ltd.* v. *Cannon*,[59] decided by Finlay P. in the same court in the previous year. In that case, Finlay P. issued a warning against disregarding the separate legal personalities of connected companies and their controllers. He said in relation to a group of companies in common beneficial ownership:

> "It seems to me however a fundamental principle of the law that if a person decides to obtain and use the benefit of trading through limited liability companies and if for any purposes whether the limitation of his liability, tax purposes or otherwise he transfers assets from one company to another or makes drawings from one company and invests them in his own name in another company that he cannot subsequently be heard to ignore the existence of the legal entities consisting of the different companies and to look upon the entire transaction as a personal one."

More specifically he decided that a debtor could not set off against a debt owed by him to a creditor, debts owed by the creditor to a com-

---

[57] *i.e.* in *D.H.N.*
[58] At p. 96.
[59] High Court; July 2, 1980, unrep.

pany of which the debtor was the effective beneficial owner, saying that

> "as a matter of law even a 100% beneficial shareholder cannot for the purposes of the settling of an account between him and another individual or company be identified with the company."[60]

The informality had arisen in this case because the debtor had controlled the creditor company before it went into liquidation and through the liquidator brought claims against him.

Since *Power Supermarkets Ltd.*, McWilliam J. has observed in *Fleming* v. *Ranks (Ireland) Ltd.*[61] that there is "no legal distinction" between "inter-company debts between parent companies, associated companies and subsidiary companies" and those owed by a company to its ordinary creditors. There has also been the important decision of Carroll J. in *The State (Thomas McInerney and Co. Ltd.)* v. *Dublin County Council*[62] in which *D.H.N.* was again urged upon the court, though *Power Supermarkets Ltd.* apparently failed to achieve a mention. Both S1 and S2 were wholly owned subsidiary companies of a parent company in the property development business, which had in fact over 30 such wholly owned subsidiaries, operating through one or more of them at various sites throughout the country as circumstances demanded. S1 bought land for development, and had it conveyed to S2 which became its registered owner. S1 applied for planning permission which was refused. Consequently, S1 then served a notice on the Council requiring it under current planning legislation to purchase the land. Upon the Council failing within a statutory time limit to refuse to purchase, S1 sought an order of mandamus against the Council compelling it to buy. Unfortunately for S1 such a right, if established, exists in favour of "the owner" of the land. S2 was the owner: hence the invitations "to lift the veil," which Carroll J. declined. It is heartening to note that she confirmed that *Smith, Stone and Knight Ltd.* v. *Birmingham Corporation*[63] turned on a finding of substantive agency, not present in the case before her. Addressing herself to *D.H.N.* she said:

> " . . . the corporate veil is not a device to be raised and lowered

---

[60] Citations from pp. 19 and 22 *et seq.* in transcript.

[61] High Court; March 16, 1983, unrep. (at p. 9 of the transcript).

[62] High Court, December 12, 1984, unrep. Citations are from pp. 11 and 12 of the transcript.

[63] See p. 46, *supra*.

at the option of the parent or group. The arm which lifts the corporate veil must always be that of *justice*."

Justice was not a concept she elaborated upon, but seemed to find that its arm should not be lifted in favour of S1 was determined conclusively by the lack of a recognised legal relationship, such as trusteeship, agency or partnership, between S2 and S1 in relation to the holding of the land so as to give rise to a proprietary interest in it, or its proceeds. S1 and S2 appeared at most to be in the non-proprietary relationship of creditor and debtor, the intention being that the purchase money provided by S1 should be repaid in due course out of the proceeds of realisation. She said:

> " . . . it appears to me that here is a group of companies operated so as to maximise the benefits to be gained from the individual corporate identity of each subsidiary. If the purchase money was to be repaid out of the proceeds of realisation, it follows that the profits (or losses) remained with the registered owner. If the development was not profitable, the loss would be confined within the assets of that one company. . . . It is not for a corporate group to claim that the veil should be lifted to illuminate one aspect of its business while it should be left *in situ* to isolate the individual actions of its subsidiaries in other respects."[65–66]

One may conclude with a warning against the attractive but dangerous simplicity of the *D.H.N.* proposition. Impatience with the web that can be woven with corporations is understandable, and the careful analysis of it can be tedious, but an unprincipled tearing of it aside, a disregard of these separate persons created by the law can

[64] She added: "If justice requires (as it did in the D.H.N. case) the courts will not be slow to treat a group of subsidiary companies and their parent company as one" a somewhat enigmatic statement because "justice" certainly did require a remedy in that case in view of the alternative, more conventional grounds available. See p. 43, *supra*.

[65–66] Among post—*Power* v. *Supermarkets Ltd.* developments, one should note also a Consent Order made on April 23, 1982 in the *Kelly's Carpetdrome Ltd.* litigation (on which see p. 519, *post*), called the "aggregation" order. Assets bought with Carpetdrome's money by an associated company were treated as Carpetdrome's, because of the trusteeship nature of the transaction and not because of the association between the two companies which merely provided the occasion for it. For this Consent Order see *Byrne* v. *U.D.T. Bank Ltd.* [1984] I.L.R.M. 418. Noted also is *Re Bray Travel Ltd.* (Supreme Court, July 13, 1981, unreported). An interlocutory injunction was granted to the liquidator of a holding company freezing the assets of subsidiaries. The liquidator was seeking to recover those assets, or to unravel transactions concerning them, in current proceedings. The injunction seems therefore sustainable on usual *Mareva* principles. The court nonetheless approved Costello J.'s "economic realities" thesis which, was both unnecessary to the decision and given in interlocutory proceedings, carries little weight.

only be unhealthy. In the interests of investors and creditors, company law proceeds on the basis that duties are owed to these creations and a disregard of them by the courts can only encourage a similar disregard in others.

The corporation and Constitutional rights

A corporation can be the object of *duties* derived from the Constitution,[67] but the courts have hesitated at the prospect of according it constitutional *rights*. The Constitution is part product of the Natural Law[68] a system within which the corporation never found a home.[69] Nowhere does the Constitution recognise the existence of corporations.[70] In bestowing personal rights it has the purpose of protecting human kind. Take equality before the law. Article 40.1 is unequivocal. It says "All citizens shall, *as human persons*, be held equal before the law."[71] The other personal rights important to corporations are also drawn from Article 40, such as the right to the protection of property[72] given by Article 40.3.2°, and the right to a livelihood,[73] an unspecified personal right judicially created from Article 40.3.1°. These are conferred simply on the "citizen" without specifically requiring humanity. Of course it *could* be argued that a corporation being capable of bearing a nationality[74] is capable of

---

[67] *e.g. Educational Co. of Ireland Ltd.* v. *Fitzpatrick* [1961] I.R. 323; *Meskell* v. *C.I.E.* [1973] I.R. 121; *Glover* v. *B.L.N. Ltd.* [1973] I.R. 388.

[68] *e.g. McGee* v. *Att.-Gen.* [1974] I.R. 284, 310, 317 *per* Walsh J.

[69] Gierke, *op. cit.* at p. 99: "the domain of Natural Law was closed to the Corporation."

[70] Unless Article 44.2.5° can be said to create a corporate status for "religious denominations."

[71] Italics supplied. Walsh J. said in *Quinn's Supermarket Ltd.* v. *Att.-Gen.* [1972] I.R. 1, 14 that "under no possible construction of the Constitutional guarantee could a body corporate or any entity but a human being be considered to be a human person for the purposes of this provision". In *Abbey Films Ltd.* v. *Att.-Gen.* [1981] I.R. 158, 166 McWilliam J. was likewise unequivocal but in the Supreme Court (at p. 172) Kenny J. sidestepped the issue saying "It was argued that [certain legislation] was repugnant to the Constitution because its operation requires a company to retain a solicitor to act for it in proceedings . . . , while a citizen may appear in person. It was contended that this was a breach of the principle of equality before the law. . . . Even if Article 40, s.1 were to be held applicable to a company (which the court refrains from deciding) the nature of a company and its difference of capacity from that of an individual are such as would justify the implied requirement in the [legislation] that it should retain a solicitor to act for it." Art 40.1 expressly allows enactments to have "due regard to differences of capacity, physical and moral, and of social function." For the representation of companies before the courts, see *Battle* v. *Irish Art Promotion Centre Ltd.* [1968] I.R. 252, discussed at p. 23, *supra*.

[72] *e.g. Blake and Madigan* v. *Att.-Gen.* [1981] I.L.R.M. 34.

[73] *e.g. Att.-Gen.* v. *Paperlink Ltd.* [1984] I.L.R.M. 373.

[74] *e.g. Daimler Co. Ltd.* v. *Continental Tyre & Rubber Co. (G.B.) Ltd.* [1916] 2 A.C. 307 (nationality in accordance with place of registration), and see p. 35, *supra*.

being a "citizen" for the purpose of these protections, but this would lead to an odd and arbitrary distinction between these rights and the right to equality before the law which immediately precedes them. As Costello J. said in *Att.-Gen.* v. *Paperlink Ltd.*[75] the courts should not in the interpretation of the Constitution "place the same significance on differences in language used in two succeeding sub-paragraphs as would, for example, be placed on differently drafted sub-sections of a Finance Act. A purposive, rather than a literal approach . . . is appropriate."

We assume therefore that personal constitutional rights are conferred only on the individual citizen.[76] It is clear that such rights may be exercised through the medium of a corporation. Costello J. held in *Att.-Gen.* v. *Paperlink Ltd.*[77] that citizens "if they are actively engaged in a business carried on by a private company of which they are shareholders and directors then they are not merely investors in a company but are exercising a constitutional right to earn a livelihood by means of a company."

It is but a short step from this position to say that the constitutional rights of members must be vindicated in accordance with the manner in which they have lawfully chosen to exercise them, *i.e.* through the medium and for the benefit of the corporation. The courts have not yet, as we shall see, taken this step. To do so would vindicate also, as the courts are obliged to do under Article 40.3.2°, the property rights of citizen members arising out of their membership of the corporation.[78] Those rights cannot truly be vindicated

---

[75] [1984] I.L.R.M. 373, 385.

[76] One must read carefully in making any general remarks about the Constitution. Therefore let it be said that we are concerned here only with the actual possession of constitutional rights, not with the quasi *"actio popularis"* by which plaintiffs of whatever sort may, it seems, seek to impugn legislation whether or not they are personally affected by it, provided they have sufficient interest in the outcome of the proceedings. *E.g.* in *Quinn's Supermarket Ltd.* v. *Att.-Gen.* [1972] I.R. 1 a corporation in attacking legislation on the grounds of alleged religious discrimination did not, and indeed could not, claim that its own religious rights and liberties had been infringed. Secondly, by "personal rights" we mean, as does the Constitution, those set out in or derived from Article 40, and thirdly, only those of them capable of being enjoyed by a business corporation. (Habeas corpus guaranteed by Article 40.4.2° in respect of the body of "any person" cannot of course be enjoyed by a corporation). Of the succeeding "fundamental rights" in Articles 41 to 44, the family rights are clearly inapplicable to corporations, the educational rights are granted to parents and children, the religious rights to individual, religious denominations and institutions. (See n. 76a, *supra*), and Article 43 headed "Private Property" (obviously of importance to business corporations) has been held to create an institution not a right: *P.M.P.S. Ltd and Moore* v. *Att.-Gen.* [1984] I.L.R.M. 88 (Supreme Court).

[77] [1984] I.L.R.M. 373, 383–384.

[78] *Central Dublin Development Association Ltd.* v. *Att.-Gen.* (1973) 109 I.L.T.R. 69; *P.M.P.S. Ltd and Moore* v. *Att.-Gen.* [1984] I.L.R.M. 88.

without giving full expression to the corporate form the members have lawfully chosen to adopt and which is the inescapable premise of all their rights in or, in relation to it.

Instead the courts will protect a corporation against unconstitutional attack by indirect means. A *member* of the corporation may maintain an action on the ground that the property rights constituted by his membership will be indirectly injured if the corporation were to suffer. This was the expedient adopted by the Supreme Court in *P.M.P.S. Ltd. and Moore* v. *Att.-Gen.*[79] There the member alleged the unconstitutionality of legislation curtailing the activities of the corporation. The action was for a declaration. Provided the relief remains declaratory, insuperable difficulties do not arise, though the device remains clumsy. But suppose a member bringing such an indirect claim seeks and is awarded personal *compensation*[80] for loss suffered by his corporation through unconstitutional action. That would give rise to the danger of double indemnity. How could the courts safeguard the defendant against the corporation itself subsequently seeking redress against him for the same loss but on the basis of a different cause of action, not dependent on a constitutional right? Also, if the corporation subsequently became insolvent might not its unsatisfied creditors pursue the same defendant for the same unconstitutionality? There is also a problem of quantification. Essentially such indirect claimants are basing their entitlements against the defendant on their rights *vis-a-vis* the corporation. Those rights may have different priorities among themselves, *i.e.* creditors before members, preferential before ordinary creditors, *etc.* On an insolvency, or apparent insolvency, the worth of these individual rights can be quantified only when all have been processed in an orderly and systematic winding up[81] of the company, and certainly not as an incident of ordinary litigation.

The way round these and other potential absurdities is to insist that the corporation itself is the proper plaintiff in respect of unconstitutional conduct adversely affecting other persons in a legal relationship with it, and whose claims are based on loss suffered or loss which might potentially be suffered by it, and the proper beneficial recipient of the proceeds of such an action. This would be an essential first step in the process of vindicating pursuant to Article 40.3

---

[79] [1984] I.L.R.M. 88. See also *Att.-Gen.* v. *Paperlink Ltd.* [1984] I.L.R.M. 373, 381 in which the constitutional claim was maintained by directors and members of the company "it being accepted that the company [had] no constitutionally guaranteed personal rights on which to found a cause of action", and *East Donegal Co-operative Livestock Marts Ltd.* v. *Att.-Gen.* [1970] I.R. 317, 333.

[80] *Meskell* v. *C.I.E.* [1973] I.R. 121.

[81] See generally Chap. 16, *infra*.

the rights of these other persons in accordance with their respective entitlements, priorities and expectations, at the centre of which was the understanding that they had entered into a legal relationship with a corporation. Taking this step is not the same as saying that a corporation has personal rights guaranteed by the Constitution. The rights invoked would remain those of the members, or on an insolvency, those of the creditors. Company law already has a procedural device of this kind. We shall see in Chapter 8 that an individual member may by a process known as the *derivative action* invoke for the company's benefit a cause of action possessed by it.

Statute

Statute, within the Constitution, can do anything. The Companies Act 1963 itself provides examples of occasions where by statute the separate legal personality of the company is disregarded, or the liabilities of the company are imposed on its controllers. As instances, group accounts prepared by a company are required to deal with the "affairs . . . of the company and the subsidiaries dealt with thereby as a whole"[82]; any person responsible for carrying on the business of a company with intent to defraud creditors may be made personally responsible for its debts[83]; and if the number of members of a company is reduced to the statutory minima, members may be personally liable for its debts.[84]

Taxation statutes are fertile source of such provisions, usually, but not always, for the benefit of the Revenue. For the purposes of capital acquisitions tax a company controlled by a donee is "regarded as being itself a relative of the donee,"[85] and gifts taken by certain companies are deemed to be taken by the beneficial owners of the shares in the company.[86] One of the measures designed to counter the use of companies as a means of avoiding taxes on income provides that land held by a company shall be treated as disposed of if there is a disposal of a shareholding in that company.[87] A loss making company may surrender trading losses to another company in the same group for the purpose of giving the latter relief from corporation tax.[88]

---

[82] s.152(1). See Chap. 11, *infra*.

[83] s.297(1). See pp. 516 *et seq.*, *post*.

[84] s.36.

[85] s.16(3), Capital Acquisitions Tax Act 1976.

[86] *Ibid.* s.34.

[87] Pt. IV of the Finance (Miscellaneous Provisions) Act 1968, as amended by s.29 of the Finance Act 1981.

[88] Pt. XI of the Corporation Tax Act 1976.

Other Irish legislation anticipates difficulties arising out of the separate personality of companies. Notable was the Land Act 1965. This statute was designed to control the ownership of agricultural land and to ensure, with certain exceptions, that such land did not come into the ownership of unqualified persons, chiefly aliens[89-90] without the consent of the Land Commission first having been obtained. The Act equates occupation of land by a corporation with occupation by the beneficial owners of its shares, and requires relevant changes in the control of a body corporate to be notified to the Land Commission.[91] The Landlord and Tenant (Amendment) Act 1980 contains provisions designed to prevent the renewal rights of tenants in occupation being thwarted by a strict application of the theory of the separate personality of corporations. These rights remain unimpaired if the premises are in fact occupied under licence by the tenant's private company which has succeeded to his business, or by a tenant company's subsidiary company, holding company or fellow subsidiary company.[92]

Section 22 of the Consumer Information Act 1978 may be interpreted as providing that offences under the Act are only committed by a company if there is a relevant fault on the part of the lawful controllers of its management available to be imputed to it.[93] If the company is guilty, then its controllers in the sense above mentioned are also *ipso facto* guilty of an offence under section 19 as members of the "controlling authority" of the company with whose "consent or connivance" the offence was committed, or to whose "neglect" it was attributable. By a neat circularity these provisions first require the imputation of the controllers' fault to the company, and then impute that same fault from the company back to the controllers.

[89-90] Subject now to the requirement of non-discrimination against nationals of the other member states of the EEC. See now the Land Act 1965 (Additional Category of Qualified Person) Regulations 1983 [S.I. 1983 No. 144].

[91] ss.35, 45 of the Land Act 1965.

[92] s.5(3); *c.f. Tunstall* v. *Steigmann* [1962] 2 Q.B. 593, p.24, *supra.*

[93] *Tesco Supermarkets Ltd.* v. *Nattrass* [1972] A.C. 153, interpreting the equivalent U.K. legislation. See text at nn. 85 *et seq., supra.*

Chapter 3. Internal Structure

THE CONSTITUTIONAL DOCUMENTS

A company's constitution is made up of two documents, the memorandum of association and the articles of association.

Though former distinctions between these two documents have been eroded by developments in the law and practice, the basic distinction remains. The memorandum is the document by the registration of which the company is formed, and the articles constitute regulations for the conduct of that company, though even this basic distinction is occasionally somewhat blurred, as we shall see. Fundamentally therefore, the articles are equivalent to the deed of settlement of the old unincorporated deed of settlement company, and the memorandum to the document used to superimpose corporate status on it.[1] This basic rôle of the memorandum is spelled out in the Companies Act 1963. Section 5 says that persons may "by subscribing their names to a memorandum of association and otherwise complying with the requirements of this Act relating to registration, form an incorporated company . . . ," and section 18 provides that after registration of the memorandum and the issue of a certificate of incorporation "the subscribers of the memorandum, together with such other persons as may from time to time become members of the company, shall be a body corporate with the name contained in the memorandum, capable forthwith of exercising all the functions of an incorporated company, and having perpetual succession and a common seal. . . ."

The memorandum of a company limited by shares must state its name,[2] its objects,[3] its authorised share capital,[4] the fact that the liability of its members is limited,[5] and the fact that it is a public

---

[1] On this transition, see pp. 19–21, *supra.*

[2] s.6(1)(a), (b), as amended by 1983 Act, Sched. 1, para. 1.

[3] s.6(1)(c) as likewise amended. For the objects clause, see Chap. 4, *Objects.*

[4] s.6(1)(4)(a). For authorised share capital, see Chap. 10 *Capital and its Maintenance.*

[5] s.6(2). For the limited liability of members, see principally pp. 18–21 and Chap. 10.

limited company, if that is the case.[6] Forms of memoranda are prescribed by the Companies Acts.[7] These are the statutory minima, and every one of them is now as a result of piecemeal developments in the law subsequently alterable by appropriate procedures: the name[7a] by section 23 of the 1963 Act, the objects by section 10,[8] the authorised share capital by sections 68 and 72,[9] the limited liability of the members to unlimited liability under section 52 of the 1983 Act, and public limited company status to that of a private company by section 14 of the 1983 Act.

But the contents of a memorandum are not necessarily confined to these statutory minima. The subscribers may on formation include other provisions as well. Doing so has the purpose of "entrenching" them in the company's constitution, or, in other words, rendering them unalterable and enforceable for the life of the company.[10] Formerly this was done solely in reliance on the fact that the Companies Acts, although always allowing the members to alter the company's *articles*[11] never contained a general provision entitling them to alter the *memorandum*, and have indeed asserted the basic contrary rule, now contained in section 9 of the Companies Act 1963:

> "A company may not alter the provisions contained in its memorandum except in the cases, in the mode and to the extent for which express provision is made in this Act."

The whittling away of this general prohibition now extends not only to all the compulsory provisions, but also under section 28 of the Companies Act 1963 to all voluntary ones as well *except* those which the memorandum itself expressly declares to be unalterable or alterations involving "the variation or abrogation of the special rights of any class of members."[12] Entrenchment of rights therefore remains

---

[6] s.2(1) of the 1983 Act.

[7] s.16 and Table B in Sched. 1, and s.4(3) of the 1983 Act and Pt. I of Sched. 2 to that Act in the case of a public company limited by shares. Technical requirements relating to printing, stamping, attestation and signature are also prescribed by s.7.

[7a] See p. 13, *supra*.

[8] See pp. 137–142, *infra*.

[9] See Chap. 10, *Capital and its Maintenance*.

[10] On the enforceability of a company's constitutional documents as between members and the company, see principally pp. 161–169, *infra*.

[11] Now s.15.

[12] s.28(3), except to the extent authorised by the memorandum itself, or by a clause in the *articles* (present from first incorporation) purporting to allow the alteration of class rights contained in the memorandum: s.38(4)(a) of the 1983 Act, a further example of the erosion of the distinction between memorandum and articles. The remarks, *infra*, about the dominance of memorandum over articles must be read subject to this small point. For examples class rights, see pp. 169 *et seq. infra*, and for the protection of minorities in their alteration, see pp. 278–288 *infra*.

possible by appropriate draftsmanship. Instances where entrenching rights in this way might be considered could include the case of a person joining in the formation of a private company on the understanding that he was to be director for life but with insufficient votes in general meeting to prevent an alteration of the articles which could therefore not be relied upon to protect his position.[13] Class rights are less obvious candidates nowadays, since even if left in the articles they now attract the special protections in the alteration process introduced by section 38 of the 1983 Act.[14]

Entrenched rights may be altered only under a scheme of arrangement sanctioned by the court under section 201[15] or pursuant to an order of the court under section 205 (which expressly contemplates alterations to the memorandum) or, in the case of class rights entrenched by the memorandum, by agreement of all members of the company.[15a]

Little is now left of the original character of the memorandum as the charter or fundamental law of the company beyond the control of the members after registration, and, ironically, the only provisions of it which maintain this character are those which need not be there. From this former immutability[16] judges of the last century drew not only the *ultra vires* rule,[17] but also the notion that the memorandum was dominant over the articles,[18] the contents of which have always been under the control of the members. In this dominance has been found the justification for the principle that provisions which by statute ought to be in the memorandum cannot be governed by provisions in the articles.[19] Resort to a theory of dominance is not necessary to this conclusion, simply on the *a priori* grounds that one cannot look elsewhere for what compulsorily ought to be in the memorandum. The dominance of the memorandum over the articles does however have a legitimate rôle where provisions which could have been placed in the articles are put in the memorandum, and the articles contain, or are altered to contain, conflicting or inconsistent provisions. Here, on the existing case law,

---

[13] For life directors of private companies, see pp. 82, 91–92 *infra*; and for the alternative of loaded voting rights, see pp. 63, 101–102 *infra*.

[14] Discussed at pp. 278 *et seq.*, *infra*.

[15] Discussed generally at pp. 289–297, *infra*.

[15a] s.38(5), 1983 Act.

[16] Under the 1862 Act only the capital was alterable.

[17] See n. 4 on p. 112.

[18] *e.g. Ashbury Railway Carriage and Iron Co. Ltd.* v. *Riche* (1875) L.R. 7 H.L. 653; *Guinness* v. *Land Corporation of Ireland* (1882) 22 Ch.D. 349.

[19] This point arose in both the *Ashbury* and *Guinness* cases, n. 18, *supra*. And see n. 12, *supra*.

the memorandum dominates. In *Re Gilmour (Duncan) and Co. Ltd.*,[20] class rights of certain preference shareholders contained in the memorandum would if construed in isolation give them no right to participate in surplus assets in winding up,[21] but the articles were apparently more generous. The memorandum prevailed. Had the memorandum been found ambiguous, then the articles could have been called upon to resolve the ambiguity,[22] a relaxation, it should be emphasised, which only applies where the ambiguous provision was not one compulsorily required to be stated in the memorandum.

Sufficient, albeit slight, vestiges of the original rationale for the dominance of the memorandum over the articles, namely the unalterability of the former, survive for one to suppose that the theory is still to be treated as good law. Furthermore, it is reinforced by section 15 of the Companies Act 1963 which states that a company's statutory power to alter its articles is "subject to . . . the conditions contained in its memorandum." Thus, in *Hennessy* v. *National Agricultural and Development Association*[23] where the memorandum contained a prohibition against the alteration of the articles without the consent of a Government Minister, purported alterations of the articles without that consent first having been obtained were void.

Although the nature of the memorandum may have changed, the articles on the other hand still remain close to early descriptions of them. They are, as Bowen L.J. observed in *Guinness* v. *Land Corporation of Ireland*,[24] "the internal regulations of the company." Their chief functions are to define the manner in which the company's powers are to be exercised and by whom, and to describe the rights of the participants in relation to each other and the company.[25] A company limited by shares is not technically obliged to register articles on formation,[26] but they almost inevitably do. If they do not, then they are deemed by section 13 of the Companies Act 1963 to have adopted the model form of articles set out in Table A[27] in the First Schedule to that Act. If they do register articles, then section 13 further provides that the regulations of Table A will nonetheless apply unless expressly modified or excluded. In practice most com-

---

[20] [1952] 2 All E.R. 871.

[21] For a full discussion of rights to participate, see pp. 174 *et seq., infra.*

[22] [1952] 2 All E.R. 871, 874, citing *Angostura Bitters Ltd.* v. *Kerr* [1933] A.C. 550, 554 (P.C.). See also *Roper* v. *Ward* [1981] I.L.R.M. 408, 410–11, *per* Carroll J.

[23] [1947] I.R. 159.

[24] (1882) 22 Ch.D. 349.

[25] On the enforceability of a company's constitutional documents as between the members and the company, see pp. 161–169, *infra.*

[26] s.11, as amended by s.2 of the 1982 Act.

[27] Or those set out in Tábla A where the memorandum is in the Irish language.

panies limited by shares adopt Table A, or more accurately Part II of Table A which is designed for private companies and therefore most companies in the State, with modifications, some of them standard[28] and others specially suited to the circumstances of the company being formed.

Since Table A is not obligatory, its regulations are not general statements of company law, save where they reflect the contents of the Companies Acts. Nevertheless, most of the regulations in Table A have a long history, going back to the 1908 Act and beyond, and therefore, though they may not be law, a body of law has grown up around them as a result of their interpretation in the many jurisdictions possessing the British company law heritage. Objections to their occasionally archaic forms of expression may be considered outweighed by the certainty which their long use has brought to company practice. The fundamental objection to Table A concerns the almost total unsuitability of the company structure built by them, and indeed by the Companies Acts themselves, for the business with only a few participants. The chief defect in this regard is the requirement that these participants, perhaps only two,[29] owning between them all the shares in the company and each participating in its management, are required on different occasions and for different purposes to constitute themselves into two separate bodies, the general meeting and the board of directors. Despite the very slight amelioration introduced by Part II, Table A remains a vehicle suited to a large number of participants of whom only a few actually manage the enterprise. A company adopting Table A remains firmly rooted in its historical origins as the deed of settlement company upon which corporate status was imposed,[30] and never in law

---

[28] Modifications commonly made on the formation of private companies include standard forms purporting to relax the restrictions on share transfers contained in art. 3 of Pt. II (for this and its doubtful efficacy, see p. 193n *infra*); amending art. 22 so that share transfers need not be executed by transferees (see p. 197 *infra*); allowing resolutions described by s.141(8) to consist of several documents (see p. 77n, *infra*); deleting directors' remuneration from the category of "special business" in art. 53 (see p. 72 *infra*); liberating the directors' borrowing powers from the restrictions in art. 79 (see pp. 67, 158–159, *infra*); freeing directors from the obligation to retire and seek re-election at *a.g.m.*'s, whether retirement by rotation (arts. 92 *et seq.*) or the retirement of an additional director appointed by the board under art. 98 (see p. 82 *infra*); modifying art. 75 to fix the maximum number of directors at seven; providing for the creation of executive directorships in addition to that of managing director; and extending a company's lien on its own shares granted by art. 11 to include a lien on fully paid shares (see p. 318 *infra*).

[29] For the requirement that there be two directors, see pp. 78–79, *infra*, and for the statutory minimum of two members on formation of a private company, see s.5(1).

[30] For this evolution, see pp. 19–21, *supra*.

becomes the corporate partnership[31] which most corporate enterprises in the State in essence are. Much trouble flows from this artificiality, not least the neglect by the participants of seemingly pointless distinctions and procedures.[32] It is in fact possible within the framework of the existing Companies Acts to draft a new set of regulations suited to the "corporate partnership," but the most that is usually done in practice, and that rarely, is to provide on formation piecemeal protection for participants within the normal structure, for example, the constitutional documents might be drafted so as to give security of tenure to directors or a particular director, a right to appoint or remove one or more directors, a guaranted dividend policy, or a veto at board level on certain decisions (*e.g.* on increases in the company's borrowing, on the disposal of certain assets, on the lending of money to persons connected with the company, and on salary levels).[33] If an individual participant will not have sufficient votes (26 percent.) to block a special resolution altering the constitutional documents (under the procedures described below) so as to remove these and like protections, then consideration will have to be given on formation to entrenching them in the memorandum, or granting him "loaded" voting rights on any such resolution.[33a]

Britain is considering the introduction of a new form of incorporation for small firms[34]; in Ireland, where the small firm predominates, the prospect should be given some thought.

THE GENERAL MEETING

The members of a company express themselves through the general meeting. This body acts by means of resolutions, either *ordinary* or *special* depending on the circumstances. An ordinary resolution must be carried by a simple majority of the votes cast either in person or by proxy.[35] A special resolution requires at least 75 per cent. of the votes cast in person or by proxy to be in favour.[36]

---

[31] For partnerships proper, see pp. 18–20, *supra*, and for "corporate partnerships" or "quasi-partnerships," see pp. 95–96, 270, *supra*.

[32] And the abuse of them when fully mastered: *e.g.* pp. 91 *et seq.* (dismissal of directors), pp. 224–228 (allotment of shares), p. 187 *et seq.* (registration of transfers) etc.

[33] See also Young, "Agreements between shareholders relating to the operation of a small company," Society of Young Solicitors, Lecture 118; and generally Butterworth's *Encyclopaedia of Forms and Precedents*.

[33a] *e.g. Bushell* v. *Faith* [1970] A.C. 1099, and p. 101, *infra*.

[34] *A New Form of Incorporation for Small Firms*, H.M.S.O., February 1981, Cmnd. 8171. This Green Paper also briefly reviews the small firm in France and Germany.

[35] For voting, voting rights and proxies, see pp. 72, 105–106, 179–180, 182–184.

[36] A special resolution is fully defined in s.141(1).

The general meeting has little to do with the everyday conduct of a company's business. This function is by common form articles vested in the board of directors, and the extent to which the company in general meeting can interfere with it is explored, *infra*.[37] This delegation to the directors is generally expressed widely, such as in the common form article 80 of Table A which states that "the business of the company shall be managed by the directors, *who . . . may exercise all such powers of the company as are not, by the Act or by these regulations,*[38] *required to be exercised by the company in general meeting. . . .*" The apparent width of the italicised passage is in fact qualified by the words which immediately precede it. As O'Connor M.R. pointed out in *Re Galway and Salthill Tramways Co.*[39]:

> "that part of the section which gives the directors all the powers of the company subject to the exception must be read along with the opening words giving powers of management, and is merely in aid of the proper and effective exercise of such powers."

What then is left to the general meeting? Four, sometimes interconnected, functions may be found: first, carrying out functions specifically reserved to it by the Companies Act or by the articles; secondly, acting as a legislature for the company; thirdly, operating as a source of power within the company structure, and, fourthly, exercising as residual authority in the company's affairs.

Reserved functions

These are found throughout the Companies Acts and the articles, and will be discussed in turn as this book proceeds. A prominent statutory example is the requirement that there be a special resolution to precede an application to the court for a reduction of capital under section 72(2) of the Companies Act 1963; another is the requirement of a special resolution to authorise the giving by a company of financial assistance towards the purchase of its own shares pursuant to section 60 of the Companies Act 1963. Prominent examples drawn from the articles are the power of the general meeting under article 76 of Table A to fix the remuneration of the directors, and the general meeting's power under article 130 to grant or withhold approval of a bonus issue proposed by the directors.

---

[37] Under the heading *Powers of management and the relationship between board and general meeting, infra*, at pp. 85, *et seq.*

[38] Meaning respectively the Companies Acts 1963 to 1983, and Table A.

[39] [1918] 1 I.R. 62, 65; cited with approval in *Re Emmadart Ltd.* [1979] Ch. 540.

Legislative functions

By this is meant the general meeting's power to amend the company's constitutional documents. Chiefly, such legislation will consist of special resolutions altering or adding to the articles of association under the power given to the general meeting by section 15 of the Companies Act 1963; less frequently, there may be alterations of the objects clause of the memorandum by a special resolution pursuant to section 10 of the Companies Act 1963,[40] and special resolutions under section 28 of the Companies Act 1963 altering provisions of the memorandum which could have been placed in the articles[41]; and there are other instances.[42] All exercises of the legislative powers of the general meeting are subject to constraints, particularly where the individual membership rights of the members are affected.[43]

A source of power

The general meeting may be regarded as a source of power, in that those who command a majority of votes in general meeting will generally be able to control the composition of the board of directors. This proposition is subject to considerable qualifications in practice, discussed below in the contexts of the appointment of directors, their dismissal, and the maintenance of control.

Residual authority

This residual authority derives from what is now section 18(2) of the Companies Act 1963 which declares that after incorporation "the members of the company . . . shall be capable forthwith of exercising all the functions of an incorporated company. . . . " We have seen that the members give up most of these plenary powers at once by adopting an article, of which article 80 of Table A is typical, delegating the powers of management to the board of directors, and we shall see that after that delegation has been made, the general meeting usually cannot interfere with the way the directors manage the business.[44] To be certain of interfering in management, the general meeting would have to alter the terms of the delegation to

---

[40] See Chap. 4, pp. 137 *et seq.*

[41] p. 59, *supra.*

[42] Including s.23 (the company's name); s.68 (authorised capital); s.14 of the 1983 Act (re-registration of plc as private company); and s.20 of the 1983 Act (authorising directors to make allotments of shares).

[43] See generally Chap. 9: Minority Protection.

[44] See *Powers of Management and the Relationship between Board and General Meeting, infra.*

the board, and that would require an alteration of the articles by special resolution.

The residual authority is found in matters not comprised in this delegation. Five instances may be isolated. First, there is the rare case of an act which the company is capable of doing but which is neither an act of management, nor expressly reserved to the general meeting by the Companies Acts or by the articles. For example, a company may present a petition to the court for its own winding up on the grounds, among others of insolvency or on the "just and equitable" ground.[45] The Acts and usual articles are silent about who within a company must act on its behalf in presenting such a petition, and killing the company is clearly not a function of management. Accordingly, the task falls to the general meeting which may itself authorise the presentation of the petition, or, on usual agency principles, ratify the presentation of an unauthorised petition.[46]

Secondly, the delegation of powers to the board supposes that there is a board in existence. If there is no board, then the general meeting may exercise all the powers of the company, including those reserved by the articles to the directors, and may on behalf of the company ratify[47] in accordance with ordinary agency principles acts done by unauthorised persons on the company's behalf during this interregnum.[48] The general meeting is also competent during such an interregnum to "hold out" as being directors persons who have not in fact been appointed, and thereby clothe them with ostensible authority to bind the company in contract.[49] The general meeting may also act on the company's behalf in matters otherwise falling within the competence of the board when that body, though in existence, is unable to act because of a procedural deadlock among its members.[50]

Thirdly, where the directors have purported to do something on behalf of the company beyond the powers delegated to them, the

---

[45] s.213(e), (f). Presentation by the company itself on these grounds is rare; usually, a creditor will present on the first ground, and a member on the second. In fact, winding is usually accomplished by voluntary relations in general meeting (voluntary liquidation) without the intervention of the court. See generally Chapter 16: Winding Up.

[46] *Re Galway and Salthill Tramways Co.*, n. 39, *supra*; *Re Cannock Ltd.* (High Court, Murphy J., September 8, 1984, unrep.) but see McHugh (1985) 3 I.L.T. (N.S.) 93.

[47] For these ordinary principles of agency, see *Firth* v. *Staines* [1897] 2 Q.B. 70, discussed at pp. 156 *et seq.*, *infra*.

[48] *Ward (Alexander) & Co. Ltd.* v. *Samyang Navigation Co. Ltd.* [1975] 1 W.L.R. 673, 678–79 *obiter* (H.L., on appeal from Scotland).

[49] *Mahony* v. *East Holyford Mining Co.* (1875) L.R. 7 H.L. 869 (H.L. on appeal from Ireland), discussed at pp. 147, 150 *infra*.

[50] *Barron* v. *Potter* [1914] 1 Ch. 895; *Foster* v. *Foster* [1916] 1 Ch. 532.

general meeting may ratify, and thereby adopt, their act on behalf of the company on the general principle stated by Kenny J. in *Re Burke Clancy & Co. Ltd.*[51] that "it is established law that the members of a company may ratify acts which are outside the powers of the directors but are *intra vires* the company."[52] In *Re Burke Clancy & Co. Ltd.*, the directors had acted beyond a limit imposed by the articles on their power to borrow on behalf of the company.[53] A company in adopting such acts is not contravening its articles, since the articles place limits on the delegation of powers to the directors, and not upon what the company in general meeting might do. If articles were clearly to state that a particular transaction could not be entered into *by the company*, then the articles would have to be altered by special resolution before the general meeting could intervene to ratify an unauthorised attempt to bind the company to that transaction. For example, in *Boschoek Proprietary Co. Ltd.* v. *Fuke*,[54] the articles limited the remuneration of the whole board to £500 per annum, and therefore an attempt by the board supported by resolutions in general meeting to remunerate one director at £700 per annum failed. This case was followed by Gavan Duffy P. in *Towey & Others* v. *Irish Live Stock Exporters' & Traders Association Ltd.*[54a] in which he had to determine which acts out of the tangle produced by years of informality had been validly ratified, and which not. Thus, the election of a non-member to the governing body of the association could not be validated by ratification whilst the articles confined membership of the governing body to members only. And in upholding another ratifying resolution in respect of a different irregularity he recognised the distinction sought to be stated here, "the broad distinction between an alteration of the articles and resolution to ratify an internal act[54b] not in terms authorised by the articles."[54c]

---

[51] High Court, May 23, 1974, unreported, at p. 9 of the transcript.

[52] Following *Irvine* v. *Union Bank of Australia* (1877) 2 App.Cas. 366; and *Grant* v. *United Kingdom Switchback Railway Co.* (1888) 40 Ch.D. 135. An act *ultra vires* the company, *i.e.* beyond its capacity as ascertained from its memorandum is on the present authorities unratifiable: see p. 131, *infra*.

[53] Under the article in question, the borrowing could have been but was not authorised in advance by an ordinary resolution in general meeting. This fact was not, and was not seen in the judgment as being, material to the general principle of ratification discussed there.

[54] [1906] 1 Ch. 148.

[54a] High Court, December 3, 1941, unreported, at p. 18 of the transcript.

[54b] *i.e.* by the board.

[54c] He referred to *Gregory* v. *Patchett* (1864) 33 Beav. 595, 606; *Pickering* v. *Stephenson* (1872) 14 Eq. 322, 339; *Grant* v. *United Kingdom Switchback Railway Co.* (1888) 40 Ch.D. 139; *Dawson* v. *African Consolidated Land and Trading Co.* [1898] 1 Ch. 6.

One of the authorities cited by Kenny J. in support of his general proposition, *supra*, the 1888 decision of *Grant v. United Kingdom Switchback Railways Co.*,[55] must now be regarded as suspect in the application of the general principles enunciated in it to its own particular facts. These were a purported decision by the board *within* its sphere of competence, which was rendered invalid because the directors who had voted in favour were disqualified by the articles from doing so, being personally interested in the outcome. The English Court of Appeal upheld the effectiveness of a later resolution in general meeting ratifying the board decision, but would probably not have done so had the twentieth century idea that the general meeting may not under common form articles interfere in matters of management then been formulated.[56] With that development the choice of the general meeting would have lain between altering the articles to withdraw the delegation of the decision to the directors, or altering them to delete their disqualification; in either event, a special resolution would have been necessary.

Fourthly, there is the delicate matter of ratification by the general meeting of wrongs done by the directors to the company, referred to by Harman L.J. in the leading English case of *Bamford v. Bamford*[57] as "absolution and forgiveness of their sins," and in characteristically robust language as the ability of the general meeting to administer "a perfectly good whitewash." The wrongs include breaches of the fiduciary and other duties which a director owes to his company, and wrongful exercises by the board of the powers delegated to them, on both of which topics see Chapter 7: *Directors' Duties*.

The delicacy of the matter arises because this fourth category is in part disputed territory, and there are important distinctions to be observed in it. Primary among them is the fact that the general meeting cannot by a simple majority vote forgive or ratify the breach of an individual membership right; such rights are beyond the reach of collective decisions whilst the constitutional documents or statutes conferring them stand unaltered. For the nature, sources and extent of these rights, see Chapter 6: *Shares and Membership*. Another important distinction is the fact that certain wrongs done to the company, known in this book as "unratifiable wrongs," are not for-

---

[55] See n. 52, *supra*.

[56] On this later growth, *Powers of Management and the Relationship between Board and General Meeting*, *infra*, particularly *Salmon* v. *Quin and Axtens Ltd.* [1909] 1 Ch. 311. For attitudes contemporary to *Grant*, see *Isle of Wight Railway* v. *Tahourdin* (1883) 25 Ch.D. 320.

[57] [1969] 1 All E.R. 969, 972–3, citing *North-West Transportation Co. Ltd.* v. *Beatty* (1887) 12 App.Cas. 589 (P.C.). See also *Hogg* v. *Gramphorn* [1967] Ch. 254; *Nash* v. *Lancegaye Safety Glass (Ireland) Ltd.* (1958) 92 I.L.T.R. 11.

giveable, and the company may always maintain an action in respect of them, even at the instance of an individual member suing on the company's behalf by a process known as the derivative action. On this, see Chapter 8: *Enforcement of Duties.*

There is no conceptual difficulty in the general meeting having the power to forgive the consequences of a breach of duty, or, in other words, deciding that the company will not seek redress for the loss suffered by it, but there is such a difficulty in taking the matter a step further, as the English authorities clearly do, and allowing the vote in general meeting to ratify in the sense of *validate* a transaction which was voidable on the grounds that the exercise by the directors of their power to enter into it was tainted with impropriety. For would this not infringe the principle[58] that matters *within* the directors' powers are their own concern under common form articles, and beyond the interference of the general meeting? The answer one must suppose at the risk of some casuistry is that the directors in exercising their powers improperly were not acting *within* them, but outside the terms of the delegation of the company's powers to them, and have therefore opened the way to a ratification by the general meeting under the general principle stated by Kenny J. in *Re Burke Clancy & Co. Ltd., supra.*

Fifthly, the general meeting may release the duties owed by directors to the company in advance of any breach of them, provided that the anticipated breach was one which could have been ratified. On this topic, see Chapter 7: *Directors' Duties.*

Over both the fourth and fifth categories, and indeed over the whole conduct of a company's affairs, there hovers the ubiquitous section 205 of the Companies Act 1963 which is discussed on many occasions in this book, and particularly in Chapter 9: *Minority Protection.* This section permits the court to give discretionary relief to a member who has established that the powers of the directors have been exercised, or the affairs of the company conducted, in a manner oppressive to him or in disregard of his interests as member. Accordingly therefore, the fact that duties may have been released or conduct exonerated under the principles above mentioned is not necessarily the end of the matter. The supervening morality of section 205 may yet afford a remedy where strictly no legal rights remain.[59]

---

[58] For the extent that this principle holds good under Table A to the 1963 Act, see pp. 85 *et seq., infra.*

[59] It may also be chosen as a remedy in preference to the enforcement of legal rights. See Chap. 8, *post.*

Meetings

There are two types of general meeting, the annual general meeting (*a.g.m.*) and the extraordinary general meeting (*e.g.m.*).

A company is obliged to hold an *a.g.m.* once in each calendar year at not more than 15 monthly intervals, except that in the calendar year of the company's incorporation and in the following calendar year it is exempt from this requirement provided that it holds its first *a.g.m.* within 18 months of incorporation.[60] The duty of convening an *a.g.m.* rests on the directors, and failure can be visited with a default fine of up to £500.[61] The Minister for Trade, Industry, Commerce and Tourism may on the application of a member where a company has failed to hold an *a.g.m.*, direct that one be held.[62]

The directors may convene an *e.g.m.*,[63] and may feel the need to do so if there are functions of the general meeting, as described above, which they would like to see discharged before the next following *a.g.m.*, but there are also occasions when they are actually *obliged* to convene an *e.g.m.* They must do so when members holding at least 10 per cent. of the paid up share capital with voting rights, present them with a signed requisition demanding a meeting, and if they fail to comply the requisitionists may themselves convene the meeting[64]; and the directors must convene an *e.g.m.* when the company has suffered a severe loss of capital.[65]

A single requisitionist qualified to call a meeting may, even when it has been convened, be thwarted by the failure, perhaps deliberate, of other members to attend, since in that event there will be no quorum,[65a] and, indeed, no meeting which by definition requires the presence of more than one person.[66] In such a case, a solution may be provided by applying to the court under section 135 of the Companies Act 1963 for an order that a meeting be held at which "one member of the company present in person or by proxy shall be

---

[60] s.131(1), (2).

[61] s.131(6); fine increased by Sched. 1 to the 1982 Act.

[62] s.131(3)–(6). He may direct that one person present in person or by proxy shall constitute "a meeting." See n. 66, *infra*. There was an instance of the Minister's powers being used in 1982.

[63] Art. 50 of Table A; and *Angelis* v. *Algemene Bank Nederland (Ireland) Ltd.* High Court, Kenny J., July 4, 1974, unreported; at p. 5 of the transcript.

[64] s.132; the plural "members" of this section has in practice allowed the requisition of one member holding sufficient shares: *Re El Sombrero Ltd.* [1958] Ch. 900. Requisitionists' rights are further discussed at pp. 183–184, *infra*.

[65] s.40 of the 1983 Act. See pp. 182, 341, 371, 379–80, *infra*.

[65a] Table A, art. 54; Part II, art. 5.

[66] *Re London Flats Ltd.* [1969] 1 W.L.R. 711, 717–20 where the authorities are reviewed.

deemed to constitute a meeting."[67] The court's jurisdiction arises "if for any reason it is impracticable to call a meeting of a company in any manner in which meetings of that company may be called or to conduct the meeting of the company in manner prescribed by the articles" or the Act, and will certainly be exercised where a majority shareholder is being thwarted in his desire to hold a meeting by the minority.[68] The court will not exercise this power if no purpose for the meeting is adduced, or if the applicant commands sufficient shares to requisition a meeting without recourse to the court and the directors have not shown themselves unwilling to comply with such a requisition if presented: *Angelis* v. *Algemene Bank Nederland (Ireland) Ltd.*[69] The court's power is also used on those rare occasions where it is not possible in law for any participants in a company to convene a meeting themselves. Common form articles provide no means of calling a meeting where there are no directors and only one member.

General meetings may be summoned with varying periods of notice. Section 133 of the Companies Act 1963 provides for at least 21 days notice in writing of an *a.g.m.*, and for *e.g.m.*'s, a minimum period of seven days for private and unlimited companies, and 14 days for the rest. Common form articles reflect these minima,[70] as indeed they must since section 133 also states that any provision in the articles for lesser notice is void. Section 133(3) provides the only exception to these statutory minima. It allows all the members entitled to attend and vote at the meeting *and the auditors* by unanimous agreement between them to deem to have been properly called a meeting summoned at shorter notice.[71] Assumedly, such an agreement may retrospectively validate a meeting.

Further notice requirements relate to the business to be despatched by the meeting. These are imposed partly by statute and partly by common form articles. Section 141(1) of the Companies Act 1963 requires that there should be at least 21 days' notice of a general meeting at which a special resolution is to be proposed, "specifying the intention to propose the resolution as a special resolution." The special resolution will be invalid unless it is substantively identical to the intended resolution in the notice; differences in expression or form of the resolution as passed are immaterial pro-

---

[67] If no *a.g.m.* has been held the single member may have resort to the Minister's power under s.131, who may similarly provide that one person constitutes a meeting.

[68] *Re El Sombrero Ltd.* [1958] Ch. 900.

[69] See n. 63, *supra.*

[70] Table A, Part I, art. 51; Pt. II, art. 4.

[71] For further discussion of s.133(3), see pp. 75–76, *infra.*

vided notice of every matter of its substance was given.[72] The Companies Act 1963 also requires what it describes as "extended notice" to be given *to* the company where resolutions are being proposed *other than* by the directors either to dismiss a director under section 182,[73] or at an *a.g.m.* to appoint under section 160[74] an auditor other than the retiring auditor or that the retiring auditor be not appointed. Section 142 requires extended notice to be given at least 28 days before the meeting at which the resolution is to be moved, and requires the company to give notice of it to the members either with the notice of the meeting itself or, if that is not practicable, by advertisement. The period of extended notice gives the affected parties their statutory opportunity to tell their side of the story to the members.

Common form articles make a distinction between *ordinary* and *special* business, and require that the general nature of special business must be stated in the notice convening the meeting.[75] If a notice fails to do this, resolutions concerned with the special business will be invalid and ineffective.[76] Article 53 of Table A provides that all business transacted at an *e.g.m.* shall be deemed special, and all business at an *a.g.m.* save "declaring a dividend, the consideration of the accounts, balance sheets and reports of the directors and auditors, the election of directors in the place of those retiring, the re-appointment of the retiring auditors and the fixing of the remuneration of the auditors," to which under a variation in common use in Ireland is added also "fixing the remuneration of the directors."

Common form articles provide that the quorum for a general meeting of a public company should be three and for a private company two,[77] the minimum possible to constitute "a meeting."[78] Such articles contain also provisions relating to the conduct of meetings, such as the election and powers of a chairman, and the procedures for voting on a show of hands and on a poll, in person or by proxy.[79]

Articles usually provide that all general meetings of a company shall be held within the State.[80] Even if the articles do not provide

---

[72] *Re Moorgate Mercantile Holdings Ltd.* [1980] 1 W.L.R. 227, where the authorities are reviewed.

[73] s. 182(3). The dismissal of directors is discussed at pp. 91 *et seq.*

[74] s. 161. The appointment and reappointment of auditors 13 treated in Chap. 11, *Accounts and Auditors.*

[75] Art. 51, Table A.

[76] *Roper* v. *Ward* [1981] I.L.R.M. 408, 415.

[77] Art. 54, Pt. I of Table A; Article 5, Pt. II; and s.134(*e*).

[78] See n. 65, *supra.*

[79] Arts. 53 *et seq.* The rights of members at meetings are further discussed at pp. 105–106, 179–180, 182–184, *infra.*

[80] *e.g.* Art. 47 of Table A.

that the *a.g.m.*'s of a company be held within the State, any business transacted at an *a.g.m.* outside the State is declared by section 140 of the Companies Act 1963 to be void unless all the members entitled to attend and vote at the *a.g.m.* have consented in writing to its being held outside the State, or a resolution to that effect was passed at the preceding *a.g.m.*

Dispensing with formalities

Before the Companies Act 1963, it was clear that members of a company might, if unanimous, act together to achieve any result attainable by the company in general meeting without the necessity of constituting themselves into a general meeting. The process began with some remarks in *Salomon's Case*[81] on the effectiveness of the consent of all the initial members of the company to release the fiduciary duties owed to it by its promoters.[82] The development continued by way of *Re Express Engineering Works Ltd.*[83] in which the promoters who held all the shares in the new company and were its directors purported to give effect to their arrangements with it by a board resolution in unconscious defiance of an article[84] which prohibited directors from voting as such in respect of contracts in which they were personally interested. Since all shareholders assented to the resolution, albeit in their character as directors, and were as shareholders competent to validate it,[85] the transaction was upheld. In *Re Oxted Motor Co.*,[86] the only two members of a company met and passed a resolution that the company should be voluntarily wound up, and signed a minute to that effect. The Companies (Consolidation) Act 1908[87] provided that such resolutions for voluntary winding up should be *extraordinary* resolutions, since abolished in Ireland,[88] which required not only a three-fourths majority but also a period of notice. No such notice was given, but nonetheless the resolution was upheld, since it was competent for all the shareholders acting together to waive the formalities prescribed by the Act. In *Parker & Cooper Ltd.* v. *Reading*,[89] certain formal defects, readily curable by a ratifying resolution by the company in general meeting,[90]

---

[81] [1897] A.C. 22, 57, *per* Lord Davey.
[82] On this fiduciary duty, and its release, see pp. 389–390, *infra*.
[83] [1920] 1 Ch. 466.
[84] See now art. 84 of Pt. I of Table A, and the contrary art.7 of Pt. II.
[85] *e.g.* by altering the articles, and see the discussion of ratification at pp. 66–69, *supra*.
[86] [1921] 3 K.B. 32.
[87] s.182(3) of the 1908 Act; now s.251(*b*) which requires a special resolution.
[88] s.141(6).
[89] [1926] Ch. 975.
[90] See pp. 66 *et seq.*, *supra*.

had occurred in the granting by the directors of a debenture to a third party. However, all the members had individually and informally consented to the transaction at different times, and those consents were held sufficient to ratify it, despite the absence of any resolution or any meeting. The principle was accepted as "settled law" in 1951 by the Supreme Court in *Buchanan Ltd* v. *McVey*,[90a] the only qualifications being that the transaction be neither *ultra vires*,[90b] nor dishonest.

The principle was sufficiently advanced to attract legislative recognition in Britain in section 118 of the Companies Act 1929 which extended the existing law requiring publication of special and extraordinary resolutions to include also:

> "resolutions which have been agreed to by all the members of a company, but which, if not so agreed to, would not have been effective for their purpose unless, as the case may be, they have been passed as special resolutions or as extraordinary resolutions."[91]

This requirement was carried forward into the British 1948 Act, and prompted the Jenkins Committee to recommend "that the position should be clarified and that there should be an express provision in the Act that a resolution in writing *signed* by or on behalf of all those who would have been entitled to vote upon it at a general meeting shall be equivalent to a special or ordinary resolution (as the case may require) passed by the appropriate majority at a general meeting convened by the appropriate notice."[92]
Britain did not follow this recommendation but Ireland has. The Companies Act 1963 not only imported the requirement that such resolutions be published,[93] but also introduced the recommended clarification, of which there may be some doubt. Section 141(8) states:

> "(a) Notwithstanding anything to the contrary in this Act, in any case in which a company is so authorised by its articles,[94] *a*

[90a] [1954] I.R. 89, 118, affirming Kingsmill Moore J. at pp. 96–97. Gavan Duffy P. had previously accepted the principle in *Re S.M. Barker Ltd.* [1950] I.R. 123, 135–7.

[90b] *i.e.* beyond the company's capacity (see Chap. 4: *Objects*), or an act prohibited by law (*e.g.* an unlawful reduction of capital on which see Chap. 10: *Capital and its Maintenance*).

[91] s.118(4)(*d*) of the Companies Act 1949 [U.K.].

[92] Paras. 460, 468(*d*).

[93] s.134(4)(*b*): "resolutions which have been agreed by all the members of a company, but which, if not so agreed to, would not have been effective for their purpose unless they had been passed as special resolutions." s.143(4)(*c*) contains similar provisions in respect of "resolutions or agreements" by a class of shareholders.

[94] *e.g.* art. 6 of Part II of Table A.

resolution in writing signed by all the members for the time being[95]
entitled to attend and vote on such resolution at a general meeting . . . shall be as valid and effective for all purposes as if the
resolution had been passed at a general meeting of the company
duly convened and held, and if described as a special resolution
shall be deemed to be a special resolution within the meaning of
this Act. (b) Any such resolution shall be deemed to have been
passed at a meeting held on a date on which it was signed by
the last member to sign, and where the resolution states a date
as being the date of his signature thereof by any member the
statement shall be *prima facie* evidence that it was signed by him
on that date."[96]

The question immediately arises whether this purported clarification has in fact cut down the principle as stated in the cases by
reducing it to instances where the members have signified their
assent in writing? Must the written document actually describe itself
as a "resolution" or a "special resolution," as the case may be? That
result will follow if the courts construe section 141(8) as having been
directed towards the existing case law, as the Jenkins Committee
intended. In *Fitzpatrick* v. *Fitzpatricks Footwear Ltd.*,[97] Kenny J.
decided that "it is permissible to look at the reports of committees
on the reform of company law to see what was the object the
draftsman of the Act had in view." In that case Kenny, J. construed the obscure section 199 of the Companies Act 1963 by reference to the intentions of the Greene Committee which had
recommended the introduction of the equivalent British provision
many years before. If this method of construction is followed, the
pre-1964 case law which included the possibility of oral assents
must be viewed as having been curtailed.

Furthermore, the English decisions were arrived at on the basis
that it is within the competence of all members to dispense with the
statutory requirements about the length of notice for the calling of
meetings. Section 133 of the Companies Act 1948 [*U.K.*] lays down
minimum periods of notice for the calling of general meetings, but

---

[95] Italics supplied.
[96] s.141(8)(c) provides that this procedure does not apply to the appointment or
removal of auditors (s.160) or the dismissal of directors (s.182).
[97] High Court, November 18, 1970, unreported, at p. 8 of the transcript; following
Lord Halsbury in *Eastman Photographic Materials Co. Ltd.* v. *Comptroller General &
Patents* [1898] A.C. 571, 576, an instance of the "mischief" rule. For a broader basis of
recourse to extra-statutory material as an aid to the construction of legislation see
Wavin Pipes Ltd. v. *Hepworth Iron Co. Ltd.*, High Court, May 8, 1981, Costello J.; (1982)
8 Fleet Street Reports 32; discussed by Casey, (1981) D.U.L.J. 110.

by section 133(3) allows in the case of *a.g.m.*'s all members entitled to attend and vote to act together to waive this requirement, and for *e.g.m.*'s the holders of 95 per cent. of the shares with voting rights are given a similar collective right of waiver. In Ireland, it is *not* within the competence of the members alone to dispense with these minimum notice requirements. The equivalent section 133(3) of the Companies Act 1963 allows a general meeting to be called at shorter notice *only if* "it is so agreed *by the auditors* of the company and by all the members entitled to attend and vote thereat," another 1963 innovation.

An alternative construction regarding section 141(8) as being merely facultative, and as not excluding other methods of arriving at collective decisions, seems in these circumstances to be untenable.

Certainly, the restrictive interpretation, if adopted, would cut a swathe through the English case law, of which the three prominent recent examples are *Re Duomatic Ltd.*,[98] *Re Horsley & Weight Ltd.*[99] and *Cane* v. *Jones*.[1] In *Re Duomatic Ltd.*, directors caused themselves to be paid remuneration without obtaining the formal approval of the general meeting as required by common form articles.[2] For one of the years in question, two directors who were also the only shareholders with voting rights[3] signed the accounts which showed the remuneration. That was regarded as tantamount to a resolution in general meeting approving the remuneration, but whether it would suffice also in Ireland is questionable since section 141(8) requires not only writing and signatures but also, apparently, a document in the form of a resolution. In a later year the accounts were not drawn up or approved, but all the voting shareholders, of whom there were now more than two, had informally agreed that a particular director could draw by way of remuneration up to a certain sum per week. That again was held to be sufficient authorisation, but would not suffice as a resolution in Ireland under a restrictive interpretation of section 141(8), since the understanding was neither in writing nor signed. In *Re Horsley & Weight Ltd.*, the sole shareholders of a company, who were also two out of its five directors, caused it to take out a pension policy for a retiring employee. In doing so, they acted

---

[98] [1969] 2 Ch. 365.

[99] [1982] 3 All E.R. 1045, 1055.

[1] [1981] 1 W.L.R. 1451.

[2] *e.g.* art. 76 of Table A.

[3] There was no need to obtain the consent of a preference shareholder who had no voting rights, but the consent of *all* voting shareholders, however small their holdings, and even if they are only nominees for assenting members must be obtained for the principle to operate: *E.B.M. Co. Ltd.* v. *Dominion Bank* [1937] 3 All E.R. 555, 561–2, 566 (P.C.).

without the necessary authority of a board resolution, but the defect could have been remedied by a ratifying resolution by the company in general meeting. The company went into liquidation without this resolution having been passed, and the liquidator claimed the benefit of the policy. He failed because the company's only shareholders had themselves done everything necessary to effect the policy, and therefore obviously assented to the transaction. These acts consisted of signing a proposal form and a cheque. Since neither of these documents purported to be a resolution it is likely that in Ireland the liquidator would have won on restrictive interpretation of section 141(8).[4] In *Cane* v. *Jones,* there was a written shareholders' agreement between all the members and signed by them that the chairman for the time being should have no casting vote at board or general meetings. The articles[5] provided that he should. This shareholders' agreement was held to have altered the articles, despite not expressly purporting to do so, on the "basic principle of company law that all corporators, acting together, can do anything which is intra vires the company," the more usual special resolution procedure[6] being regarded merely as a method whereby *some* only of the members could combine to alter the articles.[7] In Ireland section 141(8) would not have given the shareholders' agreement the status of a special resolution altering the articles since it was not "described as a special resolution" as required by that provision.

Although the extent to which the principle under discussion has survived section 141(8) has not been discussed in the Irish courts, a partial way round the problem posed by it may already have been found. In *Re Greenore Trading Co. Ltd.,*[8] the petitioner alleged that an issue of the company's shares to the respondent was invalid on the grounds that various technicalities had been disregarded, *viz.* the allotment was made by the general meeting instead of by the board of directors as provided by the articles; the allotment increased his shareholding above the maximum laid down in the articles; and it involved an increase in the company's capital without a special resolution to that effect having been passed. All members of the com-

---

[4] A standard modification in current use in Ireland of art. 6 of Pt. II of Table A purports to allow resolutions in writing within s.141(8) "to consist of several documents in the like form each signed by one or more of the members." This seems permissible provided that each document states that it is only one of a series to be construed as one resolution.

[5] Likewise arts. 61 and 107 of Table A.

[6] s.15, p. 65, *supra.*

[7] [1981] 1 W.L.R. 1451, 1452.

[8] High Court, Keane J. March 28, 1980, unreported; the comment by Ussher, (1981) D.U.L.J. 79 is misconceived insofar as it does not take account of legislative differences in Ireland.

pany were represented at the general meeting in question, and agreed to the allotment either in person or by attorney. The allotment was not challenged by the petitioner until long afterwards. In those circumstances, Keane J. decided that:

> "The Petitioner is clearly estopped in my opinion, from asserting the irregularities of a transaction which he tacitly approved of when it was being implemented, which does not offend against any principle of law and which was entirely for the benefit of the company and indeed its creditors."[9]

The learned judge did not advert to the line of authority under discussion, nor to the possibility that the assent might in fact constitute a resolution, but as between members the result of his decision was much the same. The weakness of an estoppel lies in the fact that it is not necessarily binding upon persons not party to it, such as a liquidator or receiver. In *Re Duomatic Ltd.*,[10] for example, the liquidator's claim to recover the remuneration paid without authority was defeated because the assent of the members had the force of the enabling resolution required by the articles. Had the members merely been estopped, it is difficult to see the liquidator could have been prevented from recovering from the recipient directors.[11] Consequently, the precise categorisation of the effect of the unanimous consent of the members is no mere academic exercise; it is of particular importance to that large body of Irish companies in which the niceties of company law do not enter into the participants' list of priorities.

THE BOARD OF DIRECTORS

Composition

Every company must have at least two directors.[12] The "one man company" is not possible in Ireland. Both the Cox[13] and the Jenkins Committees recommended this minimum of two. The Jenkins Com-

---

[9] At p. 17 of the transcript.

[10] [1969] 2 Ch. 365.

[11] Keane J. is by no means alone in viewing members' informal assents as founding an estoppel rather than a resolution. Buckley J. took a similar line in *Re Pearce, Duff & Co.* [1960] 1 W.L.R. 1014, 1016, the Privy Council likewise in *E.B.M. Ltd.* v. *Dominion Bank* [1937] 3 All E.R. 555, 556. In *Re Bailey, Hay & Co. Ltd.* [1971] 1 W.L.R. 1357, on the other hand, knowing acquiescence by members in the implementation of a defective resolution, was interpreted as an assent to it, thereby giving it the status of a resolution.

[12] s.174.

[13] 1958 Pr. 4523.

mittee felt "that a minimum requirement of two directors might . . . help to check the present spate of irresponsible incorporations" by which was meant companies which soon after incorporation became defunct.[14] The Cox Committee did not disclose its reasons. It is by no means obvious that the adoption of this measure in Ireland discouraged "irresponsible incorporations." Every year, a significant number of companies are struck off by the registrar under the section 311 procedure for not carrying on business.[15] In many small companies only one person is the effective proprietor, and to force upon him a cypher as second director is artificial. Whatever its effect upon irresponsible incorporations, this measure certainly proliferates directors who do not expect to be responsible. We consider the duties of individual directors in Chapter 7. Here it is enough to cite some general remarks of Carroll J. in *Re Hunting Lodges Ltd.*[15a] where she said of a wife, a nominal second director in a company *de facto* directed by her husband, that she:

> "cannot evade liability by claiming that she was only concerned with minding her house and looking after her children. If that was the limit of the responsibilities she wanted, she should not have become a director of the company, or having become one she should have resigned. . . . Any person who becomes a director takes on responsibilities and duties, particularly where there are only two . . . A director who continues as a director but abdicates all responsibility is not lightly to be excused."

If this be the law, then in the realities of life the nominal second director will either be in an impossible position, or impossible to obtain. Some companies by their articles purport to legislate all directors save the one driving force into the position of lawful cyphers by putting them in all respects under his or her control and giving him or her all the powers of the directors,[15b] whether they would truly be directors within the meaning of the 1963 Act is open to question. In other companies, the less extreme expedient of mak-

[14] Cmnd. 1749, paras. 20, 25. The measure was also designed to resolve difficulties arising on the death of a sole director.

[15] This is determined by their failure to answer his letter of enquiry. 780 companies were struck off under s.311 in 1981, 833 in 1982 and 974 in 1983. The numbers of companies entering members' voluntary liquidation are also an indication: 405 in 1981, 584 in 1982 and 475 in 1983. s.311 was slightly amended by s.11 of the 1982 Act. These statistics are given in the annual Companies Reports issued by the Department of Industry, Trade, Commerce and Tourism and its predecessors.

[15a] [1985] I.L.R.M. 75.

[15b] See *Re Westwinds Holding Co. Ltd.* (High Court, Kenny J., May 21, 1974, unreported) and *Fitzpatrick* v. *Fitzpatricks Footwear Ltd.* (High Court, Kenny J, November 18, 1970, unreported).

ing the driving force managing director with sole responsibility for managing the company's business is adopted. See *The Managing Director, infra.*[16]

A company director is not required to possess any qualifications. Many company directors do not have any notion of the fiduciary nature of their office, or of the restraints upon their conduct which company law seeks to impose for the protection of shareholders and creditors, some of whose sufferings might well be avoided if controllers of companies were required to know a little of what the law expects of them. As it is, the Companies Acts provide only ineffectual machinery for the disqualification of the obviously unsuitable potential director, rather in the manner of a Road Traffic Act requiring that the competence of drivers be assessed only after their first crash. Section 184 of the Companies Act 1963 is the relevant provision. It allows the Director of Public Prosecutions to intervene at the close of the trial of any person convicted on indictment "of any offence in connection with the promotion, formation or management of a company or any offence involving fraud or dishonesty whether in connection with the company or not" to apply for an order disqualifying that person from being a director or taking any part whether direct or indirect, in the management of any company for a fixed period. Since such prosecutions are about as common as the Irish elk, this provision is not in practice used.[17] Civil proceedings brought in the course of the winding up of a company are marginally more fruitful. Where a company is being wound up, section 184 allows the liquidator, any member or past member, or any creditor to apply for an order similarly disqualifying any person who has been guilty (whether convicted or not) of the offence under section 297 of carrying on the business of the company with intent to defraud creditors, or "has otherwise been guilty, while an officer of the company, of any fraud in relation to the company or of any breach of his duty to the company." At the conclusions of the fraudulent trading proceedings in *Re Kelly's Carpetdrome Ltd.*,[18] two respondents were on the application of the liquidator disqualified for five years. One of them, it should be noted, had held no official position in the company. The equivalent British provisions[19] have been

---

[16] For further discussion see the consultative document "A New Form of Incorporation for Small Firms" Dept of Trade U.K., February 1981, Cmnd. 8171.

[17] See p. 517n, *post.*

[18] High Court, Costello J., July 1, 1983, unreported. For fraudulent trading, see pp. 516 *et seq., post.*

[19] s.188 of the Companies Act 1948 [U.K.] as amended by s.93 of the Companies Act 1981 [U.K.]. Also, a public register of disqualified persons was established by s.29 of the Companies Act 1976 [U.K.].

much expanded and now include in particular the possibility of disqualification in respect of a company's failure to make to the Registrar the returns required by law.[20]

It is a criminal offence for an undischarged bankrupt to act as a director of a company.[21]

A body corporate cannot be a director of a company,[22] the object being to prevent the individuals responsible for the affairs of a company from sheltering behind a further corporate facade.[23] In particular, a body corporate acting as director of another company could from time to time delegate responsibility for that company to different individuals without the public being aware of the changes.

There appears to be no general principle of law that the members of the governing body of a corporation should also be members of the corporation.[24] In the case of a modern registered company, the Companies Acts require a share qualification for directors only where the articles of the company stipulate one. The common form article 77 of Table A does not require a share qualification unless the general meeting by ordinary resolution adopts one. If a director fails to obtain his qualification shares within two months after his appointment (or such shorter time as may be fixed by the articles), or if he later loses them, he automatically ceases to be a director of the company, and is not capable of becoming one until he obtains the necessary shares.[25]

Appointment of directors

Before the coming into force of section 3 of the Companies (Amendment) Act 1982, the first directors of a company were commonly named in and appointed by its articles, though this was not obligatory. Section 3 now provides for the delivery to the Registrar of particulars of the first directors as part of the formation process, and these individuals become the first directors on incorporation, regardless of what the articles may say. Subsequent appointments

---

[20] In Ireland, the company may be struck off by the registrar for failure to make annual returns: s.12 of the 1982 Act. For the annual return, see p. 444, *post*.

[21] s.183; the penalties include imprisonment and a fine of up to £2500 (fine increased by s.15 of the 1982 Act).

[22] s.176.

[23] Jenkins Committee 1962, Cmnd 1749, para. 84, following the Patton Committee on Company Law Amendment in Northern Ireland.

[24] *R.* v. *Grout* (1830) 1 B & Ad. 104; 109 E.R. 725.

[25] s.180. See also s.179 which, since it does not apply to private companies or companies which were private before becoming public, can seldom have been applied in Ireland in recent years.

are governed by the articles. Table A[26] provides for re-election by the general meeting following retirement by rotation, and for the filling of casual vacancies and the appointment of additional directors both by the general meeting and by the board. This regime is not necessarily suitable for companies with few participants. In such companies, the requirement that directors retire by rotation and stand for re-election is commonly deleted in practice. Also, the articles of such companies might appropriately provide for the appointment of life directors,[27] or for a particular shareholder or group of shareholders to have the right to appoint one or more directors.[28]

Failure by the general meeting to observe the procedural requirement imposed by section 181 of the Companies Act 1963 that the directors cannot be elected or re-elected *en bloc* results in the non-election of the directors.[29] This provision is intelligible in the case of a truly public company where the investors might wish to pick and choose among a wide range of potential directors, but in the case of private companies it seems an unnecessary procedural hazard. Indeed, the equivalent provision in Britain has always applied only to public companies.[30]

Proceedings of directors

Functions given to directors are carried out by means of resolutions of a quorate board of directors. Minutes must be kept.[30a] Under common form articles, the quorum is usually two; each member has one vote, with a casting vote to the chair; the chairman is elected by the directors, usually for a fixed period; and a convenient measure of informality is allowed by providing that a resolution in writing signed by all the directors for the time being entitled to

---

[26] Arts. 92 *et seq.* Note art. 103 by which *inter alia* a single surviving director may appoint an additional director.

[27] *e.g. Grant* v. *William Grant & Sons (Newtownards) Ltd.* (1916) 50 I.L.T.R. 189; *Bersel Manufacturing Co. Ltd* v. *Berry* [1968] 2 All E.R. 552.

[28] *e.g. Re A & B.C. Chewing Gum* [1975] 1 W.L.R. 579; *Ulster Investment Bank Ltd.* v. *Euro Estates Ltd.* [1982] I.L.R.M. 57. If the articles empower a director "to assign his office as such to another person" the obscure s.199 provides that any such assignment shall be of no effect unless and until approved by a special resolution of the company in general meeting. This provision does not apply to a power to appoint a successor on death: *Fitzpatrick* v. *Fitzpatricks Footwear Ltd.* (High Court, Kenny J., November 18, 1970, unreported); but it may apply to the appointment by a director pursuant to such a power of a successor *inter vivos.*

[29] s.181. See *Moylan* v. *Irish Whiting Manufacturers Ltd* (Hamilton J.; unreported; April 14, 1980).

[30] s.183, Companies Act 1948 [U.K.].

[30a] s.145.

receive notice of meetings ranks as if a board resolution passed at a meeting duly convened and held.[30b]

Status

"A director is not a servant. He is a person who is doing business for the company, but not upon ordinary terms," *per* Bowen L.J. in *Hutton* v. *West Cork Railway Co.*[31] He is in fact the holder of an *office*, a troublesome anachronism stemming from the old law of corporations and beyond; troublesome because, as Kenny J. remarked in *Glover* v. *B.L.N. Ltd*,[32] "The holder of an office does *not* hold it under a *contract*: he holds it under the terms of the instrument which created it." In the case of a director, this instrument is the articles of association.

The non-contractual aspect of a director's relations with his company concerns only his directorship; in other respects, he may well have a contract with his company, whether as managing director, employee under a service contract[33] or otherwise.

The courts will generally protect the office of director by giving effect to the rights incidental to it. Rights incidental to the office are found either in the constitutional documents, or in statute. The right of a director given by the articles to participate in the management of the company will be enforced by an injunction if attempts are made to exclude him from meetings whilst he still holds office. There are difficulties here occasioned by the fact that an injunction is an equitable remedy, and as such is not usually granted to enforce close personal relationships,[34] such as contracts of personal service[35] or marriage. However, in enforcing a director's right to enjoy his office, the courts allow the proprietary aspects of the office to outweigh these considerations: *Coubrough* v. *James Panton Ltd.*[36] In this case the

---

[30b] For sample articles governing the mechanics of board meetings, see arts. 101, *et seq.*, Table A.

[31] (1883) 23 Ch.D 654.

[32] [1973] I.R. 388, 414, italics supplied. The same judge in *Re Dairy Lee Ltd.* [1976] I.R. 314, 316 said: "A director holds his office under the articles of association of the company and so, as a director, is not an employee or a clerk or a servant of the company."

[33] Such a contract may be implied where the director works full time for the company, and is in receipt of regular remuneration: *Re Dairy Lee Ltd* [1976] I.R. 314, in which the respondent, in addition to being a director, was held to be a "servant" of the company, and therefore entitled to holiday remuneration as a preferred debt under s.285, despite there being no express service contract.

[34] *Thompson* v. *Park* [1944] K.B. 408.

[35] *Warner Bros. Ltd.* v. *Nelson*[1936] 3 All E.R. 160.

[36] [1965] I.R. 272; following *Pulbrook* v. *Richmond Consolidated Mining Co.*(1878) 9 Ch.D 610; and *Hayes* v. *Bristol Plant Hire Ltd.* [1957] 1 W.L.R. 499.

necessary proprietary interest was found in the fact that the director had a prospect of remuneration and a shareholding in the company, neither of which will usually be absent. Thus, the fact that the majority of members and of directors in that company did not wish him to continue was of no avail. This case arose before the enactment of section 182 of the Companies Act 1963[37] which allows for the peremptory dismissal of directors by a simple majority vote in general meeting, but the situation in *Coubrough* could still arise today in the case of a wrongly excluded life director of a private company.[38] Also, nowadays a wrongly excluded director may thereby have grounds to support a just and equitable winding up petition, if there was an understanding that he should participate in management.[39]

If the articles do contain provisions for the remuneration of directors, the rights so given will readily be enforced by the courts.[40] If these provisions are omitted from the articles, a most unusual omission, then the director has no right[41] to remuneration at all. As Bowen L.J. said: "It is not implied from the mere fact that he is a director that he is to have a right to be paid for it."[42] A usual form of article governing directors' remuneration, is article 76 of Table A which says:

> "The remuneration of the directors shall from time to time be determined by the company in general meeting. Such remuneration shall be deemed to accrue from day to day."

What if after remuneration has accrued under this or another form of article, the articles of the company were to be altered retrospectively with the object of disentitling directors to receive remuneration for a past period? Prospective alterations they can do nothing about, since they can rely only on the articles as they stand. But in the case of retrospective alterations, the courts are prepared to use the language of implied contracts to give a right to accrued remuneration, based on the articles as they were. As Lord Esher said in *Swabey* v. *Port Darwin Gold Mining Co.*,[43] a retrospective reduction case,

---

[37] pp. 91 *et seq., infra.*

[38] For life directors, see *inter alia*, pp. 82, 91, 92.

[39] *Re Murph's Restaurants Ltd* (High Court, Gannon J, unreported July 31, 1979). See pp. 95 *et seq., infra.*

[40] *Moylan* v. *Irish Whiting Manufacturers Ltd* (High Court, Hamilton J., unreported April 14, 1980).

[41] Apart, of course, from any rights he may have under a separate contract with the company. All comments on the position of directors must be taken subject to this *caveat.*

[42] *Hutton* v. *West Cork Railway Co.* (1883) 23 Ch.D. 654.

[43] (1889) I Meg. 385. See also *Re New British Iron Co*[1898] 1 Ch. 324.

"The articles do not themselves form a contract but from them you get the terms upon which the director is serving."

The articles *do* confer contractual rights, but only on the company *vis-a-vis* the members and on members as members *inter se* and against the company. This is discussed in detail in Chapter 6, but at this stage it might be observed that it seems quaint to exclude directors' rights against the company from this contract. It might be useful rationalisation of the law to provide that all rights and duties conferred by the articles sound uniformly in contract.

Section 147(3) of the Companies Act 1963 contains an example of a right given to a director by statute, the right to inspect the books of account kept by his company. In *Healy* v. *Healy Homes Ltd*[43a] this right was enforced by injunction.

The authority of the board of directors and of individual directors to bind the company in contract is dealt with in Chapter 5.

The fiduciary relationship between directors and their company, and their duties to the company are discussed in Chapter 7.

Powers of management and the relationship between board and general meeting

Although, as has been remarked, the general meeting may be the residual source of power in the company, to what, if any, extent may the members in general meeting ensure that the directors carry out their wishes in managing the affairs of the company? The answer to this question depends upon how functions have been divided between the general meeting and the board of directors in the articles of the company. It would be possible to draft the articles of a company in such a way that the board of directors would be subject to the supervision of the general meeting in all matters of management. However, the article most commonly used in these islands for over a century to delegate powers of management to the board of directors has been consistently interpreted by the courts as vesting exclusive management functions in the board. The article in question being article 71 of Table A of the Companies Act 1908 (now reproduced in Britain as article 80 of Table A of the Companies Act 1948), provides:

"The business of the company shall be managed by the directors, who . . . may exercise all such powers of the company as are not, by the Act or by these regulations, required to be exer-

---

[43a] [1973] I.R. 309. The director may exercise the right through the medium of an accountant.

cised by the company in general meeting, subject, nevertheless, to any of these regulations, to the provisions of the Act and *to such regulations*, being not inconsistent to the aforesaid regulations or provisions, as may be prescribed by the company in general meeting; but no *regulation* made by the company in general meeting shall invalidate any prior act of the directors which would have been valid if that *regulation* had not been made."[44]

The now standard interpretation of this article in effect ignores the word "regulation" italicised above, a just fate perhaps for bad draftsmanship. The interpretation proceeds upon the simple basis that the delegated powers are not to be interfered with; if interference is desired, then the terms of delegation must be altered by an alteration of the articles. In other words, a simple majority of members may not tell the directors what to do. In *John Shaw & Sons (Salford)* v. *Shaw*,[45] the board of directors of the company had caused it to commence litigation. An ordinary resolution in general meeting directing that the litigation be discontinued was held ineffective.

In *Salmon* v. *Quin and Axtens Ltd*,[46] the majority of the directors who also commanded a majority in general meeting failed to obtain a decision at board level because one director was given by the articles of the company a power to veto board decisions. The ordinary resolution which the thwarted directors subsequently obtained in their favour in general meeting was held ineffective to bind the board or the company. And in Ireland the principle has been further affirmed by Budd J. in *Nash* v. *Lancegaye Safety Glass (Ireland) Ltd.*[46a] in relation to powers of directors properly exercised by them. He said "a majority in general meeting would not have had power to undo or reverse what had been done by the directors in the exercise of powers delegated to them"[46b]

The current Irish article 80 of Table A of the Companies Act 1963 differs significantly from the older form set out above. Chiefly, it substitutes *directions* for *regulations*, so that it reads:

"The business of the company shall be managed by the directors, who . . . may exercise all such powers of the company as

---

[44] Italics supplied.

[45] [1935] 2 K.B. 113. See also *Salmon* v. *Quin & Axtens Ltd. infra; Clark* v. *Workman* [1920] I.R. 107,114 and *Automatic Self–Cleansing Filter Syndicate Co.* v. *Cunninghame* [1906] 2 Ch. 34.

[46] [1909] 1 Ch. 311.

[46a] (1958) I.L.T.R. 11.

[46b] At p. 26.

are not, by the Act or by these regulations, required to be exercised by the company in general meeting, subject nevertheless to any of these regulations, to the provisions of the Act and to such *directions* being not inconsistent with the aforesaid regulations or provisions as may be given by the company in general meeting: but no *direction* given by the company in general meeting shall invalidate any prior act of the directors which would have been valid if that *direction* had not been given."[47]

Intrinsically, this new form makes much better sense than the old. Whether it has, as one commentator has suggested,[48] "totally altered the balance of power between the shareholders and directors in relation to the management of the company" so that they may now "give instructions to the company as to how the business of the company should be run" is very doubtful. Certainly, the courts will be bound to construe "directions" as meaning an ordinary resolution in general meeting passed by a simple majority. But such "directions" are expressly required by article 80 not to be "inconsistent with the aforesaid regulations," by which is meant all the other articles in Table A. The same reasoning will apply in interpreting this requirement of consistency as applied in the interpretation of article 80 in its older, unmodified form, namely that the exercise of powers conferred on one person must not be usurped or interfered with by another person. Articles in Table A other than article 80 confer a wide variety of individual powers on the directors, such that most purported directions by the general meeting under article 80 will involve the directors in the exercise of one or more of them, and therefore cause the direction to be correspondingly inconsistent with the articles conferring these other powers.

Thus, for example, the general meeting could not force the directors to pay an interim dividend[49] (article 117) or to recommend a final dividend (article 116), or, in a private company register as member someone of whom they disapproved (article 3 of part II). Other examples are less obvious: if the direction requires the company to expend money, its fulfilment may be thwarted by the fact that the application of reserves is the concern of the directors (article 119), or by the fact that whether or not to borrow is their decision (article 79). Some of the inconsistent articles delegate powers to the

---

[47] Italics supplied.

[48] J. Temple Lang, (1973) *Gazette* I.L.S.I. 241. For a contrary view see Ussher (1975) *Gazette* I.L.S.I, December.

[49] See *Scott* v. *Scott* [1943] 1 All E.R. 582 where under an equivalent article it was held that the general meeting could not direct the directors to pay an interim dividend.

directors in terms more emphatically personal than others by the use
of such phrases as "in their absolute discretion" (article 3 of Part II)
or "as appear to the directors to be justified" (article 117),[50] but the
reasoning applies whether the powers are thus adorned or not, and
is derived from the nature of a power. In *Clark* v. *Workman*,[51] for
example, the article simply provided "the directors may elect a
chairman . . . ". In deciding that the purported election by the
general meeting of a chairman for the board of directors was invalid,
Ross J. said: "The powers given to directors are powers delegated to
the directors by the company, and when once given the company
cannot interfere in the subject of the delegation unless by special
resolution . . . . The power having been delegated by the company to the directors cannot be controlled or affected by the company, unless the contract has been altered by special resolution, but
no such special resolution has been passed."[52]

The same principle applies to a power given to a trustee. He is not
obliged to exercise it in accordance even with the unanimous wishes
of the beneficiaries.[53]

There are probably instances where an article 80 direction by the
general meeting to the board would be lawful. Possibilities are
mostly negative, and include a direction to cease trading in a certain
part of the business or with a certain country (perhaps for political
reasons), a direction to discontinue litigation,[54] or directing the destination of newly raised share capital. These instances are arbitrary
being occasioned only by the chance absence of relevant articles in
the current Table A. The new form of article 80 is best avoided by
company draftsmen, not only to avoid the uncertainties of it, but
also to fulfill the expectations of most company promoters who
would like to see matters of management exclusively the province of
the board. The older form of article, or a new form which deletes all
mention of directions from the general meeting, should therefore be
adopted.

The foregoing draws a picture of the legal inter-relationship
between the board and general meeting in matters of management,
but the directors, even when exercising their powers of management
properly within their terms of delegation, should keep a weather eye
out for the protections afforded to the individual member by the

---

[50] Some even use imperative language *e.g.* art. 5: "The shares *shall* be at the disposal of the directors," as amended by 1983 Act, Sched. 1, para. 23.

[51] [1920] I.R. 107.

[52] At pp. 114–115, See also *Kehoe* v. *Waterford and Limerick Railways* (1888–89) 21
L.R., Ir.

[53] *Re Brockbank* [1948] Ch. 206.

[54] Overturning therefore *John Shaw & Sons (Salford) Ltd* v. *Shaw*, n. 45, *supra*.

ubiquitous section 205[54a] of the Companies Act 1963, and temper their conduct accordingly. *Re Clubman Shirts Ltd.*[55] concerned a company with few substantial participants. The petitioner under section 205 held about 20 per cent. of the equity, and the board of directors from which he had been ousted some years previously, held between them about 70 per cent. The board of directors, without consulting the petitioner, and by a perfectly proper and unimpeachable transaction sold the whole undertaking of the company. The petitioner successfully alleged that this lack of consultation for so important a step constituted an exercise of the powers of the directors "oppressive" to him within the meaning of section 205. In response, the directors had contended that "as the Articles of Association entitled the directors to exercise all such powers of the company as are not by statute or by the Articles required to be exercised by the company in general meeting, they were entitled to follow the course adopted by them and dispose of the entire undertaking without having any obligation to consult the members in general meeting before doing so."[56] O'Hanlon J. disposed of this contention by saying:

> "This proposition may be correct in strict law, but it would be a highly unusual course for any board of directors to adopt when they propose to dispose of the whole business undertaking of the company for a consideration which will yield not a penny to the individual shareholder,[57] as happened in the present case. A minority shareholder is entitled to have such a transaction, completed without his knowledge or consent, subjected to the closest scrutiny to ensure that he has been dealt with fairly by those who controlled the destinies of the company."[58]

The learned judge, although expressing some unspecified reservations about putting this omission on the part of the directors into the category of oppressive conduct towards a minority, nonetheless felt that the petitioner had made out a case for limited relief, and, accordingly made an order in his favour under section 205 directing the majority shareholders to buy his shareholding at the value they had at the time when he should have been given the opportunity of being consulted.[59]

[54a] This section crops up throughout this book. There is a detailed analysis in Chapter 9: Minority Protection.
[55] [1983] I.L.R.M. 323
[56] *Per* O'Hanlon J. at p. 4 of the transcript.
[57] The company was in financial difficulties.
[58] At pp. 4–5 of the transcript.
[59] At pp. 10–11 of the transcript. Contrast *P.M.P.A. Ltd* v. *New Ireland Assurance Co. Ltd.*, October 22, 1975, *Irish Times* in which a shareholder in a *public* limited company failed in s.205 proceedings brought to obtain information about its financial affairs.

For improper exercises of the directors' powers, and the consequences thereof, see Chapters 8 and 9.

The managing director

A managing director is something of a hybrid, in part an officer of
the company and in part an employee. In this latter respect, he has
the benefit of a contract of employment.[60] He is appointed by the
board under common form powers contained in the articles,[61] the
effect of which is discussed in the context of the dismissal of directors, *infra*.

The functions of a managing director are potentially equal to
those of the board, even to the exclusion of the board. The function
of a managing director is by no means uniform from company to
company. The wide variety of possible functions is illustrated by the
common form article 112 of Table A which says:

> "The directors may entrust to and confer upon a managing
> director any of the powers exercisable by them upon such terms
> and conditions and with such restrictions as they may think fit,
> and either collaterally with or to the exclusion of their own
> powers, and may from time to time revoke, withdraw, alter or
> vary all or any of such powers."

His functions thus depend upon the terms of his appointment. In the
extreme case of *Holdsworth (Harold) & Co. (Wakefield) Ltd* v. *Caddies*,[62]
the terms of appointment of a managing director stated that he
should "perform the duties and exercise the powers in relation to the
business of the company and the businesses (howsoever carried on)
of its existing subsidiary companies . . . which may from time to
time be assigned or vested in him by the board of directors of the
company." In the fullness of time the board came to be displeased
with the managing director, and directed him to confine his attention to the business of one of the subsidiaries. The managing director, in unsuccessfully arguing that his contract had been broken,
contended in effect that a managing directorship by its very nature
had attached to it specific functions. It was held by the House of
Lords that the post of managing director does not carry with it pre-

---

[60] *Carvill* v. *Irish Industrial Banks ltd.* [1968] I.R. 325, 342. A generally accepted
statement of the status of a managing director is contained in *Anderson* v. *James Suther-
land (Peterhead) Ltd.* 1941 S.C. 203, cited to the Supreme Court in *Carvill*, and implicitly followed; and also approved by Kenny J. in *Re Dairy Lee Ltd.* [1976] I.R. 314,
317.

[61] Currently art. 110 of Table A.

[62] [1955] 1 W.L.R. 352.

scribed functions; these are left to the parties themselves to define in the terms of appointment, and in this particular case the width of those terms permitted the board's direction.

A company need not have a managing director, but having one (or an equivalent under another name) if found to be a useful method of management throughout the spectrum of Irish companies. In the smaller concerns, the appointment of a managing director can successfully obviate artificialities caused by the fact that each company must have at least two directors.[63] In the larger concerns, management structures differ widely,[64] but it is not uncommon to find a full time managing director at the head of a company's operations, subject to the supervision of a board of directors composed of fellow executives and part-time directors.

See Chapter 5 for the authority of a managing director when dealing on behalf of the company with third parties.

Dismissal of directors

Section 182(1) of the Companies Act 1963 provides:

"A company may by ordinary resolution remove a director before the expiration of his period of office notwithstanding anything in its articles or in any agreement between it and him so, however, that this sub-section shall not, in the case of a private company, authorise removal of a director holding office for life."[65]

Even a life director is vulnerable to removal under this section if he has not retained enough voting shares to block a special resolution altering the articles, since it is only the articles which give him his position. In *Shuttleworth* v. *Cox Brothers & Co. Ltd*[66] (decided in England before the peremptory dismissal provisions equivalent to section 182(1) were introduced), a director protected by the articles against dismissal except on any one of six grounds was held effectively removed after the articles had been altered to introduce a seventh ground, namely that his fellow directors should have asked him to go. Life directors of private companies apart, nothing can prevent the dismissal of a director under section 182,[67] but there are a number of factors which might in any given case deter the general meeting from exercising this power of peremptory dismissal.

---

[63] pp. 78–79, *supra*.
[64] For the management structure at one time of Arthur Guinness, Son and Co. (Dublin) Ltd., see *The Lady Gwendolen* [1965] 3 W.L.R. 91.
[65] Art. 99 of Table A echoes s.182(1).
[66] [1927] 1 K.B. 9.
[67] Provided the proper procedure is followed. See pp. 100, *infra*.

The first such deterrent is the possibility that peremptory dismissal might constitute a breach of contract, with a consequent right to damages in the dismissed director. That the company has a statutory *power* to dismiss but not necessarily a right is made clear by section 182(7):

> "Nothing in this section shall be taken as depriving a person removed thereunder of compensation or damages payable to him in respect of the determination of his appointment as director or compensation or damages payable to him in respect of the determination of any appointment terminating with that as director . . . ."

For there to be a right to damages on dismissal there must first be a contract, and secondly, its terms must be inconsistent with a right of peremptory dismissal. As has been seen,[68] the rights of the individual director as such are not considered to be contractual. Insofar as contractual rights are implied in favour of directors,[69] they do not relate to security of tenure,[70] and are, in fact, nothing more in essence than a quasi-contractual claim for an accrued sum. In a private company having life directors, the common form article 99 allowing peremptory dismissal might be omitted. Even so, any contract implied on the basis of the articles in that company would still be prospectively alterable, just as the articles are,[71] so that the implication of a contract would add nothing to the security of tenure of a life director who does not also have sufficient voting power in general meeting to prevent the alteration of the articles. One should however emphasise the starting point of this discussion, namely that in any event the *implication* of a contract affording security of tenure to ordinary, non-executive directors as such or life directors is unprecedented. Where then does one find contractual terms inconsistent with the section 182 power of peremptory dismissal? They can be found where the dismissed director had an express,[71a] independent service contract with the company, and in the case of managing directors. Directors frequently have service contracts under which they are employed by their company to perform certain duties beyond those simply of a director,[72] *e.g.* sales director, an executive director in charge of a certain division of the

---

[68] pp. 83 *et seq. supra.*[69] pp. 84–85, *supra.*

[70] The Courts resisted an invitation to imply such a contract in *Shuttleworth* v. *Cox Brothers & Co. Ltd.* [1927] 2 K.B. 9. See also text at n. 66, *supra.*

[71] *Shuttleworth* v. *Cox Brothers & Co. Ltd.*, n. 70, *supra.*

[71a] Express or implied. A service contract in favour of a director acting as an executive was implied in *Re Dairy Lee Ltd.* [1976] I.R. 314. See p. 502n, *post.*

[72] Art. 85 recognises the possibility *Glover* v. *B.L.N. Ltd.* [1973] I.R. 388 is an example.

companies operations, or technical director as the case may be. If this contract of employment contains a provision entitling the employee to remain a director throughout his period of service, naturally peremptory dismissal as a director under section 182 for a cause not contemplated by the contract will be a breach of it, to be compensated in damages.

The case of the managing director is not so easy. The task of finding terms of appointment inconsistent with a right of peremptory dismissal is made difficult by the fact that standard form articles under which managing directors are commonly appointed expressly provide that his appointment as managing director should terminate if he should for any cause cease to be a director, thereby, it seems, contemplating peremptory dismissal by the general meeting as a lawful termination of the contract. Yet, other parts of the terms of appointment may be quite to the contrary, and may, for example, state that he is to be appointed for a fixed term. The difficulties arise in reconciling these two aspects. The practical answer is, of course, an appreciation of the hazards and clear draftsmanship at the appointment stage.

The courts are in fact willing to view terms of appointment taken as a whole as being inconsistent with a right of peremptory dismissal. In Ireland, great store is set by the qualificatory words italicised below in the standard form article 110 of Table A, which states that a managing director:

> "shall not, whilst holding that office, be subject to retirement by rotation or be taken into account in determining the rotation of retirement of directors but (*without prejudice to any claim he may have for damages for breach of any contract of service between him and the company*) his appointment shall be automatically determined if he cease from any cause to be a director."[73]

O'Keefe J., dealing with similar qualificatory words in *Carvill* v. *Irish Industrial Bank Limited*.[74] said "Once these words appear, it is open to the directors to enter into a contract with the managing director the effect of which may be to deprive the company in general meeting of the power to remove him from office without paying damages . . ."

---

[73] The italicised words have not appeared in the equivalent articles in any British Table A: art. 107 of the current 1948 Act, nor in art. 68 of the 1929 Act, nor in art. 72 of the 1908 Act. The words after the italicised passage always form part of the contract and may be taken, assumedly, as a waiver pursuant to s.7 of the Minimum Notice and Terms of Employment Act 1973 of the statutory minimum period of notice of termination of employment imparted by that Act. On waiver for the purposes of s.7, see *Industrial Yarns Ltd.* v. *Greene* [1984] I.L.R.M. 15.

[74] [1968] I.R. 325, 342 (S.C.).

He gave as examples of terms of appointment inconsistent with the right of peremptory dismissal by the general meeting an appointment for a fixed term or an appointment determinable only on notice. In *Carvill's* case itself, it was held that the managing director had been appointed and employed on a yearly basis, mainly it seems, because he was remunerated on a salary quantified on a yearly basis, *i.e.* £2,000 per annum. He was therefore held entitled to at least one year's notice of termination, and corresponding damages in lieu.

Similar qualificatory words appeared in the article appointing the managing director in *Southern Foundries Ltd.* v. *Shirlaw*,[75] but that case proceeded also on a broader principle which is helpful in dealing with cases of managing directors appointed under articles where those words are omitted. This useful aid to construction is the old principle of contract law of general application stated by Cockburn C.J. in *Stirling* v. *Maitland*[76]:

> "If a party enters into an arrangement which can only take effect by the continuance of a certain existing state of circumstances, there is an implied engagement on his part that he shall do nothing of his own motion to put an end to that state of circumstances, under which alone the arrangement can be operative."

This principle was applied by Diplock J. to give a right to damages in *Shindler* v. *Northern Raincoat Co Ltd*,[77] where a managing director was appointed for a ten year term at £3,000 per annum plus commission under an article without the qualificatory words of article 110 of the 1963 Table A.[78]

It is recognised in *Carvill* that even under the new style article 110 there may be appointments of managing directors where peremptory dismissal by the general meeting would not involve a breach of contract. *Read* v. *Astoria Garage (Streatham) Ltd.*[79–80] was such a case under an old style article.[81] Here, the managing director was appointed by a board resolution which resolved simply that Mr. Read: "be and he is hereby appointed managing director of the company at a salary of £7 per week as from Monday, February 1,

---

[75] [1940] A.C. 701 (H.L.).

[76] (1864) 5 B & S 852.

[77] [1960] 1 W.L.R. 1038, 1042.

[78] For a list of such articles which have been in common use, see n. 73, *supra*.

[79–80] [1952] Ch. 637. (C.A.).

[81] Art. 68 of Table A to the 1929 Act.

1932." The English Court of Appeal was prepared to recognise that even under an older style article it would be possible to find terms inconsistent with a right of peremptory dismissal, but not on the sparse terms of appointment before them. As Jenkins L.J. said[82] "The resolution containing as it did, no other special terms beyond the fixing of the remuneration of £7 per week and nothing whatever amplifying or inconsistent with the provisions of article 68, must be taken to have been an appointment of the plaintiff as managing director on the terms of article 68, and accordingly an appointment on the terms, inter alia, that it should be subject to termination if the company in general meeting resolved that the plaintiff's tenure of office as managing director be determined."[83]

To summarise, we have seen that the terms of appointment of managing directors have when viewed as a whole been frequently irreconcilable, but that the courts when construing such terms are willing to make a mental division between those terms founded on the articles and statute on the one hand and the remaining circumstances (if any) of the appointment on the other hand, and to allow the latter to prevail if inconsistent.

A further potential deterrent against dismissing a director under section 182 is the possibility that he might be justified as shareholder in presenting a petition for the winding up of the company on the just and equitable ground.[84]

Where a company is formed on the understanding among the original members that some or all of them are to participate in its management as directors, and that understanding is violated by the dismissal of one of them as director, then the court may, whilst recognising the lawfulness of his dismissal, nonetheless visit it with the equitable consequence of winding up. This is one of the propositions one can extract from *Ebrahimi* v. *Westbourne Galleries*,[85] a decision closely followed in Ireland in *Re Murph's Restaurants Ltd*[86] In the *Murph's* case, a successful company was formed by three equal

---

[82] At p. 294.

[83] Contrast the first instance decision in the same case [1952] 1 All E.R. 922 where Harman J. characteristically said that any managing director appointed under an article such as this must "take his chance" on dismissal by the general meeting under a right which overrode whatever the rest of his terms of appointment might say to the contrary. He, in fact, unlike the Court of Appeal, was prepared to find terms of appointment to the contrary sufficient to require a reasonable period of notice if dismissal *by the board, infra,* was contemplated.

[84] s.213(f) of the Companies Act 1963. See generally Chapter 9, but like s.205 this remedy crops up throughout this work.

[85] [1973] A.C. 360.

[86] High Court, Gannon J. July 31, 1979, unreported. See Ussher (1979–80) D.U.L.J. 92.

members "on the basis that all should participate in its direction and management,"[87] and all three became directors. Gannon J. also found a "relationship of equality, mutuality, trust and confidence between the three of them which constituted the very essence of the existence of the company,"[88] evidenced for the most part by the informality, to employ a neutral term, with which the company's finances were handled. On the formulation in *Ebrahimi*,[89] a violation of either of these understandings would have sufficed for a just and equitable winding up order; furthermore it is unlikely that an understanding about equal participation in management would exist without there being a relationship of trust and confidence. The understandings were violated in *Murph's* case by two of the members informing the third that he was no longer wanted in the company, and that he could take three months salary in lieu of notice and sell his shares to them at a valuation. He was also presented with notice of an extraordinary general meeting at which it would be proposed that he be dismissed under section 182. This meeting was in fact never held, but that lack of it may be regarded in this case as an uncompleted formality, since the majority had the necessary voting power and the intent to use it. Gannon J. made an order for winding up, despite that fact that the defendants had made an offer to purchase the petitioner's shares at a valuation.[89a] This is understandable because the company represented to the petitioner more than a mere shareholding, but also a livelihood, no dividends being declared and all profits being taken by way of directors' remuneration. Gannon J. was accordingly reluctant to see the wrongdoers left in possession of the fruits of their wrongdoing. However, since an equitable jurisdiction is seldom exercised where the applicant can be adequately compensated in money, it is questionable whether a winding up order would be granted in a similar case where the wrongdoers had offered the petitioner not only a fair value for his shares but also full compensation for loss of livelihood. Another equitable principle which could prove material resisting such a winding up petition is the requirement that a seeker of an equitable remedy must come to court with "clean hands." Thus, if it can be established that the breakdown in the relationship was partly the petitioner's own fault, a winding up order might not be granted.

The equity as formulated in the foregoing cases is a personal matter between the original members of the company, but there is little

---

[87] At p.30 of the transcript.

[88] At p.18 of the transcript.

[89] [1973] A.C. 360, 379, *per* Lord Wilberforce.

[89a] In answer to an alternative petition for relief under s.205.

in principle to prevent such an understanding arising between a new member and all the continuing members.[90]

A director dismissed under section 182 may also in appropriate circumstances petition for an order under section 205 of the Companies Act 1963 on the grounds that "the affairs of the company are being conducted . . . in a manner oppressive to him."[91] This constitutes a third possible deterrent against removing a director under section 182. It is clear both from the wording of the section and from *Re Murph's Restaurants* (which contained an alternative claim under section 205) that section 205 may be invoked by a member even where he has suffered as a director. The equivalent British provision,[92] section 210 of the Companies Act 1948, required the conduct complained of to be "oppressive to some part of the members (including himself)," and a line of authority,[93] inapplicable in Ireland, established this formulation precluded complaints relating to the petitioner's status as director, such as his removal or exclusion from office, or diminution in remuneration. In *Murph's Restaurants*, Gannon J. observed that the exclusion of the petitioner by his two fellow members was "undoubtedly oppressive,"[94] but declined to make an order under section 205 for the purchase of the petitioner's shares for reasons already mentioned. In fact, there was not in the judgment any attempt to review the full range of remedies which section 205 could afford to an expelled director.[95] Under section 205(3) the Court may:

> "with a view to bringing to an end the matters complained of, make such order as it thinks fit, whether directing or prohibiting any act or cancelling or varying any transaction or for regulating the conduct of the company's affairs in future, or for the purchase of the shares of any members of the company by other

---

[90] Indeed, Lord Wilberforce in giving his purposefully inexhaustive description of the jurisdiction at [1973] A.C. 379 spoke of "an association formed or *continued* on the basis of a personal relationship."

[91] s.205(1).

[92] Now repealed; and replaced by s.75 of the Companies Act 1980 [*U.K.*].

[93] *e.g. Elder* v. *Elder and Watson* 1952 S.C. 49; *Re H.R. Harmer Ltd.* [1959] 1 W.L.R. 62 (where the difficulty was cleverly circumvented by arguing that oppression suffered by directors at board level was also suffered as members since a company's constitution confers the right to the enjoyment of office on members with sufficient votes); *Re Lundie Brothers Ltd* [1965] 1 W.L.R. 1051; *Re Westbourne Galleries Ltd*[1970] 1 W.L.R.1378 (at first instance). See also Ussher (1979–80) D.U.L.J. 92.

[94] At p.20 of the transcript.

[95] Doubtless because only the respondents appear to have been pressing for s.205 relief in resistance to the alternative of a winding up. Even so, all they appear to have contemplated was an order that they purchase the petitioner's shares.

members of the company or by the company and in the case of a purchase by the company, for the reduction accordingly of the company's capital, or otherwise."

The section is sufficiently wide to permit an order restoring the expelled director to office. In many cases, such as *Murph's Restaurants* itself, the relationship between the participants will have so irretrievably broken down that such an order would be inappropriate and futile. There is also the difficulty that such an order for reinstatement would run directly counter to the statutory power of expulsion given by section 182, and there might therefore be an argument that on the construction of the Act as a whole such an order was not in fact contemplated by section 205(3). This conflict could be avoided in private companies, where most such disputes arise anyway, by ordering, where appropriate, an alteration in the articles of the company so as to make the participants each life directors, thereby both satisfying the understanding between them and removing them from the ambit of section 182.[96] If reinstatement is inappropriate, there are other untried possibilities such as an order that a certain proportion of the profits be distributed annually by way of dividend instead of being absorbed by the continuing directors' remuneration, or an order not only that the ousted director's shares be purchased at a valuation but that he also receive from the continuing directors compensation for loss of livelihood. *Re Murphs' Restaurants* also contemplates that the winding up petition by the ousted director might be brought under section 213(*g*) of the Companies Act 1963 on the grounds of oppression.

A managing director may be dismissed by the board of directors as well. Standard form articles contemplate this possibility, such as article 110 of Table A which begins:

"The directors may from time to time appoint one or more of themselves to the office of managing director for such period and on such terms as to remuneration and otherwise as they think fit, and, *subject to the terms of any agreement entered into in any particular case, may revoke such appointment* . . . "[97]

The italicised words make it plain that the directors' power of revocation does not override a managing directors' terms of appointment. A dismissal by the board inconsistent with those terms,

---

[96] s.205(4) refers to orders altering the company's memorandum and articles, and provides "that the company concerned shall not have power without the leave of the Court to make any further alteration in or addition to the memorandum or articles inconsistent with the provisions of the order."

[97] Italics supplied.

though effective, will be a breach of contract. Even if those words did not appear, the position would be the same, since the article speaks of an appointment for a "period," and is therefore only rightfully revocable in accordance with that period as defined in the terms of appointment.[98] That definition will commonly provide for termination in the event of misconduct or other specified causes, and, occasionally, if the parties have so agreed, for termination by simple board resolution.

Where the board dismisses a managing, or other employed, director for one of the lawful causes of termination stated or implied in his contract of employment, failure to observe the requirements of fair procedure may result in the dismissal being wrongful, even if it was in all other respects justified. This emerged from the Supreme Court decision in *Glover* v. *B.L.N. Ltd.*[99] where Walsh J. observed that "public policy and the dictates of constitutional justice require that statute, regulations or agreements setting up machinery for taking decisions which may affect rights or impose liabilities should be construed as providing for fair procedures."[1] In *Glover*, the plaintiff's service contract appointing him as technical director provided that if he should be "guilty of any serious misconduct or serious neglect in the performance of his duties . . . which in the unanimous opinion of the board of directors" injuriously affected the "business or property or management" of the company, then he might be dismissed without any right to compensation. The board dismissed the plaintiff on the grounds of serious misconduct and neglect within this clause, but since they did so without giving him the opportunity to be heard on the charges against him, the dismissal was wrongful and the plaintiff was awarded damages. It is immaterial that the dismissal might on

---

[98] *Nelson* v. *James Nelson & Sons Ltd.* [1914] 2 K.B. 770. The judgments are expressed in such a way as to suggest that the board has no power to revoke an appointment otherwise than in accordance with its terms. Yet, this was an action for damages for wrongful dismissal which presupposes an effective dismissal. The text, *supra*, proceeds on the basis that there is a general power in the board to terminate contracts, albeit wrongfully.

[99] [1973] I.R. 388, 422 criticised (1975) *Annual Survey of Commonwealth Law* 389 as being "surely based on a misconception," *i.e.* a confusion between a private post as employee and the holder of a public office. The criticism continues in [1976] A.S.C.L. 298, citing *Thorpe* v. *South Australian National Football League* (1974) 10 S.A.S.R. 17 for the view that the necessity for fair procedures is restricted to the dismissal of the holder of a *public* office. Such criticisms are made in ignorance of the extent to which a requirement of constitutionality pervades dealings between citizens in Ireland. See Von Prondzynski [1979–80] D.U.L.J. 14, 20.

[1] At p.425; a statement derived from the judicial development of Art. 40(3) of the Constitution. *McDonald* v. *Bord na gCon* [1965] I.R. 265, *East Donegal Cooperative* v. *Att.-Gen.* [1970] I.R. 317, and *Re Haughey* [1971] I.R. 217 were cited.

the facts have been justified.[2-6] The Supreme Court in *Glover* left open the extent to which the parties are free to agree in their contract that fair procedures need not apply on a dismissal for cause[7]; But there seems to be no constitutional objection to waiver of this kind since rights under Article 40(3) from which the requirement of fair procedures is drawn, are not expressed to be inalienable.[8]

A board of directors dismissing a managing, or other employed director for cause, may not rely in justification on circumstances not known to it at the time of the dismissal.[9]

In the case of dismissals where no cause need be shown, there is correspondingly no need for fair procedures, there being no case to be shown or answered. No cause need be shown for the dismissal of a director under section 182 by a majority vote in general meeting. The office of director is truly one held at pleasure, and the holder of it takes it on the expectation that if he displeases the majority in general meeting he will forsake it, just as the Government is similarly answerable to the legislature.[10] Similar considerations apply to a managing, or other employed director who has expressly agreed in his service contract that he may be dismissed without cause being shown.

In fact, section 182 itself goes some way towards providing for fair procedures where a director is dismissed under that section by the general meeting. Section 182(3) requires the company to circulate to the members written representations made by the director concerned. Section 182(2) requires extended notice[11] of a dismissal resolution in order to give time for this safeguard to operate, and also entitles the director to be heard in person at the meeting.

If the dismissal of a director has involved the termination, with or

---

[2-6] *Per* Walsh J. at 423, 429. Indeed Kenny J. at first instance (p.413) held the plaintiff guilty of conduct warranting dismissal within the terms of the clause. That finding was not the subject of appeal.

[7] Walsh J. at p.425; though there is a hint of public policy to the contrary at p. 428.

[8] On waiver of constitutional rights see Kelly *The Irish Constitution*, 336–67, and Redmond, [1979–80] D.U.L.J. 104.

[9] *Carvill* v. *Irish Industrial Bank Ltd.* [1968] I.R. 325.

[10] See *Garvey* v. *Ireland* (1980) 113 I.L.T.R. 61, 68, 71, 74 and contrast the office of Garda Commissioner, apparently held at pleasure since the relevant dismissal provision, s.6(2) of the Police Force (Amalgamation) Act 1925 as amended by this Constitution (Consequential Provisions) Act 1937, stated baldly that "Every Commissioner may at any time be removed by the Government." But since the holder of it has the expectation of holding it whole until normal retiring age, and with the benefit of a pension, it is imbued with totally different characteristics which require fair procedures before dismissal. On *Garvey* see Casey [1979–80] D.U.L.J. 95.

[11] s.142 governs extended notice. It involves 28 days notice to the company of the resolution except where the directors themselves intend to move it, and, in any event, at least 21 days notice of the resolution by the company to the members.

without legal justification, of a contract of employment, he may apply for the discretionary relief of re-instatement or compensation under section 7 of the Unfair Dismissals Act 1977. This Act may therefore afford redress for dismissed managing directors or directors with service contracts. This jurisdiction, and the meaning of "unfair dismissal" within section 6 of the Act, are beyond the scope of this book.[11a]

The maintenance of control

It is proposed here to consider briefly methods, or even devices, by which individual directors or a board of directors may maintain themselves in office despite not commanding a majority of votes in general meeting. Factors which might deter a majority from exercising the section 182 power to dismiss have already been mentioned,[12] as has one method, particularly important in the context of the smaller Irish company, of circumventing section 182, namely the appointment of life directors of a private company,[13] who if they retain sufficient votes to block a special resolution altering the articles are safe from dismissal by the members.[14]

A second method involves the holding by a director of shares with "loaded" voting rights. Typically, the articles governing such shares will provide that they carry on a poll the normal one vote per share[15] on all issues arising before the general meeting, *except* when the dismissal of the director concerned is proposed, in which case the number of votes carried by each of his shares is augmented by a pre-determined amount calculated to afford him security of tenure. The validity of such an article was upheld by the House of Lords in *Bushell* v. *Faith*[16] where Lord Upjohn saw it as part of a company's freedom which "Parliament has never sought to fetter . . . to issue a share with such rights or restrictions as it may think fit."[17] Indeed, there are other commonplace examples of variations in voting rights. Preference shares commonly carry no votes unless their dividend is in arrear, and some classes of shareholders in some companies have

---

[11a] See Redmond, Dismissal Law in the Republic of Ireland, Dublin, 1982.

[12] pp. 92 *et seq., supra.*

[13] pp. 60, 82, 91–92, *supra.*

[14] 26 per cent. would therefore suffice, but common form articles appointing life directors sometimes stipulate that to continue to enjoy his security of tenure he should retain more, commonly one-third of the votes in general meeting, sometimes one-half.

[15] Art. 63 of Table A; s.134(e).

[16] [1970] A.C. 1099. See also *Re Westwinds Holding Co. Ltd.* (High Court, Kenny J., May 21, 1974, unreported; Ussher, (1978) D.U.L.J. 48).

[17] At p. 57.

no right to vote in general meeting at all.[18] One prominent Irish company has voting rights weighted in favour of the smaller shareholder.[19] Provisions loading voting rights in favour of directors are commonly adopted by the participants on the formation of a company, or by the agreement of all participants whilst it is a going concern; attempts to force such provisions upon an unwilling minority by altering the articles might encounter the difficulties discussed generally in Chapter 9: *Minority Protection*.

Shareholders' agreements are a third method. Agreements between members to support and not to vote against each other in board elections are readily enforceable by injunction.[20] Section 182 overrides only the articles and agreements between directors and the company, but not agreements between members. A shareholders' agreement of this kind may be used to reinforce articles giving a particular minority shareholder or group of shareholders the right to appoint and remove a director[21] who would otherwise be vulnerable to a section 182 removal.[22]

A fourth method involves the control by the directors of the votes on shares which they themselves do not beneficially own. The most extreme example of this practice has now been outlawed for public limited companies by section 41 and 43 of the Companies Act 1983,[23] and involves the use by the directors of the votes on shares in the company which it itself beneficially owns. Before this legislation came into force, any company could hold its own shares beneficially through a nominee,[24] provided that its funds had not been laid out in acquiring them in such a way as to break the capital maintenance rules.[25] In practice this meant that the beneficial ownership of the

---

[18] In the case of a quoted company, the Stock Exchange requires that such shares are clearly designated "non-voting"; "restricted voting" or "limited voting" as the case may be: para. K, Sched. 11, Appendix 34 to the Rules and Regulations of the Stock Exchange.

[19] See *Kinsella* v. *Alliance and Dublin Consumers Gas Co.* (High Court, Barron J. unreported, October 5, 1982) a company incorporating the Companies Clauses Consolidation Act 1845 under which weighted voting was standard.

[20] *Greenwell* v. *Porter* [1902] Ch. 530.

[21] For such articles with shareholders' agreements in support, see *Ulster Investment Bank Ltd* v. *Euro Estates Ltd.* [1982] I.L.R.M. 57, 58–59, and *Re A. & B.C. Chewing Gum Ltd.* [1975] 1 W.L.R. 579.

[22] For other aspects of shareholders' agreements, see pp. 223–224, *post.*

[23] Prompted by, but more stringent than, Arts. 18 to 22 of the Second EEC Companies Directive.

[24] *Kirby* v. *Wilkins* [1929] 2 Ch. 444 *Re Castiglione* [1958] Ch. 549; Gower (1958) 21 M.L.R. 313; Jenkins para 154. *Re Ennis and West Clare Ry.* (1879–80) 3 L.R., Ir. 187; *Re Munster Bank* (*Dillon's claim*) (1886–87) 17 L.R., Ir. 341.

[25] See Chap. 10.

shares would be acquired by the company by the gift or will of a member, perhaps on the occasion of the transfer of control from one generation of controllers to the next. Public limited companies are now required to cancel such shares[26] and pending cancellation their voting rights may not be exercised.[27] The former freedom possessed by companies other than public limited companies to retain the beneficial ownership of their own shares is preserved by the Act, which apparently even enlarges this freedom in the case of companies limited by shares by obviating the former necessity that such shares should be held through the medium of a nominee.[28] If this is the case, the former stated by Cozens-Hardy L.J. in *Bellerby* v. *Rowland & Marwood's Steamship Co*[29] that it is contrary to the nature of a company for it to be a member of itself has been abrogated for such companies.

Shares which the directors hold on trust, perhaps for the benefit of employees, their dependants or charitable objects, also fall into this fourth category. A trust instrument may be drafted in such a way as to release the director trustees from what would otherwise be their fiduciary obligation not to use the trust votes to further their own interests. If such a trust fund is established by a new issue of the company's shares (perhaps funded by the company out of reserves of profits) questions will arise about the company's capacity to pursue such generosity,[30] and about whether the directors have exercised their powers properly in making the allotment.[31] In this latter respect, the allotment may be voidable if the directors' apparent altruism is sufficently tinged with self interest, and shareholders should always look askance at any such proposals. Ratification of such a scheme by majority vote in general meeting will not necessarily render the allotment valid if it was made in bad faith.[32]

The fifth method was frowned on by the Jenkins Committee,[33] and involves interlocking shareholdings. The most obvious of these is already broadly prohibited by section 32 of the Companies Act 1963. This section prevents a subsidiary company from being a

---

[26] s.43(3) of the 198 Act.

[27] *Ibid.* s.43(4).

[28] *Ibid.* s.41(2) which states "A company limited by shares may acquire any of its own fully paid shares otherwise than for valuable consideration." The distinction made in ss.42 and 43 between a company holding its own shares beneficially and non-beneficially, and between holding itself and through a nominee clearly indicates that s.41(2) is to be construed in the manner indicated in the text.

[29] [1902] 2 Ch. 14, 25.

[30] See Chap. 4.

[31] See Chap. 7.

[32] See Chap. 8.

[33] Paras. 148 *et seq.*

member of its own holding company.[34] Were the law otherwise, directors of the holding company by means of their control of a majority shareholding in it owned by the subsidiary could maintain themselves in office indefinitely, whatever the wishes of the other shareholders. The prohibition applies also to shares held by a nominee for the subsidiary.[35] The section contains a number of relaxations all of which, except one, are not germane to the present theme, since the shares held by the subsidiary pursuant to them are disqualified from voting at meetings of the holding company.[36-37] The one exception concerns shares held by the subsidiary in a fiduciary capacity for objects other than the holding company or another subsidiary of it.[38] This means that a subsidiary could be chosen as trustee for the kind of trust fund described above.

The method under discussion therefore involves schemes for the perpetuation of directors' control which do not involve the establishment of a holding/subsidiary relationship. One might for example have three companies, each having boards of directors in common, and each owning 26 per cent of the voting shares of each other. Any two of these companies could block an ordinary resolution in the third company. The Jenkins Committee decided that any legislation prohibiting such arrangements would be arbitrary and overwhelmingly complex. They instead expressed the hope that another of their recommendations[39] made in a different context and requiring compulsory disclosure of beneficial shareholdings of 10 per cent. or more in public quoted companies would meet the case, because thereby "the existence of substantial cross (and circular) holdings [would] become public knowledge and subject to press comment so that investors and prospective investors [might] be warned."[40] Britain implemented this recommendation in 1967,[41] but Ireland never has. The closest Irish legislation comes to it is the requirement in section 158(4) of the Companies Act 1963 that the directors' report should contain:

---

[34] The holding/subsidiary relationship is defined in detail in s.155. The essence of it is *control*.

[35] s.32(7).

[36-37] s.32(6).

[38] s.32(2). The subsidiary company is not debarred from holding such shares as fiduciary where the holding company's only interest in them is "by way of security for the purposes of a transaction entered into by it in the ordinary course of business which includes the lending of money." For the interpretation of this phrase, see *Steen* v. *Law*[1964] A.C. 287 (P.C.) Certainly, no avoidance schemes could be built upon it.

[39] At para. 147.

[40] *Ibid.* para. 153.

[41] ss.33 and 34 of the Companies Act 1967 [U.K.], since repealed, and replaced by Part 1V of the Companies Act 1981 [U.K.].

"a list of bodies corporate in relation to which either of the following conditions is fulfilled at the end of the company's financial year—

(a) the body corporate is a subsidiary of the company;

(b) although the body corporate is not a subsidiary of the company, the company is beneficially entitled to more than 20% in nominal value of its shares carrying voting rights (other than voting rights which arise only in specified circumstances)."

This provision will force the disclosure of the first link in a chain of circular shareholdings of the kind described, but the other end of the chain, where it re-enters the company in question may be disguised by a nominee holding, and the intermediate links may be lost in private companies which, although they are obliged to prepare directors' reports, are not obliged as the law stands at present to publish them.

Lastly, there are in Ireland some publicly quoted companies in which, although the directors do not command a majority of potential votes in general meeting, those votes are nonetheless so widely dispersed and unorganised as not to constitute a threat to the directors. Furthermore, these uncommitted voters are a fruitful source of proxy votes for the existing board, since they tend, if not apathetic, to support established authority. Certainly, dissident members of Irish quoted companies are at a disadvantage compared to the directors in soliciting these uncommitted votes. There is no provision in Irish company law equivalent to section 140 of the Companies Act 1948 [*U.K.*] requiring the company to circulate at the members' expense copies of statements by them in support of their resolutions. Thus, the only statements emanating from the company in a fight for control will reflect the directors' viewpoint, and they may properly charge to the company the expense of communicating their views.[42] Directors might be tempted to abuse this advantage. Fortunately the law and the rules of the Stock Exchange combine to put a brake upon yielding to the more obvious temptations. The Stock Exchange now requires that proxy forms with provision for two-way voting[43] on all resolutions intended to be proposed should be sent to all members entitled to vote with the notice covening the meeting.[44] Before the Stock Exchange took a hand, the board was at

---

[42] *Peel* v. *London and North Western Railway Co.* [1907] 1 Ch. 5.

[43] Art. 71 of Table A is an example; indeed, the two-way proxy is the only form on offer in Table A. Contrast the British Table A, arts. 70 and 71.

[44] *Admission of Securities to Listing*, Listing Agreement, para. 12; (explanatory note 54–56); only procedural resolutions are excepted from this requirement.

liberty to circulate at the company's expense one-way proxies in favour of themselves. This intervention was designed to afford all members adequate opportunity to express their views, and dissidents may build upon it by circulating their own views privately to the members,[45] but, even so, the dissidents will know about the company's affairs only what the law requires to be disclosed to them,[46] and will lack therefore the board's means of making a cogent case. Secondly, it is a criminal offence for the directors to solicit at the company's expense some only of the available proxy voters, *e.g.* those which they anticipate to be favourable to themselves.[46a] And thirdly, a circular soliciting proxies may be the subject of judicial intervention. In *Jackson* v. *Munster Bank*[46b] a member obtained an injunction preventing the company from holding an *e.g.m.* on the ground that the directors had employed a misleading circular to ask for proxy votes in support of resolutions to be proposed by them. The circular was misleading in the sense of withholding information relevant to a member in making up his mind which way to give his votes. Such a circular should be "a fair and candid commentary," observed Chatterton V.-C.[46c]

THE SECRETARY

Every company must have a secretary who may be one of the directors.[47] No particular qualifications are required for the post. The only limit imposed by the Companies Act prevents one person acting as both director and secretary from effectively doing acts required to be done by each of them together.[48] In view of the failure of many companies to comply with the increasing bureaucratic burden upon them, the absence of a requirement of professional qualifications such as those offered by the Institute of Chartered Secretaries and Administrators becomes less sustainable. Although the Companies Act imposes few specific duties on the secretary as such, they do also impose upon a company numerous duties of an administrative nature which in practice the secretary should perform, and in respect of which, if he does not, he will be treated as an

[45] Their names and addresses are obtainable under ss.116 and 117.
[46] See Chap. 11, *Accounts and Auditors*, and Chap. 12, *Promoters and Prospectuses*.
[46a] s.136(5), (6), (7); penalty raised to £500 by Sched. 1, 1982 Act.
[46b] (1884–85) 13 L.R., Ir. 118.
[46c] At p. 137.
[47] s.175.
[48] s.177; such as the provisions governing the use of the seal (Art. 115); or signing the annual return (s.127).

officer in default for the purpose of penalties. There is a case for the abandonment of the post of secretary, and the substitution of the post of Responsible Officer, with a professional qualification, charged with clearly defined duties. The precedent is the post of company auditor to which the Companies Acts give close attention, and for which appropriate qualifications are required.[49] A Responsible Officer could likewise, as a profession, look after the affairs of several companies, just as some company secretaries do at present.

A new company cannot now be incorporated unless a secretary or joint secretaries have been nominated in the formation process, and persons so nominated are automatically appointed.[50] Subsequent appointments and removals are within the province of the board of directors.

The sporadic statutory duties specifically imposed upon a secretary include making the appropriate statutory declarations prerequisite to the commencement of business of public companies[51-52] and public limited companies,[53] the re-registration of old public limited companies as public limited companies[54] or public limited companies as private companies[55]; signing the annual returns and accompanying documents[56]; verifying the statement of affairs to be filed in court on a compulsory winding up[57]; verifying the statement of affairs submitted to a receiver appointed by the holders of debentures secured by a floating charge[58]; and signing the prescribed forms of application for the re-registrations of a limited company as unlimited or an unlimited company as limited.[59] Duties imposed by the Companies Acts which in practice fall within the province of the secretary, though he is not named specifically as being responsible, would appear to include keeping the register of members, allowing its inspection and supplying copies[60]; issuing share certificates[61]; keeping the register of directors and secretaries, allowing its inspection and making returns in respect of it[62]; keeping the register of directors' and secretaries' shareholdings, allowing its inspection,

---

[49] See s.162 as amended by s.6 of the 1982 Act.

[50] s.3 of the 1982 Act.

[51-52] s.115.

[53] s.6 of the 1983 Act.

[54] s.12 of the 1983 Act.

[55] s.14 of the 1983 Act.

[56] ss.127, 128 and 129. For the annual return, see Chap. 15: *The Charges Register and Other Disclosures*.

[57] s.224, and see Chap. 16, *Liquidations*.

[58] s.320, and see Chap. 14, *Floating Charges and Receivers*.

[59] ss.53 and 54 of the 1983 Act.

[60] ss.116 *et seq.*, and see Chap. 6, *Shares and Membership*.

[61] s.86.   [62] s.195 as amended by s.8 of the 1982 Act.

supplying copies of it and producing it at the annual general meeting[63]; entering directors' declarations of interest in the prescribed book, and producing the book[64]; ensuring that the business letters of the company show the required particulars about directors,[65] and that letters and order forms mention the place of registration of the company, its registered number, the address of its registered office, and do not refer to any other than paid up share capital of the company[66]; publishing in *Iris Oifigiúl* notice of the delivery to the registrar of companies of a wide variety of documents[67]; causing the registration of charges[68] and judgment mortgages[69] affecting the company's property, keeping copies of such charges and allowing inspection of them[70]; giving notice to the registrar of any change in the registered office of a company[71]; ensuring the publication of the company's name at its place of business, on its seal and business letters and other publications[72]; ensuring that a register of debentures is kept, and giving notice of its whereabouts to the registrar of companies,[73] allowing inspection of it and supplying copies of debentures[74]; issuing debenture certificates[75]; making returns to the registrar of companies of allotments[76]; delivering to the registrar copies of altered memoranda of association[77] and special and certain other resolutions[78]; delivering to the registrar of companies a state-

---

[63] s.190, and see Chap. 15.

[64] s.194, and see Chap. 7.

[65] s.196.

[66] Reg. 9 of the European Communities (Companies) Regulations 1973.

[67] The two relevant lists of documents are contained in s.55 of the 1983 Act, and in Reg. 4 of the European Communities (Companies) Regulations 1973. All failures to publish notices of s.55 documents carry penalties, as do the other duties mentioned in this paragraph, but in the case of Reg. 4 the penalty is prescribed only in respect of a failure to publish notice of the delivery of one of the specified documents, the annual return (Reg. 12).

[68] ss.100 and 101. See Chap. 15: *The Charges Register and Other Disclosures.*

[69] s.102. See Chap. 15.

[70] ss.109 and 110.

[71] s.113 as amended by s.4 of the 1982 Act.

[72] s.114.

[73] s.91.

[74] s.92.

[75] s.86.

[76] s.58, as simplified by s.31 of the 1983 Act and see Chap. 10 at p. 312.

[77] s.10 (and notice of any application to the Court for the alteration to be cancelled).

[78] s.143 as amended by s.5 of the 1982 Act and para. 14 of the Sched. 1. to the 1983 Act. It also includes resolutions made under s.20 of the 1983 Act. For the relationship between the disclosure of such resolutions and the authority of a company's agents, see Chap. 5.

ment describing the rights attached to newly alloted shares, or a variation of rights or a new designation for a new class of shares[79]; giving notice to the registrar of companies of alterations in share capital[80]; keeping minutes of meetings of directors and of general meetings, and allowing inspection of the minutes of general meetings[81]; furnishing copies of a company's balance sheet and directors' and auditors' reports to members and debenture holders,[82] and similar documents to members of a private holding company in respect of its subsidiaries.[83]

With one exception,[84] each item in the foregoing dreary and intimidating list carries a criminal sanction.[85] That is to be expected, but the oddity is that the *mens rea* required is not constant despite the offences being of a similar nature. Where, as most frequently happens, the provisions speak simply of an "officer who is in default" being liable, that means "any officer of the company who knowingly and wilfully authorises or permits the default."[86] Under such a provision, an officer ignorant of the requirements of the Companies Acts may escape liability, whereas other formulae used in other provisions such as "every person is responsible for the contravention shall . . . be liable,"[87] or "if any person without reasonable excuse makes default . . . he shall be liable,"[88] impose a stricter liability. There is a case for a uniform standard of liability. If the suggestion made above that each company must have a designated officer responsible for the fulfilment by the company of the formal requirements of the Companies Acts were to be adopted, that standard of liability could be absolute. The present "officer in default" formula reflects an uncertainty on the part of the legislature about who within a company should have the responsibility for fulfilling these functions. In effect, the Acts are saying that if an individual actually undertakes the functions, then he will be liable for failure; otherwise the only liability is on the company itself. This attitude fails to reflect the evolution over the last century of the office of company   secretary

---

[79] s.39 of the 1983 Act.

[80] s.69.

[81] ss.145 and 146.

[82] s.159; including profit and loss accounts and group accounts (where prepared): s.157.

[83] s.154.

[84] See n. 67 above.

[85] Companies Act 1963 penalties have been raised by a factor of five by s.15 and the Sched. 1. of the 1982 Act.

[86] s.383.

[87] s.115(6).

[88] s.320(5).

from that of mere servant to administrative officer[89]; with usual responsibility in these areas. Indeed, default provisions in the 1908 Act sought to impose liability in addition to that on the company itself only on *directors* and *managers* who had knowingly and wilfully authorised or permitted the default.[90] If the formal requirements of the Companies Acts are to be taken seriously, the actual practices which have evolved should be built upon by legislation.

The secretary will commonly have other ministerial functions under the direction of the board in addition to those directly connected with the performance of the company's statutory duties as set out above. It is within his usual province for example, to certificate transfers, to carry out the board's instructions to convene meetings, to witness the affixing of the company's seal to documents, and to receive notices and other communications addressed to the company.[91] Depending on the size and nature of the company, he may also be assigned by the board other administrative functions incidental to the carrying on of the company's business. The usual authority of a company's secretary to bind the company to contracts with third parties depends on the public perception of the office of company secretary, and is discussed in Chapter 5.

OTHER SERVANTS AND AGENTS

The board of directors may cause the company to employ all manner of servants and agents, according to the needs of the business. In the case of higher management posts, the board may effect the employment itself; but in many instances the function will be delegated, perhaps down a whole chain of delegation, depending on the size of the organisation. Technically, the board's authority to cause these everyday things to happen is derived from the general powers of management given to the board by Article 80 of Table A. Article 80 is so widely drafted as to permit the directors to appoint agents to conduct the company's business instead of themselves, and to execute deeds on behalf of the company under powers of attorney:

[89] Contrast Lord Esher in *Barnet, Hoares & Co.* v. *South London Tramways Co.*(1887) 18 Q.B.D. 815, 817, where a secretary is described as "a mere servant" whose function is "to do what he is told" and Salmon L.J. in *Panorama Development Guildford Ltd.* v. *Fidelis Furnishing Fabrics Ltd.* [1971] 2 Q.B. 711, 713 where a secretary is described as "the chief administrative officer of the company."

[90] s.26(5) of the Companies (Consolidation) Act 1908. See also Companies Act 1862, ss.26, 27; Companies Act 1867, s.32; Companies Act 1900, ss.19,30; Companies Act 1907, ss.7, 20, 21.

[91] Including the auditor's report: *Re Allen Craig & Co.* [1914] Ch. 483.

Industrial Development Authority v. *Moran*.[92] In practice, this extreme occurs only under the common form provisions in debentures for the appointment of receivers[93]; nevertheless, it is apparent that the maxim *delegatus non potest delegare* has little or no application to the directors' general powers of management as conferred by Table A.[94]

Auditors

The appointment of auditors and their status within a company is discussed in Chapter 11: *Accounts and Auditors*.

---

[92] [1978] I.R. 159. This proposition is amplified by s.40 which expressly permits the appointment of an attorney to act outside the State, apparently a matter of some doubt before 1862: *ibid.*, p. 164. The company in this case had at the relevant time the 1908 form of Table A which, whilst having an equivalent of art. 80, did *not* have the *express* powers to appoint attorneys given by the present day art. 81 of Table A; hence the need to imply the power as falling within the general powers of management.

[93] Though there is a practice in some companies of appointing a "chief executive" or "general manager" who is *not* a director but who has powers under his terms of appointment close to that of the board in the conduct of the company's business.

[94] *Ibid.* pp. 164–165.

Chapter 4. Objects

Since 1856,[1] a modern registered company has been obliged to state its objects, the purposes for which it is formed. This statutory requirement is now embodied in section 6(1)(*b*) of the Act: "The memorandum of every company must state . . . (*b*) the objects of the company." In the early days of the modern registered company these objects, once stated, were unalterable.[2] The objects of the company are now freely alterable,[3] but one of the consequences of the former restriction remains with us,[4] namely the judge-made rule that a company is not capable of entering into transactions outside or beyond its objects, known for convenience as the *ultra vires* rule. The *ultra vires* rule has been much modified by statute in recent years in favour of persons dealing with companies.[5]

The contents of objects clauses

The model form memorandum contained in Table B states the objects of its imaginary company with admirable brevity.[6] Such suc-

---

[1] 19 & 20, Vict. c. 47, s.V, 3.

[2] *e.g.* Companies Act 1862 s.12.

[3] s.10 of the 1963 Act.

[4] *Ashbury Railway Carriage and Iron Co.* v. *Riche* (1875) L.R. 7 H.L.C. 653, the leading case, proceeded on the basis that a corporation created by statute was to be assumed to have a general and unfettered power of contracting unless the statute by negative words curtailed that power. The negative words were found in the prohibition against alteration of objects which by construction included "within it the engagement that no object shall be pursued by the company in practice except an object which is mentioned in the memorandum of association," *per* Lord Cairns at p. 670. Such a rationale cannot be applied to the 1963 Act under which the objects are freely alterable. But s.8 thereof expressly modifies the *ultra vires* rule, thereby presupposing its continued existence, and, arguably, preserving it.

[5] s.8 of the 1963 Act; there was also purported intervention by reg.6 of the European Communities (Companies) Regulations 1973, (S.I. 1973 No. 163), *infra.*

[6] 1963 Act, Sched. 1, Form of Memorandum of Association of a Company limited by shares, para. 2: "The objects for which the company is established are the mining

cinctness, though justified in law, is seldom found in practice. Real life memoranda are more likely to follow the pattern stigmatised by Lord Wrenbury in *Cotman* v. *Brougham*[7] in 1918 as being the "pernicious practice of registering memoranda of association which, under the clause relating to objects, contained paragraph after paragraph not specifying or delimiting the proposed trade or purpose, but confusing power with purpose and indicating every class of act which a corporation is to have power to do."[8] This practice, however pernicious, has cheerfully survived the blasts of judicial criticism. For example, fifty years after *Cotman* v. *Brougham*, Buckley J. in *Re Introductions Ltd.*[9] was able to describe the memorandum before him as having been framed in accordance with the practice "whereby the draftsman assembles a number of objects or powers about as diverse in their character as the topics of conversation proposed by the walrus to the carpenter,[10] but in many a case much more numerous, then for good measure, adds, at the end, a clause to the effect that each paragraph of the objects clause shall be construed independently and shall be treated as an independent object of the company . . . ."[11]

Sometimes such prolixity was born of a fear in the draftsman that unless he enumerated expressly at the outset every possible thing which the company might thereafter wish to do within the normal ambit of the business proposed to be followed by it, there was a danger of common place transactions later being held to be *ultra vires* and therefore wholly void with the result perhaps that the company would be unable to recover payment for services rendered and goods supplied. This abundance of caution has not been completely justified for over a century. Since the *Att. Gen.* v. *Great Eastern Railway*,[12] a draftsman has been able to rely upon a company having *implied*

---

of minerals of all kinds and the doing of all such other things as are incidental or conducive to the attainment of the above object." The objects clause for a plc in the 1983 Act, Sched. 2, is similar.

[7] [1918] A.C. 514.

[8] At p. 523.

[9] [1968] 2 All E.R. 1221.

[10] Lewis Carroll, *Alice through the Looking Glass*, Chap. 4.

[11] At p. 1223.

[12] (1880) 5 App. Cas. 473; applied in *Northern Bank Finance Corporation Ltd.* v. *Quinn and Achates Investment Company*, High Court, unreported, Keane J., November 8, 1979. In *Martin* v. *Industrial Benefit Building Society* (1960) Ir.Jur.Rep. 42 (Circuit Court; Judge Barra O'Briain) it was held that furnishing a surveyor's report was reasonably incidental to the carrying on of the business of a building society, and therefore *intra vires*.

powers to do "whatever may fairly be regarded as incidental to, or consequential upon"[13] its stated objects. Thus, to give some obvious examples, any trading company engaged in a business within its objects, may for the purposes of that business do such things as employ staff, buy or lease property, run a bank account, borrow money and so on. Necessary ancillary powers of this nature will be implied if not expressly stated in the memorandum, and in so far as not expressly negatived or curtailed by the memorandum.[14]

A second motive behind excessively long objects clauses is the desire to give the company the maximum capacity so that any activities which the company may conceivably in the future wish to pursue, and which, indeed, it may never have the intention of pursuing, are nonetheless covered at the outset. It is not usually necessary to take such precautions in Ireland. In a culmination of the process begun by the Companies (Memorandum of Association) Act 1890, section 10(1) of the 1963 Act now provides that:

> "A company may, by special resolution, alter the provisions of its memorandum by abandoning, restricting or amending any existing object or by adopting a new object and any alteration so made shall be valid as if originally contained therein, and be subject to alteration in like manner."[15]

This section is sufficiently widely drafted to allow total abandonment of the existing objects clause, and the adoption of a new and unrelated clause. It is extensively used in Ireland,[16] and obviates the choice between an attempt at an initial comprehensive statement of objects or the acceptance instead of the necessity for a liquidation in the event of a future change in direction.

---

[13] *Per* Lord Selbourne L.C. at p. 478.

[14] An example of such curtailment is sometimes found in relation to borrowing powers.

[15] In other jurisdictions, such prolixity combined with the drafting expedients described *infra* is often still necessary. In Britain, for example, objects may be altered only for certain specified purposes set out in s.5 of the 1948 Act. Their continuance in Ireland might perhaps be justified by the wish on the part of controllers to ensure in advance that it will be unnecessary to refer to the general meeting in the event of a future change in direction. This justification does not apply in the common case where the promoter of a company retains voting control after formation.

[16] *e.g.* in 1980, particulars of 705 alterations were notified to the Registrar under s.10(9) of the 1963 Act, in 1981 there were 1018 notifications and in 1982 there were 688. (annual *Companies Reports*: Departments of Industry, Commerce and Tourism, and Trade, Commerce and Tourism).

Principles of construction

Old habits die hard and verbose objects clauses in memoranda of association continue to be produced in Ireland. It is accordingly necessary to review briefly the principles upon which the courts construe them. Since *Ashbury Railway Carriage and Iron Co.* v. *Riche*[17] the courts have met inflated objects clauses with the "main objects" rule of construction, a variant on the *eiusdem generis* rule. Under the "main objects" rule, if a main or dominant object can be divined from the memorandum,[18] all other capacities stated therein are subordinated to it, and can only be pursued while the main object survives and as part of the enterprise built around the pursuit of the main object.[19] Not only do generally stated capacities succumb to this rule, such as the power to act as "general contractors" in the *Ashbury Carriage* case, but also more specific purposes such as that to obtain and exploit patents in *Re German Date Coffee Co. Ltd.*[19]

In response to the "main objects" rule, draftsmen employed two main devices to circumvent it. The validity of the first was upheld only recently in *Bell Houses Ltd.* v. *City Wall Properties Ltd.*[20] though the use of *Bell Houses* clauses is in fact old established. Essentially this device renders the necessary connection between a main object and a necessarily subordinate purpose a matter for the subjective opinion of the company's directors rather than the objective judgment of the court, and, furthermore, the nature of the subordinate activity is left at large until the directors have formed the requisite opinion. A typical *Bell Houses* clause reads as follows:

> "To carry on any other trade or business whatsoever which can, in the opinion of the Board of Directors, be advantageously carried on by the company in connection with or as ancillary to any of the above businesses or the general business of the company."

In the *Bell Houses* case, the plaintiff company whose chief business was property development, had allegedly introduced the defendant to sources of finance in return for a procuration fee. When sued for

---

[17] (1875) L.R. 7 H.L.C. 653.

[18] Including, apparently, the "name" clause in the memorandum: *Re Crown Bank* (1890) 44 Ch.D. 634, 645; but only if the objects clause is of itself unclear: *Cotman* v. *Brougham* [1918] A.C. 518, 521.

[19] *Re German Date Coffee Co. Ltd* (1882) 20 Ch.D. 169; *Ashbury Railway Carriage and Iron Co.* v. *Riche, supra; Re Crown Bank, supra. Stephens* v. *Mysore Reefs (Kangundy) Mining Co.* [1902] 1 Ch. 745 also illustrates the "main objects" approach, but must now be regarded as overruled in respect of its application to the actual facts of that case. On this, see *Anglo-Overseas Agencies Ltd.* v. *Green* [1961] 1 Q.B. 1, 11.

[20] [1966] 2 Q.B. 656.

it, the defendant unsuccessfully contended that the alleged procuration contract was *ultra vires* the plaintiff company. All that was required to connect the business of property developer to that of loan broker was the honest opinion of the board of directors that the two might be advantageously combined.

The second main device used to counteract the "main objects" rule of construction is the "independent objects" clause. A typical "independent objects" clause will be tacked on as the last sub-clause of an objects clause containing a wide variety of objects, and will state:

> "It is hereby declared that the objects specified in the preceding sub-clauses of this clause shall be regarded as independent objects, and shall be construed independently of the other sub-clauses of it, and that none of the objects mentioned in any sub-clause shall be deemed to be merely subsidiary to the objects expressed in any other sub-clause."

The validity of such a clause was upheld by the House of Lords under protest in *Cotman* v. *Brougham* in 1918.[21] Thus a rubber plantation company was held to be responsible for underwriting an issue of shares.

The courts have felt themselves bound to accept and construe such devices as "independent objects" clauses and plenipotentiary clauses of the *Bell Houses* type because they have been passed by the registrar of companies in the formation process. Section 5 of the Companies (Amendment) Act 1983, and its repealed predecessors,[22] state that his certificate of incorporation shall be *conclusive evidence*

> "that all the requirements of the Companies Acts in respect of registration and of matters precedent and incidental thereto have been complied with . . . and that the association is a company authorised to be registered and is duly registered under [the Companies Act 1963]."[23]

Thus a registered objects clause, even if it does not comply with whatever might be the contemporary judicial view of what an objects clause should be, cannot be called into question. But *the registrar* may, and should if he is properly to carry out his duties under the Acts, reject such objects clauses. The propriety of an objects

---

[21] [1918] A.C. 514.

[22] *e.g.* s.19 of the 1963 Act, repealed by the 1983 Act, Sched. 3, Part I.

[23] s.5(4) of the 1983 Act. ss.9(9), 11(3), 12(7), 14(5) and 18(6) all use the same formula with regard respectively to the re-registration of a private company as a plc, an unlimited company as a plc, an old public limited company as a plc, a plc as a private company, and the registration as a plc of a joint stock company as defined by s.329.

clause, as opposed to its interpretation, has not been in issue since in 1918 in *Cotman* v. *Brougham*[24] the courts finally accepted that their role was diminished by the conclusiveness of the registrar's certificate. Thus, the contemporary judicial view is difficult to ascertain. In 1969 in *Re Introductions Ltd.*,[25] Harman L.J. remarked that "one cannot have an object to do every mortal thing one wants, because that is to have no object at all"; and in 1890 North J. observed in *Re Crown Bank*[26] that the legislation required the statement of certain, specific objects. If these statements do indeed reflect the intention of the Companies Acts, then it is open to the registrar to reject not only *Bell Houses* clauses (since they in essence leave the choice of objects to the future discretion of the directors), but also "independent" objects of too great a generality.[27]

During most of the long life of the 1983 Act as a Bill the "conclusive evidence" formula was deleted in favour of "sufficient evidence until the contrary is shown," only to be restored in the closing stages at the behest of the professions. It has been suggested that the purpose of the substitution was to avoid the constitutional difficulty founded on *Maher* v. *Att.-Gen.*[28] that legislation should not oust the jurisdiction of the courts, but that case concerned only certain courts in criminal matters. It is constitutionally permissible to delegate this judicial or quasi-judicial function to the registrar.[28a]

Could it be argued that the registrar's certificate, despite its statutory conclusiveness, is in fact amenable to judicial review? Grounds for judicial review are easily produced nowadays[28b]; it is fashionable, and so must be touched upon. For example, the registrar might in error have allowed the registration of a company whose objects were not contemplated by the Acts, or there may have been other slips. It has recently been held at first instance in England that the

---

[24] See *Cotman* v. *Brougham* at p. 523; and *Bell Houses Ltd.* v. *City Wall Properties Ltd.* at p. 685; *Re Ennis and West Clare Railway* (*ex. p. Hill*) (1879) 3 L.R., Ir. 94.

[25] [1970] Ch. 199, 200.

[26] At p.644. North J. thought that he himself could reject clauses of too great a generality but that was before the House of Lords in *Cotman* v. *Brougham* established that the judicial role was to construe and sigh.

[27] For example, the "independent" sub-clause in *Re New Finance & Mortgage Co. Ltd.* [1975] Ch. 420 "to carry on business . . . as merchants generally" was held to justify the carrying on of a petrol filling station where petrol, oil, motor accessories etc. were sold. See also the "independent" sub-clauses in *Anglo-Overseas Agencies Ltd.* v. *Green, supra*, discussed in Furmston, (1961) 24 M.L.R. 715.

[28] [1973] I.R. 140. The suggestion was made by Power, *Irish Company Law 1973–1983—A guide and handbook*, (Dublin, 1984), p.51.

[28a] Article 37 of the Constitution.

[28b] See pp. 468 *et seq., infra.*

registrar's "conclusive" certificate given in respect of the registration of company charges does yield to *certiorari*.[28c] Whatever the
slight merits of that decision in that context, the overwhelming
objection to its application to a company's certificate of incorporation is that to destroy the registrar's decision to incorporate is to
render the company a nullity.[28d] If Irish law in its present state were
to permit that consequence it would be at variance with the First
EEC Companies Directive which by Article 12(2) requires that nullity should be followed by a winding up of the company, *i.e.* the payment of its debts and the disposal of its assets. Yet Irish company
law, relying on the conclusiveness of the certificate of incorporation,
naturally does not seek to regulate the winding up of a non-existent
company. Article 12(3) of the Directive further provides that:

> "nullity shall not of itself affect the validity of any commitments
> entered into by or with the company . . . ."

Destruction of those commitments will be the objective of those
seeking nullity of the company, and for Ireland to abide by the
Directive that objective must be thwarted. The short answer to these
problems is not to allow *certiorari* of the certificate of incorporation.
In other words, Irish law in general, including the availability of *certiorari* must be interpreted as if it accorded with the Directive which
Ireland has purported to implement.[28e]

Re Introductions Ltd.[29] illustrates the limitations of both the *Bell
Houses* type of plenipotentiary clause and of the "independent
objects" clause. The former is of necessity ancillary, and the latter
cannot elevate a mere power to the status of an object. In that case,
the company's memorandum contained a *Bell Houses* type clause and
and "independent objects" clause. One of the sub-clauses of the
objects clause gave the company an express power to borrow money
upon security. The company had for some years pursued the *intra
vires* business of hiring out deck-chairs at the seaside in accordance
with an object allowing the provision of services to holidaymakers.
Then, after abandoning that business, the company went into the

---

[28c] *R.* v. *Registrar of Companies, ex p. Esal (Commodities) Ltd., The Times*, November 26,
1984. See p.468, *post.*

[28d] See *Irish Permanent Building Society* v. *Registrar of Building Societies* [1981] I.L.R.M.
242 where Costello J. at pp. 269–270 recognised the dangers involved in the inconclu-
siveness of a certificate of incorporation.

[28e] This approach was adopted for English law in *International Sales and Agencies Ltd.*
v. *Marcus* [1982] 3 All E.R. 551, and see also *Re Friedrich Haaga Gmbh* [1975] C.M.L.R.
124. Any assertion that it is unconstitutional so to fetter the consequences of judicial
review may be met by reference to the Third Amendment to the Constitution Act
1972, passed as a prerequisite to entry into the European Communities.

[29] [1968] 2 All E.R. 1221; [1970] Ch. 199 (on appeal).

clearly *ultra vires* business of inviting the public to subscribe for shares in breeding sows. A bank had advanced money upon a debenture for the pig business, knowing that it was to be used for *ultra vires* purposes, and in the company's subsequent massive insolvency sought to claim priority as a secured creditor. The bank unsuccessfully argued that the "independent objects" clause rendered the activity of borrowing money upon security an independent, and therefore *intra vires*, object of the company. It was held that money is not borrowed in isolation; it is borrowed for a purpose, and borrowing therefore cannot be an independent object: it must be ancillary to some other purpose which is required to be legitimate.[30] The *Bell Houses* sub-clause could not avail the bank since the *intra vires* deck-chair business was no longer being pursued. Had it been, who knows whether or not the directors of the company might have formed the honest opinion that the pig business could have been advantageously combined with it?

Capacity to make gifts

The capacity of a company to make gifts has been the subject of some controversy.[31] Unfortunately, a confusion in this area was introduced by certain English cases,[32] which has only recently been dispelled both in that jurisdiction, and in Ireland.

Gifts in this context include any gratuitous disposition made by a company. It may take the form of an outright transfer of the company's assets such as a charitable donation, the sponsorship of sporting events, contributions to political parties, *ex gratia* redundancy payments to former employees[33] or the endowment of educational institutions.[34] Or the "gift" might involve the gratuitous assumption of an obligation, such as the obligation to pay a pension for which no previous contractual stipulation existed,[35] or gratuitously undertaking to guarantee the debts of a third person.[36]

---

[30] Contrast the lending of money which can exist as a business on its own; or "powers" to borrow and to lend which together are the business of banking.

[31] Bastin, "Charity at the Board Room Table," 36 Conv. (N.S.) 89; Wedderburn, (1962) C.L.J. 141; Instone, "Powers and Objects," (1978) New L.J. 948.

[32] Chiefly *Re Lee, Behrens & Co. Ltd.* [1932] 2 Ch. 46 (Eve J.), and to a much lesser extent *Charterbridge Corporation* v. *Lloyd's Bank Ltd.* [1970] Ch. 62 in which Pennycuick J. in fact did much to expose the errors of the *Lee, Behrens* case.

[33] *e.g. Parke* v. *The Daily News Ltd.* [1962] Ch. 927.

[34] *e.g. Evans* v. *Brunner, Mond & Co.* [1921] 1 Ch. 359.

[35] *e.g. Re W & M Roith* [1967] 1 W.L.R. 432; *Re Horsley & Weight Ltd.* [1982] 3 All E.R. 1045.

[36] *e.g. Charterbridge Corporation* v. *Lloyd's Bank Ltd., supra*; and *Northern Bank Finance Corporation Ltd.* v. *Quinn and Achates Investment Company* High Court, unreported, Keane J., November 8, 1979; *Rolled Steel Products* v. *British Steel Corpn.* [1982] 3 All E.R. 1057.

Powers to make gifts may be either express or implied. In the case of express powers, the normal principles of construction should apply. An express power to make gifts is capable of being the "main" object of a company, as in the case of a company formed for charitable purposes, and, accordingly, an express power to make gifts is capable of being an independent object of a company formed for other purposes but possessing an "independent objects" clause.[37] An express power to make gifts contained in a memorandum *without* an "independent objects" clause will be subjected to the "main objects" rule of construction, and, accordingly, can be used only to further the main purposes of a company. Implied powers to make gifts are by definition subjected to similar constraints: they will be implied only for purposes "reasonably incidental to" the objects of the company (in accordance with the general rules for the implications of powers contained in the *Att.-Gen.* v. *Great Eastern Railway Co.*[38]). The same validity test therefore applies to ancillary express powers and implied powers.

The "reasonably incidental" test requires that a company's generosity is tempered by a sufficient measure of self interest; charity practised by companies where this test applies must be the kind of charity which is in the interests of those that practice it. As Bowen L.J. said in the leading case of *Hutton* v. *West Cork Railway Co.*[39] in qualification of his vision of railway porters being treated by a benevolent employer to a picnic in the country:

> "The law does not say there are to be no cakes and ale, but there are to be no cakes and ale except such as are required for the benefit of the company . . . "

---

[37] The making of gifts is not of necessity ancillary as was the power to borrow in *Re Introductions*; it may in reality be an "object." The power to grant a pension may be a valid independent object: *Re Horsley & Weight Ltd.* [1982] 3 All E.R. 1045. So too may be the power to give guarantees, but in this instance care must be taken to employ unequivocally clear draftsmanship in view of the questionable decision of Vinelott J. in *Rolled Steel Products* v. *British Steel Corporation* [1982] 3 All E.R. 1057. He decided that the words "as may seem expedient" in a sub-clause empowering the company "to lend and advance money or give credit to such persons, firms or companies and on such terms as may seem expedient, and in particular to customers of and others having dealings with the company, and to give guarantees or become security for any such persons, firms, or companies" indicated that the power was, despite the presence of an independent objects clause, nevertheless "ancillary to and to be exercised when expedient in the furtherance of the objects of the company and is not to be construed as an independent object" (p.1078).

[38] (1880) 5 App. Cas. 473, *supra.*, applied in *Northern Bank Finance Corporation Ltd.* v. *Quinn and Achates Investment Company*, High Court, unreported, Keane J., November 8, 1979 where a company had purported to guarantee the debts of a third party.

[39] (1883) 23 Ch. D. 654, 672 *et seq.* The use of the word "benefit" here should be treated with caution. See below.

Thus *ex gratia* redundancy payments to former employees of a business which has ceased to be a going concern are not permissible under an implied power;[40] nor are gratuitous payments to the officers of a company in the course of being wound up.[41] But where the business remains a going concern, such disbursements to departing employees and officers is readily justifiable as encouraging those who remain, and indeed any liberality to employees whilst the company remains a going concern may be justified in the interests of good labour relations. Similarly, donations to charities are "reasonably incidental" as being good for the company's "image," the sponsorship of sporting events as being advertising and contributions to political parties as tending to create or preserve the business climate in which the company would wish to operate.[42]

It should be emphasised that the test is objective, both on principle and on a careful reading of *Hutton* v. *West Cork Railway Co.*[43] Unfortunately, in the *West Cork Railway Co.* case Bowen L.J. was dealing not only with the capacity of a company to make gifts but also with the fiduciary duty of directors in exercising that capacity on behalf of the company, without always clearly distinguishing these two elements. He was describing the whole duty of directors, that of ensuring that the company acted *intra vires* and that of fulfilling their fiduciary duty of acting bona fide for the benefit of the company. Eve J. in *Re Lee, Behrens & Co.*[44] fifty years later seized upon these latter elements of bona fides and benefit, and incorporated them into his test of the limits of a company's capacity, saying that the validity of gratuitous dispositions by a company was to be tested "by the answers to three pertinent questions:

> (i) Is the transaction reasonably incidental to the carrying on of the company's business? (ii) Is it a *bona fide* transaction? (iii) Is it done for the benefit and to promote the prosperity of the company?"

---

[40] *Parke* v. *Daily News Ltd., supra.*

[41] *Hutton* v. *West Cork Railway Co., supra.*

[42] In fact, objective justification for most common-place instances of generosity can be found whilst the company remains a going concern, but a due proportion must be observed. Excessive liberality or other surrounding circumstances may indicate that the company's purposes were not the prime consideration. See *Re W. & M. Roith Ltd.* [1967] 1 W.L.R. 432, and *Re Halt Garage Ltd.* [1982] 3 All E.R. 1016.

[43] "The test must be what is reasonably incidental to, and within the reasonable scope of carrying on the business of the company," *per* Bowen L.J. at p. 671, and at p. 674: " . . . the ultimate test is not bona fides but what is necessary for carrying on the business."

[44] [1932] 2 Ch. 46, 51.

Both (ii) and (iii) are of spurious parentage; they were disapproved of by Pennycuick J. in *Charterbridge Corporation* v. *Lloyds Bank Ltd.*[45]; and it would now seem that they are not to be followed in Ireland. In *Re Metro Investment Ltd.*,[46] McWilliam J. stated that "the principle appears to be clearly established that money can only be spent by a company for purpose reasonably incidental to the carrying on of the company's business," and expressly followed the *Charterbridge Corporation* case[47] saying:

> " . . . the judgment in this case reviews the authorities very fully and it seems to be clearly indicated that a third party who enters into a transaction involving[48] a company which has power to enter into that transaction[48] is *not concerned to investigate the possibility of the transaction not being for the benefit of the company*."[49]

Furthermore, in *Northern Bank Finance Corporation Ltd.* v. *Quinn and Achates Investment Company*[50] Keane J., though unfortunately not referring to the earlier case of *Re Metro Investment Ltd.*, stated *obiter*:

> "The celebrated observations of Bowen L.J. in *Hutton* v. *West Cork Railway* that 'charity cannot sit at the boardroom table' and 'there are to be no cakes and ale except for the benefit of the company' may have been taken too far in *Re Lee, Behrens and Co.*; . . . its authority as a persuasive precedent would require reconsideration today in the light of the decision in *Charterbridge Corporation Ltd.* v. *Lloyd's Bank*."

And the capstone has been put on the matter in England by *Re Halt Garage Ltd.*[50a] and *Re Horsley & Weight Ltd.*[50b] which each affirm that elements (ii) and (iii) relate to the directors' exercise of their fiduciary powers, and do not form part of the definition of a company's capacity.

---

[45] [1970] Ch. 62.

[46] High Court, unreported, May 26, 1977. The company gave a promissory note to the creditor of an associated company in consideration of the creditor's forbearance in relation to that company. The only element connecting the two companies was the fact that they were under common control. There had been no business dealings between them. In these circumstances, it is very difficult to see how the giving of the promissory note could be "reasonably incidental to the carrying on of the company's business," but such was the finding.

[47] *Hutton* v. *West Cork Railway Co.*, *supra*; *Re Lee, Behrens, supra* were cited with other cases in the judgment, but none of them were analysed.

[48] The learned judge is here either begging the question or dismissing it.

[49] Italics supplied.

[50] High Court, unreported, November 8, 1979.

[50a] [1982] 3 All E.R. 1016, 1029, 1034j.

[50b] [1982] 3 All E.R. 1045, 1054.

The consequences of an ultra vires transaction

At common law an *ultra vires* transaction was wholly void.[51] It conferred neither rights nor duties; it passed no property, and the courts would not enforce it either directly or indirectly. The plight of the outsider[52] seeking to recover the price of goods delivered to a company under an *ultra vires* contract or the cost of services rendered led to effective legislative intervention in his favour by section 8 of the 1963 Act.[53] There was also purported further intervention by Regulation 6 of the European Communities (Companies) Regulations 1973[54] which, it will be submitted, was ineffective in this area.[55]

It is necessary to consider the consequences of an *ultra vires* transaction from four different view points: the outsider protected by section 8, the outsider without the protection of section 8, the company seeking to enforce an *ultra vires* transaction and the position of an insider (*i.e.* a member or shareholder).

The outsider protected by section 8

Section 8(1) of the 1963 Act provides:

"Any act or thing done by a company which if the company had been empowered to do the same would have been lawfully and effectively done, shall, notwithstanding that the company had no power to do such act or thing, be effective in favour of any person relying on such act or thing who is not shown to have been *actually aware*,[56] at the time when he so relied thereon,

---

[51] *Ashbury Railway Carriage and Iron Co.* v. *Riche* L.R. 7 H.L. 653; *Hennessy* v. *National Agricultural and Industrial Development Association* [1947] I.R. 159, 203.

[52] A useful term meaning the other party to any transaction with a company.

[53] Prompted no doubt by paras. 42(c) of the Report of the Jenkins Committee (1962, Cmnd. 1749). The Company Law Reform Committee reporting in Ireland in 1958 (Pr. 4523) had said that there was "much in favour of the view that the [*ultra vires*] doctrine should now be wholly abolished and that every company should now have the same powers as an individual whether these are conferred by the memorandum or not" (para. 49), but did not recommend its abolition on the grounds that it had "been a distinctive feature of our company law for a long time," and that the British had not abolished it, despite the recommendations of the Cohen Committee (Cmnd. 6659 (1945)) that it should go, and "we must assume that there were strong reasons for this decision." (para. 50).

[54] S.I. 1973, No. 163.

[55] *Infra.* p. 134 *et seq.*

[56] Italics supplied.

that such act or thing was not within the powers of the company . . . "[57]

The section applies only to acts or things "which if the company had been empowered to do the same would have been *lawfully* . . . done." Thus the section does not operate to increase a company's capacity beyond what would be lawfully possible. For example in *Trevor* v. *Whitworth*[58] a company by its Memorandum was expressly authorised to purchase its own shares, an act which would constitute an unlawful reduction of capital, and no capacity to do so was thereby conferred. Similarly in *Bank of Ireland Finance Ltd.* v. *Rockfield Ltd.* at first instance[59] it was unsuccessfully argued that section 8 might operate to validate in favour of an outsider a transaction involving the unlawful provision of finance to a company to purchase its own shares.[60]

Section 8 will most commonly be invoked against a company seeking to escape from an *ultra vires* contract, but it is sufficiently widely drafted to allow an outsider to keep the benefits of an *ultra vires* gift or other gratuitous disposition. All that is required of the outsider is *reliance* on the act or thing done by the company, and the donee of a gift might well be said to *rely* on it once he has taken it, or altered his position on the footing that it is his. Section 8 will not however render a company bound by a mere promise to make a gift,[61] any more than an individual in like circumstances would be bound, for lack of consideration moving from the promisee (however much he may have relied upon the promise). The section supplies the necessary capacity; it does not obviate the normal principles of the law of contract.

In the case of contracts, the "act or thing" relied upon by the outsider is the purported entry into the contract by the company. The outsider will be adversely affected by the company's lack of capacity only if it can be proved that he was *actually aware* of it at the time of contracting. The heavy burden of proving actual awareness lies on

---

[57] s.8 is extensively analysed in Ussher, "Questions of Capacity: the Implementation in the Republic of Ireland and in the United Kingdom of the First EEC Companies Directive," (1975) *Irish Jurist*, 39, from which some of the following treatment is drawn. See also Ussher, (1981) D.U.L.J. 76.

[58] (1887) 12 App. Cas. 409. Such purchases are now prohibited by s.72 of the 1963 Act, and by s.41 of the 1983 Act.

[59] [1979] I.R. 21, 26.

[60] For this prohibition, see s.60 of the 1963 Act, as amended by para. 10, Sched. 1, 1983 Act.

[61] As in *Parke* v. *The Daily News Ltd.*, *supra*.

the company[62]; all the outsider need prove is reliance, a negligible requirement in the case of a purported contract.

Actual awareness (or, in other words, knowledge) must be distinguished from actual notice. Though one is not often required to make the distinction, the terms are not synonymous. Lord Evershed M.R. has said: "The word 'notice' to a lawyer . . . means something less than full knowledge. It means no doubt that the thing of which a man must have notice must be brought clearly to his attention."[63] And in another case[64] Hodson L.J. said:

> "I do not myself regard the word 'notice' as a synonym for the word 'knowledge.' Notice is a word which involves that knowledge may be imparted by notice, but 'notice' and 'knowledge' are not the same thing, although loosely one sometimes talks as if to act with notice and to act with knowledge were indeed the same."

One can conceive of cases where an outsider may have had actual notice of a restriction in a company's Memorandum of Association, and yet not on the plain words of the section have been "actually aware . . . that such act or thing was not within the powers of the company." For example, an outsider, unversed in the subtleties of construing memoranda of association, might, after wading through the memorandum of Introductions Ltd. *supra*, have concluded that an apparently independent power to borrow money meant what it said. He would have had actual notice of the restriction, but not having understood it, could not be said to have been actually aware that the company lacked capacity and would accordingly, it is submitted,[65] remain protected by section 8. Indeed, the requirement of *actual awareness* of the lack of capacity should, it is submitted,[65] preclude any imputation of knowledge by construction of law, whether arising from a duty to comprehend matters of which an outsider has actual notice, or arising from the old idea of constructive notice of

---

[62] s.8 states that the transaction is to be effective in favour of any person "who is not shown to have been actually aware." Such language points to a burden of proof on the company. This proposition said Keane J. in *Northern Bank Finance Corporation Ltd.* v. *Quinn and Achates Investment Company*, (High Court, unreported, November 8, 1979), "may very well be so," (p.16 of the transcript), but he did not find it necessary to decide the point. In order to interpret Irish legislation as conforming to the 1st EEC Companies Directive the burden of proof must be construed as lying on the company: *International Sales and Agencies Ltd.* v. *Marcus* [1982] 3 All E.R. 551, 559–560.

[63] *Goodyear Tyre & Rubber Co. (G.B.) Ltd.* v. *Lancashire Batteries Ltd.* [1958] 1 W.L.R. 857, 860 (notice of resale price condition under Section 25(1) of the Restrictive Trade Practices Act, [U.K.]).

[64] *Cresta Holdings Ltd.* v. *Karlin* [1959] 1 W.L.R. 1055 (point of pleading).

[65] But see the discussion *infra* of the contrary view expressed by Keane J. in *Northern Bank Finance Corporation* v. *Quinn and Achates Investment Company*.

the memorandum as a public document,[66] or from an underlying duty to investigate either generally[67] or in suspicious circumstances only.[68] Section 8 does not tell us that the outsider *ought* to be aware of anything; it is only concerned with the actuality and it contains no words from which a duty to investigate could in any circumstances be inferred. It seems that the outsider dealing with the company may, under section 8, wilfully shut his eyes to questions of capacity,[69] and indeed it may be arguable that an agent, such as a solicitor in a conveyancing transaction, acting for an outsider might be under a duty to his principal *not* to investigate the company's capacity to enter into the proposed transaction, since his consequent awareness of lack of capacity might put into jeopardy what would otherwise have been an advantageous transaction. Conveyancing practice in this area has, however, not responded to the revolutionary changes introduced by section 8; objects clauses are still perused on behalf of prospective purchasers, but it may well be that solicitors should no more dream of doing this than their counterparts in England would consider delving for equities behind the curtain lowered by the 1925 property legislation.

Into this tidy structure built upon the plain words and ordinary language of the Act, there intrudes the decision of Keane J. in *Northern Bank Finance Corporation Ltd.* v. *Quinn and Achates Investment Company*.[70] Here the defendant company acting *ultra vires* purported to guarantee the debts of another to the plaintiff bank, and executed a charge in support thereof over its lands in favour of the plaintiff bank. Keane J. found as a fact (on the balance of probabilities) that the solicitor acting for the bank in the transaction did read the company's objects clause, yet mistakenly believed that it empowered the company to enter into the transaction. Keane J. stated himself to be "satisfied that, where a party is shown to have been actually aware of the contents of the memorandum but failed to appreciate that the Company were not empowered thereby to enter into the transaction in issue, section 8(1) has no application." But section 8(1), with all

---

[66] *Ernest* v. *Nicholls* (1857) 6 H.L. Cas 401, 418–419.

[67] As in a conveyancing situation where the purchaser in investigating title is required to display the diligence of the competent conveyancer.

[68] As in the acquisition for value of a negotiable instrument (*London Joint Stock Bank* v. *Simmons* [1892] A.C. 201); or when, under English law, a stranger to a trust is about to become implicated in a potential breach of it (*Selangor United Rubber Estates Ltd.* v. *Cradock (No. 3)* [1968] 1 W.L.R. 1555.).

[69] Note that the Jenkins Committee (Cmnd, 1749 (1962)), para. 42(c), in recommending a similar provision for England thought that the outsider should *not* have to investigate suspicious circumstances.

[70] High Court, unreported, November 8, 1979, analysed in Ussher, "Company Law—Validation of Ultra Vires Transactions," [1981] D.U.L.J. 76.

respect to the learned judge, runs directly counter to this: it speaks not of the outsider being actually aware of the contents of the memorandum, but of the outsider being "actually aware . . . that such act or thing was not within the powers of the Company . . . " It does not seem permissible on these words to hold, as did Keane J., that once there are "no further facts of which [an outsider] could be put upon notice"[71] he is deemed to have drawn the correct inference from them on the principle *ignorantia juris haud neminem excusat.*[72] This is a form of constructive knowledge, and confuses notice with knowledge. It would be sounder and more in accord with the words of the section to achieve much the same result in most cases by raising an evidential presumption that an outsider who has actually read the objects clause in fact understood it,[73] unless he can adduce cogent evidence to the contrary. Such cogent evidence might surely be found where the application of the rules of construction render an objects clause misleading, for example where the "main objects" rule causes a stated object to be nonetheless *ultra vires,*[74] or where a clearly-stated apparent independent object fails to attain that status through being a necessarily ancillary power.[75]

As matters stand however,[76] Keane J. has drawn a distinction, based chiefly upon an incredulity that the legislature could have

---

[71] At p. 18 of the transcript.

[72] *Ibid*, pp. 19–20. Contrast the opinion of the Judicial Committee of the Privy Council delivered by Lord Denning in *Kiriri Cotton Co. Ltd.* v. *Ranchoddas Keshaviji Dewani* [1960] A.C. 192, 204: "It is not correct to say that everyone is presumed to know the law. The true proposition is that no man can excuse himself from doing his duty by saying that he did not know the law on the matter." s.8 casts no duties upon the outsider. This dictum was carried into Irish law in *Dolan* v. *Neligan* [1967] I.R. 247, 260, and confirmed by the Supreme Court in *Rogers* v. *Louth County Council* [1981] I.L.R.M. 144, 147.

[73] One would in effect be saying, in the words of the EEC First Directive that he "could not in view of the circumstances have been unaware of" the lack of capacity. See Lord Esher, M.R. in *English and Scottish Mercantile Investment Co. Ltd.* v. *Brunton* [1892] 2 Q.B. 700, 707–708: "When a man has statements made to him, or has knowledge of facts, which do not expressly tell him of something which is against him, and he abstains from making further inquiry because he knows what the result would be—or, as the phrase is, he "wilfully shuts his eyes"—then judges are in the habit of telling juries that they may infer that he did know what was against him. It is an inference of fact drawn because you cannot look into a man's mind, but you can infer from his conduct whether he is speaking truly or not when he says he did not know of particular facts. *There is no question of constructive notice or constructive knowledge involved in that inference; it is actual knowledge which is inferred.*" [Emphasis supplied]. For the text of the Directive see *Purported intervention under Regulation 6, post.*

[74] See n.19, *supra.*

[75] *Re Introductions Ltd., supra.*

[76] An appeal to the Supreme Court was lodged by the Northern Bank Finance Corporation, but was not pursued.

intended the contrary,[77] between cases where the outsider has read
the memorandum before entering into the transaction and those
where he has not. In the former he will be deemed to have understood it, and in the latter he will remain fully protected by section 8.
It should be emphasised that this case has imposed only a duty to
comprehend; there still remains no duty to investigate.

The knowledge gained by an agent acting for an outsider will be
imputed to his principal under the normal principles of agency.[78] If
the knowledge came to the agent in the course of some other transaction when he was working on his own account or for a different
principal, knowledge so gained will not be imputed to the principal
for the purposes of section 8: such knowledge is imputed only if the
agent has a duty to that principal to make the kind of enquiry which
would lead to the acquisition of the knowledge,[79] and as has been
seen there appears to be no duty of enquiry or investigation under
section 8.

Assuming that actual awareness is not proved in the outsider, the
contract is enforceable against the company by an action for
damages or specific performance in the normal way, and merits no
further comment here.

The outsider without the protection of section 8

As stated above the transaction is void.

In the case of a void contract, there are, naturally, no contractual
remedies available to the outsider, but they are in effect granted
where the *ultra vires* creditor can avail of the anomalous right akin to
subrogation, whereby his debt is validated to the extent that the
money advanced by him was used by the company to pay off legitimate *intra vires* creditors. This principle is illustrated by *Re Lough
Neagh Ship Co.*[80] Here, a company formed for the purposes of having
a ship built borrowed *ultra vires* in order to pay the builder, an *intra*

---

[77] The legislative context is further pursued in Ussher, [1981] D.U.L.J. 76; and *cf.*
Lord Wilberforce in *Midland Bank Trust Co. Ltd.* v. *Green* [1980] 1 All E.R. 153, 159
where he said that *Re Monolithic Building Co.*[1915] 1 Ch. 643, 663 had disposed "for
the future of the old arguments . . . for reading equitable doctrines (as to notice etc.)
into modern Acts of Parliament; it makes it clear that it is not 'fraud' to rely on legal
rights conferred by Act of Parliament; it confirms the validity of interpreting clear
enactments . . . according to their tenor."

[78] *e.g. Northern Bank Finance Corporation Ltd.* v. *Quinn and Achates Investment Company*,
High Court, unreported, November 8, 1979, at p. 18 of the transcript.

[79] *Re David Payne* [1904] 2 Ch. 608; *Re Cummins, Barton* v. *Bank of Ireland* [1939] I.R.
60.

[80] [1895] 1 I.R. 533; though the provenance is English. See, *inter alia*, *Blackburn
Building Society* v. *Cunliffe, Brooks & Co.* (1883) 22 Ch. D. 61, and *Sinclair* v. *Brougham*
[1914] A.C. 398.

vires creditor. The lender's claim was accordingly validated.[81] The right is not a full subrogation since the claimant is not subrogated to any securities held by the *intra vires* creditor, but *ultra vires* securities held by the claimant are validated as part of the process.[82]

The courts will not grant a quasi-contractual remedy to the outsider if the effect would be that of indirectly enforcing the contract.[83] Thus, an outsider who has lent money to a company under an *ultra vires* borrowing contract may not recover these in a quasi-contractual action for moneys had and received since repayment was exactly what the purported contract envisaged.

Non-contractual remedies may, however, be invoked, in essence to undo the transaction. An applicant for such relief will be granted it only on condition that he restores, sets off or accounts for all benefits received by him under the *ultra vires* transaction.[84] He cannot "approbate and reprobate" the transaction.[85]

A personal remedy in quasi-contract is available where to grant it would not involve indirect enforcement. For example, premiums paid under *ultra vires* contracts of life assurance would be so recoverable,[86] as would the price paid for undelivered goods or unrendered services. If the outsider has parted with identifiable chattels, the remedies in tort of detinue and conversion will be available to him. There is also the possibility of a discretionary order for the specific restitution of goods. The outsider may further vindicate his rights *in rem* by tracing at common law, and into a mixed fund in equity by securing a charge thereon.[87]

The foregoing summary of the rag bag of remedies available to an

---

[81] But not completely. He had purported to lend at 7 per cent. interest: this was disallowed since the *intra vires* creditor to whose rights he was subrogated had not stipulated for interest. However, interest at the Court rate is allowable from the date of validation: *Baroness Wenlock* v. *River Dee Co.* 19 Q.B.D. 155.

[82] *Re Wrexham, Mold & Connah's Quay Railway* [1899] 1 Ch. 440.

[83] *Sinclair* v. *Brougham* [1914] A.C. 398, a refusal based essentially on considerations of public policy. These must have weakened in today's climate of easy alterability of objects. Nonetheless, the case remains a direct and binding authority in Ireland.

[84] *Re Irish Provident Assurance Co. Ltd.* [1913] 1 I.R. 352 365, 377; these were the winding up proceedings consequent upon *Flood's Case, infra.* The company was the applicant for restitution, but the principle must be applicable to outsiders *mutatis mutandis.* See *Buggy* v. *Maher* [1926] I.R. 487 for a statement by Murnaghan J. of the principle that he who seeks equity must first do equity by disgorging benefits wrongly received.

[85] *Per* Palles C. B., at p.365.

[86] *Flood* v. *Irish Provident Assurance Co.* 46 I.L.T.R. 214; *Re Phoenix Life Assurance Co.* 2 J. & H. 441.

[87] See *Shanahan's Stamp Auctions Ltd.* v. *Farrelly and Dawson* [1962] I.R. 386 in which the tracing principles laid down in *Re Hallett's Estate* (1880) 13 Ch. D. 696, 705, *Sinclair* v. *Brougham, supra,* and *Re Diplock* [1948] Ch. 465 were applied.

ultra vires creditor unprotected by section 8 shows that it is possible in many instances for him to claw back some benefit. Since none of them allow a claim for loss of profit[88] they are almost invariably inferior to the forfeited contractual remedies, though, in some instances where the company is insolvent, a claim *in rem* (tracing) in respect of the price paid for goods undelivered or services unrendered, or in respect of goods delivered but not paid for may be superior to the *in personam* contractual claim available to an *intra vires* creditor in like circumstances, securing priority over him in the liquidation. The right akin to subrogation is by definition superior to tracing where that process is halted by the use of the funds to pay an *intra vires* creditor.[89]

The remedies afforded to the *ultra vires* claimant are piecemeal and arbitrary. The unpaid supplier of services fares worse than the unpaid supplier of the goods, and yet morally there is nothing to choose between them; the tracer's prospects of success depend upon haphazard chances which may result in his doing better or worse in relation to other claimants against the company with whom he has an equal moral claim; and the examples could be multiplied. The only measure of reform appropriate to remove these anomalies would be to confer on the company in its dealings with outsiders the same capacity as that possessed by individuals.[90]

If a company has parted with property in purported pursuance of a gift or other gratuitous disposition which it had no capacity to make, it would seem on principle that the outsider in possession thereof must be treated as if in possession without right or title of property belonging to the company, and accordingly remedies in tort or in tracing (in respect of the property and its product) should lie against him. Insofar as the company purported to confer such benefit by deed or other instrument, it is ineffective through lack of the capacity to execute it. If it purported to confer the benefits by physical delivery, no property passed through a lack of the capacity to form the requisite intention to give.[91]

The company seeking to enforce an ultra vires transaction

Where a company's agent exceeds his authority to contract on its behalf, it has always been possible for the company to adopt the

---

[88] But see n.81, *supra*, for the recovery of interest.

[89] Tracing in equity is not available against a bona fide purchaser for value without notice, which such a creditor will usually be.

[90] It is submitted that internally the position should remain as it is. See *The internal position as between member and company*, *infra*.

[91] For the necessity for such an intention, see Crossley Vaines, *Personal Property*, (3rd ed., London, 1962), p.263.

agent's acts by ratification on normal agency principles, thereby precluding the outsider from pleading the want of authority as avoiding the contract. An *ultra vires* transaction however is incapable of acquiring validity through ratification by the company.[92] This rule flowed from the fact that the capacity of a company was conferred, not by the collective will of the members, but by statute, and once so conferred was immutable. This rationale has departed with the advent of alterability of objects by the members in general meeting,[93] and it may well be that the company, having by special resolution made a prospective alteration of objects sufficient to permit the existing and disputed transaction for the future, may then have the capacity to adopt it by ratification, all the more so if the alteration purports to confer an *express* capacity to adopt past transactions. There is no specific authority for the foregoing proposition, but the Supreme Court in *Bank of Ireland Finance Ltd.* v. *Rockfield Ltd.*[94] has observed *obiter* that it is "*at the time of ratification* [that] the principal must have been legally capable of doing the act himself." The existing authorities[95] are clear however that an alteration of objects does not *ipso facto* have a retrospective ratifying effect, despite the words in section 10 which state that such alteration to the objects clause shall be as valid as if originally contained therein.

Turning now to consider whether the outsider can plead *ultra vires* against the company at all, the traditional view is that such a contract, being void, is enforceable neither by the company nor by the outsider.[96] Latterly, this view has begun to be questioned in respect of contracts where the company has executed its part. For example, in *Bell Houses Ltd.* v. *City Wall Properties Ltd.* Salmon L.J. doubted *obiter* whether a doctrine manifestly for the benefit of the share-

---

[92] *Ashbury Railway Carriage and Iron Co.* v. *Riche* (1875) L.R. 7 H.L.C. 653; *Re Bansha Woollen Mills* 21 L.R.; Ir. 181; *Re Balgooley Distillery Co.* (1886) 17 L.R., Ir. 239, 258, 267; *Buchanan Ltd.* v. *McVey* [1954] I.R. 89, 98.

[93] s.10 of the 1963 Act.

[94] [1979] I.R. 21, 35 (emphasis supplied), citing *Firth* v. *Staines* [1897] 2 Q.B. 70, 75 and at p.156, *infra. Cf.* Chatterton V.-C. in *Holmes* v. *Trench* [1898] 1 I.R. 319, 333: "The principle of ratification cannot apply to an act which was in itself a nullity."

[95] *Northern Bank Finance Corporation Ltd.* v. *Quinn and Achates Investment Company*, High Court, Keane J., November 8, 1979 unreported and *Securities Trust Ltd.* v. *Associated Properties Ltd.* High Court, McWilliam J., November 19, 1980, unreported. These words in s.10 mean that the altered objects are to have the same qualities as originally contained objects, and *per* Keane J. in the former case "relieve the company from the necessity of having the Memorandum in its altered form signed again by the subscribers and attesting witness and reprinted." s.7 of the 1963 Act imposes such requirements in respect of original memoranda.

[96] See Furmston, (1961) 24 M.L.R. 715.

holder[97] should allow outsiders to gain the benefit of the company's services without any prospect of paying for them.[98] Certainly the courts could construct some equity to the effect that the outsider should not take the benefit of a transaction without also taking the burden.[99] In the reverse situation, *supra*, where the company seeks to escape it can be argued that it has no capacity to undertake the burden; not so with the outsider.

Since the enactment of section 8 of the 1963 Act, there has been a new dimension to this discussion in Ireland.[1] Section 8 is expressed to be "in favour of" the outsider so that it seems only he and not the company may invoke it; it therefore seems that an outsider having an *ultra vires* contract with a company may at his option, depending on how matters turn out, either enforce that contract against the company under section 8 or resist the company's enforcement of it on the grounds that it is void. Such legislative partiality to the outsider may seem unfair but it is not unprecedented: unilaterally void contracts may also occur under the Infants Relief Act 1874. Nonetheless, this situation does illustrate the absurdity of the retention of the vestiges of the *ultra vires* rule in so far as they affect the external relations of a company.

There seems to be no doubt that an outsider may invoke the *ultra*

---

[97] [1966] 2 Q.B. 656, Historically, the judicial view was that the *ultra vires* rule served the two-fold purpose of protecting subscribers and *intra vires* creditors. See Lord Parker in *Cotman* v. *Brougham* [1918] A.C. 514, 520, and Lord Hatherley in the *Ashbury Railway Carriage* case: (1875) L.R. 7 H.L.C. 653, 687. For an original view of *ultra vires* as having a purely internal rôle as between the company and the members, see Berwick J. in *Re Bagenalstown and Wexford Ry. Co.* (1867) 1 L.R. Eq. 275, 281.

[98] Mocatta J., at first instance, [1966] 1 Q.B. 207, entertained no such doubts saying that "to hold the defendant liable on a non-existent contract would be contrary to all principle."

[99] This principle is encapsulated in the maxim *qui sentit commodum sentire debet et onus* acknowledged in the common law in *Dean and Chapter of Windsor* v. *Hyde* (1601) 5 Co. Rep. 24a; 77 E.R. 87, and corresponding to the rule of Scots law that a person may not "approbate and reprobate." The equitable doctrine of election is based on just such a broad principle: see Snell, *Principles of Equity*, 27th ed. p. 484. Other applications are found in the rule that a person who enjoys the benefit of a deed must also submit to its burdens: *Halsall* v. *Brizell* [1957] Ch. 169. It should also be noted that Commonwealth jurisdictions have shown a willingness actually to enforce transactions *ultra vires* a public authority against the other party to them where the former has performed its part. See *Breckenridge Speedway Ltd.* v. *The Queen (in right of Alberta)* (1967) 64 D.L.R. 2d. 488, affirmed by the Supreme Court of Canada (1970) 9 D.L.R. 3d. 142 (recovery of loan and interest); followed in *Provincial Treasurer of Alberta* v. *Long* (1975) 49 D.L.R. 3d. 695 (recovery of loan and interest). *Re K. L. Tractors* 106 C.L.R. 318, High Court of Australia, (recovery of the price of goods supplied).

[1] And also in Britain since the enactment of s.9 of the European Communities Act 1972. See Prentice, 89 L.Q.R. 518, 524.

vires against the company in the case of contracts which remain wholly executory. The lack of any binding promise moving from the company results in there being no consideration to support any reciprocal promise moving from the outsider.[2] Here again the outsider would have the option of enforcing the contract under section 8 or of freeing himself by setting up the total failure of consideration.

Finally, the company will in appropriate circumstances, and subject to similar qualifications, have the same remedies in tort,[3] quasi-contract, and *in rem* as those afforded to an outsider without the protection of section 8, save that the courts are possibly readier to grant quasi-contractual remedies to a company in cases where doing so might indirectly enforce the contract.[4] In *Brougham* v. *Dwyer*[5] the company recovered in quasi-contract, money advanced to an outsider under an *ultra vires* lending contract. Admittedly the promise of the outsider to repay was not *ultra vires* the outsider but by indirectly enforcing it, it may be argued that the *ultra vires* contract as a whole, of which that promise formed part, was enforced. *Brougham* v. *Dwyer* is now overshadowed by the later, and technically more authoritative, House of Lords decision in *Sinclair* v. *Brougham* where, as has been said,[4] their Lordships declined indirectly to enforce an *ultra vires* contract *against* a company by quasi-contractual means.[6]

The internal position as between member and company.

Section 8 increases the capacity of the company in favour of appropriately qualified outsiders. Internally, the *ultra vires* rule remains in full force. The company's capacity is enforceable as between a member and the company as part of the shareholder's contract,[7] and section 8(2) expressly declares that any member[8] may apply for an injunction against the company to restrain the commission by it of *ultra vires* acts. He may also apply for a declar-

---

[2] *Re Staines U.D.C.'s Agreement* [1968] 2 W.L.R. 1433, 1439.

[3] Including deceit and orders for reparation in criminal proceedings where the outsider takes services without ever having the intention of paying for them.

[4] *Sinclair* v. *Brougham* [1914] A.C. 398. See text at n.83, *supra*.

[5] (1913) 108 L.T. 504. See also *Caledonia Community Credit Union Ltd.* v. *Haldimand Feed Mill Ltd.* (1974) D.L.R. 3d. 676, 679 where a company lending *ultra vires* was held entitled to recover "as a promise to repay will be imputed to the borrower who is unjustly enriched."

[6] See Goff and Jones, *The Law of Restitution*, (1st ed.) p. 324.

[7] s.25 of the 1963 Act; Chap. 6, *infra*.

[8] A debenture holder may also apply. The Act here recognises the traditional view that creditors have an interest in restraining *ultra vires* transactions. See n.97, *supra*.

ation.[9] Section 8(1) makes it clear that any director or officer of a company who was responsible for the entry by that company into *ultra vires* transactions, even those externally validated by section 8 itself, "shall be liable to the company for any loss or damage suffered by the company in consequence thereof." It should be noted however that a member seeking to invoke this provision on behalf of the company against an erring director or officer will be subjected to the normal constraints of the derivative actions.[10]

Purported intervention under regulation 6[11]

This sorry story arose out of a desire to implement the First Council Directive[12] on the harmonization of company law in the member states of the European Economic Community, which Ireland became obliged to implement upon entry into that Community on January 1, 1973. The Directive required that the company law of Ireland be changed in a number of areas, but Irish law through section 8 of the Companies Act 1963, discussed above, was already in conformity with the Directive's requirements concerning the validation of a company's *ultra vires* contracts in favour of outsiders. The Directive had the stated object of ensuring that outsiders should be protected to the greatest possible extent against subsequent invalidation of obligations entered into in the name of the company,[13] and accordingly Article 9(1) states:

> "Acts done by the organs of the company shall be binding upon it even if those acts are not within the objects of the company, unless such acts exceed the powers that the law confers or allows to be conferred on those organs.
>
> However, Member States may provide that the company shall not be bound where such acts are outside the objects of the company, if it proves that the third party knew that the act was outside those objects or could not in view of the circumstances have been unaware of it; disclosure of the statutes[14] shall not of itself be sufficient proof thereof."

[9] *Hennessy* v. *National Agricultural and Industrial Development Association* [1947] I.R. 159.

[10] Chap. 8, *infra.*

[11] See Ussher, "Questions of Capacity: the implementation in the Republic of Ireland and in the United Kingdom of the First EEC Companies Directive," (1975) *Irish Jurist*, 39.

[12] Council Directive of March 9, 1968, 68/151; O.J.E.C. Special English ed., Dec. 1972, 1968 (I) p. 41.

[13] See the preamble to the Directive.

[14] The company's constitution (*i.e.* memorandum, articles and special resolutions).

Thus, the primary desire of the Directive was that the *ultra vires* rule be wholly abrogated in favour of outsiders, and the maximum deviation allowed to Member States from this standard was the line already taken by section 8 with its requirement that the company prove actual awareness on the part of the outsider. The expression "actually aware," standing on its own as in section 8, allows a court to infer that an outside was in fact "actually aware" if, despite his denial, other evidence on the balance of probability points towards this conclusion. Thus, the rider in the Directive, "or could not in view of the circumstances have been unaware of it" must be regarded as cautious surplusage, adding nothing to the formula already employed in section 8.1[14a]

Nevertheless the Minister for Industry and Commerce on June 20, 1973 proceeded to enact regulation 6 of the European Communities (Companies) Regulations 1973[15] as follows:

> "(1) In favour of a person dealing with a company in good faith, any transaction entered into by any organ of the company, being its board of directors or any person registered under these regulations as a person authorised to bind a company, shall be deemed to be within the capacity of the company and any limitation of the powers of that board or person, whether imposed by the memorandum or articles of association or otherwise, may not be relied upon as against any person so dealing with the company.
>
> (2) Any such person shall be presumed to have acted in good faith unless the contrary is proved."

This regulation deals both with the authority of agents to represent a company and with the capacity of the company itself. One is concerned here only with the latter.[16]

The regulation requires "good faith" on the part of the outsider,[17] and in this respect goes beyond the latitude allowed to Member States in the Directive. Good faith imposes subjective standards; it requires honesty on the part of the outsider, and imposes upon him a duty to investigate should suspicious circumstances come to his

[14a] See n. 73, *supra*.

[15] S.I. 1973, No. 163 made by him pursuant to s.3 of the European Communities Act 1972 which conferred a general enabling power on Ministers of State to implement European Communities requirements by delegated legislation.

[16] The authority of a company's agents is discussed in Chap. 5, *infra*.

[17] Influenced, no doubt by the formulation adopted across the water. See s.9 of the European Communities Act 1972. [*U.K.*].

attention.[18] Thus, an outsider whilst not actually aware of the company's lack of capacity will not be in good faith if he allows to remain unresolved any suspicions which he may actually have about the company's capacity. Such suspicions may arise from a discrepancy between the company's name and the nature of the business conducted by it, or by a change in the nature of the company's business of which the outsider is aware from previous dealings with it, or from doubts on points of construction arising from a reading of the company's memorandum, and the examples could be multiplied. Most concern the outsider who knows some company law. He, to maintain his bona fides, may be bound to pause and investigate, whilst his rival unhindered by such learning may go ahead and transact business. The Directive would free both of them from a duty to investigate, and so does section 8.

It is patent that we are dealing here with a legislative blunder.[19] The regulations nowhere expressly amend or repeal section 8, and, indeed, expressly apply it to unregistered companies to which it had not previously applied.[20] Accordingly, the courts are free to construe regulation 6 as not amending section 8 and would be assisted to such conclusion by the following considerations. The legislation as a whole may be construed on the assumption that Ireland did not wish to fall short of the requirements of the Directive[21] and that the Minister did not intend to act *ultra vires* in that he had no power to alter domestic law other than to make it accord with the Directive. Also, it would be odd if the law were to be amended only where the

---

[18] Ussher, *op. cit.*, pp. 44–46; *London Joint Stock Bank* v. *Simmons* [1892] A.C. 201, 217, and *Jones* v. *Gordon* 2 App. Cas. 616, 628–629 (cases concerning negotiable instruments), and *Midland Bank Trust Co. Ltd.* v. *Green* [1981] 1 All E.R. 153 in which Lord Wilberforce said (at 158): "Addition of a requirement that a purchaser should be in good faith would bring with it the necessity of inquiring into the purchaser's motives and state of mind . . . ," No objective standard is imposed: "The reasonable man sets himself a higher standard than to act in good faith," *per* O'Dálaigh C.J. in *Holoham* v. *Friends Provident and Century Life Office* [1966] I.R. 1, 21.

[19] See the deliberations (Vol. 1, No.7, February 7, 1974) and *Report* (Prl. 3841) of the Oireachtas Joint Committee on the Secondary Legislation of the European Communities.

[20] See Reg.8 of the 1973 Regulations where in the Table is found: "Subject matter: Acts done by company *(ultra vires* rule) . . . Provisions applied: s.8." An unregistered company is, broadly speaking, any trading corporation having a place of business in the State and incorporated therein otherwise than by a public general statute: s.377 of the 1963 Act.

[21] This principle is adopted by the German Federal Supreme Court. See *Friedrich Haaga Gmbh* [1975] C.M.L.R. 124 where the effect of the German implementation of the EEC First Directive on company law was considered. Similarly in *International Sales and Agencies Ltd.* v. *Marcus* [1982] 3 All E.R. 551 the equivalent British legislation was construed so as to give effect to the court's interpretation of the directive. In particular "good faith" was defined as meaning the formula set out in the Directive.

outsider deals with the board of directors or a person registered under the regulations leaving section 8 to apply to dealings with the other, and often lesser, agents to whom a company may act. Similarly, regulation 6 appears to apply only to commercial dealings like its British model, and it would be peculiar to leave section 8 in a truncated form to deal with gratuitous dispositions. Finally, regulation 6 is not actually inconsistent with section 8: each applies in favour of persons with differing characteristics, the one to be in good faith and the other not to be actually aware.[22] It just so happens that all outsiders in good faith will also not be actually aware, whereas the reverse is not true.

The practical result of the foregoing interpretation will be that Regulation 6 will remain a dead letter[23] so far as the company's capacity is concerned. It does however have a role in circumventing limitations on the authority of certain of a company's agents.[24]

The alteration of objects and the protection of dissentients

Section 10(1) of the 1963 Act provides that[25]:

" . . . a company may, by special resolution, alter the provisions of its memorandum by abandoning, restricting or amending any existing object or by adopting a new object and any alteration so made shall be as valid as if originally contained therein, and be subject to alteration in like manner."

The ensuing sub-sections give a procedure[26] under which dissent-

---

[22] In this connection note Lord Cranworth's observation in *O'Flaherty* v. *M'Dowell* 6 H.L.C. 142, 10 E.R. 1248, on appeal from Ireland, citing at p.162 Lord Clare in *Hayden* v. *Carroll* 3 Ridg. Parl. Cases 545: "if there be two affirmative statutes, and 'the provisions in the subsequent affirmative statute are not contrariant,' as he terms it to those of the prior affirmative statute, those provisions not so contradicted by the subsequent statute must stand."

[23] Indeed, this may already have happened. Reg.6 was not even mentioned in the judgment in *Northern Bank Finance Corporation Ltd.* v. *Quinn and Achates Investment Company* High Court, unreported, Keane J., November 8, 1979. It was not strictly material since that case concerned an unlimited company to which Reg.6 does not apply, but immaterial English legislation *was* discussed.

[24] There was a possibility of legislative clarification. The Government's fifth and sixth *Reports on Developments in the European Communities* (Prl. 4663 and Prl. 5118) stated that "consideration is being given to the steps to be taken to amend" the 1973 Regulations in the light not only of opinions given by the Joint Committee, but also by the EEC Commission.

[25] Such alterations do not *per se* have a retrospective effect. See text at n.95, *supra*.

[26] The procedure is largely self-explanatory, and is in most respects identical to that contained in s.5(2) *et seq* of the 1948 Act [U.K.]. Unlike s.10 the British statute still requires grounds for the alterations: s.5(1).

ing shareholders[27] may apply to the court for the alteration to be cancelled. In such a case, the alteration has effect only in so far as it is confirmed by the court, but in all other cases the special resolution itself is sufficient to effect the alteration. The dissentients must either have or represent at least 15 per cent. of the company's nominal share capital or of any particular class thereof (or, not less than 15 per cent. of the members if the company is not limited by shares).

An application to the court is therefore the first line of defence (apart from voting against the special resolution) for a member who finds that his company is about to change direction in a manner not to his liking. The court then has a wide discretion under which it may cancel the alteration, or confirm it either in whole or in part, or impose terms and conditions, including a condition requiring the majority to purchase the shares of the dissenting minority if that is what the dissentients wish, or a condition that the company itself purchase the shares of any members, and reduce its share capital accordingly. The legislation[28] is however silent on what factors should influence the court in exercising this discretion. Assumedly, the court should be satisfied that the new object is proper within the construction of the Acts. On this occasion there is no registrar's "conclusive" certificate interposed between the courts and their view of a proper object.[28a] For the rest, Irish case law on the alteration of objects, in so far as material nowadays,[29] states that the objection of the dissentient member must be made *qua* member, and not in some other capacity. In *Re Munster and Leinster Bank*[30] the seven objecting shareholders who were also solicitors failed to prevent an alteration in the Bank objects, enabling the Bank to undertake executorship and trusteeship work in addition to its banking activities. The objections were designed more to preserve a traditional area of profit for solicitors rather than to safeguard their interests as shareholders. A more general statement of the principles affecting the court's discretion is found in the English case of *Re Jewish Colonial Trust*.[31] It can be deduced from this case that the court is

---

[27] And also debenture-holders, but only if their debentures were issued before April 1, 1964, or form part of a series so issued.

[28] s.10(6), as amended by para. 3, Sched. 1, 1983 Act. For reduction of capital, see pp.283–288, 338–340, *infra*.

[28a] See pp.116, *et seq*.

[29] Mostly not, in view of the changes introduced by the 1963 Act. The cases concern the ambit of the former restricted power, and procedural points under the former system which required positive confirmation of alterations by the court. See s.9 of the 1908 Act.

[30] [1907] 1 I.R. 237.

[31] [1908] 2 Ch. 287.

not concerned with the business merits of a proposed alteration. That is a matter for the requisite majority of members. The court is however concerned with "unfairness" between individual shareholders or between individual classes of shareholders. Most changes in trading direction will affect all members alike, and most objections to them will accordingly fail. It is however just possible to conceive of instances where objections under this principle might be sustained. For example, if a company formed for the purpose of acquiring assets for capital appreciation were to change to activities concentrating on the generating of income, a class of shareholders without income participating rights might legitimately object[32]; or, where a special majority within a trading company wished to discharge their moral or charitable obligations through the medium of a company by enabling it to distribute its assets as largesse.[33]

In the case of non-commercial companies where its activities directly affect the members, an objection by a member on the ground of unfairness might be easier to sustain. In the *Jewish Colonial Trust* case, an alteration in objects restricting the Trust's colonisation and aid work to the Middle East only (as opposed to the worldwide scale of activities originally envisaged) was held to be unfair to those members living in other parts of the world.

Another line of defence may be found in a principle which considerably antedates the statutory alteration of objects, but which, nonetheless, appears still to thrive. This is the possibility of a member's petition for the winding up of the company on the just and equitable ground[34] for failure of substratum. Substratum may be defined as the understanding between subscribers and company of the type of business to be carried on by the company. It must be sharply distinguished from the company's capacity. As Lord Parker said in *Cotman* v. *Brougham*[35]:

> "The question whether or not a company can be wound up for failure of substratum is a question of equity between a company and its shareholders. The question whether or not a transaction is *ultra vires* is a question of law between the company and a third party . . ."

Doubtless in the earlier cases[36] a company's substratum was

---

[32] *e.g.* the share structure in *Re Saltdean Estate Co. Ltd.* [1968] 1 W.L.R. 1844.
[33] Such altruism is not unknown. See the conduct of the Cadbury family in *Parke* v. *The Daily News Ltd.* [1962] Ch. 927.
[34] s.213(*f*) of the 1963 Act.
[35] [1918] A.C. 514, 520.
[36] *Re German Date Coffee Co.*(1882) 20 Ch. D. 169; *Re Crown Bank* (1890) 44 Ch. D. 634: *Re Haven Gold Mining Co.* (1882) 20 Ch. D. 151.

treated as synonymous with its capacity, as it often is where the main objects rule of construction of capacity is to be applied. This is no longer so. In a case from the State of Victoria, *Re Tivoli Freeholds Ltd.*,[37] a company was wound up for failure of substratum whilst pursuing the *intra vires* business of money lending after selling its theatres and other assets for the running of which it was originally formed. Were the law otherwise, a statutory alteration of objects would be conclusive and the dissentients would have only the statutory right of objection. However, courts exercising the just and equitable jurisdiction recognise the lawful exercise of rights given by the Companies Acts but nonetheless visit them with equitable consequences; and, indeed, the exercise of such a right may be the precipitating event.[38]

How then does one find a company's substratum? Formerly, there were attempts to divine the substratum by an analysis of the objects clause of the memorandum,[39] but now after the restatement of the principles informing the just and equitable jurisdiction by Lord Wilberforce in *Ebrahimi* v. *Westbourne Galleries Ltd.*,[40] (a restatement adopted wholesale into Irish law by Gannon J. in *Re Murph's Restaurants Ltd.*),[41] a different approach is necessary. The former approach was part of a tendency, now to be discarded, to create separate and exclusive categories within the just and equitable jurisdiction. The new approach requires recognition of the fact that behind a limited company "or amongst it, there are individuals, with rights, expectations and obligations *inter se* which are not necessarily submerged in the company's structure. That structure is defined by the Companies Act . . . and by the articles of association by which shareholders agree to be bound. In most companies and in most contexts, this definition is sufficient and exhaustive . . . . The 'just and equitable' provision does not . . . entitle one party to disregard the obligation he assumes by entering a company, nor the court to dispense him from it. It does, as equity always does, enable the court to subject the exercise of legal rights to equitable considerations; considerations, that is of a personal character arising between one individual

---

[37] [1972] V.R. 338, [1973] A.S.C.L. 610, see Prentice, (1973) 89 L.Q.R. 107.

[38] In *Ebrahimi* v. *Westbourne Galleries Ltd.* [1973] A.C. 360, the lawful expulsion of a company director under s.184 of the 1948 Act led to a winding up on the just and equitable ground where there was an understanding between participants that all should take part in management.

[39] See for examples *Re Kitson & Co. Ltd.* [1946] 1 All E.R. 435; *Re Taldua Rubber Co.* [1946] 2 All E.R. 763.

[40] [1973] A.C. 360.

[41] High Court, unreported, July 31, 1979, Ussher, (1979–1980) D.U.L.J. 92.

and another, which may make it unjust, or inequitable, to insist on legal rights, or to exercise them in a particular way."[42]

Thus, a company may not have a substratum at all. There may be no particular understanding on the basis of which the money was subscribed, and which would be violated by an alteration of objects and the assumption of a fresh direction. But commonly there will be such an understanding, particularly where a company has been formed to take over and manage an existing family business or family assets.

Although the substratum is usually stated to be a matter of equity between the original subscribers and the company, it seems on principle that a transferee of shares may by the transfer acquire the benefit of it just as equities travel within a conveyance. Or fresh equities may arise during the life of a company. These aspects are free from authority. How then does substratum fail? Formerly, it was said to fail if the resumption of the original purpose was as a practical matter impossible. Thus a ship owning company might have sold all its ships, become an investment company, and thirty years later, without having bought any replacement ships, might yet still deny a shareholder the pleasure of a liquidation of assets and distribution of funds because it might yet revert to its original purpose, despite the absence of any intention on the part of its controllers to do so.[43] The modern approach, exemplified in *Re Tivoli Freeholds Ltd., supra* is to ask whether the understanding has been violated, and if it has, then the just and equitable consequence follows whether the violation be wilful or inescapable. Indeed one might consider intervention in the former case more justifiable.

Since the just and equitable jurisdiction is subject to the usual equitable considerations, a member should lose his remedy if he or his predecessor in title have acquiesced in an alteration of objects or change of direction. Also, the courts may not be inclined to grant the devastating remedy of a winding up in loss of substratum cases where the complainant has been made a fair offer for his shares.[44]

---

[42] *Per* Lord Wilberforce at [1973] A.C. 360, 379; echoed by Gannon J. in *Re Murph's Restaurants Ltd., supra.*

[43] *Galbraith* v. *Merito Shipping Co.* [1947] S.C. 446; McPherson, (1964) 27 M.L.R. 282. *Cf. Re Chinese Estates Ltd.* [1976] H.K.L.R. 369 in which a winding-up was refused where a building, held as the company's main asset since its formation, had been sold but the directors intended to pursue the *intra vires* activity of investing in other land.

[44] Such an offer is not always sufficient to secure the dismissal of just and equitable petitions; in some circumstances, *e.g.* those of *Re Murph's Restaurants Ltd. supra*, it may be unfair that the respondents should remain in control of the company. Such considerations are unlikely to apply where the complaint is loss of substratum.

Monetary compensation to the full "assets" or "break-up" value of his shares should usually satisfy the equity.[45] Often, the hope of such an offer will be the motive for the proceedings.

Unlike the statutory procedure for dissentients, there is no minimum share qualification required to found a petition on the just and equitable ground. In *Bryanston Finance Ltd.* v. *de Vries (No. 2)*,[46] a petitioner under the equivalent English jurisdiction was not non-suited for holding only 62 shares out of a total issued capital of 7,414,938. Nor is there any provision for the company itself to buy out the dissentient.[47]

---

[45] *Cf.* the power of the court under s.10(6) to adjourn a dissentient members' application under the statutory procedure "in order that an arrangement may be made to the satisfaction of the Court for the purchase of" their interests.

[46] [1976] Ch. 63.

[47] s.10(6), as amended by para. 3, Sched. 1, 1983 Act. See p.138, *supra*.

Chapter 5. Contract and Tort

This chapter concerns the responsibility of a company in contract and in tort for the acts of its agents.[1]

CONTRACT

A company must act through agents. We are concerned here with the authority of agents to bind a company to a contract *within its capacity*.[2] The dominant role is played by the ordinary rules of agency, but they are considerably complicated by a network of subsidiary rules special to companies.

The ordinary law of agency

Actual and ostensible authority
    The company as principal is obviously bound if the agent had *actual* authority to conclude the contract on its behalf. The common law has however long held the view that commerce would grind to a halt if persons dealing with an agent were required scrupulously to check the precise limits of his actual authority before entering into the contract through him. Accordingly, as with so much commercial law, the person dealing with an agent is entitled to rely upon appearances without verifying the actuality. The principal is bound if the act is one within the *ostensible* authority of the agent even if no actual authority exists.[3] To this must be entered the usual *caveat* that the outsider must not have known or have had actual notice (in the sense of being put on enquiry) that the agent was exceeding his

---

[1] For criminal responsibility, see pp.39 *et seq.*, *supra*.

[2] This chapter is written on the footing that no question of *ultra vires* arises. For that, and the capacity of a company to contract and make gifts, see Chap. 4.

[3] For an early Irish statement of the principle of ostensible authority, see *Page* v. *G.N.R.* (1868) I.R. 2 C.L. 228, 233; and for general statements of principle the standard works such as Bowstead, *Agency*, and Halsbury's *Laws of England*.

actual authority, for that would destroy the semblance of authority upon which the outsider was seeking to rely.

Ostensible authority may be viewed as an impression given by the principal to the world upon which the world is entitled to rely, and indeed in the leading English case of *Freeman & Lockyer* v. *Buckhurst Park Properties (Mangal) Ltd.*,[4] Diplock L.J. rationalised this area of the law in terms of a representation, express or implied, from which the principal is estopped from resiling. One may ask three questions about such representations. *What* is their content? *How* are they made? *By whom* are they made?

Contents of the representation

The representation may be that the agent held a particular post or position, and that he possessed the *usual* authority of someone in that position; or, the contents of the representation may go further by asserting that his authority is greater than the usual. It is often important in company law to distinguish this element of usual authority: it not only frequently accords with the actuality, but also serves as an indication to the outsider of the normal limits outside of which he is certainly not safe in dealing through the agent. One should consider therefore the usual authority of a company's agents within the Table A type company structure.[5] Structures other than Table A are not sufficiently widespread to found a usual authority upon them.

The usual authority of *the directors, acting as a board*, is as wide as the usual articles delegating functions to it. The widest of these is article 80 giving the board the management of the company's business, but other articles throughout Table A entrust other specific functions to it. All these things are therefore within the usual authority of the board. However, this usual authority may in actuality have been cut down in a number of ways. For example, the articles of a particular company may not be in common form in that certain decision making powers ordinarily left to the board may be reserved for the approval of the general meeting[6] or the general meeting may have made an effective direction to the board under article 80,[7] or the board may under article 112 have taken the unusual course of

---

[4] [1964] 2 Q.B. 480; Rice, [1965] J.B.L. 317.

[5] Their relative functions were reviewed in Chap. 3: *Internal Structure.*

[6] *e.g.* in *Re Burke Clancy & Co. Ltd.* (High Court, May 23, 1974, Kenny J., unreported) the articles required that the exercise of directors' borrowing powers be approved of by the company in general meeting. The common qualification such as that in Art. 79 of Table A that outsiders need not be concerned with this restriction was not present. In fact, in common practice, the Table A restriction is deleted.

[7] For this possibility see pp.87 *et seq., supra.*

appointing a managing director "to the exclusion of their own powers."

The usual authority of a *managing director* is potentially commensurate with that of the board in running the business of the company. But again, behind the scenes it may have been cut down in actuality. Perhaps his terms of appointment provide that his areas of responsibility shall from time to time be determined by the board as in *Holdsworth (Harold) & Co. (Wakefield) Ltd.* v. *Caddies.*[8]

The usual authority of an *individual director* acting *as such* is minimal. He cannot be assumed to have authority to contract on behalf of the company.[9] It is within his usual authority in view of the common form article 115 to witness the affixing of the company's seal to a document which requires it, but even here in actuality, his authority to do so may not exist, since the same article provides that the seal shall only be used by authority of the board of directors.

A *chairman of the board of directors* may be either a figurehead or the driving force behind the company.[10] Consequently, the chairman of the board as such has no settled role in the representation of the company, and therefore no settled usual authority save in one respect. It is part of the usual function of a chairman of the board to sign minutes of previous board meetings. If he does so, they constitute a standing representation until disproved that the meeting was duly held and convened and of what occurred at it: section 145(3) of the Companies Act 1963. The chairman's minute may thus constitute a sufficient memorandum to bind the company to a contract previously unenforceable because of the Statute of Frauds 1695.[11]

---

[8] [1955] 1 W.L.R. 352; discussed at pp.90–91, *supra.*

[9] *Freeman & Lockyer, supra; Hazlewood* v. *West Coast Securities Ltd.* (1975) 49 D.L.R. 3d 46, 61.

[10] In *Hely-Hutchinson* v. *Brayhead Ltd.* [1968] 1 Q.B. 549, the chairman was found by the English Court of Appeal on the facts of that case to have actual authority to bind the company. Again, actual authority with an equal ostensible authority was found in a chairman in *Kilgobbin Mink & Stud Farms Ltd* v. *National Credit Co. Ltd.* [1980] I.R. 175. The ostensible authority seems to have been founded on a course of dealing. In *British Thomson-Houston Co. Ltd.* v. *Federated European Bank Ltd.* [1932] 2 K.B. 176 there was an ostensible authority founded on the chairman's having been allowed to act as if a sole managing director. In *Nash* v. *Lancegaye Safety Glass (Ireland) Ltd.* (1958) 92 I.L.T.R. 11, 18 a chairman was entrusted by the board with "full and complete plenipotentiary powers." Some standard form modifications of Table A in common use in Ireland allow the board to appoint a director to "any executive office in the management of the business . . . including the office of Chairman or Deputy Chairman . . . as the directors may decide, and on such terms as they think fit, and if no period or terms are fixed, then such executive shall comply with such directions as may be given to him by the directors from time to time." The functions of such an appointee are so variable that no usual authority can be built on the prevalence of this article.

[11] *Jones* v. *Victoria Graving Dock Co.* (1877) 2 Q.B.D. 314; *Re Strathblaine Estates Ltd.* [1948] 1 Ch. 228.

The mere fact that a person is a *controlling shareholder* of a company does not entitle the outsider to assume that he has any usual authority[12] for to do so would of necessity disregard the company's constitution, but doubtless the court was helped towards a finding of actual authority in *Kilgobbin Mink & Stud Farms Ltd. v. National Credit Co.Ltd.*[13] by the fact that the agent in question held 49,999 of the 50,000 issued shares of the company.

As far as the usual authority of the *company secretary* is concerned, the world has moved on since Lord Esher said in *Barnett, Hoares & Co. v.South London Tramways Co.*[14] "A secretary is a mere servant: his position is that he is what he is told, and no person can assume that he has any authority to represent anything at all . . . " The outsider may certainly now assume that it is within the usual authority of a company secretary to enter into contracts on its behalf concerning administrative matters ancillary to the carrying on of the company's business and its internal functioning. In *Panorama Developments (Guildford) v. Fidelis Furnishing Fabric Ltd.*[15] a company was held liable upon contracts entered into by a company secretary on his company's behalf for the hire of cars which he used for his own purposes. The secretary's role has evolved from that of a mere hand to do the directors' bidding. Older authorities are therefore unreliable insofar as they tend to limit a secretary's ostensible authority within areas which are now his established province, such as the issuing of share certificates[16] and the certification of transfers[17] so as in each case to make a representation effectively estopping the company as against an outsider.

---

[12] *I.R.C.* v. *Ufitec Group Ltd.* [1977] 3 All E.R. 924, 937.

[13] [1980] I.R. 175.

[14] [1887] 18 Q.B.D. 815, 817.

[15] [1971] 2 Q.B. 711; see also *Re Maidstone Buildings Provisions Ltd.* [1971] 1 W.L.R. 1085, 1092–1093.

[16] Cases where the secretary *had* actual authority to issue certificates and the company *was* estopped include *Re Bahia & San Francisco Railway Co.* (1868) L.R. 3 Q.B. 584; *Re Ottos Kopje Diamond Mines Ltd.* [1893] 1 Ch. 618; *Balkis Consolidated Co.* v. *Tomkin* [1893] A.C. 396. Cases where the secretary acted unauthorisedly include *Bank of Ireland* v. *Evans Charities Trustees* (1855) H.L. Cas 389; 10 E.R. 950 (chartered corporation); *Ruben* v. *Great Fingall Consolidated* [1906] A.C. 439; *South London Greyhound Racecourses Ltd.* v. *Wake* [1931] 1 Ch. 496. s.26 of the 1983 Act now operates to prevent a company being estopped from claiming that shares certified as fully paid on allotment were not in fact paid up. See p.307, *post.*

[17] By s.79, where a secretary *has* general authority to certify transfers a certification by him estops the company even where a share certificate had not been lodged with him. *George Whitechurch Ltd.* v. *Cavanagh* [1902] A.C. 117 and *Kleinwort* v. *Associated Automatic Machine Corporation Ltd.* [1934] W.N. 65 are now therefore overruled by statute. Where unusually the secretary in a particular case has not in fact even the actual authority, the outsider must rely on the evolution described in the text.

Auditors do not as such have any authority to make representations on behalf of the company.[18]

Other agents with power to bind the company in contract will commonly also be employed. Their usual authority will depend upon their functions, whether they be shop assistants, purchasing officers, sales managers, salesmen, foremen, or whatever. These essentially are not company law questions. Certainly, at the higher levels within a company, the employee may also be a director, but that fact of itself is not sufficient to found usual authority in contract.

The maker of the representation

By whom may a representation of ostensible authority effectively be made? Obviously, the mere assumption by the purported agent himself of the power in question is not sufficient; neither are any representations made by him about the extent of his own powers.[19] What is necessary is a representation by a person or body of persons within the company with actual power to confer the authority in question. Thus in the *Freeman & Lockyer* case where an individual director acted as managing director though not appointed as such, the representation of his authority was found in the board of directors who did have power to appoint a managing director, and had allowed the individual to act as one. Sometimes it is necessary to go back further than the board of directors within the structure of the company to find persons capable of making the representation. In *Mahony* v. *East Holyford Mining Co.Ltd.*[20] persons purporting to be directors had entered into contracts on behalf of the company. The necessary representation of authority was found from the general body of members who had power to appoint directors.

Method of making the representation

How then are the representations made? They will usually be passive in the sense of standing by with knowledge of the purported agent's activities or allowing a course of dealing to develop (*e.g. Mahony* and *Freeman & Lockyer*), or the representation may be a posi-

---

[18] *Re Transplanters (Holding Co.) Ltd.* [1958] 1 W.L.R. 822.

[19] *Beloff* v. *Pressdram Ltd.* [1973] 1 All E.R. 241.

[20] (1875) L.R. 7H.L. 869; affirming (1871) I.R., 5 C.L. 508. Since the enactment of s.20 of the Companies Act 1900, a public register of directors of a company limited by shares has been compulsory with the result that on the facts of *Mahony*, the outsider would have been put upon enquiry about the existence of a board of directors. The present law concening this register is contained in s.195 as amended by s.8 of the 1982 Act and amplified by s.3 of that Act and by reg. 4(1)(*e*) of the European Communities (Companies) Regulations 1973. See *Company Law Modifications, infra.*

tive "holding out" by which the outsider is given to understand that the agent holds a particular position, or has a particular authority.

COMPANY LAW MODIFICATIONS

The ordinary rules of agency are in the case of companies modified by the idea of constructive notice which in turn is qualified by the "indoor management" rule[21] and severely restricted by Regulation 6 of the European Communities (Companies) Regulations 1973.[22]

Constructive notice

The constructive notice rule proceeds upon the impractical hypothesis that persons about to deal with a company will consult in the public registry those documents concerning it which a beneficient legislature has decided should be displayed there. "If they do not choose to acquaint themselves . . . it is their own fault"declared Lord Wensleydale in 1857,[23] thus raising opportunity to the level of duty, a robust attitude which it has taken over a century to mitigate, and even then only partially. Furthermore, and this is the most unsustainable aspect of the constructive notice rule, the outsider is deemed to understand the documents which he has notionally consulted. The doctrine in its unmodified form failed to take account not only of the practicalities of business life where non-perusal of public documents is the norm, but was also at variance with those corner stones of the commercial law which in the interests of the efficient operation of the market place say that in favour of persons dealing honestly, appearances should be given the force of reality, *e.g.* the ostensible authority of agents in the ordinary law of agency, the rights of a holder in due course of a bill of exchange, the powers of a seller in possession, the outlawing of secret security interests in chattels etc.. The list is longer,[24] and is indicative of a philosophy recently expressed in Ireland by Kenny J., unfortunately in a different context, in giving the judgment of the Supreme Court in *Bank of Ireland Finance Ltd.* v. *Rockfield Ltd.* that "the doctrine of constructive

---

[21] *Royal British Bank* v. *Turquand* (1856) 6 E. & B 327; *Mahony* v. *East Holyford Mining Co.*, n.20.

[22] S.I. 1973 No. 163.

[23] *Ernest* v. *Nichols* (1857) 6 H.L. Cas. 401, 418–419. The public right to inspect is now embodied in s.370 and for an equally robust criticism, see Sealy, *Company Law and Commercial Reality* (London, 1984). It is salutary to note that the registration of a deed under the Registration of Deeds (Ireland) Act 1707 does *not* constitute constructive notice of it, or its contents: *Latouche* v. *Dunsany* (1808) 1 Sch. & Lef. 137.

[24] The examples given in the text are drawn from the Bills of Exchange Act 1882; s.25 of the Sale of Goods Act 1893 and Bills of Sale (Ireland) Acts 1879–83.

notice is not to be extended to commercial transactions"[25] Its inclusion in company law was and remains at variance with this philosophy. There is also the comment of Parke J. in the Supreme Court decision of *Welch* v. *Bowmaker (Ireland) Ltd.*[26] that "The doctrine of constructive or implied notice, like that of public policy, is an unruly horse and should be ridden with a firm hand." Doubtless; but insofar as its rôle in the representation of companies in commercial dealings is concerned, if horse it be, it should be shot.

Whatever the utility of the public documents to those positively seeking information about a company, few would now doubt that deeming the public to be aware of the contents of every document filed in the Companies Registry is unrealistic. Whilst both the courts[27] and the legislature[28] have intervened substantively to qualify the doctrine, it remains at present the bedrock of the company law modifications of the ordinary law of agency.

Constructive notice has the effect of cutting down the ostensible authority of a company's agent. By no means all the public documents will be relevant to an outsiders' deemed perception of the authority of a company's agents. Those that may in a particular case be relevant are likely to be the documents forming part of a company's constitution, notifications to the registrar of the identity of certain officers, and certain resolutions.

Let us look at these sources of constructive notice, bearing in mind however that its consequences have been tempered judicially by the indoor management rule, *infra* and restricted statutorily by the European Communities (Companies) Regulations 1973, *infra*. But to understand these modifications one must first appreciate what would be the consequence of the doctrine's undiluted application, because the modifications assume the fact of constructive notice as a conceptual foundation upon which to build.

Taking first the constitutional documents, the articles of association may specifically have limited the powers of the agent to less than the usual, of which limitation the outsider would be deemed to be aware with a corresponding diminution in the ostensible authority of the agent. For example, the usual powers of the board to borrow might be dependent on the passing of a resolution in general

---

[25] [1979] I.R. 21, 35.

[26] [1980] I.R. 251. An outsider has constructive notice of charges created by a company and of which particulars are registered against it in the Companies Registry pursuant to ss.99 *et seq.* This case decided that the outsider did *not* thereby have constructive notice of a clause in the charge *not* forming part of the registered particulars even though such clauses are common place. The topic is discussed at pp. 423–429, *post.*

[27] See *The Indoor Management Rule, infra.*

[28] See *European Communities (Companies) Regulations, infra.*

meeting.[29] Or the outsider may be deemed to be aware from the articles of certain preliminary requirements necessary to perfect the usual authority of the agent. For example, the director who under article 115 witnesses the affixing of the company's seal to a document is required to be authorised by the board to do so. There are also internal procedural requirements of which the outsider will have notice. For example, the articles commonly require that there be a quorum at board meetings.[30]

Secondly, the Companies Acts require public notification of directors and secretaries,[31] with the result that an outsider dealing with a person purporting to be a director or secretary may be put upon enquiry if that person is not registered as such. In this respect, statute appears to have overtaken *Mahony* v.*East Holyford Mining Co.*[32] in which the outsider was able to rely upon the existence of an ostensible board held out as such by the members. The public register of directors of a company limited by shares came in after *Mahony* with section 20 of the Companies Act 1900. There is not yet in Irish company law any requirement that the identities of all agents authorised to bind a company be publicly disclosed.

Thirdly, with some minor exceptions,[33] the only resolutions which have to be registered, and therefore the only ones of which an outsider can have constructive notice are resolutions required to be passed by a special majority. These are predominantly special resolutions in general meeting, or agreements in lieu of them.[34] Broadly speaking therefore, the outsider will not have constructive notice of an ordinary resolution in general meeting or of a board resolution. An appreciation of this is vital to the understanding of the *Indoor Management Rule*, below. One must also appreciate that there are other internal matters apart from board and ordinary resolutions which may have a bearing upon the actual authority of a company's agents, but of which, again, the outsider will not have constructive notice. In particular the

---

[29] See *Re Burke Clancy & Co. Ltd.* (High Court, May 23, 1974, Kenny J; unreported).

[30] See *Allied Irish Banks Ltd.* v. *Ardmorre Studios International* (1972) *Ltd.* (High Court May 30, 1973, Finlay J; unreported).

[31] s.195, as amended and amplified by ss.3, 8 of the 1982 Act and reg. 4(1)(*e*) of the European Communities (Companies) Regulations 1973. Likewise, the appointment of a receiver or a liquidator must be notified to the registrar: see p. 430, n. 50, *infra*.

[32] (1875) L.R. 7 H.L. 869; affirming (1871) I.R., 5 C.L. 508.

[33] The exceptions are certain resolutions for voluntary winding up: s.251 (1) (*a*), (*c*); resolutions described by s.143(4)(*f*)—(*i*) (added by s.5 of the 1982 Act) insofar as they relate to unissued share capital; ordinary resolutions relating to the directors' authority to allot share capital passed pursuant to s.20 of the 1983 Act and the directors' resolutions described in Sched. 1, para. 14 of the 1983 Act relating to changes in the company's status which are added as s.143(4)(*j*).

[34] s.143(4).

outsider will not have constructive notice of the contractual terms of appointment of a managing director which may limit his authority to less than the usual. His contract may for example require him to submit all contracts for sales or purchases above a certain value to the board for approval. The outsider will have no constructive notice of that limitation, since his contract is not a public document.

The indoor management rule

The doctrine of constructive notice is tempered by the indoor management rule, known also as the rule in *Turquand's case*.[35] This allows an outsider to assume that all steps necessary to perfect or confer the *usual* authority of a company's agent have been taken, provided that the step itself was not one of which the outsider would have had constructive notice. For example, the agent concerned might be the board of directors itself, and the question might be whether that board was properly constituted. In *Allied Irish Banks Ltd.* v. *Ardmore Studios International (1972) Ltd.*,[36] the outsider had constructive notice that the company had three directors and that the quorum for board meetings was two. It did not matter that the third director might not have been given the notice to which he was entitled of the board meeting which adopted the transaction from which the company was now seeking to escape.[37] The giving or withholding of notices convening meetings was not something of which the outsider could constructively have had notice. Similarly, article 115 of Table A requires that the usual authority of a director and secretary to affix the company's seal to a document must be conferred by a resolution of the board. The outsider will have had no constructive notice of such a board resolution, and may assume that it has been passed.[38] For example, in *Ulster Investment Bank Ltd.* v. *Euro Estates Ltd.*[39] a mortgagee had notice of articles requiring a special quorum at board meetings of the mortgagor company. An inquorate meeting authorised the execution of the mortgage deed, and in upholding its validity, Carroll J. said:

> "In the ordinary way a mortgagee dealing with a company is entitled to rely on the rule in *Royal British Bank* v. *Turquand* and

[35] *Royal British Bank* v. *Turquand* (1856) 6 E. & B. 327.
[36] High Court, May 30, 1973, Finlay J. unreported.
[37] In reaching this conclusion, Finlay J. relied upon *Duck* v. *Tower Galvanising Ltd.* [1901] 2 K.B. 314.
[38] *Aliter* if any of the signatures are forged: *Ruben* v. *Great Fingall Consolidated* [1906] A.C. 439. See also the text at nn.16 and 17 *supra*.
[39] [1982] I.L.R.M. 57, following *County of Gloucester Bank* v. *Rudry Merthyr Steam and House Coal Colliery Co.* [1895] 1 Ch. 629.

is not obliged to call for copies of resolutions appointing directors or authorising the borrowing (where it is within the directors' powers[40]) or approving the form of the mortgage or
authorising the affixing of the seal. All these are matters of
internal management."[41]

Indeed, the reports abound in such general statements. In *Cox* v.
Dublin City Distillery (No. 2),[42] Palles C.B. said:

"It has been decided by a long line of cases, extending back certainly for fifty years, that an outsider taking debentures . . . ,
which are invalid merely by reason of a matter of internal management, is entitled to rely on the seal of the company as showing that everything connected with such management is right,
unless he has notice to the contrary . . . of any irregularity."

Likewise with most ordinary resolutions in general meeting: if the
directors' usual authority to borrow is subjected by the articles to
prior approval of a simple majority in general meeting, the proposed
lender may assume that such an approval has been obtained.[43] No
such assumption could be made if the approval were required to be
by special resolution since that would be a public document, and
therefore within the ambit of constructive notice.

The indoor management affects only *usual* authority. It cannot be
relied upon to perfect a potential authority wider than the usual. A
moment's reflection will confirm this. The board has the implied
power to appoint all manner of agents to carry on the company's

[40] See n.43, *infra.*

[41] At p.65.

[42] [1915] 1 I.R. 345, 373–374. The reference by Palles C.B. to the *seal* is coincidental. It just happens to be the method, necessary in that case, by which the company
entered into the transaction. For the non–necessity of the seal in most transactions,
see *Forms of Contracts, infra.* Unfortunately, this case was not cited in any of the more
recent Irish authorities above-mentioned.

[43] Though Kenny J. in dealing with this point *obiter* in *Re Burke Clancy & Co. Ltd.*
(High Court, May 23, 1974, unreported) reserved "for future consideration the question whether when the articles of association limit the borrowing powers of the directors and prescribe that the directors may not borrow more than the authorised or
issued share capital without the consent of the company in general meeting and an
application is made to a lender for a loan which will exceed that limit, he may assume
that the necessary resolution has been passed by the company giving the directors
these powers. When articles contain such a provision, it would, I think, be prudent for
lenders to get proof that such a resolution has been passed by the company in general
meeting." This question is largely academic, since the common form article 79 provides that "no lender or other person dealing with the company shall be concerned to
see or inquire whether" the limit is observed, and also because limitations on the
usual powers of the board will seldom now be resolved by an application of the indoor
management rule in view of the width of reg. 6 of the European Communities (Companies) Regulations, *infra.*

business: potentially therefore, a clerk might have been authorised by the board to bind the company to an important contract, but the outsider cannot rely upon that. Equally, an express power to delegate cannot be relied upon as perfecting in the proposed delegate an authority greater than the usual. Suppose, for example, that a company's articles contain the following unusual provision: "An ordinary individual director may if authorised by the board enter into contracts affecting all areas of the company's business." If the outsider were able to rely upon any potential beyond the usual, whether express or implied, as having been perfected then, according to Sargant L.J. in *Houghton & Co.* v. *Nothard, Lowe & Wills Ltd.*,[44] "Not only a director of limited company with articles founded on Table A, but a secretary or any subordinate officer might be treated by a third party acting in good faith as capable of binding the company by any sort of contract, however exceptional, on the ground that a power of making such a contract might conceivably have been entrusted to him."

An outsider cannot rely upon the indoor management rule where facts come to his attention indicating that the authority in question might not have been perfected. Such suspicious circumstances would be sufficient to put the outsider on enquiry, and negate the ostensible authority of the agent in question.

The practical effect of the indoor management rule has been much diminished by regulation 6 of the European Communities (Companies) Regulations 1973 since it operates to relieve the outsider of the consequences of limitations upon the authority of the board of seem to arise most in practice.

European Communities (Companies) Regulations 1973

These regulations apply only to companies with limited liability and cut down the doctrine of constructive notice in two ways. First, regulation 10 prevents the company from relying upon a variety of documents of which the outsider would otherwise have had constructive notice, unless notice of delivery of these documents to the registrar of companies has been published in *Iris Oifigiúil* or unless the company proves that the outsider had knowledge of them. The documents in question are set out for the most part in regulation 4, and include the memorandum and articles of association and alterations therein, and particulars of the directors. Furthermore, regulation 10 provides that "with regard to transactions taking place before the sixteenth day after the date of publication," the published directors, in respect of which the indoor management rule would documents "shall not be relied upon against a person who proves that it was

[44] [1927] 1 K.B. 246, 267. See also the *Freeman, Lockyer* case at [1964] 2 Q.B. 480, 507.

impossible for him to have had knowledge of them." The registry itself publishes the required particulars in *Iris Oifigiúil* as a matter of course. It has long been judicially determined that the insertion of an item in *Iris Oifigiúil* cannot be considered a sufficient publication of it if it is to affect rights; such an insertion is notice, as said Kennedy C.J. in *Re Mountcharles' Estate*,[44a] only to "that comparatively small and very select class, the regular readers of *Iris Oifigiúil*." Even without judicial support, it is obvious that publication in this organ is not an effective means of communication with the public at large and that such publication adds nothing to the disclosure requirements already in the Acts. We owe this absurd consumption of paper to Article 3 of the First EEC Companies Directive.

Regulation 6 strikes a more fundamental blow at constructive notice. It states:

"Organs authorised to bind company

6.(1) In favour of a person dealing with a company in good faith, any transaction entered into by any organ of the company, being its board of directors or any person registered under these regulations as a person authorised to bind the company, shall be deemed to be within the capacity of the company and any limitation of the powers of that board or person, whether imposed by the memorandum or articles of association or otherwise, may not be relied upon as against any person so dealing with the company.

(2) Any such person shall be presumed to have acted in good faith unless the contrary is proved.

(3) For the purpose of this Regulation, the registration of a person authorised to bind the company shall be effected by delivering to the registrar of companies a notice giving the name and description of the person concerned."

We have already looked at this regulation in Chapter 4 in the context of a company's capacity, and have, in particular explored the concept of "good faith."[45] Much said there need not be repeated here. We should however note again that regulation 6 applies only where the outsider is dealing with the board of directors, or a person specifically registered under the regulations. Suppose that the board is obliged by the company's articles to obtain a special resolution in power. Formerly, the outsider would have been deemed constructively to know of the necessity for that resolution, a public document, and would have been debarred by that constructive knowledge from relying on the board's ostensible authority to deal. Now by virtue of regulation 6 the board's ostensible authority is

---

[44a] [1935] I.R. 163, 166.   [45] At pp. 135 *et seq., supra.*

destroyed only if the outsider is actually put upon enquiry. Similarly, if the company has complied, as it should, with section 20 of
the Companies (Amendment) Act 1983 by placing limits on the
authority of the board to allot shares, the outsider would, but for
regulation 6, have had constructive notice of those limits since all
documents imposing them are public.[45a] By regulation 6, whether or
not an outsider may insist on the validity of an unauthorised allotment to him will depend on such factors as whether he was aware of
section 20, or otherwise put upon enquiry.[45b]

Article 9 of the First EEC Companies Directive is somewhat
opaque in communicating what it intended should be done about
limitations on the authority of the board to act in matters *intra vires*
the company. It *does* say in Article 9(2) that

> "The limits on the powers of the organs of the company, arising
> under the statutes[45c] or from a decision of the competent
> organs, may never be relied on as against third parties, even if
> they have been disclosed."

This does rather imply that an outsider when entering into transactions with a company through its board may assume that it has
plenipotentiary powers to bind it to acts within its capacity, and need
not be in good faith as to the existence of those powers. Such an interpretation of the Directive may be carried into Irish law by a purposive interpretation of the Regulations purporting to implement it.[45d]

The Directive *seems* to have it in mind that an outsider may continue to have constructive notice of limits on the powers of managing
directors,[46] but also indicates that there should, in accordance with
the German pattern[47] be compulsory disclosure and registration of
managing directors as well as ordinary individual directors. Article
2 of the Directive says, where material:

[45a] s.20(6) of the 1983 Act.

[45b] s.20(8) of the 1983 Act which states that nothing in s.20 should "affect the validity of any allotment of relevant securities" relates assumedly to non–compliance
with the section through failure to limit the authority of the directors, and not to acts
by them in excess of their authority as so limited. It has alway been open to an outsider dealing with a board which has exercised its powers improperly, and if not in
complicity with the board, to rely on the indoor management rule, and now *semble*,
reg. 6. See *Bamford* v. *Bamford* [1969] 1 All E.R. 969, 975–976, and *Nash* v. *Lancegaye
Safety Glass (Ireland) Ltd.* (1958) 92 I.L.T.R. 11, 27.

[45c] i.e. the Company's constitutional documents.

[45d] As in *International Sales Ltd.* v. *Marcus* [1982] 3 All E.R. 551, and *Re Friedrich
Haaga Gmbh* [1975] C.M.L.R. 124.

[46] Art. 9(3).

[47] *AKtG*, 78, 81 (September 6, 1965).

"1. Member States shall take the measures required to ensure compulsory disclosure by companies of . . .
(d) the appointment, termination of office and particulars of the persons who either as a body constituted pursuant to law or as members of any such body . . . are authorised to represent the company in dealings with third parties . . . It must appear from the disclosure whether the persons authorised to represent the company *may do so alone* or must act jointly."

Whatever the intention of the Directive, Ireland does not require registration of directors who individually are able to bind the company. The 1973 Regulations are merely facultative in this regard, and permit the registration of such a person should the company so wish. This lack of compulsion does not matter particularly in an Irish context, since a purported managing director will usually have been "held out" as such, and will thus be clothed with an ostensible authority which the company will be estopped from denying. It is unfortunate that the First Directive, adopted before Ireland and the United Kingdom joined the European Communities, was not subsequently modified to reflect the assumptions of agency at common law.

Ratification

A company may ratify unauthorised transactions entered into on its behalf, and thereby adopt them as its own.[48] The Supreme Court in *Bank of Ireland Finance Ltd.* v. *Rockfield Ltd.*[49] adopted the three conditions of ratification set out by Wright J. in the well known passage from his judgment in *Firth* v.*Staines*,[50] a somewhat surprising adoption in 1979, since the second condition had long been falsified insofar as it relates to pre-incorporation contracts by section 37 of the Companies Act 1963 of which more below. Wright J. said:

"To constitute a valid ratification three conditions must be satisfied. First, the agent whose act is sought to be ratified must have purported to act for the principal; Secondly, at the time the act was done the agent must have had a competent principal; and thirdly, at the time of the ratification the principal must be legally capable of doing the act himself."

---

[48] In the absence of ratification, the outsider may sue the purported agent for breach of warranty of authority as in *e.g. Chapleo* v. *Brunswick P.B. Building Society* (1881) 6 Q.B.D. 696, 715.

[49] [1979] I.R. 21, 35 *per* Kenny J.

[50] [1897] 2 Q.B. 70, 75; followed by the House of Lords (on appeal from Scotland) in *Alexander Ward Ltd.* v. *Samyang Navigaton Co. Ltd.* [1975] 2 All E.R. 424 in which a liquidator was held able to ratify on behalf of the company.

Thus in the *Rockfield* case, two persons who were not yet either members or directors of Rockfield Ltd. signed a promissory note "for and on behalf of Rockfield Ltd.," and thereby satisfied the first condition. The second condition is, as stated above, no longer wholly true in Ireland, since section 37 of the Companies Act 1963 permits a company to ratify contracts purportedly made on its behalf before it came into existence.

Section 37(1) follows a Jenkins Committee recommendation,[51] and states:

> "37(1) Any contract or other transaction purporting to be entered into by a company prior to its formation or by any person on behalf of the company prior to its formation may be ratified by the company after its formation and thereupon the company shall become bound by it and entitled to the benefit thereof as if it had been in existence at the date of such contract or other transaction and had been a party thereto."[52]

Delays of necessity occur in the formation process. Formerly, the promoter if he wished the company to be a party to a contract would have to wait until the certificate of incorporation had been issued before contracting on its behalf, or, if that proved impracticable,[53] he would be forced to contract in his own name, thereby incurring personal liability, and later transfer the benefit of the contract to the that difficulty. Despite the use of the word "transaction" it was held by the Supreme Court in *The State (Finglas Industrial Estates Ltd.)* v. *Dublin County Council*[53a] that the purported grant of planning permission to an applicant company not yet in existence at the date of the grant could not be adopted by the company after its incorporation. This decision flowed from the public policy consideration that the planning code assumes that both the planning authority and the public should have the "opportunity of vetting the planning application in the light of, among other matters, the identity of a named and legally existing applicant."[53b] Section 37 also obviates another question which used to embarass the courts before its enactment: has the purported agent contracted in such a way as to become himself personally liable on the contract? Answering this question led to

---

[51] 1962, Cmnd. 1749, para. 44. Britain has not yet an equivalent of s.37 (1).

[52] The form of s.37 is identical to the Ghana Companies Code, Act 179, s.13, drafted by Professor L.C.B. Gower. See his Report on Company Law in Ghana, p.32.

[53] *e.g.* land which the promoter intends the company ultimately to own may be offered for sale by its vendor before formation is complete.

[53a] February 17, 1983.

[53b] At p.3 of the transcript.

fine distinctions[54] which have been swept away by section 37(2) which says:

> "37(2) Prior to ratification by the company the person or persons who purported to act in the name or on behalf of the company shall in the absence of express agreement to the contrary be personally bound by the contract or other transaction and entitled to the benefit thereof."

Section 9(2) of the European Communities Act 1972 [*U.K.*][55] which is broadly equivalent to section 37(2) has been interpreted by the English Court of Appeal in *Phonogram Ltd.* v. *Lane*.[56] According to this interpretation the word 'purported'[57] does not imply that there is any need for there to have been a representation by the agent that the company was already in existence; indeed, *per* Lord Denning M.R. "a contract can purport to be made on behalf of a company, or by a company, even though that company is known by both parties not to be formed . . . "[58] More importantly, an "agreement to the contrary" cannot be inferred by the agent's having expressed himself to contract as agent or on behalf of the company. That would defeat the whole purpose of the section. There must be a clear exclusion of personal liability.[59]

The third condition in *Firth* v. *Staines* concerns mainly the capacity of the company itself; this aspect is dealt with elsewhere.[60] This third condition when applied to a company also requires that the ratifying body within the company could have conferred the missing authority in the first place. Occasionally, this body will not be the board of directors. In *Re Burke Clancy & Co. Ltd.*,[61] the articles limited the authority of the board of directors to borrow on behalf of the company "without the consent of the company in general meeting." The general meeting could bind the company to the excess borrowing by ratifying it after it had been incurred by the directors. This was a case where the articles expressly required the board of directors to obtain the authority of the general meeting before entering into the transaction. The general meeting may also under its residual power ratify, and thereby adopt on behalf of the company,

---

[54] See *Phonogram Ltd.* v. *Lane* [1981] 3 W.L.R. 736 and compare *Kelner* v. *Baxter* (1886) L.R. 2 C.P. 174 with *Newborne* v. *Sensolid (Great Britain) Ltd.* [1954] 1 Q.B. 45.
[55] Enacted pursuant to Art. 7 of Council Directive 68/151.
[56] [1981] 3 All E.R. 182.
[57] "Purports" in the British section.
[58] At p. 186g.
[59] At pp. 187e, 188.
[60] At p. 131, *supra*.
[61] High Court, Kenny J., May 23, 1974, unreported.

other unauthorised transactions of the board.[62] There are some transactions which are not ratifiable.[63]

Re Burke Clancy & Co. Ltd. shows that the ratification need not be explicit. In that case, approval by the general meeting of the company's annual accounts in which the unauthorised borrowing was reflected was held to be a sufficient ratification of the borrowing to bind the company.

Form of contracts

A company in making contracts is subject to the same formal constraints as a human individual in like circumstances. If the individual would have been required to use a seal or writing, then so will the company; otherwise, parol contracts will suffice.[64] The only constant point of difference between the company and an individual is that the company will always be acting through agents.

A person acting for a company under a power of attorney, such as a receiver disposing of its assets pursuant to powers given by common form debentures, has no power to use the company's seal where its articles are in the form of Table A, article 115: *Industrial Development Authority* v. *Moran*.[65] He may however execute deeds on its behalf by using his own name and seal, or by writing the name of the company alongside his own seal, or, apparently, by doing both.[66]

LIABILITY IN TORT

A corporation is no exception to the principle of vicarious liability in tort. It is vicariously liable as principal or employer for the tortious acts of its agents or servants acting within the scope of their employment just as any other principal or employer would be. This automatic assumption of liability stems from the relationship of principal and agent and master and servant, and there is no more need to impute to the corporation any complicity, mental or physical, than there is in the case of a human individual employer or principal who, however oblivious or innocent, is nonetheless deemed responsible in law.

---

[62] see p. 66 *et seq.*, *supra.*

[63] see p. 68 *et seq.*, *supra*, and pp.246–255, *infra.*

[64] s.38; likewise s.39 for negotiable instruments. See *Holmes* v. *Trench* [1898] 1 I.R. 319, 333.

[65] [1978] I.R. 159 (Supreme Court, on a reference by the Registrar of Titles).

[66] *Ibid.*, *per* Kenny J. at p. 166. The use of the attorney's own name is permitted by s.46 of the Conveyancing Act 1881. When executing in the name of the company, it is the better practice to write also that it is acting through its named attorney.

There was at one time some doubt about the extension of the principle of vicarious liability to what might be termed the higher classes of tort, such as fraud, as opposed to ordinary, everyday negligence. It was felt that there should be some element of complicity on the part of the principal before he could be liable, and it will be appreciated that if the principal was a corporation, the imputation of such fault to it would present great difficulties, particularly if the wrongdoer was a minor servant of it.[67] This matter was finally laid to rest in Ireland in *Pearson* v. *Corporation of Dublin*,[68] an appeal from Ireland to the House of Lords, in respect of his own part in which as a judge below Palles C.B. felt able to say in a later case that he "did not express any doubt (nor, I may add, did any of the judges in Ireland) as to the liability of the principals for the fraud of their agent, acting within the scope of his employment,"[69] and proceeded to consolidate the position by holding in the case in question, *Fitzsimons* v. *Duncan and Kemp & Co.*,[70] that a company was capable of being vicariously liable for libel. Often cited in this connection are Lord Selborne in *Houldsworth* v. *City of Glasgow Bank*[71] where he said that "with respect to the question whether a principal is answerable for the act of his agent in the course of his master's business, no sensible distinction can be drawn between the case of fraud and the case of any other wrong," and Lord Cranworth who observed in *Ranger* v. *Great Western Railway*[72] that in the imposition of vicarious liability for fraud "the same principles must prevail when the principal under whom the agent acts is a corporation" as apply in the case of other employers or principals.

---

[67] On the imputation of fault, and for the occasions when it is necessary, see pp. 36 *et seq.*, *supra*.

[68] [1907] A.C. 351; [1907] 2 I.R. 537.

[69] *Fitzsimons* v. *Duncan and Kemp & Co.* [1908] 2 I.R. 483, 491, but some slight confusion notwithstanding is still apparent in his judgment.

[70] [1908] 2 I.R. 483, 491.

[71] (1880) 5 App. Cas. 317.

[72] (1854) 5 H.L.C. 72, 86; though at that time vicarious liability was not fully developed for all torts, including fraud.

Chapter 6: Shares and Membership

The nature of a share

We have seen that as a consequence of the separate personality of the company, a shareholder cannot be said to own its property or have any sort of proprietary interest in it.[1] The courts have felt bound to repeat this message on several occasions. For example, Kenny J. in *Att.-Gen. for Ireland* v. *Jameson*[2] said "No shareholder has a right to any specific portion of the company's property . . . ," and Evershed L.J. in *Short* v. *Treasury Commissioners*[3] said "The shareholders are not in the eye of the law part-owners of the undertaking. The undertaking is something different from the totality of the shareholdings." Nor, to state the obvious, is the nature of a share in the company affected by the nature of the assets held by the company; in other words, a share in a company owning land does not for that reason become realty.[4]

What then is a share? One definition, accepted repeatedly in Ireland,[5] is that of Farwell J. in *Borland's Trustees* v. *Steel Brothers & Co. Ltd.*[6] where he describes a share as being:

> "the interest of the shareholder in the company measured by a sum of money, for the purpose of liability in the first place, and of interest in the second, but also consisting of a series of mutual covenants entered into by all shareholders *inter se* in accordance with section 16 of the Companies Act 1862."

This respected definition is useful but incomplete; it nonetheless

---

[1] See Chap. 2: *Incorporation and its Consequences.*

[2] [1904] 2 I.R. 644, 671.

[3] [1948] 1 K.B. 116, 124.

[4] *Lee and Company (Dublin) Ltd.* v. *Egan (Wholesale) Ltd.* (High Court, unreported, Kenny J. October 18, 1979) at p.3 of the transcript; see Rice, "The Legal Nature of a Share," (1957) 21 Conv. N.S. 433; and see s.79 which states shares to be personalty.

[5] *Casey* v. *Bentley* [1902] 1 I.R. 376, 393; *Att.-Gen. for Ireland* v. *Jameson* [1904] 2 I.R. 644, 699. *Provincial Bank of Ireland Ltd.* v. *O'Connor* (High Court, unreported, Kenny J., October 10, 1974).

[6] [1901] 1 Ch. 288.

provides a starting point for the discussion. The money measure of a shareholder's liability is dealt with elsewhere.[7] The money measure of what is called his "interest" refers to the fact that dividends are declared by reference to the nominal value of his share, and the nominal value provides a basis for the distribution of the net assets in a winding up.[8] The "series of mutual covenants entered into by all shareholders *inter se*" is nowadays to be found in section 25 of the Companies Act 1963 which says:

> "the memorandum and articles shall, when registered, bind the company and the members thereof to the same extent as if they respectively had been signed and sealed by each member, and contained covenants by each member to observe all the provisions of the memorandum and of the articles."

The somewhat archaic wording of this section can be explained by the fact that, with some variations, it goes all the way back to the Act of 1844 and has its origins before that in the form of deed entered into by members of the old unincorporated deed of settlement company. In everyday speech, section 25 is saying that the company's constitution, chiefly the articles in fact, are a source of contractual rights and duties which constitute "inseparable incidents"[9] of a share. A share may be viewed therefore as a bundle of rights and duties, most of which flow from section 25. To complete the picture, one should add that the Companies Acts independently confer on members numerous rights, an element not mentioned in Farwell J.'s definition. Perhaps therefore Lord Russell of Killowen in *I.R.C.* v. *Crossman*[10] provides a more satisfactory summary of a share:

> "It is the interest of a person in the company, that interest being composed of rights and obligations which are defined by the Companies Act and by the memorandum and articles of association of the company."

The rights given to an individual member by the section 25 contract, and by statute, are enforceable regardless of the will of the majority to the contrary. These individual membership rights constitute a most important exception in the increasing catalogue of exceptions to the general, but diminishing, principle that in the conduct of the

---

[7] See Chap. 2, pp.18 *et seq.*, and Chap. 10, pp.302 *et seq.*

[8] [1904] 2 I.R. 669–670. For nominal value, see p.306; and for rights in a winding up, see pp.174 *et seq.*

[9] [1904] 2 I.R. 670, *per* Kenny J.

[10] [1937] A.C. 26, 66. Lord Macmillan at pp.69–70 said "a share in a joint stock company is an entirely conventional creation; the congeries of rights and liabilities of which it consists is the creature of the Companies Acts and the memorandum and articles of the particular company."

company's affairs the will of the majority prevails.[11] It is important therefore to examine in detail the extent of individual membership rights.

The section 25 contract

This contract has been dubbed by Ross J. in *Clark* v. *Workman*[12] "a contract of the most sacred character" for the worldly reason that "it is on the faith of it that each shareholder advances his money," a somewhat misleading statement, because, first, this contract even if sacred is scarcely sacrosant since its terms are alterable by alterations in the memorandum or articles, and, secondly, because the contract extends not only to the initial subscribers for shares but also to any person who subsequently becomes a member.

The contents and extent of the section 25 contract have received considerable judicial attention, the results of which may be summarised by stating that insofar as the constitution of the company purports to confer lawful rights on an individual member *in his capacity as member*, he may enforce those rights both as against the company and against fellow members, and duties imposed upon him *in his capacity as member* are likewise enforceable by the company and fellow members. Aspects of this statement of principle which may now be regarded as settled have not been considered as beyond argument in England during this century. In *Hickman's Case*[13] in 1915 it was strenuously argued that provisions in the articles could not be enforced *by* members against the company. The article in that case provided that disputes between members and the company should be referred to arbitration. Astbury J. in a judgment which is regarded as a classic found it necessary painstakingly to review all the authorities before finding in favour of the members. A similar painstaking process of review occurred in *Rayfield* v. *Hands*[14] where one of the issues was whether or not particular provisions of the memorandum and articles were enforceable directly between the members themselves, or was the company the necessary and proper party to enforce obligations against members? It was held that the rights and duties under the section 25 contract flowed directly between the members themselves as well as between the company and members. Such fine distinctions do not appear to have troubled the Irish courts. In the broadest statement of principle, Ross, J. in *Clark* v. *Workman*[15] said:

[11] See pp.166–169, 244.
[12] [1920] I.R. 107, 112.
[13] *Hickman* v. *Kent or Romney Marsh Sheepbreeders' Association* [1915] 1 Ch. 881.
[14] [1958] 2 W.L.R. 851.
[15] [1920] I.R. 107, 112.

"Now, what do the articles of association amount to in point of law? They constitute a contract between every shareholder and all the others, and between the company itself and all the shareholders."

In *Lee & Co. (Dublin) Ltd.* v. *Egan (Wholesale) Ltd.*[16] Kenny J. declined to order specific performance of a contract for the sale of shares in the company to an outsider without giving existing members[17] an opportunity to exercise their pre-emption rights in respect of them given by the articles, and, indeed, ordered the vendor to put the pre-emption machinery into action. In another pre-emption rights case, *Att. Gen. for Ireland* v. *Jameson,*[18] the majority judgments accept the enforceability of the articles as between the members, Kenny J. saying:

> "in becoming a member of the company . . . he is deemed to have simultaneously entered into a contract under seal to conform to the regulations contained in the articles of association . . . . Whatever obligations are contained in these articles, he accepts the ownership of the shares and the position of member of the Company, bound and controlled by them. He cannot divorce his money interest, whatever it may amount to, from these obligations. They are inseparable incidents attached to his rights, and the idea of a share cannot, in my judgment, be complete without their inclusion."[19]

It was emphasised in the above definition of the rights and duties within the section 25 contract that they included only those given or imposed on a member *in his capacity as member.* In *Eley's Case,*[20] the

---

[16] High Court, Kenny J, unreported, April 27, 1978.

[17] Who were not in fact even parties to the action.

[18] [1904] 2 I.R. 644 (K.B. Division); [1905] 2 I.R. 218 (C.A.). The validity of the articles was not in issue on the appeal (p.237), but Lord Ashbourne C. did say: "the share cannot be split up and considered apart from its contractual incidents. The articles are part and parcel of the share, and not collateral and separate. The shareholder must be assumed to have absolutely bound himself to obey and conform to the articles."(p.226)

[19] [1904] 2 I.R. 664, 670. Palles C.B. in his dissent on the main questions in the case (valuation of shares for estate duty) adds: "I have assumed the provisions affecting the transferability of these shares contained in the articles of association to be valid, and enforceable at the suit of the members designated by the articles as "the purchasing members"; and . . . it is immaterial for me to consider whether these provisions are so enforceable. Upon this question, which, in my opinion, involves grave and difficult questions . . . , I shall not enter." He had in fact found the provisions of the articles to be "collateral to . . . the character and nature of a share" (p.690), in which respect he is destined now to remain in a minority of one. His judgment was respectfully analysed in *I.R.C.* v. *Crossman* [1937] A.C. 26 *supra.*

[20] (1876) 1 Ex.D. 88.

articles contained a clause providing that the plaintiff should be employed for life *as solicitor* to the company, and should be dismissable for misconduct only. He became a member of the company, and later was dismissed as its solicitor. The English Court of Appeal dealt cursorily with his claim for breach of contract, saying that the relevant article constituted an agreement between the members that they would employ him, and not an agreement with him to that effect, apparently ignoring the fact the he *was* a member. The *Eley* case was followed in *Browne* v. *La Trinidad*[21] where again the plaintiff was a member of the company, and yet denied rights which the articles conferred on him, it was said, in his capacity *as promoter*. By the time *Hickman's Case*[22] was decided in 1915, Astbury J. was able to put the principle in the form of the following generalisations:

> "I think this much is clear, first that no article can constitute a contract between the company and a third person; secondly, that no right merely purporting to be given by an article to a person whether a member or not, in a capacity other than that of member, as for instance, solicitor, promoter, director, can be enforced against the company. . . ."

This doctrine is easy enough to state, but difficult to apply. The difficulty lies in the fact that the rights of members within a company are not required to be uniform. We have seen affirmed in *Bushell* v. *Faith*[23] the liberty which a company has to create shares with widely differing rights. Therefore the possibility of making the only firm and logically sustainable distinction, namely that between rights possessed by all members of a company and those purported to be granted to only some, disappears. The present difficulty can be explained by the fact that the unfortunate doctrine has its roots in a period before the nature of a share was fully perceived as a collection of rights and duties derived mainly from the company's articles and memorandum, with all the potential for variety which that implies. It is submitted that Irish law is free to take account of this development, and to eschew the artificialties introduced by *Eley's Case* and its successors. By doing so, the Irish courts would be freed from the impossibilities inherent in such cases as *Rayfield* v. *Hands*[24] in which Vaisey J. was required to decide whether it was merely coincidental that certain members upon whom the articles purported to impose a duty to buy the shares of another members were also directors.[25]

---

[21] (1887) 37 Ch.D. 1.
[22] [1915] 1 Ch. 881.
[23] [1970] A.C. 1099, discussed at pp.101–102, *supra*.
[24] [1958] 2 W.L.R. 851.
[25] He held that the duty to buy was imposed *qua member*.

Essentially, the suggestion is that once section 25 privity is established by membership, the member should be able to enforce against the company and fellow members all duties which the company's constitution states that they respectively owe to him, without attempting to distinguish the capacity in which his corresponding rights are conferred. This approach would, in particular, enable the courts to deal with the entitlements of directors[26] in a more straightforward manner, without recourse to the fiction of implying contracts "on the basis of" the articles,[27] and without being hampered by the uneasy and anachronistic classification of a director as an office holder,[28] a concept which belongs more properly in the public domain than in the commercial world, and even in the former has been largely superseded by contract.

There is thus, as matters stand, no general right in members to have the articles observed. This proceeds not only from the fact that rights to be enforceable must be conferred upon the member as such, but also from the fact that many duties imposed by the articles are construed as being owed not to the members but to the company itself. For these the rule in *Foss* v. *Harbottle*[29] quite logically prescribes that the company itself, the separate person in the law, is the proper plaintiff. Chief among these duties are those owed by the directors in the conduct of the company's business.[30] We shall see[31] that only occasionally may individual shareholders cause a company to enforce these duties, and it should be emphasised that even then they are enforcing not their own rights, but those of the company.

The facts of *Foss* v. *Harbottle*, decided over 140 years ago, concerned alleged breaches of duty owed by directors to the company in their management of the company's business, and it would have been decided in the same way today, unless the plaintiffs could have brought themselves within certain modern refinements.[32] However, following *Foss* v. *Harbottle* it became customary to categorise *other* internal irregularities in a company as breaches of duties owed to the company, with the consequent non-suit of an individual or represen-

---

[26] The Courts would not be able to take this step in the rare instances where directors are not members. Legislative intervention would be required to make qualification shares compulsory. See p.81, *supra*.

[27] See pp.83 *et seq.*, 92 *supra*.

[28] See p.83, *supra*; and *per, e.g. Glover* v. *B.L.N.* [1973] I.R. 338. It is noteworthy that the principles of natural justice applied in that case were at first instance confined to office holders but in the Supreme Court were based on contract, it being considered fortuitous that the complainant was also an office holder.

[29] (1843) 2 Hare 461.

[30] See Chap. 7. Directors' Duties.

[31] See Chap. 8. Enforcement of duties.

[32] *Ibid.*

tative shareholder plaintiff. High points in this judicial attitude were reached in *Mozley* v. *Alston*[33] where directors who had failed to retire by rotation in accordance with the articles were treated exclusively as having wronged the corporation by usurping office rather than also having wronged individual members by denying them their right under the articles to elect directors, and *Macdougall* v. *Gardiner*,[34] perhaps the flimsiest of such cases, in which the court refused to recognise as enforceable an individual shareholder's right to demand a poll. Doubtless, influencing the decisions was the attitude that it is pointless to insist upon the niceties of procedure and strict adherence to rights if, at the end of the litigation, the majority will get its own way on the substantive matter in issue, that is to say, would in *Mozley* v. *Alston* have properly elected the usurping board and in *Macdougall* v. *Gardiner* have carried the vote on the denied poll. Be this as it may, the tendency for some considerable time in the case of internal irregularities has been mostly the other way. There is now a judicial willingness in such cases to categorise the provisions of the articles as giving individual membership rights, and to enforce them. This tendency is likely to be reinforced in Ireland by the individual's Constitutional right to have his personal rights of property vindicated,[35] and by the willingness of the Irish courts to insist on Constitutional grounds that proper procedures be followed.[36] The erosion of the high point described above, and therefore the process whereby the 19th century procedural irregularity is becoming today's infringement of an individual membership right, came about through judicial decisions[37] of which the following are illustrations. In *Pender* v. *Lushington*,[38] a significant early case, a member whose nominees' votes had been refused by the chairman at a general meeting obtained an injunction against the directors restraining them from acting on the resolutions passed at the meeting. Jessel M.R said:

> "This is an action by Mr. Pender for himself. He is a member of the company, and whether he votes with the majority or the

[33] (1847) 1 Ph. 790.

[34] (1875) 1 Ch.D. 13.

[35] Art. 40.3 of the Constitution. Shareholders' rights have frequently been classified as "rights of property" *e.g.* Jessel M.R. in *Pender* v. *Lushington* (1877) 6 Ch.D. 70, *infra* and for the same classification in a constitutional context see *P.M.P.S. Ltd. and Moore* v. *Att.-Gen.* [1984] I.L.R.M. 88, and *Central Dublin Development Association Ltd.* v. *Att.-Gen.* (1973) 109 I.L.T.R. 69, 84.

[36] *e.g. Re Haughey* [1971] I.R. 217.

[37] There is now a statutory membership right to demand a poll in s.137, though, ironically, it does not extend to a poll on the question of an adjournment, the point at issue in *Macdougall* v. *Gardiner, supra.*

[38] (1877) 6 Ch.D. 70.

minority he is entitled to have his vote recorded—an individual
right in respect of which he has a right to sue. That has nothing
to do with the question like that raised in *Foss* v. *Harbottle* and
that line of cases. He has a right to say, "whether I vote in the
majority or minority you shall record my vote, as that is a right
of property belonging to my interest in this company, and if you
refuse to record my vote I will institute legal proceedings
against you to compel you." What is the answer to such an
action? It seems to me it can be maintained as a matter of substance, and that there is no technical difficulty in maintaining
it . . . ."[39]

In *Clark* v. *Workman*,[40] minority shareholders, suing as such,
obtained an injunction restraining the directors from acting on a
board resolution carried by the casting vote of the chairman of the
board. One of the grounds was that the board itself had not properly
appointed the chairman in accordance with the articles. Of this Ross
J., after reviewing the relevant articles said: "There you have the
precise contract with the shareholders, and it is essential that the
chairman should be elected by the machinery provided by that contract, and in no other way,"[41] and thus enforced as an individual
membership right procedures laid down by the articles for the conduct of business at board level. *Hennessy* v. *National Agricultural &
Industrial Development Association*[42] treats the requirement under the
articles of a quorum in general meeting as an individual membership right, so that a member could obtain a declaration that the
actions of inquorate meetings were ineffective.

The best modern authority on the inter-relationship between the
rule in *Foss* v. *Harbottle* and individual membership rights is the
judgment of Jenkins L.J. in *Edwards* v. *Halliwell*.[43] This case concerned a trade union whose rules stated that members' contributions
were not to be altered unless a ballot-vote of all members had been
taken, and a two-thirds majority in favour obtained. A meeting of
union delegates purported by resolution to increase the contributions without taking a ballot. Two individual members of the union
obtained a declaration that the increase was ineffective, the rule concerning ballots being readily interpreted as an individual membership right. Jenkins L.J. said:

"It is not a case where what is complained of is a wrong done to

[39] *Ibid.* at pp.80–81.
[40] [1920] 1 I.R. 107.
[41] At pp. 114, 115.
[42] [1947] I.R. 159.
[43] [1950] 2 All E.R. 1064.

the union, a matter in respect of which the cause of action would primarily and properly belong to the union. . . . The gist of the case is that the personal and individual rights of membership of each of them have been invaded by a purported, but invalid, alteration of the tables of contribution. In those circumstances, it seems to me that the rule in *Foss* v. *Harbottle* has not application at all, for the individual members who are suing sue, not in the right of the union, but in their own right to protect from invasion their own individual rights as members."[44]

So influential has this judgment been that its generalisations have been relied upon even to overturn the leading early case of *Mozley* v. *Alston, supra.*[45] This occurred in *Kraus* v. *J.G. Lloyd Pty. Ltd.,*[46] where the Supreme Court of Victoria granted an injunction to an individual shareholder restraining an invalidly appointed director from acting as such. Doubtless, a similar result could have been achieved by relying on the earlier Irish authority of *Clark* v. *Workman, supra.*

In England the tendency to enlarge the ambit of matters affecting members as members spread to the statutory provisions allowing discretionary relief from oppression, the former section 210 of the Companies Act 1948. This section required the matters complained of to be suffered by the complainant in his character as member. Nonetheless, in *Re H.R. Harmer Ltd.*[47] disregard by an oppressively octogenarian director and controlling shareholder of his fellow director sons at board level was held to constitute oppression *qua* member as denying them their right to have the company's affairs conducted in accordance with its articles of association. Although the Irish equivalent section 205 of the Companies Act 1963 does not suffer from this limitation of section 210,[48] *Re H.R. Harmer Ltd.* can be taken as a further indication of the general trend.

For the protection of the minority in the alteration of individual membership rights, and for considerations affecting the choice of whether to pursue an individual membership right as opposed to some other head of minority protection, see Chapter 9. Minority Protection.

Particular rights

We shall now look more closely at certain prominent rights commonly forming part of the shareholders' contract. The extent of

[44] At p. 1067.
[45] n. 33, *supra.*
[46] [1965] V.R. 232.
[47] [1959] 1 W.L.R. 62.
[48] Chapter 9. Minority Protection.

those rights depends in each case upon the interpretation of the contract, and it will be seen that the courts have frequently found difficulty in construing the relevant provisions of the documents in which that contract is contained, chiefly the articles of association and documents deriving authority from them,[49] and occasionally the memorandum, all of which may be described collectively as the terms of issue. So frequently have the courts been confronted with what Gavan Duffy P. described in *Re Imperial Hotel (Cork) Ltd.*,[50] as "the perplexing effort of a sadly perplexed draftsman" that certain canons of construction have grown up, mainly with regard to the right to participate in surplus assets on a winding up, which may not always reflect the true intention of the parties. The remedy is, of course, clear draftsmanship, and, as a spur to this, section 39[51] of the Companies Act 1983 provides on pain of criminal penalties that particulars of the rights attached to newly allotted shares should be given to the registrar of companies, insofar as not contained in its other published documents. Since section 5 of the Companies (Amendment) Act 1982 now requires these published documents to include every conceivable type of resolution concerning shares, section 39 can only be directed towards the omission of sufficient particularity in the description of shareholders' rights in them. Furthermore, section 5(2) of the 1982 Act requires every company to "forward to the registrar of companies a return containing particulars not previously forwarded to him of any right or restriction attaching to shares" in existence upon the coming into force of that section.[52]

Dividends

A dividend is a distribution which a company may make to its members out of its profits. Entitlement to a dividend can arise only before the company goes into liquidation.[53] The profits available for this purpose are described in Chapter 10.[54] Under common form

---

[49] *e.g.* a resolution under art. 2 of Table A which provides that "any share in the company may be issued with such preferred, deferred or other special rights or restrictions, whether in regard to "dividend, voting, return of capital or otherwise as the company may from time to time by ordinary resolution determine."

[50] [1950] I.R. 115, 116.

[51] "Unless the shares are in all respects uniform with shares previously allotted": s.39(1).

[52] Insofar as there is a hiatus between s.5(2) of the 1982 Act and s.39(1) of the 1983 Act, the requirements of the Second Directive (which relates only to public limited companies) have not been fully observed, since it is expressed so as to require rights to be stated regardless of when they were created.

[53] See n. 72, *infra.*

[54] At pp.327–336.

articles of association, including Table A, the mere availability of profits does not entitle a member to a dividend. To found that entitlement the dividend must first be *declared*. As Lord Davey said in *Burland* v. *Earle*[55]:

> "Their Lordships are not aware of any principle which compels a joint stock company while a going concern to divide the whole of its profits among its shareholders. Whether the whole or any part should be divided, or what portion should be divided and what portion retained, are entirely questions of internal management . . . , and the court has no jurisdiction to control or review their decision or to say what is a "fair" or "reasonable" sum to retain undivided, or what reserve fund may "properly" be required . . . "

Under Table A dividends are declared by the general meeting but must not exceed an amount recommended by the directors; and the directors themselves may pay interim dividends should they think fit.[56] As we have seen,[57] where the articles are in the form of Table A the members cannot force the directors to recommend a dividend. The member's only legal right in the declaration process under such articles is to have his vote counted when voting whether or not to accept the recommendation of the directors. However, this strictly legal position is overshadowed by section 205 of the Companies Act 1963. When the Cohen Committee recommended in 1945 the introduction of the British forerunner of this remedy, section 210 of the Companies Act 1948 [*U.K.*], they had in mind, as one of the mischiefs it was intended to mitigate, cases where controlling directors of a company caused themselves to be appointed to paid posts within it at excessive rates of remuneration, thereby absorbing the profits and leaving little or nothing for the minority shareholders by way of dividend.[58]

The Jenkins Committee took up the same theme[59] in 1962 and there is little doubt that such conduct on the part of the controllers would constitute, in the words of section 205, an exercise of "the powers of the directors of the company . . . in a manner oppressive to the complaining members or in disregard of . . . their interests as members." The wide variety of discretionary relief available under this section under which "the court may, with a view to bringing to

---

[55] [1902] A.C. 83, 95. (P.C.).
[56] Arts. 116, 117.
[57] See Chap. 3, at p.87. *et seq.*
[58] Para. 60 of the Cohen Report.
[59] Para. 205 of the Jenkins Report.

an end the matters complained of, make such order as it thinks fit, whether directing . . . any act . . . or for regulating the conduct of the company's affairs in future . . . ," would surely include an order that a dividend be declared. Thus, the supervening morality of this section must be taken now to have tempered the strict statement of legal rights described above by Lord Davey in *Burland* v. *Earle*.

Once a dividend has been declared, the member has a right to receive it arising out of the section 25 contract, and it constitutes therefore a debt owed by the company to him. This proposition has been established by several Irish authorities, the earliest being *Smith* v. *Cort & Bandon Railway Co.*[60] in 1870 and the latest being *Re Belfast Empire Theatre of Varieties*[61] in 1963.

The dividends on preference shares, so called because they have preferential rights to dividends and usually also priority in the return of capital in a winding up (*infra*), are likewise under usual terms of issue dependent upon a dividend actually being declared. Of necessity the preferential dividend is defined by the terms of issue as a fixed entitlement, almost invariably by reference to a percentage of the nominal value of the share, payable annually. The judicial principles of construction include a presumption that preference shares are not income participating. By this is meant that preferential dividend rights are construed as an exhaustive definition of the preference shareholders' entitlement in the year in question. In the leading case of *Will* v. *United Lankat Plantations*,[62] preference shareholders who were entitled to and had received their preferential dividend of 10 per cent. *per annum* in a particular year claimed equal participation with the ordinary shareholders in the rest of the dividends declared in that year after they too had received their 10 per cent. Undoubtedly the rejection by the House of Lords of this contention reflects the everyday understanding in the business community of the nature of a preference share. However, the claimants in making their assertion were relying upon a notion of basic equality between shares even where a preference has been given. This notion, though dead in the English jurisdiction and alien to the businessman's understanding of a preference share, may still have some vigour in the Irish courts in the context of preference shareholders' rights in a winding up, (*infra*).

There is a willingness in the courts, again as a matter of construc-

---

[60] (1870) 5 I.R., Eq. 65.

[61] [1963] I.R. 41. Others include *Re Drogheda Steampacket Co. Ltd.* [1903] 1 I.R. 512, and *Ward* v. *Dublin North City Milling Co. Ltd.* [1919] 1 I.R. 5, 12. A leading English authority is *Bond* v. *Barrow Haematite Steel Co.* [1902] 1 Ch. 353

[62] [1914] A.C. 11.

tion, to find that a preference dividend is cumulative,[63] even if not expressed to be so. A cumulative entitlement carries the right to be paid arrears of preference dividends missed in previous years when dividends are declared in subsequent years, and in priority to the ordinary shareholders.

We have dealt so far with common form articles and usual terms of issue. There is nothing to prevent the parties expressly making a different bargain. In *Re Saltdean Estate Co. Ltd.*[64] the articles expressly and validly provided that the preference shares should be income participating; likewise the terms of issue in *Webb v. Earle.*[63] Express terms may even declare that the entitlement to a dividend is not dependent on a declaration, but only on the existence of profits. As Kingsmill Moore J. pointed out in *Re Lafayette*,[65] none of the authorities

"lay down that articles may not give to preference shareholders an absolute right to be paid their fixed dividend and arrears out of profits without any previous declaration of dividend by the directors or the company. They do lay down that certain forms of articles require a dividend to be declared before it is presently payable."

Under common form articles the entitlement of members to bonus shares (or, in other words, capitalisation issues) is decided in accordance with their entitlement to dividends. For example, article 130 of Table A allows the company's reserves and credit balances in its profit and loss account to be applied in paying up bonus shares "on behalf of the members who would have been entitled to receive the same if the same had been distributed by way of dividend." The process is illustrated in *Re Faris deceased*[66] where Meredith M.R. describes a shareholder who had received a bonus issue as being "in the same position as before, except that he had to sell two shares instead of one, if he wanted to realise his money."[67] In fact, bonus issues often have more significance than that. They may be used to counter a take-over bid[68] or to enable ordinary shareholders to steal a march

---

[63] *Webb* v. *Earle* (1875) L.R. 20 Eq. 556. The passing of a non-cumulative preferential dividend where profits *are* available may be a cause for a petition under s.205. See Jenkins Report para. 205.

[64] [1968] 1 W.L.R. 1844.

[65] [1950] I.R. 100, 111; following *Re Imperial Hotel (Cork) Ltd.* [1950] I.R. 115. Also, the constitutions of Irish railway companies incorporated by statute commonly provided for guaranteed dividends supported by a baronial guarantee in lieu, *e.g. Re Castleisland Railway* [1896] 2 I.R. 661.

[66] [1911] 1 I.R. 165.

[67] *Ibid.* p. 174.

[68] See pp. 320–321.

on preference shareholders when a winding up is in prospect and the articles are such that the preference shares are not income participating whilst the company is a going concern, but do participate in the surplus in a winding up. (See *Rights in a Winding up, infra*).

Rights in a winding up

After the affairs of a company have been wound up and all its creditors paid, the members are entitled to have what remains of its assets divided among themselves. If all shareholders have the same rights in a winding up, no problem arises. Where, however, the shares are divided into different classes, there is a prospect of competition between them in a winding up, and where, as has often been the case, the terms of issue have not clearly defined their respective entitlements, the most excruciating problems of construction have arisen. In Ireland the judicial authorities are in such a state that clarity of draftsmanship is absolutely imperative.

Potential rights of a member in a winding up are, insofar as assets are sufficient to satisfy them, a right to receive an amount equal to his nominal capital in the company (return of capital), a right in a preference shareholder to receive an amount equal to the arrears of preference dividend unpaid during the life of the company (the right to arrears), and the right to participate in surplus assets, if any, after the foregoing two items have been satisfied (the right to participate in surplus assets). The chief difficulties of construction have arisen in connection with this last right, and it will be discussed first.

It is essential to grasp the fact that the concept of "profits" does not survive into a winding up. All assets in a winding up are treated simply as "assets" without any attempt being made to differentiate their origin, and, consequently, this principle serves to counteract the logical inconsistency involved in a finding that preference shareholders are entitled in a winding up to assets representing profits to which they would *not* have been entitled by way of dividend whilst the company remained a going concern. Authority for this principle is widespread. The most recent Irish authority is *Wilson (Inspector of Taxes)* v. *Dunnes Stores (Cork)Ltd.*[69] in which Kenny J. said:

"The fallacy of the Inspector's argument is that while what is

---

[69] High Court, January 22, 1976, unreported; following *I.R.C.* v. *Blott* [1920] 2 K.B. 657, and *I.R.C.* v. *Burrell* [1924] 2 K.B. 52, 67. There are similar dicta in *I.R.C.* v. *Pollock & Peel Ltd.* [1956] 1 W.L.R. at 963, *per* Upjohn J.; *Scottish Insurance Corporation Ltd.* v. *Wilsons & Clyde Coal Co. Ltd.*, *infra*, *per* Lord Simonds, and in two Irish cases likewise unfortunately not mentioned by Kenny J., *Re Lafayette Ltd.* [1950] I.R. 100, 106 and *Re Imperial Hotel (Cork) Ltd.*, *infra*.

distributed to members in a winding up may be identified as having been profits, it is not distributed as profits . . . What remains after discharge of liabilities is distributed among the shareholders not as profits but as surplus assets or as a distribution in the winding up. All the cases are consistent with this view and, on close examination, they refute the contention that what is distributed in a winding up is in any sense profits of the company."[70]

And in *Re Imperial Hotel (Cork) Ltd.*[71] Gavan Duffy P. said that he had not overlooked:

"the rule that dividends, properly so called, are not payable on a winding up, when, after payment of the liabilities, the mass of a company's assets, whatever their separate provenance, comes to be allocated among the members entitled . . . "[72]

Perhaps the most succinct statement is that of Lord Simonds in *Scottish Insurance Corporation Ltd.* v. *Wilson & Clyde Coal Co.*[73]:

"I am unwilling to suppose that the parties intended a bargain which would involve an investigation of an artificial and elaborate character into the nature and origin of separate assets."

Competing rights to participate in surplus assets must be considered against this background. Where the terms of issue do not express any preference or priority for the preference shareholders in a winding up, the position is straightforward. All shareholders, whether preference or ordinary, participate in a winding up on equal terms, and each receive rateably what is due to them in accordance with the nominal value of their shares. This manner of proceeding is in accordance with the rule of construction stated chiefly in *Birch* v. *Cropper*[74] presuming equality between shares in the absence of a contrary indication. The difficulties arise where the terms of issue are not wholly silent on the rights of preference shareholders in a winding up, but expressly state that they are to have priority in the return of capital without saying whether or not they are also to have the right to participate in surplus assets. The usual business under-

---

[70] At p. 8 of the transcript.
[71] [1950] I.R. 115, 118; not cited in the judgment in *Wilson* v. *Dunnes Stores (Cork) Ltd., supra.*
[72] There is ample further authority for the proposition that entitlement to a dividend can arise only before the winding up commences, *e.g. Re Foster (W.) & Son, Ltd.* [1942] 1 All E.R. 314.
[73] [1949] A.C. 462, 481, cited with approval by Buckley J. in *Dimbula Valley (Ceylon) Tea Co. Ltd.* v. *Laurie* [1961] Ch. 353, 369.
[74] (1889) 14 App. Cas. 525.

standing of such an article is that the rights of preference shareholders in a winding up are confined to the fixed entitlement of no
more than a return of nominal capital, and the British courts are
now in agreement with this view: *inter alia, Scottish Insurance Corporation* v. *Wilson & Clyde Coal Co.*[73] and *Re Isle of Thanet Electricity Supply
Co. Ltd.*.[75] These British decisions of 1949 represent the culmination
of an evolution which as assimilated the construction of preference
shareholders' rights in a winding up to that pertaining in the case of
dividends under the long established case *Will* v. *United Lankat Plantations*,[76] *supra.* which decided that any statement of preference in the
payment of dividends should be construed as an exhaustive statement of the whole entitlement to dividends in the absence of express
words to the contrary. Perhaps this evolution may still occur in Ireland, but for the moment it must be considered as arrested by a
decision of the Supreme Court in 1931, *Re Cork Electric Supply Co.
Ltd.*.[77] In that case, the preference shareholders were entitled by the
terms of issue to a preferential dividend, and expressly no further
dividend. They were expressly given priority in the return of capital
in a winding up, and the rest was silence. The Supreme Court held
that the preference shareholders *were* entitled to participate in the
distribution of surplus assets in a winding up, and in doing so relied
upon the presumption of equality in *Birch* v. *Cropper*, particularly the
passage in which Lord Herschell says:

> "When the whole of the capital has been returned both classes
> of shareholders are on the same footing, equally members and
> holding equal shares in the company, and it appears to me they
> ought to be equally entitled to its property."[78]

Kennedy C.J. considered the decision to be "very important for the
elementary principles it affirmed . . . Preference shareholders are
holders of shares in the capital of the company in the same way as
ordinary shareholders are holders of shares in its capital . . . . Their
respective positions are differentiated only to the extent to which the
rights and privileges attaching to their respective shares are qualified contractually by the memorandum and articles."[79] And looking
at the memorandum and articles he did not find that the prima facie
right of the preference shareholder to participate in surplus assets
had been "abrogated, cut down or qualified in any way." The strik-

---

[75] [1949] 2 All E.R. 1060 (English C.A.). See generally Pickering, "The Problem of
the Preference Share" (1963) 26 M.L.R. 499.

[76] See n. 62, *supra*.

[77] [1932] I.R. 314.

[78] (1889) 14 App. Cas. 525, 538.

[79] [1932] I.R. at p. 327.

ing difference between this attitude and the modern British position is exemplified by Fitzgibbon J. who found that the preference shareholders' right to priority in the return of nominal capital did *not*:

> "by implication negative or restrict their right to a share in the surplus, if any. It is *a definition of the amount of preferential treatment which they are to receive, not a deprivation or restriction of any other right to which they are, prima facie, entitled.*"[80]

Fitzgibbon J. in this passage may in fact provide the key to reconciling *Cork Electric* with *Will* v. *United Lankat*, since he is categorising rights in a winding up as not one but several, such that preference accorded in one cannot affect the possession of the others, whereas the right to a dividend may be regarded as a single right.

There is no doubt that the British courts in reaching their conclusion were influenced by the fact that under such articles as those in *Cork Electric*, the ordinary shareholders whilst the company remains a going concern could appropriate to themselves exclusively, either by way of dividend or bonus issue, the profits which would otherwise go to make up the disputed surplus assets in a winding up. There is therefore a logical consistency in giving those assets to the ordinary shareholders in a winding up, albeit that they have by then lost their character as profits. In *Cork Electric*, the court expressly repudiated the suggestion that there should necessarily be a "logical consistency" between rights enjoyed whilst the company remained a going concern and rights in a winding up.[81] That, they felt, would be contrary to the wide variety of bargains a company can enter into when creating different classes of shares, and, indeed, support is gained for this view from cases where the draftsman has expressly and plainly provided for such an inconsistency. Modern examples include *Dimbula Valley (Ceylon) Tea Co.* v. *Laurie*[82] where the preference shareholders had an express right to participate in the surplus in a winding up but were non-participating beyond a fixed dividend whilst the company was a going concern, and *Re Saltdean Estate Co. Ltd.*[83] where the preference shares were income participating whilst the company was a going concern but had expressly no rights to participate in the surplus in a winding up.

What then are the practical consequences of this preference for equality over logic? None whatsoever, if careful draftsmanship is employed in the terms of issue; but if it is not, and the problem is

---

[80] *Ibid* at pp.332–333. Author's emphasis.
[81] *Ibid* at pp.333–334.
[82] [1961] Ch. 353.
[83] [1968] 1 W.L.R. 1844.

spotted before the winding up commences, the ordinary share-holders may consider capitalising the reserves of profits by making a bonus issue exclusively for themselves in accordance with their dividend entitlement, as was done in the *Dimbula Valley* case,[84] thereby ensuring that they exclusively will receive the surplus assets on a winding up, but as a return of nominal capital.

Cumulative preference shareholders commonly have a right to receive as part of their entitlement in a winding up an amount equal to the "arrears" of preference dividend which accrued whilst the company was a going concern; sometimes this right is express,[85] and, if not, the courts are willing to imply it.[86] One should distinguish this right from the rare situation where the preference shareholders' entitlement to dividends depends only on the existence of profits.[87] In this case the preference shareholders' right to arrears is a liability on the company incurred before the commencement of the winding up,[88] and is a deferred debt in the liquidation.[89]

Pre-emption rights

There are two types of pre-emption right, the first in respect of shares which members wish to transfer, and the second in respect of shares about to be allotted for the first time.

The first is frequently contained in the articles of companies with few shareholders, usually family companies, and provides a machinery whereby the company on behalf of the member wishing to transfer offers the shares to existing members *pro rata* in accordance with their existing shareholding. Typical articles may be found in *Att. Gen. for Ireland* v. *Jameson*,[90] and in *Lee and Co. (Dublin) Ltd.* v. *Egan (Wholesale) Ltd..*[91] The usual article giving effect to the compulsory restriction on the transfer of shares in private companies,[92] article 3 of Part II of Table A, leaves the acceptability of a transferee

---

[84] See p.173, *supra*.

[85] *e.g.* in the *Dimbula Valley* case, *supra*.

[86] *Re F. de Jong & Co. Ltd.* [1946] Ch. 211.

[87] See p.173, *supra*.

[88] *per* Kenny J, at p. 8 of the transcript of *Wilson (Inspector of Taxes)* v. *Dunnes Stores (Cork) Ltd.* (High Court, January 22, 1976, unreported) where a number of authorities on this type of entitlement are reviewed, as they are also in *Re Lafayette Ltd.* [1950] I.R. 100 and *Re Imperial Hotel (Cork) Ltd.* [1950] I.R. 115, in each of which entitlements of this kind were found after exhaustive construction of the articles.

[89] *Re Imperial Hotel (Cork) Ltd.*, *supra* at p. 119. "Deferred" means deferred to the claims of non–members: s.207(1)(g).

[90] [1904] 2 I.R. 644; see p.164, *supra*.

[91] High Court, Kenny J., April 27, 1978, unreported. See p.164, *supra*.

[92] s.33(1)(*c*); for the operation of art. 3 in practice, see pp. 187 *et seq.*, *infra*.

entirely in the discretion of the directors; articles giving pre–emption rights pass a significant measure of control over admission to membership from the directors to the members.

The second type of pre-emption right gives existing members the right to subscribe for new issues *pro rata* in accordance with their existing shareholdings. The object of such provisions is that of allowing members to ensure that the balance of control within a company is not altered by a new issue.[93] Companies with a Stock Exchange quotation have long been under an extra-legal obligation to give their members this opportunity,[94] and articles of association occasionally do so as well, but there is *no* such requirement in Table A. There is however now a statutory right of pre-emption of this type given by sections 23 *et seq.* of the Companies Act 1983, discussed in *Statutory rights, infra.*

Voting rights

As we have seen,[95] there is a possibility of great variety in voting rights. Normality, as represented by article 63 of Table A, gives one vote per share on a poll; and common terms of issue of preference shares entitle them to attend, receive notice of, and vote in general meetings only when their dividend is in arrear.[95a]

True voting strength comes out only on a poll, and the right to demand one is an important necessary preliminary to the exercise of voting rights. In the absence of a demand for a poll, resolutions are decided on a show of hands under the usual form of article, article 59 of Table A. Though Table A gives the right to demand a poll on all issues, its exercise by individual members is qualified by the necessity of having the support of at least two other members present in person or by proxy, or by the need to command the support of at least 10 per cent. of the total voting strength of the company, whether represented at the meeting or not (article 59). Individual members who command less than this proportion of the potential votes and who wish to ensure that a poll will be taken on a particular issue should take the precaution of vesting at least two of their shares in nominees, and obtaining their proxies for the meeting. In the case of publicly quoted companies, this presents little difficulty since the

---

[93] This matter is further discussed in the context of directors' fiduciary duties in the issue of shares in Chap. 7. Directors' Duties.

[94] Para. 22, *Admission of Securities to Listing.*

[95] See pp.101–102 *supra.*

[95a] Each member of a company is entitled to receive notice of general meetings whether or not he has rights to attend and vote, unless the articles provide to the contrary: s.134(*a*). Art. 136(*a*) of Table A reflects s.134(*a*).

Stock Exchange requires the articles of such companies to be "free from any restriction on the right of transfer" of fully paid shares.[96] In other companies, there is the obstacle of the directors' discretion to overcome.[97]

Once a vote is being taken, whether on a show of hands or on a poll, there is an enforceable individual membership right in a member to have his vote counted towards the result: *Pender* v. *Lushington*.[98]

Statute also confers individual membership rights in relation to voting and meeting, designed to entrench or supplement the articles. See *Statutory rights, infra*.

Statutory rights

Generally, the Companies Acts leave it to the company itself through its constitutional documents to determine what rights a member shall and shall not have.[99] There has, however, been statutory intervention of a sporadic nature which has resulted in some individual and some collective statutory rights of membership independent of the constitutional documents.

Foremost among the individual rights are those which allow the individual member to seek the intervention of the court, or, at any rate, to threaten to do so, where there is sufficient misconduct in the company's affairs. Under section 205 he may petition for an order bringing to an end oppressive conduct, and under section 215 he may, as a contributory, petition for the company's winding up, usually on the grounds that it is "just and equitable" to do so, or that there has been oppressive conduct.[1]

We consider next statutory rights to information about the company's financial affairs. Each member of a company whether entitled to attend and vote at meetings or not, is entitled to be sent before the annual general meeting copies of the accounts which will be laid before it.[2] These accounts comprise the annual balance sheet, the profit and loss account, the directors' and auditors' reports, and the separate group accounts, if any.[3] If the group accounts of a company do not deal with the affairs of any subsidi-

---

[96] Appendix 34 to the Rules and Regulations of the Stock Exchange, Sched. VII, Pt. A, A2.

[97] See pp.187 *et seq., infra*.

[98] (1877) 6 Ch.D. 70; and see pp.167–168, *supra*.

[99] *Bushell* v. *Faith* [1970] A.C. 1099.

[1] s.213(*e*) and 213(*f*) respectively. In this context, "contributory" means member (see p.479n. *post*).

[2] s.159.

[3] ss.159, 157; 148; 150. For the content of these documents see Chap. 11: *Accounts and Auditors*.

ary,[4] then any member of the company is entitled on demand to receive the subsidiary's latest balance sheet, profit and loss account, directors' and auditors' reports, and the group accounts (if any) prepared by the subsidiary.[5] Members of private companies which have not prepared full group accounts are entitled not only to the latest documents described above but also on demand and at nominal charge to all such documents affecting a subsidairy for the preceding ten years.[6] With some qualifications, these statutory rights represent the limits on a member's entitlement to information on his company's financial standing, and the information thus accorded to him is in some respects imperfect. The information recorded in these documents may be up to nine months out of date[7] when received by him; the accounts may lawfully be prepared on accounting assumptions which may actually mislead[8]; and the directors' report on the period covered by the accounts may not only be out of date but also, in practice, reticent, a tendency encouraged by section 158 of the Companies Act 1963 itself which requires the directors merely to report generally "on the state of the company's affairs" and those of "its subsidiaries as a group," without requiring in this aspect of the report any more by way of specific information than a statement of "any change during the financial year in the nature of the business" in which the company or its subsidiaries are directly or indirectly interested.[9] The individual member will usually not be successful in an attempt to supplement these statutory rights by fishing for further information under section 205. In *P.M.P.A. Insurance Co. Ltd.* v. *New Ireland Assurance Co. Ltd.,*[10] a substantial minority shareholder failed to obtain an order under section 205 that the company divulge to it information about a certain aspect of its business. Indeed, the sense of this decision is particularly apparent where the petitioning member is a rival concern or interested in one. Where, however, such considerations are not present, and the directors are proposing to carry out radical action in a financial crisis, then an individual

---

[4] For exoneration from the obligation to prepare group accounts: see s.150(2); s.154. For the holding/subsidiary relationship, see s.155.

[5] ss.150(3); 154(2); 157.

[6] s.154(3).   [7] s.148(1).

[8] *e.g.* the "historic cost" assumption See Chap. 11: *Accounts and Auditors.*

[9] Contrast on this aspect of the directors' report the general formula now inserted in the equivalent s.157 of the 1948 Act [*U.K.*] by s.13 of the 1981 Act [*U.K.*] and the *specific* information on the company's business to be disclosed in directors' reports under s.16 of the 1967 Act [*U.K.*] as amended by s.13 of the 1981 Act [*U.K.*], and note the changes to be introduced by the 1985 Bill, described in Chap. 11: *Accounts and Auditors,* at pp. 353–356.

[10] High Court, Kenny J. October 22, 1975, reported in the *Irish Times* October 23, 1975; and noted (1978) D.U.L.J. 50: no transcript exists.

member who was not fully informed or consulted may be granted a remedy under section 205, as witness the case *Re Clubman Shirts Ltd.*[11] Another opportunity for members to be consulted and to be given current financial information may arise under section 40 of the Companies (Amendment) Act 1983. This requires the directors to summon an *e.g.m.* "where the net assets of a company are half or less of the amount of the company's called-up share capital" so that the members may consider "whether any, and if so what, measures should be taken to deal with the situation" not that there appears to be any compulsion on the directors to take heed of these deliberations.[12]

It may be important for a member, particularly a dissatisfied member of a publicly quoted company, to know what a director's stake in that company is, not least his voting strength. To this end, section 190 of the Companies Act 1963 is designed to prevent a director from sheltering behind nominee holdings, or more complex arrangements. It requires the company to keep and gives a member the right to inspect, a register of the beneficial shareholdings of each of a company's directors and its secretary. There must be recorded on this register not only the shares held by him, but also those held "in trust for . . . him or his spouse or any child of his or . . . which he or they have any right to become the holder." Any interest under a trust suffices, including being the object of a discretionary trust. Shares held by a body corporate which is or whose directors are, accustomed to act in accordance with the instructions of any person are deemed to be held by that person; likewise, if that person controls the exercise of one-third or more of the voting power at general meetings of that body corporate. The disclosure must extend to shares held in the company's subsidiary company, fellow subsidiary, and holding company.[12a]

The member also has access, as does the public, to the register of members which section 116 of the 1963 Act requires the company to keep. The member is thus in a position to circularise fellow members.

In relation to the meetings of a company, whether general meetings or the meetings of a class of members, section 136 of the Companies Act 1963 gives to any member entitled to attend and vote at that meeting the individual statutory right to appoint any other per-

---

[11] [1983] I.L.R.M. 323 discussed primarily at p.89, *supra.*

[12] This meeting is further discussed in Chap. 11: *Accounts and Auditors.*

[12a] There are further details in s.190. It extends to debentures, and deems any person "in accordance with whose directions or instructions the directors of a company are accustomed to act" to be a director.

son as his proxy to attend and speak instead of him, and to vote instead of him, whether on a show of hands or on a poll.[13] There is a collective statutory right to demand a poll given by section 137 of the Companies Act 1963, couched in such terms that the individual member who wishes to be sure that the true voting strength on a particular issue comes out must between himself and his supporters to command at least 10 per cent. of the votes entitled to be cast on the particular issue, *i.e.* 10 per cent. of the voting strength in the company or class as the case may be, whether represented at the meeting or not, or, the individual member must have the support of at least four others in his demand for a poll. For a shareholder commanding less than 10 per cent. of the voting strength of a publicly quoted company, the way round this difficulty is found in vesting part of his shareholding in four separate nominees. For other companies, the restrictions on transfer provide an obstacle.[14] There is a collective right given by section 132 of the Companies Act 1963 given to members holding at least one tenth of the paid-up capital carrying voting rights to requisition a general meeting of the company.[14a] Though this right is expressed to be given to "members" in the plural, in *Re El Sombrero Ltd.*[15] a requisition by a single member holding the requisite shares was accepted as valid without comment. The single requisitionist's problems arise later when no one else turns up to the meeting he has requisitioned so that there can be neither a meeting nor a quorum.[16] Table A effectively gives the directors control of the agenda at general meetings summoned by them on their own initiative.[16a] This comes about not because individual members have no right to propose resolutions but because article 51 requires notice of any special business,[16b] in this instance the member's resolution, to be given *with* the notice convening the meeting, a matter ordinarily beyond the control of the individual member unless he has the voting strength to requisition a meeting of the company expressly for the purpose of considering his resolution.[16c] There is no general duty on directors to give notice of members' resolutions when convening general meetings on their own

---

[13] There are ancillary provisions in s.138 and in arts. 63 *et seq.* of Table A and for practical uses of proxy voting see Chap. 3. Internal Structure, under the heading *The Maintenance of Control.*

[14] See *Becoming registered, infra.*

[14a] Also s.134(*b*) and art. 50 of Table A.

[15] [1958] Ch. 900.

[16] See pp. 70–71, *supra.*

[16a] Art. 51, and see p.70, *supra.*

[16b] For the nature of special business, see p.72, *supra.*

[16c] See s.132, *supra.*

initiative.[16d] One possible exception to this impasse relates to resolutions requiring extended notice within the meaning of section 142, *i.e.* resolutions to dismiss directors, or that the company's auditors be not re–appointed.[16e] Section 142 says

> " . . . where . . . extended notice is required of a resolution, the resolution shall not be effective unless (except when the directors of the company have resolved to submit it) notice of the intention to move it has been given to the company not less than 28 days before the meeting at which it is moved, and *the company shall give its members notice of any such resolution at the same time and in the same manner as it gives notice of the meeting* or, if that is not practicable, shall give them notice thereof, either by advertisement . . . or in any other mode allowed by the articles, not less than 21 days before the meeting."[16f]

Thus, if a member gives notice to the company well before its next *a.g.m.* of an intention to propose such a resolution it is arguable that the company must give effective notice of it to enable it to be proposed at the meeting. This argument failed to convince Slade J. in *Pedley* v. *Inland Waterways Association Ltd*.[16g] chiefly on the ground that so to construe the British equivalent of section 142 would give an individual member more extensive rights thereunder than are given by section 140 of the Companies Act 1948 [*U.K.*], a provision obliging the company at the behest of at least 5 per cent. of voting members (or of 100 members holding on average per member paid up share capital of not less than £100) to circulate in advance of an *a.g.m.* notice of any resolution to be proposed at it. But Ireland has no equivalent of section 140 of the 1948 Act.

Individual members have statutory rights[17] to be supplied on demand with copies of its memorandum and articles, copies of all resolutions which the company is obliged to forward to the Registrar under section 143 of the Companies Act 1963 as amended,[18] and copies of all minutes of general meetings which a company is obliged to keep under section 145(1), and which a member may also inspect at the company's registered office.

Sections 23 to 25 of the Companies (Amendment) Act 1983 give individual members statutory rights of pre-emption when the com-

---

[16d] Contrast s.140 of the Companies Act 1948 [*U.K.*], *infra*.
[16e] s.182 and s.161, respectively.
[16f] Italics supplied.
[16g] [1977] 1 All E.R. 209.
[17] Respectively contained in ss.29, 143(3), 146(2).
[18] For the present ramifications of this section, see pp. 449–451, *infra*.

pany is proposing to allot unissued equity securities which are to be wholly paid up in cash.[19] The definition of equity securities contained in section 23(13) excludes the usual type of preference share (on which see pp. 172–178 *supra.*) since it excludes shares which after issue are to have restricted rights in the distribution of dividends and capital. By excluding shares which are to be issued otherwise than for cash, there is excluded also from the members' pre-emption rights shares issued in a company in exchange for shares in another company, a common transaction in takeovers with variants for amalgamations, on all of which see Chapter 9. Essentially, what the new provisions seek to guard against is the abuse in companies without a Stock Exchange quotation, where pre-emption provisions have been the norm for some time, of directors exercising their powers to allot shares for cash in such a way as to dilute the value of the existing holdings of existing members. The abuse of the directors' power of allotment, and the extent to which that power may survive untrammelled by these new rights of pre-emption is discussed in Chapter 7 at pp.225–226, and the standard of conduct to be observed by the general meeting in suspending that right is mentioned in Chapter 9 at p.277.

Definition of member

The general rule is that in order to be a member a person must either be an original subscriber to the memorandum of association[20] or, more commonly, have agreed to become a member *and* had his name entered on the register of members.[21]

Entitlement to be registered as member

Apart from original subscription, a person may become entitled to be placed upon the register of members and thereby become a member if he has the benefit of a contract of *allotment* in respect of shares in the company, or if he has acquired title to them by *transfer* or by *transmission*. Under a contract of allotment a subscriber agrees to take from the company newly issued shares. Transfer refers to the disposition *inter vivos* from transferor to transferee of the right to a share by a written instrument of transfer. Transmission involves the passing of the entitlement to a share by operation of law, *i.e.* on the

---

[19] s.23(4) of the 1983 Act.

[20] ss.18(2), 31(1); *Alexander* v. *Automatic Telephone Co.* [1900] 2 Ch. 56; *Tangney* v. *Clarence Hotels Ltd.* [1933] I.R. 51, 64.

[21] s.31(2). For the contents of the register of members, see ss.116 *et seq.* Entry on the register may now consist of giving the appropriate instructions to a computer: s.378(1) as amended by s.4 of the Companies (Amendment) Act 1977.

death of a member to his personal representative or on his bankruptcy to his assignee in bankruptcy.

Position pending registration

An unregistered transferee has, save in one instance, none of the rights of membership, "since a transfer is not legally complete until the transferee has been registered in the books of the company."[22] In *Kinsella* v. *Alliance & Dublin Consumers Gas Co.*,[23] unregistered transferees unsuccessfully contended that once their transfers had been lodged for registration with the company they had the right to attend and vote at its general meeting. The one exception is the unregistered transferee who in the terms of section 205(6) is the "trustee of, or person beneficially interested in, the shares of a company by virtue of the will or intestacy of any . . . person" who at the date of his death was a member of the company. Section 205(6) equates such a person to a full member for the purpose of making an application to the court under section 205.[24]

A person becoming entitled to a share by transmission has under most common form articles whilst still unregistered somewhat fuller rights than those possessed by the unregistered transferee. For example, article 32 of Table A provides that such a person "shall be entitled to the same dividends and other advantages to which he would be entitled if he were the registered holder of the share, except that he shall *not*, before being registered as a member in respect of the share, be entitled in respect of it to exercise any right conferred by membership in relation to meetings of the company. . . . ," but by article 136(*b*) he is entitled to receive notice of such meetings. Consequently, under such articles, a person becoming entitled to a share by transmission cannot vote until he is registered as holder, and can therefore have no part in the control of the company, and, in particular, in the appointment of directors. But, again, the position is modified for the personal representative of deceased members. Section 205(6) equates him to a member for the purpose of making an application under section 205.[25]

An unregistered allottee has none of the rights of membership.

---

[22] *Per* Johnson J. in *Tangney* v. *Clarence Hotels Ltd.* [1933] I.R. 51, 61.

[23] High Court, October 5, 1982, Barron J., unreported, which concerned a company governed by the Company Clauses Consolidation Act 1845, a fact which has no bearing on the proposition stated in the text.

[24] Such applications under s.205 by unregistered transferees are discussed *infra* at pp. 193–195, *infra.*

[25] Likewise discussed at pp. 193–195, *infra.*

Becoming registered

This presents few problems in the small minority of Irish companies whose articles contain no restrictions on transfer. These will mostly be those public companies whose shares are quoted on the Stock Exchange which outlaws restrictions on transfer in respect of fully paid shares.[26] Here the person entitled to registration who has complied with the necessary preliminaries and put in an application in proper form[27] to the company may apply to the court for an order under section 122 of the Companies Act 1963 for an order that the register by rectified by the inclusion of his name. He must show that his name has been omitted "without sufficient cause,"[28] and such a cause may well be that the company requires further time to process his application. It is clear that the company is entitled to "a reasonable time": *Kinsella* v. *Alliance & Dublin Consumers Gas Co.*[29]; as ever what is reasonable depends upon the circumstances, but it seems that the courts are prepared to accept as the outer limit of reasonableness the two months within which the company is obliged under section 84 of the Companies Act 1963 on pain of criminal penalties to inform a transferee that his application for registration has been refused, if that be the case.[30]

The vast majority of Irish companies do however have restrictions in their articles on the free transferability of their shares. These restrictions stem partly from a desire natural in the participants in family companies and others with few original members not to have membership thrown open to all comers[31]; the other reason for their presence is that such restrictions are an essential condition for private company status.[32] The form of restriction suggested by article 3 of Part II of Table A baldly states:

---

[26] Appendix 34 to the Rules and Regulations of the Stock Exchange, Schedule VII, Pt. A,A.

[27] As to which matters see *Mechanics of transfer, infra*.

[28] s.122(1)(a).

[29] *Per* Barron J. at p. 16 of the transcript, High Court, October 5, 1982, unreported.

[30] *Re Swaledale Cleaners Ltd.* [1968] 1 W.L.R. 1710 (English C.A.). See also s.86 which requires the share certificate to be ready for delivery to the transferee within two months of the lodgment of a valid transfer, except in the case of such transfers as "the company is, for any reason, entitled to refuse to register and does not register." The transferee must also take into account the fact that s.121 and most articles entitle companies to close their membership register for 30 days in every year: Art. 27 of Table A.

[31] See *Att. Gen.* v. *Jameson* [1904] 2 I.R. 644, 665 (*per* Kenny J.); 680 (*per* Boyd J.).

[32] s.33(1)(b). Britain has abandoned all statutory conditions for private company status, which is now the residual category of company in that country. Instead, a U.K. private company is forbidden on pain of criminal penalties from inviting the public to subscribe for its shares or debentures: s.15 Companies Act 1980 [U.K.].

> "The directors may, in their absolute discretion, and without assigning any reason therefor decline to register any transfer of any share, whether or not it is fully paid share."[33]

Such an article concentrates the power of determining whom to admit to membership into the hands of the directors, and therefore of the controlling group for the time being. Difficulties consequently arising with this and similar articles in common use are discussed below. It should be observed however that less extreme forms of restriction may be adopted without jeopardising private company status. Among them there are articles such as those employed in *Tangney* v. *Clarence Hotels Ltd.*[34] which allowed free transferability of shares among its existing members and sought in the words of Johnson J.:

> "to place no restrictions upon the circulation of the shares amongst members of the company, but to enable the heavy hand of the Directors to come down when a stranger seeks to enter into the charmed circle."[35]

Or free transferability and transmissibility may be extended to include certain relatives of existing members as in *Att.-Gen.* v. *Jameson*[36]; or to include companies controlled by specified classes of persons, such as existing members or their descendants or to include trustees of trusts for beneficiaries similarly defined; or, indeed, any other variations according to the needs and expectations of the participants. In fact, it is submitted that the statutory requirement that the shares of private companies be subjected to restrictions on transfer will be satisfied by any provision in the articles which departs from "the elements of free and uncontrolled disposition . . . the absolute right to go into the open market and sell to any outsider and for the best price."[37] In that event, the mere inclusion in the articles of rights of pre-emption in favour of existing members in the event of another member wishing to transfer should suffice to satisfy the statutory condition,[38] and the expectations of most participants if properly advised on formation. It would certainly obviate the diffi-

---

[33] The equivalent in Pt. I of Table A, art. 24 is obsolete, depending for its form on *inter alia*, erstwhile protectionist trade policies (*i.e.* the Control of Manufacturers Acts 1932–34) and the former discriminatory stamp duties against foreigners.

[34] [1933] I.R. 51.

[35] *Ibid.* p. 63.

[36] [1904] 2 I.R. 644.

[37] *Ibid.* at p. 673, *per* Kenny J. See also Johnston J. in *Tangney* v. *Clarence Hotels Ltd.* [1932] I.R. 51, 63, where he states that "the right of an owner of shares to get rid of them is absolute except in so far as it is restricted by contract *inter socios*."

[38] For rights of pre-emption of existing shares, see pp. 178–179.

culties and abuses arising from leaving transferability in the discretion of the directors under articles such as article 3 of Table A (and its variants), to the operation of which we now turn.

Not only are transferees faced with the hurdle of the directors' discretion, but, almost invariably, so also are persons acquiring title by transmission. Articles 30 and 31 of Table A give such a person an election either to have himself registered as member or some other person nominated by him, such as, for example, in the case of transmission on death the person ultimately entitled under the deceased's will or intestacy. In either event, these articles treat the applicant for membership as a transferee of the member from whom transmission occurred, and provide that "all the limitations, restrictions and provisions of these regulations relating to the right to transfer and the registration of transfer of shares shall be applicable."[39] In the absence of such articles, a person taking by transmission has an unqualified right to be registered as member.[40]

Unregistered transferees facing the directors' discretion fall into three possible categories. First there is the situation where the board does nothing after receipt of the application. If this inactivity is sufficiently prolonged, the company will lose its opportunity to refuse the applicant, and he will be entitled to an order for rectification of the register under section 122. This comes about because the transferee's position *vis-à-vis* the company is categorised as a *right* capable of being defeated by the directors' *power*, if exercised, and powers, if unexercised, lapse after a reasonable time. That the transferee has a direct right against the company to be registered is most trenchantly put by Johnston J. in *Tangney* v. *Clarence Hotels Ltd.*, where he said:

> "It is quite idle for the Company and the Directors to contend, as they both have done, that a person to whom a member of a company has transferred his stock or his share has no such privity with the company as would entitle him to go to the company with his deed of transfer and insist upon his being registered as the owner of the shares."[41]

The provenance of this right is the early principle of the free transferability of shares[42] which even now can be spelled out from section 79 of the Companies Act 1963 which states: "The shares . . . in a

---

[39] Art. 31. There is a similar statement in Art. 30.
[40] *Safeguard Industrial Investments Ltd.* v. *National Westminster Bank Ltd.* [1982] 1 All E.R. 449, 451. (English C.A.). *Re Ray-Ger Ltd.* (High Court, Costello J., April 28, 1983, unreported) at pp.37 and 39 of the transcript.
[41] [1933] I.R. 51, 59.
[42] *Weston's Case* (1868) L.R. 4 Ch.App. 20; *Lindlar's Case* [1910] 1 Ch. 312.

company shall be . . . transferable." A right of alienation is necessarily incomplete unless it includes an ability to ensure that the alienated property is effectively passed to the alienee; one must suppose that this right passes from transferor to transferee by the transfer itself. So much is the right to be registered considered to be that of the transferee, that statute intervened under what is now section 83 of the Companies Act 1963 to give a transferor *locus standi* to apply for the transferee's name to be placed upon the register.[43] Such a right is of obvious importance to the transferor of shares in an unlimited company.[44]

Authority for the proposition that the directors' power of veto must be exercised in order to be effective may be found in *Re Hackney Pavilion Ltd.*[45] and *Moodie* v. *W. & J. Shepherd (Bookbinders) Ltd.*[46] in each of which there was deadlock on the board, and in *Re Swaledale Cleaners Ltd.*[47] in which an attempt was made to define the time within which the power of veto would lapse. In that case the two months a company has under section 84 of the Companies Act 1963 to notify refusal to an applicant was taken as a guideline, but it should be emphasised that whether or not a power has lapsed depends upon what is "reasonable" in all the circumstances, sometimes a very nebulous concept.[48] It is unlikely, for example, that lapse would readily be assumed if a company had no directors, or none able to act. Section 122 proceedings brought in such a case might be stood over until a general meeting had been held to appoint directors.[49]

The second category concerns the situation where the transferee does not have the benefit of section 205, *i.e.* is neither an existing member nor within section 205(6),[50] and has been refused by the directors within a reasonable time. Here the transferee in his application for rectification of the register under section 122 will have to show that the directors exercised their discretion against him either

---

[43] *Tangney* v. *Clarence Hotels Ltd.* [1933] I.R. 51, 60, citing *Skinner's Case* (1885) 14 Q.B.D. 882.

[44] As in *Casey* v. *Bentley* [1902] 1 I.R. 376.

[45] [1924] 1 Ch. 276.

[46] [1949] 2 All E.R. 1044 (H.L.).

[47] [1968] 1 W.L.R. 1710. See n. 30, *supra*.

[48] For lapse of powers generally see *Re Allen—Meyrick's W.T.* [1966] 1 W.L.R. 499 (trustees' power to distribute income held to have lapsed); *Re Gulbenkian's S.T.* (*No. 2*) [1970] Ch. 408 (uncertainties over validity of settlement prevented trustees' powers over income lapsing during many years of litigation).

[49] The meeting could be convened by the Court itself on its own motion under s.135.

[50] These fall into the third category, *infra*.

for an improper purpose or in bad faith. Bad faith involves a finding that the directors did not genuinely think that what they were doing was for the benefit of the company. Directors are required to observe these standards in the exercise of all their fiduciary powers, of which the power to refuse transferees is merely one instance. The matter is more fully discussed in Chapter 7. Proving an abuse of fiduciary powers is difficult. The difficulties are compounded by the general principle that a person exercising such a power is not obliged to give his reasons, and, in this particular instance, by the very width with which the power to refuse transferees is generally drawn.

As a first step one must analyse the ambit of the power.[51] Article 3 of Part II of Table A is drafted in such sweeping terms as to justify the directors taking into consideration matters in the general interests of the company beyond the personal characteristics of the transferee such as, according to Lord Greene, M.R. in *Re Smith & Fawcett Ltd.*,[52] "whether by passing a particular transfer the transferee would obtain too great a weight in the affairs of the company or might even obtain control." This statement should not be regarded as surprising, since, after all, such articles are designed to secure a closed society. Other forms of article are narrower. Some are construed as confining legitimate considerations to the personal attributes of the transferee[53]; others as excluding existing members from their operation.[54] Some motives for refusal will clearly be improper even under the widest article, such as a desire on the part of the directors to force the transferee to sell his shares to the directors at an undervalue,[55] or a desire on the part of the directors to maintain themselves in a position of wrongdoing in relation to the company with which the new member might interfere.[56]

Article 3 of Part II of Table A states that the directors may take their decision on transfers "without assigning any reason therefor." These words are in fact surplusage. Directors exercising wide discretions are assimilated in this respect to the position of trustees,[57] and even where these words do not appear may, as Meredith M.R. put it in *Re Dublin North City Milling Co. Ltd.*,[58] nevertheless "hold their tongues." They may resist cross-examination, and are immune

---

[51] *Re Dublin North City Milling Co. Ltd.* [1909] 1 I.R. 179, 183 *per* Meredith M.R.
[52] [1942] Ch. 304, 309.
[53] *Re Bede Shipping Co. Ltd.* [1917] 1 Ch. 123.
[54] *Tangney* v. *Clarence Hotels Ltd.* [1933] I.R. 51.
[55] *Re Smith & Fawcett Ltd.* [1942] Ch. 304, 309.
[56] *Re Hafner* [1943] I.R. 426, *infra*.
[57] *e.g. Re Londonderry's Settlement* [1965] Ch. 918.
[58] [1909] 1 I.R. 179, 184.

from interrogatories.[59] The position of the directors was summarised by Black J. in *Re Hafner*[60]:

> "They are not bound to assign their reasons, and the court is not entitled to infer merely from their omission to do so that their reasons were not legitimate. Hedged around with the privilege of remaining mute and the prima facie presumption of rectitude the astutely silent director who wishes to exercise this power illegitimately may well consider himself all but invulnerable. . . . "

How then does the claimant in this second category discharge the apparently impossible burden[61] of displaying the state of mind which he is prohibited from examining? The answer according to *Re Hafner*,[60] one of the few cases of success for applicants in this category, is for the applicant to produce *some* evidence, not necessarily sufficient of itself to discharge the burden of proof, tending to indicate *mala fides* or improper purpose. If such allegations remain uncontroverted, the court is *then* prepared to draw an adverse inference from the directors' silence, sufficient in fact, to substantiate the allegations. In *Re Hafner* itself, the applicant was able to show that the refusing directors had given themselves exorbitant service contracts with the company, such that "the bloated emoluments would convert the flourishing company from a dividend-paying concern into a director remunerating enterprise."[62] Black J. drew an inference from the directors' continuing silence in the face of this evidence that they wished to exclude the applicant from membership because, if admitted, he might wish to question these over comfortable arrangements. In *Clark* v. *Workman*,[63] Ross J. overturned the directors' approval of a proposed transfer of a controlling interest on the grounds, *inter alia*, that the directors had failed to refute an unsubstantiated allegation that the new controllers intended to use the assets of the company to finance their own business: "It was a challenge that required some answer, and no answer has been given."[64] An adverse inference will not necessarily be drawn from

---

[59] *Berry and Stewart* v. *Tottenham Hotspur Football & Athletic Co. Ltd.* [1935] 1 Ch. 718.

[60] [1943] I.R. 426, 439, 440, unanimously upheld by the Supreme Court on the aspects under discussion at [1943] I.R. 462.

[61] For the burden of proof being on the applicant, see *Re Dublin North City Milling Co. Ltd.* [1909] 1 I.R. 179, 183.

[62] *Per* Black J. at pp.443–444.

[63] [1920] 1 I.R. 107.

[64] *Ibid.* p. 118.

the fact that the transferee is already a member, or that a previous transfer to him had but recently been approved.[65]

The third category arose in, part out of the difficulties caused by the second. Particularly disturbing was the ease with which the directors' discretion could be used to prevent shareholdings in family companies from being passed down the generations. Such companies might on formation have had only one or two effective participants who did not anticipate by inserting appropriate provisions in the articles[66] the difficulties arising on the fragmentation of their original shareholdings after their deaths, and, indeed, the deaths of their immediate successors. Companies of this kind may often with the passage of time degenerate into warring groups struggling to acquire or maintain control. In this struggle, the directors' discretion to refuse to admit transferees to membership can be a potent weapon. Since 1964, as has been observed,[67] the successors to the share of a deceased member on his death, whether the ultimate beneficiary, a trustee for him or the personal representative himself, are treated by section 205(6) as being entitled to petition for a remedy under section 205. These, and an existing member who has taken a transfer of further shares, form the third category, namely persons with the benefit of section 205. The jurisdiction is founded in this context by the applicant's establishing "that the powers of the directors of the company are being exercised in a manner oppressive to him . . . or in disregard of his . . . interests as member. . . . " Although exclusion from membership may in most cases of applicants in this category be regarded as "oppressive,"[68] it seems more appropriate and straightforward in this context for the applicant to rely simply on a "disregard of his interests." What greater disregard for a person in his position could there be than a refusal to admit

---

[65] *Re Dublin North City Milling Co. Ltd.* [1909] 1 I.R. 179. He would be entitled to seek a remedy under s.205 *infra*.

[66] *e.g.* by providing guaranteed directorships for the representatives of particular groups of shareholders, and for free transferability of shares within the family. A standard form modification of Table A commonly made on the formation of private companies in Ireland states: "Any share of a deceased member may be transferred by his executor or administrator to the widow or widower, child or grandchild of such deceased member and regulation 3 of Part II of Table A shall be amended accordingly." This form suffers from two defects. First, it may not reflect the family circumstances of the deceased member, or his choice of legatee; and secondly, it is not expressed to modify the directors' power to refuse to *register* transfers, and could be construed as restricting the class of potential transferees to those mentioned, and not as touching at all on the directors' powers to refuse even them, a very different result, one would suppose from that intended by the draftsman. Specific instructions should always be taken on the question of transferability.

[67] At p. 186, *supra*.

[68] This expression is analysed in Chap. 9. Likewise, "disregard of interests."

him to the circle of membership with its attendant rights? Also, preventing an existing member from enjoying the further rights to
which he is entitled as a transferee of further shares may be considered a disregard of his interests .

Once the jurisdiction has been established, then under section
205(3) "the court may, with a view to bringing to an end the matters
complained of, make such order as it thinks fit. . . . " In carrying out
this function, the court is not reviewing the discretion of the directors, as in the second category; it is exercising its own fresh discretion on the evidence before it. If the directors fail to contribute to
that evidence factors adverse to the applicant, he will inevitably be
ordered to be registered as a member. If they do, the court may, if it
thinks fit, order that the directors buy the applicant's shares at a fair
value, or since the granting of relief is discretionary, it may make no
order at all despite the presence of jurisdiction. It is submitted that
the evidence to be produced by the directors must in order to outweigh their disregard of the interests of the applicant be such as to
show that his admission to membership would be strongly adverse
to the interests of the company; perhaps, in the case of an applicant
entitled to a majority holding that he had a proven record of dishonesty, or intended after gaining control of the company to pursue
a course of wrongdoing in relation to it or its members. Certain personal attributes of the applicant, such as his or her sex or religion,
cannot on constitutional grounds[69-70] be considered by the court in
exercising its discretion.

The transferor *inter vivos* remains technically a member of the company until his name is removed from the register. Technically, therefore, he remains a member for the purpose of making a section 205
application *if* he should wish to lend his aid to an unregistered transferee of the second category, or *if* his contract of sale to the transferee
expressly obliges him to do so. That he, being merely a bare trustee
for the transferee retains no benefical interest capable of being disregarded or no sufficient stake in the company to render the actions
oppressive to him, cannot be a sufficient objection to his bringing
proceedings under section 205. To do so would exclude all

[69-70] Art. 40 of the Constitution: equality before the law; Art. 44, 2: religious freedom. Such considerations should not sway the directors either; on the effect of constitutional provisions *between* citizens, see *inter alia* Von Prondzynski:, (1979–80)
D.U.L.J. 20 *et seq.* Nor, *semble* should political views as such be taken into account
(Art. 40.6.1 of the Constitution: rights of free expression and association). If an applicant after admission to membership possesses such a commanding majority as to be
able to attempt to force political and economic theories damaging to the company
upon it, the minority will have appropriate redress. See Chap. 9: *Minority Protection.*

fiduciaries from its benefits. A company is generally not concerned with the capacity in which the members hold their shares.[71]

The position of an unregistered allottee under a lawful allotment is straightforward. The company of whatever kind must pursuant to section 116(2) of the Companies Act 1963 register him as member within 28 days of the conclusion of the contract of allotment or face an application for rectification.

Protection of equitable interests

Generally a company is not concerned with equitable interests subsisting in its shares. Section 123 of the Companies Act 1963 states this general rule:

> "No notice of any trust, express, implied or constructive, shall be entered on the register or be receivable by the registrar."

The "register" there referred to is the register of members which a company is obliged to keep under section 116 and the "registrar" is the person deputed by the company to keep it, usually its secretary. Most companies augment this section by adopting article 7 of Table A which provides:

> "Except as required by law, no person shall be recognised by the company as holding any share upon any trust, and the company shall not be bound or be compelled in any way to recognise, even when having notice thereof, any equitable, contingent, future or partial interest in any share . . . or (except only as by these regulations or by law otherwise provided) any other rights in respect of any share except an absolute right to the entirety thereof in the registered holder: this shall not preclude the company from requiring the members or a transferee of shares to furnish the company with information as to the beneficial ownership of any share when such information is reasonably required by the company."

Provisions such as these encourage nominee holdings and reinforce the conclusion arrived at in *Salomon's Case*[72] that persons making up the statutory minima to form a company need not be independent of one another. The nominee, though holding the whole beneficial interest in the shares upon trust for the beneficial owner (or nominator) and being under a duty to him to exercise all rights attached to the shares in accordance with his directions, is nonetheless the

---

[71] See *Protection of equitable interests, infra.*

[72] [1897] A.C. 22; the equivalent statutory provision at that time was s.30 of the Companies Act 1862.

member in the eye of the law and of the company, having all the
benefits and burdens[73] of membership. A transferor who has been
paid is in the position of a nominee for the transferee.[74] Other persons with less absolute beneficial interests in shares include beneficiaries under trusts of shares giving, as is usual, powers of
management to the trustees, and equitable mortgagees of shares, *i.e.*
persons who have had deposited with them a share certificate by
way of security.

Prima facie, all these and other persons possessing beneficial
interests in a company's shares remain screened off from the company in a state of equitable limbo until, if at all, their titles are perfected by registration. But there are occasional chinks in the screen.
Some persons having equitable interests may have the benefit of section 205(6), as we have already seen.[75] Other instances should be
noted briefly. Order 46 of the Rules of the Superior Courts contains
a procedure under which persons beneficially interested in shares
may give formal notice to the company of their interest. A company
in receipt of such a notice must notify the beneficiary of any attempt
by the legal owner to transfer the shares, and must delay the transfer
for eight days during which time, the beneficiary may take steps to
safeguard his position.[76] Since, nowadays, share certificates almost
invariably have to be produced to a company on transfer, this procedure will generally only be useful where the beneficial owner is not
in possession of the certificate, such as, perhaps, the purchaser of
shares under an uncompleted or instalment contract of sale.[77]
Secondly, there is another rarity. Where the share certificate does
not on the face of it state that is must be produced on a transfer, then
an equitable mortgagee who has taken a deposit of a share certificate
by way of security should give notice of his interest to the company.
If he does not, there is a danger that the security may be defeated on
the registered owner's subsequent bankruptcy since the shares will
have continued in his reputed ownership pursuant to section 313 of
the Irish Bankrupt and Insolvent Act 1857.[78] Thirdly, if the company has a lien on its shares in respect of money owed to it by the
holder of them, an equitable mortgagee of those shares may give
effective notice to the company so as to prevent the company claim-

---

[73] *e.g. Re Munster Bank: (Dillon's Claim)* (1886–87) 17 L.R., Ir. 341.
[74] *Casey* v. *Bentley* [1902] 1 I.R. 376, 387. For unpaid transferors, and generally, see
Musselwhite v. *C.H. Musselwhite & Son Ltd.* [1962] Ch. 964.
[75] At pp. 186, 193, *supra.*
[76] The notice may also extend to the payment of dividends.
[77] For his position see *Musselwhite* v. *C.H. Musselwhite & Son Ltd.* n. 74 *supra.*
[78] *Re Morrissey* [1961] I.R. 442; *Re McClement* [1960] I.R. 141; *Bankruptcy Law Committee Report*, 1972, Prl. 2714, Ch. 61.

ing priority in respect of debts incurred by the holder after the date of that notice.[79]

Mechanics of transfer

Section 81 of the Companies Act 1963 requires a transfer to be effected by "a proper instrument of transfer," thereby furnishing a document to which stamp duty can attach, which, one supposes, is the main purpose of the section. The supplementary provisions of Table A no longer fully reflect current practice. Article 22 purports to require the instrument of transfer to be "executed by or on behalf of the transferor *and transferee*. . . . " Yet the Stock Transfer Act 1963 introduced for fully paid shares a simplified form of transfer which may be used and executed by the transferor alone, notwithstanding anything in the company's articles.[80] Article 23 of Table A which states that "any member may transfer all or any of his shares by instrument in writing in any usual or common form or any other form which the directors may approve," is also misleading insofar as it may suggest that the directors may prescribe a form of transfer which is exclusively to be used. They may not in fact prohibit the use of forms of transfer authorised by the Stock Transfer Act 1963, and, indeed, these are the forms in common use. The Act does not however actually prohibit the use of other forms.

Further new forms were recently introduced[81] to be used in the new Talisman computer system for the settling of Stock Exchange transactions. This system involves the transfer of shares sold on the Stock Exchange to the stock exchange nominee, Sepon Ltd.[82] and a transfer by Sepon Ltd. to the ultimate transferee. Only the latter transfer attracts stamp duty.[83] Companies are not obliged to issue share certificates in respect of their shares transferred to Sepon Ltd.,[84] since these holdings are not intended to be permanent and will fluctuate from time to time depending on the course of dealing

---

[79] *Rearden* v. *Provincial Bank of Ireland* [1896] 1 I.R. 532; following *Bradford Banking Co. Ltd.* v. *Briggs* (1887) 12 App.Cas. 29.

[80] s.2 of the Stock Transfer Act 1963. The Act has no application to partly paid shares. Art. 22 is commonly modified on formation to reflect the changes introduced by this Act.

[81] By S.I. 1980, No. 139 made pursuant to s.5 of the Stock Transfer Act 1963 as amended by the Companies (Amendment) Act 1977.

[82] Designated nominee of the Stock Exchange for the purposes of the 1977 Act by S.I. 1979, No. 121. Sepon Ltd. is an English registered company formed by the Stock Exchange.

[83] S.I. 1979, No. 121 which also contains authority for composition procedures to streamline the collection of duty.

[84] s.2 of the 1977 Act amended s.86 of the 1963 Act in this respect.

and progress in the completion of bargain. Transfers of Irish registered securities from Sepon Ltd. to the ultimate transferee are
executed by the two Stock Exchange-Irish officials who represent
this regional Exchange on the board of Sepon Ltd.[85]

A share certificate made under the seal[86] the company is defined
by section 87 of the Companies Act 1963 as being *"prima facie* evidence of the title of the member to the share."* Section 86 imposes a
duty on the company to issue a share certificate to an allottee or
registered transferee in respect of his holding. This "voucher of
ownership"[87] is invariably required by a company's articles to be
produced on an application for registration of a transfer,[88] and will,
if it is in common form, state this requirement on its face. Where a
shareholder has sold the whole of the shareholding to which his certificate relates, he will cause it to be delivered to the transferee or his
agent together with the executed transfer, leaving it to the latter to
pursue registration and the issue of a new certificate to the transferee. Where the vendor is transferring only part of the holding
covered by his certificate, he will obviously not wish to part with it to
the transferee. In these circumstances, it became the practice and
the transferor's duty to lodge his certificate and his executed transfer
of the part holding with the company so that it might endorse "certificate lodged" or some such formula on the transfer as a form of
proof to the transferee that the transferor had a certificate in respect
of the shares comprised in the transaction. This process is known as
the certification of transfers. The transferor fulfills his obligations to
the transferee by causing to be delivered to him a certificated
transfer, and the company retains the original certificate pending
the completion of the transaction whereupon new certificates are
issued for the split holdings. Since the introduction of the Talisman
system for the settling of Stock Exchange transactions, the Stock
Exchange has itself undertaken certification of transfers. Certification by companies has therefore fallen into disuse in the majority
of cases where it would have been necessary. Correspondingly diminished in importance is section 85 of the Companies Act 1963. This

---

[85] Facsimile signatures are permitted: S.I. 1980, No. 139. For further information
on the working of Talisman, see Abrams, "Talisman: a legal analysis" (1980) 1 Co.
Law 17. Readers of this article interested in the system from the Irish viewpoint
should note that there are no jobbers on the Stock Exchange—Irish. In fact, a
"dummy" jobber is written into the computer programme to accommodate Irish
Stock Exchange transactions.

[86] The share certificate need no longer be executed under the common seal of the
company. s.3 of the 1977 Act makes provision for the use of a separate seal for share
certificates.

[87] *Per* Fitzgerald L.J. in *Kelly* v. *Munster & Leinster Bank* (1892–93) 29 L.R.Ir. 19, 52.

[88] *e.g.* art. 25(*b*) of Table A.

section describes the effect of a certification as being a representation that there have been produced to the company "such documents as on the face of them show a *prima facie* title to the shares"; the company does not by certification warrant the transferor's title to the shares. Section 85 also gives a somewhat circumscribed statutory action for compensation to any person who "acts on the faith of a false certification by a company made negligently." The claimant must prove that the certificated transfer was issued by a person *authorised* to do so on the company's behalf, and that it was signed by a person likewise *authorised* to do so.[89] The section unfortunately leaves unanswered the question whether proof of ostensible authority will suffice for this purpose, or whether actual authority must be proved.[90] Although section 85(3)(*c*) contains a presumption in favour of the claimant that a certification is signed by any person if "it purports to be authenticated by his signature or initials (whether handwritten or not)," it also allows the company to escape liability if it can prove that "they were placed there neither by himself nor by any person *authorised* to use the signature or initials."[91] In these circumstances, the claimant may be better advised to proceed against the company in tort where developments, particularly in the area of negligent misstatement, seem to have overtaken this statutory remedy.

---

[89] s.85(3).
[90] On the usual authority of a company secretary in this respect, see p. 146, *supra*.
[91] Italics supplied.

Chapter 7: Directors' Duties

INTRODUCTION

An individual director stands in a *fiduciary* relationship to his company. A fiduciary has power to deal with the property of another, and is assumed therefore to occupy a position of trust and confidence in relation to that other, whom we might loosely call the beneficiary. In our case, the beneficiary is the company. To protect the relationship from abuse, the courts will prevent the fiduciary from making any personal profit from it without the informed consent of the beneficiary. They will curb acts of the fiduciary beyond the powers delegated to him, but they will be reluctant to interfere with decisions honestly made by him within his powers, since the discretion is his, and not the court's. They will impose personal responsibility on him to compensate the beneficiary for loss caused through his dereliction of the duties which he undertook.[1] These are broad generalisations; their particular application to company directors will be elaborated in this Chapter.

The term "fiduciary" is of comparatively recent coinage[2]; it is a generic term covering a variety of relationships, most of which are species of agency, and of which that between a director and his company is only one. A trustee is also a fiduciary, and in earlier cases one often sees the term "trustee" being used to describe the relationship between an officer holder and the corporation in which he holds office,[3] assumedly for want of a better word. The tendency continued with modern registered companies, probably aided by the fact that the property of their immediate forerunners, the unincor-

---

[1] On fiduciary obligations, see generally P.D. Finn, *Fiduciary Obligations*, Sydney Law Book Co., 1977; L.S. Sealy, "Fiduciary Relationships," (1962) C.L.J. 69, and "Some Principles of Fiduciary Obligation," (1963) C.L.J. 119.

[2] Sealy, *op. cit.*; it begins to occur with some frequency in the 1840s. Common also are generic paraphrases of the sort used by Sir Michael O'Loghlen, M.R. in *Alven* v. *Bond* (1841) Fl. & Ky. 196, 211: "persons filling a confidential office in relation to the properties to be sold." The fiduciary in that case was a receiver.

[3] *e.g. Att.-Gen.* v. *Belfast Corporation* (1855) 4 Ir. Ch. Rep. 119, 160 *per* Maziere Brady L.C.

porated deed of settlement company, was vested in trustees, there
being no corporation to hold it. The slack use of the term "trustee"
is by no means confined to this context.[4] Of its use in relation to
company directors Farwell J. said in *Re City Equitable Fire Insurance
Co. Ltd.*[5]:

> "It has sometimes been said that directors are trustees. If this
> means no more than that the directors in the performance of
> their duties stand in a fiduciary relationship to the company,
> the statement is true enough. But if the statement is meant to be
> an indication by way of analogy of what those duties are, it
> appears to me to be wholly misleading."

If one were to seek a model in antiquity for the contents of the
fiduciary relationship between a director and his company, and
indeed between other fiduciary agents having the management of
property and their principals, it would be found in the post-classical
form of the Roman institution of *mandatum*,[6] which was adopted by
the Common Law to govern the duties of that species of bailee who
gratuitously undertook tasks in relation to the money or chattels of
another at his request.[7] Explicit references back to these antecedents
can scarcely be found in English and Irish cases seeking to define a
director's relationship to his company, even though the answers
given are in accordance with them; in fact, the authorities when
grappling with the problems of the degrees of skill and diligence
required of a company director often give the impression of dealing
with them in an *a priori* fashion, striving thereby to give effect to the
business community's understanding of the rôle of a company director. The connection was however drawn by Sharwood J. in *Spering's
Appeal*,[8] an American authority, in which he says of directors: "They
are undoubtedly said in many authorities to be trustees, but that, as
I apprehend, is only in a general sense, as we term an agent or any
other bailee intrusted with the care or management of the property

---

[4] Lord Holt, for example, uses it as loosely descriptive of the relationship between
bailor and bailee in *Coggs* v. *Bernard* (1703) 2 Ld. Raym. 909.

[5] [1925] Ch. 407. See also Sealy, "The Director as Trustee" (1967) C.L.J. 83.

[6] For *mandatum*, see such standard works as Buckland, *A Manual of Roman Private
Law*, Cambridge, 1939, p. 300; Leage, *Roman Private Law*, 3rd ed. 1961, pp. 367 *et seq*,
and generally Watson, *Contract of Mandate in Roman Law*, Oxford, 1961.

[7] See *Coggs* v. *Bernard* (1703) 2 Ld. Raym. 909. A good description of the subsequent development of the institution in the Common Law is given in Halsbury,
Laws of England, 1st ed. (1907), pp. 535–37: *Mandate*.

[8] 71 Pa. 11; cited with approval by Fuller C.J. in the U.S. Supreme Court in *Briggs*
v. *Spaulding* (1891) 141 U.S. 132; 35 Law. Ed. 662, 669. Lord Chelmsford in *Overend &
Gurney Co.* v. *Gibb* (1872) 5 L.R., H.L. 480, 502 refers to the directors in that case as
having been "mandataries."

of another. It is certain that they are not technical trustees. They can only be regarded as mandataries, persons who have gratuitously undertaken to perform certain duties . . . ."[9]

Directors may still be described in this way; their services are still prima facie gratuitous, even though they will nonetheless expect their fees,[10] just as the late Roman mandatary would generally expect an *honorarium* under a separate arrangement.[11]

To whom are the duties owed?

It is well established law that the director owes the duties arising out of his office to the company itself, the separate person, and to no one else. Accordingly, as a necessary corollary, and as the central core of the rule in *Foss* v. *Harbottle*,[12] the company exclusively will be the proper plaintiff in the event of the breach of any such duty. This fundamental proposition is not altered by the fact that the directors in exercising their functions owe a duty to the company to take into account the interests of the members,[13] nor by the fact that the members in certain circumstances may for the company's benefit and on its behalf invoke the company's cause of action against wrongdoing directors.[14] But in four other respects, two of them peculiarly Irish, developments have occurred in which a weakening of the fundamental proposition may be perceived.

First, there is the quasi-duty imposed by section 205 of the Companies Act 1963 on the directors when acting collectively not to exercise their powers "in a manner oppressive" to any member. Even though the oppressed member is the proper plaintiff, it is difficult to term the directors' obligation to him a full duty since the discretion of the court is interposed between him and a remedy.

Secondly, there may be an erosion in Ireland of the fundamental principle inherent in *Foss* v. *Harbottle* that a member may not maintain a personal action in respect of loss indirectly caused to him, such as the diminution in the value of his shareholding, by an unredressed wrong committed against the company. That wrong may arise out of a breach by directors of duties owed to the company by virtue of their office, or from other causes of action possessed by the

---

[9] Having thus classified the directors, the learned judge fixed the level of skill and diligence required of them at that required, in his opinion, of mandataries.

[10] This is explained at pp. 84–85, *supra*.

[11] See the works cited in n. 6, *supra*.

[12] (1843) 2 Hare 461.

[13] See p. 220, *infra*. For further discussion of the company as proper plaintiff, see Chapter 8: *Enforcement of Duties*.

[14] For a contrary view, see *Volkswagen Canada Ltd.* v. *Spicer* (1978) 91 D.L.R. 3d 42, 62. (Nova Scotia Supreme Court)

company against directors or others. This principle was recently strongly affirmed by the Court of Appeal in England in *Prudential Assurance Co. Ltd.* v. *Newman Industries Ltd.* (*No.* 2).[15] In this action a plaintiff shareholder alleged that two directors had injured the company by a tortious conspiracy, and claimed personally damages in tort for the consequences of that conspiracy on him, a diminished market value of his shares and a likely diminution in dividends, both heads being merely intertwined reflections at one remove of the loss directly suffered by the company. The plaintiff was non-suited in this personal claim. To have allowed it would have transformed the contractual rights of members in relation to the company[16] into proprietary rights over its property, and would have sown the seeds of subversion over a wide area of the law. Suppose, for example, that *B* with whom *A* is in contractual relations is robbed by *C*, with the result that *B* no longer has the funds to perform his contract with *A*. *A* cannot sue *C* in respect of the fruits of the robbery: that is *B*'s privilege. Essentially, the English Court of Appeal was protecting the separate legal personality of the company; it also adverted to the danger of double recovery if after the member had been compensated by the wrongdoer the company elected to sue, and to the difficulty of quantifying the member's loss.[17] In Ireland, on the other hand, the Supreme Court in *P.M.P.S. Ltd. and Moore* v. *Att.-Gen.*[18] has held that the property rights of a member constituted by his shareholding,[19] and protected by Article 40.3 of the Constitution, are capable of being harmed by an injury done to the incorporated society of which he is a member.[20] In that case the apprehended injury to the member's property rights came from legislation affecting the incorporated society. Whether the Courts will employ this decision when the injury to the corporation comes from some other quarter such as, say, a tortfeasor or a director in breach of his duties to the company can scarcely be predicted. To do so would be to lose sight of the fact that the formulation in *P.M.P.S.* was adopted because of doubts whether the corporation possessed constitutional rights. A way of resolving those doubts is suggested in Chapter 1. Extending the expedient to causes of action which the corporation

---

[15] [1982] 2 W.L.R. 31.

[16] See *The Nature of a Share*, at pp. 161 *et seq. supra.*

[17] [1982] 2 W.L.R. 31, 48–9.

[18] [1984] I.L.R.M. 88.

[19] Also *Central Dublin Development Association* v. *Att.-Gen.* (1973) 109 I.L.T.R. 69,

[20] The society was incorporated under the Industrial and Provident Societies Acts. The observations of the Supreme Court are applicable *mutatis mutandis* to a company incorporated under the Companies Acts, and to its members.

undoubtedly does possess will rob the corporation of its separate personality. The Constitutional obligation on the Courts under Article 40.3 to vindicate the property rights of citizens does not include extending them to include those of other persons.

Thirdly, there are recent indications that Irish and other courts are nowadays more willing to find that company directors have assumed direct obligations to the members, independent of those owed to the company. It has long been established that such independent obligations may be *expressly* assumed where the shareholders constitute the directors their agents in a transaction, for example, in negotiations with a third party who has made a takeover bid for their shares.[21] Or, unsurprisingly, the independent obligations may flow from the ordinary law of tort, from which, of course, directors are not immune, such as the duty to be honest and careful when making statements upon which the members might reasonably be expected to act,[22] provided, as has been pointed out above,[23] the members are not seeking recompense for loss suffered Article 40.3 to vindicate the property rights of citizens does not by them indirectly as a consequence of the loss suffered by the company through a tort of which it was also the victim.

Express agency apart, the courts have until recently set their faces firmly against implying an independent fiduciary relationship between a company director and the members. Christian L.J. in *Smith* v. *Cork and Bandon Railway Co.*[24] in rejecting an assertion that directors were "trustees" for individual members said:

> "I am aware that there have been cases in which, for some purposes, directors of joint stock companies have been assimilated to trustees—as, for example, in the not permitting them to make their office a source of private profit—but that they are actually trustees, for each individual shareholder, is a proposition which presents itself to my mind with all the effect of novelty . . . ."

And a rejected novelty it remained in the subsequent leading case of

---

[21] *e.g. Allen* v. *Hyatt* (1914) 30 T.L.R. 444 (Privy Council on appeal from Ontario).

[22] *e.g. Gething* v. *Kilner* [1972] 1 W.L.R. 337 (alleged deceit); *Prudential Assurance Co. Ltd.* v. *Newman Industries Ltd.* (*No.* 2) [1982] 2 W.L.R. 31, 48, (alleged conspiracy to defraud); *Coleman* v. *Myers* [1977] N.Z.L.R. 225, 340 (duty of care).

[23] At p. 203, *supra*.

[24] (1870) 5 I.R., Eq. 65, 75: it had been asserted that directors were trustees for members of unpaid dividends. "Novelty" and the mind of Christian L.J. were not fully compatible. In *Re Nixon's Estate* (1874) I.R. 9 Eq. 7, 13 he said "It is better that the law should be certain than that it should be abstractedly correct." For further comments on him see (1910) I.L.T. & S.J. and Harpum (1983) 24 L.Q.R. 32–5.

Percival v. *Wright*.[25] The members in that case had sold their shares to directors who had secret knowledge of an imminent take-over bid for them by a third party at a higher price. Had a fiduciary relationship been found to exist between the directors and the members, the former would have been bound to disclose this "price-sensitive" fact,[26] and the sale to them would have been voidable through their failure to do so.

These traditional authorities are now on the retreat. In *Securities Trust Ltd.* v. *Associated Properties Ltd.*,[27] the fact that the takeover of a company was to be financed by it itself was suppressed in the offer documents addressed to its shareholders by the bidder company. McWilliam J. thought that that and other facts ought to have been disclosed by their directors to the members of the company bid for, saying:

> "I have not been addressed on the duty of directors towards their own members or their position as agents or otherwise vis a vis the shareholders on such a transaction but, although a director is not a trustee for the shareholders, directors are to some extent in a fiduciary position and I am of opinion that, on a transaction such as this, the shareholders are entitled to given reasonably full particulars by their directors. . . ."[28]

This, although only a tentative statement untested by ar nonetheless constitutes a departure from *Percival* v. *Wright* like authority. A far more comprehensive and carefu departure has taken place in the New Zealand Cou the case of *Coleman* v. *Myers*,[29] which concerned members' shares by the directors, and in whi owed by the latter to the former *was* found to quent duty on the directors to disclose "price-sens during the negotiations to purchase. This was a fa fact which assisted the Court towards its conclusion long been familiar with the fiduciary duty arising bet

---

[25] [1902] 2 Ch. 421.

[26] This is the terminology used in the extra-legal *City Code on Takeovers and M. rule 30, applicable to Irish resident public companies which are either listed on Stock Exchange or traded on the Unlisted Securities Market. The conduct of th directors in *Percival* v. *Wright* would contravene rule 30(2). Furthermore, the Companies Act 1980 [U.K.], Part V (Insider Dealing) contains provisions designed to prevent the abuse of "price sensitive" information. Similar legislation must be expected in Ireland.

[27] High Court, McWilliam J., November 19, 1980, unreported.

[28] At p. 10 of the transcript.

[29] [1977] 2 N.Z.L.R. 225.

of a family coming to an arrangement about family property,[30] but the roots lie deeper than a mere blood relationship; it just so happens that the pre-requisites for the existence of such a duty are often found where members of a family do business together. In *Coleman* v. *Myers*, the fiduciary relationship was found in the trust and confidence which the members *actually had* in the directors not to abuse their exclusive inside knowledge of the company's affairs in their dealings with the members.[31] "The existence of such a relationship," said Woodhouse J. "must depend upon all the facts of a particular case," and "the mere status of a company director should not produce that sort of responsibility to a shareholder."[32]

In summary, one may discern from *Securities Trust Ltd.* v. *Associated Properties Ltd.* and from *Coleman* v. *Myers* an emergent fiduciary duty owed by directors to members to disclose material facts when the members' rights are to be directly affected by proposals to which the directors are party or privy, provided that the directors are trusted and relied upon to do so by the members, which will not, of course, always be the case.

And, finally, there is the limited statutory intervention introduced by sections 188 and 189 of the Companies Act 1963.[32a] These sections can impose on a company director both a duty of disclosure owed directly to members and a trust of which members may be the direct beneficial object. These broadly drawn sections operate when a director has received or been promised any payment in connection with certain full or partial takeover bids for shares in the company, which have actually resulted in shares in the company being transferred. The bid must either be addressed to the general body of shareholders, or be by a body corporate for controlling interest,[32b] or be by an individual with a view to his obtaining not less than one-third of the voting power in general meeting, or any bid conditional on a certain level of acceptances. The payment includes any excess obtained by the director for his shares over the price which could at

---

[30] *e.g. Leonard* v. *Leonard* (1812) 2 Ball. & B. 171.

[31] [1977] 2 N.Z.L.R. 276–78, 325–26, 330–33, 370–71. For another modern justification of similar equitable intervention, see *Lloyd's Bank Ltd.* v. *Bundy* [1974] 3 W.L.R. 1279, particularly the judgment of Sachs L.J. *cf.* Gavan Duffy P. in *Grealish* v. *Murphy* [1946] I.R. 35, and Napier C.S. in *King* v. *Anderson* (1874) I.R., 8 Eq. 628.

[32] [1977] 2 N.Z.L.R.225.

[32a] For the related ss. 186 and 187, to which s.189 is also ancillary, see pp. 213, 217–218, 252–253, *infra*. The text, *supra*, contains only a précis of the cumbrously drafted ss.188 and 189. For further details, see the Act.

[32b] *i.e.* an offer to establish the holding subsidiary company relationship between the bidder (or its holding company) and the company: s.188(1)(*b*). For the holding subsidiary relationship, see s.155.

the time have been obtained by other holders of the like shares,[32c] and any valuable consideration given to the director,[32d] (including all payments in compensation for loss of office or as a consideration for or in connection with his retirement from office, except *bona fide* payment by way of damages for breach of contract or by way of pension for past services.[32e] Unless the director takes all reasonable steps to secure that the proposed payment is disclosed in the offer document to shareholders or sent with it, and unless before any shares have been transferred he obtains the approval of a meeting of the holders of the shares to which the offer relates (and other holders of shares of the same class), he will hold his payment on trust for any persons who sold their shares as a result of the bid.[32f] There are ancillary provisions designed to ease the burden of proof on claimants.[32g]

Conflict of interest

The law reports of the common law world abound in statements of the consequences to a fiduciary of putting himself in a position where his personal interests and his duty to his principal may conflict, and in them we find stated a rule "not . . . founded on principles of morality,"[33] but rather as a precaution against the abuse of power, a preventive jurisprudence. As the Supreme Court of Canada put it in *Canadian Aero Service Ltd.* v. *O'Malley*,[34] strict application of this rule:

> "against directors and senior management officials is simply recognition of the degree of control which their positions give them in corporate operations, a control which arises above . . . accountability to owning shareholders and which comes under some scrutiny only at annual general or at special meetings. It is a necessary supplement, in the public interest, of statutory regulation and accountability which themselves are . . . an acknowledgment of the importance of the corporation in the life of the community and of the need to compel obedience by it and

---

[32c] s.189(2)(*a*).

[32d] s.189(2)(*b*).

[32e] s.188(1) and s.189(3). For entitlement to damages, see Chapter 3: Internal Structure, *Dismissal of Directors.*

[32f] s.188(1), (3).

[32g] s.189(1).

[33] *Per* Lord Herschell in *Bray* v. *Ford* [1896] A.C. 44, 51.

[34] (1973) 40 D.L.R. 3d 371, 384; judgment of the Court delivered by Laskin J.; followed in *Christie W.J. & Co. Ltd.* v. *Greer* (1981) 121 D.L.R. 3d 472 (Manitoba C.A.), *Alberts* v. *Mountjoy* (1977) 79 D.L.R. 3d 108 (Ontario H.C.).

by its promoters, directors and managers to norms of exemplary behaviour."

What then is this rule? The leading Irish case of *Gabbett* v. *Lawder*[35] concerned a personal representative who had been offered in his fiduciary capacity the reversion on the lease held by him as such, and which he had honestly declined to purchase. He subsequently bought it for himself at public auction. Chatterton V.-C., in deciding that the personal representative held the reversion for the benefit of his beneficiaries, subject to their discharging the costs of its acquisition, said:

"The fundamental principle upon which the doctrine of constructive trusts proceeds is that no person in a fiduciary capacity shall be allowed to retain any advantage gained by him in his character as trustee. His cestuis que trust[36] are entitled to the benefit of any advantage so gained by him, to any addition or accretion to the trust estate which he may have acquired, and to all profit he may have made by any dealing with it . . . . If his position could have caused or even contributed to his obtaining the advantage, it is in my opinion enough; and the Court will not undertake the difficult and often impossible task of investigating the motives of the parties to the transaction. If it results in either gain to the trustee, or loss to the cestuis que trust, the trustee is liable to hand over to them the one, or to make good the other . . . . It was urged here that the circumstances of the purchase show that the administrator did not buy in his fiduciary capacity but for his own personal benefit. It was contended that the statutory offer of pre-emption having been refused, he was at liberty to bid for the estate as any other member of the public could. If this were so it would open a wide door to fraud, for a trustee whose duty is to secure for his cestuis que trust every advantage incident to the trust property would be at liberty for his own purposes to decline the right of pre-emption, and thus secure the setting up of the estate by public auction, and then buy, as he did here, at a less price and hold property as his own. . . . [E]very advantage which may possibly arise from the fiduciary position shall enure for the benefit of the cestuis que trust."[37]

---

[35] (1883) 11 L.R., Ir. 295.

[36] *i.e.* the beneficiaries.

[37] (1883) 11 L.R., Ir. 295, 299, 304, 309. See also *Patten* v. *Hamilton* [1911] 1 I.R. 47; *Moore* v. *M'Glynn* [1894] 1 I.R. 74; *Sherrard* v. *Barron* [1923] 1 I.R. 21; *O'Herlihy* v. *Hedges* (1803) 1 Sch. & Lef. 123; *Armstrong* v. *Armstrong* (1880) 7 L.R., Ir. 207, 216, 218.

This passage has been set out at some length not least because it is the leading Irish expression of these principles; but also because some of the points there made are perennially topical in the application of these principles to company directors, and will be referred to later.

The principle is designed to secure that fiduciaries act disinterestedly. Thus, as will appear particularly strongly in its application to company directors, the fiduciary must still account for profits even where the opportunity of which he took advantage could not have been availed of by his principal.[38] That may seem unfair, but fairness is not the object. Deterrence, and the avoidance of temptation is. As Lord Cranworth L.C. said in *Aberdeen Rail Co.* v. *Blaikie Bros.*[39] of a contract entered into by a director with his own company:

> "A corporate body can only act by agents. . . . Such an agent has duties to discharge of a fiduciary character towards his principal, and it is a rule of universal application that no one having such duties to discharge shall be allowed to enter into engagements in which he has or can have a personal interest conflicting or which possibly may conflict with the interests of those whom he is bound to protect. So strictly is this principle adhered to that no question is allowed to be raised as to the fairness or unfairness of a contract so entered into."

This potentially devastating principle was devised for the protection of principals, and they may release their fiduciaries from the full rigours of it, and frequently do so, either by defining the terms of appointment of the fiduciary in such a way that some or all of what would otherwise be the fiduciary consequences of the relationship do not apply to him, *or* by consenting in advance to the fiduciary's proceeding in the matter which gives rise to the conflict of interest after the fiduciary has made a full disclosure of it to him.[40]

Turning now to explore the application of these general principles to the relationship between a director and his company, we find that the former type of release, namely, subtracting what would otherwise be the fiduciary consequences by a redefinition of the relationship, is almost invariable for dealings *between* a director and his company. Were it not so, commonplace transactions between a

---

[38] *e.g. Regal (Hastings) Ltd.* v. *Gulliver* [1942] 1 All E.R. 378 (H.L.); *Industrial Development Consultants Ltd.* v. *Cooley* [1972] 1 W.L.R. 445, *Canadian Aero Service Ltd.* v. *O'-Malley*, n. 34, *supra*; also *Boardman* v. *Phipps* [1967] 2 A.C. 46.

[39] H.L. (1854) 1 Macq. 461; 2 Eq. Rep. 1281; see also *Bray* v. *Ford* [1896] A.C. 44, 51; *Glover* v. *B.L.N. Ltd.* [1973] I.R. 388, 406.

[40] *e.g. Sherrard* v. *Barron* [1923] 1 I.R. 21, 24, 26.

director and his company, such as the entry by him into a service contract with it, would automatically be struck down. On the other hand, the external aspect of the relationship is usually released, if at all,[40a] by the latter method: full, prior disclosure and consent. By external aspect is meant the use by the company director of his position to gain advantages for himself through dealings with outsiders.

Taking first the internal aspect, that is to say, dealings to which the company is itself a party, companies have for many years redefined the fiduciary relationship by adopting an article such as the present article 85 of Table A:

"A director may hold any other office or place of profit under the company (other than the office of auditor) in conjunction with his office of director for such period and on such terms as to remuneration and otherwise as the directors may determine, and no director or intending director shall be disqualified by his office from contracting with the company either with regard to his tenure of any such other office or place of profit or as vendor, purchaser or otherwise, nor shall any such contract or any contract or arrangement entered into by or on behalf of the company in which any director is in any way interested, be liable to be avoided, nor shall any director so contracting or being so interested be liable to account to the company for any profit realised by any such contract or arrangement by reason of such director holding that office or of the fiduciary relation thereby established."

Articles of this type were the business community's response to such early decisions as *Aberdeen Rail Co.* v. *Blaikie Bros.*[41] which were perceived to be intolerably incompatible with prevailing commercial morality, and doubtless still are. In that case, a contract between the plaintiff partnership and the defendant company for the supply of goods was set aside because a member of the former was a director of the latter. Were it not for articles such as article 85, the fiduciary principle would apply in untrammelled vigour to render voidable all everyday dealings between a director and his company, and him accountable for profits, unless the other method of release, the obtaining of consent after full, prior disclosure, had been employed. This latter method is cumbersome where it is sought to release a *director* from fiduciary duties, since the board of directors itself is

---

[40a] But see Part II of Table A, art. 8 under which a director may participate in exercising the company's votes on shares in another company to secure him remuneration, *etc.*, as officer of the latter company, without by implication, there being a duty to account to the former.

[41] See n. 39, *supra*.

incapable of acting on behalf of the principal, the company, to release one of their own number: in this instance, the disclosure and release must be obtained from the company in general meeting.[42]

Legislative concern at the effective atrophy of the fiduciary principle in internal dealings brought about by the universal adoption of articles of the article 85 type led to statutory intervention, first in Britain in 1929 and later in Ireland in the form of section 194 of the Companies Act 1963, to compel some measure of disclosure by directors of their interests in contracts with their own company. Section 194(1) requires:

> "a director of a company who is in any way, whether directly or indirectly, interested in a contract or proposed contract with the company to declare the nature of his interest at a meeting of the directors of the company."

This falls short of the disclosure to the general meeting demanded by the unmodified fiduciary principle, but this objection is partly met by section 194(5) which provides that declarations of interest made under the section should be entered in a book kept for the purpose, which should be available for inspection without charge by any director, secretary, auditor or member of the company at its registered office, and at every *a.g.m.* A declarant director may mask the full nature of his interest in any contract by making a general declaration under section 194(3):

> "to the effect that he is a member of a specified company or firm and is to be regarded as interested in any contract which may, after the date of the notice, be made with that company or firm [which] shall be deemed to be a sufficient declaration of interest in relation to any contract so made."

Section 194 is concerned only with disclosure; there is no statutory requirement that the company consent to the director having the competing interest, or statutory accountability in respect of profits made from it. If the contrary interest thus disclosed is unacceptable to a majority in the company, they may seek to dismiss the director under section 182 of the Companies Act 1963,[43] or if the majority in

---

[42] *Furs Ltd.* v. *Tomkies* (1936) C.L.R. 583, 590, 592. (High Ct. of Australia). Fiduciaries other than directors may be released by the board (n. 63, *infra*) except that in the case of promoters the board must be independent of them: see Chapter 12, *Promoters and Prospectuses*.

[43] Discussed generally at pp. 91, *et seq.*, *supra*. If the director has a service contract, peremptory dismissal under s.182 may constitute a breach of it by the company, entitling him to damages. Kenny J. has said in *Glover* v. *B.L.N.* [1973] I.R. 388, 406 that mere possession of a conflicting interest does not constitute conduct justifying dismissal.

general meeting (including, perhaps, the director himself) obstruct
this, then the minority, if the company is being damaged by the
director's activities, may perhaps apply for remedy under section
205 on the grounds that the shielding of the director by the majority
constitutes conduct of the affairs of the company in a manner
oppressive to them.

The only sanction imposed by section 194 for failure to make the
disclosures required by it is the criminal penalty of a fine not exceeding £500.[44] There is however English authority for the proposition
that failure to comply with the statutory disclosure requirements
leaves the director in default unprotected by articles of the article 85
type. "Non-disclosure," said Lord Denning M.R. in *Hely-Hutchinson*
v. *Brayhead Ltd.*,[45] "does not render the contract void or a nullity. It
renders the contract voidable at the instance of the company and
makes the director accountable for any secret profit he has made."
But the relieving article in that case was drafted so as to be expressly
dependent upon statutory disclosure having been made, unlike
article 85 which makes no mention of section 194. To arrive at the
same conclusion under Table A in Ireland, the Courts would be
obliged to find that article 83 which says:

> "A director who is in any way, whether directly or indirectly,
> interested in a contract or proposed contract with a company
> shall declare the nature of his interest at a meeting of the direc-
> tors in accordance with section 194 of the Act"

qualifies in all respects the relief given by article 85, a construction
which is by no means self-evident.

Common form articles make other modifications to what would
otherwise be the fiduciary assumption. Article 7 of Part II of Table
A allows directors of private companies to vote at board meetings in
respect of any matter in which they are interested and to be counted
for the quorum, and article 84 of Part I allows such voting in more
restricted circumstances. Were it not for these relaxations by redefinition, the consequences would remain as they were in *Cox* v.
Dublin City Distillery (No. 2)[46] in which directors, though at liberty
under the articles to contract with their company, made the mistake of
voting in favour of a proposal to issue debentures to themselves, with
the result that the debentures were held void *per* Palles C.B. "on the
ordinary principle of equity, that a director, being a trustee for the

---

[44] s.194(5), (6); penalty raised by s.15 of the 1982 Act.
[45] [1967] 3 All E.R. 98, 103. See also Lord Wilberforce at p. 103, and Lord Pearson
at p. 109.
[46] [1915] 1 I.R. 345.

company, cannot vote upon a matter in which he himself has an interest."[47]

The internal aspect of the fiduciary relationship is supplemented by section 186 of the Companies Act 1963. No payment to a director "by way of compensation for loss of office, or in consideration for or in connection with his retirement from office" shall be lawful, unless the proposed payment shall have been disclosed to all the members, and approved by a simple majority vote in general meeting. The ancillary section 189(3) makes it clear that section 186 is confined to gratuitous, or "uncovenanted," payments, an expression employed both by the Jenkins Committee[48] and by Lord Wilberforce in giving the opinion of the Privy Council in *Taupo Totara Timber Co.* v. *Rowe*[49] in which similar legislation was construed to like effect. Such uncovenanted payments may have to surmount the additional hurdle of being proved *intra vires* the company, particularly if it is in the course of dissolution.[50] Excessive gratuities of this kind, carried perhaps by the votes in general meeting of the recipients, could provide an occasion for intervention under section 205, as with the payment of excessive directors' fees.[51]

Section 189(3), following a recommendation of the Jenkins Committee,[52] extends section 186 to cover payments made to a director "for the loss . . . of any other office in connection with the management of the company's affairs or of any office as director or otherwise in connection with the management of the affairs of any subsidiary company." The loss of a managing directorship is an obvious example.[53]

The external aspect of conflict of interest, that is to say, the use by the company director of his position to gain advantages for himself through dealings with outsiders, has been a lively jurisdiction in recent years. The leading case in the Common Law world is *Regal (Hastings) Ltd.* v. *Gulliver*.[54] The facts baldly were that the company ("Regal") had a cinema which its directors decided that it should sell. They also decided that the sale price would be enhanced if the cinema were to be sold as one of a chain. Accordingly, they caused

---

[47] At p. 366.
[48] Paras. 93, 99.
[49] [1977] 3 W.L.R. 466.
[50] *e.g. Hutton* v. *West Cork Ry. Co.* (1883) 23 Ch.D. 654. The capacity of a company to make gratuitous payments is discussed at pp. 119 *et seq., supra*.
[51] See pp. 171–172, *supra*.
[52] Paras. 93, 99.
[53] *Cf. Taupo Totara Timber Co. Ltd.* v. *Rowe*, n. 49 *supra*, in which legislation identical save for the omission of the express extension in s.189(3) was construed nonetheless to cover payments made in respect of the loss of office of managing director.
[54] [1942] 1 All E.R. 378 (H.L.).

Regal to form another company, Amalgamated, to acquire the leases of two other cinemas to be sold in conjunction with Regal's. The proposed lessor of these two cinemas to Amalgamated would not grant it the lease unless it had a paid up capital of at least £5000. Regal itself could not take more than 2000 £1 shares in Amalgamated, which it took and for which it paid. The remaining 3000 £1 shares in Amalgamated were taken and paid for by the directors of Regal themselves, their friends and associates, and in due course, the lessor's condition being fulfilled, Amalgamated obtained a lease of the two extra cinemas. There was then a change of plan. It was decided that instead of the two companies selling the cinemas the companies themselves should be sold, or, put more accurately, it was decided that the totality of the shareholdings in the two companies should be sold, the cinemas thus being disposed of indirectly. This was done, and the directors of Regal disposed of their shares in Amalgamated at a handsome profit. The new controllers of Regal then caused it to sue its former directors for the profit they had made on the sale of their shares in Amalgamated. In economic reality, ignoring the separate personalities of the companies interposed between the vendors and the purchasers, the latter were seeking to recover a part of the purchase price of the cinemas from the former. Regal won. The former directors had "entered in the course of their management into a transaction in which they utilised the position and knowledge possessed by them in virtue of their office as directors, and . . . the transaction resulted in a profit to themselves."[55]

The fact that the original directors of Regal had decided in good faith that it could not itself take up the shares was considered to be immaterial to this conclusion.[56] To admit its materiality would permit the directors themselves to be the arbiters of the limits of their own fiduciary duty, and would, as Chatterton V.-C. said in *Gabbett* v. *Lawder*[57] "open a wide door to fraud." The Supreme Court of Canada was prepared to open that door a chink in *Peso Silver Mines Ltd.* v. *Cropper.*[58] There the board of a company honestly rejected a business opportunity. An individual director who had participated in this decision subsequently took part in a syndicate which exploited the opportunity for themselves. The company failed in its attempt to make him disgorge his profit, the Court preferring to follow Lord Greene M.R. in the English Court of Appeal in the *Regal (Hastings) Ltd.* case, and also to believe that a proposition he put had

---

[55] *Per* Lord Russell of Killowen at p. 386, and *per* Lord Macmillan at p. 391.
[56] See, in particular Lord Wright at p. 394.
[57] At p. 208, *supra.*
[58] (1966) 58 D.L.R. (2d) 1.

not been answered in the negative by the House of Lords. That proposition, and Lord Greene's answer to it, were:

> "To say that the company was entitled to claim the benefit of those shares would involve this proposition. Where a board of directors considers an investment which is offered to their company and bona fide comes to the conclusion that it is not an investment which their company ought to make, any director, after that resolution is come to and bona fide come to, who chooses to put up the money for that investment himself must be treated as having done it on behalf of the company, so that the company can claim any profit that results to him from it. That is a proposition for which no particle of authority was cited; and goes, as it seems to me, far beyond anything that has ever been suggested as to the duty of directors, agents, or persons in a position of that kind."[59]

This approach suffers from a practical difficulty: it requires an examination of the motives for the decision of the board, and motives are always difficult to pin down, and may be disguised. "The Court," said Chatterton V.-C. in *Gabbett* v. *Lawder*[60] "will not undertake the difficult and often impossible task of investigating the motives of the parties to the transaction." The undiluted principle has the object of *preventing* "underhand dealing"[61]; to excuse underhand dealing by which the beneficiary is not harmed is to destroy the principle. *Peso* was a hard case, and to follow it would make bad law; *Regal (Hastings) Ltd.* was likewise a hard case, but much of the apparent hardship evaporates when one considers that in each of them the directors could have been released by taking the precaution of making prior disclosure to the general meeting, and obtaining its consent.[62] In each case that consent would undoubtedly have been obtainable, since in each case the vindictive attitude of the company manifested itself only after a subsequent change in its controllers.

---

[59] Unreported, but transcript cited in *Peso, supra*.

[60] At p. 208, *supra*; likewise Lord Eldon L.C. in *Ex p. James* (1803) 8 Ves. 337, 345.

[61] "The underlying principle upon which all these cases are based is that it is of paramount importance in all transactions between . . . parties who stand in a fiduciary relationship to one another . . . that there should be nothing in the nature of underhand dealing" *per* Andrews L.J. in *Sherrard* v. *Barron* [1923] 1 I.R. 21, 26.

[62] [1942] 1 All E.R. 378, 389 (*per* Lord Russell of Killowen), 394 (*per* Lord Wright), affirming that the disclosure of directors must be to the general meeting, and its assent obtained: directors cannot release themselves. See also *Furs Ltd.* v. *Tomkies* (1936) 54 C.L.R. 583 (High Ct. of Australia). For the power of the board or its equivalent to release lesser fiduciaries, see *New Zealand Society "Oranje" Inc.* v. *Kuys* [1973] 1 W.L.R. 1126 (P.C.).

Where the board has not had the chance even to consider the opportunity exploited by the director, the attitude of the Courts is unequivocal. He must account for profits, even if the company itself could not have used the opportunity for itself. Two recent cases illustrate this. In *Industrial Development Consultants Ltd.* v. *Cooley*[63] the defendant managing director of the plaintiff company had tried very hard on behalf of the company to obtain for it a contract with a public body which, nonetheless, remained unimpressed by the company and unwilling to do business with it. They were however most impressed with the managing director, Mr. Cooley; so much so, that he was able to resign from the company on the pretext of ill-health, and pursue and obtain the contract for himself, and with it a good profit for which he had ultimately to account to his former company. In *Canadian Aero Service Ltd.* v. *O'Malley*[64] the story was similar. Officers of a company who had been negotiating on its behalf a contract with a foreign government resigned their posts, and subsequently continued the negotiations on behalf of their own newly-formed company which obtained the contract. It was held that their fiduciary duty survived the termination of their relationship with the original company so as to visit fiduciary consequences upon their subsequent pursuit of a business opportunity actively nurtured by them whilst still in office. It did not matter that the company might not ultimately have secured the contract for itself: "liability to account does not depend on *proof* of an *actual* conflict of duty and self-interest,"[65] thereby unconsciously echoing Chatterton V.-C. in *Gabbett* v. *Lawder*[66]:

> "If his position *could have caused or even contributed* to his obtaining the advantage, it is in my opinion enough. . . . [E]very advantage which *may possibly* arise from the fiduciary position shall enure for the benefit of the cestuis que trust."

There should be no doubt that this is a principle designed to cause "the pervasiveness of a strict ethic,"[67] and to operate *in terrorem* to secure that end, a "terror without which virtue is impotent," to quote Robespierre severely out of context.[68]

Had Mr. Cooley or the directors in the *Canadian Aero Service* case

---

[63] [1972] 1 W.L.R. 445.

[64] (1973) 40 D.L.R. (3d) 371 (Supreme Ct. of Canada).

[65] Italics supplied; judgment of Court, *per* Laskin J. at p. 384, relying heavily on *Boardman* v. *Phipps* [1967] 2 A.C. 46 (H.L.): solicitor who used information gained whilst acting as such to make a profitable investment for himself held accountable to principal. Sceptics should read the dissenting judgments.

[66] At p. 208 *supra*. Italics supplied.

[67] (1973) 40 D.L.R. (3d) 371, 382.

[68] *Discourses et Rapports de Robespierre*, Paris, 1908, G. Vellay (ed.), p. 132.

disclosed their plans to their respective companies, and had they, even if satisfied that they would not obtain the contracts for themselves, adopted a "dog in the manger attitude" and refused to allow these reluctant fiduciaries to go ahead on their own account, what could the latter do about it? In some fiduciary cases, particularly where the beneficiary is an infant incapable therefore of assenting, the fiduciary may well find himself in the unfortunate position of being "the only person in the world who could not avail himself of the opportunity."[69] This is not however necessarily the case where the principal is a company. The thwarted fiduciary may, it seems, apply to the Court for relief under section 391(2) of the Companies Act 1963. This permits any officer of a company who:

> "has reason to apprehend that any claim will or might be made against him in respect of any negligence, default, breach of duty or breach of trust, [to] . . . apply to the court for relief . . . ."

The grounds for relief are set out in section 391(1). They are that the officer

> "has acted honestly and reasonably, and that, having regard to all the circumstances of the case, . . . ought fairly to be excused for the negligence, default, breach of duty or breach of trust."

The jurisdiction appears to be conferred only in respect of a breach of duty which has already occurred. Perhaps it should be amended to permit prospective clearance in the circumstances under discussion. As matters stand, it is suggested that the cautious fiduciary should enter into the contract which precipitates the breach of duty before applying to the court, but should reserve in that contract a right of rescission exercisable in the event of the application being unsuccessful. The efficacy of this proposition is as yet untested.

The fiduciary principle may be brought into operation by a great variety of dealings between the fiduciary and outsiders, ranging from the blatancy of a bribe[70] to the less obvious transgression in the *Regal (Hastings) Ltd.* case. One such instance is the subject of the partly declaratory section 187 of the Companies Act 1963. If a director is to lose office[71] in connection with the disposal by the company "of the whole or any part of [its] undertaking or property" any payment to him in that regard is declared to be unlawful, unless prior

---

[69] *Per* Lord Wright in *Regal (Hastings) Ltd.* v. *Gulliver* [1942] 1 All E.R. 378, 394 referring to an observation of Lord King L.C. in *Keech* v. *Sandford* (1726) Sel. Cas. Ch. 61, 62.

[70] *e.g. Reading* v. *Att.-Gen.* [1951] A.C. 507. And *cf.* s.188, discussed at pp. 206–207 supra.

[71] As defined in s.189(3).

disclosure thereof shall have been made to all the members, and the proposal approved by the company in general meeting. Payments rendered illegal by the section are held by the director on trust for the company. Sales of this kind are obvious occasions for corruption, since they may often involve the directors in being put out of a job, and therefore the payment by the purchaser to them of an inducement to agree to the sale of the company's assets may be made a pre-condition. The situation is further discussed in Chapter 8: Enforcement of Duties at pp. 252–253, *infra*.

Competition

For a company director to be concerned in a competing business, whether as a director of another company or otherwise, is not of itself a breach of his duty to the company. The leading Irish case is another decision of Chatterton V.-C., *Moore* v. *M'Glynn*.[72] Here an executor and trustee had been left the testator's business upon trust to run it for the beneficiaries. He later set up a rival business of his own. Chatterton V.-C., said:

> "The chief complaint is for setting up in business in the same town which, to a considerable extent, was of the same nature as that carried on in the testator's house of business. I have not been referred to, nor am I aware of, any case deciding that an executor or trustee of a will carrying on the business of the testator is disabled from setting up a similar business in the same locality on his own account. If he in any way represents to the public that his own business is the same concern as that of which he is trustee, as by using the name of the testator's concern in connexion with his own business, or otherwise seeking to draw away the customers to his own shop, there might be some ground for an application to restrain him from so doing. But I am not prepared to hold that a trustee is guilty of a breach of trust in setting himself up in a similar line of business in the neighbourhood, provided that he does not resort to deception, or solicitation of custom from persons dealing at the old shop."[73]

A similar approach was taken by the House of Lords in relation to company directors trading on their own account in *Bell* v. *Lever Bros Ltd.*[74]

---

[72] [1894] 1 I.R. 74.
[73] *Ibid.* at p. 89. Contrast the performance of Clauson J. in *Re Thomson* [1930] 1 Ch. 203.
[74] [1932] A.C. 161, 195 *per* Lord Blanesburgh.

Any fiduciary trading in competition skirts a fine line; if he diverts the principal's business opportunities to himself or in any other way uses his fiduciary position to gain advantages for his own trade, he oversteps it, and must account. Furthermore, controlling company directors face also the hazard of proceedings under section 205 if they deliberately run down or neglect the business of one company for the benefit of another business.[75] In *Moore* v. *M'Glynn*, Chatterton V.-C., though holding that the competing fiduciary had not committed a breach of trust by so doing, nonetheless felt that there was an inconsistency between his duties "as trustee and manager of the testator's business, and the necessary personal interest which he must take in his own,"[76] and accordingly removed him from the trusteeship. Unlike the case of trustees, the Court possesses no independent jurisdiction to remove company directors. A case for that, if at all, must be made under section 205.[76a]

Abuse of power

Courts in reviewing the exercise by fiduciaries of their powers take the broad view that they must not abuse them or act outside them, but that, provided these limits are observed, they are not overmuch concerned with the actual content of the fiduciary's decision. This broad distinction is captured in the judgment of Maziere Brady L.C. in *Att.-Gen.* v. *Belfast Corporation*[77]:

> "So long as a corporator acts within the scope of his powers, although he does so irregularly, and perhaps mistakenly, he is not responsible, unless he was influenced by malice; but if he do a wrongful act not within his power—if he exceed them—there, I consider he is responsible just as any private person would be."

Ross J. speaking of a modern registered company in *Clark* v. *Workman*[78] said:

> "[Counsel] contended that the Court has no jurisdiction to interfere in a question of internal management. That proposition cannot be disputed. The Court has no right to say how much is to be distributed in dividends, or how much is to be

---

[75] *Per* Lord Denning in *Scottish Co-operative Wholesale Society Ltd.* v. *Meyer* [1958] A.C. 324.

[76] [1894] 1 I.R. 74, 90.

[76a] For the possibility of the suspension of directors under the inherent jurisdiction to appoint a receiver, see *Trade Auxiliary Co.* v. *Vickers* (1873) L.R. 16 Eq. 298.

[77] (1855) 4 Ir. Ch. Rep. 119, 161; also p. 160; see also *Armstrong* v. *Armstrong* (1880) 7 L.R., Ir. 207.

[78] [1920] 1 I.R. 107, 116.

added to the reserve account; what contracts for material are to be accepted, what remuneration is to be paid to their employees, and such like. All these things must be dealt with by the directors, and no Court can interfere so long as they are acting within their powers."

More recently, the Privy Council in *Smith (Howard) Ltd.* v. *Ampol Petroleum Ltd.*[79] affirmed that in matters of management "it would be wrong for the court to substitute its opinion for that of the management, or indeed to question the correctness of the management's decision . . . , *if bona fide arrived at*. There is no appeal on merits from management decisions to courts of law: nor will courts of law assume to act as a kind of supervisory board over decisions within the powers of management *honestly arrived at*."

These statements convey a broad truth, but the Courts *do* occasionally and reluctantly impose responsibility on directors for bad management decisions, as we shall see, *infra*, under the heading *Duties of diligence skill and care*; also the statements must nowadays be read subject to the supervening morality of section 205. A failure to recommend dividends, for example, may constitute oppression.[80]

For the moment however we are concerned with abuse of power. Company directors must exercise their powers bona fide (*i.e.* in good faith, honestly) for the benefit of the company as a whole, and for their proper purpose.[81] Since all cases involving this definition have been concerned with the attempt to prove conduct falling outside it, the periphery is better explored than the contents.

What is meant by the "company as a whole" in this definition? Obviously, the separate person in the law, the abstraction, is included in it: it stands to benefit or suffer detriment depending upon the manner in which management powers are exercised. But the expression includes more than that; it includes also the general body of shareholders, for whom ultimately the company exists. There are things which may legitimately be done by the company which are nonetheless bad for the abstraction: distributing profits by way of dividend, for example. And the directors have some powers to the exercise of which the abstraction is indifferent, but of which a wrongful exercise might matter very much to individual shareholders.[82] No one else, no other interest group, comes within the

---

[79] [1974] A.C. 821, 831 (on appeal from New South Wales); italics supplied.

[80] See pp. 171–172.

[81] *e.g. Re Smith & Fawcett Ltd.* [1942] 1 All E.R. 542, 543; or as Ross J. put it in *Clark* v. *Workman* [1920] 1 I.R. 107, 113: "There must be bona fides. There must be no indirect motives."

[82] Particularly the power to allot shares, discussed at pp. 225–228. *infra*.

definition of the company as a whole, and, in particular, the employees of the company do not. In this respect, the law still regards the modern registered company as a capitalist capsule, a last survivor of laissez-faire, insulated from divergent economic and social theories and compromises, current in society as a whole. Whether this is desirable is not for this book to judge. Britain has enacted[83] section 46 of the Companies Act 1980 [*U.K.*] purporting to modify this state of affairs, and it is likely that Ireland will follow suit. Section 46 says:

> "(1) The matters to which the directors of a company are to have regard in the performance of their functions shall include the interests of the company's employees in general as well as the interests of its members. (2) Accordingly, the duty imposed by subsection (1) above on the directors of a company is owed by them to the company (and the company alone) and is enforceable in the same way as any other fiduciary duty owed to a company by its directors."

This enactment may be criticised as being a mere cosmetic. The duty is owed to the company, and not the employees; it is not enforceable by them; any breach of it could be absolved by the company in general meeting, the competing interest group.[84] Also, if there is a clash between the profitability of a non-State enterprise and its function in creating employment, no amount of lip service to the latter will save jobs without cash to back it. On the other hand, generous treatment of the employees of a going concern has always been capable of being both within the company's capacity and a proper exercise of the directors' powers, since a policy of good labour relations will enure to the benefit of the company and its members.[85] The move towards the enactment of section 46 started with the reaction to the English High Court decision of *Parke* v. *Daily News Ltd.*[86] in which an attempt by the company, backed by the overwhelming majority in value of its shareholders, to make substantial *ex gratia* payments to employees who were to become redundant upon the abandonment by the company of a substantial and distinct part of its business, was foiled by Plowman J. Such a proposal could not be

---

[83] Foreshadowed by the Department of Trade White Paper, *The Conduct of Company Directors*, H.M.S.O., 1977, Cmnd. 7037.

[84] For the general principles of ratification, see pp. 66–69, *supra* and pp. 243 *et seq.*, *infra*.

[85] See the judgment of Bowen L.J. in *Hutton* v. *West Cork Rly Co.* (1883) 23 Ch.D. 654, and pp. 120–121, *supra*.

[86] [1962] Ch. 927.

regarded as reasonably incidental to the carrying on of the company's business and therefore within its capacity, since the relevant part of the business was being discontinued.[87] As far as the proper exercise of the directors' powers was concerned, the key passage politically in Plowman J.'s judgment was:

> "The view that directors, in having regard to the question what is in the best interests of the company, are entitled to take into account the interests of the employees, *irrespective of any consequential benefit to the company*, is one which may be widely held . . . But no authority to support that proposition has been cited to me; I know of none, and in my judgment such is not the law."[88]

The actual decision in *Parke* has now been reversed in Britain, not by section 46, but by section 74 of the Companies Act 1980 [*U.K.*] which allows a company to make gratuitous provisions for employees or former employees on the cessation or transfer of its business. Few could quibble at the adoption of such a provision in Ireland.[88a]

Are creditors comprehended within the term "company as a whole"? Probably not, despite an essay in that direction by the High Court of Australia.[88b] Duties owed directly to creditors to act honestly in relation to them and fairly between them can be constructed out of Sections 297 and 286 of the Companies Act 1963, sections respectively concerned with fraudulent trading and fraudulent preference.[88c]

Next we consider "good faith." Good faith is subjective. In this context it implies as Lord Greene M.R. said in *Re Smith & Fawcett Ltd.*[89] that the directors "must exercise their discretion *bona fide* in what they consider—not what the court may consider—to be in the interests of the company . . . " Now, whilst it is true, as Lord Finlay pointed out in *Hindle* v. *John Cotton Ltd.*[90]:

> "Where the question is one of abuse of powers, the state of mind of those who acted, and the motive in which they acted, are all important, and you may go into the question of what their

[87] See p. 121, *supra*.

[88] At p. 948; italics supplied.

[88a] Note also that a duty owed directly to employees to inform and consult them may yet be born out of the "Vredeling" initiative within the E.C. Commission. See p. 5, n.26 *supra*.

[88b] See *Walker* v. *Wimborne* (1976) A.L.J.R. 446; Barrett, (1977) 40 M.L.R. 226; Forde, (1983) *Irish Jurist*, 289, 296; and Buckley L.J. in *Re Horsley & Weight Ltd.* [1982] 3 All E.R. 1045, 1055.

[88c] See pp. 516 *et seq.*, and p. 504 *et seq.* respectively.

[89] [1942] 2 All E.R. 542, 543.

[90] (1919) 56 S.L.R. 625, 630, adopted in *Clark* v. *Workman* [1920] 1 I.R. 107, 117.

intention was, collecting from the surrounding circumstances all the materials which genuinely throw light upon that question of the state of mind of the directors, so as to show whether they were honestly acting in the discharge of their powers in the interests of the company"

nonetheless it is by no means easy to establish bad faith because the surrounding circumstances may not oblige by being forthcoming, and the directors themselves are not required to offer an explanation of their conduct. *Re Dublin North City Milling Co. Ltd.*[91] establishes that the onus of proving bad faith lies on the plaintiff, and, furthermore, Meredith M.R. declared himself

> "of opinion that the law allows the directors to hold their tongues. It allows them to say that everything was done honestly and *bona fide* in the interests of the company; . . . and according to my view I have no power to make them say more."

Of the surrounding circumstances indicative of bad faith, Ross J. in *Clark* v. *Workman*[92] was prepared to find that the making of a decision without adequate time for consideration, and voting at a board meeting in accordance with a prior promise to an outsider, both qualified. In that case, the chairman of the board had promised the proposed transferee of a controlling interest in the company that he would use his best endeavours to obtain the board's approval, and this he did by casting his own and his casting vote in favour. Ross J. said that:

> "By acting thus he had fettered himself by a promise to the [transferee], and had disqualified himself from acting bona fide in the interests of the company. . . ."[93]

One must not suppose from this case that the board itself is powerless to resolve how it will vote on a future question; it frequently, and validly, does.[94] Nor one must suppose that the courts will refuse to enforce a voting agreement operative at board level made between all the participants in a company. In *T.M.G. Group Ltd.* v. *Al Babtain*

---

[91] [1909] 1 I.R. 179, 183–34, further discussed with *Re Hafner* in which the burden was discharged, at p. 192, *supra*.

[92] [1920] 1 I.R. 107.

[93] *Ibid.* p. 118. Other circumstances indicating bad faith in this case have been mentioned at p. 192, *supra*.

[94] *e.g.* to take an example from the same context as *Clark* v. *Workman*, it is standard practice for a company which is the subject of an "agreed bid" to undertake to register all transfers submitted in favour of the transferee: *Re Savoy Hotel Ltd.* [1981] 3 W.L.R. 441, 445, *et seq.*

Trading & Contracting Co.[95] two participants had formed a company, Datsun Ltd., had taken unequal shareholdings in it, and had entered into a collateral shareholders' agreement governing the running of this joint enterprise. The minority shareholder in Datsun Ltd. obtained an interlocutory injunction restraining the majority shareholders from exercising their voting rights so as to cause the company to enter into certain contracts prohibited by the agreement. The voting rights in question were those possessed by the defendants at board level in Datsun Ltd.

The proof of bad faith usually involves clutching at straws. Attempts to prove infringements of the latter part of the definition, namely that the directors' powers should be exercised for their proper purpose, are altogether more productive. Here the courts have attempted a systematic approach. "The first general proposition is that you must ascertain the power of the directors from the very words of the articles," said Meredith M.R. in *Re Dublin North City Milling Co. Ltd.*[96] And Lord Wilberforce said much the same in giving the opinion of the Board in the Privy Council case of *Smith (Howard) Ltd.* v. *Ampol Petroleum Ltd.*[97]: "it is necessary to start with a consideration of the power whose exercise is in question. . . . " and to define "as best can be done in the light of modern conditions the, or some, limits within which it may be exercised." This initial consideration of the ambit of the power will of necessity be imprecise, and can only properly be phrased in generalities, since, as Lord Wilberforce admitted earlier in the opinion:

> "To define in advance exact limits beyond which directors must not pass is, in their Lordships' view, impossible. This clearly cannot be done by enumeration, since the variety of situations facing directors of different types of company in different situations cannot be anticipated."[98]

Some powers are wider than others; among the widest is the common form power to register transfers of shares, discussed at pp. 189 *et seq.*, *supra*, where we saw that the directors may legitimately take into account a very wide variety of circumstances in refusing to register a transferee. Another is the power to allot shares, where, as we shall see, the need for fresh capital is by no means the only legitimate consideration.

Have determined the ambit of the power, the Court must then, in the opinion of the Privy Council:

---

[95] High Court, Keane J., March 24, 1980, unreported.
[96] [1909] 1 I.R. 179, 183.
[97] [1974] A.C. 821, 835 (on appeal from New South Wales).
[98] *Ibid.* at p. 835.

"examine the *substantial* purpose for which it was exercised, and. . . . reach a conclusion whether that purpose was proper or not. In doing so it will necessarily give credit to the bona fide opinion of the directors, if such is found to exist, and will respect their judgment as to matters of management; having done this, the ultimate conclusion has to be as to the side of a *fairly broad line* on which the case falls."[99]

Assuming the acceptability of this formulation, the courts do not insist on an absolute propriety in the exercise of directors' powers; the exercise may be tinged with impropriety, particularly self-interest, provided that substantial purpose is proper. This attitude reflects the fact that directors, especially of private companies, are usually beneficially interested in the enterprise as members; to require a *wholly* detached altruism in those circumstances would be unreal. Consequently, as Dixon J. observed in the leading Australian case of *Mills* v. *Mills*[1] "the application of the general equitable principle[2] to the acts of directors managing the affairs of a company cannot be as nice as it is in the case of a trustee exercising a special power of appointment."

Turning now to some examples of the foregoing principles in action, one finds that many of them concern the directors' power to allot unissued shares, usually pursuant to an article such as article 5 of Table A which declares:

"the shares shall be at the disposal of the directors, and they may (subject to the provisions of the Companies Acts, 1963 to 1983) allot, grant options over or otherwise dispose of them to such persons, on such terms and conditions as they may consider to be in the best interests of the company and its shareholders. . . . "[3]

Abuses of this power will in future be somewhat inhibited by sections 20 and 23 of the Companies (Amendment) Act 1983 which respectively subject the directors' power to allot shares to periodic authorisation by the general meeting, and create pre-emption rights in favour of existing members over shares proposed to be allotted.[4] Section 20 offers no threat where the directors have the support in person or by proxy of a majority in general meeting, since their auth-

---

[99] *Ibid.* at p. 835; italics supplied.

[1] (1938) 60 C.L.R. 150.

[2] *i.e.* that fiduciary powers be exercised only for their proper purpose.

[3] As amended by para. 23, First Sched., 1983 Act.

[4] The statutory pre-emption right and the authority to allot are discussed in Forde, "The Companies (Amendment) Act 1983," (1983) *Irish Jurist* 289, and see pp. 184–185 *supra* and p.277 *infra*.

ority to allot is to be given, varied, revoked or renewed by an ordinary resolution.[4a] Its restrictions will thus be useless where a majority
through the directors are attempting so to dilute the voting strength
of a minority opposition that they would no longer be able to block a
special resolution. Section 20 has no application at all to the allotment of shares "in pursuance of an employees' share scheme,"[4b] a
term which includes schemes under which shares are held "by *or for
the benefit of* employees."[4c] The italicised words show that a favourite
abuse remains open still, the issue of a controlling block of shares to
the trustees of such a scheme, the trustees being the directors, or
their associates. An allotment made in contravention of section 20 is
not for that reason alone invalid,[4d] but the criminal consequences
may deter.[4e] A private company may opt wholly out of the system of
pre-emption rights given by section 23 simply by having a contrary,
or inconsistent provision in its memorandum or articles.[4f] For all
companies, including *p.l.c.*'s, the pre-emption rights may be avoided
either by an express provision in the articles if there is also in force a
general authority in the directors for the purposes of section 20, or
by special resolution.[4g]

The examples drawn from pre-1983 Act litigation must be read on
the assumption that the new statutory hurdles had in each case been
overcome.

Re Jermyn Street Turkish Baths Ltd.[5] illustrates that the power to allot
unissued shares may legitimately be exercised for purposes other
than the raising of money by the issue: the ambit of the power
includes the attainment of financial stability for the company. In
that case a director had caused to be issued to herself 100 £1 shares
in the company, thereby converting her holding from a 50 per cent.
to a 75 per cent. stake, as part of a "package deal" under which she
advanced several thousand pounds by way of loan to the company
which was sorely in need of funds. The power extends to the raising
by a share issue of money in excess of the immediate needs of the
company, again, in the cause of financial stability: *Harlowe's Nominees
Pty. Ltd.* v. *Woodside (Lake Entrance) Oil Co.*[6]

[4a] s.20(6) of the 1983 Act.
[4b] *Ibid.* s.20(10)(*a*).
[4c] *Ibid.* s.2(1). Italics supplied.
[4d] *Ibid.* s.20(8).
[4e] *Ibid.* s.20(7), and s.57(1),(4): on indictment or fine not exceeding £2,500, or,
summarily not exceeding £500.
[4f] *Ibid.* s.23(10). See also s.25(3).
[4g] *Ibid.* s.24 for the precise details.
[5] [1971] 1 W.L.R. 1042, 1057.
[6] (1968) 121 C.L.R. 483.

Most reported cases of mixed motivation fall on the wrong side of the "fairly broad line" drawn by Lord Wilberforce. Thus, though it may be admirable and proper to set up a trust fund of newly issued shares for the benefit of employees, the issue is voidable if the substantial purpose is to fend off a takeover bid by the use of the trust votes thereby created: *Hogg* v. *Cramphorn Ltd.*[7] Similarly, the issue of shares to long serving service directors at a fair value and the issue of shares to trustees to create a share incentive scheme for employees fail if the substantial purpose is to reduce a minority shareholder's holding from nearly half to less than a quarter: *Clemens* v. *Clemens Bros. Ltd.*[8] Indeed, numerous cases testify that the deliberate creation or dilution of voting strength in general meeting is never a proper substantial purpose, however honestly in the best interests of the company the creators or diluters may consider their own majority to be.[9] Such bona fides is irrelevant to a consideration of the propriety of the purpose.[10] One of the more blatant cases of this kind happens also to be Irish. In *Nash* v. *Lancegaye Safety Glass (Ireland) Ltd.*,[11] attempts by one Daniel Breen to persuade the court that the proceeds of the issue of shares by the directors to a friendly recipient were "manna from heaven" to a company sorely in need of cash were to no avail, and contrasted curiously with a contemporaneous directors' report which in appealing to the members for their proxy votes at a forthcoming general meeting had stated that the company "had never been in a sounder position nor run on more efficient lines." The purpose of the issue was in fact to confer a benefit on the recipient, and to increase the voting strength of the controlling group whose tenure of office was under threat.

There are rarer reported instances of share issues being upheld despite voting strengths in general meeting being altered by them. In these cases, the shifting of the balance of control in general meeting was found to be only an incidental consequence of the issue, its substantial purpose falling on the right side of Lord Wilberforce's "fairly broad line." A common example in practice is the joint venture, in which one or both proposed corporate partners issue shares

---

[7] [1966] 3 W.L.R. 254.

[8] [1976] 2 All E.R. 268.

[9] *Smith (Howard) Ltd.* v. *Ampol Petroleum Ltd.*, n. 97, *supra* (majority receptive to takeover bid created); *Bamford* v. *Bamford* [1969] 2 W.L.R. 1107 (majority hostile to bid created); *Punt* v. *Symons & Co. Ltd.* [1903] 2 Ch. 506 (special majority created to pass special resolution); *Piercy* v. *S. Mills & Co. Ltd.* [1920] 1 Ch. 77 (shares issued in an attempt to retain office).

[10] Though it may be relevant to the question whether the impropriety is ratifiable in general meeting: see Chapter 8, at pp. 253–255.

[11] (1958) 92 I.L.T.R. 11.

in themselves to the other as part of the agreement for participation. An unsuccessful challenge to such an arrangement was made in *Teck Corporation Ltd.* v. *Millar*.[12] The directors of a company declined to cause it to enter into an agreement with its majority shareholders for the joint exploitation of its mineral rights, and, instead, before the majority could dismiss them, caused the company to enter into a similar agreement with another company. Under this agreement the new partner subscribed for a substantial block of the company's shares, thereby fortuitously converting the threatening majority into a litigious minority. The directors' power to capitalise profits by making a bonus issue to the ordinary shareholders who would have been entitled to them if distributed by way of dividend affords another example.[13] The bonus shares carry votes in general meeting. In *Mills* v. *Mills*[14] the conversion by such an issue of preference shareholders holding a dominant position in general meeting into a less effectual minority was held to be only incidental to the substantial purpose. Such an issue exclusively to the ordinary shareholders is under common form articles within the reasonable expectation of *all* members.[15] A rights issue, on the other hand, addressed to part only of the voting shareholders, would almost inevitably be an improper favouritism of one section of voting shareholders as against another, and therefore an abuse of power.[16]

DUTIES OF DILIGENCE, SKILL AND CARE

We have under the heading *Abuse of power* been concerned with the validity of decisions of directors acting as a board. We now consider the extent to which the company may, if so minded, force the individual director to make recompense to it for losses suffered through the imperfect conduct of its affairs. We are here concerned with the individual director's duties of diligence, skill and care, imposed by the general law and drawn primarily from the fiduciary regime applicable to gratuitous agents, with some adaptations suited to companies.[17]

---

[12] (1973) 33 D.L.R. (3d) 288 (Supreme Court of British Columbia).
[13] See articles 130, 130A of Table A (as amended by para. 23, First Sched., 1983 Act), and pp. 173–174, *supra*.
[14] (1938) 60 C.L.R. 150.
[15] *e.g. Dimbula Valley (Ceylon) Tea Co. Ltd.* v. *Laurie* [1961] Ch. 353.
[16] On sectionalism, see the discussion in *Smith (Howard) Ltd.* v. *Ampol Petroleum Ltd.* [1974] A.C. 821, 835 of *Mills* v. *Mills*, n. 14, *supra*.
[17] For the statutory consequences on directors of breach of duty to creditors by "fraudulent trading" within the meaning of s.297, see Chap. 16: *Liquidations* at pp. 516 *et seq.*

Diligence

The constitution of a modern registered company envisages that its affairs may be conducted without the participation of all the directors. The board is a quorate body; under common form articles the quorum may be as low as two,[18] and decisions effectively taken by a board so constituted whatever the total number of directors may be. Trusteeships by contrast usually require unanimity. The question most often arising in relation to a non-participant director is whether or not he is to be implicated in the wrongdoing of those to whom the management is left. Has there been such a lack of the diligence required of him as to constitute complicity in the wrongdoing? Had he been as concerned in the affairs of the company as he ought to have been, would the wrongdoing have occurred? In answer to these questions one can no longer say absolutely as Maziere Brady L.C. did in 1855 in relation to the executive of a municipal corporation:

" . . . this Court holds that persons who withdraw themselves from the duties of their office may be rendered equally answerable for the acts of those whom they allow, by their absence, to have exclusive dominion over the corporate property. Lord Hardwicke, in establishing that principle, presents it as a warning to gentlemen assuming corporate functions; since, by their negligence, they may become quite as responsible as the others, to whom they have committed the sole control, and who did the wrongful acts."[19]

Instead, the law now recognises the understanding of the business community that a director is *not* necessarily appointed to exert a constant surveillance over all aspects of a company's business.[20] The degree of diligence required of him depends very much on what may be perceived as the assumptions on which he was appointed. Very seldom does he assume an absolute liability of the kind described by Maziere Brady L.C. The point is neatly illustrated by the leading Irish case of *Jackson* v. *Munster Bank Ltd., ex p. Dease*.[21] The bank had contrary to its articles lent money to some of its directors, and, worse, some of it was irrecoverable. Was one of the directors, Mr.

---

[18] *e.g.* art. 102, Table A.

[19] *Att.-Gen.* v. *Belfast Corporation* (1855) 4 Ir. Ch. Rep. 119, 160. The Lord Chancellor used the word "negligence" here in the sense of "neglect." The citation of Lord Hardwicke refers to his decision in *Charitable Corporation* v. *Sutton* (1742) 2 Atk. 400.

[20] For this development, see Sealy "The director as trustee" (1967) C.L.J. 83. A turning point was *Land Credit Co. of Ireland* v. *Lord Fermoy* (1869) L.R. 8 Eq. 7; (1869–70) L.R. 5 Ch. App. 763.

[21] (1885) 15 L.R., Ir. 356.

Dease, to be held responsible to the company for this loss? He had received none of the money himself, and had not taken part in any of the board meetings sanctioning the loans. The bank operated in both Cork and Dublin, and Mr. Dease was appointed a director on February 11, 1881 for the purpose of controlling with another director the Dublin end of the business. He regularly attended the weekly meetings of directors in Dublin which were concerned with the conduct of the Dublin business. Meanwhile, the malversations were occurring in Cork, sanctioned by board meetings held in that city. Mr. Dease had attended one or two meetings in Cork, at which nothing untoward had occurred. Chatterton V.-C. held that:

> "There can be no doubt that it was intended at the time[22] that his services were to be made use of principally, at any rate, in Dublin. . . . It was expected of him that he would remain in Dublin, and there certainly was plenty of business to occupy him there."[23]

Accordingly, Mr. Dease did not incur responsibility for wrongdoing in Cork of which he was unaware at the time of its commission. *But,* in January 1883 he was shown a letter written by one of the plaintiffs, setting forth suspicions that large, unsecured loans were being made to directors. From that moment all was different. If he had then investigated, said Chatterton V.-C., he would have found out:

> "that there had been a systematic fraudulent misappropriation of the property of the bank . . . extending over a period of years conducted principally by the Chairman . . . . A firm man going down in the execution of his duty, mastering the facts, and remonstrating with his brother directors, could have put a stop to this infamous system."[24]

Instead, he stood by silently, and did nothing. Accordingly, he incurred personal responsibility for the defaults from and after February 1883, dereliction of duty and a causal connection between it and the loss having each been established.[25]

What is expected by way of diligence from an individual director depends therefore very much on the rôle that it might reasonably be

---

[22] *i.e.* at the time of his appointment.
[23] *Ibid.* pp. 360, 361.
[24] *Ibid.* at p. 361.
[25] For the necessity of proving causation, see *Barnes* v. *Andrews* (1924) 298 Fed. Rep. 614.

envisaged at the time of his appointment he will play.[26] Nothing much was expected, and nothing much was obtained from the Marquis of Bute[27] who at the age of six months was appointed to a position in a trustee savings bank[28] equivalent to that of a company director, in fact its president, attended one meeting shortly after attaining his majority, and thereafter forgot all about the bank until, some 20 years later, its liquidator sought to make him personally responsible for money embezzled by its chief paid official. There were 55 other "directors" in a like position to the Marquis; it is scarcely surprising therefore that regular attendance from any of them was not expected, and that he was exonerated. He received regular notices of the meetings of the bank, even though he could not recollect having done so. Had he not received these notices, he would have been put on enquiry as to whether they were being held at all, and upon a failure to act, might have been implicated in any wrongdoing which was proceeding.[29] Few companies however are constituted as was this savings bank. In most companies persistent neglect to attend will constitute a breach of duty, and loss which might have been forestalled but for that neglect will be attributable to the non-participating director.[30] *Dorchester Finance Co. Ltd.* v. *Stebbing*[31] illustrates the perils lying in wait for non-executive directors who fail to interest themselves to any significant degree in the affairs of their company. Two directors had left the conduct of the company's moneylending business to a third; there were no board meetings, and the two directors seldom visited the company's offices. The third director caused loss to the company by making irrecoverable loans on its behalf.[32] All three were held jointly and severally liable for the loss. The two neglectful directors were skilled, professional men, such that had they concerned themselves with the conduct of the company's business, the losses would probably have been avoided. Had they been unskilled, as are many of the mere cyphers

---

[26] " . . . diligence must depend on the nature of the undertaking," *per* Judge Porter in *Percy* v. *Millaudon* 8 Mart. N.S. 68 (Supreme Court of Louisiana), cited as a "leading case for more than 60 years" in *Briggs* v. *Spaulding* (1891) 141 U.S. 132; 35 Law. Ed. 662, 669 (U.S. Supreme Court).

[27] *Marquis of Bute's Case* [1892] 2 Ch. 100.

[28] The office and liability was governed by the Trustee Savings Bank Act 1863.

[29] *Ibid. per* Stirling J. at p. 109.

[30] English formulations of the duty to attend may be found in *Perry's Case* (1876) 34 L.T. 716; *Re Forest of Dean Co.* (1878) 10 Ch.D. 450; *Re Denham & Co.* (1883) 25 Ch.D. 752; *Re City Equitable Fire Insurance Co. Ltd.* [1925] Ch. 407.

[31] High Court (England), Chancery Division, Foster J., July 22, 1977, unreported; but noted (1980) 1 Co. Law. 38.

[32] Though failure to comply with the formalities prescribed by the notorious Moneylenders Acts 1900–1927 *[U.K.]*.

or dummies appointed directors in Irish companies to bring the directorship up to the statutory minimum of two,[33] it is doubtful whether they would have incurred liability since their intervention would not have averted the loss. The causal connection between breach of the duty of diligence and the loss to the company was made in this case by the breach of another duty on a director, discussed below, to exert when taking part in the management of the company such skills that he happens to possess, and, as we shall see, if he possesses none, he need display none.

Active participation in Acts beyond the powers of the board

We have seen that the courts are zealous to ensure that directors do not overstep the limits of their powers, whilst not being over concerned with the content of decisions made within them.[34] This latter aspect arises again in *Acts within their powers*, below, in which the extent to which the directors must bear personal responsibility for bad business decisions is discussed.

Where an individual director is party to an act beyond the powers of the board by which the company suffers, such as the wrongful declaration of a dividend at the expense of capital, or some act in breach of the company's constitution, he is clearly personally responsible for the consequential loss if he knew the facts which constituted the act a misfeasance.[35] Nor can he plead ignorance of the existence of the legal duty, the breach of which rendered the act a wrong: *ignorantia iuris haud neminem excusat*. But if he did not know the facts which constituted the act a breach of duty there is a possibility of exoneration. To escape personal responsibility[36] the directors must have taken "reasonable care" to ensure that they were not exceeding their powers,[37] a higher standard of conduct than that required of them when acting within their powers. In practice, this standard relieves directors of the consequences of being deceived. In the House of Lords decision of *Dovey* v. *Cory*[38] the director of a bank had participated in board decisions to pay dividends on false profits contained in falsified accounts. He had failed to find out "what was fraudulently withheld from his knowledge," and it was sought to

---

[33] s.174.

[34] The standard response to fiduciaries, upon which see pp. 200, 219–220, *supra*.

[35] *e.g. Dovey* v. *Cory* [1901 A.C. 477, 482.

[36] The act itself remains voidable: its validity is often the only material point in proceedings against directors. See *Abuse of power, supra*.

[37] *Leeds Estates Building and Investments Co.* v. *Shepherd* (1887) 36 Ch. D. 787, 798 *et seq.*; approved by the House of Lords in *Dovey* v. *Cory* [1901] A.C. 477, 490.

[38] [1901] A.C. 477.

make him "responsible because he did not find out the fraudulent knaves by whom he was surrounded,"[39] chiefly his brother, chairman of the board, who was in combination with the general manager. In exonerating him, Lord Halsbury L.C. said that if individual directors were:

> "called upon to distrust and be on their guard against the possibility of fraud being committed by their subordinates of every degree . . . anything like an intelligent devolution of labour [would be] impossible. Was Mr. Cory to turn himself into an auditor, a managing director, a chairman, and find out whether auditors, managing directors, and chairmen were all alike deceiving him?"[40]

Of course, if the director's suspicions are aroused, or ought, depending on the skills which he brought to the job, to have been aroused, and he then fails to investigate, then there might well be a lack of reasonable care on his part: *Jackson* v. *Munster Bank, ex p. Dease, supra.*

The finding in *Dovey* v. *Cory* presupposed that the directors had adopted a reasonable system of management, culminating in the board, and that they had done so was not in issue in the case. In *Re City Equitable Fire Insurance Co. Ltd.*,[41] on the other hand, such a system had not in all respects been adopted. Directors had left the investment of large sums of money to the general manager of the company who turned out, too late, to be "a daring and unprincipled scoundrel." The function of investment should, it was held, have been retained by the board, calling upon the advice of the scoundrel if so desired. The directors responsible for so delegating it that control of it passed out of the hands of the board were accordingly found to be in breach of duty. No proper system of management under the control of the board was established in *Dorchester Finance Co. Ltd.* v. *Stebbing*,[42] and this lack contributed to the finding of dereliction in that case.

Skill

It is generally accepted that a company director when acting as such is not required to exercise any greater degree of skill than may

---

[39] *Per* Lord Halsbury, L.C. at p. 484.

[40] *Ibid.* p. 485. See also Lord Davey to like effect at p. 492, and *Land Credit Co. of Ireland* v. *Lord Fermoy* n. 20, *supra.* (director not liable for being defrauded by lawful delegate).

[41] [1925] Ch. 407; often cited for Romer J.'s useful summary of the duties of directors as drawn from the English authorities.

[42] n. 31, *supra.*

reasonably be expected from a person of *his* knowledge and experience.[43] As Neville J. put it in a famous passage in *Re Brazilian Rubber Plantations and Estates Ltd.*[44]:

> "He is, I think, not bound to bring any special qualifications to his office. He may undertake the management of a rubber company in complete ignorance of everything connected with rubber, without incurring responsibility for the mistakes which may result from such ignorance; while if he is acquainted with the rubber business he must give the company the advantage of his knowledge when transacting the company's business."

To the above formulation should be added the case of a director who has put himself forward as an expert in a particular field, and been appointed as such, but does not in fact have his professed skill. Such a director will be judged, not on his actual knowledge and experience, but on what he professed. Nothing short of that could reasonably be expected of him.[45]

These standards are identical to those long established as appropriate to the gratuitous bailee,[46] though, with the inevitability nowadays that directors are in practice remunerated and are no longer the unpaid, gentlemen agents which they remain in at least one eye of the law, the analogy has considerably weakened. Nonetheless, the standards do reflect the understanding of the business community of the risks assumed when undertaking a directorship, and that understanding at present does not include an expectation that a director will find his conduct measured against a minimum, objective stan-

---

[43] *Re City Equitable Fire Insurance Co. Ltd.* [1925] Ch. 407; and also the formulation adopted by the United Kingdom Dept. of Trade White Paper "The Conduct of Company Directors," 1977 Cmnd. 7037. The *Re City Equitable* formulation was derived from a statement by Lindley M.R. in *Lagunas Nitrate Co.* v. *Langunas Syndicate* [1899] 2 Ch. 392, 435: "If directors . . . act with such care *as is reasonably to be expected from them,* having regard to their knowledge and experience . . . they discharge . . . their duty" (italics supplied). "Care" in this context encompassed "skill."

[44] [1911] 1 Ch. 425, 437.

[45] See the passage from the judgment of Lindley M.R. in n. 43, *supra.*

[46] And indeed other unpaid agents generally, *e.g. Wilson* v. *Brett* (1843) 11 M. & W. 113 (person conversant with horses obliged to horse owner to use such skill as a person conversant with horses might reasonably be expected to use); *O'Hanlon* v. *Murray* (1860) 12 I.C.L.R. 161, 164 where on the assumption that an attorney had been acting gratuitously (which was not in fact the case) counsel said: "Where a party holds himself out as filling an office, or acting in a character which implies the existence of a certain amount of skill in the exercise of that office, or the fulfilling of that character, he is bound to bring a fair amount of skill to the performance of his duties." See also *Finlay* v. *Murtagh* [1979] I.R. 249, 257 (Supreme Court) in which *per* Henchy J. *nem. diss.* a solicitor undertaking "to act professionally without reward" owes duties in tort of professional skill and care; followed in *Wall* v. *Hegarty* (High Court, Barrington J., June 19, 1980, unreported).

dard such as that of "a reasonably skilled man of business," however much that may be preferred by a wider public. He may be a butcher, and still conduct surgery. One may reconcile this attitude of both law and business with that to negligence displayed by the general law of tort by viewing the company as having consented to unskilled management: *volenti non fit injuria.*[47]

A failure by directors to display skills actually possessed by them resulted in liability in *Dorchester Finance Co. Ltd.* v. *Stebbing, supra,*[48] as we have seen.

Acts within their powers

We have seen that the courts have set their faces against passing judgment on management decisions made by directors acting within their powers[49] in which "they may safely proceed as their judgment dictates."[50]

But, despite these disavowals, there would seem to be a residual but low standard below which directors taking management decisions within their powers must not fall without risking intervention by the courts. Kenny J. is reported to have said in *P.M.P.A. Insurance Co. Ltd.* v. *New Ireland Assurance Co. Ltd.*[51] that the management of a company entrusted to the directors "would not be interfered with unless it was in breach of the articles of association or was dishonest or *grossly incompetent.*"

One may put some flesh on this notion of gross incompetence by referring to the judgment of the House of Lords in *Overend & Gurney Co.* v. *Gibb*[52] in which the only substantive allegation was that the directors, acting within their powers, had lost most of the company's money by entering into a contract on its behalf which turned out very badly for it. Lord Hatherley L.C. said that their personal liability depended upon the answer to this question:

> "whether if they did not . . . exceed their powers they were cognisant of circumstances of such a character, so plain, so manifest, and so simple of appreciation, that no men with any

---

[47] See Lindley M.R. in *Lagunas Nitrate Co.* v. *Lagunas Syndicate* [1899] 2 Ch. 392, 426.

[48] n. 31, *supra.*

[49] See the excerpts from *Att.-Gen.* v. *Belfast Corporation, Clark* v. *Workman, Smith (Howard) Ltd.* v. *Ampol Petroleum Ltd.* set out on pp. 219–220, *supra,* and *Turquand* v. *Marshall* (1869) L.R. 4 Ch. App. 376.

[50] *Per* Maziere Brady L.C. in *Att.-Gen.* v. *Belfast Corporation* (1855) 4 Ir. Ch. Rep. 119, 160.

[51] High Court, *ex tempore* judgment delivered October 22, 1975; no official transcript available; reported *Irish Times,* October 23, 1975. (Italics supplied).

[52] (1872) 5 L.R., H.L. 480.

ordinary degree of prudence, acting on their own behalf, would have entered into such a transaction as they entered into?"[53]

This is a difficult standard *not* to live up to; all the more so, when one adds to it the fact directors are permitted, indeed expected, to take risks. Prudence and caution are not the watchwords of commercial success. Lord Hatherley L.C. later in his judgment qualifies his test by introducing the element of risk, saying:

" . . . there is a great deal more trust, a great deal more speculation, and a great deal more readiness to confide in the probabilities of things, with regard to success in mercantile transactions, than there is on the part of those whose habits of life are of an entirely different character. . . . "[54]

And "the probabilities of things" can go horribly awry, even after the most copious market research. "Funds embarked in a trading company . . . are placed under the control of the directors in order that they may be employed for the acquisition of gain, and *risk* (greater or less, according to the circumstances) *is of the very essence of such employment*": *per* Sterling J. in *Leeds Estates Building and Investment Co.* v. *Shepherd*.[55]

Liability under this test is illustrated by *Re New Mashonaland Exploration Co. Ltd.*[56] There Vaughan Williams J. gave it as his opinion that directors who had decided to make a loan on security and then proceeded to hand over the money to the borrower without taking the security would be guilty "of so unbusinesslike an act that it [could not] be called a mere error of judgment or imprudent act."

Managing and service directors

This discussion has been concerned with members of the board as such. Far more will be expected by way of diligence from a managing director since he functions singly, and not as a member of a quorate group; management skills are also usually to be expected. These matters are usually defined specifically by the terms of his appointment. Likewise, the extra duties undertaken by service direc-

---

[53] *Ibid.* at pp. 486–87. *Cf.* the *diligentia quam suis rebus* required at one time of a mandatory in Roman law: Leage, *op. cit.* 328, 371; and Christian L.J. in *McNamara* v. *Carey* (1867) I.R., 1 Eq. at p. 31: "a trustee must exert precisely the same care and solicitude on behalf of his *cestuis que trust* as he would do for himself."

[54] *Ibid.* at p. 495.

[55] (1887) 36 Ch. D. 787, 798; italics supplied; followed in *Re City Equitable Fire Insurance Co. Ltd.* [1925] Ch. 407, 428.

[56] [1892] 3 Ch. 577, 586.

tors are implicit in the nature of the job or are defined by their contracts of employment.

Exemption clauses

It used to be common practice for companies to have in their articles of association a provision exempting each director from personal liability in respect of acts or defaults arising out of his directorship, unless the loss or damage complained of was caused by his "own wilful default or wrongdoing,"[57] or "his own dishonesty."[58] Notorious escapes from liability, particularly in *Re City Equitable Fire Insurance Co. Ltd.*[59] led to legislative intervention in Britain, copied some decades later in Ireland by section 200 of the Companies Act 1963:

> " . . . any provision whether contained in the articles of a company or in any contract with a company or otherwise for exempting any officer of the company or any person employed by the company as auditor from, or indemnifying him against, any liability which by virtue of any rule of law would otherwise attach to him in respect of any negligence, default, breach of duty or breach of trust of which he may be guilty in relation to the company shall be void. . . . "[60]

This section gives rise to considerable conceptual difficulty. It prevents the parties from getting rid of an accrued liability, but to what, if any, extent does it prevent the parties from so defining their relationship that the liability does not arise in the first place, or, in other words varying what would otherwise be the duty? We have seen that what would otherwise be the whole fiduciary duty owed by a director to his company is modifiable by subtracting parts of it in advance by an appropriate form of article; this happens most prominently by use of the common form article 85 of Table A.[61] Furthermore, the content of a director's duties of diligence and, particularly, of skill varies, as we have seen, *supra*, according to the expectations of the parties, and is therefore, it would seem to follow, controllable by them. There are no absolutes here. On this reasoning it would seem

---

[57] As used in *Re City Equitable Fire Insurance Co. Ltd.* [1925] Ch. 407.

[58] *e.g. Re Brazilian Rubber Plantantions and Estates Ltd.* [1911] 1 Ch. 425.

[59] n. 57, *supra*.

[60] There is a proviso allowing officers and auditors to be indemnified against costs incurred in defending successfully civil or criminal proceedings, or making a successful application for relief under s.391.

[61] See p. 210, *supra*.

possible by the use of an appropriate article so to define a director's duty to a company that he incurs personal responsibility only if he is dishonest. In the face of such an article, section 200 would be of no avail since there would be no liability other than that for fraud to excuse. These questions are as yet unanswered.[62]

---

[62] For a useful discussion, see Birds, "The permissible scope of articles excluding the duties of company directors" (1976) 39 M.L.R. 394.

Chapter 8: Enforcement of Duties

This chapter describes the enforcement of the duties which directors individually or collectively owe to their company.[1]

Since the duties are owed to the company, it is the proper plaintiff to seek a remedy against directors in breach. Whether or not the company should litigate is whilst the company is a going concern a management decision delegated to the board under common form articles.[2] Where the board is hostile to the alleged wrongdoer, few problems in practice arise. They simply cause the company to sue him. *Regal (Hastings) Ltd.* v. *Gulliver*,[3] *Industrial Development Consultants Ltd.* v. *Cooley*[4] and *Canadian Aero Service Ltd.* v. *O'Malley*[5] all discussed in Chapter 7 are each examples of this. Most of the present chapter concerns the resolution of the difficulties which arise when the wrongdoers themselves remain in control of the company, and are disinclined to allow it to sue them.

But first we must look briefly at what happens when the company has gone into liquidation. Here the directors are *functus officio*,[6] and the task of pursuing malefactors falls primarily upon the liquidator. He will usually proceed by way of the summary procedure afforded by section 298 of the Companies Act 1963 known as "the misfeasance summons" which provides:

> "If in the course of winding up a company it appears that any person who has taken part in the formation or promotion of the company, or any past or present director or liquidator, or any

---

[1] For the content of those duties, see Chap. 7.

[2] *e.g. John Shaw & Sons (Salford) Ltd.* v. *Shaw* [1935] 2 K.B. 113. For the extent to which under the Irish form of art. 80 of Table A, a majority in general meeting may interfere with management decisions, see *Powers of Management and the Relationship between Board and General Meeting* in Chapter 3.

[3] [1942] 1 All E.R. 378.

[4] [1972] 1 W.L.R. 443.

[5] (1973) 40 D.L.R. (3d) 371.

[6] ss.258, 269 and *Gosling* v. *Gaskell* (1897) A.C. 575, 587.

officer of the company, has misapplied or retained or become liable or accountable for any money or property of the company, or been guilty of any misfeasance or breach of trust in relation to the company, the court may, on the application of the liquidator or of any creditor or contributory, examine the conduct of the promoter, director, liquidator or officer, and compel him to repay or restore the money or property or any part thereof respectively with interest at such rate as the court thinks just, or to contribute such sums to the assets of the company by way of compensation in respect of the misapplication, retainer, misfeasance or breach of trust as the court thinks just.''

This provision has been on the statute books for over 120 years,[7] and litigation on it in that period has established that it is purely procedural, conferring no new rights, and that it may be used against a director only where the company is seeking to recover pecuniary loss suffered as a result of the breach by the director of duties owed by him to the company by virtue of his office.[8] Thus, in *Re Irish Provident Assurance Co.*[9] the only relief to which the company was entitled independently of the section was rescission of an *ultra vires* contract and the restoration by the company and the other party to the contract of the benefits respectively received by them under it. Multilateral relief of this kind was not available under the section. Also, since the company had in any event suffered no pecuniary loss, the impugned transaction being fair, though *ultra vires*, the liquidator was not to be allowed to obtain for the company by the section relief which it could not have obtained by other means.

The pecuniary loss claimed must be suffered as a result of the breach of duty. In *Re S.M. Barker Ltd.*[10] a company discharged its controllers' debts to it on the footing that its new controllers would put it in funds to like extent. In so far as they did not do so, the loss to the company was not caused by the original controllers' breach of duty, if any,[11] as directors.

That the breach must be of duties imposed *virtute officii* rules out the use of the section to obtain compensation for the breach of duties

---

[7] It succeeds s.165 of the 1862 Act, and s.215 of the 1908 Act.

[8] *Re Irish Provident Assurance Co.* [1913] 1 I.R. 352, 374, following in particular *Cavendish-Bentinck* v. *Fenn* (1887) 12 App.Cas. 652, 661–62, 669.

[9] [1913] 1 I.R. 352.

[10] [1950] I.R. 123.

[11] No breach of duty was in fact found. The explanation in the text is perhaps the one satisfactory way out of a confusing judgment in which a number of important distinctions are blurred. Another might be that s.298 relief is discretionary.

arising independently of the office, in particular, duties in tort arising at common law.[12]

If directors have been guilty of misconduct or irregularities in their handling of the company's assets such that there is a prima facie case to be investigated under section 298, the costs even of an unfruitful application under the section may be awarded against the directors pesonally: *Re David Ireland & Co. Ltd.*[13] There is thus a judicial encouragement to use the procedure, and a deterrent against even innocuous wrongdoing. In *Re David Ireland & Co. Ltd.* the controller of a company who was the sole beneficial owner of its shares, had caused its bank account to be used as if it were his own, he and his fellow directors making payments out for his own private purposes, but in fact always making sure that the company was ultimately reimbursed. Fitzgibbon, L.J. affirmed the order that the directors should personally pay the costs of the proceedings on the ground that this is the usual consequence "where a party in a fiduciary position has, by misconduct, made litigation necessary," and added:

> "It has been said that this is "an extremely hard order." The hardship, if any, is the result of the "one-man Company" system. In my opinion anyone who chooses to give the support of his name as a Director to a Company of that class, and who neglects his duty by allowing the "one man" to do as he pleases, and actively assists him by paying away the Company's money at will, deserves to bear the expense of investigating what has been done, and any practical judicial lesson against undertaking such directorships should not be lightly set aside by a Court of Appeal."[14]

This remains a salutary reminder in the Ireland of today in which mere figurehead second directors are compulsory.[15]

Although the liquidator will usually bring a misfeasance summons, any creditor or contributory (*i.e.* a member) may likewise apply: the rule in *Foss* v. *Harbottle* has no application in a winding up. Also, any interested party may apply to the court for an order

---

[12] *Re Johnson B. & Co. (Builders) Ltd.* [1955] Ch. 634. The general remarks *obiter* by Evershed M.R. at p. 648 on the applicability of the section to "negligence" were made in the course of refuting the liability of a receiver, held in any event not to be within the section. The section must not be interpreted as being inapplicable to breaches of the directors' duties of skill, care and diligence. For the common law liability of receivers for negligence, see now Chapter 14: *Floating Charges and Receivers* at pp. 439–443.

[13] [1905] 1 I.R. 133.

[14] At p. 141.

[15] s.174, and see pp. 78–79, *supra*.

that the liquidator exercise his powers to recover the assets of the company. In *Provincial Bank of Ireland Ltd.* v. *O'Connor*,[16] the assignee of a member's entitlement in a voluntary winding up obtained an order that the liquidator takes steps to recover a debt from a debtor. *Semble*, a similar application can be made where any creditor, member, or other interested party wishes the liquidator to pursue a misfeasance summons.

It seems high time that the archaic form of section 298 was recast in contemporary language to give a summary procedure to any interested person (but the liquidator to have the first right of proceeding where he is not to be the defendant) the opportunity of having investigated in a summary way in a winding up any cause of complaint arising out of the conduct of the company's affairs with the object of securing any appropriate form of redress for the company. The amended section could also provide that costs are to be awarded against the defendants, unless they shall have given satisfactory and verifiable explanations before the commencement of the proceedings. Pleadings could be ordered where there are complicated issues of fact to be resolved.

We now turn to the difficulties which arise when the company remains a going concern and the board is unwilling to act against the alleged delinquents, either because they themselves are the alleged wrongdoers, or because they are prepared to condone the alleged wrongdoing of some of their number. What can the individual aggrieved shareholder do in these circumstances? The cause of action is the company's, not his. Initiating litigation is under common form articles the function of the board,[17] not the general meeting. If he can muster a majority in general meeting, he will usually be able to alter the composition of the board so as to secure a majority on it.[18] We will assume that this solution is not open to him; commonly, the board will command a majority in general meeting, and sometimes articles will have been adopted under which the composition of the board does not reflect majority voting power in general meeting.[19] The answer is that save in limited circumstances the individual member can do nothing about the enforcement of the duties owed to the company. Within those limited circumstances, the courts are prepared to cut through the corporate decision making process, and to allow the individual member to bring an action on behalf of the company against the wrongdoers. This is the *derivative*

---

[16] High Court, Kenny J., unreported October 10, 1974.

[17] See n. 2, *supra*.

[18] See pp. 65, 91 *et seq.*, *supra*.

[19] *e.g.* these may be life directors, or directors with "loaded" voting rights, etc. See Chapter 3: *Internal Structure*.

action, so called because the cause of action is derived from the company. In older decisions, the action was often referred to as the *representative action* since the plaintiff would invoke the company's cause of action on behalf of himself and all other members of the company,[20] and, indeed, this manner of proceeding is still a usual, if unnecessary feature of such actions.[21] The company itself is joined as a defendant to make it a party to the proceedings so as to bind it by their conclusions, but despite the slight confusion introduced by this technicality, and whatever the nomenclature, the essence of the action remains one brought on behalf of and for the company, the separate person, to whom all benefits of it accrue. The plaintiff's only benefit is indirect, through his participation in the company, and if his stake in it is small he would have to be endowed with altruism to an uncommon degree to undertake the burden of such litigation. But the very fact that such plaintiffs are not acting on their own behalf has led the English Court of Appeal in *Wallersteiner* v. *Moir (No. 2)*[22] to encourage them by stating that in principle they ought to be indemnified against their costs by their principal, the company, and that to safeguard themselves they ought to make an interlocutory application to the court at the commencement of the proceedings to obtain its sanction to their continuing the proceedings on the basis that they will be indemnified, rather in the way that a trustee should when about to bring proceedings in the interests of his trust.[23]

We now consider the limited circumstances in which an individual shareholder may bring a derivative action against directors. We have seen that the general meeting may ratify wrongs committed by the directors against the company[24]; certainly, they may not absolve themselves or one of their number by a decision at board level.[25] Not all such wrongs are ratifiable in general meeting; some are incapable of being ratified. Where it is alleged that a director or the directors have committed an unratifiable wrong, a derivative action will lie in respect of it. Categorising the wrong into ratifiable or unratifiable is

---

[20] The representation being constituted in Ireland under R.S.C., Ord. 15, r. 9.

[21] *Per* Lord Denning M.R. in *Wallersteiner* v. *Moir (No. 2)* [1975] 1 Q.B. 373, 358. Contrast the derivative action (presented representatively) and the truly representative action in *Prudential Assurance Co. Ltd.* v. *Newman Industries Ltd. (No. 2)* [1982] 2 W.L.R. 31. See also *Estmanco (Kilner House) Ltd.* v. *G.L.C.* [1982] 1 All E.R. 437, 443c.

[22] [1975]1 Q.B. 373, 391.

[23] *Re Beddoe* [1893] 1 Ch. 547.

[24] See pp. 66 *et seq.*, *supra*.

[25] *Furs Ltd.* v. *Tomkies* (1936) 54 C.L.R. 583; and see pp. 210–211, *supra*. The English Court of Appeal in the *Prudential Assurance Co. Ltd.* case, n. 21 *supra*, did not make this important distinction (particularly at pp. 41–42).

a key to the availability of the derivative action. If the wrong is categorised as ratifiable, it is pointless to allow an action founded on it to proceed without first ascertaining the wishes of the majority in general meeting since they may at any time ratify, thereby rendering the proceedings nugatory. This is a central truth of the rule in *Foss* v. *Harbottle*. As Wigram V.-C. said in that case:

> "Whilst the Court may be declaring the acts complained of to be void at the suit of the present Plaintiffs, who in fact may be the only proprietors who disapprove of them, the governing body of proprietors may defeat the decree by lawfully resolving upon the confirmation of the very acts which are the subject of the suit. The very fact that the governing body of proprietors assembled at the special general meeting may so bind even a reluctant minority is decisive to shew that the frame of this suit cannot be sustained whilst that body retains its functions."[26]

Formerly, it was the practice immediately to non-suit a plaintiff bringing in respect of a ratifiable wrong a derivative action to which the majority in general meeting might be opposed. But in recent years the occasional practice has grown up in England of allowing the case to proceed to judgment on the question whether or not a wrong has been committed, and if in fact it is found that there has been, and that it is of the ratifiable variety, of adjourning the proceedings so that the company in general meeting might decide whether or not to ratify: *Hogg* v. *Cramphorn Ltd.*[27] The waste involved in such a manner of proceeding is well illustrated by *Prudential Assurance Co. Ltd.* v. *Newman Industries Ltd.* *(No. 2)*[28] in which at huge expense after 71 hearing days at first instance a wrong stated by the English Court of Appeal to be ratifiable[29] was found by Vinelott J. The Court of Appeal was firmly of the view that whether or not a derivative action was permissible should be determined before the trial, if at all, of the substantive issues of the wrongdoing.[30] This was done in both *Bamford* v. *Bamford*[31] and in *Daniels* v. *Daniels*[32] as a pre-

---

[26] (1843) 2 Hare 461, 493–95; most recently analysed in the *Prudential Assurance Co. Ltd.* case, n. 21 *supra*.

[27] [1966] 3 W.L.R. 995, 1006.

[28] [1980] 2 All E.R. 841; in fact the learned judge did not order the matter to go to general meeting ruling at p. 875 erroneously (see [1982] 1 All E.R. 354, 362, and pp. 245–246, *infra*) that it was a pre-requisite to a proper ratification that "the majority could be relied upon to determine in a disinterested way whether it is truly in the interests of the company that proceedings be brought," and finding these conditions to be absent.

[29] [1982] 2 W.L.R. 31, 41.

[30] *Ibid.* at p. 38.

[31] [1970] Ch. 212 (trial of preliminary question of law ordered).

[32] [1978] Ch. 73 (point determined on an application to strike out).

liminary question to be decided on the footing that the plaintiff's allegations of misconduct would be substantiated. As we shall see, the boundaries of ratifiability cannot be regarded as settled, and in fact the area of unratifiable conduct seems to be expanding; consequently, these preliminary frontier skirmishes on the law must be expected to continue. If the alleged wrong is considered clearly to be ratifiable, the proposed plaintiff should be advised to requisition an *e.g.m.* of the company with the object of getting it to pass a resolution that the conduct in question be *not* ratified,[33] and in the unlikely event of the directors not commanding a majority there, he may, armed with this resolution, assumedly proceed[34]; if he fails to take this precaution he must expect the court to order such a meeting[35] (and if he is defeated at it, he will have thrown away his costs of launching the action, and incurred those of his opponents), or to be non-suited.

It is implicit in the foregoing, and has been repeatedly affirmed in the courts, that a director guilty of a ratifiable wrong against the company may cast his votes *as member* in general meeting in favour of his own absolution. He is not debarred from casting his vote simply by his own personal interest in the outcome. Two Privy Council cases are most often relied upon in support of this proposition.[36] In the first, *North-West Transportation Co. Ltd.* v. *Beatty*[37] it was said:

" . . . the resolution of a majority of the shareholders, duly convened, upon any question with which the company is legally competent to deal, is binding upon the minority, and consequently upon the company, and every shareholder has a perfect right to vote upon any such question, although he may have a personal interest in the subject-matter opposed to, or different from the general or particular interests of the company."

a statement confirmed in the second, *Burland* v. *Earle*[38] in which it was said:

---

[33] For the requisitioning of meetings, see pp. 70–71, 183–184, *supra*. If he fails to secure the support of the 10 per cent. necessary to requisition a meeting, it is unlikely that his resolution would have been passed.

[34] Uncertainties remain; what would the court's attitude be to the possibility of the general meeting changing its mind, as of course it may, and deciding to release the directors after all?

[35] As in *East Pant Du United Lead Mining Co. Ltd.* v. *Merryweather* (1864) 2 Hem. & M. 254.

[36] See also *Regal (Hastings) Ltd.* v. *Gulliver* [1942] 1 All E.R. 378, 389; *Bamford* v. *Bamford* [1970] Ch. 212, 238.

[37] (1887) 12 App.Cas. 589, 593.

[38] [1902] A.C. 83, 94.

" . . . a shareholder is not debarred from voting or using his voting power to carry a resolution by the circumstance of his having a particular interest in the subject-matter of the vote."

Furthermore, there is in Ireland a constitutional dimension to this question. The Supreme Court in *P.M.P.S. Ltd. and Moore* v. *Att.-Gen.*[39] has decided that a shareholder's individual rights are personal rights of property protected by Article 40.3 of the Constitution, which therefore the courts are bound to vindicate. Among these individual rights, there is, as we have seen,[40] the right to vote in general meetings. As the law stands, the courts will prevent votes being cast on a ratification resolution only where the very existence of those votes is the subject of the ratification, *e.g.* where the general meeting is voting to ratify a voidable share issue the votes on the shares in dispute must not be cast.[41]

What wrongful acts of the directors are *unratifiable* in general meeting? First, we have seen in Chapter 4[42] that the general meeting cannot by a ratifying resolution validate a transaction which the company has entered into *ultra vires*. By the declaratory section 8(2) of the Companies Act 1963, the individual member[43] is permitted to apply to the court for an injunction to restrain his "company from doing any act or thing which the company has no power to do"; the individual member may also obtain a declaration that conduct was *ultra vires*.[44] The justification for the freedom given to the individual member here is simply that no organ of the company possesses the ability to confer capacity on it retrospectively, but other aspects of *ultra vires* transactions are potentially within the control of the majority, such as the power to forgive the directors their responsibility for the loss to the company caused by its having entered into the *ultra vires* transaction.[45]

Secondly, as O'Brien L.C. put it in *Cockburn* v. *Newbridge Sanitary Steam Laundry Co. Ltd.*[46] "a company cannot ratify its own criminality." The facts were bizarre. The managing director of the com-

---

[39] [1984] I.L.R.M. 88, following *Central Dublin Development Association* v. *Att-Gen.* (1973) 109 I.L.T.R. 69, 84.

[40] See pp. 167–168, 179–180, *supra.*

[41] *Hogg* v. *Cramphorn Ltd.* [1966] 3 W.L.R. 995, 1006, approved in *Bamford* v. *Bamford* [1970] Ch. 212, 240.

[42] At p. 131.

[43] Or debenture holder.

[44] *Hennessy* v. *National Agricultural and Industrial Development Association* [1947] I.R. 159.

[45] Their responsibility to the company for loss incurred as a consequence of *ultra vires* transactions validated by s.8 is expressly preserved by s.8(1).

[46] [1915] 1 I.R. 237.

pany had on its behalf entered into contracts with the War Office to do laundry work for the military establishments on the Curragh. The company did the work, and the managing director received the money, £3,268 in all of which he paid over only £1,038 to the company, refusing to account for the balance, heavily hinting without quite admitting (on the grounds that he would thereby incriminate himself) that the balance had with the consent of the company been disbursed in necessary bribes among War Office personnel to secure the contracts. Though the Court of Appeal found it "hard to understand, even on the wildest scheme of bribery, that £2,230 out of £3,268 [had been] paid in secret commissions,"[47] it nonetheless accepted this as the probable explanation and accordingly allowed a derivative action at the suit of two minority shareholders on the ground that the general meeting was incapable of ratifying such a criminal transaction between the company and its managing director. The remaining history of the company is told two years later in the sequel, *Re Newbridge Sanitary Steam Laundry Ltd.*[48–49] The managing director had refused to comply with the order made in the earlier proceedings that he account to the company; in this refusal he had been wholeheartedly supported by a resolution passed by a majority of the shareholders, he himself not being in a controlling position; and the board had at all times been and remained opposed to pursuing the managing director. Faced with this obduracy, the court wound up the company on the just and equitable ground in order to bring to an end its vicious career. Another example of this second category of unratifiable wrongs is found in *Buchanan Ltd.* v. *McVey*[50] in which it was held that it was not within the power of the members of the company, even if acting unanimously, to sanction a dispersal of the company's property if so to do involved "dishonesty," in this case a scheme to work a fraud upon the Scottish Revenue.

Thirdly, we come to the matter of "fraud on the minority," a shorthand for overstepping the limits of tolerance allowed to majority rule, and a somewhat inappropriate expression in this context where the wrong is technically suffered by the company itself, and the minority suffers only indirectly and incidentally in the process. The expression is also used more appositely where the majority is behaving improperly in the use of its voting power to alter individual membership rights, an entirely distinct matter, discussed in Chapter 9, *post*, at p. 274 *et seq*. In the present context, the misnomer is compounded since "fraud on the minority" is by no means confined to

---

[47] *Per* O'Brien L.C. at p. 254.
[48–49] [1917] 1 I.R. 67 and see pp. 268 *et seq., infra.*
[50] [1954] I.R. 89, 100 (Kingsmill Moore J.); aff'd by the Supreme Court at p. 118.

the meaning of dishonest conduct or the intention to deprive by deceit which it bears in the Common Law[51]; nor does it equate to fraud in Equity since some matters which the fastidious equitable conscience might find unpalatable are nonetheless ratifiable. In short, it is a *sui generis* expression describing the instances recognised by the courts in the last 140 years as falling within the admission in *Foss* v. *Harbottle* itself that the "claims of justice"[52] might demand exceptions, true exceptions since they concern situations in which the majority in general meeting, though acting within its capacity, is not allowed to prevail in forgiving a wrong done to the company.

As matters stand at present in this slowly evolving area of the law, "fraud on the minority" consists certainly of one category of cases, and less certainly of another. The "expropriation" cases form the certain category, though, as we shall see, its boundaries are difficult to draw; exercises by the directors of their powers *in bad faith, i.e.* without a genuine belief on their part that in so doing they are acting for the benefit of the company form the less certain category.

The "expropriation" cases

Here, in the language of James L.J. in *Menier* v. *Hooper's Telegraph Works*,[53] "the majority have put something into their pockets at the expense of the minority." Put more compendiously later in the Privy Council case of *Burland* v. *Earle*[54] this category concerns cases where:

> "the majority are endeavouring directly or indirectly to appropriate to themselves money, property, or advantages which *belong* to the company . . ."

In *Menier* v. *Hooper's Telegraph Works* itself, the controllers of the company had caused its directors to settle an action pending by it against a third party on terms that the company gave up its cause of action in return for substantial benefits to the controllers in their personal capacities. The minority were allowed to pursue a derivative action to untangle this transaction on the company's behalf. In

---

[51] If it were, it would fall into the second category abovementioned.

[52] *Per* Wigram V.-C. at p. 492; see also *Russell* v. *Wakefield Waterworks Co.* (1875) L.R. 20 Eq. 474, 480; *Cotter* v. *National Union of Seamen* [1929] 2 Ch. 58, 69; *Edwards* v. *Halliwell* [1950] 2 All E.R. 1064, 1067; *Heyting* v. *Dupont* [1964] 1 W.L.R. 843, 851; *Prudential Assurance Co. Ltd.* v. *Newman Industries Ltd. (No. 2)* [1982] 2 W.L.R. 31, 43; *Estmanco (Kilner House) Ltd.* v. *G.L.C.* [1982] 1 All E.R. 437, 444.

[53] (1874) L.R. 9 Ch. App. 350, following *Atwool* v. *Merryweather* (1867) 5 Eq. 464.

[54] [1902] A.C. 83, 93; following *Menier* v. *Hooper's Telegraph Works* n. 53 *supra.* Italics supplied.

Estmanco (Kilner House) Ltd. v. *Greater London Council*[55] the G.L.C. was contractually obliged to the proposed management company of a block to sell all the flats in it to the sitting tenants. Before all the sales had been completed, the G.L.C. decided for political reasons deliberately to break this contract, and not to proceed. The company issued a writ against the G.L.C. to restrain this breach, and for specific performance. The G.L.C. which, pending the completion of the scheme, held the only voting shares in the company responded by causing the general meeting to pass unanimously a resolution instructing the directors to discontinue the action, and the directors acquiesced.[56] A minority shareholder, a flat owner whose purchase had been completed before the change in policy, was substituted as plaintiff to continue the action against the G.L.C. in derivative form on behalf of the company, Sir Robert Megarry V.-C. saying:

> "No right of a shareholder to vote in his own selfish interests or to ignore the interests of the company entitle him with impunity to injure his voteless fellow shareholders by depriving the company of a cause of action and stultifying the purpose for which the company was formed."[57]

The expropriation of the company's property by its controllers need not be part of a scheme of deliberate wrongdoing in order to justify a minority action. "Fraud," as has been said above, is a misnomer. In *Daniels* v. *Daniels*,[58] a derivative action brought by minority shareholders against a company's two directors who were also its majority shareholders was allowed to proceed, it being alleged that they had in breach of their duty as directors caused the company to sell some of its land to one of them at a gross undervalue. Fraud was not alleged. To qualify the minority as proper plaintiffs to sue on the company's behalf, it sufficed to allege that its property had been channelled off for the benefit of the majority, or, in other words, had been expropriated. The mental state of the majority in thus acquir-

---

[55] [1982] 1 All E.R. 437. Sir Robert Megarry V.-C. did not in these Long Vacation interlocutory proceedings find it "a suitable occasion on which to probe the intricacies of the rule in *Foss* v. *Harbottle* and its exceptions, or to attempt to discover and expound the principles to be found in the exceptions." (at p. 447).

[56] Technically, whether the directors need have responded to this *diktat* depends on the form of the company's articles (which are not reported). In practice, resistance would have been useless since at this stage of the company's life the directors were to be G.L.C. nominees.

[57] At p. 448.

[58] [1978] Ch. 406.

ing the company's property whether "intentionally or unintentionally, fraudulently or negligently"[59] was not material to the question of who should be allowed to sue in respect of it on the company's behalf, but might of course be a relevant ingredient of the company's actual cause of action against the majority, a separate matter.

The expropriation category can include cases where the controllers have diverted a business opportunity from the company to themselves, or otherwise for their own benefit such as to another company in which they are beneficially interested. In *Cook* v. *Deeks*,[60] another Privy Council case, the company had carried out several large construction contracts for the Canadian Pacific Railway Company. Another such contract was coming up. Had the company tendered, one can see with the benefit of hindsight that it certainly would have obtained it; instead, three of the company's four directors, holding between them 75 per cent. of the company's shares, bid for it themselves, and after securing it arranged for it to be transferred to and executed by a new company formed by the three of them for the purpose. Their object in proceeding in this way was to sever their business relationship with the Plaintiff who was the fourth director, holding the remaining 25 per cent. of the shares, and with whom they had quarrelled. Although the three took the precaution of using their majority votes in general meeting to pass a resolution purporting to absolve themselves, the plaintiff succeeded in maintaining a derivative action against them and their new company for an account of the profits of the transaction. The Privy Council treated the contract as *belonging* in equity to the company, its *property* which they held on its behalf, and of which they could not make a present to themselves.[61] The new company was likewise bound by the equity since it took the contract with knowledge (imputed via its controllers) of the circumstances of its acquisition.[62] The controllers in *Cook* v. *Deeks* had diverted to themselves a business opportunity arising out of the company's continuing business connections; they had, in other words, been trespassing on the company's goodwill, readily regarded in the business world as an asset, if somewhat nebulous, but nonetheless capable of valuation and transfer.

One must contrast with the diversion of property involved in the

---

[59] *Ibid.* at p. 414, *per* Templeman J.

[60] [1916] 1 A.C. 554.

[61] *Ibid.* at p. 562–64, *passim.*

[62] *Ibid.* at p. 565. The imputation of mental attributes to a corporation is discussed in Chapter 2 at pp. 33, *et seq.*

expropriation cases the ratifiable wrongs arising out of abuses of a fiduciary position. This distinction between abuses of property and position is well known in the law. In *Lister & Co. v. Stubbs,*[63] principals claimed as their own the investments into which their corrupt agent had salted away the bribes he had received whilst acting on their behalf, and attempted to obtain an injunction to prevent him from dealing with the investments. They failed on the ground that they did not have and never had a proprietary interest in the bribes or their product; the abuse by the agent of his fiduciary position had not led to the creation of a trust over the bribes in favour of the principals but to a personal duty on him to account to them for their amount. The plaintiffs' claim was "confounding ownership with obligation."[64] The distinction was carefully preserved in *Archer's Case*[65] in which the principal was a company. Mr. Archer had secretly accepted a financial inducement to become a director of the company. The inducement was not made at the expense of the company but by a third party. Nonetheless, since he had received it as a consequence of his fiduciary position he was bound to account for the amount of it to the company.[66] Lindley L.J. emphasised that the claim was only personal:

> "Has not Mr. Archer obtained, in respect of his agency, a sum of money which . . . is payable by him to the company? To say it is the company's money is to use an ambiguous expression. In one sense it may be said to be the company's money—that is to say in the sense that the company are entitled to get it. In another sense it is not the company's money—that is to say, the company cannot follow it into investments of it, nor, in the event of Mr. Archer's bankruptcy, could they withdraw the money from his assets instead of ranking as creditors against his estate."[67]

The distinction made in *Lister* v. *Stubbs* between abuses of position and of property has now been eroded in its own particular context by the growth of the *Mareva* injunction by which assets may be frozen regardless of whether the applicant claims a proprietary interest

---

[63] (1890) 45 Ch.D. 1.

[64] *Per* Lindley L.J. at p. 15.

[65] [1892] 1 Ch. 322.

[66] " . . . the director is really a watch-dog, and the watch-dog has no right, without the knowledge of his master, to take a sop from a possible wolf": *ibid. per* Bowen L.J. at p. 341. This general principle is discussed in Chap. 7.

[67] *Ibid.* at p. 338.

in them,[68] but in the context of the derivative action the distinction
retains its importance even though it is sometimes difficult to draw.
In *Regal (Hastings) Ltd.* v. *Gulliver*[69] the directors were in breach of
fiduciary duty by utilising for themselves an opportunity which had
come their way by virtue of their position as directors. The breach
was ratifiable.[70] The fact that the company could not take the
opportunity for itself, or that the board had bona fide decided that it
should not, must be regarded as having taken the opportunity out of
the category of the company's "property." In *Cook* v. *Deeks*[71] where
the opportunity taken by the directors was looked upon as being the
company's property, the Privy Council was careful to add that had
the directors decided their course of conduct after having "exercised
a discretion or decided on a matter of policy . . . different results
would ensue."[72]

Section 187 of the Companies Act 1963 declares that a situation
which might otherwise fall on the awkward borderline between an
abuse of position and a diversion of property is in fact ratifiable. The
section concerns payments to be made to directors who are about to
retire from office upon the sale of the whole or any part of the company's undertaking or property, typically its business, lock, stock
and barrel. In effect, such payments to the directors could be categorised as diversions of the company's property since, had the directors not secured the money for themselves, the purchaser could
probably have been persuaded to use it to augment the purchase
price payable to the company. As the worldly-wise Vaughan
Williams L.J. observed in *Kaye* v. *Croydon Tramways Co.*[73]:

> "I cannot help thinking that anybody familiar with business
> would be very slow in believing that the purchasing company
> was willing to pay what in effect is a larger price if the money

---

[68] *Mareva* injunctions have now become a major industry in both England and Ireland. The development of the jurisdiction and its relationship to *Lister* v. *Stubbs* are
discussed in *Barclay-Johnson* v. *Yuill* [1980] 1 W.L.R. 1259; *Faith Panton Property Plan
Ltd.* v. *Hodgetts* [1981] 1 W.L.R. 927; *Z Ltd.* v. *A* [1982] Q.B. 588; *Powerscourt Estates* v.
Gallagher (High Court, McWilliam J., May 18, 1982, unreported; at pp. 4 *et seq.* of the
transcript); *Fleming* v. *Ranks (Ireland) Ltd. and O'Donoghue* [1983] I.L.R.M. 541, 545,
and its relationship to a proprietary claim in *P.C.W. Ltd.* v. *Dixon* [1983] 2 All E.R.
158.

[69] [1942] 1 All E.R. 378; the facts are given at pp. 213–214, *supra.*

[70] *Ibid.* at pp. 389, 394.

[71] [1916] 1 A.C. 554; p. 250, *supra.*

[72] *Ibid.* at p. 565; see also p. 562. Such conduct would still, it is submitted at p. 215,
supra, be a breach of duty.

[73] [1898] 1 Ch. 358, 376. See also *Furs Ltd.* v. *Tomkies* (1936) 54 C.L.R. 583.

went into the pockets of the directors, than it would be willing to pay if it went into the coffers of the company."

Section 187 declares that such payments unless disclosed in advance to the members and approved by the company in general meeting are unlawful, and are held by the recipients on trust for the company.

Acts of negligence or neglect constituting a breach of duty, but not as alleged in *Daniels* v. *Daniels*[74] a diversion of the company's property to its controllers, are ratifiable. In *Pavlides* v. *Jensen*[75] it was alleged that the directors had been grossly incompetent, but not that they had thereby lined their pockets, or those of their associates. The substance of the complaint against them was that they had sold a mine at a huge undervalue. A derivative action brought by a minority shareholder was struck out on the ground that "it was open to the company by a vote of the majority to decide that, if the directors by their negligence or error of judgment had sold the company's mine at an undervalue, proceedings should not be taken by the company against the directors."[76] In *Heyting* v. *Dupont*,[77] characterised by Harman L.J. as "perhaps the most barren and futile litigation that it has ever been my lot to encounter,"[78] a director had withheld from the company a document necessary for the patenting of an invention which the company had been formed to exploit. The dismissal of a derivative action against him for compensation for the loss allegedly caused to the company by his neglect was upheld on the ground that the misfeasance "had not put any money or property into his pocket."[79]

Powers exercised in bad faith

The English decisions though not clear cut, on balance favour the view that a board resolution voidable for impropriety may be vali-

---

[74] [1978] Ch. 406.

[75] [1956] Ch. 565.

[76] *Ibid.* p. 576, *per* Danckwerts J. In *Re Horsley & Weight Ltd.* [1982] 3 All E.R. 1045, 1056, Templeman L.J. doubted *obiter* whether an actionably negligent breach of the duty owed by a director to his company was in fact ratifiable. See also Cumming-Bruce L.J. at p. 1055.

[77] [1964] 1 W.L.R. 843.

[78] *Ibid.* p. 852.

[79] *Ibid.* p. 854 *per* Harman L.J. There was probably in fact no causal connection between the breach of duty and the loss to the company. Even if the defendant had not delayed, it is unlikely that the company would have been able to exploit the invention because its functioning had been paralysed by the bad blood between its two participants, the plaintiff and the defendant. (See Russell L.J. at p. 851).

dated by a ratifying resolution in general meeting, even if the board resolution was passed in bad faith, or, in other words without a belief that it was for the benefit of the company. *Bamford* v. *Bamford*[80] in which the improper allotment was to be held by the Court of Appeal to be ratifiable, was tried on the express "assumption that the allotment by the board . . . was not made bona fide in the interests" of the company.[81] On the other hand, in the later first instance decision of *Clemens* v. *Clemens Bros. Ltd.*[82] Foster J. declined to recognise the ability of a controlling shareholder to authorise a proposed allotment which had the main purpose of so diluting the minority shareholding of the plaintiff as to deprive her of her position of "negative control," *i.e.* her power to block a special resolution. Though it is tolerably clear that the allotment was to be made in bad faith, the judge specifically refused to base his decision on that ground, or indeed on any ground other than "equitable considerations."[83] There are hints in *Re Horsley & Weight Ltd.*[83a] that acts of the board done in bad faith are not ratifiable in general meeting. Whatever the position in England, *Nash* v. *Lancegaye Safety Glass (Ireland) Ltd.*[84] may be taken as authority in Ireland for the proposition that the element of bad faith in the exercise of directors' powers will render the acts in question unratifiable. Certainly, the judgment of Budd J.[85] in this case is confused, and therefore confusing, but the clear inference from it is that bad faith in the exercise of a fiduciary power is some species of a fraud on the minority, and unratifiable.

Resolutions of the board made in good faith but voidable through

---

[80] [1970] Ch. 212; p. 227, n. 9 *supra*.

[81] *Ibid.* pp. 229 *et seq.*: terms of preliminary point of law. In actuality, the board certainly acted in good faith.

[82] [1976] 2 All E.R. 268.

[83] *Ibid.* at p. 282; an eclectic decision, authorities being cited from a number of differing contexts, including *Ebrahimi* v. *Westbourne Galleries Ltd.* [1973] A.C. 360 (breach of understanding between participants in a company visited with the consequence of a just and equitable winding up: see pp. 95 *et seq.*, *supra*, and pp. 270–271, *infra*), *Allen* v. *Gold Reefs of West Africa Ltd.* [1900] 1 Ch. 656 and *Greenhalgh* v. *Arderne Cinemas Ltd.* [1951] Ch. 286 (each concerned with the standards to be observed by the majority when voting in a general meeting to alter individual membership rights: see pp. 274 *et seq.*, *infra*) and *Scottish Co-operative Wholesale Society Ltd.* v. *Meyer* [1959] A.C. 324 (a claim for a discretionary remedy under s.210 of the Company Act 1948 *[U.K.]*: see p. 264, *infra*). s.210 of the 1948 Act was not in fact specifically invoked in *Clemens*. Its successor, s.75 of the Company Act 1980 *[U.K.]* would undoubtedly give a remedy for the "unfairly prejudicial" conduct complained of in this case, even if ratifiable, as would s.205.

[83a] *e.g.* Buckley L.J. at [1982] 3 All E.R. 1045, 1055e.

[84] (1958) 92 I.L.T.R. 11, discussed at p. 227, *supra*.

[85] The report states that the judge was Dixon J.

being exercises of power for an improper purpose are clearly ratifiable in England, as witness *Hogg* v. *Cramphorn Ltd.*[86] in which the directors genuinely believed that the defeat of a takeover bid would be for the benefit of their company, and accordingly their defensive measures involving the wrongful allotment of unissued shares to friendly holders were held to be ratifiable. No doubt the Irish courts would take a similar line towards powers exercised wrongly but honestly for the benefit of the company.

Section 205

This chapter constitutes an attempt to state the strict legal position on the enforcement of the duties owed by directors to their company. In the opening section of the next chapter we explore the extent to which in practice a complainant in pursuit of a personal and discretionary remedy may invoke the supervening morality of section 205 of the Companies Act 1963. We will see that such a remedy may be given even where a derivative action would lie.

---

[86] [1966] 3 W.L.R. 995.

Chapter 9: Minority Protection

Section 205: a general consideration

Section 205 of the Companies Act 1963 crops up throughout this book. It is intended here to discuss the remedy generally, without, it is hoped, being too repetitive.

Section 205, said Kenny J. in *Re Westwinds Holding Co. Ltd.*,[1] "made a profound change in the remedies available to a shareholder." For the first time in Ireland the court was given a discretion to remedy unprincipled conduct in the company even where no legal rights had been infringed, and a flexibility to suit the remedy to the matters of which complaint was made. Section 205 was broadly modelled upon section 210 of the Companies Act 1948 *[U.K.]*, now repealed,[2] but with modifications in part suggested by the Jenkins Committee, in part by the draftsman's own perception of defects in section 210 brought to light by British interpretations of it, and in part without any recognisable provenance. The chief Jenkins Committee recommendation followed (and by no means all were) is that the Irish courts in exercising jurisdiction under section 205 are liberated from the necessity, present in section 210, of finding grounds justifying a just and equitable winding up of the company. This was the most fundamental departure from the British model, and British authorities, occasionally referred to in Ireland as aids to the construction of section 205, should always be treated with caution because of the absence of this restrictive element from the Irish jurisdiction. Other departures will become apparent as this analysis proceeds.

Section 205 can be parsed into four separate limbs. The court is given jurisdiction in each of the following four situations:

    (i) if the affairs of the company are being conducted in a man-

---

[1] High Court, unreported, May 21, 1974; Ussher, (1978) D.U.L.J. 48. For a view of s.205 before the emergence of any case law on it, see J. Temple Lang, "Minority Shareholder Protection under Irish Legislation," (1974) 25 N.I.L.Q. 387.

[2] And replaced by s.75 of the Companies Act 1980 *[U.K.]* in which the principal recommendation of the Jenkins Committee, para. 212, was followed.

ner oppressive to the complainant member or any of the members (including himself);

(ii) if the powers of the directors of the company are being exercised in a manner oppressive to the complainant member or any of the members (including himself);

(iii) if the affairs of the company are being conducted in disregard of the interests of the complainant as member or of the interests of any of the members (including himself) as members;

(iv) if the powers of the directors of the company are being exercised in disregard of the interests of the complainant as member or of the interests of any of the members (including himself) as members.

Limb (i) standing alone is the equivalent of the British section 210, and even then it is broader. The British equivalent said that the conduct complained of must be "oppressive to some part of the members (including himself)," thereby making it clear that the oppression must be suffered *qua* member. For example, in *Elder* v. *Elder and Watson*,[3] *Re Lundie Bros. Ltd.*,[4] and in *Re Westbourne Galleries Ltd.*,[5] expelled and excluded directors all failed on this ground to found jurisdiction under section 210. In *Re H.R. Harmer Ltd.*,[6] this difficulty was circumvented by the argument that an overwhelming majority shareholder who proceeded on the strength of it to disregard his fellow directors at board level, had nonetheless caused them to suffer as members, in which character they had an expectation that the company's constitution would be observed. Such ingenuity is unnecessary in Ireland, since the obstacle to relief does not apply. Section 205 is significantly different in wording. Under limb (i) and (ii) the complainant may allege conduct "oppressive *to him* or any of the members (including himself)."[7]

Of course, he must be a member to complain, but the significant divergence in wording from the British model does not necessitate his complaining in any particular character. In *Re Murph's Restaurants Ltd.*,[7a] an excluded director claimed relief under section 205, and alternatively for a just and equitable winding up. Gannon J. preferred the latter course as the more appropriate remedy in the circumstances, after weighing it against the possibilities afforded by section 205. He expressed no doubts about his jurisdiction on the

---

[3] 1952 S.C. 49.
[4] [1965] 1 W.L.R. 1051.
[5] [1971] 2 W.L.R. 618 (at first instance: this aspect was not pursued on appeal).
[6] [1959] 1 W.L.R. 62.
[7] Italics supplied.
[7a] Gannon J. High Court, unreported, July 31, 1979. Ussher, (1979–80) D.U.L.J. 92.

facts before him to make an order under section 205, and it is implicit in his judgment that he considered he did have that ability.[7b] Against this must be inserted one *caveat*. The complaint must arise out of some matter internal to the company's structure. In *Re Irish Visiting Motorists Bureau Ltd.*,[8] the first case decided under section 205, and not mentioned in *Re Murph's Restaurants Ltd.* or in any other case in which section 205 has arisen (indeed, it being a characteristic of this jurisdiction that no decision on it is ever mentioned in any other decision), a complaint by a member that the company had broken an agreement with him independent of the company's constitution was said to be insufficient to found jurisdiction under section 205.[9]

Both limbs (i) and (ii) concern oppressive conduct. The definition most often cited is the dictionary meaning given by Lord Simonds in *Scottish Co-operative Wholesale Society Ltd.* v. *Meyer*,[10] and accepted in Ireland by Keane J. in *Re Greenore Trading Co. Ltd.*[11] By this definition oppressive conduct is "burdensome, harsh and wrongful." Though these are strong words, the primary definition of "oppressive" given by the *Oxford English Dictionary* is even stronger, showing it to be a word altogether too strong for its purpose of protecting a minority within a company. It says:

> "Of the nature of oppression or tyrannous treatment of subjects, inferiors, etc.; unjustly burdensome, harsh, or merciless; tyrannical."

"Oppressive" has now been abandoned in Britain in favour of the "unfairly prejudicial" formula recommended by the Jenkins Com-

---

[7b] Contrast the earlier interlocutory judgment of McWilliam J. in the same case (High Court, April 5, 1979; unreported) on an unsuccessful motion by the company to restrain the petitioner from advertising his winding up petition on the grounds, *inter alia*, that s.205 relief would be more appropriate than a winding up. This interlocutory judgment might be interpreted as stating *obiter* that s.205 relief was *not* more appropriate since it applied only "to members of a company as members" (p. 5 of the transcript). In the event, McWilliam J. refused the application on the ground that genuine prima facie grounds for winding up did appear to exist.

[8] Kenny J. High Court, unreported, January 27, 1972.

[9] His comment at p. 32 of the transcript that "the conduct or exercise of the powers complained of must affect the person making the complaint in his character as a member and not as a creditor or as a person having commercial dealings with the company" must be confined to the distinction he was making there, and not be extended to finer distinctions such as that between complaints *qua* member and those *qua* director.

[10] [1959] A.C. 324, 342.

[11] High Court, unreported, March 28, 1980, at p. 19 of the transcript. See generally on this case Ussher, (1981) D.U.L.J. 179.

mittee,[12] and there have been judicial attempts in British and other jurisdictions to inject into the definition a milder element, particularly such formulations as "a visible departure from the standards of fair dealing, and a violation of the conditions of fair play"[13] and a lack of "that degree of probity which [members] are entitled to expect in the conduct of the company's affairs."[14] Fortunately, except for the instance recorded above, the Irish courts have discarded the dictionary in their application of section 205, and, indeed, any attempt at a comprehensive paraphrase, the imprudence of which was recognised by Buckley L.J. in *Re Jermyn Street Turkish Baths Ltd.*[15] on the ground that "the affairs of life are so diverse that it is dangerous to attempt a universal definition." A similar fear of hampering jurisdiction has rendered some judges reluctant to define "fraud" in the context of equitable intervention.[16] In *Re Clubman Shirts Ltd.*[17] a mere failure by the directors to consult a principal shareholder at a time of crisis in the company's affairs was held to be conduct oppressive of him. In other cases, wrongs which were plainly remediable by means other than section 205 were held noneLtd.,[18] the exercise by a governing director of his powers in such a way as to expropriate the company's property for his own benefit justified intervention under section 205, even though the minority shareholder could have righted the wrong to the company by means of a derivative action.[19] In *Re Greenore Trading Co. Ltd.,*[20] the misapplication of the company's money in the purchase of its own shares contrary to section 60 of the Companies Act 1963 was held to be sufficiently oppressive to justify a remedy under section 205, despite the fact that the money was easily recoverable by the company at the suit of the petitioner.[21] Thus, a notion central to the ordinary meaning of oppression, and to the development of this term in the English courts, that it involves suffering under wrongs which are *without* a lawful remedy, is lacking in Ireland. By contrast,

---

[12] Paras. 204, 212(*a*); s.75 of the Companies Act 1980 [*U.K.*].

[13] *Per* Lord Cooper in *Elder* v. *Elder & Watson Ltd.*, 1952 S.C. 49, 55; Jenkins, para. 204.

[14] *Per* Buckley L.J. in *Re Jermyn Street Turkish Baths Ltd.* [1971] 1 W.L.R. 1042, 1059. *Re Tivoli Freeholds Ltd.* [1972] V.R. 445; (1973) A.S.C.L. 610.

[15] [1971] 1 W.L.R. 1042, 1059.

[16] Snell, *Principles of Equity*, (28th ed. 1982) p. 538 where Lord Hardwicke's observations on this topic are set out.

[17] [1983] I.L.R.M. 323. See p. 89, *supra.*

[18] See n. 1, *supra.*

[19] See pp. 248 *et seq., supra.*

[20] See n. 11, *supra.*

[21] See Ussher, (1981) D.U.L.J. 79, 81.

oppression was seen by the leading English case of *Re Jermyn Street Turkish Baths Ltd.*[22] as involving the overbearing but lawful exercise of a dominant power in the company, such that the sufferer would be "constrained to submit" to it but for section 210.

Though unlawful conduct, whether in relation to the company or the individual members, may found jurisdiction under section 205, it is not a pre-condition. One of the primary functions of the section is to provide redress where no legal rights have actually been infringed, as witness *Re Clubman Shirts Ltd.*[23] The word "wrongful" in Lord Simonds' definition, *supra*, does not import the necessity of unlawfulness. Equally, not every unlawfulness will result in the section 205 remedy being available. A mere indolent neglect of statutory duties will not suffice to constitute oppression.[24] In *Re Clubman Shirts Ltd.*, O'Hanlon J. found that "as happens unfortunately, with many private companies where the entire shareholding is vested in a few people, a completely cavalier attitude [appeared] to have been adopted to the need to have proper accounts prepared annually and to have them duly audited and placed before the general meetings of the members." There had also been a failure to file annual returns. The petitioner asserted that these, and other alleged failures to comply with the Companies Acts, by depriving him of information to which he was statutorily entitled constituted oppression. O'Hanlon J. held that of themselves they did not:

> "These were examples of negligence, carelessness, irregularity in the conduct of the affairs of the company, but the evidence does not suggest that these defaults or any of them formed part of a deliberate scheme to deprive the Petitioner of his rights or to cause him loss or damage."[25]

The inference clearly is that neglect which is designed purposefully to harass or harm the petitioner may constitute oppressive conduct.

It is sometimes said that an isolated act cannot constitute oppression.[26] This statement has some small element of truth in it but must not be misunderstood. Its justification is the statute itself which requires that the complainant should show "that the affairs of the company *are being* conducted or that the powers of the directors

---

[22] See n. 15, *supra*.

[23] See n. 17, *supra*.

[24] But see the discussion of "disregard of interests" *infra*.

[25] [1983] I.L.R.M. 323, 327. *cf. Re Five Minute Car Wash Service Ltd.* [1966] 1 W.L.R. 745.

[26] *Re Westbourne Galleries Ltd.* [1970] 3 All E.R. 374, 385 *Re Greenore Trading Co. Ltd.*, High Court, Keane J., March 28, 1980, unreported, at p. 19 of the transcript.

of the company *are being* exercised" in an oppressive manner at the time when the complaint is made, *i.e.* at the date of presentation of the petition. These words imply a continuous course of conduct up to that date. It is however clear that a single, *unlawful* act which remains unredressed at that date can in Ireland satisfy the section. In *Re Westwinds Holding Co. Ltd.*,[27] Kenny J., in dealing with the first of several acts of unlawfulness perpetrated on the company, said:

> "On this ground alone the conditions of the exercise of the powers of the Court under section 205(3) have been fulfilled."

It would not seem necessary to find, as Keane J. did in *Re Greenore Trading Co. Ltd.*,[28] a multiplicity of unlawfulness in the same one act in order to raise it to the level of oppressive conduct. The learned judge did however hold that unlawful acts which remained unredressed at the date of the petition could constitute oppression operative at that date.[29] Where, however, the acts relied upon to constitute oppression are *not* of themselves unlawful, the English authorities[30] on section 210 state that these acts must be "operative" at the date when the petition is launched. If and insofar as such statements mean that the petitioner must still be suffering the consequences of the allegedly oppressive act when the petition is launched, that seems obvious and acceptable, for he has no continuing unredressed legal wrong to rely on. Reading more into these statements, and hence giving birth to the "isolated act" difficulty, appears to stem from something Roxburgh J. said in *Re H.R. Harmer Ltd.*[31]:

> "The section does not say 'who complains of acts of oppression'; it says 'that the affairs of the company are being conducted in a manner oppressive' . . . . In other words, I think it invites attention, not to events considered in isolation, but to events considered as part of a consecutive story; and it is because I take the view that I have not dealt (and do not propose to deal) with each of the items which I have enumerated one by one."

In other words, where the petitioner alleges that he has suffered from an oppressive course of conduct, he is relieved from establishing that each isolated act in a chain of events was itself oppressive.

---

[27] High Court, May 21, 1974, unreported, at p. 17 of the transcript.
[28] At p. 19 of the transcript.
[29] At p. 20 of the transcript.
[30] *Re Westbourne Galleries Ltd.* n. 26, *supra*; *Re Jermyn Street Turkish Baths Ltd.* [1971] 3 All E.R. 184, 198.
[31] Repeated by Jenkins L.J. at [1958] 3 All E.R. 689, 704–705 from the first instance transcript.

If this statement is the origin of the "isolated act" difficulty, as it appears to be, it has become somewhat perverted in the repetition, a clearly intended help to complainants being transformed into a hindrance. In Britain now the new form of section 210, contained in section 75 of the Companies Act 1980 [*U.K.*], affords relief whenever "the affairs of the company are being or *have been* conducted in a manner . . . unfairly prejudicial . . . " or whenever "any actual or proposed act or omission of the company is or would be so prejudicial." Some such clarificatory amendment would do no harm in Ireland.

Limb (ii) extends section 205 to oppressive exercises of the powers of the directors. Section 210 of the Companies Act 1948 [*U.K.*] was confined to oppressive conduct of the affairs of the company, and, consequently, statements from the English courts which define oppression in terms of the use of superior voting power in the general meeting, or the threat of it, must not be regarded in Ireland as exclusive formulations.[32] Oppressive exercises of the powers of the directors include not only those which may be voidable in law, and therefore independently remediable,[33] such as the misapplication of funds in *Re Greenore Trading Co. Ltd.*[34] or the sale of property in *Re Westwinds Holding Co. Ltd.*,[35] but also exercises of power by the directors which are not tainted with unlawfulness. Kenny J. in *Re Irish Visiting Motorists Bureau Ltd.*[36] was prepared to find that a resolution of the board of directors, whilst not being a voidable exercise of their powers, was nonetheless oppressive. He said:

> "the affairs of a company may be conducted or the powers of
> the directors may be exercised in a manner oppressive to any of
> the members although those in charge of the company are act-
> ing honestly and in good faith . . . . One of the most terrifying
> aspects of human history is that many of those whom we now
> regard as having been oppressors had a fanatical belief in the
> rightness of what they were doing. The question then when
> deciding whether the conduct of the affairs of a company or the
> passing of a resolution is oppressive is whether, judged by
> objective standards, it is."[37]

Mismanagement by the directors in the exercise of their powers of

---

[32] See in particular *Re Jermyn Street Turkish Baths Ltd.* [1971] 1 W.L.R. 1042, 1059.
[33] See p. 259, *supra*.
[34] See n. 11, *supra*.
[35] See n. 1, *supra*.
[36] See n. 8, *supra*.
[37] At p. 38 of the transcript. These observations apply likewise to limb (i). For voidable exercises of directors' powers see Chapter 7 at pp. 219 *et seq.*

running the business does not constitute oppressive conduct. Mac-William J. said in *McCormick* v. *Cameo Investments Ltd.*:

> "It is not oppression for the directors to make an unsatisfactory decision in the conduct of the business of a company."[38]

Similarly, it is not oppression for company directors to neglect technical statutory duties of the kind in issue in *Re Clubman Shirts Ltd.*, unless their doing so constituted part of a deliberate plan to harm the petitioner.[39] Incompetent management and neglect of statutory duties may possibly, however, constitute a disregard of interests under limbs (iii) and (iv), discussed below.

Limb (ii) applies in its terms only to collective exercises of power by the board of directors. It does not as such apply to individual wrongdoing by an individual director. In such case the oppression would be found, if at all, in the attempts by the controllers of the company to shield him from the consequences of his acts, whether by forebearing to sue or by purporting to absolve him by a resolution in general meeting. However, a managing director who under usual terms of appointment such as article 112 of Table A is entrusted with powers exercisable by the board of directors "either collaterally with or to the exclusion of their own powers," would appear to be within the ambit of section 205 in his exercise of them.[40] Conduct of an individual director, such as being a director of a competing company, which a complaining member might regard as reprehensible, but which does *not* of itself involve a breach of the director's duty to the company, does not appear of itself to be within the ambit of section 205.[41]

It is not really necessary to state that for there to be oppression the allegedly oppressed must have suffered directly or indirectly from the conduct of which complaint is made. Suppose that after a successful takeover bid the bidder company has acquired all the ordinary shares in a company, but, as is common, has not sought to

---

[38] High Court unreported, October 27, 1978, at p. 9 of the transcript. Admittedly, this was not a case on s.205, but see *Re Five Minute Car Wash Services Ltd.* [1966] 1 W.L.R. 745.

[39] See text at n. 25, *supra.*

[40] In *Re Westwinds Holding Co. Ltd.* n. 1, *supra*, the individual wrongdoer was vested by the company's articles with all the powers of the board and was there exercising the "powers of the directors," and he had overwhelming voting power in general meeting.

[41] See the discussion in Chapter 7 at pp. 218–219, *supra.* Keane J. in *Re Greenore Trading Co. Ltd.* n. 11, *supra*, at p. 11 of the transcript envisages that the activities of an individual director, conducted outside the framework of the company and having a detrimental effect on its trade, might be within s.205. The allegations were unsubstantiated, and the observations *obiter.*

acquire a class of non-voting, non-participating preference shares in it. The bidder company then proceeds to run down for its own benefit the business of its newly acquired subsidiary, usually, by diverting under one guise or another its assets to its new holding company in order to stimulate the cash flow of the latter. It is doubtful whether preference shareholders could complain that this was oppressive of them, provided that their fixed dividend and their fixed rights in a winding up were suitably safeguarded. If the bidder company had left some of the ordinary shares outstanding, their holders could of course allege oppression since they would have a direct interest in the profitability of the company, their entitlements not being fixed, and would probably succeed on the model of *Scottish Co-operative Wholesale Society Ltd.* v. *Meyer*[42] which concerned the deliberate running down of the business of a subsidiary. Curiously, the preference shareholders in such a case, though unable to allege oppression, could, it would seem, maintain a derivative action on the company's behalf in respect of any wrongs done to it, and could also, if matters had gone far enough, attempt to wind up the company on the just and equitable ground for loss of substratum.[43] Bringing such proceedings, or threatening to do so, could lead to a bid by the controllers for the preference shares, or to their redemption by the company at par (through the reduction of capital procedure given by section 72), which, in the case of low coupon preference shareholders "locked in" a company in this way, is usually what they most desire.

Limbs (iii) and (iv) of section 205 concern disregard of interests. Here, unlike limbs (i) and (ii), it is clear from the words of the section that members may complain only in their character as members. The relevant words, "in disregard of his or their interests as members," have achieved a perfection in ambiguity upon the question whether a member's "interest" or "interests" was intended. If the former, then there might be the suggestion that these limbs are to apply only to disregard of the member's rights in the strictly legal sense, since the "interest" of a member is an expression well established in company law to describe just that.[44] The restrictive consequences of such a construction can readily be appreciated. For example, a member has no right to have a dividend declared, but only a hope and expectation that the directors might do so if in their view there are sufficient profits.[45] "Interests," on the other hand,

---

[42] [1959] A.C. 324 (on appeal from Scotland).
[43] See pp. 139–142, *supra*.
[44] See pp. 161 *et seq.*, *supra*.
[45] See pp. 170, *et seq.*, *supra*.

does not have this connotation. It is unequivocally closer to the meaning of the word as used in such expressions as: "Will it be in A's interests to do this?" or, indeed, "Will it be in A's interest to do this?" since the singular is capable of bearing the broader meaning as well. These two questions are asking simply whether the proposed course of conduct is for A's *benefit*. It is submitted that this is the meaning intended in section 205. The related section 213(*g*) of the Companies Act 1963, which allows a company to be wound up on the grounds of oppression or disregard of interests despite the existence of an alternative remedy under section 205, refers in relation to the petitioning member to conduct "in disregard of his *interests* as a member," thus indicating the broader meaning. And Kenny J. in *P.M.P.A. Insurance Co. Ltd.* v. *New Ireland Assurance Co. Ltd.*,[46] a case in which a substantial minority shareholder in a public company sought unsuccessfully under section 205 to obtain current information on its business, said:

> "The interest of a member of a public company is first that the company should be carried on successfully, that the maximum of dividends should be paid consistent with commercial prudence, and that the assets should if possible be increased."

He thus favoured the broader meaning, though in the earlier case concerning the same petitioner, *Re Irish Visiting Motorists' Bureau Ltd.*[47] he had, in referring to the purpose of section 205, apparently preferred the narrower view. He had said:

> "This section, which had not been in any of the earlier Companies Acts, provides a remedy for a shareholder whose *rights* as a shareholder are affected by the way in which the affairs of the company are being conducted or in which the powers of the directors are being exercised. The shareholders' rights come from the Companies Act, the equitable principles which have become part of company law and the memorandum and articles of association viewed as a contract created by membership of the company. See s.25 sub-s.1 of the Act of 1963 . . ."[48]

Kenny J. consistently uses the singular "interest" in this context[49]; Keane J. prefers the plural.[50]

---

[46] *Irish Times*, October 23, 1975. No official record of the judgment survives.
[47] High Court, January 27, 1972, unreported.
[48] At p. 31 of the transcript. Italics supplied.
[49] See also *Re Westwinds Holding Co. Ltd.* n. 1, *supra* at pp. 17, 18 and 20 of the transcript.
[50] *Re Greenore Trading Co. Ltd.*, n. 11, *supra*, at p. 9 of the transcript.

Assuming that the statute intends the broader sense, what then constitutes a disregard of a member's interests? Save in one respect, it is doubtful whether limbs (iii) and (iv) add any remedy where none otherwise exists, whether under limbs (i) and (ii) or by the law outside section 205. In particular, one must doubt whether a decision properly taken by the board of directors or a resolution affecting the rights of members properly carried in a general meeting can either of them be categorised as made in disregard of the interests of members, since each of them as a condition of its propriety is required to be made bona fide for the benefit of the company.[51] "Company" in this context includes the general body of members or put more succinctly, the individual hypothetical member whose characteristics all members share. If these have not been ignored in the taking of a particular decision or the passing of a particular resolution, it becomes difficult for an individual member to say that his interests have been *disregarded*, another strong word, just because he would have preferred a different decision or resolution, or, indeed, none at all, which might have suited his own personal interests better. For example, if the directors decide one year honestly and for the benefit of the company to plough back its profits into the business rather than using them to pay a dividend to the members, an individual member in whose own personal interests it was to receive the cash, can scarcely allege that his interests have been disregarded since he, as with the other members, stands to benefit ultimately from the re-investment. Different considerations would apply to preference shareholders having no prospect of participating in capital growth; such conduct in relation to them could, in appropriate circumstances, constitute oppression,[52] as well as a disregard of interests.

We have seen that incompetent management of a company's business does not of itself constitute oppression. It lacks that overbearing quality[53] which is an ingredient central to oppressive conduct; manifest incompetence is by definition not purposeful or deliberate. It might, however, in a case of extreme recklessness where an uncaring attitude was displayed towards the consequences of business decisions taken amount to a disregard of the interests of members. The point is undecided. Such conduct would probably also be a breach of the duties of care and skill[54] owed by the directors to the

---

[51] See pp. 220, *et seq.*, *supra*, and pp. 274, *et seq.*, *infra*.

[52] See Jenkins Committee, para. 205, and p. 171, *supra*, in respect of profits being unduly devoted to directors' remuneration.

[53] *Re Five Minute Car Wash Service Ltd.* [1966] 1 W.L.R. 745.

[54] See pp. 233, *et seq.*, *supra*.

company, but such a breach would be absolvable by means of a resolution passed by the controllers in general meeting. Proceedings under section 205 might be used to sidestep that absolving resolution and, despite it, to seek compensation for the company, or, whether absolution had occurred or not, might be used to secure the dismissal of the incompetent board.

Section 205 as a whole possesses the great advantage over other proceedings of a flexibility of remedies. The court may under section 205(3), make any conceivable order affecting the participants in the company:

> "with a view to bringing to an end the matters complained of . . . , whether directing or prohibiting any act or cancelling or varying any transaction or for regulating the conduct of the company's affairs in future, or for the purchase of the shares of any member of the company by other members of the company or by the company . . . , or otherwise."

The remedy usually preferred by petitioners where relationships have broken down within the company is an order that their shares be purchased by the wrongdoers. They are valued as if the impugned transactions had not occurred.[55] The courts stipulate that a fair value should be fixed, either by the court after, if necessary, an inquiry in chambers, or by an independent valuer appointed by the court in default of agreement between the parties. In any event, the courts envisage a fair value as being market value, making in the case of a private company the assumption of marketability.[56] Thus Keane J. in *Re Greenore Trading Co. Ltd.*,[57] in determining the value of a minority holding distinguished it from a majority holding, a distinction which relates solely to market value. Some petitioners might prefer a "break-up" or "assets" valuation, that is to say what they would receive on a liquidation. It may therefore, as matters stand, be a wise precaution to include, in appropriate cases, an alternative plea for a winding up of the company on the just and equitable ground.

This common form of order that the majority buy out the minority leaves the wrongdoers in sole control of the field of battle. To a mem-

---

[55] *Re Westwinds Holding Co. Ltd.* n. 1, *supra*; *Re Greenore Trading Co. Ltd.* n. 11, *supra*. In *re Clubman Shirts Ltd.*, n. 17, *supra*, their value at the date of the proceedings was close to nil, the company's undertaking having been disposed of by the directors on terms which left the company without assets. The shares were ordered to be valued as at the date on which the directors ought to have consulted the petitioner before making this disposal.

[56] *Re Westwinds Holding Co. Ltd.* n. 1, *supra*, at p. 21 of the transcript.

[57] At pp. 21 *et seq.* of the transcript.

ber who ideally would have wished to remain involved in the company, this smacks of being forced into a position where he has no choice but to consent to be expropriated. In *Re Murph's Restaurants Ltd.*[58] therefore, Gannon J. declined to order that the excluded director's shares be purchased by those who had excluded him. Instead, he ordered that the company be wound up, with the idea that all should suffer alike in the collapse of the relationship between the participants in the enterprise. Taking the matter a step further, there is no reason in theory why an oppressed minority should not be allowed under section 205 to expropriate the oppressing majority, imposing on them usual covenants against competition in the sale agreement, since, after all, it is they, rather than those they oppressed, who have by their conduct forfeited their right to participate in the enterprise.[59] The possibility of such an outcome would certainly deter the majority from alleging, as they usually do in such proceedings, that the shares in the company have little value.

Section 205 is discretionary. Accordingly, where there is an independently remediable wrong, whether arising out of the breach of shareholders' individual or collective rights or out of wrongs done to the company in respect of which a derivative action lies, the claimants under section 205 would be well advised to join as alternative claims for relief the appropriate damages, restitution and declarations, suited to the circumstances. Their entitlement to these is independent of the discretion of the court.

Winding up on the just and equitable ground: general principles

This remedy, conferred by section 213(*f*) of the Companies Act 1963, likewise crops up throughout this work. It is proposed here to discuss some of the general principles applicable to it. Since the introduction of this remedy in the middle of the nineteenth century, there has been a battle between those who would formalise the jurisdiction into classes and categories, and those who would maintain the broad intent of the words "just and equitable." The three Irish decisions discussed here show that the Irish courts have chosen to maintain the more liberal interpretation.

Sir Ignatius O'Brien L.C., after an exhaustive review of the auth-

---

[58] See n. 7, *supra*.

[59] In *Re H.R. Harmer Ltd.* [1959] 1 W.L.R. 62, the oppressively octogenarian stamp dealer was, under s.210 [*U.K.*], compulsorily retired from the board, ordered not to interfere with the affairs of the company, and appointed a figurehead president for life, without powers, duties or rights.

orities, came to the conclusion in *Re Newbridge Sanitary Steam Laundry Ltd.*[60] that what is now section 213(*f*) of the Companies Act 1963, ought to be construed as allowing the winding up of the company "where, having regard to the established principles of courts of equity, justice and equity require a company to be wound up."[61] In making this statement, the Lord Chancellor was purposefully disassociating Irish law from a line of English authorities which had held that the "just and equitable" clause appearing in the section[62] then conferring jurisdiction on the court to wind up a company should be construed *eiusdem generis* with the preceding clauses of that section conferring jurisdiction in other circumstances; he was also stating furthermore that once that departure had been made the courts should not think of the "just and equitable" jurisdiction in terms of particular categories. Freely interpreting an *obiter* reference by Lord Cairns in an earlier case[63] to two of these, Sir Ignatius O'Brien L.C. said that he thought Lord Cairns

> "was clearly of opinion that a company might be wound up under this "just and equitable" clause, not only when it was a bubble company, or when the substratum of the company had disappeared, but also when the general principles on which Courts of equity act required it."[64]

Applying these broad principles in *Re Newbridge Sanitary Steam Laundry Ltd.*[65] itself, the court wound up a profitable company against the express wishes of the majority of shareholders. The managing director of the company had been ordered in previous proceedings[66] to account for money he had received on behalf of the company. He had nonetheless refused to do so, and had been supported in this refusal by a resolution of confidence in him passed by a majority in general meeting. The basis of the decision seems to have been that it would be intolerable to leave the petitioners locked into an enterprise of which the controllers had shown themselves to be incurably dishonest.[67] Nowadays, perhaps a more appropriate

---

[60] [1917] 1 I.R. 67.

[61] *Ibid.* at p. 90.

[62] Then s.129 of the Companies Act 1908 [*U.K.*].

[63] *Re Suburban Hotel Co.* [1867] 2 Ch. App. 737.

[64] For "loss of substratum," see pp. 139–142 *et seq.*, *supra*.

[65] [1917] 1 I.R. 67, 68.

[66] *Cockburn* v. *Newbridge Sanitary Steam Laundry Ltd.* [1915] 1 I.R. 237, discussed, *supra*, at pp. 246 *et seq.*, *supra*.

[67] It seems that the full story never came out in court, where it was suggested in exoneration of the managing director that the money had been disbursed by him in necessary bribes among the War Office personnel at the Curragh, not circumstances which it would have been prudent for him conclusively to prove.

remedy would have been found under section 205 which undoubtedly covers the facts of the case.

Had the persons who formed this laundry company been asked hypothetically on formation whether their company should be allowed to survive the state of affairs which ultimately developed, they would almost certainly have answered that it should not. Lord Wilberforce in *Ebrahimi* v. *Westbourne Galleries Ltd.*[68] has rationalised much of the courts' intervention on the "just and equitable" ground as being a response to violations within the company of understandings upon which it was formed or continued. Often that understanding reflects what would have been the position between the participants had they been associated in a partnership, instead of through the medium of a modern registered company, the authorities rationalised by him being often therefore called the partnership analogy cases. A vital point of the jurisdiction is that even, and, indeed usually, the *lawful* exercise by one or more participants of powers given to them by the company's constitution or by statute can constitute the violation of the understanding which leads to the equitable consequence of a winding up. In *Ebrahimi* itself, a director had been dismissed by the majority under the British equivalent of section 182 of the Companies Act 1963, but there had been an understanding between the participants on formation that each would participate in management, an understanding echoed in relation to true partners by section 24(5) of the Partnership Act 1890. Passages from the judgment of Lord Wilberforce were adopted by Gannon J. in *Re Murph's Restaurants Ltd.*,[69] a case in which the understanding had been violated by the exclusion of one of three directors, and, in particular the following key extract on the nature of the jurisdiction conferred by the words "just and equitable":

> "The words are a recognition of the fact that a limited company is more than a mere legal entity, with a personality in law of its own: that there is room in company law for recognition of the fact that behind it, or amongst it, there are individuals, with rights, expectations and obligations inter se which are not necessarily submerged in the company structure. That structure is defined by the Companies Act 1948 and by the articles of association by which shareholders agree to be bound. In most companies and in most contexts, this definition is sufficient and exhaustive, equally so whether the company is large or small. The 'just and equitable' provision does not, as the respondents

---

[68] [1973] A.C. 360.
[69] High Court, July 31, 1979, unreported; Ussher, (1979–80) D.U.L.J. 92. *Re Newbridge Sanitary Steam Laundry Ltd.* was not cited in the judgment.

suggest, entitle one party to disregard the obligation he assumes by entering a company, nor the court to dispense him from it. It does, as equity always does, enable the court to subject the exercise of legal rights to equitable considerations; considerations, that is, of a personal character arising between one individual and another, which may make it unjust, or inequitable, to insist on legal rights or to exercise them in a particular way."[70]

Most cases in which the jurisdiction is invoked will involve the breakdown of a personal relationship upon which the company was founded or continued. In some such cases, the relationship has deteriorated into deadlock. In *Re Irish Tourist Promotions Ltd.*,[71] Kenny J. wound up a company in which the two directors could not meet without the risk of unruly scenes, and the business of the company could not be conducted. In *Re Yenidje Tobacco Company Ltd.*[72]; the two participants in the company which was wound up were not only not on speaking terms but also not on hearing terms such that conversations between them could not take place unless an intermediary was also present. And in *Re A. & B.C. Chewing Gum Ltd.*,[73] the majority had refused to accord to the minority the right which they had under the articles to appoint a director, this refusal being based on a genuine but false belief that that right had been abrogated by mutual agreement. Even though the majority declared themselves willing to give effect to this right once it had been found by the court still to survive, the minority secured a winding up on the just and equitable ground because the dispute had caused the working relationship on the basis of which the company had been founded to be destroyed. Other examples of windings up on the just and equitable ground concern the failure or violation of understandings other than those arising out of the quality of the relationship between the participants envisaged on formation. For example, there are the loss of substratum cases, discussed elsewhere,[74] concerning understandings about the type of business to be engaged in by the company. In fact it is most important to heed the following words of Lord Wilberforce in relation to his own judgment. They were also adopted by Gannon J. in *Re Murph's Restaurants Ltd.*[75] They are:

---

[70] [1973] A.C. 360, 379, repeated in *Murph's* case at pp. 26, 27 of the transcript.
[71] High Court, April 22, 1974, unreported. No authorities were cited in the judgment.
[72] [1916] 2 Ch. 426.
[73] [1975] 1 W.L.R. 579.
[74] At pp. 139–142, *supra*.
[75] At p. 23 of the transcript.

"There has been a tendency to create categories or headings under which cases must be brought if the clause is to apply. This is wrong. Illustrations may be used, but general words should remain general and not be reduced to the sum of particular instances."[76]

Thus, even the principles constructed by Lord Wilberforce as justifying a "just and equitable" intervention should not be regarded as exclusive. The jurisdiction remains open to the extent pointed out above by Sir Ignatius O'Brien. The court may intervene whenever "the general principles on which Courts of equity act"[77] require it, however they may develop.

The petitioner must not have misbehaved in such a way as to justify the other parties to the understanding breaking it. As Lord Cross says in *Ebrahimi* v. *Westbourne Galleries Ltd.*[78]:

'A petitioner who relies on the 'just and equitable' clause must come to court with clean hands, and if the breakdown in confidence between him and the other parties to the dispute appears to have been due to his misconduct he cannot insist on the company being wound up if they wish it to continue."

It seems however that misconduct in relation to the company in which all participants acquiesce will not prevent the petitioner from obtaining his remedy. In *Re Murph's Restaurants Ltd.* the hands of each participant were far from clean. Each set of hands was regularly in the till taking the company's money. This siphoning off of the "slush money" as it was called,[79] whilst unrecorded as against the company, nonetheless proceeded on the basis of a strictly drawn equality between the participants, so much so that it contributed to the judge's finding that there was a "relationship of equality, mutu-

---

[76] [1973] A.C. 360, 374.

[77] See n. 64, *supra*. *O'Flanagan* v. *Ray-Ger Ltd.* (High Court, Costello J., April 28, 1983; unreported) may be an example of this approach. The principal defendant had been an equal "partner" in the company with the deceased. The plaintiffs (being the deceased's personal representative and widow) obtained orders (i) setting aside on the ground of undue influence exerted by the defendant over the deceased an agreement where by the latter had purported to acquire all the former's share capital; and (ii) declaring that the company held certain property on trust for the widow. Both claims had been strenuously resisted by the defendant. Costello J. indicated (at p. 40 of the transcript) that upon registration of the deceased's personal representative as a member he would, if he so petitioned, be entitled to a winding up order on the just and equitable ground, *Ebrahimi* v. *Westbourne Galleries Ltd.* being cited.

[78] [1973] A.C. 360.

[79] At p. 4 of the transcript.

ality, trust and confidence between the three of them which constituted the very essence of the existence of the company,"[80] the repu-
diation of which led to the winding up order.

It has long been established in the English jurisdiction that a
shareholder petitioning for the winding up of a company must show
that he has a "tangible interest" in the proceedings.[81] To establish a
tangible interest, the petitioning member will usually have to aver
that the winding up will yield a surplus of assets over liabilities, such
that he as member will receive something for his pains.[82] A member
of an unlimited company will always have a tangible interest in view
of his unlimited liability to contribute towards the satisfaction of its
debts; *semble*, so will a member of a limited company whose shares
are partly paid. This principle has operated in an unnecessarily
obstructive manner. In *Re Othery Construction Ltd.*,[83] a company had
been pursuing a course of dealing prejudicial to the creditors, but
since it was insolvent a member failed to bring its career to an end.
In *Re Chesterfield Catering Co. Ltd.*,[84] unopposed but unsuccessful petitioners to wind up a defunct company wished to have a liquidator
appointed so that he could deal with property of which it was technically the tenant of the petitioners. This restrictive principle has been
ignored in Ireland. In *Re Irish Tourist Promotions Ltd.*[85] a member succeeded in having a deadlocked company wound up on the just and
equitable ground, despite the fact that it was insolvent, and that the
majority of creditors were against a winding up. No authorities were
cited, but the case is consistent with section 216(1) which states that:

> "On hearing a winding up petition . . . the court shall not
> refuse to make a winding up order on the ground only that the
> assets of the company have been mortgaged to an amount equal
> to or in excess of those assets, or that the company has no
> assets."

The English authorities have expressly held that this provision first
introduced in 1908 was not intended to alter the tangible interest
rule in the case of a member's petition.[86]

---

[80] At p. 18 of the transcript.
[81] *Re Rica Gold Washing Co.* [1879] 11 Ch.D. 36.
[82] Unless he is unable to make that averment through the company's own default
in supplying accounts: *Re Newman and Howard Ltd.* [1961] W.L.R. 192.
[83] [1966] 1 W.L.R. 69.
[84] [1976] 3 W.L.R. 879.
[85] High Court, Kenny J, April 22, 1974, unreported, at p. 6 of the transcript.
[86] See *Re Chesterfield Catering Co. Ltd.* [1976] 3 W.L.R. 879. See also Jenkins Committee, para. 503 (*h*).

One should also note that Meredith M.R. in *Re Belfast Tailors' Co-partnership Ltd.*,[86a] admittedly not a member's petition, observed *obiter*:

> "I lay down no rule that meagreness of assets in itself justifies the Court in refusing an order. . . . An order for winding up may be made by the Court even if the company has no assets at all."

In the alteration of individual membership rights

We have seen that there has been an increasing tendency to categorise rights afforded by the memorandum and articles as individual membership rights.[87] It is not within the collective power to override them, but it is within the collective power to alter them. Section 15(1) of the Companies Act 1963 states:

> "(1) Subject to the provisions of this Act and to the conditions contained in its memorandum,[88] a company may by special resolution alter or add to its articles."

Membership rights given by the memorandum are likewise alterable by special resolution pursuant to section 28 of the Companies Act 1963 if, as is almost[89] invariably the case, they "could lawfully have been contained in articles of association instead of in the memorandum," *unless* they are "entrenched" by a declaration in the memorandum itself that they are to be unalterable, or are class rights, or are the subject of an express alteration procedure laid down in the memorandum itself. Class rights are often alterable but they are subject to separate considerations, and are therefore discussed separately. See *In the variation of class rights*, at pp. 278–283, *infra*. If the memorandum prescribes its own alteration process for individual membership rights, that must be followed to the exclusion of statute.

We are concerned for the moment only with alterations in individual membership rights sought to be brought about pursuant to a decision collectively taken in general meeting by special resolution.

Traditionally, by which is meant before the advent of section 205 of the Companies Act 1963, the standard of conduct required of the majority in the alteration of individual membership rights has been expressed in the bland formula that they must act bona fide for the

---

[86a] [1909] 1 I.R. 49, 54.

[87] See pp. 167 *et seq., supra*.

[88] For the general dominance of the memorandum, see pp. 60–61, *supra*.

[89] One exception is the right to restrain the company from acting beyond its objects which may be categorised as a membership right flowing exclusively from the memorandum, now given statutory recognition by s.8(2).

benefit of the company as a whole. An Irish expression of this principle is found in *Clark* v. *Workman*[90] where Ross J. says:

> "I refer . . . to the weighty observations of Lord Lindley when Master of the Rolls in *Allen* v. *Gold Reefs Co. of West Africa.*[91] Even statutory powers of altering articles of association by a special resolution must be exercised subject to those general principles of law and equity which are applicable to all powers enabling majorities to bind minorities. They 'must be exercised,' says the learned Master of the Rolls, 'not only in the manner required by law, but also bona fide for the benefit of the company as a whole, and must not be exceeded. These conditions are always implied, and are seldom if ever expressed.' These observations refer to the exercise of powers by shareholders."

This is not a principle that the minority should not suffer. They may, provided that the majority genuinely perceive it to be for the benefit of the company that they should. The test was elaborated in the leading English case of *Greenhalgh* v. *Arderne Cinemas Ltd.*[92] According to Evershed M.R., "the company as a whole" in this context does not mean the separate abstraction:

> "It means the corporators as a general body. That is to say, you take the case of an individual hypothetical member and ask whether what is proposed is, in the honest opinion of those who voted in its favour, for that person's benefit."[93]

Protestations of honesty and genuineness of purpose still have to be tested however, and, since motivation is extraordinarily difficult to pin down, Evershed M.R. preferred to reformulate the test

> "by looking at the converse and by saying that a special resolution of this kind would be liable to be impeached if the effect of it were to discriminate between the majority shareholders and the minority shareholders so as to give the former an advantage of which the latter were deprived."[94]

In essence therefore, the test resolves itself into providing an objective answer to a single question: was the proposal discriminatory? A benefit to the majority from the proposal is permissible insofar as it benefits them in their character as "individual hypothetical mem-

---

[90] [1920] 1 I.R. 107, 114.
[91] [1900] 1 Ch. 656, 671.
[92] [1951] Ch. 286.
[93] *Ibid.* p. 291. Evershed M.R. delivered the unanimous judgment of the Court.
[94] *Ibid.*

bers." The interests of "justice" do not have a separate role to play.[95]

The actual application of this test in the *Greenhalgh Case* itself must have been desolating. Mr. Greenhalgh had been fighting the controllers of the company for years, and in fact this was the seventh action over the company in ten years, and the fifth to go to the Court of Appeal. His opponents had decided to quit the field, and had wished to sell their shares to a third party, but a right of pre-emption in the articles[96] under which Mr. Greenhalgh was entitled to buy them stood in the way. The majority responded by altering the articles to excise the pre-emption right. The Court of Appeal held that this removal of the fetter on free alienation enured to the benefit of all members and was accordingly not discriminatory against Mr. Greenhalgh. His response is not recorded.

This traditional approach may well now have been modified where section 205 of the Companies Act 1963 is invoked by a minority shareholder. The general stance of section 205 is to look at the situation complained of squarely from the point of view of the suffering incurred by the minority shareholder, as opposed to treating that suffering as an unavoidable incident of a general benefit to the company. The minority shareholder will wish to found jurisdiction under that limb of section 205 which applies when "the affairs of the company are being conducted . . . in a manner oppressive to him or any of the members (including himself)." Insofar as he may also allege alternatively that the majority's conduct in altering his rights constitutes conduct "in disregard of his . . . interests" as member, he is unlikely to have added anything not already covered by the traditional test. "Disregard" is a strong word, and if the majority has had regard to the interests of the "individual hypothetical member," thereby satisfying the traditional test, they are likely also to have satisfied this limb of section 205, since the complainant can scarcely argue that his interests have been *disregarded* simply because some, but not all of them, have been taken into account. Authorities showing no discrimination under the traditional test may, it would seem, be used to refute a charge of disregard of interests. Support for the view that a complainant alleging *oppressive* conduct may well succeed

---

[95] *Sidebottom* v. *Kershaw, Leese & Co. Ltd.* [1920] 1 Ch. 154 (C.A.), disapproving in this respect of *Brown* v. *British Abrasive Wheel Co.* [1919] 1 Ch. 290. See also on the evolution of the test *Dafen Tinplate* v. *Llanelly Steel Co.* (1907) *Ltd.* [1920] 2 Ch. 124; *Shuttleworth* v. *Cox Bros. & Co. (Maidenhead) Ltd.* [1927] 2 K.B. 9. All save the last involved the insertion of articles entitling the shares of the minority to be expropriated. The Courts will enforce an expropriation clause, once it is safely in the articles, with equanimity (*e.g. Walsh* v. *Cassidy* (1951) Ir. Jur. Rep. 47.).

[96] For these, see pp. 178–179, *supra*.

where he might fail under the traditional test is gained from the supplementary judgement given by Kenny J. in *Lee & Co. (Dublin) Ltd. v. Egan (Wholesale) Ltd.*[97] In that case, specific performance was claimed against a defendant that he perform a contract to sell certain shares in a company to the plaintiffs, but there was a pre-emption clause in the company's articles under which the defendant was obliged to offer those shares to his fellow members first. Kenny J. declined to order the defendant to use his majority voting power in the company to alter its articles to excise this right of pre-emption on the ground that special resolution doing so "could be set aside by the other shareholders as being oppressive. It would be an abuse of his majority position."[98] Consequently, if the actual facts of the *Greenhalgh Case* were to come up for decision in Ireland, and if this aspect of section 205 were to be invoked, there are good grounds for thinking the decision would go the other way.

All the foregoing principles imposing standards of conduct on the majority in the alteration of alterable individual membership rights given by the constitutional documents apply also, one must suppose, to alterable statutory rights, in particular, to alterations of the right of pre-emption given to members by section 23 of the Companies (Amendment) Act 1983.[99] By section 24(1), (2) of that Act the company in general meeting has a power to suspend the pre-emption rights either generally for a limited period, or in respect of a specific allotment.

Where the individual membership rights are conferred by the memorandum of a company and are altered pursuant to section 28 of the Companies Act 1963, statute itself purports to regulate the right of dissent. Section 28(2) provides that if an application is made to the court for the alteration to be cancelled, it shall not have effect except insofar as it is confirmed by the court. Section 28(4) imposes the same limits on such an application as apply under Section 10 of the 1963 Act on an application under that section to defeat an alteration of objects, *i.e.* time limits and quantitative limits requiring a dissentient to be a holder of, or to have the support of the holders of, at least 15 per cent. of the company's nominal capital or of any class thereof. On a superficial view it might be inferred that the section seeks to debar any objector outside these limits from contesting the alteration in his rights.[1] Drawing such an inference would result in the unconstitutionality of this aspect of section 28, in that persons

---

[97] High Court, supplemental judgment delivered May 23, 1979, unreported.
[98] At p. 3 of the transcript.
[99] For this right, see pp. 184–185, 225–226, *supra*.
[1] *Cf.* s.5(9) of the Companies Act 1948 [*U.K.*].

wishing to vindicate their property rights would be denied access to the courts.[2] Accordingly, objectors who are out of time or who possess too few shares to avail of section 28 may nonetheless bring an action for a declaration on the traditional grounds, or a petition under section 205. The only differences between such proceedings and an application under section 28 is that under the latter the alteration will not have effect until confirmed by the court, whereas in the former cases an interim injunction to restrain its operation may be necessary and that section 28 has now been amended by the 1983 Act[3] to allow the court to order that the company's own money be used to buy out the shares of any dissentient applicants, and its capital reduced accordingly. If applicants under section 28 successfully overturn the alteration, the court may restrain the company from making it again without its leave.

Alterations in individual rights given by the memorandum or the articles may give the aggrieved party a justification for seeking the dissolution of the company on the just and equitable ground, if the altered provision was one on the basis of which the company was established, such as a provision entitling the aggrieved party to security of tenure as a director or to appoint a director.[4] In such circumstances, even if attempted alterations of the memorandum or of the articles ultimately prove unsuccessful, the resultant breakdown in trust and confidence may likewise lead to a winding up.[5]

In the variation of class rights

Shares are divided into different classes whenever there is any differentiation between the rights attached to them. An alteration of any of the rights of whatever nature attached to a class of shares is an alteration of class rights.

The alterability of class rights has been a confused topic for many years, and remains complex even after the clarificatory provisions introduced by section 38 of the Companies (Amendment) Act 1983. Before the 1983 Act, class rights contained in the *memorandum* were alterable only in accordance with provisions for their alteration expressly contained in or referred to in the memorandum itself, or by a scheme of arrangement under section 201 of the Companies Act

---

[2] *Constitution of Ireland*, Art. 40.3. See *O'Brien* v. *Keogh* [1972] I.R. 144, 155; *O'Brien* v. *Manufacturing Engineering Co. Ltd.* [1973] I.R. 334, 364.

[3] First Sched., paras. 2,4.

[4] *Cf. Ebrahimi* v. *Westbourne Galleries Ltd.* [1973] A.C. 360; *Re Murph's Restaurants Ltd.* (High Court, Gannon, J., unreported, July 31, 1979).

[5] *Re A. & B.C. Chewing Gum* [1975] 1 W.L.R. 579.

1963. The 1983 Act, following Jenkins Committee recommendations, adds two further methods of altering class rights contained in the memorandum: first by the agreement of all the members of the company[6]; and secondly, where the memorandum contains no procedure for alteration but the articles do and have done so since the company's incorporation, then the procedure in the articles may effectively be followed.[7] It has been clear since *Andrews* v. *Gas Meter Co.*[8] decided in 1897 that class rights contained in the *articles* are alterable by a special resolution pursuant to the statutory power of altering articles under what is now section 15 of the Companies Act 1963. Before this decision, uncertainties on the alterability of class rights contained in the articles had led to the insertion in articles of association of facultative provisions enabling alteration. These are called "variation of rights clauses." Despite *Andrews* v. *Gas Meter Co.*, these clauses continued to be drafted in a facultative form, even when they appeared in Table A. The present article 3 of Table A is an example. Most variation of rights clauses provided, as does article 3 of Table A, that:

> "The rights attached to any class may . . . be varied or abrogated with the consent in writing of the holders of three-fourths of the issued shares of that class, or with the sanction of a special resolution passed at a separate general meeting of the holders of the shares of the class . . . ."

Statute built upon the form of such clauses, by allowing a dissenting minority at the class meeting summoned to consent to the variation of rights to apply to the court to have the variation cancelled. The current Irish provision, section 78 of the Companies Act 1963, follows the British models of 1929 and 1948 with some Jenkins Committee modifications, and states that a dissentient minority of at least 10 per cent. of the class of shares affected by the variation may apply to the court where:

> "provision is made by the memorandum or articles for *authorising* the variation of the rights attached to any class of shares in the company, subject to the consent of any specified proportion of the holders of the issued shares of that class or the sanction of a resolution passed at a separate meeting of the holders of those

---

[6] s.38(5), 1983 Act. Jenkins Committee, para. 190.

[7] s.38(4), 1983 Act (other than an alteration of rights connected with a reduction of capital or an authority to issue shares under s.20, 1983 Act); s.38(4) introduces the Scottish authority of *Re Marshall Fleming & Co. Ltd.* (1938) S.C. 873 into Irish Law. See Jenkins Committee, para. 190.

[8] [1897] 1 Ch. 361 (English Court of Appeal).

shares, *and in pursuance of the said provision* the rights attached to any such class of shares are at any time varied."[9]

Section 78 was flawed by being restricted to cases where the class rights were varied "in pursuance of" the variation of rights clause. The majority could in reliance on *Andrews* v. *Gas Meter Co.* bypass both the clause and the statute by altering the articles first to excise the clause, and secondly to vary the class rights, at risk, of course, of an accusation that such proceedings should be set aside as discriminatory or oppressive, since the same standards of conduct apply to a majority seeking to alter class rights as apply to a majority seeking to alter individual membership rights. Whether section 78 and variation of rights clauses could be bypassed in this way was controversial; there were, in particular, two conflicting decisions on the equivalent Australian provisions.[10] But the point is now resolved by the 1983 Act on lines recommended by the Jenkins Committee.[11] Some Jenkins Committee recommendations, covering such matters as the percentage of shareholders necessary for an application and the time limits within which it should be brought, were in fact followed in the drafting of section 78 of the 1963 Act; it is a pity, and scarcely explicable, that the opportunity was not then taken to clear up this vital point.

Section 38 of the 1983 Act resolves this problem by providing in subsection (7) that any alteration of a variation of rights clause in the articles shall itself be treated as a variation of rights, with the result that the procedures laid down by that clause must be followed on that occasion, including, if the clause so stipulates (as it usually will), obtaining the consent of a specified proportion of the class.[12-14] Where the articles do not contain a variation of rights clause, section 38(2) implies one so that any alteration of the articles bringing about an alteration in class rights will only be effective if:–

"(*a*) The holders of three-quarters in nominal value of the issued shares of that class consent in writing to the variation; or
(*b*) a special resolution passed at a separate general meeting of the holders of that class sanctions the variation . . . ."

Section 78 of the 1963 Act applies to dissentients under this statutory procedure as it does to dissentients under express clauses.

[9] Italics supplied.
[10] *Crumpton* v. *Morrine Hall (Pty) Ltd.* [1965] N.S.W.R. 240; *Fisher* v. *Easthaven Ltd.* [1964] N.S.W.R. 261, each a decision of the New South Wales Supreme Court.
[11] Para. 192.
[12-14] s.38(4)(*b*) contains an independent provision stating that where there is a variation of rights clause in the articles rights attached otherwise than by the memorandum may be varied only in accordance with it.

Section 38 does not import the statutory safeguard of a separate class meeting in all cases. If a company has adopted an express provision in its constitutional documents authorising the variation of class rights, then the statutory safeguards are ousted, save in two instances. Section 38(3) states these as being variations "connected with" a reduction of the company's share capital,[15] or "connected with the giving, variation, revocation or renewal of an authority for the purposes of section 20" of the 1983 Act which concerns the authority of directors to allot shares.[16] With these two exceptions, a company may effectively remove the necessity for separate class meetings by inserting in its articles[17] a variation procedure which does not require them. This precaution should be taken before or at the same time as the shares are divided into separate classes, since by section 38(7) the insertion of such a clause in the articles where none existed before is in itself a variation of rights, attracting the statutory protections, as is the alteration of an existing clause, such as article 3 of Table A.[18]

The standard of conduct traditionally required of the majority in voting on a special resolution in general meeting to alter class rights is the same as in the alteration of individual membership rights, *i.e.* to vote bona fide for the benefit of the company as a whole, and the comments at pp. 274 *et seq., supra* on the utility of the test and its interrelationship with section 205 are likewise applicable in this context. More important in practice is the standard of conduct imposed on the majority in the class in voting to give the consent required by the statutory or express variation of rights clauses. According to Megarry J. in *Re Holders Investment Trust Ltd.*[19] they must honestly endeavour "to decide and act for the benefit of the class as a whole rather than with a view to the interests of some of the class and against that of others."[20] In that case, the overwhelming majority of preference shareholders who voted in the class meeting to consent to the proposed variation in their rights also held a substantial block of ordinary shares, and their correspondence with their advisers showed that they had been actuated in voting by a belief that the variation would benefit their ordinary shareholding, and accord-

---

[15] See pp. 283–288, 338–340, *infra.*

[16] Discussed at pp. 225–226, *supra.*

[17] Such a desire would not in practice arise where class rights are inserted in the *memorandum*, since doing so usually indicates a desire to protect them from alterability, or to allow it subject only to a stringent variation of rights clause.

[18] As amended in the case of new incorporations by para. 23(*a*), First Sched., 1983 Act.

[19] [1971] 1 W.L.R. 583.

[20] *Ibid.* p. 586.

ingly the consent of the class meeting was held to be invalid. Motivation, which is usually difficult to prove, was rendered comparatively easy in this case because the deliberations of the majority before voting had been recorded in writing. The requirement that preference shareholders voting in these class meetings should have regard to their sectional interests rather than those of the company as a whole seems legitimate as a purposive interpretation of variation of rights clauses in accordance with their function, namely the protection of the class.

Assuming a valid decision by the class meeting, a dissentient minority, if representing at least 10 per cent. of those who dissented, may apply to the court under section 78 of the Companies Act 1963 for an order that the variation be set aside as one which would "unfairly prejudice" them. The notion of unfair prejudice is obviously of wide import,[21] but, this said, it will be difficult for a minority to establish prejudice where a 75 per cent. majority of the class has bona fide and in the interests of the class voted in favour of the proposed variation. It may be that section 78, which was based on a British model going back to 1929, was enacted on the assumption that a vote of the kind disqualified in 1971 in *Re Holders Investment Trust Ltd.* was in fact valid. Section 78 may therefore have been overtaken by events.

Dissentients who represent less than 10 per cent. of their class or who are outside the time limits imposed by section 78 are nonetheless, it is submitted, free to attack the resolution under section 205. Holding otherwise would deprive them of their constitutional rights.[22] Proceedings to challenge the *validity* of a resolution of the class meeting, whether on the grounds that the correct standard of voting was not observed or otherwise, are not by definition within the ambit of section 78, and, accordingly, the time and quantitative limits imposed by that section have no application.

There remains the question of what constitutes a variation of rights anyway. Section 38(9) of the 1983 Act declares that a variation of rights includes their abrogation, but for the rest leaves untouched the disappointing jurisprudence which has grown up on this question. In *White* v. *Bristol Aeroplane Co. Ltd.*,[23] there was a variation of rights clause drafted in far wider terms than article 3 of Table A. The preference shareholders were to be entitled to give or to withhold their consent in a separate class meeting if "the rights or

---

[21] Indeed it has been adopted in Britain in s.75 of the Companies Act 1980 [*U.K.*] to replace the concept of "oppression" in the British equivalent of s.205.

[22] See text at n. 2, *supra.*

[23] [1953] Ch. 65 (English Court of Appeal); see also *Re John Smith's Tadcaster Brewery Co. Ltd.* [1953] 2 W.L.R. 516.

privileges" attached to those shares were proposed to be "*affected, modified, varied, dealt with, or abrogated in any manner.*"[24] Profits were to be capitalised by a bonus issue to ordinary shareholders. Some of the bonus shares to be issued to the ordinary shareholders were to rank as *preference* shares *pari passu* with an existing class of preference shares. The preference shareholders unsuccessfully contended that since this admixture of ordinary shareholders would dilute their existing voting power as a class, their rights had been "affected" and they were therefore entitled to vote upon the proposal at a separate class meeting. It was held that although the existing preference shareholders might lose power and influence when the proposal had been implemented, their rights as such would not be "affected," and would remain the same after as before implementation. A more extreme example of such reasoning is found in another case concerning the unfortunate Mr. Greenhalgh in his battle over Arderne cinemas,[25] *Greenhalgh* v. *Arderne Cinemas Ltd (No. 1)*.[26] Each share in that company carried one vote, but some were 10s. shares and some were 2s. shares. Pursuant to the power of subdivision equivalent to that contained in section 68 of the Companies Act 1963 (and in article 44 of Table A), the 10s. shares were subdivided into 2s. shares, effectively multiplying the number of votes per share by a factor of five. It was held that the rights attached to the existing 2s. shares had not been varied. Those rights remained as a matter of law as they always have been — a right to one vote per share. Such conduct would nowadays invite proceedings under section 205.

In the reduction of capital

Members have a right to be heard by the court in a reduction under section 72(2), although they are not specifically mentioned in the statutory machinery. Reductions of capital are described in Chapter 10 at pp. 338–340, *et seq.*

In dealing with the objections of members the court ostensibly asks itself whether the reduction is unfair or inequitable either as between different classes of shareholders or as between shareholders of the same class, being the test laid down by the House of Lords in *Poole* v. *National Bank of China Ltd*[27] and in *British and American Trustee and Finance Corporation Ltd.* v. *Couper*,[28] and accepted by the Supreme

---

[24] Emphasis supplied.
[25] See text at n. 92 *supra*.
[26] [1946] 1 All E.R. 512.
[27] [1907] A.C. 229.
[28] [1894] A.C. 399.

Court in Ireland in *Re John Power & Son Ltd.*[29] In practice, fairness and equity in this context are held to be satisfied where each member within a class is treated alike, and the reduction itself is not contrary to the rights[29a] and expectations of the class itself. Subject to these considerations, majority rule as expressed in the special resolution will carry the day.

There are few reported instances of attempts to reduce share capital unequally within a class. One such occurred in *Re Robert Stephen Holdings Ltd.*[30] where only some of the ordinary shareholders were being paid off, but since no member appeared before the court to object, the judge allowed the reduction, with some misgivings.

The different treatment of different classes of shareholders frequently occurs, and is a fertile source of litigation. Such proposals usually involve the payment off of preference shareholders and the cancellation of their shares, and usually the ordinary shareholders stand to benefit from the departure of their fellow members. Sometimes the advantage to ordinary shareholders lies in the fact that the company will be able after the reduction to resume dividend payments to them without the profits being skimmed off by the preference shareholders[31] or the ordinary shareholders might be tempted to get rid of income participating preference shares having rights equal to or greater than theirs to dividends and bonus issues.[32]

What then are the reductions in capital which treat preference shares differently, and yet accord with their class rights and the expectations of their holders, thereby earning the stamp of judicial approval? The mere fact of reduction is not of itself, without more, contrary to class expectations. The reports abound with statements such as that of Asquith L.J. in *Re Chatterley-Whitfield Collieries Ltd.*,[33] dealing with the reasonable expectations of a preference shareholder:

> "He must be taken to know of section 55 of the Companies Act 1929 [i.e. in Ireland, section 72 of the 1963 Act]. He must be taken, in my view to know more, namely, that a prudent company will cut the millstone of onerous prior charges or senior

---

[29] [1934] I.R. 412, 425.

[29a] Chiefly rights in a winding up. For them see Chapter 6 at pp. 174 *et seq.*

[30] [1968] 1 W.L.R. 522.

[31] As in *Re John Power & Son Ltd.*, n. 29, *supra.*

[32] For income participating preference shares, see p. 173, *supra.* and *Re Saltdean Estate Co. Ltd.* [1968] 1 W.L.R. 1844. Articles generally give rights to bonus shares in accordance with dividend rights: arts. 130, 130A (added by para. 23(*f*), First Sched., 1983 Act) of Table A.

[33] [1948] 2 All E.R. 593, 601, later affirmed by the House of Lords at [1949] 1 All E.R. 1094.

stocks from its neck as soon as money becomes cheaper or the company finds itself in possession of a surplus of cash not needed to carry on its business. This risk is the price the preference shareholder pays for solid advantages, namely, for what is in the present case a high, as well as a well-secured, rate of fixed dividend and a first charge on the assets in a liquidation . . . "

Buckley J. put the same matter in more lawyer-like terms in *Re Salt-dean Estate Co. Ltd.*[34]:

> "It is part of the bargain between the shareholders and forms an integral part of the definition or delimitation of the bundle of rights which make up a preferred share."

This said, a reduction in accordance with class rights and expectation boils down to one made in the right order, in the right manner, and for the right amount. The right order includes giving the same priorities in a reduction as would pertain in a winding up. Thus, if losses are being written off by the cancellation of capital and preference shareholders have priority in the return of capital in a winding up, those losses must be borne by the ordinary shares, as witness *Re John Power & Son Ltd.* in which it was stated that "as a matter of right between the preference and ordinary shares . . . the loss of capital should be borne by the ordinary shares."[35] If the reduction involves a repayment of capital and the preference shareholders have priority in a winding up, then that priority may be used as a justification for bidding them farewell earlier on a reduction.[36] The right manner means payment in a form to which the preference shareholders would have been entitled in a winding up, usually cash, and not some species of deferred obligation, such as a debenture redeemable at a later date.[37] The right amount is satisfied by paying what the preference shareholders would have been entitled to in a winding up, usually, by common terms of issue,[38] simply a return of the nominal capital paid up on the shares, though it should be noted that some publicly quoted companies have adopted terms

---

[34] [1968] 1 W.L.R. 1844.

[35] [1934] I.R. 412, 431; *Re Fowlers Vacola Manufacturing Co. Ltd.* [1966] V.R. 97.

[36] *e.g. Re Chatterley—Whitfield Collieries* [1948] 2 All E.R. 593, 596; *Re Saltdean Estate Co. Ltd.* [1968] 1 W.L.R. 1844.

[37] *Re Holders Investment Trust Ltd.* [1971] 1 W.L.R. 583; *Re John Power & Son Ltd.* [1934] I.R. 412, in which, to allow repayment in a form other than cash, a scheme of arrangement under the contemporary equivalent of s.201 was first entered into abrogating the rights of the preference shareholders contained in the memorandum. See pp. 289–297, *infra.*

[38] See pp. 174 *et seq., supra.*

of issue of preference shares which require greater amounts to be paid in a winding up or on an earlier reduction, by reference to their quoted market price.[39] Since, in recent years, low coupon stocks have invariably stood at discounts in the market, these formulae have not often been operative. Where preference shares are entitled, in addition to priority in the return of nominal capital, to participate in the distribution of surplus assets in a winding up[40] and the articles do *not* allow those profits to be diverted away from them by way of dividends or a bonus issue exclusively in favour of the ordinary shareholders, then it would seem that an amount reflecting a reasonable estimate of the value of that right should be included in the repayment, if it is to remain in accordance with class rights and expectations. An *obiter* statement by Lord Simonds in *Scottish Insurance Corporation Ltd.* v. *Wilsons & Clyde Coal Co. Ltd.*[41] to the effect that the preference shareholders' right to participate in the surplus might be disregarded in quantifying their entitlement on a reduction must not be severed from what prompted him to make it, namely that in that company the surplus could be channelled into the pockets of the ordinary shareholders to the exclusion of the preference shareholders by a dividend or a bonus issue, such that they had no reasonable expectation of participating in it to be confounded.

The application of these principles in practice, although decried by some as involving over reliance on "a desolating logic,"[42] would seem to be fair in most cases. The sense of injustice engendered by some of them arises more from the idiosyncratic terms upon which the preference shares were issued. *Re Saltdean Estate Co. Ltd.*[43] is an extreme example. There, by curious draftsmanship, each £1 income-participating preference shareholder had been receiving on average £1 per annum per share by way of dividend, but on a winding up would be entitled to the return of nominal capital only, namely £1 per share. Their reduction by being paid off at a gratuitous premium of 50 pence per share was acknowledged to be disappointing, but not held to be unfair.

Let us suppose that the reduction is not in accordance with class rights in the sense described above. The consequence, according to *Re Holders Investment Trust Ltd.*,[44] is to reverse the burden of proof,

---

[39] *e.g.* the Spens formula.

[40] See pp. 174 *et seq., supra*.

[41] [1949] A.C. 462, 485 *et seq*.

[42] Lord Cooper in *Scottish Insurance Corporation Ltd.* v. *Wilsons & Clyde Coal Co. Ltd.*, 1948 S.C. 360, 376, echoing Lord Dunedin in *Balmenach—Glenlivet Distillery Co. Ltd.* v. *Croall* (1906) 8 F. 1135, 1142.

[43] [1968] 1 W.L.R. 1844.

[44] [1971] 1 W.L.R. 583.

thereby putting the onus of proving fairness on the proponents of the scheme. In that case, where it was proposed to repay the preference shareholders with an unsecured loan stock worth less on the market than the cash to which they were entitled, the burden was not discharged.

Controllers of companies wishing to push through a reduction of preference share capital contrary to the rights of that class will usually therefore wish to alter those class rights before the reduction so that they accord with the scheme. This is no longer practicably possible if any serious degree of opposition is anticipated from within the class. By section 38(2), (3) of the Companies (Amendment) act 1983 an alteration of alterable class rights "connected with the reduction of the company's share capital" requires in all cases, and whatever the company's constitutional documents may say to the contrary, the separate consent of the class concerned; and, as we have seen, the courts insist that members of the class in giving that consent should vote bona fide in the interests of the class itself. These questions and the alterability generally of class rights are discussed *In the variation of class rights, supra.*[45]

Also difficult to shift, may be equitable considerations which may have arisen between the class of preference shareholders and the company in relation to the proposed reduction, such that the court would find it inequitable to confirm the reduction even if it accorded with class rights, unless the equity was in some way satisfied. There is an example in *Re Old Silkstone Collieries*.[46] There, preference shareholders had consented to an earlier partial reduction in capital on the assurance of the company that they would continue to have the benefit of a somewhat doubtful statutory right given to them as long as they remained members of the company by the Coal Industry Nationalisation Act 1946 [*U.K.*]. Under the proposed further reduction, they would cease to be members of the company, and therefore no longer have the opportunity of claiming under this statutory right. The English Court of Appeal refused to confirm the reduction on the ground, *inter alia*, that the company should not be allowed to go back on its word. This decision is but one thread in a broad band of equitable principle which states that understandings arrived at and acted upon should, if violated, be visited with some appropriate equitable response.[47] The prime current example in company law is

---

[45] At pp. 278 *et seq.*

[46] [1954] 2 W.L.R. 77.

[47] A useful starting point for an investigation into the myriad of cases from which this principle can be extracted is *Crabb* v. *Arun D.C.* [1975] 3 W.L.R. 847 (English C.A.).

Ebrahimi v. *Westbourne Galleries Ltd.*,[48] the broad principles of which
were carried into Irish law in *Re Murph's Restaurants Ltd.*[49]

In reconstructions by voluntary liquidation

Section 260 of the Companies Act 1963 authorises the liquidator
of a company which is being or about to be wound up voluntarily by
the members[50] ("the transferor company") to sell with the sanction
of a special resolution all or any part of its assets to another company
("the transferee company") in exchange for shares in the transferee
company. These shares are then distributed to the members of the
transferor company as part of their entitlement in its winding up. By
this means, an amalgamation of the two companies may be
achieved. Under a common variant, a new company is formed to act
as transferee company and to issue its shares to the liquidators of the
two existing companies. Upon their dissolution, the new company
often changes its name to that of one of them.[51]

Reconstructions under section 260 do not require the intervention
of the court. Dissentient members are protected by giving them
rights which may in practice amount to a veto on the whole scheme.
By section 260(3) the holder of any shares in the transferor company
in respect of which "the voting rights . . . were not cast in favour of
the special resolution . . . may require the liquidator either to
abstain from carrying the resolution into effect or to purchase that
part of his interest which those shares represent at a price to be
determined by agreement or arbitration . . . ." There is no way
round this right of dissent. The company cannot in any way abro-
gate it by inserting provisions to the contrary in its articles or its
memorandum: to do so would be repugnant to statute.[52] If faced
with a sufficient volume of dissent, the liquidator may well be forced
to abandon the scheme, since in order to finance the purchase of the
dissentients' shares, he may have to market the shares in the transferee company which they would have received, and this may prove

---

[48] [1973] A.C. 360.
[49] Gannon J., High court, unreported, July 31, 1979; (1979–80) D.U.L.J. 92.
[50] Section 260 may also be used in a creditors' voluntary winding up, but only with
the consent of the court or the committee of inspection: s.271. Apart from some minor
improvements in draftmanship, s.260 is identical to s.287 of the Companies Act 1948
[U.K.]. In addition to the standard works, readers are referred to Weinberg and
Blank, *Takeovers and Mergers*, (4th ed. 1979). For voluntary liquidations generally, see
Chapter 16: *Liquidations*.
[51] Under s.23 by special resolution and with the consent of the Minister.
[52] *Bisgood* v. *Henderson's Transvaal Estates Ltd.* [1908] 1 Ch. 743.

not to be practicable. Therefore, if much dissent is anticipated, the controllers of the company may be better advised to initiate a scheme for the amalgamation of the companies under sections 201–203 of the Companies Act 1963, but, as we shall see, the court may in fact be reluctant to sanction a scheme under sections 201–203 which could have been accomplished under section 260 without giving its opponents the same rights of dissent as they would have had under the latter section.[53]

If within 12 months of the passing of the special resolution, the company is ordered to be compulsorily wound up by the court, then by section 260(5) the special resolution, and therefore the reconstruction, will have effect only if sanctioned by the court. This year of uncertainty is imposed primarily for the protection of creditors so that they may, if they feel that their prospects of being paid are being jeopardised by the disappearance of the company's assets in exchange for the mere paper of the transferee company, bring the reconstruction to a halt until they are satisfied that proper provision had been made for them. Members also may technically present a petition for compulsory winding up with the object of stopping the reconstruction, or controlling one being unfairly or oppressively administered.[54]

In schemes of arrangement

Section 201 of the Companies Act 1963 provides a means whereby a dissenting minority of creditors or members may with the sanction of the court be bound to a scheme which varies their rights. The forerunner[55] of this section was concerned only with compromises and arrangements arrived at between a company and its creditors. Even now, the section has an important function in allowing a company to get rid of its debts, or to defer them, and continue trading. For example, it has been used for schemes under which creditors have given up their securities and accepted instead fully paid shares in the company,[56] or have given up their priority under an existing debenture in favour of a fresh charge on the company's assets,[57] or

---

[53] See the discussion at pp. 000–000, *infra* of *Re Anglo-Continental Supply Co. Ltd.* [1922] Ch. 723.

[54] *Re Consolidated South Rand Mines Deep* [1909] 1 Ch. 491.

[55] For the history of its predecessors, see *Re Savoy Hotel Ltd.* [1981] 3 W.L.R. 441, 446–448.

[56] *Re Empire Mining Co.* (1890) 44 Ch.D. 402.

[57] *Re Dominion of Canada Freehold Estate and Timber Co.* (1886) 55 L.T. 347.

have had the immediate enforcement of their rights against the company deferred pending an advantageous development and realisation of the company's assets which would not have been possible in a liquidation.[57a]

But we are primarily concerned here with its application to members. It may be used to vary even those class rights which have been "entrenched" in the company's memorandum of association, that is to say class rights set out in and conferred by a memorandum which contains no express procedure for altering them.[58] In the absence of the consent of *all* the members of the company, a relaxation introduced by section 38(5) of the Companies (Amendment) Act 1983,[58a] they may be altered only by a scheme of arrangement under section 201. The section may also be used for reconstructions and amalgamations.[59] These may be very sophisticated, but the rudiments of most involve either an amalgamation by a share for share exchange or an amalgamation by the acquisition of assets. Under a share for share exchange, the company applying for the scheme of arrangement (S.co.[60]) becomes the wholly owned subsidiary of another company (H.co.[60]). All shares in S.co. other than those already held by H.co. are cancelled; shares in H.co. are issued to the shareholders in S.co. by way of compensation for their cancelled shares; and new shares in S.co. are allotted to H.co. in lieu of those cancelled.[61] An amalgamation under section 201 by acquisition of assets usually involves H.co. acquiring not merely the assets of S.co. but also its liabilities, in fact its whole undertaking. Ancillary powers are given to the court by section 203 to effect the transfer of liabilities as well as assets. The bare bones of this type of scheme involve the transfer of all assets and liabilities of S.co. to H.co. by a vesting order made under section 203; the allotment[62] of shares in H.co. to the shareholders of S.co. in compensation for the fact that S.co. has been

---

[57a] *Re Pye* (*Ireland*) *Ltd.* (Supreme Court, April 17, 1985; unreported).

[58] s.28(3) and see pp. 59–60, *supra*.

[58a] Or by a variation of rights clause present in the *articles* from first formation and purporting to allow variations of rights contained in the memorandum: s.38(4)(*a*), 1983 Act.

[59] See, in addition to the standard works, Weinberg and Blank, *Takeovers and Mergers* (4th ed., 1979) on the comparable British legislation.

[60] Being the terminology adopted in Weinberg and Blank, *op. cit.*

[61] The independent valuation provisions introduced for plc's by the 1983 Act will generally not apply to this allotment: *ibid.* s.30(2), (3); and see Chapter 10 at pp. 309 *et seq.* But the Third and Sixth EEC Companies Directive will, when implemented, introduce independent assessment requirements in respect of schemes between plc's: 78/855/EEC, art. 10 and 82/891/EEC, art. 8.

[62] Likewise exempt from independent valuation: *ibid.* s.30(4).

stripped of all its net assets; and the dissolution by the court under section 203 of S.co. which, since it has been left without assets or liabilities, is dispensed from the necessity of going through a winding up. Proceedings under sections 201–203 possess two solid advantages over an acquisition by H.co. in exchange for its shares of S.co.'s undertaking without statutory help: the new block of shares issued by H.co. is from H.co's point of view gratifyingly dispersed among S.co's members instead of being concentrated in the hands of S.co., perhaps even to the extent of making S.co. H.co.'s holding company, and secondly, S.co.'s liabilities are satisfactorily shifted to H.co. In the absence of a statutory scheme of arrangement, they would have been left untidily with S.co., subject to an indemnity by H.co.

These then are typical "arrangements" entered into under sections 201–203. The word "arrangement" in section 201 "has for many years been treated as being one of very wide import,"[63] not limited to the notion of a "compromise" which also founds jurisdiction under section 201 and involves the prerequisite of a dispute. However, since the jurisdiction arises "where a compromise or arrangement is proposed *between* a company and its creditors or any class of them or *between* the company and its members or any class or them,"[64] something must be required of the company if the scheme is to qualify as an "arrangement" within the meaning of the section. This may be something very slight, such as an undertaking to register share transfers to give effect to a scheme.[65] Where the company contributes nothing to the scheme, it does not qualify as an "arrangement"; there must be some element of give and take on all sides.[66]

The company itself must consent to the scheme independently of the section. There is no provision of dispensing with the company's consent, and the lack of it would disqualify the scheme from being an arrangement *between* the company and the other parties to it.[67] Thus the consent of the company must be manifested by a resolution of the board of directors, and, if the scheme involves more than merely an adjustment of rights, further internal procedures will be required, such as in a share for share exchange, a special resolution

---

[63] *Re Savoy Hotel Ltd.* [1981] 3 W.L.R. 441, 448; *Re Calgary and Edmonton Land Co. Ltd.* [1975] 1 W.L.R. 355.

[64] s.201(1): italics supplied.

[65] *Re Savoy Hotel Ltd.* [1981] 3 W.L.R. 441, 445 *et seq.*

[66] *Re NFU Development Trust Ltd.* [1973] 1 All E.R. 135 where a proposal that members should give up all rights and cease to be members did not qualify as an "arrangement."

[67] *Re Savoy Hotel Ltd.* n. 65, *supra.*

for the reduction of capital integral to the scheme. It follows that sections 201–203 are totally unsuited to proposed amalgamations opposed by the controllers of S.co.[68] In fact, for all schemes of arrangement the affected company is usually the applicant.

The company sets about binding those whose rights are to be affected by the proposed scheme by asking the court to direct that meetings of them be held so that they may vote on the proposals. By section 201(3) dissentients will be bound if a majority in number representing three-fourths in value of those present and voting either in person or by proxy vote in favour, and if the court later sanctions the scheme. The company must be careful about the composition of the meetings which it causes to be summoned. Obviously, all whose rights are to be affected by the proposed scheme must be given the opportunity of voting at a meeting, but each meeting must be composed in such a way that it consists only of:

> "those persons whose rights are not so dissimilar as to make it impossible for them to consult together with a view to their common interest . . . ."

This is a much quoted quotation from the judgment of Bowen L.J. in *Sovereign Life Assurance* v. *Dodd*,[69] a case involving a scheme of arrangement between a life assurance company and its creditors, but some had matured rights under their policies, and some had not. The failure to hold separate meetings between these two classes within the class of creditors resulted in the court's refusal to sanction the scheme on the ground that the meetings required by statute had not in fact been held. Some divisions into classes are obvious. Secured and unsecured creditors should not be asked to vote together; nor should preference and ordinary shareholders. Others are not so obvious. In *Re Hellenic & General Trust Ltd.*[70] one ordinary shareholder was held to have interests sufficiently different from the other ordinary shareholders as not to be in the same class as them. The scheme proposed in that case involved the cancellation of all existing ordinary shares in the company, the allotment of a like amount of new shares to a bank, and payment of compensation by the bank to the former ordinary shareholders. It so happened that over half of these ordinary shares belonged to a wholly-owned subsidiary of the bank, which naturally voted in favour of the scheme.

---

[68] That situation is met by the takeover bid: see pp. 297–301, *post*.
[69] [1892] 2 Q.B. 573, 583.
[70] [1976] 1 W.L.R. 123.

Templeman J., in holding that this shareholder did not have a sufficient community of interest to form a class with the others, said:

"Vendors consulting together with a view to their common interest in an offer made by a purchaser would look askance at the presence among them of a wholly owned subsidiary of the purchaser . . . . It is incongruous that the loudest voice in theory and the most significant vote in practice should come from the wholly owned subsidiary of the purchaser."[71]

The same principle received a passing glance in the Supreme Court decision of *Re John Power & Son Ltd.* where the preference shareholders' rights were being affected by a scheme which it was to the advantage of the ordinary shareholders that they should accept. FitzGibbon J. observed that

"it has been stated without challenge or contradiction that the required majority of preference shareholders was obtained without reckoning the votes of any preference shareholders who were also holders of ordinary shares."[72]

By confining class meetings to those with a common interest, less pressure is put on the principle that those voting in the class meeting must vote bona fide the interests of the class as a whole, which applies in this context, as we shall see, as much as it does in the different context of class meetings called to consider a variation of class rights to be effected outside the scheme of arrangement procedure.[73] In that context, it is not possible to exclude those lacking a common interest with the rest of the class because those meetings concern classes of *shares*, a classification determined by their terms of issue; whereas schemes of arrangement are concerned with classes of *members*, and, of course, creditors if their rights are affected, classifications determined by a community of interest. The common interest between persons affected in a similar way by a scheme is not destroyed just because there are relevant distinctions between them. In *Re Pye (Ireland) Ltd.*,[74] an unsecured creditor voting for a scheme to defer payment of a company's debts happened also to hold 25 per cent. of the shares in the company. This creditor had an extra inter-

---

[71] *Ibid.* at p. 126.
[72] [1934] I.R. 412, 429.
[73] See pp. 281–282, *supra.*
[74] Supreme Court, April 17, 1985; unreported, reversing High Court, Costello J., March 11, 1985; unreported.

est in voting for the scheme because the breathing space being
allowed to the company advantageously to develop its assets could,
if successful, enure to the benefit of members as well as creditors.
Nonetheless, the Supreme Court held that the inclusion of this creditor in the same class meeting as the other unsecured creditors did
not render it improperly constituted, in the absence of proof that
these others had been prejudiced by the inclusion. Assumedly, the
decision would have gone the other way upon proof that the creditor's interests as member were such as to predominate.[74a] Earlier in
the same litigation, Costello J. at first instance[74b] said that the Collector-General was not to be regarded in respect of Revenue debts[74c]
due

> "as just another creditor similar to other creditors; he is
> charged with the collection of monies due to the State. . . . [If]
> the Collector-General has decided that this scheme is not in the
> public interest, I should be very slow indeed to order these
> meetings given the opposition of the Collector-General. . . . He
> has the duty of deciding how the Public Interest is best served
> and he has considered the public interest and has decided that
> the Public Interest would not be served by postponing the
> State's debt. I must therefore refuse this application. . . . "

The learned judge may be interpreted as saying that the Collector-
General was in effect in a class of his own for the purposes of assenting to the scheme. Fortunately, this notion has been firmly rejected
by the Supreme Court, Henchy J. saying of the Collector-General:

> "He has very fairly stated that he does not wish to be treated as
> a separate category of unsecured creditor. He is an ordinary
> unsecured creditor and indeed if he were to be so treated as a
> separate class of unsecured creditor on his own, no scheme
> might even succeed."[74d]

Of course as a trustee for the public he would have to make up his
mind on the scheme accordingly. One may deduce that the holding

---

[74a] There is no official transcript of the judgments which were delivered *ex tempore*.
The statements in the text are an attempt to extract a coherent *ratio* from an unofficial
transcript taken by one of the parties.

[74b] High Court November 12, 1984; unreported.

[74c] Not being preferential debts under s.285. See Chapter 16, at pp. 501 *et seq.*

[74d] April 17, 1985, according to an unofficial transcript in the possession of the
author. See also the Supreme Court's order of November 22, 1984.

in a fiduciary capacity if rights to be affected by a scheme is not a relevant criterion for determining the composition of classes.

We now turn to consider the factors which influence the court in granting or withholding its sanction to a scheme of arrangement. The tests laid down by Lindley L.J. in *Re Alabama, New Orleans, Texas and Pacific Junction Railway Co.*[75] were adopted in Ireland in the Supreme Court decision of *Re John Power & Son Ltd.*.[76] First, the court must be satisfied that the provisions of the statute have been observed. Here the court will concern itself with such matters as the convening and composition of class meetings; and, there is also the matter of circulars. Section 202 of the Companies Act 1963 requires notices convening the necessary meetings to be accompanied by a statement explaining the effect of the scheme of arrangement, and, in particular stating any material interests of the directors, and the extent, if any to which they as members, creditors, or otherwise, are being treated differently by the scheme from other persons with like interests. These provisions will be amplified for plc's after the implementation of the Third and Sixth EEC Companies Directives. In particular, the draft scheme together with the directors' explanations of it and an independent assessment of it by experts must be available to members for inspection at the plc's registered office a month before the relevant meeting.[76a] If the circulars do not comply with section 202, or are otherwise so misleading as to have caused meetings to have voted under a material misapprehension the scheme will not be sanctioned.[77] Secondly, those voting at the meetings must vote bona fide in the interests of the class, or as Lindley L.J. put it in the *Alabama case*:

> "The Court must look at the scheme, and see whether . . . the majority are acting *bona fide*, and whether they are coercing the minority in order to promote interests adverse to those of the class they purport to represent."[78]

As we have seen, adverse interests of this kind are to be weeded out in the composition of the class itself. Before *Re Pye (Ireland) Ltd., supra*, one might have said that any which survived that process were unlikely to be detectable, and that this second requirement was

---

[75] [1891] 1 Ch. 213.

[76] [1934] I.R. 412, 424.

[76a] See 78/855/EEC, arts. 5, 9, 10, 11, and 82/891/EEC, arts. 3, 7, 8, 9.

[77] *Ibid.* pp. 427–8, 433. *Re National Bank Ltd.* [1966] 1 W.L.R. 819. See also *Jackson v. Munster Bank Ltd.* (1884–5) 13 L.R., Ir. 118.

[78] *Ibid.* p. 424.

becoming otiose. Thirdly, there is an objective test, summarised by Murnaghan J. in *Re John Power & Son Ltd.*:

> "In my opinion the Court under this section can give all due weight to the opinion of the majority of the shareholders but the Court is in no way bound merely to register the opinion of this majority. The sanction to be given by the Court must be a real sanction, and to my mind the meaning of the section clearly is that no majority under the section can carry an arrangement which a fair and impartial mind would not sanction."[79]

English courts have adopted further tests which the Irish courts are free to find unwarranted. Each involves a cross-fertilisation from other statutory provisions. Thus, in *Re Anglo-Continental Supply Co. Ltd.*[80] Astbury J. felt able to state that a scheme of arrangement under the equivalent of section 201 which could have been carried out as a reconstruction under the equivalent of section 260[81] should incorporate the same safeguards for dissentients as exist under the latter section, and that even where section 260 was not available but the proposed scheme under section 201 was of similar effect, the court might in its discretion still insist on the section 260 safeguards being given. Further, in *Re Hellenic & General Trust Ltd.*[82] the court's sanction under the equivalent of section 201 was refused on the grounds, *inter alia*, that the same scheme could have been brought under the equivalent of section 204,[83] and could in that event have been successfully blocked by the dissentient under that machinery in that section. Judicial opinion in England is by no means unanimously behind these developments. Plowman J. in *Re National Bank Ltd.*[84] declined to accede to such an argument in relation to a scheme which could have been carried out under the equivalent of section 204. To do so would:

> "involve imposing a limitation or qualification either on the generality of the word "arrangement" in [the equivalent of sec-

---

[79] *Ibid.* p. 432. For the adoption by Fitzgibbon J. of remarks by Lindley L.J. to similar effect, see *ibid.* 424. *Re Dorman, Long & Co. Ltd.* [1934] Ch. 635 is similar. See also *Carruth* v. *Imperial Chemical Industries Ltd.* [1937] 2 All E.R. 422.

[80] [1922] 2 Ch. 723.

[81] See pp. 288–289, *supra*.

[82] [1976] 1 W.L.R. 123.

[83] Concerning compulsory acquisition of outstanding shares following a partially successful takeover bid: see below.

[84] [1966] 1 W.L.R. 819 concerning banks operating in Ireland.

tion 201] or else on the discretion of the court under that section. The legislature has not seen fit to impose any such limitation in terms and I see no reason for implying any."[85]

The Irish courts may well be of a similar view, if the occasion arises to express it.

In relation to the compulsory acquisition powers after a take-over bid

Under section 204 of the Companies Act 1963 a company (here called "the bidder company") which has made a partially successful bid for the shares of another company (called here "the offeree company") is given the power compulsorily to acquire the shares of those shareholders in the offeree company who did not accept the offer.[86] The power is carefully circumscribed by the section, but in some respects, as we shall see, not as carefully as one might wish.

There are three statutory pre-requisites to the power arising. Firstly, the section, unlike the equivalent section 209 of the Companies Act 1948 [*U.K.*], does not apply to partial bids; the offer must relate either to *all* the shares in the offeree company other than those already in the beneficial ownership of the bidder company or any of its subsidiaries or to all the shares in a particular class other than those already beneficially owned as aforesaid.[87] These are the "shares affected" by a bid within the section.[88] Secondly, the bidder company must have received 80 per cent. acceptances in respect of the "shares affected." Thirdly, there is a condition imposed by section 204(2) in those cases in which at the date of the offer the bidder company and its subsidiaries are already the beneficial owners of 20 per cent. of all the shares in the company, or of 20 per cent. of any class of them if only that class is the subject of the bid. In these circumstances, the assenting shareholders should hold not only 80 per

---

[85] *Ibid.* p. 829.
[86] See in addition to the standard works, Weinberg and Blank, *Takeovers and Mergers* (4th ed., 1979) for the comparable s.209 of the Companies Act 1948 [*U.K.*] from which it should be noted that the Irish section differs in some material respects. It is sometimes suggested that this compulsory acquisition power is unconstitutional as not being necessitated by the "common good" in Article 43 of the Constitution. Against this it may be said that a share consists of a bundle of statutory and other rights and duties (see Chapter 6) of which this statutory duty to sell is but one, and that therefore this susceptibility to compulsory purchase is an integral part of the nature of a share. See also s.205(3).
[87] s.204(1), (11).
[88] s.204(3), (8).

cent. of the shares affected but should comprise also at least 75 per cent. of the holders of them.[89]

Provided that these statutory conditions are satisfied and the bidder company follows the correct procedures laid down in section 204, the only thing standing between the dissenting shareholder and compulsory acquisition of his shares is the discretion of the court to which he may apply for relief. In dealing with these applications the courts reflect the attitude of the section itself which is, put bluntly, that 80 per cent. of the offerees cannot be wrong, or, put another way, the resisting minority are merely being difficult. That rationale is destroyed if some part of the assenting 80 per cent. is not genuinely independent of the bidder company. In such a case it is irrelevant and of little consolation to an expropriated minority who wished to continue as members that the price paid to them was fair. The Jenkins Committee recommended[90] that the equivalent British section be amended in effect to exclude from the "shares affected" any shares held by a company *in the same group* as the bidder company. Although section 204 is influenced by the Jenkins Committee in some other respects, this recommendation was not adopted. For example, though shares held by a subsidiary of the bidder company are excluded from "the shares affected," shares held by its holding company are not; nor are the shares held by a fellow subsidiary. It is possible by an astute choice of bidder company to ensure not only that the additional hurdle erected by section 204(2) is avoided but that a large proportion of the acceptances will come from a majority shareholder closely connected with the controllers of the bidder company. Fortunately, the courts have shown themselves prepared in the exercise of their statutory discretion to look through the separate legal personalities of assenting shareholders and to equate them, where necessary, with the bidder company, certainly in extreme cases. As we have seen, in *Re Bugle Press Ltd.*[91] a bidder company was formed by the controlling shareholders of the offeree company in order to expropriate a 10 per cent. minority shareholder. The statute was satisfied in that 90 per cent acceptances came from the controlling shareholders themselves, but the court in its discretion declined to allow the compulsory acquisition of the remaining 10 per cent. Lord Evershed M.R. saying that the equivalent British section:

"is directed to a case where there is a scheme or contract for the

---

[89] The Jenkins Committee, para. 288 recommended the repeal of the equivalent British provision.

[90] Paras. 291, 294(1)(*v*).

[91] [1961] Ch. 270.

acquisition of a company, its amalgamation, re-organisation or the like, and where the offeror is independent of the shareholders in the transferor company or at least independent of that part or fraction of them from which the ninety per cent.[92] is to be derived. Even, therefore, though the present case falls strictly within the terms of s.209,[93] the fact that the offeror, the transferee company, is for all practical purposes entirely equivalent to the nine-tenths of the shareholders who have accepted the offer, makes it in my judgment a case in which, for the purpose of exercising the court's discretion, the circumstances are special . . . ."[94]

In *Esso Standard (Inter-America) Inc.* v. *J.W. Enterprises*[95] the holding company of the bidder company held 96 per cent. of the shares in the offeree company and, unsurprisingly accepted its bid with alacrity. The Supreme Court of Canada disregarded this acceptance as not being independent of the bidder, and disallowed the compulsory acquisition of the minority. Effectively, the courts in these cases are subtracting the non-independent acceptances from "the shares affected." Doing so is consistent with the reasoning employed by the courts when deciding the composition of class meetings under section 201—only those with common interests should vote together. But this analogy must not be regarded as secure, and it is open to an Irish court to depart from it, since requiring separate class meetings under section 201 is merely applying the statute, whereas it might be argued that the legislature in section 204 had defined what categories of acceptances should be considered independent, and that it is not the function of the judiciary to diminish them.

If no question of the independence of the acceptances arises, the attitude of the courts to dissentients is akin to that of the Beadle to Oliver Twist. There is no question of asking for more if the offer price reflects their present value, and the fact that this might involve a dissenting shareholder parting with them at a loss is immaterial: *McCormick* v. *Cameo Investments Ltd.*[96] In this case, as in others like it, the court showed itself to be strongly influenced by the fact that a large majority of the holders of the shares affected were not disposed to quarrel with the terms of the offer, McWilliam J. saying:

---

[92] 90 per cent. is the level of acceptances required under the British equivalent s.209 of the Companies Act 1948 [*U.K.*].

[93] See n. 86, *supra*.

[94] At p. 286.

[95] (1963) 37 D.L.R. 2 (*d*) 598.

[96] High Court, McWilliam J., unreported October 27, 1978, at pp. 9–10 of the transcript. See also *Re Grierson, Oldham and Adams Ltd.* [1968] Ch. 17.

"Here there were several active and fairly substantial shareholders well informed in business matters who have accepted
the scheme, to whose views I should pay the greatest attention."[97]

In fact, the onus firmly placed on the dissentients[98] of proving
unfairness is extremely difficult to discharge. A slight lightening of
the burden is however afforded by the same judge in *Securities Trust
Ltd.* v. *Associated Properties Ltd.*[99] where he said:

"I do not know what is the reason for the provisions of section
204 of the 1963 Act or why it should be thought desirable that
minority shareholders may be compulsorily bought out, but I
am of opinion that, on a compulsory purchase of this nature the
people whose shares are being compulsorily purchased are
entitled to be given full particulars of the transaction, its purpose, the method of carrying it out and its consequences . . . .
The shareholders are entitled to be given reasonably full particulars by their directors about the matters I have just mentioned."

The English cases impose no duty upon the directors of the offeree
company to make such disclosure as may be necessary to help an
offeree in making up his mind.[1] In *Re Evertite Lock Nuts (1938) Ltd.*[2]
the compulsory acquisition was upheld of the shares of an offeree
who had wished to obtain but had been denied information about
the value and prospects of a subsidiary of the offeree company before
deciding whether to accept the offer. MacWilliam J.'s assertion may
be the beginning of a reversal of this attitude. As far as takeovers of
public companies, whether quoted on the Stock Exchange (Irish) or
on the Unlisted Securities Market, are concerned, the *City Code on
Take-overs and Mergers* already provides extra-legally for a high level
of disclosure.

Section 204(4) of the Companies Act 1963 gives shareholders in
the offeree company the right to be bought out by the bidder company where it has acquired *some* shares in the offeree company as a

---

[97] *Ibid.* pp. 8–9 of the transcript. See also *Re Hoare & Co. Ltd.* (1934) 150 L.T. 374,
Re Grierson, Oldham & Adams Ltd., n. 95, *supra* each of which were cited in the judgment.

[98] *Ibid.* pp. 6–7, citing the authorities in n. 97.

[99] High Court, McWilliam J., November 19, 1980, unreported, at pp. 9–10 of the
transcript.

[1] *Cf. Gething* v. *Kilner* [1972] 1 All E.R. 1166 in which a duty on the part of the
directors of the offeree company to make disclosure to their members was not
acknowledged. They must be honest and not actively mislead but that involves no
more than the usual duty in tort (deceit).

[2] [1945] Ch. 220.

consequence of a "scheme, contract or offer" *within* the section, and following such acquisition the totality of its holding amounts to 80 per cent. of all shares in the offeree company (or of a class of them, if the bid related only to a class.[3]) Since section 204 does not apply to partial bids,[4] this right to be bought out serves no greater purpose than that of giving dissenting shareholders a second bite at the cherry,[5] and the possibility of securing a better price than that obtained by their fellows. The original offer price prevails unless a different price is agreed by the parties, or the court on the application of either of them fixed a different price. Because of this possibility, a bidder company, intent on buying cheaply or not at all, may make the original offer conditional on acceptance by the holders of a specified proportion of the shares affected, or the right to be bought out may be avoided by an astute choice of bidder company. For example, shares in the beneficial ownership of the bidder company's holding company are not aggregated with those of the bidder company in determining whether it has the beneficial ownership of 80 per cent.[6]

In the alteration of objects

See Chapter 4 at pp. 137–142, *et seq.*

---

[3] s.204(11).
[4] s.204(1).
[5] After they have been warned by the bidder company by a notice pursuant to s.204(4)(a) that they are in a 20 per cent. minority or less within the company.
[6] See Jenkins Committee, paras. 291, 294(1)(xi).

Chapter 10: Capital and its Maintenance

We have seen how the anomalous full liability of the members of a modern registered company for its debts was reduced to a limited liability to contribute to its assets.[1] Nowadays, this limitation of liability is brought about by several interrelated statutory provisions. In the case of a company limited by shares,[2] these provide that the memorandum of a company must "state the amount of share capital with which the company proposes to be registered, and the division thereof into shares of a fixed amount"[3]; that a company may have "the liability of its members limited by the memorandum to the amount, if any, unpaid on the shares respectively held by them"[4]; and that in the case of the winding up "of a company limited by shares, no contribution shall be required from any member exceeding the amount, if any, unpaid on the shares in respect of which he is liable."[5] A corner stone of this statutory structure is found in section 27 of the Companies Act 1963. This declares that the individual member shall not be bound by any alteration in the memorandum or articles to which he has not actually agreed in writing:

> "if and so far as the alteration requires him to take or subscribe for more shares than the number held by him at the date on which the alteration is made, or in any way increases his liability as at that date to contribute to the share capital of, or otherwise to pay money to, the company."

To judges brought up on partnerships and their derivatives, such as the old deed of settlement companies, where each participant was

---

[1] See Chapter 2 at pp. 18, *et seq.*
[2] For companies limited by guarantee, see Chapter 1 at pp. 7–9, *et seq.*
[3] s.6(4)(a).
[4] s.5(2)(a).
[5] s.207(1)(d).

fully liable for the debts of the enterprise, the notion of limited liability must have been disturbing, even distasteful. They conceived of the money which the members had subscribed, or agreed to subscribe, as being in a sense "a creditors' fund" to take the place, albeit inadequately, of the former full liability of the members. Accordingly, they interpreted the Companies Acts to devise several rules known collectively as the capital maintenance rules, designed to protect this "fund" from the depredations of the members. It is, of course, inaccurate to talk of a "creditors' fund" as if the money was in some way set aside for them. Money derived from the issued shares is employed in the business as much as money derived from other sources. As Fitzgibbon L.J. observed in *Dale* v. *Martin*,[6] "payments out of capital in discharge of lawful obligations do not 'reduce the capital'." The capital maintenance rules did not seek to create a static fund, but rather to impose constraints upon what might otherwise have been the company's liberty to make payments to its members whether by dividend, purchase of their shares, or otherwise, or to release them from their obligation to contribute to its assets. The judicial capital maintenance rules have now been superseded by express statutory provisions, for the most part declaratory of the pre-existing law which may therefore be resorted to as an aid to interpretation. In some respects, however, statute now reverses the line of judicial development, particularly in the law relating to the distributability of profits (or, in other words, dividends) which, as we will see, had in the hands of the judges almost lost sight of the capital maintenance idea. Statute has also amplified the judicial rules.

Before discussing the individual capital maintenance rules, it is as well to explore the extent to which the law requires a company to have capital at all. To the extent that it does not, the capital maintenance rules become mere window dressing. By capital in this context is meant assets acquired by a company in exchange for the issue of its shares. This, the *issued* share capital, must be distinguished from the *authorised* share capital. The latter is purely potential, and, indeed the compulsory statement[7] of authorised capital in a company's memorandum such as that in Table B which says that "the share capital of the company is £200,000 divided into 200,000 shares of £1 each" may actually mislead the unwary. This statement means only that the company may issue shares up to that amount and not that it has done so; if it wishes to issue more, it will have to increase its authorised capital by passing an ordinary resolution under section 68 of the Companies Act 1963 (and article 44 of Table A). To

---

[6] (1883–84) 11 L.R., Ir. 371, 376.
[7] s.6(4)(*a*).

find out how much share capital a company has actually issued, one can consult its last annual return filed in the Companies Registry.[8] Issued capital must also be distinguished from other sources of finance. Statistics have shown that on average only one-fifth of the activities of Irish private companies are financed by issued share capital, most of the balance being provided more or less equally by trade creditors, reserves (or, in other words, profits from previous activities ploughed back into the business), and loans.[9] In fact, in many private companies the position is more extreme. All that the law requires by way of risk capital is that the two initial subscribers take one share each,[10] and the denomination of these may be as low as one penny each, though £1 is more commonly chosen. Such enterprises are often launched on loans. These may be loans from the company's promoters incurred perhaps in the purchase from them of assets, such as an existing business. If those promoters truly wish to emulate Mr. Salomon,[11] they will cause their loan to the company to be secured by a debenture on its assets so that if the enterprise founders they themselves may be able to salvage something something from the wreck to the detriment of later, unsecured creditors. Or the loans may come from outside sources, such as a bank, in which case the promoters will usually be required personally to guarantee the repayment.

Although there is a widely held feeling that an entrepreneur trading through the medium of a limited liability company should not be able to put the public (*i.e.* its creditors and their creditors and so on) at risk without first having risked his own capital, it appears still to be government policy in both Britain and Ireland that the prospect of limited liability acts as a spur to economic activity, even though the evidence seems to be that most businesses in fact start off in an unincorporated form. Another argument put forward in favour of a requirement that each company should on formation have a minimum paid-up capital is that under-capitalised businesses tend to go under, that loan capital with its servicing burdens of interest and repayments may often hasten the process, whereas share capital upon which no dividend need be paid[12] and which generally may

---

[8] s.125; para. 3, Fifth Sched. For the annual return, see pp. 444 *et seq., post.*

[9] Regrettably, somewhat elderly statistics: *Company Taxation in Ireland*, 1972, Prl. 2628, at p. 52; the information is as at 1967. State grants on average provided 1.2%, though in the case of an individual company in receipt of a grant this proportion will be much higher.

[10] s.6(4)(*b*).

[11] *Salomon* v. *Salomon & Co.* [1897] A.C. 22. See pp. 21–22, *ante.*

[12] See pp. 170 *et seq., ante.*

not be returned to the investor whilst the company remains a going concern, is in a sense free money.[13]

Before the passing of the Companies Act 1983, the closest statute got to requiring a minimum capital was "the minimum subscription" requirement imposed by section 53 of the Companies Act 1963. This provides that when a public company has invited the public to subscribe for its shares, it may not proceed to allot shares to the applicants unless the public response has produced enough money to cover, *inter alia*, the price of property to be purchased out of the proceeds of the issue, preliminary expenses, commissions and working capital.[14] The section is commonly bypassed in practice by having the issue underwritten, so that no minimum subscription is required since the funds will in any event be produced.

The Companies Act 1983 introduces for the first time a general minimum share capital requirement, but only for public limited companies. This requirement, introduced to comply with article 6 of the EEC Second Directive on company law reform,[15] prescribes for the moment a minimum of £IR 30,000.[16] Not all of this has to be paid up on issue: the payment of only a quarter of the nominal value and the whole of any premium[17] suffices to qualify the company to commence business as a newly formed public limited company,[18] or to be converted from a private into a public limited company.[19] A contravention does not avoid the allotment but the allottee is immediately liable to pay up the share to the required extent.[20] Any share taken by a subscriber to the memorandum of a public limited company in pursuance of an undertaking of his *in the memorandum* and any premium on the shares must be paid up *in cash*.[21] This requirement is of only slight importance, contravention being visited by a default fine only,[22] since it will in practice relate only to the seven shares required to be subscribed *on formation* of a public limited company[23]: the allotment of the authorised minimum of £IR30,000 may,

---

[13] For a general discussion of these and related issues, see Kahn-Freund, "Some Reflections on Company Law Reform," (1944) 7 M.L.R. 54.

[14] For full details, see para. 4 of the Third Sched. s.53 is now amplified for plc's by s.22 of the 1983 Act.

[15] 77/91/EEC; December 13, 1976.

[16] s.19 of the 1983 Act.

[17] A premium is that part of the issue price in excess of the nominal value. For premiums generally, see pp. 324 *et seq.* Nominal value is described below.

[18] s.28(1) and s.6(3)(*b*) of the 1983 Act.

[19] *Ibid.* s.10(1)(*b*).

[20] 1983 Act, s.28(2).

[21] *Ibid.* s.35.

[22] *Ibid.* s.36(1).

[23] *Ibid.* ss.5(1), 6(4)(*b*), (*c*).

and in practice, will occur after formation and before the commencement of business,[24] and may therefore be allotted for a non-cash consideration, a topic discussed below. Existing public companies which opted for public limited status were given a transitional period of three years to conform to these capital requirements.[25]

Payment for shares: prohibition on issues at a discount

We have seen that the share capital of a company must be divided into shares of a *fixed* amount.[26] This is known as the *nominal* or *par* value of a share. This indicates that the company has received or is entitled to receive at least that amount in respect of each share, but is not an indication of the amount for which a share may be sold in the open market (market value) or the amount which the shareholder may receive on the company going into liquidation (assets value), each of which may be more or less depending on the fortunes of the company. The fact that a £1 share may after its issue be worth more or less than £1 has led to recommendations that companies should be permitted to issue shares of "no-par value" in order "to remove a suggestion of value which is untrue and unreal,"[27] a somewhat patronising recommendation since it is difficult to believe that investors putting their minds to the distinctions involved, could fail to grasp them. Furthermore, dividends are often declared as a percentage of the nominal value of a share, and in a winding up it is often important to distinguish between a right to the return of capital, or, in other words a repayment of the nominal value, and a right to participate in the surplus generally.[28]

Shares may not be issued at a discount, *i.e.* the company in exchange for the allotment must receive at least the nominal value or a promise to pay it. This is one of the judicial rules of capital maintenance which has now been embodied in statute in the form of a simple prohibition made in section 27 (1) of the Companies Act 1983. The rationale of the prohibition is stated by Lord MacNaghten in the leading case of *Ooregum Gold Mining Co. of India Ltd.* v. *Roper*[29] as being that the investor may "purchase immunity from liability beyond a certain limit on terms that there shall be and

---

[24] *Ibid.* s.6.
[25] *Ibid.* s.2(1): s.12(8), (9).
[26] s.6(4)(a).
[27] Report of the Committee on Shares of No-Par Value (Gedge) 1954, Cmnd 9112 [*U.K.*].
[28] See pp. 174 *et seq., ante.*
[29] [1892] A.C. 92, citing the then current Buckley on the Companies Acts.

remain a liability up to that limit." The liability "up to that limit" is generally viewed with extraordinary strictness. For example, in *Re Munster Bank (Dillon's Claim)*[30] a bank manager had as a matter of convenience become registered as holder of partly paid shares in the bank charged to the bank by a borrower by way of security for an advance. He was held personally liable for the calls[31] on the shares. In the case of shares issued at a discount however, there has always been some mitigation in favour of the holder of shares who became a member without being aware that the shares had originally been issued otherwise than as fully paid. Thus a person becoming a member on the faith of a share certificate issued by the company stating the shares to be fully paid, could allege that the company was thereby estopped from claiming the unpaid balance.[32] Such an estoppel by share certificate was always a doubtful doctrine since it was not clear that the company had a capacity to be estopped. Now however section 27 of the Companies Act 1983 sets out to regulate the whole matter. The primary liability rests on the allottee who by section 27(2) "shall be liable to pay to the company an amount equal to the amount of the discount,"[33] and as a spur to prompt payment is liable also to pay "interest thereon at the appropriate rate," currently only five per cent. per annum.[34] Subsequent purchasers for value of the shares who did not have actual notice of the discount or who derive title from such a purchaser are exonerated from liability to pay up the discount,[35] but all other holders including "any person who has an unconditional right to be included in the company's register of members in respect of those shares or to have an instrument of transfer of the shares executed in his favour" become jointly and severally liable with the transferee.[36] The court has power under section 34(5) of the Companies Act 1983 to adjust the contributions between themselves of those persons jointly liable for the payment to the company, having regard to their "respective culpability." There is nothing in the Companies Act 1983 to relieve persons liable for the payment of discounts simply on the ground

---

[30] (1886–87) 17 L.R., Ir. 341.

[31] *i.e.* the lawful request made by directors whilst the company is a going concern (art. 15 of Table A) or the liquidator during a winding up that unpaid balances due on shares be paid.

[32] *e.g. Burkinshaw* v. *Nicholls* (1878) 3 App. Cas. 1004.

[33] Thus putting paid to the idea invoked by Porter M.R. in *Re Leinster Contract Corporation* [1902] 1 I.R. 349 that an allotment at a discount might for that reason be voidable or rescindable, an approach which ignored the prejudice to creditors. See *Tennent* v. *City of Glasgow Bank* (1879) 4 App.Cas. 615.

[34] 1983 Act, s.2(1), (7).

[35] *Ibid.* ss.27(3), 26(4).

[36] *Ibid.* ss.27(3), 26(4), (6).

that the company is in liquidation and its creditors will be satisfied without the payment. In this respect the pre-1983 position is preserved.[37] Also, assumedly if the company fails to obtain payment of the discount from any of the persons statutorily liable, it may still turn as a last resort to the directors responsible for the issue, and secure satisfaction from them.[38] The difficulties which a company may suffer under the prohibition against the issue of shares at a discount are illustrated by the *Ooregum Case* itself. The company had suffered reverses, and its £1 shares stood at only 12-and-a-half pence in the market. It needed fresh capital to continue, and created a new class of £1 preference shares and allotted them at a discount of 75 pence each, leaving the allottee with only 25 pence to pay. It is doubtful whether the company would have got fresh subscriptions on any other basis. The subscribers were held liable for the full amount. The prohibition on the issue of shares at a discount renders it impossible in practice for a company to raise fresh money by an issue of shares ranking equally with existing shares standing at a discount in the market. There was formerly a procedure under section 63 of the Companies Act 1963, now repealed,[39] under which discounts in such circumstances were permitted with the sanction of the court. Now a company wishing to pursue such a course must first apply to the court for a reduction of capital under procedure afforded by sections 72(2) *et seq.* of the Companies Act 1963 to bring the nominal value of the existing share capital into line with its market value. This procedure is discussed at pp. 338 *et seq.*

Hidden discounts

Companies frequently issue shares not for cash, but for money's worth. This is permissible, but there is a danger that the consideration given by the allottee may be so inadequate as to result in the shares being issued at a hidden discount. The Companies Act 1983[40] now requires an independent valuation of the non-cash consideration given in exchange for an allotment of the shares of a public limited company, of which more below. The extent to which the consideration given for the allotment of shares in *private* companies is subjected to scrutiny prima facie remains unchanged. Here the courts have had the attitude that they will not question the valuation put by the directors on the consideration unless there is on the face

[37] *Re Newtownards Gas Co.* (1885–86) 15 L.R., Ir. 51; *Welton* v. *Saffery* [1897} A.C. 299.

[38] *Hirsche* v. *Sims* [1894] A.C. 654.

[39] 1983 Act, s.3(2), Third Sched. and s.27(4) (transitional provisions).

[40] s.29 *et seq.* of the 1983 Act.

of the issuing transaction some obvious "money measure" which shows without further investigation the probability of a discount having being allowed. Thus, in *Mosely* v. *Koffyfontein Mines Co.*[41] it was found to be manifest on the face of the transaction, that the allottee could have been paying less than the nominal value of the shares. There debentures had been issued at a discount, but they were to be convertible into shares in the company one for one at par at the option of the holder at a later date. It was obvious on the face of the transaction that the debentures might still have been standing below par at that date, and the issue was accordingly held to have been made at a discount. This abdication by the courts in matters of valuation may have been born of a desire to avoid ruling on contentious matters of opinion (which in essence a valuation is), and also may have been influenced by the then prevailing notion, since much eroded, that matters of business should be left exclusively to business men. One must question whether Irish courts are free to take the same attitude today since now, for the first time, the 1983 statute contains an express prohibition against the issue of shares at a discount, and it would seem that that prohibition must be administered whatever form the discount takes.[42] The earlier English cases are unsatisfactory in other respects too. A recurring phrase in two of them, the *Ooregum Case* itself and in *Re Wragg Ltd.*,[43] is that the adequacy of the consideration will only be investigated when the transaction is shown to be "colourable," a perplexing description since, if the "colouring" or disguise has been successful, there will not be the open money measure which in the *Molsely Case* was held to be the essential prelude to an investigation.

The plc and non-cash considerations

The Companies Act 1983 now restricts the power of a public limited company to issue shares for non-cash considerations. Cer-

---

[41] [1904] 2 Ch. 108.

[42] Porter M.R. seemed *obiter* to share this view in *Re Leinster Contract Corporation* [1902] 1 I.R. 349, 358 where he suggested without qualifications that an allegation that the consideration furnished by an allottee was inadequate would result in "a question for inquiry what value he gave in money or money's worth; and, as he agreed to become a shareholder, he would have been liable to pay up the difference between what he gave for the shares and their nominal amount." That approach was not adopted in the case on the clearly wrong ground that an allotment expressly authorised in the memorandum could not be impugned as being made at a discount, thus confusing illegality and incapacity: see *Trevor* v. *Whitworth* (1887) 12 App. Cas. 409. For another unsatisfactory aspect of *Re Leinster Contract Corporation* see n. 33, *supra*.

[43] [1897] 1 Ch. 796.

tain non-cash considerations are outlawed and all non-cash considerations are subjected to the safeguard of an independent scrutiny.

Taking first unlawful non-cash considerations, a public limited company may not accept in payment for its shares "an undertaking given by any person that he or another should do work or perform services for the company or any other person,"[44] but this does not preclude the sale of expertise in a capital form, *i.e.* "know-how" in exchange for shares.[45] A public limited company is also forbidden from issuing shares in exchange wholly or partly for "an undertaking which is to be or may be performed more than five years after the date of the allotment."[46] In each case, the allottee is liable to pay to the company cash in respect of that part of the issue price covered by the undertaking,[47] and there are provisions for successors in title other than purchasers for value without actual notice to be jointly liable.[48] Curiously, the undertakings given by the allottees in contravention of these provisions remain valid[49] but the consequent double liability of the allottee both to pay and to perform is mitigated by provisions under which he may apply to the court for relief.[50] In exercising this jurisdiction, the court is to have regard to two overriding principles[51]: firstly, that the company should have received value in money or money's worth at least equal to the cash which should have been paid, which means in effect that the court will investigate the adequacy of the unlawful consideration; and, secondly, where the company has more than one remedy against a particular person, it is for the company to decide which one it should remain entitled to pursue. Where two or more persons are liable to a company in respect of a single obligation, the court may adjust the contribution between them so as wholly or partially to exonerate one to the detriment of the other.[52]

Secondly, we look at the independent scrutiny of non-cash considerations. The Companies Act 1983 requires that the consideration "otherwise than in cash" given for the allotment of shares in a

---

[44] s.26(2) of the 1983 Act. The consideration of *past* services rendered is insufficient for any kind of company: *Re Eddystone Marine Insurance Co.* [1893] 3 Ch. 9; approved in *Re Leinster Contract Corporation* [1902] 1 I.R. 349, 361.

[45] *Ibid.* s.26(1) which also contains a statutory declaration of the general principle that shares may be paid up "in money or money's worth (including goodwill and expertise)."

[46] 1983 Act, s.29(1).

[47] *Ibid.* ss.26(3), 29(2).

[48] *Ibid.* ss.26(4), 29(6).

[49] *Ibid.* s.36.

[50] *Ibid.* s.34.

[51] *Ibid.* s.34(4).

[52] *Ibid.* s.35(5).

public limited company must be verified by an independent person, and a report containing his valuation must be given to the company and to the proposed allottee before allotment.[53] If the shares are allotted without these conditions being satisfied, and the allottee did not receive a copy of the report or otherwise knew or ought to have known that there had been a contravention of the section, he is immediately liable to pay up in cash the whole of the nominal value of the shares plus any premium on them, less "such proportion of that amount as is treated as paid up by the consideration,"[54] or such proportion of the issue price as was treated in the transaction as having been paid up by the non-cash consideration. In addition, the allottee's undertaking to provide the non-cash consideration remains in force,[55] subject to his right to apply to the court for relief, as outlined above.[56] His successors in title are also liable to the extent outlined above.[57] There need be no independent valuation where a company as part of an offer to all holders of shares in another company (or a particular class of them) proposes to allot its shares to them in exchange for their shares, or their cancellation, or all the assets of their company.[58] This topic of mergers and amalgamations is discussed in Chapter 9 at pp. 289, *et seq.* Nor do the provisions apply where the company's reserves, or a credit balance on its profit and loss account are applied to pay up any shares allotted to members.[59] Most commonly these will be bonus or capitalisation issues.[60]

To be a person sufficiently "independent" within the meaning of the 1983 Act to conduct the required valuations, a person need simply possess qualifications entitling him to act as auditor to the company[61] but in fact, as we shall see[62] auditors are not necessarily wholly independent of the company whose affairs they are examining. "Independent" is therefore not wholly apt in this context. The possibility that an auditor might not be competent to value all items of property is covered by allowing him to delegate whole or part of his function to someone who "appears to him to have the requisite knowledge and experience," provided that he is not an officer or servant of the company, or of its holding, subsidiary or fellow subsidi-

---

[53] *Ibid.* ss.30 and 31.
[54] *Ibid.* s.30(10).
[55] *Ibid.* s.36(2).
[56] *Ibid.* s.34. See p. 310, *supra.*
[57] *Ibid.* s.30(11), 26(4), and see p. 310, *supra.*
[58] *Ibid.* s.30(2), (3), (4).
[59] *Ibid.* s.30(10).
[60] As to which see pp. 173–174, *supra*, and p. 334, *infra.*
[61] 1983 Act, s.30(5).
[62] Chapter 11 at pp. 366–368 *et seq.*

ary companies, or the partner or employee of anyone being such an officer or employee.[63]

Since section 30 of the Companies Act 1983, the provision imposing the foregoing system of compulsory valuation, applies only when a public limited company is proposing to allot shares for a consideration "otherwise than in cash," it is important to determine what that expression means. Section 2(3) of the 1983 Act defines an allotment for cash, and guidance is also found in the judicial interpretations of section 58 of the Companies Act 1963 which concerns allotments paid up "otherwise than in cash." Section 2(3) states that a share:

> "shall be taken to have been . . . allotted for cash if the consideration for the allotment . . . is cash received by the company or is a cheque received by the company in good faith . . . or is *the release of a liability of the company for a liquidated sum* or is an undertaking to pay cash to a company at a future date. . . ."[63a]

Section 58 requires limited companies to make a return to the Registrar of Companies of any allotment of its shares, stating, *inter alia* the nominal value of the shares comprised in the allotment and the amount, if any, paid on them, and to deliver to him:

> "in the case of shares alloted as fully or partly paid up *otherwise than in cash*, a contract in writing constituting the title of the allottee to the allotment together with any contract of sale, or for services or other consideration in respect of which that allotment was made . . . and a return stating the number and nominal amount of the shares so allotted, the extent to which they are to be treated as paid up and the consideration for which they have been allotted."[64]

These duties are now amplified by section 31(2) of the Companies Act 1983 which requires the independent person's report to accompany the return of allotments. The expression "otherwise than in cash" in section 58 has been interpreted in practice as not requiring a return of the non-cash consideration or the delivery of contracts when the share issue has been arranged by two separate contacts, one selling shares in the company to the allottee in exchange for cash, and the other selling the allottee's property to the company in exchange for a like sum in cash. The two sums are then set off, or occasionally there is the barren formality of an exchange of cheques

---

[63] 1983 Act, s.30(5) (*a*), (*b*).

[63a] If the contract is not in writing, particulars of it must be delivered: s.58(2).

[64] Italics supplied. The sub-section further provides that payments or undertakings to pay persons other than the company are included, and that "cash" includes foreign currency. See also 1983 Act, s.2(4)(*b*).

which are then destroyed. This understanding of what constitutes an issue for cash has been established for over a century, and arises from judicial interpretations of a predecessor[65] of Section 58. As Chatterton V.-C. said in the leading Irish case of *Re Gibson, Little & Co. Ltd.*[66]:

> "In order to constitute a payment in cash . . . , the amount of the shares must either pass in actual cash or must be paid by setting against that amount an equal sum due and presently payable in cash to the allottee by the company, which sum by agreement between these parties must be given by the allottee and accepted by the company in discharge of the amount due on the shares . . . ."

It is vital that there be nothing in the contracts themselves providing for the set-off. In *Re Gibson, Little & Co. Ltd.* itself, the parties had agreed that an asset should be sold to the company for £2,000, but then the agreement proceeded to say that this liability should be satisfied by the issue of shares in the company. There was accordingly no cash sum payable by the company available as a set-off against the allottee's liability in respect of the shares, and on this ground the allotment was held not to be for cash. That part of section 2(3) of the 1983 Act which provides that a share in a company "shall be taken to have been . . . allotted for cash if the consideration for the allotment . . . is the release of a liability of the company for a liquidated sum" does not appear to alter this reasoning. A set-off is not a release of an obligation[66a]; and if the barren formality of an exchange of cheques is observed, each independent obligation will have been discharged by payment, not release.

The possibility of avoidance by arrangements such as these certainly takes the teeth out of section 30 of the Companies Act 1983, and appears to afford the reason for the different draftsmanship employed in the closely related section 32 of the Companies Act 1983. This applies the independent valuation system to certain agreements between a newly formed public limited company or an existing company registered or re-registered as such[67] and any subscriber to the memorandum (in the case of a newly formed plc) or any member at the time of registration or re-registration in the case of the other companies. The agreements covered by section 32 are

---

[65] s.25 of the Companies Act 1867.

[66] (1880–81) 5 L.R., Ir. 139, 155, following *Spargo's Case* (1873) L.R. 8 Ch. App. 407.

[66a] *Re Hiram Maxim Lamp Co.* [1903] 1 Ch. 70.

[67] Other than "old public limited companies" as defined by s.12 of the 1983 Act.

those entered into between any of the persons described above and the public limited company within two years of its obtaining its certificate entitling it to commence business [68] (in the case of a newly formed plc) or within two years of the date of registration or re-registration in the other cases under which it is agreed that there should be:

> "the transfer by him . . . of one or more non-cash assets to the company or another for a consideration to be given by the company equal in value at the time of the agreement to at least one-tenth of the nominal value of the company's share capital issued at that time."

The non-cash consideration is to be independently valued, as described above in relation to section 30, a copy of the independent person's report is to be delivered to the company, the agreement is to be approved by an ordinary resolution of the company after copies of the report and the proposed resolution have been circulated to all the members; furthermore section 33 of the Companies Act 1983 requires a copy of the report and the resolution to be delivered to the registrar of companies. Section 32 applies to a wider range of transactions than the allotment of shares by the public limited company[69] in exchange for assets, but insofar as it does relate to allotments it provides an independent scrutiny in one of the areas where it has traditionally been tempting for promoters to receive shares in exchange for inflatedly valued assets, namely the formation of a company to take over an existing business, and the preliminaries to the launch of a company or its shares upon an unsuspecting public. These topics are discussed elsewhere in this book. See Chapter 12: *Promoters and Prospectuses.*

Where a company has entered into an agreement for the allotment of shares without observing the procedures laid down in section 32, the other party to it if he had not received the valuation report or if he knew or ought to have known of any other contravention of the section, is liable to the company to pay up the shares in cash to the extent required by section 30 as if there had been a breach of that section,[70] in addition to performing his part of the bargain.[71] The

---

[68] s.6 of the 1983 Act.

[69] Not that that appears to have been the purpose of article of the EEC Second Directive (77/91/EEC) in compliance with which s.32 was enacted. Art. 11 speaks o the acquisition by the company of assets "for a consideration of not less than one tenth of the subscribed capital."

[70] s.32(7), (8) and 30(10) of the 1983 Act.

[71] *Ibid.* s.36(2).

provisions entitling the allottee to apply to the court for relief,[72] and governing the liability of successors in title likewise apply.[73] There is an exception in section 32(4) for assets acquired in the ordinary course of business by a company whose business includes the acquisition of assets of that type. The acquisition of assets from a subscriber or member in exchange for the allotment of its shares would not therefore qualify unless the company ordinarily acquired assets in this way.

Prohibition on a company purchasing its own shares

Irish company legislation now contains two distinct provisions prohibiting a limited company from purchasing its own shares. Section 72(1) of the Companies Act 1963 declares:

> "Except insofar as this Act expressly permits, it shall not be lawful for a company limited by shares . . . *to purchase any of its shares* or to reduce its share capital in any way."

Section 41 of the Companies Act 1983 puts the same point somewhat more cumbrously:

> "(1) Subject to the following provisions of this section, no company limited by shares . . . shall acquire its own shares (whether by purchase, subscription or otherwise). (2) A company limited by shares may acquire any of its own fully paid shares otherwise than for valuable consideration."[74]

Statute is not required to repeat itself for emphasis. The explanation for the repetition here seems simply to be that the draftsman modelled section 41 on the corresponding provision in the British Companies Act 1980,[75] as indeed was most of the rest of the 1983 Act, without in this instance taking into account the fact that Irish legislation already contained an express prohibition, which the British pre-1980 legislation did not.

These provisions are statutory expressions of the judicial rule in *Trevor* v. *Whitworth*,[76] first acknowledged in Ireland in *Re General Finance Co. Ltd.*,[77] in which relief was given to the participants

---

[72] *Ibid.* s.34.
[73] *Ibid.* s.32(8), 26(4).
[74] The omitted words in each case extend the prohibition to companies limited by guarantee and having a share capital.
[75] s.35 of the Companies Act 1980 [*U.K.*] as amended by s.119, and Sched. 3 of the Companies Act 1981 [*U.K.*].
[76] (1887) 12 App. Cas. 409.
[77] (1889–90) 23 L.R., I.R. 173. The earlier case of *Re Balgooley Distillery Co.* (1886–87) 17 L.R., IR.239 went the other way with strong expressions of doubt from Fitzgibbon L.J. (at p.263), and Barry L.J. (at p. 268).

because of the novelty of the rule. A stricter Irish application is to be found in *Re Irish Provident Assurance Co. Ltd.*[78] Here, an agreement for the parting of the ways between a company and its managing director and for the settlement of all outstanding differences between them had provided that the company should pay him £2,000, and in return he had entered into covenants not to compete, had given up various valuable claims, and had agreed to surrender his shares in the company to it. It was held that the consideration provided by him was not severable, and that the whole agreement was void because of the company's incapacity to purchase its own shares.

The justification for the rule was originally the same common thread which runs through the whole topic of capital maintenance, the idea that money subscribed or agreed to be subscribed for share capital was in a sense "a creditors' fund," not to be diminished by the return of the limited company's assets to its members or by the release of their obligation to pay up unpaid balances on their shares.[79] In fact, the rule is broader than this justification, and prohibits one particular disbursement of the company's funds to its members in exchange for their shares, which would be perfectly proper if carried out by other means. A limited company may not generally[80] use its profits to purchase its own shares; yet it is the expectation of every member that those profits will lawfully be used to fund the payment to them of dividends.[81] The present rationale of the rule therefore goes beyond capital maintenance, and includes at least two further propositions, of which the first is that it is undesirable for a company to use its funds to acquire control of itself.[82] Doing so would diminish the members' prospects of a dividend and would divert funds from the business towards the illegitimate task of maintaining the present directors in control through their use of the company's votes on its own shares.[82a] Secondly, the prohibition prevents a publicly quoted company from trafficking in its own shares in the market, by which means it might artificially influence the share price, a matter of great importance to a company contemplat-

---

[78] [1913] 1 I.R. 352.

[79] See pp. 302–303, *supra* and the speeches in *Trevor* v. *Whitworth* itself, particularly Lord Herschell at (1887) 12 App. Cas. 409.

[80] For an exception, see redeemable preference shares discussed *infra* at p. 326, *infra*.

[81] The capital maintenance aspect of the dividend rules is discussed at pp. 326–338 *infra*.

[82] For devices used in the maintenance of control, see Chapter 3 at pp. 101 *et seq.*

[82a] It also opens up a publicly quoted company to the possibility of "greenmail," a U.S. term. This describes the situation in which a potentially disruptive outsider has secretly built up a substantial holding in the company with the object of applying pressure on the company to buy him out at a profit, often massive.

ing a rights issue (under which existing members are given the opportunity to subscribe for further shares in the company), or to a company on the takeover trail in which, under a variety of arrangements,[83] its own shares will be issued in exchange for the shares in or assets of other companies.

Section 41 of the Companies Act 1983 declares, as heretofore, a purported purchase by a limited company of its own shares to be void, and sets out other recognised exceptions to the prohibition: the redemption of redeemable preference shares,[84] the purchase of shares pursuant to an order of the court,[85] or the forfeiture of partly paid shares for non-payment of calls (or the acceptance of a surrender of shares liable to be forfeited).[86]

Forfeiture

The release of a shareholder from his obligation to pay up the sums outstanding on his partly paid shares constitutes a reduction of capital. As Collins M.R. said in *Bellerby* v. *Rowland & Marwood's Steamship Co.*,[87] there is "no distinction in principle between returning to a shareholder part of the paid-up capital in return for his shares and wiping out his liability for the uncalled-up sum payable thereon." Nonetheless, articles of limited companies have from the earliest time made provision for the forfeiture of partly paid shares on which sums due have not been paid. Such provisions gained statutory authority by their inclusion in Table A to the Companies Act 1862, the present equivalent being articles 33 to 39 inclusive of Table A to the Companies Act 1963.[88] There is now express statutory recognition of the right of forfeiture in section 41(4)(d) of the Companies Act 1983.

Upon forfeiture a shareholder ceases to be a member in respect of the forfeited shares, and under common form articles[89] remains liable only for the instalments actually payable at the time of the forfeiture. By statute, he retains a secondary liability as a past member in respect of all sums unpaid on his former shares in the event of a

---

[83] For takeovers and amalgamations, see Chapter 9 at pp. 289, *et seq.*

[84] p. 326, *infra.*

[85] s.72(2) (in a reduction of capital); s.10, as amended by para. 2, Sched. 1, 1983 Act (as relief for a dissentient on an alteration of objects); s.205 (as a possible remedy for the petitioner); s.15 of the 1983 Act (reduction of membership on the re-registration of a plc as a private company).

[86] See below.

[87] [1902] 2 Ch. 14, 25

[88] The total number of shares forfeited is to be stated in the annual return: para. 3(i), Fifth Sched. For disclosures in accounts, see p. 354, n. 33c, *infra.*

[89] Art. 37 of Table A.

winding up commencing within a year of the forfeiture,[90] but
beyond that year the past member will, as far as statute is concerned, have escaped liability for instalments or calls not yet payable
at the time of forfeiture and the company's capital will correspondingly have been reduced. Forfeitures are not of frequent occurrence
in practice,[91] owing to the scarcity of partly paid shares. Hitherto,
when forfeitures have occurred in public companies, the forfeited
shares have been disposed of on the market, but now by section 43 of
the Companies Act 1983 companies registered as public limited
companies are obliged to cancel the forfeited shares, and reduce
their nominal capital accordingly. This may be done without the
intervention of the court, but if as a result their nominal capital falls
below the authorised minimum, the directors are obliged to secure
re-registration as a private company.

Liens

Most articles of association provide that the company shall have a
lien, *i.e.* an equitable security interest, over its own shares in respect
of all or some of any money owed to it by the registered holder. The
enforcement of this security by sale does not break the rules of capital maintenance, since no obligation is thereby released.[91a] Enforcement is usually by means of an express power of sale given by the
articles.[91b] If that power is omitted, it is likely that the company
would have the power of sale implied by section 19 of the Conveyancing Act 1881 favour of mortgagees *by deed*, and thus be saved
recourse to the courts. We have seen[91c] that the section 25 contract
of which the article imposing the lien forms part takes effect as if
"signed and sealed by each member," *i.e.* as a deed.

Table A confers a lien in respect of all debts owed by a member to
the company but confines it to partly paid shares.[91d] A standard
modification in common use in private companies extends it to fully
paid shares.

Section 44 of the 1983 Act restricts the use of the lien by plc's[91da].
They are to be void except in respect of amounts unpaid on partly
paid shares, or unless they arose in the ordinary course of the company's moneylending, credit providing or hire purchase business[91e];

---

[90] s.207(1) *(a)*, *(b)*, *(c)*, *(d)*.

[91] For an instance of forfeiture, see the *Irish Times*, October 29, 1976.

[91a] *Cf. Re Balgooley Distillery Co.* (1886–7) 17 L.R., Ir. 239, 263 *per* Fitzgibbon L.J.

[91b] *e.g.* Art. 12 of Table A.   [91c] Chapter 6, at pp. 162 *et seq.*

[91d] Table A, Art. 11 1983 Act, Third. Sched., confines this lien to payments owed
on partly paid shares, *i.e.* calls, etc.

[91da] For accounting disclosures, see 1983 Act Sched. 1, para 27, and p. 354, n. 33c,
infra.

[91e] *Cf.* s.60. *Steen* v. *Law* [1964] A.C. 287 could be applicable here.

or unless they were liens in existence before the company applied to become a plc.

We have already seen how equitable mortgagees in competition with the company's lien may protect themselves by giving notice to the company.[91f]

Prohibition against a company assisting the purchase of its own shares

This topic now has a tangled history in Ireland. Briefly, section 3 of the Companies Act 1959 introduced a general prohibition against a company giving financial assistance towards the purchase of its own shares; that provision was replaced by section 60 of the Companies Act 1963 which substantially liberalised the general prohibition in accordance with a recommendation of the Jenkins Committee which Britain itself did not follow; this liberalisation was repealed by the Companies Act 1983 in relation only to public limited companies in accordance with the dictates of article 23 of the Second EEC Companies Directive; and there are other aspects of section 60 which are not paralleled in Britain or in other jurisdictions.

Legislation of this type is designed to prevent a company financing its own takeover. At its simplest, this might involve a person borrowing money from a bank to purchase a controlling interest in the share capital of the company, and, after the acquisition of control, arranging that the company's funds are used to repay the bank. The sophistication of the methods employed to channel the money back to the bank depends upon the awareness of the participants of the legal hazards involved. Where there is this awareness, the funds will start their journey from the company suitably disguised as payments to an intermediary for non-existent services rendered, worthless property purchased, or as a loan which is never intended to be repaid. The most sophisticated series of disguises of any in the law reports was employed in the English case of *Wallersteiner* v. *Moir*[92] where Lord Denning M.R. felt able to cut through the mass of transactions employed in this channelling process in order to find a contravention of the English equivalent legislation. He said:

> "The transactions are extremely complicated, but the end result is clear. You look to the company's money and see what

---

[91f] Chapter 6 at pp. 196–197: *Rearden* v. *Provincial Bank of Ireland* [1896] 1 I.R. 352; also *Champagne Perrier-Jouet S.A.* v. *H. M. Finch Ltd.* [1982] 1 W.L.R. 1359.

[92] [1974] 1 W.L.R. 991. For a simple infringement, see *Re Greenore Trading Co. Ltd.* (High Court, Keane J., March 28, 1980, unreported; (1981) D.U.L.J. (N.S.) 79).

has become of it. You look to the company's shares and see into whose hands they have got. You will then soon see if the company's money has been used to finance the purchase."[93]

Other examples of the kind of conduct at which such legislation is aimed are found in *Selangor Rubber Estates Ltd.* v. *Cradock (No. 3)*[94] and *Karak Rubber Co. Ltd.* v. *Burden.*[95]

Some of these transactions, if genuine, do not of themselves reduce the company's capital. In the case, for example, of a realisation of its assets in order to lend money to its new controller, it has technically only switched investments. But, as the Jenkins committee observed:

"If people who cannot provide the funds necessary to acquire control of a company from their own resources, or by borrowing on their own credit, gain control of a company with large assets on the understanding that they will use the funds of the company to pay for their shares, it seems to us all too likely, that in many cases the company will be made to part with its funds either on inadequate security or for an illusory consideration. If the speculation succeeds, the company and therefore its creditors and minority shareholders may suffer no loss, although their interests will have been subjected to an illegitimate risk . . ."[96]

And as part of the failure of that "illegitimate risk," the company's share capital may disappear. That the Irish measures are directed towards the protection of share capital is made clear by section 60(12) which still applies to all types of Irish companies:

"(12) Nothing in this section shall be taken to prohibit the payment of a dividend properly declared by a company or the discharge of a liability lawfully incurred by it."

It is, as we shall see,[97] a cardinal rule that dividends be paid only out of profits, and not at the expense of share capital. If the directors of a company are worried that a takeover bidder might be intending to finance his acquisition of its shares by declaring a dividend on them after their acquisition (as indeed he may under section 60(12)), the appropriate defence is to capitalise its profits by using

---

[93] At p. 1014. In England even if the initial step is commercially fair to the company there is still a contravention if it is part of a scheme to provide assistance: *Belmont Finance Corporation* v. *Williams Furniture Ltd. (No. 2)* [1980] 1 All E.R. 393, 402, but in Ireland, see s.60(12) at n. 98, *infra*.

[94] [1968] 1 W.L.R. 1555.

[95] [1971] 1 W.L.R. 1748.

[96] 1962, Cmnd. 1749, para. 173. See also *Re V.G.M. Holdings* [1942] Ch. 235, 238.

[97] At pp. 326, *et seq.*

them to pay up an issue of bonus shares, thereby rendering them no longer available to fund a dividend. By "the discharge of a liability lawfully incurred by it," section 60(12) assumedly means an intra vires debt properly incurred in the course of its business,[98] and not the type of bogus transaction characteristic of attempts to evade legislation of this kind.

The general prohibition against the giving of financial assistance is modelled on section 54 of the Companies Act 1948 [*U.K.*],[99] and is contained in section 60(1) of the Companies Act 1963:

> "Subject to subsections (2), (12) and (13), it shall not be lawful for a company to give, whether directly or indirectly, and whether by means of a loan, guarantee, the provision of security, or otherwise, any financial assistance for the purpose of or in connection with a purchase or subscription made or to be made by any person of or for any shares in the company, or where the company is a subsidiary company, in its holding company."

The exceptions contained in subsection (13) relate to all companies, with the proviso in the case of public limited companies that assistance given in accordance with subsection (13) should, insofar as gratuitous, be provided out of profits available for dividends.[1] The subsection (13) exceptions concern the establishment of share incentive schemes for the benefit of employees, this being the area where there is a gratuitous element present; the making of loans to employees other than directors to enable them to purchase or subscribe for shares in the company; and "where the lending of money is part of the ordinary business of the company, the lending of money by the company in the ordinary course of its business." This last exception protects transactions in which money borrowed from a genuine banking or moneylending company happens to be applied in the purchase of its shares. Any relaxation of the safeguards normally required by lenders of borrowers would prima facie take the loan out of the ordinary course of business.[2]

The exception provided by subsection (2) no longer applies to public limited companies.[3] The exception came about because it

---

[98] See *Dale* v *Martin*, p. 303, *supra*, and see n. 93, *supra*.
[99] Since repealed, and replaced by ss.42 *et seq.* of the Companies Act 1981 [*U.K.*].
[1] s.60(15B), 15(C), added by para. 9, First Sched. 1983 Act.
[2] See generally *Steen* v. *Law* [1964] A.C. 287. (P.C.).
[3] s.15(A) of s.60, added by para. 9 of the First Sched., 1983 Act, in response to art. 23, 2nd EEC Directive: unless the special resolution initiating the subsection (2) procedure was passed by an existing company before registration or re-registration as a plc.

was perceived by the Jenkins Committee that there are occasions when the giving of financial assistance is both convenient and reasonable.[4] The unqualified prohibition, as it existed in both Britain and Ireland before the enactment of section 60, was according to this Committee "an occasional embarrassment to the honest without being a serious inconvenience to the unscrupulous,"[5] and, broadly following the recommendations of the Jenkins Committee, subsection (2) authorised the giving of financial assistance provided that procedures involving the consultation of members and compulsory advance publicity for the protection of creditors were followed. At the same time, the previously derisory criminal penalties for infringement were raised to include the possibility of imprisonment for a term of two years or a substantial fine, now £2,500,[6] or both.[7] The consultation of the members takes the form of requiring that the financial assistance be given with the authority of a special resolution of the company passed not more than 12 months previously. Unless the special resolution is passed unanimously by every shareholder entitled to vote, an extreme requirement, there is to be a delay of 30 days before the financial assistance is actually given.[8] This delay gives dissentient shareholders the opportunity to exercise the right given to the holders of at least 10 per cent. in nominal value of the company's issued share capital (or any class thereof) to apply to the court for the cancellation of the special resolution,[9] in which proceedings anything suspect in the proposal may be fully investigated. The protection of creditors is attempted by requiring the directors shortly before the meeting at which the special resolution is to be proposed to make and to deliver to the registrar of companies for filing a statutory declaration describing the form of the proposed financial assistance, persons to whom it is to be given, its purpose, and, most importantly, a statement by the declarants that the company will after giving the assistance be able to pay its debts in full as they become due.[10] Any director making this declaration of solvency without reasonable grounds for his opinion, is made personally liable for the company's debts in full as they become due and also to criminal penalties including imprisonment; furthermore, if the com-

---

[4] Examples are given at 1962, Cmnd. 1749, paras. 175 *et seq.*

[5] *Ibid.* para. 176.

[6] Fine increased by s.15 of and by First Sched. to the 1982 Act.

[7] s.60(15).

[8] s.60(7).

[9] s.60(7)–(11). Such an application was made in *Securities Trust Ltd.* v. *Associated Properties Ltd.* (High Court, McWilliam J.; November 19, 1980) in which the exercise of the Court's discretion under s.60 did not arise since the special resolution was held to be *ultra vires* in any event.

[10] s.60(2)(*b*), (3), (4).

pany is wound up within 12 months of the making of the declaration and its debts are not paid or provided for within the ensuing 12 months, there is a presumption that the director did not have reasonable grounds for his opinion.[11]

Section 60(14) states the civil consequences of transactions contravening this section in these terms:

> "Any transaction in breach of this section shall be voidable at the instance of the company against any person (whether a party to the transaction or not) who had notice of the facts which constitute such a breach."

When this subsection was enacted it was generally understood on the authority of *Victor Battery Co. Ltd.* v. *Curry's Ltd.*[12] that a security given by a company in contravention of the section guaranteeing the repayment of a loan taken out by a purchaser to acquire its shares was valid. Subsection (14) was a necessary measure of reform suggested by the Jenkins Committee to reverse that decision.[13] In England and in other jurisdictions where this legislative step was not taken, the case law has evolved not only to overrule *Victor Battery Co. Ltd.* v. *Curry's Ltd*, but to declare any such security to be void,[14] whereas in Ireland such developments have been frozen by section 60(14). The consequences are illustrated by the Supreme Court decision of *Bank of Ireland Finance Ltd.* v. *Rockfield Ltd.*[15] There, a company had created in favour of the bank an equitable mortgage over its assets to secure an advance made for the purchase of its shares. The mortgage was declared to be valid since the bank, it was held, did not know that the advance was to be used for this purpose, and "notice" in subsection (14) was construed as meaning *actual* notice, it being considered undesirable that notions of constructive notice should be extended to commercial transactions. Had the case been decided in England, the mortgage would have been void. If the company had paid money under it to the bank, then the likelihood in England and other jurisdictions, but not in Ireland, is that the bank would have been accountable for that money as constructive trustee to the company,[16] the constructive trusteeship arising through the

---

[11] s.60(5).

[12] [1946] Ch. 242.

[13] 1962, Cmnd. 1749, para. 181.

[14] *Selangor United Rubber Estates* v. *Cradock* (*No.* 3) [1968] 1 W.L.R. 1555, 1656–57, *Heald* v. *O'Connor* [1971] 1 W.L.R. 748; prompted by misgivings in Australian jurisdictions.

[15] [1979] I.R. 21; Ussher, (1978) D.U.L.J. 44.

[16] *e.g. The Selangor case,* n. 14, *supra; Karak Rubber Co. Ltd.* v. *Burden* (*No.* 2) [1972] 1 W.L.R. 602; *Belmont Finance Corporation Ltd.* v. *Williams Furniture Ltd.* (*No.* 2) [1980] 1 All E.R. 393 (C.A.).

bank being deemed to know all that a reasonable and prudent banker would have known and discovered in the circumstances. Such post-Jenkins developments are thwarted in Ireland by the present form of section 60(14).

Share premiums

A share premium is the excess in the issue price of a share over its nominal value. For example, a £1 share issued for £1.50 is issued at a premium of 50 pence. Formerly, share premiums were regarded as a source of funds for the payment of dividends, undifferentiated from other profits.[17] Now, however, a company may not pay a dividend if the consequent adjustments to the account result in a diminution of the share premium account.

Section 62(1) of the Companies Act 1963 now provides:

> "Where a company issues shares at a premium, whether for cash or otherwise, a sum equal to the aggregate amount or value of the premiums on those shares shall be transferred to an account, to be called 'the share premium account,' and the provisions of this Act relating to the reduction of share capital of a company shall, except as provided in this section, apply as if the share premium account were paid up share capital of the company."

For those unfamiliar with the language of accountancy, it should be observed that this talk of the transfer of a sum equal to the premiums to a separate account, does not mean that the assets for the time being representing the share premiums are in some sense to be a static fund, or in some way earmarked or differentiated from other assets derived from other sources, any more than any such thing is required of share capital itself. In balance sheet language, all assets are derived from certain sources of finance, or, put more archaically all assets are derived from liabilities. The share premium account is one of those sources of finance, and appears on the liabilities side; there is not required to be an actual physical correspondence between any item on the liabilities side and any particular asset, although in the early stages of an enterprise one might coincidentally be able to say that a particular asset does in fact physically represent a certain source of finance, but such dissection is both unnecessary and misleading. It is particularly important to grasp this when considering the lawfulness of the payment of dividends. This involves the distribution of assets, and, accordingly, there must be a corresponding diminution on the liabilities side of the balance

---

[17] *e.g. Drown* v. *Gaumont—British Picture Corporation Ltd.* [1937] 2 All E.R. 609.

sheet. As we shall see,[18] the only items available for this purpose on the liabilities side are a credit balance on the profit and loss account, and revenue reserves: a distribution of assets by way of dividend which results in the writing down of the share premium account or the amount of nominal share capital is unlawful. But the proceeds of a fresh issue of shares may physically be used to pay a dividend, as indeed may borrowed money, provided that there exists on the liabilities side other appropriate items to finance it.

The share premium account may, as a matter of balance sheet accounting, be used to pay up unissued shares of the company to be allotted to members of the company as fully paid bonus shares, or, in other words capitalised or converted into issued share capital; or it may be correspondingly diminished if the preliminary expenses of the company are expunged from the assets side of the balance sheet (considered by many to be a curious form of asset in any event[18a]); or it may be used to finance the expenses of an issue of shares or debentures, and commissions and discounts lawfully allowed on those occasions[19]; or, it may be correspondingly written down if a premium has been paid on the redemption of any redeemable preference shares[20] or on the repayment of any debentures.[21]

Section 62 of the Companies Act 1963 applies where a company issues shares for cash "or otherwise." Thus, where a company allots shares for a consideration other than cash that consideration must be valued, and if that calculation shows that the shares were issued at a price in excess of their nominal value, a corresponding share premium account must be created. This proposition has been clearly established since *Head Henry & Co. Ltd.* v. *Ropner Holdings Ltd.*[22] recently followed in *Shearer* v. *Bercain Ltd.*[23] Each of these cases involved the acquisition by a holding company of the whole share capital of other companies under a share for share exchange. In each case the nominal value of the shares issued by the holding company was very much less than the value of the shares in the newly acquired subsidiaries obtained in exchange. The creation of a share premium account in the holding company to reflect this difference has given rise to acute problems in determining whether the pre-

---

[18] At pp. 326 *et seq., infra.*

[18a] See now 1985 Bill, s.4(12) which states that preliminary expenses (*inter alia*) "shall not be treated as assets in the balance sheet of a company."

[19] As to which see pp. 340 *et seq., infra.*

[20] On redeemable preference shares, see p. 326, *infra.*

[21] All these uses of the share premium account are set out in s.62(2), as amended by para. 10, First Sched. 1983 Act.

[22] [1952] Ch. 124.

[23] [1980] 3 All E.R. 295, criticised in Ussher, "Doubts remain on Shearer v. Bercain," (1982), 3 *Company Lawyer* 28.

acquisition profits of the subsidiaries may, after they have been distributed by way of dividend to the holding company, be distributed by *it* in turn to its members, since to do may be seen as trenching upon the holding company's share premium account, the amount of which was partly determined by the value of the pre-acquisition profits whilst they remained in the hands of the subsidiaries. The resolution of this problem is discussed at pp. 335–336 under the heading *Dividends*.

Redeemable preference shares

A limited company may, if authorised by its articles, issue preference shares on terms that they be redeemable during the life of the company, constituting therefore an exception to the general rule prohibiting a limited company from purchasing its own shares.[24] The governing section 64 of the Companies Act 1963[25] ensures that the capital yardstick is maintained despite redemption, since the redemption may be made only out of the proceeds of a fresh issue of shares, or out of profits otherwise available for dividends. In the latter event, a further sum of profits available to fund dividends must be transferred on the liabilities side of the balance sheet to a "capital redemption reserve fund" which is to be treated in all respects as paid up capital and may in fact be capitalised by being applied in paying up unissued capital to be allotted as bonus shares to the members.

Redeemable preference shares are akin to debentures in that they offer a fixed return and the prospect of repayment during the life of a company, but differ in that debentures for their servicing and repayment are not dependant on a particular source of finance, and give rise to the debtor/creditor relationship, whereas redeemable preference shares always take second place to creditors, both as to servicing, since there is an overriding condition of solvency as a preliminary to the lawful payment of a dividend,[26] and in a winding up where the claims of shareholders are always deferred to those of creditors.[27]

Dividends

It is a fundamental rule of capital maintenance that dividends may be paid only out of profits. The law governing what constitutes

[24] s.41(4)(a), s.51(2)(b) of the 1983 Act, s.64 of the 1963 Act, as amended by para. 11, First Sched., 1983 Act.
[25] As amended by para. 11, First Sched., 1983 Act.
[26] See the definition of "profits" available for dividend, as pp. 328–329.
[27] s.207(1)(g).

a divisible profit has for some time been in a state of transition, dictated mainly by the Second and to a much lesser extent, by the Fourth EEC Companies Directive. The Second Directive was enacted in Ireland by the Companies (Amendment) Act 1983. Its provisions relating to the payment of dividends are now fully in force.[28] Though the Second Directive applied only to plc's, the 1983 Act extends most of its revision of the law of dividends to other Companies as well. The topic is treated here with sufficient backward glances at the pre-1983 Act law to help in problems governed by that law arising in practice. The Fourth Directive has not yet been implemented in Ireland, but a Bill to do so was introduced on May 29, 1985.[28a] It is unlikely to be enacted before November 1985. Once enacted, it will probably be brought into force in relation to companies' accounting years beginning on or after January 1, 1986, or, possibly, ending after July 31, 1986. This book indicates the changes to be made by the 1985 Bill.

The cardinal rule is now contained in section 45(1) of the Companies (Amendment) Act 1983 which states:

> "A company shall not make a distribution[29] . . . except out of profits available for the purpose."

Statute formerly contented itself with a broad statement to similar effect in Table A,[30] and relied upon the background of judicial rules. These rules had as their high point the famous statement in 1882 by Jessel M.R. in *Flitcroft's Case*[31] that:

> "The creditor has no debtor but that impalpable thing the corporation which has no property except the assets of the business. The creditor, therefore, I may say, gives credit to that capital, gives credit to the company on the faith of the representation that the capital shall be applied only for the purposes of the business, and he has therefore a right to say that the corporation shall keep its capital and not return it to the shareholders . . ."

Insofar as this high point may be interpreted as requiring that no dividend be paid to members whilst the net assets of the company

---

[28] s.2(1), s.51(6) of the 1983 Act; and see p. 2, n. 4, *supra*.

[28a] Companies (Amendment) Bill 1985.

[29] Defined by s.51(2) of the 1983 Act.

[30] Art. 118 formerly stated: "No dividend shall be paid otherwise than out of profits." It has now been replaced by a reference to the new statutory code contained in Part IV of the 1983 Act (*ibid.* First Sched., para. 23(*e*)).

[31] (1882) 21 Ch. D. 519; approved in Ireland by Porter M.R. in *Kehoe* v. *Waterford & Limerick Railways.* (1888–89) L.R., Ir. 221, 235–6

remain less than the amount of its share capital, it was considerably
eroded, as we shall see, by subsequent judicial pronouncements.
The statutory intervention inspired by the EEC Directives seeks to
repair most of these judicial breaches in the wall of capital maintenance. Interestingly, the preamble to the Second Directive almost
echoes *Flitcroft's Case*:

> "Whereas Community provisions should be adopted for main-
> taining the capital, which constitutes the creditors' secur-
> ity . . . ."

Taking the law back to *Flitcroft's Case* broadly accords with contemporary accountancy opinion, evidenced by the uniform standards
now set by that profession. Not that the judges in setting these now
archaic guidelines sought generally to fly in the face of responsible
business opinion; it is just that that opinion was formerly more in
disarray on those matters than it is at present.[32] Indeed, one of these
earlier cases, the decision of the House of Lords in *Dovey* v. *Corey*[33]
could arguably be used today as authority for the proposition that
the uniform standards now set by the accountancy profession do, so
far as not covered by statute, represent the legally permissible limit
of distributable profits, since that case can be interpreted as saying
in effect that responsible business opinion for the time being should
be the arbiter of the propriety of dividend payments and, whatever
the position formerly, the undivided views of the accountancy profession may now be said to represent responsible business opinion.
Be this as it may, such an argument is now rendered unnecessary by
section 49 of the 1983 Act which makes the accountancy profession
the arbiter of the propriety of a dividend payment by requiring that
dividends be declared only by reference to relevant items in "properly prepared" accounts. As we shall see,[33a] for accounts to be
"properly prepared" the standards of that profession must necessarily be observed.

A company's profits available for dividend are now defined by
section 45(2)[33b] as "its accumulated realised profits, so far as not
previously utilised by distribution[34] or capitalisation,[35] less its accu-

---

[32] For an excellent account of the history of the judicial rules set against the background of contemporary accounting comment, see B.S. Yamey, "Aspects of the Law
relating to Company Dividends," (1941) 4 M.L.R. 273.

[33] [1901] A.C. 493.

[33a] See p. 332 *infra*, and Chapter 11: *Accounts and Auditors*.

[33b] See generally "The determination of distributable profits in the context of the
Companies Act 1948 to 1981" (T.R. 482): Consultative Committee of Accountancy
Bodies.

[34] Defined by s.51(2) of the 1983 Act.

[35] Usually a bonus issue. See definition of "capitalisation," *ibid*. s.51(3).

mulated, realised losses, so far as not previously written off in a reduction or reorganisation of capital duly made."[36]

This definition is amplified by section 51(4) of the 1983 Act which states, *inter alia* that these references to profits and losses are "references respectively to revenue and capital profits and revenue and capital losses."

Thus, for the purpose of ascertaining the availability of profits for the payment of dividends, the company's affairs are treated without reference to individual accounting periods, and as being continuous. In one respect, there is nothing new about this statement. A company has always been free to carry forward profits from previous years, either as a credit balance on the profit and loss account or as a revenue reserve, to fund dividend payments in later years, and this ability forms an important element in ensuring the continuity of dividend payments. But in respect of previous revenue losses, the judicial attitude was anomalously different. Revenue losses might be put into the water-tight compartments of separate accounting years, and a company which had traded at a loss, and therefore accumulated a deficit on the profit and loss account, might nonetheless have distributed revenue profits of subsequent years without setting off the subsequent profits against the previous losses, even if those losses were such as to have eroded the net asset value of the company to below that of its share capital and items similarly treated. The chief authority for this proposition was *Ammonia Soda Company Ltd.* v. *Chamberlain*,[37] and its somewhat specious rationale was that the dividend was not being paid at the expense of capital since that had already been lost before the year began. Modern accountancy opinion, the Jenkins Committee,[38] and the Second Directive[39] were united against the rule which has now been changed for all companies. Nowadays therefore, a company with an accumulated loss on revenue account which wishes to resume dividend payments must either find profits to set against them, or extinguish them by going through the reduction of capital procedure given by section 72 of the Companies Act 1963.

The *Ammonia Soda Co. Ltd.* rule, now corrected, referred to past losses in current assets. A company in drawing up its accounts is

---

[36] *i.e.* a reduction of capital by order of the court under s.72 or as part of a scheme under ss.201–203.

[37] [1918] 1 Ch. 266; also *Re National Bank of Wales Ltd.* [1899] 2 Ch. 629. Some contrary indications are found in the Irish case of *Re Castleisland Railway Co* [1896] 2 I.R. 661, 669–70.

[38] Para. 341.

[39] Second Directive, art. 15.1.(*c*), in fact applying, as with the rest of the Directive, only to plc's.

required to distinguish between two types of asset: fixed and current.[40] Neither of these terms is yet defined by the Companies Acts, but the broad distinction between them is easily understood and stated. Fixed assets are those held by a company for purposes other than sale or conversion into cash. They "are intended for use on a continuing basis for the purposes of the undertaking's activities."[41] Current assets, on the other hand comprise cash and assets acquired for the purpose of conversion into cash in the normal course of business. Whether an asset is fixed or current depends upon the nature of the company's business, and not upon any inherent characteristic of the asset itself. A factory in the hands of a manufacturer is a fixed asset since it is used for the purpose of generating revenue without actually itself being realised; in the hands of a property dealer it is a current asset if held for the purpose of re-sale; a lorry to its manufacturer was a current asset but to the ultimate consumer it is fixed. As the law stands at present, the distinction is easy enough to state, but its application in some instances "may well embarass the business man and the accountant as well as the lawyer."[42] For example, an ore smelting company might own lead mines to assure itself of supplies of ore. Suppose the mines are destroyed. Is that the loss of a fixed or of a current asset?[42a] Also, a trade debt is a current asset, but if long term credit at interest is given, does it not become an investment akin to a fixed asset? The Fourth Directive, as it is being implemented by the 1985 Bill, helps to resolve such questions by defining fixed assets as above and relegating all other assets to the category of current assets,[43] so that it will be easier to classify assets which are neither obviously fixed nor obviously current as falling within the latter category.

[40] Para. 4. Sixth Sched.
[41] EEC Fourth Directive, art. 15(2).
[42] *Per* Peterson J. in *Ammonia Soda Co. Ltd.* [1918] 1 Ch. 266.
[42a] A current asset, held Farwell J in *Bond* v. *Barrow Haematite Steel Co* [1902] 1 Ch. 353.
[43] 1985 Bill, Sched., para. 60 (applying 4th Directive, Art. 15(2). On the other hand, the 1985 Bill as introduced leaves intact s.45(9) of the 1983 Act which, for the purposes of determining profits available for distribution makes fixed assets the residual category. Section 45(9) says that a fixed asset "includes any other asset which is not a current asset." The balance sheet formats permitted by the Bill (and by the 4th Directive) elaborate the fixed asset current asset distinction by requiring the former to be divided into intangible assets, tangible assets and financial assets, and the latter into stocks, debtors, investments and cash at bank and in hand, each category save the last being further sub-divided. The problem of long term trade credit is not resolved, but the balance sheet notes are required to state the amount of current trade debt falling due after more than one year.

The distinction between fixed and current assets is important because if there is a diminution in current assets in any accounting year, there will of necessity be no revenue profit in that year, and as we have seen, losses in current assets in previous accounting years are now to be brought forward.

What of losses in fixed assets? Before the 1983 Act, the judicial attitude was encapsulated in the much repeated statement of Lindley L.J. in *Verner* v. *General and Commercial Investment Trust*:[44]

> "Fixed capital may be sunk and lost, and yet . . . the excess of current receipts over current payments may be divided . . ."

This case concerned an investment company which had made revenue profits in its current accounting year, *i.e.* income from investments had exceeded current expenditure, but the value of those investments, its fixed assets, had slumped. It was held that a dividend could be declared out of current revenue profits without first making a provision from them to cover the diminution in value of the fixed assets, even if the depreciation of the fixed assets resulted in the net asset value of the company being less than its share capital.[45] This major breach in the wall of capital maintenance began with *Lee* v. *Neuchatel Asphalte Co.*[46] which decided that the depreciation of a wasting fixed asset, *i.e.* one which of necessity diminished in value, in this case the leasehold concession to work a mine, need not be made good out of profits before declaring a dividend, and the same principle was later applied in *Bolton* v. *Natal Land and Colonisation Co.*[47] to land, a fixed asset not of a wasting character, and ultimately in *Verner* to investments. In *Re John Power & Son Ltd.*[48] dividend payments were maintained for many years by the expedient of not providing for the depreciation of fixed assets. Eventually, this led to the cancellation by the company of share capital lost, under the contemporary equivalent of section 72 of the Companies Act 1963.

Irish company law does not yet, even after the 1983 Act, expressly require that provision be made out of profits for the depreciation of fixed assets.[49] If no such provision is made, depreciation of fixed assets remains an unrealised loss which need not be deducted before the ascertainment of profits in accordance with the new section 45

---

[44] [1894] 2 Ch. 239.

[45] To which subsequently one would add items akin to share capital, such as the share premium account and the capital redemption reserve fund.

[46] [1889] 41 Ch. D. 1. The asset had probably not in fact depreciated in this case.

[47] [1892] 2 Ch. 124.

[48] [1934] I.R. 412.

[49] See para. 14(3), Sixth Sched.

formula. This statutory omission is not, however, as dangerous as it might at first seem. As stated above, the agreed standards of the accounting profession have by virtue of the 1983 Act become an arbiter, together, with the specific statutory requirements, of the propriety of a dividend payment. Section 49 of the 1983 Act accomplishes this somewhat obliquely. Dividends are to be paid only in accordance with items appearing in "properly prepared" accounts, which are defined as accounts giving a "true and fair view," in the case of a balance sheet, "of the state of the company's affairs as at the balance sheet date," and in the case of a profit and loss account, "of the company's profit or loss for the period in respect of which the accounts were prepared.[49a] These items are defined as including: "profits, losses, assets, liabilities, provisions . . . , share capital and reserves."[49b] The agreed standards and conventions of the accountancy profession are directed towards attaining the "true and fair view," and whilst few would disagree that these attempts have not yet been completely successful, it is generally accepted that a flouting of these agreed standards and conventions in order to maximise distributable profits would result in a "true and fair view" not being given. Turning therefore to the accountancy profession's present understanding of when provision for depreciation of fixed assets ought to be made, we find in the relevant Statement of Standard Accounting Practice[49c] that provision should be made for depreciation of all[49d] fixed assets having a finite useful life . . . by allocating the cost (or revalued amount) less estimated residual values of the assets as fairly as possible to the periods expected to benefit from their use."

The present position depends therefore on current accountancy practice. Compulsory depreciation by statute of fixed assets, and compulsory provision out of profits for that depreciation, should however be introduced in response to article 35 of the Fourth EEC Companies Directive. This requires the writing down not only of the value of "fixed assets with limited useful economic lives" but also that:

"(bb) Value adjustments must be made in respect of fixed assets, whether their useful economic lives are limited or not, so that they are valued at the lower figure to be attributed to them

---

[49a] ss.49(1), 3(a), 5(a), 6(a), 9(c) of the 1983 Act.
[49b] *Ibid.* s.49(9).
[49c] S.S.A.P No. 12: *Accounting for depreciation.*
[49d] S.S.A.P. 6; *extraordinary items* is also relevant, as is the standard governing "investment."

at the balance sheet date if it is expected that the reduction in their value will be permanent.

(cc) The value adjustments referred to in (aa)[50] and (bb) must be charged to the profit and loss account . . . ."

Though the loose style of this excerpt reflects its origins, it would seem difficult to interpret it otherwise than requiring that wasting fixed assets and fixed assets which have suffered a permanent loss of value should be depreciated, and provision made out of the profit and loss account for that depreciation. In anticipation of these developments section 45(4) of the Companies Act 1983 states that any provision[51] (including one for depreciation) shall be treated as a "realised loss," and therefore as deductible from the realised profits in ascertaining the amount available for distribution by way of dividend. It is perplexing in view of the apparent intent of the Directive to find an exception in section 45(4) for provisions out of profits "in respect of any diminution in value of a fixed asset appearing on a revaluation of all the fixed assets or of all the fixed assets other than goodwill of the company." This exception, modelled on the equivalent British provisions,[52] allows unrealised losses in fixed assets to be disregarded in the computation of profits available for dividend provided that that loss has been ascertained by a revaluation of all fixed assets, or, by way of derogation, where the directors can say of those not actually revalued that they are in the aggregate at least equal to their book value.[53] In its practical application, section 45(4) of the 1983 Act allows a diminution in fixed assets revealed by a revaluation to be accommodated by writing down unrealised profits recorded in a capital reserve, thereby not diminishing the profit available for dividend.

The 1985 Bill[53a] gives effect to article 35 of the Directive without purporting to modify section 45(4) of the 1983 Act. If reconciliation of these apparently conflicting provisions proves necessary, paramountcy must be given to the intent of the Directive.[53b]

---

[50] Para. (aa) is a facultative provision allowing the writing down of "financial fixed assets" as defined in arts. 9 and 10 even if the diminution in value is not permanent.

[51] Defined in para. 27 of the Sixth Sched., and paras. 69–70, Sched., 1985 Bill.

[52] s.39(4) (4a) of the Companies Act 1980 [U.K.] as amended by s.119 of the Companies Act 1981 [U.K.].

[53] s.45(5) of the 1983 Act. There must be a corresponding note in the accounts: *ibid.* s.49(8).

[53a] 1985 Bill, Sched., Part II, paras. 5–7.

[53b] See pp. 136, 155, *supra*.

A loss actually incurred on the disposal of a fixed asset is a realised loss insofar as not otherwise provided for.[54]

The new definition[55] of profits available for dividend includes not only revenue profits, by which is meant profits derived from the circulation of current assets or trading stock, but also realised profits of a capital nature, such as arise on the disposal of a fixed asset. Before the 1983 Companies Act, such a realised capital profit could have been utilised for the purpose of funding a dividend, provided that the book value of the net assets remaining exceeded the share capital and items akin to share capital, such as the share premium account and the capital redemption reserve fund.[56] Whether the directors were obliged to revalue these remaining assets to ensure such an excess existed, or were allowed to be content with their book value, was uncertain.[57] The new statutory rules contained in the 1983 Act do not require such a separate revaluation.

Before the coming into force of the 1983 Act, section 149(6) of the Companies Act 1963 allowed a company to utilise unrealised capital profits, established by revaluation of all the fixed assets of the company, in paying up unissued shares of the company as fully paid bonus shares to be issued to the members. Section 149(6) is now repealed by the 1983 Act[58]; however, the availability of unrealised profits to fund a bonus issue remains, but with less clarity of draftsmanship, under the 1983 Act. First, by section 51(2)(a) a bonus issue is not a "distribution" so as to attract the new rules; secondly, section 51(1) declares that provisions existing in a company's articles when the 1983 Act comes into force allowing unrealised profits to be used to pay up a bonus issue shall continue to be sufficient authority for that purpose; and, thirdly, the First Schedule, para. 23(f) adds a new capitalisation article to Table A, drafted to accord with the expressions employed in the 1983 Act, and allowing the use of unrealised profits.

Section 45(3) of the 1983 Act prohibits the use of unrealised profits to pay up the unpaid part of any share capital already *issued*, or any debentures.

The former prohibition in section 149(6) against the use of unrealised capital profits arising on the revaluation of fixed assets to fund

---

[54] Development costs are a realised revenue loss: 1985 Bill, s.20.

[55] At pp. 328–329, *supra*.

[56] *Lubbock* v *British Bank of South America* [1892] 2 Ch. 198; *Foster* v. *New Trinidad Lake Asphalte Co. Ltd.* [1901] 1 Ch. 208.

[57] See Jenkins Committee, paras. 337, 350(a).

[58] 1983 Act, s.3 and Third Sched.

a dividend[59] continues in another guise in the general rule that only realised profits are available for this purpose. An unrealised surplus on the revaluation of fixed assets will now be represented on the liabilities side of the balance sheet in the capital reserve,[60] pending realisation, or capitalisation.

As we have seen,[61] the pre-acquisition profits of a subsidiary company acquired by a holding company under a share for share exchange will be reflected in the capital structure of the holding company, usually by the creation of a share premium account. Those profits are then distributed by the subsidiary to the holding company, and the question arises whether the holding company can treat them as its realised profits available for distribution? The fear is that such a distribution will be made at the expense of the holding company's capital since the value of the pre-acquisition profits while still in the hands of the subsidiary went partly to make up the value of the share premium account which the holding company was obliged to establish on the acquisition. Irish company law does not invariably freeze such profits in the hands of the holding company. Section 149(5) of the Companies Act 1963, enacted as a modified response to the Jenkins Committee recommendations,[62] states:

> "(5) The profits or losses attributable to any shares in a subsidiary for the time being held by a holding company . . . shall not, for any purpose, be treated in the holding company's accounts as revenue profits or losses so far as they are profits or losses for the period before the date on or as from which the shares were acquired by the company . . . . Provided, however, that where the directors and the auditors are satisfied and so certify that it would be fair and reasonable and would not prejudice the rights and interests of any person, the profits or losses attributable to any shares in a subsidiary may be treated in a manner otherwise than in accordance with this subsection."

Circumstances bringing the proviso into operation could include the case where, after a reconstruction or amalgamation, the shareholders in a new holding company remained substantially the same people as held shares in the newly acquired subsidiaries.[63] The

---

[59] s.149(6)(a), reversing *Dimbula Valley (Ceylon) Tea Co. Ltd.* v. *Laurie* [1961] Ch. 353, and see *Buchanan Ltd.* v. *McVey* [1954] I.R. 89, 97.

[60] Para. 27(1)(c, Sixth Sched. "the expression 'capital reserve' shall not include any amount regard as free for distribution through the profit and loss account, and the expression 'revenue reserve' shall mean any reserve other than a capital reserve."

[61] pp. 325–326, *supra.*

[62] Paras. 342 *et seq.*

[63] *e.g.* as in *Head Henry & Co. Ltd.* v. *Ropner Holdings Ltd.* [1951] Ch. 124.

argument that such distributions might be prohibited independently of section 149(5) because they would necessarily involve a diminution in the share premium account[64] may be dismissed on the ground that the loss of value in the shares of the subsidiary occasioned by its distribution may be regarded as a depreciation in the value of a fixed asset held by the holding company, which, as the law stands, does not have to be made good out of its profits. It does not matter that the assets channelled into the pockets of the shareholders of the holding company might be the very assets whose value established its share premium account in the first place: the physical correspondence or lack of it between profit items on the liabilities side of the balance sheet reduced in order to fund a dividend and the items on the assets side actually used to pay it is immaterial.[65] Indeed, money may be borrowed for the actual payment of the dividend, provided profits exist on the liabilities side to fund it. If and when compulsory provision for fixed assets permanently reduced in value becomes law in Ireland, the operation of section 149(5) will be much curtailed, unless amendments are made to take account of the point under discussion.[66] Even now, distributability under section 149(5) must be in doubt for public limited companies, since they are obliged by section 46 of that Act, as we shall see below, to maintain their assets at a value which exceeds their paid up share capital and undistributable reserves, including the share premium account.

Asset base for plc's

There is a further overriding test which public limited companies are required to satisfy before paying a dividend. This test introduced by section 46 of the Companies Act 1983, in response to the Second Directive,[67] brings the law for these companies overtly back to the ideas which informed *Flitcroft's Case*[68]; in other words, the capital yardstick must be maintained. Section 46 accomplishes this by stating that:

---

[64] *e.g.* the premise upon which *Shearer* v. *Bercain Ltd.* [1980] 3 All E.R. 295; Ussher, (1982) 3 Co. Law. 28. proceeded.

[65] For an extreme example see *Dimbula Valley (Ceylon) Tea Co. Ltd.* v. *Laurie* [1961] Ch. 353, where *unrealised* gains were used to fund a dividend (a possibility scotched in Ireland by s.149(6): see p. 334, *supra*.)

[66] At present a provision for depreciation is not required since the shares in the subsidiary are not assets having "a finite useful life" within the meaning of S.S.A.P. 12 (n. 49c *supra*), but the diminution in value will be "permanent" and therefore within the ambit of 1985 Bill, Sched., para. 7(2) implementing Art. 35(1)(*c*)(*bb*), 4 Ha Directive.

[67] Art. 15(1)(*a*).

[68] (1882) 21 Ch. D. 519. See pp. 327–328, *supra*.

"A public limited company may only make a distribution at any time—(a) if at that time the amount of its net assets is not less than the aggregate of the company's called-up share capital and its undistributable reserves; and (b) if, and to the extent that, the distribution does not reduce the amount of those assets to less than that aggregate."

The undistributable reserves are defined as the share premium account,[69] the capital redemption reserve fund,[70] the amount by which the company's accumulated, unrealised profits, so far as not previously utilised by any capitalisation,[71] exceed its accumulated, unrealised losses, so far as not previously written off in a reduction or reorganisation of capital duly made,[72] and any other reserve[73] which the company is prohibited from distributing by any enactment other than one contained in Part IV of the 1983 Act, or by its memorandum or articles.

Derogation for investment companies

The Second Directive permitted a derogation[74] for investment companies of the *Verner*[75] type, that is to say, a company whose shares are available to the public and which invests its funds in a wide variety of stocks and shares, and perhaps other assets, which it then proceeds to manage as its exclusive activity, the idea being that its members should through it be able to participate in a wide variety of investments. It was recognised that temporary fluctuations in the value of these investments should not inhibit its ability to pay a dividend to its members out of current income. The derogation substituted for the net assets safeguard a requirement that the investment company's assets after the payment of the dividend be at least one-and-a-half times its liabilities to its creditors. This exception was broadly carried into effect by section 47 of the Companies Act 1983, in which the nature of the exception and an investment company is more particularly defined. It is to be noted that in the case of a *private* company holding investments, temporary fluctuations in their value will not affect its ability to pay a dividend, even after the implementation of the Fourth Directive, since they will be fixed assets whose depreciation is not permanent.

---

[69] See pp. 324 *et seq.*
[70] See pp. 326 *et seq.*
[71] *e.g.* under s.149(6) before its repeal by the 1983 Act.
[72] See pp. 338 *et seq., infra.*
[73] *i.e.* the capital *reserve* as defined by para. 27(1)(c) of the Sixth Sched.
[74] Art. 15(4).
[75] [1894] 2 Ch. 239.; p. 331, *supra.*

It is curious that the Second Directive did not allow a further derogation for public limited companies formed specifically to work one wasting asset. Under the present rules, such a company will when the asset is exhausted be left with a sinking fund, not for the purpose of replacing the asset but for distribution in a winding up, unless it has been through the section 72 procedure to reduce capital during its life.

Repayment of unlawful dividends

Members who receive a dividend knowing, or have reasonable grounds for believing, that it is unlawful must repay it to the company, or, in the case of a dividend paid otherwise than in cash, an amount equal to its value at the time of payment.[76-79]

The reduction of capital by an order of the court

The primary jurisdiction under which the court may sanction a reduction of capital by a limited company is section 72(2) of the Companies Act 1963.[80] The section states that such a company "subject to confirmation by the court . . . may, if so authorised by its articles,[81] by special resolution reduce its share capital in any way." The section then proceeds to a number of particular instances, but it is important to note that these are merely examples; the jurisdiction is founded merely by the passing of the special resolution: *Poole* v. *National Bank of China Ltd.*[82]

The particular examples given by section 72(2) itself cover over-capitalisation, where the company wishes to return surplus capital to the members, or to release them from their liability for calls on their partly paid shares,[83] and the situation where the company has suffered a loss of capital, and wishes to re-introduce some reality into the balance sheet. The presence of past losses may render a reduction of capital imperative if the company is to be able to pay dividends. A loss making company may be freed by a reduction in capital from the obligation to make provision out of profits for the depreciation of fixed assets, or from the obligation to set current profits against a debit balance on the profit and loss account occurred in previous trading; or it may release for dividends a pro-

---

[76-79] 1983 Act, s. 50.

[80] This and the ensuing ancillary sections are in all substantive respects the same as ss.66 *et seq.* of the Companies Act 1948 [*U.K.*].

[81] *e.g.* art. 46 of Table A.

[82] [1907] A.C. 229.

[83] ss.72(2)(*c*) and 72(2)(*a*) respectively.

vision in fact made out of profits for depreciation.[84] Past losses will also prevent a company from raising fresh capital on the market by an issue of shares to rank *pari passu* with existing shares which are standing at a discount. In this situation, the reduction procedure may be used to reduce the nominal value of the existing shares to their market value as a preliminary to the new issue.[85]

Even reductions involving a return of capital to the members may be motivated by a desire to resume dividend payments, and not out of a spirit of largesse. The profits available for dividend may be wholly absorbed by the prior claims of preference shareholders, leaving the ordinary shareholders the prospect of no return on their investment unless profits improve. Reductions are most often contested where different classes of shareholders are treated differently as a result of motivations such as this. The extent to which members of a company may successfully thwart a reduction is discussed in Chapter 9: *Minority Protection*, at pp. 283 *et seq.*

The Act itself is expressly concerned only with the protection of creditors on a reduction. This accords with the philosophy which views the subscribed capital as "the creditors" fund."[86] Where the proposed reduction involves either a diminution of liability in respect of unpaid share capital, or the payment to any shareholder of any paid up share capital, the court must be satisfied that creditors either have consented to the reduction or that provision has been made for their debts. Every creditor is in these cases given an express statutory right to object to the reduction. Even after the reduction, it is not conclusive as against any creditor who could have objected but by reason of his ignorance of the proceedings, or of their nature and effect, was not entered on the list of creditors in the reduction process. Such a creditor may in the subsequent winding up of the company insist that members contribute to its assets the amount they would have been liable to contribute but for the reduction.[87]

Reductions of capital under section 72 are occasionally combined with schemes of arrangement under sections 201–203. This might occur when preference shareholders are to be repaid otherwise than

---

[84] See *Re John Power & Son Ltd.* [1934] I.R. 412. For the effect on distributable profits of provisions for depreciation of upwardly revalued fixed assets, see 1983 Act, s.45(6).

[85] For the prohibition on the issue of shares at a discount, see pp. 306 *et seq., supra.*

[86] See p. 303. An aspect of the same reasoning requires a plc whose allotted capital is reduced by order of the court to below the authorised minimum to seek private company status: 1983 Act, ss. 14, 17.

[87] The foregoing represents a paraphrase of the salient points of the statutory procedure. For full details, see ss.73–77. Full investigation of creditors' claims may occasionally be dispensed with: s.73(3); *Re Lucania Temperance Billiards Halls Ltd.* [1966] Ch. 98.

in cash, their prima facie entitlement,[88] or where as an integral part of a reconstruction or amalgamation, share capital of one of the companies involved is to be reduced by cancellation.[89] Reconstructions, amalgamations and arrangements are generally described at pp. 288 *et seq.*

The court may order that the shares of members be purchased by the company, and therefore that its capital be correspondingly reduced, in proceedings for relief under section 205, and in applications by dissentient members on the alteration of objects or of the memorandum pursuant to section 28 of the 1963 Act, and on a resolution by a public limited company to re-register as a private company.[90]

Commissions

A company making a public issue of shares will usually attempt to have that issue underwritten, that is to say, will enter into an agreement whereby the underwriter will subscribe to the shares in the event of the public failing to do so. The underwriting agreement will usually provide for the payment of a commission to the underwriter. Such commissions, provided that they do not exceed 10 per cent. of the issue price of the shares, are declared to be lawful by section 59(1) of the Companies Act 1963. It is tolerably clear from section 59(2) which begins:

> "Save as aforesaid no company shall apply any of its shares or capital money either directly or indirectly in payment of any commission, discount or allowance to any person in consideration of his subscribing or agreeing to subscribe . . . for any shares in the company . . . "

that the payment of lawful commissions may allow shares effectively to be issued at a discount. Furthermore, by section 62(2)(*b*) the share premium account may be used in writing off, *inter alia*," the commission paid or discount allowed on, any issue of shares . . . of the company."[90a] There would appear to be nothing in section 59 to prohibit the commission being paid from other sources, such a profits.

Moreover, it is of considerable importance to underwriters that a

---

[88] *e.g. Re John Power & Son Ltd.* [1934] I.R. 312; *cf. Re Robert Stephen Holdings Ltd.* [1968] 1 W.L.R. 522.

[89] *Re Hellenic & General Trust Ltd.* [1976] 1 W.L.R. 123.

[90] Respectively, s.205(3); s.10(6A)(B)(C) as added by para. 2 (*b*), First Sched. 1983 Act; *ibid.*, para. 5 amending s.28; s.15(7), 1983 Act.

[90a] But the 1985 Bill, s.4(12) disallows commissions and expenses as balance sheet assets.

agreement under which they agree to subscribe at par to an issue being offered to the public at a premium is not construed as giving them a "commission" within the meaning of section 59. It would seem not, because the company is parting with no money; nor, by definition, is there a discount.[91] Thus, an underwriter may by such an arrangement procure considerably more than the 10 per cent. advantage over the public obtainable by transactions within the section.

Section 59 applies likewise to an issue of shares by a private company.

Compulsory meeting after serious loss of capital

If a director of a company knows that its net assets[92] have fallen to half or less of its issued share capital, then by section 40 of the 1983 Act, the board must within 28 days summon an *egm* of the company for the "purpose of considering whether any, and if so what, measures should be taken to 'deal with' the situation."[93]

There is no indication that the board is bound to abide by the recommendations, if any, of the meeting. The prudence of this measure, particularly its application to private companies is questioned in Chapter 11: *Accounts and Auditors* at pp. 378–380.

---

[91] *Hilder* v. *Dexter* [1902] A.C. 474, decided on s.8(2) of the Companies Act 1900, the predecessor of s.59. The case concerned an option as opposed to the definite commitment to purchase posited in the text, but there seems to be no difference in principle.

[92] "Net assets" are defined by 1983 Act, s.2(4)(*b*) as being "the aggregate of its assets less the aggregate of its liabilities."

[93] The meeting must be held within 56 days of a director's first learning of the loss.

Chapter 11: Accounts and Auditors

ACCOUNTS

Keeping proper books of account

Section 147 of the Companies Act 1963 requires every company to keep proper books of account recording "all sums of money received and expended by the company and the matters in respect of which the receipt and expenditure takes place; . . . all sales and purchases of goods by the company; [and] the assets and liabilities of the company," and to preserve them for at least six years.[1] Such records will be sufficient only if they "give a true and fair view of the state of a company's affairs and . . . explain its transactions."[2] The auditor is required to certify annually in his report whether or not the company has complied with these requirements.[3] Failure by a director to take all reasonable steps to secure compliance with the section is punishable by a fine not exceeding £500,[4] and, if the default is wilful, there is the additional possibility of imprisonment for a term of up to six months.

The related section 296 of the Companies Act 1963 carries even greater deterrents. Here failure to keep proper books of account throughout the period of two years immediately preceding the commencement of a company's winding up may be visited with imprisonment for a term not exceeding two years, or a fine of up to £2,500, or both.[5] This section goes into greater detail on what is meant by proper books of account for its purposes, namely those:

> "necessary to exhibit and explain the transactions and financial position of the trade or business of the company, including books containing entries from day to day in sufficient detail of all cash received and cash paid, and, where the trade or busi-

---

[1] s.147(1), (5).
[2] s.147(2).
[3] Para. 2, Sched. 7.
[4] s.147(6); fine increased by 1982 Act, Sched. 1.
[5] Fine increased by 1982 Act, Sched. 1. For further offences relating to books of account, see p. 517, n. 5 *infra*, and for suggested remedies arising out of a failure to keep proper books, see pp. 529–530, *infra*.

ness has involved dealings in goods, statements of the annual stocktakings and (except in the case of goods sold by way of ordinary retail trade) of all goods sold and purchased, showing the goods and the buyers and sellers thereof in sufficient detail to enable those goods and those buyers and sellers to be identified."

It is time that these two provisions, of different provenance but similar effect, were assimilated.

Although "books of account" are spoken of in these sections, one need not make the relevant entries in an actual bound book in order to comply with them. Section 378 of the Companies Act 1963 states that:

"any register, index, minute book or book of account required by this Act to be kept by a company . . . may be kept either by making entries in bound books or by recording the matters in question in any other manner."

It has now been declared by section 4 of the Companies (Amendment) Act 1977 that these other permissible methods of recording information include "recording the matters in question otherwise than in a legible form so long as the recording is capable of being reproduced in a legible form," allowing therefore storage on a disc, or other computer accessible form.

The obligation to prepare annual accounts

Section 148(1) of the Companies Act 1963 states that:

"The directors of every company shall at some date not later than 18 months after the incorporation of the company and subsequently once at least in every calendar year lay before the annual general meeting of the company *a profit and loss account* . . . for the period, in the case of the first account, since the incorporation of the company, and in any other case, since the preceding account, made up to a date not earlier than the date of the meeting by more than 9 months,"

and section 148(2) requires them also to:

"cause to be made out in every calendar year and to be laid before the annual general meeting of the company *a balance sheet* as at the date to which the profit and loss account . . . is made up."

Furthermore, where a company has subsidiaries there may be an additional obligation under section 150 to prepare *group accounts*, comprising a *consolidated balance sheet* and a *consolidated profit and loss account*,[6] dealing with the state of affairs and the profit and loss of the company and the subsidiaries dealt with as a whole.[7] The holding subsidiary relationship is described by section 155. The essence of the relationship is control. Put broadly, a company will be another's subsidiary if the latter holds in it more than half its unrestricted voting shares, or more than half its equity share capital (*i.e.* excluding any part of the share capital which, neither as respects dividends nor as respects capital, carries any right to participate beyond a specified amount in a distribution,[8]) or is a member of it and has an unfettered power to appoint or veto the appointment of its directors (or a majority of them), or to remove them (or a majority of them); or, if it is a subsidiary of another subsidiary of the other company.[9] A private company need not prepare group accounts in relation to its subsidiaries[10]; neither need any company which is itself the wholly owned subsidiary of another body corporate incorporated in the State[11]; nor need they be prepared in relation to any particular subsidiary if only insignificant amounts are involved and the directors are consequently of the view that their preparation would be impracticable or of no real value to the members of the company, or if the directors think that their preparation would involve expense or delay out of proportion to the value to the members of the company, or if they think the result would be misleading.[12]

Attached to the foregoing annual accounts there should also be the *directors' report*,[13] and the *auditors' report*.[14] Failures by the directors to present annual accounts and their report, or to attach it to the accounts, are offences of a gravity similar to a failure to keep proper accounting records pursuant to section 147, *supra*, and attract like sanctions.[15] Further criminal penalties may be exacted if a balance sheet is issued, circulated or published without having first having

[6] s.151. The preparation of a consolidated profit and loss account may exonerate a company from preparing a separate profit and loss account relating to its own affairs: s.149(4), *infra*.

[7] s.152.

[8] s.155(5). For differing rights of participation, see Chap. 6, *supra*.

[9] There is further detail in s.155 itself. The parent subsidiary relationship will be redefined for the purpose of group accounts upon implementation of the 7th EEC Directive (83/349/EEC: O.J. L193/1 of July 18, 1983). See section 1 thereof. Ireland must carry this Directive into law by January 1, 1988.

[10] s.154(1).

[11] s.150(2)(*a*); "wholly owned" is defined in s.150(5).

[12] The text is partly interpretative of s.150(2)(*b*) in which the significance to be attached to the use of commas is not altogether clear.

[13] s.157(1), s.158 and s.164.

[14] For the auditors' report, see the discussion of auditors.

[15] s.148(3), s.150(4), and s.158(7).

been signed on behalf of the board by two of the directors,[16] or without first there having been annexed to it the profit and loss account and any group accounts (not already incorporated in the balance sheet or profit and loss account), and attached to it the auditors' report.[17]

The content of the annual accounts

The Sixth Schedule to the Companies Act 1963 contains details of matters required to be stated in a company's balance sheet, profit and loss account,[18] and group accounts,[19] if any. However, mere compliance with these intricacies will not necessarily be enough to satisfy the Act. Section 149(1) imposes an overriding requirement that:

> "every balance sheet of a company shall give a *true and fair view* of the state of affairs of the company as at the end of its financial year, and every profit and loss account of a company shall give a *true and fair view* of the profit or loss of the company for the financial year"[20]

and group accounts likewise are required by section 152(1) to give:

> "a *true and fair view* of the state of affairs and profit or loss of the company and the subsidiaries dealt with thereby as a whole, so far as concerns the members of the company."[21]

If a company's profit and loss account is framed as a consolidated profit and loss account dealing with all or any of the company's subsidiaries as well as the company, it is exonerated by section 149(4) from preparing a separate profit and loss account relating to the company. The consolidated profit and loss account should however meet the standards imposed by the Act for group accounts, and should show how much of the profit or loss is dealt with in the accounts of the company.[21a]

---

[16] s.156.

[17] s.157. Documents "annexed" are an integral part of the document: s.149(8)(*a*). If information required to be given in annual accounts is given instead, as it may be, in the directors' report, it becomes correspondingly annexed: s.164(2). Apart from that directors' and auditors' reports are described as being only "attached," and are therefore not integral.

[18] s.149(2).

[19] s.152(3).

[20] Italics supplied. The dominance of the "true and fair view" is secured by s.149(3).

[21] The dominance of the "true and fair view" is secured by s.152(3).

[21a] The 1985 Bill, s.3(2), (3) carries over this relaxation a course permitted by Article 58 of the 4th Directive.

Even after the implementation of the Fourth EEC Directive which requires Ireland considerably to revise and amplify the Schedule 6, the dominance of the"true and fair view" will be maintained.[22] The 1985 Bill, introduced on May 29, 1985 to implement the Directive, spells out the dominance of the "true and fair view." Section 3 of the Bill, replacing the relevant parts of section 149, states that where compliance with the specific requirements of the Bill would not result in a true and fair view, additional information must be provided in the accounts or by way of note to them in order to do so; *and* it states also that if compliance with those specific requirements would prevent the attainment of the true and fair view, then the company must depart from them in order to attain it (saying so and explaining why in a note to the accounts).

This expression, "the true and fair view," though declared by the Act to be of paramount importance, is nowhere explained in it. The closest one gets to a comprehensive statement of its content is in the Statements of Standard Accounting Practice (S.S.A.P.s) issued jointly by the main branches of the accountancy profession. The *Explanatory Foreword* to these state them to be "methods of accounting approved . . . for application to all financial accounts intended to give a true and fair view of financial position and profit or loss." Yet an S.S.A.P is not as such of legal effect; the courts will always have the last word. There are as yet no judicial decisions on the probative value to be put on the united views of the accountancy profession, whether communicated by an S.S.A.P. or otherwise, on what in any given circumstances constitutes the correct method of conveying a "true and fair view." Judges have, however, given their opinions on the closely analogous question of the status to be accorded to uniform accountancy practice in determining for tax purposes whether a profit or loss has been correctly arrived at. In *Dolan* v. *A.B. Co. Ltd.*,[23] the majority in the Supreme Court concurred with the judgment of Budd J. in which he said:

> " . . . the uncontradicted evidence of what is proper to be done from the point of view of business accountancy is a factor weighing heavily in favour of the appellants. . . ."[24]

Compliance with accountancy standards will thus not be conclusive

---

[22] Arts. 2(3), 2(4) of the Directive. See (1982) 3 Co. Law 19.

[23] [1969] I.R. 282 (deductibility by an oil company of payments under solus agreements).

[24] *Ibid.* at p. 380. For an English pronouncement to similar effect, see Lord Reid in *I.R.C.* v. *Duple Motor Bodies Ltd.* [1961] 1 W.L.R. 739, 752. In the Supreme Court, O Dalaigh C.J. (at p. 348) and Walsh, J. (at pp. 361–2) were less enthusiastic than the majority view. Teevan, J. at first instance (at p. 324) was even cooler.

evidence that the accounts give a true and fair view; nor will deviance from the standards inevitably mean that they do not.[25] Yet since the law and the accounting standards have an identical objective and since the sole purpose of the accountancy profession is to attain it, the law is usually prepared to concede, as it should, that accountancy practice, although it may "appear elaborate and artificial to a lawyer, . . . is aimed almost always successfully, at arriving at an aspect of the truth . . . "[26] The prospect of divergence is diminishing as statute incorporates into law the specific standards hammered out by the accountancy profession. A major step in this direction is being taken by the 1985 Bill. And, as we have seen,[26a] the standards of the accountancy profession have become in large part the arbiter of the propriety of a dividend payment, and necessarily also the arbiter of the propriety of key items in the calculation: profits, losses, assets, liabilities, provisions and reserves.[26b]

But there still remains a difficulty however "true and fair" accounts as presented may be in the eyes of the accountancy profession, and however precisely they may satisfy the technical requirements of Schedule 6 and its replacements. They may still fall so short of the whole truth as to mislead the unskilled or the unwary. The classic example is the acceptability in law and in accounting practice of stating certain fixed assets in the balance sheet at their acquisition cost (historic cost) less depreciation when in truth the value of those assets may be considerably greater. In *Re Press Caps Ltd.*[27] freehold property was stated in the balance sheet at one third of its market value, and other fixed assets at a figure way in excess of it. Shareholders who sought to avoid being compulsorily bought out under the British equivalent of section 204 of the Companies Act 1963[28] following a takeover bid in which the primary indication to the offerees of the worth of their company, and hence of their shares in it, were accounts drawn up in this manner, were told in effect by the English Court of Appeal that no one should be misled by the misleading conventions of accountancy. In substance accounts are addressed to specialists, and specialists know the rules. Historic cost

---

[25] See Pennycuick, V.-C. in *Odeon Associated Theatres Ltd.* v. *Jones (Inspector of Taxes)* [1971] 1 W.L.R. 442, 454.

[26] *Per* Salmon L.J. in *B.S.C. Footwear Ltd.* v. *Ridgway* [1970] 2 W.L.R. 888, 892–893.

[26a] See Chap. 10 at pp. 328, 332.

[26b] 1983 Act, s.49(1), (3), (9).

[27] [1949] 1 Ch. 434. For historic cost entries in respect of fixed assets, see para. 5, 6th Sched. For the meaning of "fixed assets," see p. 330, *supra.*

[28] As to which see Chap. 9 at pp. 297 *et seq.*

will be retained as a permissible option even after the implementation of the Fourth EEC Directive.[28a]

This is not a book on the principles of accounting as such. It is unnecessary to rehearse here the detailed content of Schedule 6, but it might be salutary to give examples of occasions where according to good accountancy practice a "true and fair view" will not be attained despite observing its requirements. For example, S.S.A.P. 12: *Accounting for Depreciation* says in para. 17 that "provision for depreciation of fixed assets having a finite useful life *should* be made"[29]; yet, surprisingly, Schedule 6 contains no such positive obligation,[30] but the 1985 Bill sets out to change all that.[30a] Another example may be found in the interrelationship between S.S.A.P. 19: *Accounting for Investment Properties* and Schedule 6. This accounting standard requires interests in developed land held for its investment potential to be valued and included in the balance sheet at their open market value. There is no such obligation in Schedule 6, and it remains only an option in the 1985 Bill.[30b]

Schedule 6 is amplified by sections 191 and 192 of the Companies Act 1963. We look at each in greater detail because each attempts to resolve through the accounts a potential abuse of a position of control, through which minorities and creditors may suffer. Section 191 is designed to elicit disclosure in the accounts (or in a statement annexed to them) of the benefits accruing to a person from his directorship. Section 192 requires disclosure in the accounts of loans to directors.

Section 191 casts its net widely, and its draftsmanship is finely meshed. The three areas of disclosure are emoluments, pensions and compensation for loss of office. It is not material that the company itself may not bear the cost of these rewards. Sums paid by or receivable from any person must be disclosed. The only connection between the payment and the company must be, in the case of emoluments and pensions, that they are in respect of services as director of the company, or services while a director of the company as director of any of its subsidiaries, or are otherwise in connection with the management of the affairs of the company or any of its subsidiaries. The connection in the case of payments for loss of office is similar: the office lost must be a directorship of the company itself, or the loss, whilst still a director of the company or on ceasing to be its

---

[28a] 1985 Bill, Sched., Pt. II.

[29] Italics supplied.

[30] Para. 5, Sched. 6, notwithstanding. This describes the treatment of fixed assets if provision *is* made for depreciation. See para. 14(2), Sched. 6.

[30a] See Chap. 10 at pp. 331–333 *et seq.*

[30b] 1985 Bill, Sched., Pt. III.

director or in connection with his ceasing to be its director, of any other office in connection with the management of its affairs or those of any of its subsidiaries. The definition of subsidiary is enlarged to include a corporation to the board of which a director is nominated by the company, *e.g.* under a power of appointment contained in the fomer's articles of association. Emoluments include not only fees, percentages, and pension contributions, but also expense allowances (insofar as chargeable to income tax) and the money value of benefits in kind. Pensions include benefits receivable by the director's nominee, his dependants, or by persons otherwise connected with him; pension includes a lump sum gratuity, but excludes a pension fully founded on a contributory pension scheme, since contributions to it made otherwise than by the director will be disclosed as emoluments. Section 191 requires the disclosure of the aggregate amount of the directors' emoluments, of directors' and past-directors' pensions, and of any compensation to directors or past directors for loss of office.

A company lending money to its own directors may tend not to require the safeguards that another lender would. Such a loan may therefore prejudice the company's creditors; also, if the company is not wholly owned by the recipient director, minority shareholders may suffer. To avert these dangers, a legislature might either prohibit loans to directors, or demand that they be disclosed to those who might suffer as a consequence. Section 192 of the Companies Act 1963 chooses the disclosure option, but since the disclosure is to be made in the company's accounts, it is confined to those entitled to see those accounts. As the law stands at present, the accounts of a private company may be confined to its members and debenture holders. When the 1985 Bill is enacted and in force they will become available to the public, including therefore creditors and potential creditors, but as we shall see under the heading *Disclosure of the financial statements, infra,* the efficacy of such disclosures as a means of protection may be doubted. Perhaps the alternative of a prohibition against loans to directors should be reconsidered. Section 192 requires the accounts to state the amount not only of loans by the company but also by any of its subsidiaries. Loan includes guaranteeing the repayment of a loan, or providing security for a loan. The loans included are those to a director, or a person becoming a director after the loan had been made to him, and, significantly, loans to a body corporate in which the directors or any of them are beneficially entitled to 20 per cent. or more of the shares carrying voting rights.

Also, so as to prevent this book departing from its proper province, we do not consider in the abstract the close detail of the changes in the accounting rules to be introduced by the 1985 Bill. We have already in reviewing the dividend rules seen the practical consequences of some of these changes.[30c] Nonetheless, a broad description of the changes in approach might be helpful.

Section 5 of the Bill will introduce into law, with slightly different terminology and language, the fundamental accounting concepts developed by the profession as the bedrock of modern accounting. As described by S.S.A.P. 2: *Disclosure of accounting policies*, issued in January 1971, these are the concepts of *going concern, accruals, consistency* and *prudence*. The going concern concept assumes that the enterprise will continue in operational existence for the foreseeable future, and is further discussed at p. 359 *infra*, and under the heading *Auditors* at pp. 379–380. Under the accruals concept, revenue and costs are recognised as they are earned or incurred, and not as money is received or paid. The consistency concept requires that like items be treated consistently within each accounting period, and from one period to the next. By the concept of prudence, revenue and profits are not anticipated until realised, but expenses and losses are provided for whether or not the amount is known with certainty. If a company's directors consider there are special reasons for departing from the accounting principles set out in section 5, then by section 6 they may do so provided that the extent of the departure, the reasons for it and its effect on the accounts is explained in a note to them.

The Schedule[30d] has a stricter approach to the format of accounts than Schedule 6, but allows a freedom of choice between a vertical and horizontal balance sheet, and two vertical and two horizontal forms of profit and loss account. Generally, Irish accounts are vertically presented; the continentals prefer the horizontal.

The Schedule considerably amplifies the content of the accounts over the requirements of Schedule 6. This is particularly so in the notes to the accounts prescribed by Part IV of the Schedule. Here we find that a wide variety of information has to be given supplementing the balance sheet and profit and loss account. To take but a few examples, a company must in the notes give reasons for allotting shares,[30e] and the reasons for issuing debentures[30f]; it must closely particularise the changes shown in the value of fixed assets and each of them[30g]; it must categorise its creditors, distinguishing between long term and short term debts, unsecured and secured, describing

[30c] See Chap. 10 at pp. 326 *et seq.*
[30d] Made applicable by 1985 Bill, s.4, and to be read in conjunction with it.
[30e] 1985 Bill, Schedule, para. 27(*a*).
[30f] *Ibid.* para. 28(1)(*a*).
[30g] *Ibid.* paras. 29–30.

the security[30h]; it must describe its pension scheme, guarantees to third parties, and financial commitments about which the accounts are silent, distinguishing commitments to associated companies[30i]; it must reveal the aggregate amount of the directors' emoluments and compensation for loss of office[30j]; it must give particulars of its turnover, segregating turnover in different sorts of business and geographical markets[30k]; and it must state its average number of employees and categorise them.[30l]

In the valuation of assets, the Schedule gives most attention to an amplification of the rules of historical cost accounting,[30m] but it does allow the option of current cost accounting.[30n] In this latter respect, it paints with a broader brush, leaving practitioners to rely for further detail on S.S.A.P. 16: *Current cost accounting.* This Accounting Standard requires large companies to prepare current cost accounts in addition to historical cost accounts.

The Schedule describes how provisions actually made by investment companies in respect of depreciated financial fixed assets are to be treated. And it addresses itself to accounting for the group of companies, including such matters as the valuation and treatment in a holding company's accounts of interests in its subsidiaries, the preparation of consolidated accounts, and the explanation of the omission of any subsidiary.

Some companies are to be fully or partially spared compliance with these new rules for the preparation of accounts. Some also are to be spared full publication of accounts as prepared. That topic is treated at pp. 356 *et seq., infra* under the heading *Disclosure of the financial statements.* We are concerned for the moment only with exemptions in respect of the content of accounts, though, as will appear they have considerable ground in common with the exemptions from publication.

The Bill does not apply at all to unlimited companies; neither did the Directive.[30o] Their accounts may still therefore be prepared in accordance with Schedule 6.

[30h] *Ibid.* para. 34.

[30i] *Ibid.* para. 36.

[30j] *Ibid.* para. 39(6). This, and para. 36(4) relating to pensions, to some extent duplicate s.191, *supra.*

[30k] *Ibid.* para. 41, but see para. 40(5) which allows directors not to disclose these facts if in their opinion to do so would be severely prejudicial to the interests of the company.

[30l] *Ibid.* para. 42.

[30m] 1985 Bill, Sched., Pt. II, and see pp. 347–348, *supra.*

[30n] 1985 Bill, Sched., Pt. III.

[30o] 1985 Bill, s.1(1). For unlimited companies, see Chap. 1 at pp. 9–10.

In addition, still to be governed by Schedule 6, are companies not trading for profit,[30p] limited companies without share capital formed for a charitable object and controlled by certain religions,[30q] limited companies without a share capital formed for charitable purposes and exempted by the Commissioners for Charitable Donations and Bequests from publishing accounts,[30r] and banking, finance and similar companies.[30s] The companies in this last category are not wholly to escape modifications in their financial statements. They are to be affected by changes in the content of the directors' report, discussed *infra* under the heading *Content of the directors' report.* Schedule 6 treats banking and discount companies more leniently than other trading companies remaining within it.[30t] Insurance companies likewise will remain subject to the former regime governing the content of their accounts,[30u] save that they too are to be affected by changes in the content of the directors' report. These exemptions, determined by the nature of the company's activities, apply to both public and private limited companies.

The foregoing apart, the Bill gives no exemptions on content to the public limited company. The exemptions based on the size of the company and envisaged by the Directive as being available, should a Member State so wish, to any qualified limited company, have been reserved by the Bill for private limited companies. These exemptions distinguish between the *small* and *medium sized* private limited company. The small company is by Irish standards really rather large. It is a company which has not for two consecutive years exceeded on its balance sheet date two of the following three criteria: a total on the assets side of the balance sheet of £IR1,250,000, a net turnover of £IR2,500,000, and an average number of employees during the financial year of 50.[30v] For a medium sized company the limits are respectively enlarged to £IR5,000,000 and £IR10,000,000, and 250 employees.[30w] The Bill contains ancillary provisions governing the classification of newly formed and existing companies,

---

[30p] *Ibid.* s.2(1)(*a*).

[30q] s.2(1)(*b*), and see n. 65, *infra.*

[30r] s.2(1)(*c*), and see n. 65, *infra.*

[30s] More particularly described in 1985 Bill, s.2(2).

[30t] Schedule 6, Part III.

[30u] Schedule 6, Part III, para. 24.

[30v] 4th Directive, Art. 11, as implemented by the 1985 Bill, s.8(1), (2). The monetary figures are stated in the Directive in terms of European Units of Account, (respectively 1m. EUA and 2m. EUA) against which the Irish currency has depreciated in recent times.

[30w] 4th Directive, Art. 27 as implemented by 1985 Bill, s.8(1), s.8(3). The EUA figures (see n. 30v, *supra*) for medium sized companies are respectively 4m. and 8m.

and the reclassification of companies whose size has altered.[30x] The Bill proposes that small companies be obliged to prepare only an abridged balance sheet,[30y] an abridged profit and loss account,[30z] and far fewer notes to the accounts.[31] The abridgements exonerate the company from breaking down key headings into their components. Relieving small companies from preparing of most of the notes to the accounts required by the 1985 Bill will result in the accounting burden on such companies not being significantly increased over Schedule 6 levels. Relief given by the 1985 Bill to the medium sized company in the preparation of accounts is only slight. They may abridge the profit and loss account to the same extent as small companies,[31a] but are neither relieved on the content of the balance sheet, nor in respect of the notes to the accounts, save that they need not break down their turnover by stating the volume of business done in particular geographical markets or in particular classes of business, such information being of particular value to competitors.[31b]

Content of the directors' report

Section 158 of the Companies Act 1963 prescribes the content of the directors' report. They must report on:

> "the state of the company's affairs and if the company is a holding company, on the state of affairs of the company and its subsidiaries as a group, the amount, if any which they recommend should be paid by way of dividend and the amount, if any, which they propose to carry to reserves within the meaning of the Sixth Schedule."

The report should deal so far as material with any change during the financial year in the nature of the company's business or that of its subsidiaries, or in the classes of business in which the company has an interest whether as a member of another company or otherwise.[31c] The report should also contain a list not only of the company's

---

[30x] 1985 Bill, s.8(7), (8); s.9.

[30y] *Ibid.* s.10(1).

[30z] *Ibid.* s.11(1) which is expressed as an exemption for medium sized companies, but small companies *a fortiori* fulfil the qualifications for medium sized companies. The exemption originates in 4th Directive, Art. 27.

[31] 1985 Bill, s.12(1).

[31a] *Ibid.* s.11(1).

[31b] *Ibid.* s.11(2), referring to Sched., para. 41.

[31c] s.158(2). The Fourth EEC Directive, art. 46, will require explicitly "an indication of . . . any important events that have occurred since the end of the financial year, . . . the company's likely future development . . . [and] activities in the field of research and development."

subsidiaries, but also of associated companies in which it "is beneficially entitled to more than 20 per cent. in nominal value of shares carrying voting rights (other than voting rights which arise only in specified circumstances),[32] giving the name of each such company, its place of incorporation, and the nature of the business carried on by it.[33]

The Fourth Directive, as implemented by the 1985 Bill, enlarges and, to an extent, repeats the existing function of the directors' report. The Bill also diminishes that function in one important respect.[33a]

The enlargement and repetition are found in sections 13 and 14. Section 13 requires as well as a "fair review of the development of the business of the company and of its subsidiaries, if any," that "any important events affecting" them during the financial year be described, and that "likely future developments" in their business and their "activities . . . in the field of research and development" be indicated.[33b] Section 14 requires disclosure of shares in itself held by the company or on its behalf, or by way of permitted security interest, all matters of relatively minor importance in this jurisdiction.[33c]

The diminution comes in section 16 by which details of holdings in subsidiary and associated companies[33d] are transferred from the directors' report to the notes to the accounts, and those details are to be expanded there. In particular, the nature of the company's shareholding must be described in the notes, and, subject to a few exceptions, the aggregate amount of the capital and reserves of each subsidiary and associated company must be stated, together with its profit and loss.[33e] The principal exception relieves the company

[32] s.158(4). For the significance of this disclosure in relation to circular voting arrangements, see Chap. 3 at pp. 104–105.

[33] s.158(5). For fuller details, see the section.

[33a] But only in respect of companies to which the 1985 Bill applies, *i.e.* excluding unlimited companies and those described in 1985 Bill, s.2(1).

[33b] Following 4th Directive, Art. 46.1, 2(*a*), (*b*), (*c*).

[33c] Following 4th Directive, Art. 46.2(*d*). The methods of acquisition are forfeiture (pp. 317–318, *supra*) or surrender in lieu, shares acquired otherwise than by purchase (pp. 102–103, *supra*), or shares in which a plc has a beneficial interest in the circumstances described by the 1983 Act, s.43(1), (*c*), (*d*), and which fall to be cancelled under s.43(3). The permitted security interests affected are described in the 1983 Act, s.44(2)(*a*), (*c*), (*d*). See also 1983 Act, Sched. 1, para 27.

[33d] As described above, *i.e.* a body corporate in which the company is beneficially entitled to more than 20 per cent. in nominal value of the shares carrying voting rights (other than voting rights arising only in specified circumstances: s.158(4)(*b*), as repeated in 1985 Bill, s.16(1)(*b*); to which are now added bodies corporate in which the company is entitled "to more than 20 per cent. in nominal value of the allotted share capital": 1985 Bill, s.16(1)(*b*).

[33e] 1985 Bill, s.16(1)(*b*)(iii), (iv).

from giving financial information about its subsidiaries if it is itself a wholly owned subsidiary,[33f] or if the subsidiary's accounts are included in the group accounts of the company, or if the shares in the subsidiary held by the company are treated in its accounts by the equity method of valuation,[33g] *i.e.* a method by which the value of those shares, though inserted initially at cost in the company's balance sheet, is adjusted according to the share attributable to the company of the subsidiary's post-acquisition retained profits and reserves.[33h] Also, a company will be exempt from disclosing financial information about its associated companies if it employs the equity method of valuation for its shares in them[33i]; it need not disclose financial information about a subsidiary or associated company which is not required to publish its accounts and in which it does not hold a half or more of its allotted share capital,[33j] and it need not disclose the information if it is not material.[33k]

A small private limited company is, as we shall see under the heading *Disclosure of the financial statements*, to be obliged by the 1985 Bill to publish an abridged balance sheet but is to be exempted from publishing its directors' report. Requiring information about subsidiaries and associated companies to be stated in notes to the accounts rather than in the directors' report will mean, it seems, that that information must be published with its balance sheet, since by section 1(2) of the 1985 Bill

> "a reference to a balance sheet or profit and loss account shall include a reference to any notes or documents annexed to the accounts in question giving information which is required by any provision of the Companies Acts 1963 to 1985, and required or allowed by any such provision to be given in a note to or a document annexed to a company's accounts."

That publication is the legislative purpose behind requiring that information about subsidiary and associated companies be given in notes to the accounts is made plain by section 16(3) of the 1985 Bill which allows the information not to be incorporated in a note to the accounts at all if the note would in the opinion of the company's directors be of excessive length; in those circumstances the infor-

---

[33f] s.150(2)(*a*), and 1985 Bill, s.16(2)(*a*).
[33g] 1985 Bill, s.16(2)(*a*)(i), (ii).
[33h] See S.S.A.P. 14: *Group Accounts,* and S.S.A.P. 1: *Accounting for results of associated companies.*
[33i] 1985 Bill, s.16(2)(*b*).
[33j] *Ibid.* s.16(2)(*b*).
[33k] *Ibid.* s.16(2)(*c*).

mation may be given in a statement to be annexed to the company's next annual return to the registrar.[331]

Disclosure of the financial statements

All companies without exception must disclose their annual accounts (balance sheets and profit and loss accounts), and their directors' and auditors' reports to their members and debenture holders.[34] Furthermore, any member is entitled to be furnished with the latest annual accounts, and directors' and auditors' reports of a subsidiary company not dealt with in group accounts,[35] or, in the case of a private holding company, where group accounts have not been prepared.[36] Members of private companies may in addition requisition previous annual accounts, directors' and auditors' reports of any of its subsidiaries going back over a period of ten years from the date of the request.

As the law stands at present, only public companies need disclose their financial statements[37] to a wider public. They are obliged to submit them to the registrar of companies with their annual return,[38] and he will place them on file open to public inspection. Private companies are exempt from this requirement, and must instead submit with their returns a certificate affirming that they still fulfill the conditions of private company status.[39] There has been some debate over the years about whether private companies should retain this privilege. The Cox Committee, reporting in 1958, declined to recommend that the privilege be relinquished, chiefly on the ground that compulsory disclosure by small private companies would place them at an unfair disadvantage in relation to their unincorporated trade competitors.[40] The Committee considered also whether the most obvious potential abuse of private company status then existed in Ireland, namely the carrying on by public companies of their business through the medium of private subsidiaries

---

[331] Unless "the financial state of the subsidiary or associated company, as disclosed by its accounts, has in the opinion of the directors of [the company] a substantial effect on the profit or loss, or the amount of the assets" of the company and its subsidiaries: s.16(3)(*b*).

[34] s.159 (in person); and s.148, s.150(1) (at *a.g.m's*).

[35] s.150(3).

[36] s.154(2).

[37] Used in this discussion to signify the annual balance sheet, profit and loss account, and the director's and auditors' reports.

[38] s.128.

[39] s.128(5); s.129.

[40] Para. 118.

and thereby hiding all but the most peripheral information about the state of affairs of their business as a whole, and found that it did not.[41] The Committee nonetheless recommended the adoption of a remedy designed to curtail such an abuse, the imposition of a duty on a public holding company to prepare and disclose group accounts, which, as we have seen,[42] has been carried into law.[43] With the advent of the Fourth Directive which required the publication of the accounts of all limited companies, but left member states with a latitude to exempt some companies from full publication, then debate narrowed to a discussion of the extent to which the Government has now made its choices in the 1985 Bill. Once this is enacted, will the debate be over? Not necessarily. There is a body of opinion throughout the member states in favour of deregulation, which would question, among many other things, the premise of the Fourth Directive that publication of accounts is desirable. Before turning to the course actually taken by the Government in the 1985 Bill, let us for a moment examine the premise of the Fourth Directive by considering against an Irish background the utility of published accounts in the protection of the public. The public in this context may be fairly considered to comprise potential investors and potential unsecured creditors. To these two groups some would wish to add trade unions and employees generally, on the ground that disclosure is essential to fair negotiations on the subject of wages and other conditions of employment. However, any such development would logically have to come about as part of legislation imposing a duty to disclose for these purposes on employers generally, not just on employers who happened to be incorporated, and this interest group will therefore be disregarded in this discussion.[44] The legislative needs of the class of potential investors diminishes almost to vanishing point when one considers the actual facts of business life. Companies listed on the Stock Exchange will in any event be issuing their annual financial statements, and more, in compliance with the Listing Agreement; these will be widely circulated, commented upon in the Press, and the potential investor may examine the copies retained by the broker through whom he deals. The purchaser of shares in a private company will be dealing face to face with the vendor or his agent, and may demand to be shown the financial state-

---

[41] Para. 114.

[42] At pp. 343–344, *supra.*

[43] The state of affairs of individual subsidiaries still need not be disclosed separately: paras. 16, 17 of the Sched. 6, but no more need the profits and losses of distinct operating divisions within a single company.

[44] For proposals from the EEC on informing and consulting employees, see p. 5, n. 26, *supra.*

ments received by him in his right as member, or if he is negotiating
for a majority interest will be able to ensure even greater disclosure
from the company itself.[45] Even in the unlisted securities market, the
danger of dealings occurring in the shares of a company without disclosed accounts is more theoretical than practical: in practice the
unlisted public company will have made disclosure in order to create
a market for its shares; and, anyway, an investor who buys blind and
who has not actually been misled has only himself to blame if his
speculation in this market goes wrong.

The legislative claims of the potential unsecured creditor have a
less vacuous quality. We consider only unsecured creditors since the
secured creditor will have investigated the company's position
before sanctioning the advance, demanding such disclosures and
reports as were considered necessary, and will have been entitled to
receive the company's subsequent annual financial statements.[46]
Conventional wisdom, which in this context has some merit, states
that those who have the benefit of limited liability must as part of the
price of this privilege make maximum disclosure of their company's
financial affairs so that potential unsecured creditors, being those
most likely to suffer from its failure may be warned, and thence stay
clear or take precautions.[47] Requiring publication of a company's
compulsory financial statements obviously assists towards this end.
But it is by no means a complete panacea. Concentration upon it to
the exclusion of other reforms misses the mark, and there are on the
statute book other measures specifically for the protection of
unsecured creditors, of far greater use, if invoked. These possible
reforms and existing measures are discussed in Chapter 15: *The
Charges Register and Other Disclosures*. Comment here will be confined
to briefly questioning the utility to a potential unsecured creditor of
published accounts, on the assumption, a large one, that he goes to
the Companies Registry and looks at them. The three main criticisms are that the information will be out of date, that it will be communicated in a manner requiring interpretation by specialists, and
that it will not necessarily be predictive of failure.

The information contained in accounts on public file may be up to
nearly two years out of date at the moment of inspection, without the
company in question having committed a default in its filing obli-

---

[45] *Subscribers* for shares in private companies need not, of course, be considered,
since private companies are debarred from making public issues, and fresh subscribers to public companies will be protected by the prospectus requirements. See
Chap. 12: *Promoters and Prospectuses*.

[46] s.159.

[47] *e.g.* directors' or other guarantees for the company's debts, the use of retention of
title clauses by a supplier, etc.

gations. One gets this alarming figure simply by totting up the 60 days which may lawfully elapse between the *a.g.m.* at which the accounts were presented and their submission to the Companies Registry[48] the nine months which may lawfully elapse from the date to which the accounts are made up and the date of the *a.g.m.* at which they are presented,[49] and the year during which the accounts may have remained on file.

The remaining two criticisms are interrelated, and must be considered from the point of view of what the prospective unsecured creditor most wants to know, namely, "Will the company collapse before I am paid?" Cahill[50] has shown in his pioneer studies on Irish company failure, that the accounts in the last year before failure of 10 out of 11 of the Irish Stock Exchange listed public companies which failed in the period 1970 to 1980 were *not* qualified by their auditors on the ground of uncertainty as to whether it was going to remain a "going concern,"[51] a fundamental accounting concept on the basis of which all accounts are drawn up unless the contrary is clearly stated. It is further discussed under *Auditors, infra*. Furthermore, in one particular case highlighted by Cahill[52] the accounts of a public listed company in the year before its collapse showed increasing and apparently healthy sales, assets, profits and dividends, and little overt indication of imminent collapse. There were however certain ratios between items set out in the accounts from which a possibility of failure might have been predicted. Models using such ratios have been constructed from data drawn from business failure in other countries.[53] If such a model could be con-

---

[48] s.127.

[49] s.148(1).

[50] Edward Cahill, Senior Lecturer in Accounting in the School of Business and Administrative Studies at Trinity College, Dublin.

[51] Cahill, "Irish Listed Company Failure, Financial Ratios, Accounts and Auditors' Opinions," (1981) *Journal of Irish Business and Administrative Research*, 19.

[52] Cahill, "Corporate Financial Distress," *Accountancy Ireland*, Feb 1982, p.8.

[53] See, *inter alia*, J.O. Horrigan, "A Short History of Financial Ratio Analysis," (1968), *The Accounting Review*, 284; W.H. Beaver, "Financial Ratios as Predictors of Failure," (1966) *Journal of Accounting Research*, 71; E.I. Altman, "Financial Ratios Discriminant Analysis and the Prediction of Corporate Bankruptcy," (1968) *Journal of Finance*, 589; E.B. Deakin, "A Discriminant Analysis of Predictors of Business Failure," (1972) *Journal of Accounting Research*, 167; M. Blum, "Failing Company Discriminant Analysis," (1974) *Journal of Accounting Research*, 1; E.I. Altman, M. Margaine, M. Schlosser and P. Vernimmen "Financial and Statistical Analysis for Commercial Loan Evaluation: A French Experience," (1974) *Journal of Financial and Quantitative Analysis*, 151; R. Taffler and H. Tisshaw, "Going, going, gone—four factors which predict," *Accountancy*, March 1977, p. 50; E.I. Altman, R.G. Haldeman and P. Naraganan, "ZETA Analysis. A new model to detect bankruptcy risk of corporations,"(1977) *Journal of Banking and Finance*, 29.

structed from Irish business conditions and its worth proven, its application to any given Irish company could give a credit rating which could be published to the exclusion of all other material. Perhaps this is the direction in which legislative intervention should be travelling. As matters stand, not only is specialist knowledge required to gain from published accounts what they are actually seeking to communicate,[54] but further specialist analysis is necessary to extrapolate from them indications of failure, this latter being the only concern of those who have a claim to legislative intervention.

We come now to the manner in which the publication requirements of the Fourth Directive are proposed to be implemented by the 1985 Bill. The Directive makes, as we have seen, a distinction between content and publication. Content we have already touched upon, as well as the distinction made by the Directive between small, medium sized and other limited companies, and the way in which that distinction is proposed to be carried into Irish law.[55] The Bill proposes that none of the concessions on publication allowed by the Directive be granted to public limited companies whatever their size, even though size as opposed to the fact of public participation was the criterion for exemption chosen by the Directive, its object being the protection of creditors rather than investors. Public limited companies must publish their balance sheets, profit and loss accounts, notes to the accounts and directors' and auditors' reports in full as prepared.[55a] This hard attitude towards the Irish public limited company stands uneasily against the indulgence accorded by the Bill to foreign enterprises trading in the State, discussed below.

We turn to the concessions granted by the Bill to private limited companies, firstly those determined by the company's size. The Directive allows Member States to permit a small limited company to publish a balance sheet only, abridged to the extent permitted by the rules governing the content of accounts together with notes to it similarly abridged[56]; there is no obligation on member states to enforce the publication by a small limited company of the other financial statements to be prepared by it, its profit and loss account, and directors' and auditors' reports.[57] The Bill allows small private limited companies all but one of these concessions.[58] Small private

---

[54] See pp. 347–348, *supra.*

[55] 4th Directive, Arts. 11 and 27; 1985 Bill, s.8; and see pp. 352–353, *supra.*

[55a] 1985 Bill, s.7, replacing s.128. But see the separate publication requirements for insurance companies, *infra.*

[56] 4th Directive, Art. 47(2).

[57] *Ibid.*

[58] 1985 Bill, s.7, s.10(2), s.12(1).

limited companies are to publish their auditors' reports. This publication is to take the form of a special report of the auditors accompanying the company's annual return to the Registrar; the special report must contain the usual auditors' report on the company's full accounts prepared pursuant to section 163 of the Companies Act 1963,[59] and a statement that the small company is entitled to the exemption claimed both as to content and publication, and the accounts have been properly prepared in accordance with the terms of the exemption.[60]

Member states may permit a medium sized limited company to publish an abridged form of its balance sheet as prepared and the notes to its accounts as prepared, but it must publish its profit and loss account, directors' and auditors' reports in full.[60a] These minor concessions are carried into effect by the 1985 Bill for the medium sized private company.[60b] The special auditors' report provisions, *supra*, are to apply the medium sized company *mutatis mutandis*.[60c]

Secondly, the 1985 Bill gives concessions to private limited companies determined by the nature of its activities. It wholly exempts from publication the accounts of limited companies not trading for profit,[60d] limited companies without share capital formed for a charitable object and controlled by certain religions,[60e] and limited companies without a share capital formed for charitable purposes and specifically exempted by the Commissioners for Charitable Donations and Bequests from publishing accounts.[60f] Although, as we have seen,[60g] the 1985 Bill does not extend the new rules for the preparation of accounts to banking, finance and similar companies except in some limited respects, they are not to be exempt from the publication requirements,[60h] and there are to be no concessions based on their size. Insurance companies on the other hand are to be exempt from the publication requirements of the Companies Acts,

---

[59] Discussed *infra* at pp. 369 *et seq.* under the heading *Auditors*; and see Savage, (1981) 3 Co.Law. 23.

[60] For the special auditors' report, see 1985 Bill, s.18(3), (4).

[60a] 4th Directive, Art. 47(3).

[60b] 1985 Bill, s.11(), s.12(2).

[60c] *Ibid.* s.18(3), (4).

[60d] *Ibid.* s.2(1)(*a*). This and the charitable and religious exemptions, *infra*, apply to plc's as well.

[60e] s.128(4)(*b*); 1985 Bill, s.2(1)(*b*). For limited companies without share capital, *i.e.* companies limited by guarantee, see Chap. 1 at pp. 7–9. The bill appears to consider that charitable and religious companies trading for profit are outside the scope of the Directive. This is questionable.

[60f] s.128(5); 1985 Bill, s.2(1)(*c*).

[60g] At p. 352, *supra*.

[60h] 1985 Bill, s.2(2).

being subject to stringent disclosure requirements under separate legislation.[60i]

Section 17 of the 1985 Bill empowers the Minister to exempt from publishing its accounts for a particular financial year any private limited company which is the subsidiary of another body corporate formed and registered in a Member State of the European Communities. Before granting exemption, the Minister must be satisfied that certain conditions have been or will be fulfilled, some of them curious. He must be satisfied that the company's accounts are to be consolidated into group accounts by the holding company prepared and audited in accordance with the requirements of the Fourth Directive, and that those group accounts are to be annexed to the annual return made by the subsidiary to the Registrar of Companies. He must be satisfied that every shareholder of the subsidiary has consented to the exemption. This is odd because the shareholder is entitled to those accounts in any event[60j]: the subsidiary is not being exempted from that requirement, and the shareholder would not therefore suffer through section 17. This oddity comes about because Article 57 of the Directive (from which section 17 is drawn) permits exemption not only from publishing the accounts of the subsidiary but from preparing and auditing them as well. The Bill repeats the full range of safeguards for only a partial exemption. The Minister must also be satisfied that the holding company has declared "in a notice sent *to every shareholder* of the [subsidiary] that it guarantees the liabilities of the [subsidiary]."[60k] This condition is designed for the protection of the *creditors* of the subsidiary. Why then require the declaration to be communicated to the subsidiary's shareholders? The Directive contains no such requirement; it requires the declaration to be filed with the annual return to the Registrar.[60l] It must be doubted whether such a guarantee gives rise to an obligation on the holding company to creditors of the subsidiary if the creditor did not actually rely on it when contracting with the subsidiary. In those circumstances, it might be elevated to a contractual promise; otherwise it remains a gratuitous declaration. Implementation of the Directive would appear therefore to demand that a statutory liability be expressly imposed on a holding company making such a declaration, in effect making the subsidiary an unlimited company to the extent of the holding company's resources. Finally, what if the subsidiary of an Irish holding company applies

[60i] s.128(4)(*b*); 1985 Bill, s.2(3); and see Assurance Companies Act 1909, s.7(4).
[60j] See pp. 180–181, *supra*.
[60k] 1985 Bill, s.17(*b*); italics supplied.
[60l] Art. 57(1)(*d*).

for a section 17 exemption? Must not the Minister grant it if in like circumstances he would to the subsidiary of a company formed in another Member State? Not to do so would appear to discriminate on grounds of nationality contrary to Article 7 of the Treaty of Rome.

The 1985 Bill does not apply to *unlimited* companies at all,[60m] whether public or private; neither did the Fourth Directive. The existing private company exemption continues therefore for private unlimited companies.[60n]

The 1985 Bill applies to unregistered companies with limited liability as if they were registered.[60o] Put broadly, unregistered companies are corporations incorporated otherwise than under the Companies Acts, and having a principal place of business in the State.[60p] The most prominent example is the Bank of Ireland.

The 1985 Bill contains provisions[60q] designed to prevent the public from being misled by published accounts, "published" being used here in the sense of making them available to the public, such as having them printed in a newspaper. A company publishing its full accounts in this way will be obliged to publish with them the auditors' report on them, and, if they purport to be abridged in a manner permitted by law, a statement by the auditors that they have nonetheless been properly prepared.[60r] If a company publishes in this way accounts containing less than the legal norms, it must clearly say so, and state also whether the proper accounts have been submitted with the annual return, whether the auditors reported on them, and, if so, whether the auditors report was in any way qualified.[60s]

Leaving now corporations formed under Irish law, we turn to foreign corporations. A foreign corporation having a place of business within the State is obliged by section 354 of the Companies Act 1963 both to prepare and publish accounts as if it were a company incorporated under the Companies Acts, *unless* "it has provisions in its constitution that would entitle it to rank as a private company if it had been registered in the State."[60t] This exemption is to remain, doubtless to avoid scaring off foreign enterprises which, not unsurprisingly, value their confidentiality as much as domestic concerns,

---

[60m] 1985 Bill, s.1(1). For unlimited companies, see Chap. 1 at pp. 9–10.
[60n] s.128(4)(*a*), (6).
[60o] 1985 Bill, s.21.
[60p] s.377.
[60q] 1985 Bill, s.19.
[60r] *Ibid.* s.19(1).
[60s] *Ibid.* s.19(2).
[60t] s.351, s.354(4).

and sometimes more so. Who, for example, would wish to embarrass a foreign manufacturing enterprise by forcing it to reveal the proportion of profit artificially taken in Ireland by false transfer pricing in order to avail of Ireland's low corporate tax rates on manufacturing industry? In everyday speech these exempt foreign corporations are spoken of as having established "branches" within the State. This is inaccurate. The Act exempts simply companies "incorporated outside the State which establish a place of business within the State. . . . "[60u] The company's sole business might therefore be within the State, not merely the "branch" of a wider enterprise. A foreign corporation will obtain the exemption even if it is the subsidiary, perhaps wholly owned, of a public corporation, multinational or otherwise. Private company status is more concerned with the number of participants than their quality.[60v]

AUDITORS

Section 163 of the Companies Act 1963 requires that the accounts of every company, large or small, which are to be laid before its annual general meeting must first be audited.[61] We shall now explore the effectiveness of this system of independent verification.[62]

Appointment and tenure of office

All types of newly formed company, save one, are free to commence business without first having appointed an auditor. The exception, by a legislative caprice, is the public unlimited company.[63]

Section 160(1) of the Companies Act 1963 imposes a duty on every company "at each annual general meeting [to] appoint an auditor or auditors to hold office from the conclusion of that until the conclusion of the next annual general meeting." The directors, and if they fail to act, the general meeting, are given powers by section

---

[60u] s.351.

[60v] See Chap. 1 at pp. 10–11.

[61] *i.e.* the balance sheet, profit and loss account and group accounts, if any and by 1985 Bill, s.15 the directors' report is in effect to be audited as well. The financial statements to be laid before the *a.g.m.* are described in ss.148, 150, 154, 157–158.

[62] On this theme, see Calvert (1962) 4 *Malaya Law Review* 87; Baxt (1974) 33 M.L.R. 413 and Savage, (1983) 4 Co.Law 187.

[63] There is an example in Table E. For the requirement that it have an auditor before being permitted to trade, see s.115 (as amended by para. 13, 1st Sched., 1983 Act), and para. 29, 4th Sched.

160(6) to appoint the company's first auditors to hold office until the conclusion of the first annual general meeting.

Companies are themselves required to police the performance of their duty to appoint an auditor at each *a.g.m.*; if they fail to do so, they must inform the Minister for Industry, Trade, Commerce and Tourism within one week of the failure on pain of a fine not exceeding £250.[64] The Minister has power by section 160(4) to fill the vacancy.

Under present companies legislation, a private company will never actually be asked officially to confirm that it has an auditor. Such enquiries of companies will be made only where a public unlimited company is seeking authority to commence business,[65] where a private company is in the process of being converted into a public company,[66] and where a public company is making its annual return, since on that occasion it is required to submit the auditors' report on the accounts accompanying the return.[67] Considerable uniformity will be imposed on this presently haphazard disclosure when private companies are required to publish their accounts.[68]

Auditors, as we have seen, hold office until the conclusion of the annual general meeting next following their appointment. Their tenure of office is however nearer continuous than periodic, since the Companies Act 1963 contains a bias in favour of the reappointment of existing auditors. Section 160 (2) provides that:

> "at any general meeting a retiring auditor, however appointed, shall be re-appointed without any resolution being passed unless—(*b*) a resolution has been passed at that meeting appointing somebody instead of him or providing expressly that he shall not be re-appointed. . . ."[69]

The incumbent auditor is entitled under section 161 to receive an advance copy of any such intended resolution, and to have the company circularise the members at its expense with a statement of his case, or, failing that to have his representations read at the *a.g.m.* He also has a right to be heard orally on this issue, and generally.[70] These provisions are designed to counteract the temptation upon directors to engineer the dismissal of an auditor for being too *good* at

---

[64] s.160(5); fine increased by 2nd Sched. 1982 Act.

[65] See the legislation cited in n. 63, *supra*.

[66] s.5, as amended by para. 5, 1st Sched., 1983 Act; para. 17, Part I, 2nd Sched., or para. 15, Third Sched.

[67] s.128(1)(*b*).

[68] See *Disclosure of the financial statements* at pp. 356 *et seq.*, *supra*.

[69] Or is not qualified for re-appointment, or has resigned: s.160(2)(*a*), (*c*).

[70] s.161(3), s.163(4).

his job. Any disinterested observer who hears that a company is attempting not to reappoint its existing auditor must as his first thought wonder whether this is indeed the motivation.

Qualifications

Persons undertaking company audit work in Ireland must possess qualifications as accountants.[71] Usually, they will be a member of a body of accountants recognised by the Minister for Industry, Trade, Commerce and Tourism[72]; exceptionally, they may be persons individually authorised by the Minister either "as having obtained similar qualifications otherwise than from such a body,"[73] or "as having obtained adequate knowledge and experience" before April 1, 1964 "in the course of his employment by, or under the supervision of, a member" of a recognised body of accountants[74]; or as having before April 1, 1964 "practised in the State as an accountant."[75] These last two categories are now closed. Applications for inclusion within them had to be made to the Minister before November 10, 1982, and he was to respond before January 10, 1983.[76]

Independence

As Meredith J. said in *Leech* v. *Stokes*,[77] "the business of an accountant and auditor is innately unsympathetic, and it is liable to suffer in efficiency when undertaken in a more or less obliging and friendly spirit." The law now makes an attempt to ensure that an auditor is not too closely connected with the company whose accounts he is auditing, but the distance could and should be further. Fortunately, ethical rules of practice of professional accountancy bodies, applicable, of course, only to those auditors who are members, go some way towards filling the gaps.

---

[71] s.162, as amended by s.6 of the 1982 Act. The 8th EEC Directive (84/253/EEC O.J. L 126/20 of May 12, 1984) lays down qualifications for auditors, including educational standards. It must be fully implemented in Ireland by January 1, 1990.

[72] s.162(1)(a). The 1983 *Report* of the Department of Industry, Trade, Commerce and Tourism specifies these bodies as being The Institute of Chartered Accountants in Ireland, The Institute of Certified Public Accountants in Ireland, The Association of Certified Accountants, The Institute of Chartered Accounts in England and Wales and The Institute of Chartered Accountants of Scotland.

[73] s.162(1)(b)(i).

[74] s.162(1)(b)(ii), as amended by s.6 of the 1982 Act.

[75] s.162(1)(b)(iii), as amended by s.6 of the 1982 Act.

[76] s.162(2), as amended by s.6 of the 1982 Act. The dates are reached by reference to the coming into force of the 1982 Act, August 10, 1982 (S.I. 1982 No. 255).

[77] [1937] I.R. 787, 832.

Statute satisfies itself with disqualifying[78] any officer or servant of the company, the term "officer" covering a director, any person occupying the position of director by whatever name called, and the secretary[79]; any person who is a partner of or in the employment of an officer or servant of the company (except where the company is a private company); a person disqualified on the foregoing grounds from being the auditor of the company's subsidiary or holding company or another subsidiary of the holding company, or would be so disqualified if the related company were a modern registered company; a person disqualified from being the public auditor[80] of an Industrial and Provident Society which is a subsidiary or holding society of the company, or a subsidiary of the company's holding society; and any body corporate.

The most startling omission from this statutory list of disqualifications is any requirement that the auditor be free of a beneficial shareholding in the audit client. It is beyond argument that such a financial stake in the enterprise will affect the objectivity of the auditor. Rules of good accountancy practice dictate that no partner in the auditing firm, nor the spouse or minor child of any such partner, should be the beneficial holder of shares in the audit client; nor should the firm employ on the audit any member of staff who is a beneficial holder of such shares.[81] Likewise, a partner or employee of an officer or servant of a private company, presently free in law to audit its accounts, would risk in doing so falling foul of professional rules of practice designed to ensure that the objectivity of the audit is not endangered by any personal relationship,[82] including one of mutual business interest. Also disquieting, and not at present subject to any legal disqualification, is the case of an auditor overly dependent upon his client company for his livelihood. Such an auditor may be tempted more than one less dependent to allow his objectivity to be softened by a desire not to displease his client: keeping the account becomes more important than fearless reporting on the accounts. Rules of professional practice recommend that an

---

[78] All these disqualifications are contained in s.162(5), as amended by s.6 of the 1982 Act.

[79] s.2.; s.162(5).

[80] These disqualifications are contained in s.162(6), as amended by s.6 of the 1982 Act.

[81] *e.g.* Institute of Chartered Accountants in Ireland, *Ethical Guide for Members*, p. 14.

[82] *e.g.* Institute of Chartered Accountants in Ireland, *op. cit.*, p. 13. Repeal of the equivalent British private company exemption (s.161(2), proviso, of the 1948 Act [U.K.]) was recommended in 1945 by the Cohen Committee, para. 56, and was carried into effect by the Companies Act 1967 [U.K.], s.2.

accountancy practice should try to ensure that the recurring fees paid by one client or group of connected clients do not exceed 15 per cent. of the gross fees of the practice.[83] The E.E.C. Directive on company auditors,[84] so far as it specifically addresses itself to the independence of auditors, seems at first sight to seek to add nothing to whatever domestic laws happen to be in force in Member States. It says in Article 24: "Member States shall prescribe that [auditors] shall not carry out statutory audits . . . if [they] are not independent in accordance with the law of the Member State. . . . " But, the Directive's seemingly nebulous more general provisions may be interrupted as requiring that Member States give professional rules of good conduct, such as those set out above, the force of law. Article 23 says: "Member States shall prescribe that [auditors] shall carry out . . . audits with professional integrity" and by Article 26 Member States must impose sanctions on auditors who fail to comply.

Honesty

Section 162(4) of the Companies Act 1963[85] provides that:

> "if an auditor is convicted of a criminal offence arising out of or connected with the performance of his duties or his conduct as an auditor, he shall not be qualified for appointment as auditor of a company . . . without the permission of the court."

What such offences are there. Most prominent is the making of a wilfully false audit report. Schedule 10 to the Companies Act 1963 lists a wide variety of documents including the auditor's report, and by section 380 "any person" who in any such document "wilfully makes a statement false in any material particular, knowing it to be false" is liable if convicted on indictment to imprisonment for up to three years, or to a fine not exceeding £2,500, or both.[85a] Secondly, there are the numerous offences created by Sections 293 *et seq.* of the Companies Act 1963, concerning companies which go, or have gone, into liquidation, and which may be committed by an "officer of a company." An auditor is not *per se* an officer of the company of which he is auditor, so that for example his certification of the accounts does not as such constitute a representation made on behalf of the company.[86] Nonetheless, it was decided in *R. v*

---

[83] *e.g.* Institute of Chartered Accountants in Ireland, *op. cit.*, p. 13.

[84] See n. 71, *supra*.

[85] As amended by s.6 of the 1982 Act.

[85a] Or if convicted summarily, to 6 months imprisonment or a fine of £500, or both. Fines reached by 1982 Act, Sched. 1.

[86] *Re Transplanters Ltd.* [1958] 1 W.L.R. 822; certification of accounts by auditor no acknowledgment of statute barred debt.

Shacter[87] that he is an "officer" for the purpose of the abovementioned offences, just as he is for the purposes of the misfeasance summons under section 298.[88] Thus, in *R.* v. *Shacter*, a company auditor was convicted *inter alia* of making a false entry in the profit and loss account which in Ireland would be contrary to section 293(1)(*j*), of inducing a bank by false pretences to give credit to the company contrary, in Ireland, to section 295(*a*), and of being party to the failure of the company to keep proper books of account contrary, in Ireland, to section 296. Thirdly, there are offences created by other statutes, such as the falsification of accounts,[88a] to which he might be a party.

Proven neglect of duty or proven incompetence does not, provided that it falls short of criminality, of itself disqualify an auditor, but, where the auditor is a member of a professional body of accountants, it may in theory lead to his expulsion or suspension from that body following appropriate disciplinary proceedings, thereby disqualifying him from company audit work. Such disciplinary proceedings suffer the disadvantage of being conducted without the powers and privileges of a court: there is no effective power to compel the attendance of witnesses or the production of documents, and since allegations and evidence before the professional body do not have the absolute privilege from defamation enjoyed by proceedings before a court, but only qualified privilege, genuine complainants and witnesses may be deterred from participating.[89] The operation of such bodies is therefore inhibited, and so correspondingly is their rôle in the protection of the public.

Duties

Statute satisfies itself with imposing on a company's auditor a duty to report on certain specified matters, but this statutory formu-

---

[87] [1960] 2.Q.B. 252.

[88] See pp. 239–242, *supra*, and p. 491, *infra*, and *Re London & General Bank* [1895] 2 Ch. 166; *Re Kingston Cotton Mill* [1896] 1 Ch. 6.

[88a] Larceny Act 1861, ss. 82 *et seq.*; Falsification of Accounts Act 1875, ss.1 *et seq.*; *R.* v. *Kylsant* [1932] 1 K.B. 442.

[89] No one needs to be told that threatening defamation proceedings, however unjustifiably, is a well worn method of silencing criticism. A witness, however free of malice (and therefore the subject of qualified privilege before the disciplinary committee) would prefer if thus threatened not to be involved. On qualified privilege in respect of complaints and their preliminary investigation, see *Lincoln* v. *Daniels* [1962] Q.B. 237. In Ireland, the substantive hearing before the disciplinary committee is not, it seems, absolutely privileged because the committee would not be a court recognised by law. For its proceedings to be valid at all, it must be categorised merely as a domestic tribunal founded as a contract between the members: *Re Solicitors Act 1954* [1960] I.R. 410.

lation by no means reflects the whole duty of an auditor to his company. Implicit in the duty to report, there is a duty first to investigate, and over both there is a gloss of case law imposing standards of professional conduct on the auditor.

The statutory duty to report is set out in section 163 of the Companies Act 1963, and in Schedule 7 to that Act, as amended.[90] Section 163(1) states:

> "The auditors shall make a report to the members on the accounts examined by them, and on every balance sheet, every profit and loss account and all group accounts laid before the company in general meeting during their tenure of office, and the report shall contain statements as to the matters mentioned in the Seventh Schedule."

Schedule 7 contains the following list of "matters to be expressly stated in the auditors' report":

> "1. Whether they have obtained all the information and explanations *which to the best of their knowledge and belief* were necessary for the purposes of their audit.
>
> 2. Whether *in their opinion*, proper books of account have been kept by the company, so far as appears from their examination of those books, and proper returns adequate for the purposes of their audit have been received from branches not visited by them.
>
> 3. (1) Whether the company's balance sheet and (unless it is framed as a consolidated profit and loss account) profit and loss account dealt with by the report are in agreement with the books of account and returns.
>
> (2) Whether, *in their opinion and to the best of their information and according to the explanations given to them*, the said accounts give the information required by this Act in the manner so required and give a true and fair view—
>
> (*a*) in the case of the balance sheet, of the state of the company's affairs as at the end of its financial year; and
>
> (*b*) in the case of the profit and loss account, of the profit and loss for its financial year; . . . ."[91]

---

[90] Para. 5 was added by the 1983 Act, 2nd Sched., para. 27. The 1985 Bill, s.15 will impose a further duty on auditors in preparing their s.163 report to consider and state whether the directors' report is consistent with the accounts. Note also that ss.191 and 192 (see pp. 348–349 *et seq.*) impose a duty on auditors to include in their report the amount of benefits and loans required to be disclosed by those sections, if they are not disclosed in the accounts and insofar as the auditors are reasonably able to do so.

[91] The omitted material relates to the special classes of company (banking, discount and assurance) covered by Part III of the 6th Sched.

4. In the case of a company which is a holding company and which submits group accounts whether, *in their opinion*, the group accounts have been properly prepared in accordance with the provisions of this Act so as to give a true and fair view of the state of affairs and profit or loss of the company and its subsidiaries dealt with thereby, so far as concerns members of the company . . . .[92]

5. Whether, *in their opinion*, there exists at the balance sheet date within the meaning of the Companies (Amendment) Act 1983 a financial situation which under section 40(1) of that Act would require the convening of an extraordinary general meeting of the company."[93]

It will be observed from the italicised passages that the duty to report is hedged about with qualifications, but these are not to be taken at their face value. Pennycuick J. said in *Re Thomas Gerrard & Son Ltd.*[94] of the equivalent words in the British 1948 Act[95] that they must not be taken as having diminished the obligations on auditors established by judicial decisions made before their introduction to the statute book.[96] These established, in the often repeated words of Lopes L.J. in *Re Kingston Cotton Mill Co. (No. 2)* decided in 1896,[97] that:

> "It is the duty of an auditor to bring to bear on the work he has to perform that skill, care and caution which a reasonably competent, careful, and cautious auditor would use. What is reasonable skill, care and caution must depend on the particular circumstances of each case."

There is the same, if not greater, emphasis on professional standards in the Irish authorities. Hanna J. in a formulation affirmed by the Supreme Court,[98] said in *Leech* v. *Stokes*[99] after reviewing the earlier authorities on company audit:

---

[92] *Ibid.*

[93] Italics supplied.

[94] [1968] Ch. 455, 471.

[95] Sched. 9, since repealed and replaced by Companies Act 1967 [*U.K.*], s.14, as amended.

[96] By the 1907 Act, s.19(2), later the 1908 Act, s.113(2), preceded by the attenuated 1900 Act, s.23.

[97] [1896] 2 Ch. 279, 288 (audit requirement imposed by the articles). See also the other leading cases of *Re London and General Bank* [1895] 2 Ch. 673 (a statutory audit imposed on banking companies by the Companies Act 1879), *Leeds, etc., Co.* v. *Shepherd* (1887) 36 Ch. D. 787 (audit imposed by the articles), and *Re City Equitable Fire Insurance Co. Ltd.* [1925] Ch. 407.

[98] [1937] I.R. 823.

[99] [1937] I.R. 787, 798.

"The cases which I have cited have clearly established that the duty upon an auditor is, under the circumstances of the particular case and of his employment, to exercise such skill and care as a diligent, skilled and cautious auditor would exercise *according to the practice of the profession.*"[1]

He echoes here Fitzgibbon L.J. in *Irish Woollen Co. Ltd.* v. *Tyson*[2] where he points out that an auditor is not to be differentiated from other professionals:" . . . the result is the same . . . in all cases in which professional skill is employed. . . . The measure of duty is the bringing of reasonable care and skill to the performance of the business directed to be done. . . . "

As stated above, these standards of professional conduct have not been diminished by the apparent words of qualification in the Schedule 7. As Pennycuick J. said in *Re Thomas Gerrard & Son Ltd.*[3]:

"it is clear that the auditor . . . when he forms the "belief" mentioned in para. 1, when he forms the "opinion" mentioned in para. 2 . . . , and again when he forms the "opinion" mentioned in para. 3 (2) . . . , must exercise reasonable care and skill. Equally, if he performs these mental operations without exercising reasonable care and skill and then proceeds to give an unqualified statement, in other words a clean certificate, he is in breach of his statutory duty as an officer of the company."

One might also add with equal accuracy that the "knowledge" in para. 1 must not fall short of what a competent professional would know, that the "information" in para. 3 (2) must not be less than he would have obtained, and the "explanations" in para. 3 (2) must be such that he would have accepted them.

Where does one find these professional standards? Formerly, what an auditor ought or ought not to have done in particular circumstances was frequently the subject of a conflict in expert evidence. Nowadays, much of the opportunity for dissension is being removed by the adoption by the accounting profession of uniform *Auditing Standards* and their related *Guidelines.*[4] One looks primarily to the

---

[1] Italics supplied.
[2] Decided by the Court of Appeal in Ireland, Jan. 20th 1900; reported in (190 The Accountant L.R. 13. Various editions of Dicksee, *Auditing*, carry this report.
[3] [1968] Ch. 435, 471.
[4] Promulgated jointly by the Councils of the Institute of Chartered Accountants Ireland, the Institute of Chartered Accountants in England and Wales, the Instit of Chartered Accountants in Scotland and the Association of Certified Accountan consequent upon exposure drafts prepared by the Auditing Practices Committee the C.C.A.B. Current developments are reported in *True and Fair*, the bulletin of Auditing Practices Committee. See particularly Issue No. 15, Spring 1980.

to ascertain whether an auditor has in any particular instance fulfilled his duty to the company; old judicial decisions, on the other hand, cannot be relied upon as doing any more than stating what the rules of good practice were at a particular time, describing generally the function of an auditor, and, as we have seen, defining his duty as one of compliance with professional standards for the time being. His function as broadly stated in the language of the old authorities is more verification than detection,[5] or, in the now tired metaphor coined by Lopes L.J. in *Re Kingston Cotton Mill Co. (No. 2)*[6] and much repeated since: an auditor "is a watch-dog, but not a bloodhound."[7] The *Auditing Standards and Guidelines* less colourfully but more accurately describe the function of an auditor, or, in other words, an audit as being:

"the independent examination of, and expression of opinion on, the financial statements of an enterprise by an appointed auditor in pursuance of that appointment and in compliance with any relevant statutory obligation. The responsibility for the preparation of the financial statements and the presentation of the information included therein rests with the management of the enterprise (in the case of a company, the directors). The auditor's responsibility is to report on the financial statements as presented by management. . . . The responsibility for the prevention and detection of irregularities and fraud rests with the management. . . . The auditor's duties do not require him specifically to search for fraud. . . . However, the auditor should recognise the possibility of material irregularities or fraud which could, unless adequately disclosed, distort the results or state of affairs shown by the financial statements. The auditor should, therefore, plan his audit so that he has a reasonable expectation of detecting material misstatements in the financial statements resulting from irregularities or fraud. . . . "[8]

This statement accords well also with judicial pronouncements on what an auditor is *not*. Thus, "he is not to be written off as a professional 'adder-upper and subtractor,' "[9] free "to confine himself to

---

[5] *Re City Equitable Fire Insurance Co. Ltd.* [1925] 1 Ch. 407, 509, *per* Pollock M.R.

[6] [1896] 2 Ch. 279, 288.

[7] Fitzgibbon L.J. remarked in *Irish Woollen Co. Ltd.* v. *Tyson*, n. 2 *supra*, that this analogy "was very unfair to the bloodhound, who was just as little likely to have his sense of suspicion aroused as the watch-dog."

[8] Excerpts from paras. 2, 8, 9 and 10 of the Explanatory Foreword to the *Auditing Standards and Guidelines*, which is to be read "in conjunction with" them.

[9] *Per* Lord Denning in *Fomento Ltd.* v. *Selsdon Fountain Pen Co. Ltd.* [1958] 1 W.L.R. 5, 61. (not a Companies Act audit).

the task of verifying the arithmetical accuracy of the balance-sheet"[10]; for that would render the audit "worse than an idle farce."[11]

Auditing is an evolving science. Though the level of an auditor's duty is still accurately stated by the judicial decisions, the content of that duty is the subject of continual change as professional practice evolves: there has been not only a marked raising of standards over the course of this century, but also an adaptation to the changing conditions of business life, such as, latterly, computerisation. We turn to some examples of how the content of the duty has changed. "There was certainly no duty cast on the auditor to take stock," says Holmes L.J. in *Irish Woollen Co. Ltd.* v. *Tyson*,[12] echoing Lindley L.J. in *Re Kingston Cotton Mill (No. 2.)*[13]:

> "It is no part of an auditor's duty to take stock. No one contends that it is. He must rely on other people for the details of the stock-in-trade on hand. In the case of a cotton mill he must rely on some skilled person for the materials necessary to enable him to enter the stock-in-trade at its proper value in the balance sheet. In this case the auditors relied on the manager."

Yet, nowadays we find that in pursuance of an auditor's duty to "obtain relevant and reliable audit evidence sufficient to enable him to draw reasonable conclusions therefrom,"[14] he should when "placing reliance upon the management's stocktake in order to provide evidence of existence [of stocks], . . . attend the stocktaking . . . because attendance at stocktaking is normally the best way of providing evidence of the proper functioning of management's stocktaking procedures, and hence of the existence of stocks and their condition."[15] During the stocktaking, the auditor should carry out a number of tests[16] to evaluate the system including *inter alia* tests designed to ensure that "movements into, within and out of stocks

---

[10] *Per* Stirling J. in *Leeds etc. Co.* v. *Shepherd* (1887) 36 Ch. D. 787, 802.

[11] *Per* Lindley L.J. in *Re London & General Bank (No. 2)* [1895] 2 Ch. 673, 683.

[12] See n. 2, *supra*.

[13] [1896] 2 Ch. 279, 286.

[14] *Auditing Standard*: "The Auditor's Operational Standard," para. 4; amplified in *Auditing Guideline*: "Audit Evidence."

[15] *Auditing Guideline*: "Attendance at Stocktaking," para. 5, to be read in conjunction with "The Auditor's Operational Standard," and "Audit Evidence," n. 14, *supra*. For examples of specific problems which might be encountered in particular businesses, see *True and Fair*, Issue No. 12, Summer 1979: retail jewellery, and Issue No. 14, Winter 1979/80: scrap metal dealers.

[16] *Ibid.* paras. 14–19.

are properly identified and reflected in the accounting records."[17] Several judicial decisions on auditor's duties have concerned falsification by the management of stock records in an effort to inflate profits, thereby contenting the shareholders (whose dividends, as well as the value of their shares, depend upon profits), and assuring the creditors of the solvency of the enterprise.[18] These cases turned upon whether the auditor ought to have had his suspicions aroused by irregularities on the face of the company's accounting records, and the extent to which he should have followed up those suspicions. Now that the auditor is to be no longer *exclusively* dependent on documentary evidence, and is to be physically involved with the ascertainment of the company's assets, the rationale of these cases has been destroyed, superseded by an evolution in auditing practice.

As a second instance of the case law no longer truly reflecting the content of the auditor's duty, one may take the statement of Holmes L.J. in *Irish Woollen Co. Ltd.* v. *Tyson*[19] that whilst the auditor is entitled to see the company's books, and the materials upon which they are based, and also to ask for explanations, "he is not called on to seek for knowledge outside the company, or to communicate with customers or creditors." This statement has been false for several decades. In *Re Thomas Gerrard & Son Ltd.*,[20] for example, it was held that an auditor who had been put on enquiry by irregularities in the dating of stock invoices ought not to have accepted the explanations of the managing director of the company, but should have gone outside it and made enquiries directly of the suppliers in question. In fact, under good auditing practice enquiries of outsiders are by no means confined to the investigation of transactions about which the internal evidence has raised suspicions. According to the *Auditing Guideline*, "Audit Evidence," the sources of such evidence include not only "the accounting systems and underlying documentation of the enterprise, its tangible assets, management and employees" but also "its customers, suppliers and other third parties who have deal-

---

[17] *Ibid.* para. 17.

[18] *e.g. Irish Woollen Co. Ltd.* v. *Tyson*, n. 2, *supra*; *Re Kingston Cotton Mill (No. 2)* [1896] Ch. 279; *Re Thomas Gerrard & Son Ltd.* [1968] Ch. 455.

[19] n. 2. *supra.* He was reluctantly forced to this conclusion by the evidence of then current auditing practice. He said: "There is no doubt that both the suppression and carrying over of invoices would have been detected if the auditor had called for the creditors' statements of accounts upon which payment was ordered, and compared them with the ledger. I should have thought that this was part of the auditor's duty for many reasons; but all the accountants examined, except Mr. Southworth, stated that such a course is never taken unless there is something to arouse suspicion. Mr. Bixley, the eminent London accountant, says it could not well be done except in the case of a very small concern."

[20] [1968] Ch. 455.

ings with, or knowledge of, the enterprise or its business." Some at least of the audit evidence will be sought from outside the enterprise; how much and from whom is a matter of professional judgment for the auditor depending on the circumstances of the audit. The factors the auditor must take into account in deciding whether he has sufficient audit evidence are expanded upon in the *Guideline*, which, unsurprisingly, observes that " 'evidence' obtained from independent sources outside the enterprise is more reliable than that secured from solely within the enterprise."[21] It is, incidentally, a common practice for auditors when verifying the validity and accuracy of the company's debtor balances to circularise the company's apparent trade debtors as part of the process of evaluating the system of internal control over sales.[22]

As a final example of the way an auditor's duty has filled up over the course of this century, we come to the question of how much law an auditor ought to know. In 1914, Astbury J. in *Re Republic of Bolivia Exploration Syndicate Ltd.*[23] allowed himself this shaky pronouncement:

> "Now, there are some legal matters which an auditor must obviously know, as there are others which it is equally obvious he could not be held responsible for not knowing, and it may not always be easy to say in which category any particular case falls."

By 1958, in *Fomento Ltd.* v. *Selsdon Fountain Pen Co. Ltd.*[24] we find Lord Denning making remarks which in substance require an auditor to have sufficient legal knowledge to recognise whether a legal problem exists on the facts before him. Problem recognition is the greater part of a practising lawyer's work. Lord Denning said:

> "Take, for instance, a point of law arising in the course of auditing a company's accounts. He may come on a payment which it appears to him, may be unlawful, in that it may not be within the powers of the corporation, or improper in that it may have no warrant or justification. He is, then, not only entitled but bound to enquire into it and, if need be, disallow it; . . . It may be, of course, that he has sufficient knowledge to deal with i

---

[21] Para. 6(*e*).
[22] For the problems encountered in practice, see "Dumb Debtors," *True & Fai* Issue No. 9, Autumn 1978.
[23] [1914] 1 Ch. 139, 171.
[24] [1958] 1 W.L.R. 45.

himself, as many accountants have, but, if it is beyond him, he is entitled to take legal advice. . . . "[25]

If one adds to the foregoing the fact that nowadays the auditing branches of the accountancy profession hold themselves out as experts in company law, and have imposed on themselves rigorous examinations[25a] in it as part of the qualification process, it is difficult to see how they can be excused ignorance of it any more than a specialist solicitor would be in like circumstances.

In summary therefore, as Pennycuick J. said in *Re Thomas Gerrard & Son Ltd.*,[26] "the standards of reasonable care and skill are, on the expert evidence, more exacting than those which prevailed in 1896." The duty may be stated in the same terms, but its content has changed. The higher the standards the auditors impose on themselves, the law follows.

This book does not pretend to be a text on auditing as such. We must nonetheless see in briefest outline how the *Auditing Standards* and their related *Guidelines* expect the "reasonably competent, careful and cautious auditor"[27] to go about his task of investigation and verification. He must adequately plan, control and record his work.[28] The extent of the planning depends on the nature of the enterprise; control relates mainly to the direction and supervision of the auditor's staff to whom audit tasks are delegated; recording the audit in working papers affords a means of checking that delegated functions have been properly performed by audit staff, and of providing evidence and justifying the opinions formed in the audit. The auditor should ascertain the enterprise's system of recording and processing transactions and assess its adequacy as a basis for the preparation of the financial statements.[29] The adequacy of an accounting system depends upon the nature of the enterprise: in a small business dealing primarily with cash sales and with only a few suppliers the accounting system may need to consist only of an analysed cash book and a list of unpaid invoices; in more complex concerns, the system should be correspondingly more complex, often

---

[25] *Ibid.* at p. 61.

[25a] See the subjects in which the 8th EEC Directive (84/253/EEC; O.J., L 126/20 of May 12, 1984), Art. 6 states that prospective auditors must be examined.

[26] [1968] Ch. 455, 471.

[27] See p. 000, *supra.*

[28] *The Auditor's Operational Standard*, para. 2, amplified in the *Auditing Guideline*: "Planning, Controlling and Recording."

[29] *The Auditor's Operational Standard*, para. 3, amplified in the *Auditing Guideline*: "Accounting Systems." This work may also be used to satisfy the distinct statutory duty imposed by para. 2 of the Sched. 7 to report whether proper books of account have been kept by the company.

including internal controls to ensure the recording of transactions which should be recorded, the discovery of irregularities, and that recorded assets and liabilities actually exist. In any event, whatever the enterprise, the accounting system must provide for the orderly assembly of accounting information and appropriate analyses to enable financial statements to be prepared. The auditor should obtain relevant and reliable audit evidence sufficient to enable him to draw reasonable conclusions therefrom.[30] Audit evidence is obtained by carrying out audit tests, which are termed either "substantive" or "compliance" tests depending on their purpose. Substantive tests are directed towards the completeness, accuracy and validity of the information contained in the accounting records, or in the financial statements; compliance tests seek to show whether or not internal control procedures are being applied as they should. Audit tests consist of inspecting records, documents and tangible assets, observing procedures within the enterprise, making enquiries of knowledgeable persons inside or outside the enterprise, checking the arithmetical accuracy of accounting records, making independent calculations and studying significant ratios, trends and other statistics and investigating any unusual or unexpected variations (analytical review procedures). Which and how many audit tests to employ is very much a matter for the auditor's informed judgment. If an auditor wishes to place reliance on any internal controls, he should ascertain and evaluate those controls and perform compliance tests on their operation.[31] Finally, the auditor should carry out such a review of the financial statements as is sufficient, in conjunction with the conclusions drawn from the other audit evidence, to give him a reasonable basis for his opinion on the financial statements.[32] In the course of this review the auditor will determine whether acceptable accounting policies have been adopted by the enterprise.

No auditing Guideline has at the time of writing yet been issued in respect of the auditor's duties under the new paragraph 5 of Schedule 7.[33] The auditor is required to report whether in his opinion "the net assets of a company are half or less of the amount of a company's

---

[30] *The Auditor's Operational Standard*, para. 4, amplified in the *Auditing Guideline* "Audit Evidence."

[31] *The Auditor's Operational Standard*, para. 5, amplified in the *Auditing Guideline* "Internal Controls."

[32] *The Auditor's Operational Standard*, para. 6, amplified in the *Auditing Guideline* "Review of Financial Statements."

[33] For the text, see p. 371, *supra*.

called-up share capital,"[34] thereby, if they have fallen below half, precipitating a duty on the directors, under section 40 of the Companies (Amendment) Act 1983, to convene an *e.g.m.* of the company "for the purpose of considering whether any, and if so what, measures should be taken to deal with the situation." Section 40 was passed in response to Article 17 of the Second EEC Directive[35] which required a general meeting to be called "in the case of a serious loss of the subscribed capital," Member States being obliged to treat a loss of more than half as "serious." The Directive did not apply to Irish *private* companies. Yet section 40 does, despite the fact that private companies, unlike plcs, are not in law required to have any significant paid up share capital.[36] In a private company with minimal share capital and financed by other means (such as by long term loans) the slightest loss before it has had time to build up reserves will send it over the section 40 limit; yet, perfectly viable enterprises commonly sustain losses in their early years. Simply, a loss in share capital in an enterprise which is not in any significant measure financed by share capital cannot be regarded as a criterion of its performance. Britain, it should be noted, in its implementation of the Second Directive confined the operation of Article 17 to public companies.[37] Even in companies significantly financed by share capital, section 40 is to an extent otiose. An auditor who under current accounting practice unqualifiedly certifies that the accounts examined by him give a "true and fair view" of the state of a company's affairs[38] is doing so on the basis that those who use the company's accounts may assume that:

> "the enterprise will continue in operational existence for the forseeable future. This means in particular that the profit and loss account and balance sheet assume no intention or necessity to liquidate or curtail significantly the scale of operation."[39]

This passage describes the fundamental accounting concept of *going concern*; if in the opinion of the auditor the enterprise is not a going concern within this meaning, the onus would seem to be on him to disclose that fact. Observance of this concept is presumed unless the

---

[34] s.40 of the 1983 Act. "Called-up share capital" is defined in s.2(1), and "net assets" in s.2(4)(1) thereof.

[35] Case 77/91/ EEC; December 13th, 1976.

[36] See generally pp. 303, *et seq.*, *supra*.

[37] s.34 of the Companies Act 1980 [*U.K.*].

[38] Sched. 7, para. 3.

[39] Statement of Standard Accounting Practice (S.S.A.P.), No. 2: "Disclosure of Accounting Policies," para. 14 (*a*), definition of "going concern."

contrary is stated.[40] How far this duty goes in practice has not yet at the time of writing been standardised; particularly, there remains the problem that an auditor by expressing doubts about an enterprise may, through the consequent loss of confidence in it, precipitate the very disaster against the possibility of which he was warning, a self-fulfilling prophecy.[41] Section 40 with its arbitrary and arithmetical early warning system may well, in appropriate cases, relieve auditors from this unpleasant responsibility.

If an auditor wishes in any way to qualify his report to the members, he should do so clearly. The members in *Re London and General Bank (No. 2)*[42] could not have been expected to extract the warning implicit in the statement made by the auditors that "the value of the assets as shewn on the balance-sheet is dependent upon realisation," by which they intended to convey, but in a form which spared the feelings of the management, that the company had lent money on inadequate security. As Lindley L.J. said:

> "A person whose duty it is to convey information to others does not discharge that duty by simply giving them so much information as is calculated to induce them, or some of them, to ask for more. Information and means of information are by no means equivalent terms."[43]

In fact, qualifications to audit reports have now been standardised

---

[40] *Ibid.* para. 2; also, para. 5, *Explanatory Foreword* to the Statements of Standard Accounting Practice states that where accountants "act as auditors . . . the onus will be on them . . . to ensure disclosure of significant departures," *i.e.* from applicable accounting standards. See also *Auditing Standard*: 'The Audit Report', para. 6 which says "when expressing an opinion that financial statements give a true and fair view the auditor should be satisfied, inter alia, that . . . all relevant Statements of Standard Accounting Practice have been complied with . . . " Example 7 of the *Auditing Guideline*: 'Audit Report Examples (Supplement for the Republic of Ireland and Northern Ireland)' contains a qualification expressly assuming that the company is a going concern, and giving the reasons for doubt. The argument in the text derives from E. Cahill, "Irish Listed Company Failure, Financial Ratios, Accounts and Auditors' Opinions," *Journal of Irish Business and Administrative Research*, Vol. 3. April 1981, p. 19. These principles are now to be given statutory expression: the 1985 Bill, s.5(*a*) requires that a company's accounts be drawn up on this basis that "the company shall be presumed to be carrying on business as a going concern," and, by s.6, departures from this and the other fundamental accounting principles listed in s.5 must be stated and explained.

[41] An exposure draft for an *Auditing Guideline* on these problems was issued by the Auditing Practices Committee on September 28, 1983. See *True & Fair*, Issue No. 25 Autumn 1983.

[42] [1895] 2 Ch. 673.

[43] *Ibid.* at p. 684.

in ascending degrees of severity.[44] Material but not fundamental uncertainty will produce a "subject to" opinion; material but not fundamental disagreement will produce an "except"opinion; a fundamental uncertainty will result in a "disclaimer of opinion," and a fundamental disagreement will be recorded in an "adverse opinion." As examples, a small company might earn a standardised "subject to" qualification pointing out that "in common with many businesses of similar size and organisation the company's system of control is dependent upon the close involvement of the directors who are major shareholders. Where independent confirmation of the completeness of the accounting records was therefore not available we have accepted assurances from the directors that all the company's transactions have been reflected in the records," but "subject to" this qualification the company's financial statements give a true and fair view of its affairs. Failure to make provision for a doubtful debt which the auditors think unlikely to be paid could lead to a report that the accounts give a true and fair view "except" in that respect. The destruction of a significant part of the company's accounting records will result in the auditors' reporting that they have been unable to form the opinion whether or not the financial statements give a true and fair view, *i.e.* they will make a "disclaimer." In an "adverse opinion" the auditors actually say that the financial statements do not give a true and fair view. An example might be a refusal by the directors to make provision for losses expected to arise on existing long-term contracts because future, but as yet unearned profits, are expected on other such contracts, an approach which is contrary to standard accounting practice.[45]

Although the auditors' duty is expressed in section 163(1) as being that of making "a report to the members," the auditors incur no responsibility if the report does not in fact reach the members[46] or if the *a.g.m.* at which it should be read[47] is not held, or the report omitted, provided that the auditors have despatched the report to the proper authority within the company, usually the secretary.[48]

Liability to the company

If the auditors fall short of the professional standards laid upon them they will be liable in breach of contract to the company for

---

[44] *Auditing Standard*: "Qualifications in Audit Reports," and *Auditing Guideline*: "Audit Report Examples (Supplement for the Republic of Ireland and Northern Ireland)" from which the ensuing examples in the text are drawn.

[45] S.S.A.P. No. 9: "Stocks and Work in Progress," August 1980.

[46] Pursuant to s.159(1).

[47] Pursuant to s.163(2).

[48] *Re Allen, Craig & Co. (London) Ltd.* [1934] Ch. 483.

consequent loss. If the company is in liquidation, the liquidator may pursue this cause of action through the medium of a misfeasance summons under section 298 of the Companies Act 1963.[49] Typical recoverable loss includes the amount of the dividends paid out of false profits, and the amount of the taxes paid on them.[50]

Auditors are precluded by section 200 of the Companies Act 1963 from stipulating in their contract with the company that they should be exempted from "any liability which by virtue of any rule of law would otherwise attach to [them] in respect of any negligence, default, breach of duty or breach of trust of which [they] may be guilty in relation to the company." Since the content of their contractual duty to the company is statutorily fixed, they may not in respect of that fixed content find a way round the section as directors may, whose duties to the company are variable by individual agreement and by the articles.[51]

A parallel duty in tort with identical content to the contractual duty may also be constructed.[52]

Liability to others

The auditor's report is addressed to the members. There is little doubt that he must have them in contemplation when making his report, and must realise that it will be relied upon by them as having been made as a result of the exercise of a proper measure of professional skill and care. Accordingly, on the well known principle in *Hedley Byrne & Co. Ltd.* v. *Heller & Partners Ltd.*,[53] if a member allows his conduct to be materially influenced by a report falling short of these standards, and suffers loss as a consequence, he should be able to maintain an action in tort for compensation against the auditor.[54] There are, of course, no contractual relations between him and the

---

[49] See the authorities cited at n. 88, *supra*.

[50] *e.g. Re London and General Bank (No. 2)* [1895] 2 Ch. 673; *Re Kingston Cotton Mill (No. 2)* [1896] 2 Ch. 279; and *Re Thomas Gerrard & Son Ltd.* [1968] Ch. 455 all involved claims by the company for compensation for the payment of excessive dividends, and, in the latter case, overpaid tax. *Semble*, the company has a duty to mitigate damage by claiming repayment of overpaid tax from the Revenue Commissioners: *Re Thomas Gerrard & Son Ltd.*, at p. 478. If so, similar principles should apply to unlawfully paid dividends. For the recovery by the company of unlawful dividends from the recipients, see s.50 of the 1983 Act.

[51] See the discussion at pp. 237–238, *supra*.

[52] *Finlay* v. *Murtagh* [1979] I.R. 249, 257 (solicitor's concurrent duty to client in tort).

[53] [1964] A.C. 465; first accepted into Ireland in *Securities Trust Ltd.* v. *Moore & Alexander Ltd.* [1964] I.R. 417, and presaged, according to McGrath in (1983) 2 D.U.L.J., by *Macken* v. *Munster & Leinster Bank.*

[54] Or an action in tort founded on breach of statutory duty?

auditor. The reliance by the member on the report might, for example, consist of buying more shares in the company, or failing to take steps to arrest a deteriorating situation.

The doubts and difficulties arise with other potential plaintiffs. In the English case of *J.E.B. Fasteners Ltd.* v. *Marks, Bloom & Co.*[55] a duty of professional care and skill was found to exist between an auditor of a company's annual accounts and a subsequent purchaser of the company's whole share capital. Fortunately for the auditor who had negligently allowed an inflated stock figure to pass without comment in his report, the purchaser would have bought the company even if the true position had been revealed in the accounts, or the auditor's certificate. There was thus, on the facts, no causal connection between the auditor's breach of duty and the purchaser's loss. It was held that but for this missing element, the purchaser's cause of action was complete. One cannot be certain that the case would have gone the same way before an Irish Court. The auditor in *J.E.B. Fasteners Ltd.* did not actually know that the subsequent purchaser would be relying on his audit work; neither did he expressly assume responsibility towards him or persons of his kind, in the sense that he did not feel when carrying out his tasks that he was "working for" anyone other than the company and its members.[56] Nonetheless, a duty of care and skill was erected on the basis that the subsequent purchaser was one of a class of persons, whether known or unknown to him, which he ought to have forseen might rely on the quality of his work. In Ireland, on the other hand, there is discernible a reluctance by the courts to extend the ability to sue on negligent mis-statements beyond the persons for whom they were specifically prepared. In *McSweeney* v. *Bourke*,[57] a professed expert in financial matters had advised a group of companies on a method of resolving a liquidity problem. The advice involved a proposal, *inter alia*, that the principal shareholders should inject fresh risk capital, which they did. Unfortunately, the companies did not pull through. Upon the shareholders suing the financial adviser, it was held by Carroll J. that the adviser, if not negligent in relation to his client, the group (as indeed he was not), could not in respect of that same work be found negligent in relation to third parties, unless he actually purported to advise them as well. Determinative of this latter point was the fact that the adviser "did not *hold himself out* as

---

[55] [1981] 3 All E.R. 289, a first instance decision, relying chiefly on dicta in *Anns* v. *London Borough of Merton* [1978] A.C. 728, 751; *Scott Group Ltd.* v. *McFarlane* [1978] 1 N.Z.L.R. 553, and *Ross* v. *Caunters* [1980] Ch. 279, 313–314.

[56] In their case, gratuitously.

[57] High Court, Carroll J., November 25 1980, unreported.

advising the shareholders as well as the group."[58] There was no evidence that he "*undertook* an additional and separate duty of advising shareholders, as such . . . "; he had no additional duty imposed on him "to add any words of warning in relation to the risks attached to further capital investment in the group"; if the shareholders assumed "that he was advising them as shareholders this was not a reasonable assumption"; and, "if they placed reliance on the advice they could only do so in the context that it was advice for the benefit of the group. . . . " An earlier example of this reluctance is found in *Securities Trust Ltd.* v. *Hugh Moore & Alexander Ltd.*.[59] A company had pursuant to its statutory duty contained in what is now section 29 of the Companies Act 1963 supplied a member with a copy of its articles. That copy contained a serious misprint which gave the false impression that preference shareholders were entitled to participate in the distribution of surplus assets in a winding up.[60] The member held as nominee for the plaintiff which then bought up large quantities preference shares on faith of the statement. The plaintiff's action for compensation failed. *Hedley Byrne & Co. Ltd.* v. *Heller & Partners Ltd.*[61] was interpreted as requiring a "special relationship" between the maker and the recipient of the statement, and the plaintiff, it was held, stood in no different relationship to the company:

> "than such as would exist between the defendant Company and any person (other than [the member] who might chance to read the copy supplied to him; or, indeed, between that Company and any member of the community at large, individual or corporate, who chanced to become aware of . . . the defective reprint. It can hardly be seriously contended that the defendant Company owed a duty to the world at large to take care to avoid mistakes and printers' errors in the reprint of their Articles."[62]

According to Kenny J. in *Bank of Ireland* v. *Smith*,[63] decided two years later, this special relationship requires that there be on the part of the defendant "an assumption of responsibility in circumstances in which, but for the absence of consideration, there would be a contract." And ten years later in the Supreme Court decision of *Dublin Port and Docks Board* v. *Bank of Ireland*,[64] he remarked that "commer-

---

[58] All citations are from pp. 18 and 22 of the transcript. Italics supplied.
[59] [1964] I.R. 417.
[60] See pp. 174, *et seq., ante.*
[61] [1964] A.C. 465.
[62] *Per* Davitt P. at [1964] I.R. 422.
[63] [1966] I.R. 646, 660 citing Lord Devlin in *Hedley Byrne* at [1964] A.C. 465, 528.
[64] [1976] I.R. 118, 141.

cial life would become impossible if forseeability that one's action or inaction would cause economic loss to another were to create liability." For that liability to arise, he said, there must be that "special relationship between the parties as there was in *Hedley Byrne & Co. Ltd.* v. *Heller & Partners Ltd.*"

One finds therefore in Ireland at present a climate of judicial opinion contrary to the generalisations of *J.E.B. Fasteners Ltd.*, the attitude being closer to that expressed by Cardozo C.J. in his famous judgment in *Ultramares Corporation* v. *Touche*[65] which concerned a claim by creditors against auditors:

> "If liability for negligence exists, a thoughtless slip or blunder, the failure to detect a theft or forgery beneath the cover of deceptive entries, may expose accountants to a liability in an indeterminate amount for an indeterminate time to an indeterminate class. The hazards of a business conducted on these terms are so extreme as to enkindle doubt whether a flaw may not exist in the implication of a duty that exposes to these consequences."[66]

Underlying the present approach of the Irish courts is the practical attitude that commercial life should not be stifled by the counsels of perfection. Another instance is found in the hostile stance of the judiciary to the introduction of constructive notice to commercial transactions.[67]

But attitudes change, and against that day auditors may wish to state in their audit report that they assume responsibility to the audit client and its members and no one else. Such a disclaimer should suffice to prevent a duty in tort arising in favour of a wider public.

The auditor as arbiter

Scattered through the Companies Acts are a number of provisions which constitute a company's auditor the judge of the propriety of actions undertaken by or within a company. There is section 133(3) of the Companies Act 1963 which allows notice requirements for the summoning of meetings to be waived provided that the auditors agree.[68] Section 149(5) of the Companies Act 1963 allows the pre-

---

[65] (1931) 174 N.E. 441.

[66] *Ibid.* at p. 444.

[67] *Bank of Ireland Finance Ltd.* v. *Rockfield Ltd.* [1979] I.R. 21; *Welch* v. *Bowmaker (Ireland) Ltd.* [1980] I.R. 251; and, contrast Keane J. in *Northern Bank Finance Corporation Ltd.* v. *Quinn*, High Court, November 8, 1979, unreported.

[68] But not so as to waive the minima in s.133(1).

acquisition profits of a subsidiary to be distributed via its new holding company if *inter alia* "the auditors are satisfied and so certify that it would be fair and reasonable and would not prejudice the rights and interests of any person."[69] The latest example is found in section 49 of the Companies (Amendment) Act 1983 which provides, *inter alia*, that where dividends are declared by reference to a company's last annual accounts, the auditors must have reported on them, and if they have qualified their report in any way, they must also have stated whether the qualification affects the propriety of the proposed distribution.[70]

---

[69] s.149(5) is discussed at pp. 335–336, *supra*.
[70] s.49 is further discussed at pp. 332, 337, *supra*.

Chapter 12: Promoters and Prospectuses

PROMOTERS

Company law is concerned with promoters in two distinct contexts. The first is his relationship with the company he has promoted, and his liability to it. Here, he occupies the centre of the stage. The second context concerns his liability to investors who have parted with their money on the faith of statements made by him. Here, the promoter no longer has the star rôle: he is merely one of a chorus of other characters who incur a similar liability, and therefore the part he plays will be treated with theirs under the general heading *Prospectuses, infra*.

The promoter and his company

He may here occupy the centre of the stage, but the spotlights have dimmed. This branch of the law is not as commercially relevant as it once was. Reading the cases one becomes aware of a certain period charm. Rogues form a company which purchases from them dubious assets at inflated prices; the rogues concoct a prospectus shot through with hyperbole and whose hallmark is the judicious suppression of material facts; and, with its aid floats off the company onto a gullible,[1] avaricious, and, may it be said, monied investing public; the company pays the rogues for the assets with the proceeds of the issue; and the rogues disappear to fresh fields of endeavour, leaving dummy and likewise gullible directors to cope inadequately with the ensuing fracas. Such predatory activities are nowadays rendered difficult by companies legislation. In particular, an invitation to the public to subscribe for shares, or, in other words, a *prospectus*, is required as we shall see, *infra*, to contain the answers to all sorts of

---

[1] See the remarks of Porter M.R in *Re Leinster Contract Corporation* [1902] 1 I.R. 349, 362.

pertinent questions, not least a requirement that the content of material contracts with promoters be disclosed. Also aiding the disappearance of the Victorian promoter as a distinct breed has been a huge diminution in the number of available victims, the leisured classes, and their replacement in the market by professional, institutional investors.

Who is a promoter? He is not in this context defined by the Companies Acts.[2] There is, however, a considerable body of case law[3] establishing whether or not in particular instances a person was a promoter in relation to a company. One may distill the results by stating that the term "promoter" describes anyone who, acting as a principal,[4] "gets a company going" whether by actually forming it, taking a part in the raising of its initial capital, procuring directors for it, introducing prospective vendors of property to a syndicate who might be interested in exploiting it, or otherwise.

A promoter stands in a fiduciary relationship to the company he promotes.[5] We have already seen in the context of directors' duties the nature and consequences of such a relationship.[6] The fiduciary must disclose to his principal any advantage to himself derived from the relationship, and obtain its assent to his retaining it. Otherwise, he must account for benefits to his principal and any arrangements between him and it are, if *restitutio in integrum* remains possible, voidable at the instance of the latter. Directors cannot acting as a board release themselves from their fiduciary duty to the company,[7] but they may release other fiduciaries. It was however early perceived that the directors of newly formed companies are likely to be mere puppets of the promoters, if not the same or partially the same people.

Accordingly, it was established that the disclosure and release in order to be effective must be made to a board capable of exercising an independent and intelligent judgment on the transaction, or to

---

[2] But he is defined in the context of prospectuses, at p. 000, *infra*.

[3] *Twycross* v. *Grant* (1877) 2 C.P.D 469 and *Whaley Bridge Calico Printing Co. Ltd.* v. *Green & Smith* (1879) 5 Q.B.D. 109 are representative examples. The point also aros in the judgment of Palles C.B. in *Components Tube Co. Ltd.* v. *Naylor* [1900] 2 I.R. 1, 6?

[4] *i.e.* not as an agent such as a solicitor or accountant employed only to advise o perform purely ministerial acts, nor as a supplier of services, such as a printer, nc involved in the broader design.

[5] *Erlanger* v. *New Sombrero Phosphate Co.* (1878) 3 App.Cas. 1218 (and in the Englis C.A. at 5 Ch.D. 73) both reports being cited with approval in *Components Tube Co. Lt.* v. *Naylor* [1900] 2 I.R. 1, *passim*.

[6] Chap. 7, *supra*.

[7] See p. 215, n. 62, *supra*.

the members of the company. Authority for the first proposition, that disclosure must be made to a board capable of exercising an independent and intelligent judgment is found in a number of monuments to Victorian jurisprudence, chiefly *Erlanger* v. *New Sombrero Phosphate Co.*[8] and *Gluckstein* v. *Barnes*,[9] each couched in that blend of condemnation, condescension and sentimentality which these less certain times seem less willing to emulate. Take Lord MacNaghten in *Gluckstein* v. *Barnes*[10]:

> "These gentlemen set about forming a company to pay them a handsome sum for taking off their hands a property which they had contracted to buy with that end in view. They bring the company into existence by means of the usual machinery. They appoint themselves sole guardians and protectors of this creature of theirs, half-fledged and just struggling into life, bound hand and foot while yet unborn by contracts tending to their private advantage, and so fashioned by its makers that it could only act by their hands and see through their eyes . . ."

Authority for the second proposition, that disclosure may be made to the members of the company, and the release obtained from them is to be found in *Salomon* v. *Salomon & Co.*[11] in which, it will be recollected, that Mr. Salomon sold his leather business to the company he had promoted for the purpose of buying it from him. The price was over £39,000 which, again in the words of Lord MacNaghten[12] was "a sum which represented the sanguine expectations of a fond owner rather than anything that can be called a business-like or reasonable estimate of value . . . ." Yet, all the members of the company has assented, albeit as mere "dummies" for Mr. Salomon, to the transaction and its execution, and had thereby released the company's rights against the promoter. In principle, such a release could be effected by a majority decision in general meeting provided that the infringement of the fiduciary relationship has not involved a "fraud on the minority."[13]

Salomon's Case therefore supplies the reason why claims by a com-

---

[8] (1878) 3 App.Cas. 1218, and see n. 5, *supra*.
[9] [1900] A.C. 240.
[10] *Ibid.* at p. 248.
[11] [1897] A.C. 22, more generally discussed at pp. 21–22, *supra*.
[12] *Ibid.* at p. 49.
[13] As to which see pp. 247–255, *supra*. *Atwool* v. *Merryweather* (1868) L.R. 5 Eq. 464n involved a failed attempt to ratify wrongdoing by a promoter amounting to a "fraud on the minority."

pany against its promoters are rare to the point of extinction nowadays. Most new incorporations in which the new company is to acquire property from its promoters tend to be of companies formed to take over existing partnership or individual businesses or to hold family assets, or to be operating subsidiaries formed by a holding company, or other situations involving few participants both before and after incorporation, all of whom are fully aware of all aspects of the transaction, and who by their participation assent to it.

Promoters may coincidentally find their dealing with a public limited company (plc) subjected to the scrutiny of an independent valuation if they have allowed themselves to fall within the conditions of section 32 of the Companies (Amendment) Act 1983, by being either a subscriber to the memorandum of a company formed as a plc, or a member of a company subsequently converted into a plc.[14]

PROSPECTUSES

Introduction

The Companies Act 1963 contains a code on prospectuses. Its object is the protection of the investing public. Its chief weapon is compulsory disclosure of material facts upon the occasion of any invitation to members of the public to subscribe for shares or debentures in a company. There are criminal sanctions for breach of the code.

The Act interests itself also in the civil consequences of a misleading prospectus. There is a statutory right of compensation against a wide class of defendants for those who have suffered as a result. Outside the Act, there is the possibility that a contract of allotment founded on a misleading prospectus might be rescinded; also, but only technically, available are the rights of compensation in tort in respect of misleading statements in a prospectus.

The statutory code

The statutory code on prospectuses is to be found in sections 43 to 52 inclusive of the Companies Act 1963, and in the massed detail of Schedule 3 of that Act.

---

[14] See pp. 313–315 *supra*, and also the 1983 Act, s.30 at pp. 310 *et seq.*, *supra*: independent valuation of the non-cash consideration received for shares.

A prospectus is defined as meaning:

> "any prospectus, notice, circular, advertisement or other invitation, offering to the public for subscription or purchase any shares or debentures of a company."[15]

With some qualifications, any document coming within this broad description must make the disclosures set out in Schedule 3.[16] And the Act operates in a pincer movement to declare, again with some qualifications, that no form of application for shares in or debentures of a company which are being offered to the public shall be issued without being accompanied by a prospectus complying with the Act.[17]

Central to these provisions is the notion of an offer or invitation being made or a form of application being issued to the *public*. This term is given a specialised meaning in the Act; its vague everyday meaning is widened to include narrower classes of persons. It is to be construed by section 61(1) as including an offer:

> "to any section of the public whether selected as members or debenture holders of the company concerned or as clients of the person issuing the prospectus or in any other manner. . . . "

but, by section 61(2) as excluding any offer which:

> "can properly be regarded in all the circumstances, as not being calculated to result, directly or indirectly, in the shares or debentures becoming available for subscription or purchase by persons other than those receiving the offer or invitation, or otherwise as being a domestic concern of the persons making and receiving it. . . . "

Thus, a takeover bidder offering to issue shares in itself in exchange for the shares of the shareholders in the company bid for is prima facie making an offer to the public and must issue a prospectus, unless it can bring the offer within section 61(2). It may accomplish this by issuing non-renounceable letters of allotment[18] in exchange

---

[15] The definition s.2.

[16] s.44(1). If issued by or on behalf of a company, or by or on behalf of any person who is or has been engaged or interested in the formation of the company. The issue by a company is amplified by s.51, discussed *infra*.

[17] s.44(3); s.44(4)(*b*). The prohibition applies by whomsoever the application form is issued.

[18] *i.e.* a contract of allotment of which the benefit is not assignable. Letters of allotment in respect of new issues are frequently renounceable to render them marketable.

for the acceptance forms in respect of shares acquired,[19] thus ensuring that the whole process of issue, including registration of the allottees as holders is completed before any outsider becomes capable of acquiring any legal interest in them.

The Act excludes from Schedule 3 disclosures some circumstances which would otherwise fall within the catchment area mapped out above. A "rights" issue to existing members or debenture holders is exempt, even though the benefits are inevitably marketable by renunciation.[20] No prospectus need be issued in connection with an application to underwriters to underwrite an issue.[21] Underwriters are deemed well able to take care of themselves. A new issue of shares or debentures which are to be in all respects uniform with shares or debentures issued within the preceding two years and, for the time being dealt with on the Stock Exchange are likewise exempt.[21a] This exemption reflects a justifiable readiness to trust in the self-regulatory processes of the Stock Exchange, and the substantial disclosures exacted by that body, to which we now turn.

A most significant exemption is given by regulation 12 of the European Communities (Stock Exchange) Regulations 1984[21b] which came into operation on January 1, 1985. This exemption relates to securities for which an application has been made to the Committee of the Irish Unit of the Stock Exchange for official listing, and in respect of which that Committee has approved the listing particulars which the company is obliged to supply on that occasion.[21c] Here, a document setting out the listing particulars as approved (or saying where they may be obtained or inspected) may

---

[19] *Government Stock and Other Securities Investment Co. Ltd.* v. *Christopher* [1956] 1 All E.R. 490. Insofar as this case states that a share for share exchange does not involve the bidder's shares being offered "for subscription" (since no cash changes hands) it may be regarded as faulty. Shares have always been subscribable for a non-cash consideration (see pp. 308 *et seq., supra*), and now the 1983 Act, s.26(1) expressly declares: "shares allotted by a company and any premium payable on them may be paid up in money or money's worth (including goodwill and expertise)."

[20] s.44(7)(*a*).

[21] s.44(4)(*a*).

[21a] s.44(7)(*b*). In fact, by Article 6.3(a) of the Listing Particulars Directive (80/390/EEC) carried into law by the European Communities (Stock Exchange) Regulations 1984 (S.I. 1984 No. 282), reg. 7(1), the Stock Exchange will be obliged (in the absence of some other applicable exemption) to receive listing particulars in respect of such shares unless their nominal value amounts to less than 10 per cent. of the shares already listed. Listing particulars, and their interrelationship with the prospectus requirements are described, *infra.*

[21b] S.I. 1984 No. 282, implementing three EEC Directives, the Admissions Directive (79/279/EEC), the Listing Particulars Directive (80/390/EEC) and the Interim Reports Directive (82/121/EEC).

[21c] Listing Particulars Directive, Arts. 1 and 3; 1984 Regulations, reg. 3(1)(*b*).

take the place of the Schedule 3 prospectus which otherwise sh(
accompany any application form for the shares or debenture
question. In that event, this document ranks as a prospectus fo
the purposes of the Companies Act 1963, save for the requirem
of that Act in respect of dating, content and registration.[21d] In
ticular, it continues to attract the statutory civil liability and cr
nal sanctions, each described below, imposed by the Companies
1963 in respect of misleading and false statements in prospectus(

The Stock Exchange has for many years been developing
imposing its own stringent extra-legal requirements governing
admission of securities to listing on the Exchange, including the
closures to be made in a prospectus.[21e] Indeed, the content of Sc
ule 3 which now in some respects lags behind the Stock Exch:
was in part inspired by these extra-legal developments, as well a
early judicial decisions. The intervention from the EEC is desi;
to ensure that each stock market in the Community exacts a uni
minimum of information concerning securities quoted on it.
Stock Exchange may and will however continue to exact its
additional disclosures.[21f]

The 1984 Regulations give the Stock Exchange power to dispense
with the publication of listing particulars, or to abridge them, in a
variety of circumstances.[22] If they are *wholly* dispensed with, the
exemptions from the 1963 Act given by the 1984 Regulations will not
apply. There may be circumstances in that event, when section 45 of
the Companies Act 1963 which before the coming into force of the
1984 Regulations was in practice used to authorise the issue of an

---

[21d] The 1984 Regulations, reg. 12(3) exempts the document from section 43 (date),
s.44(1) (content) and s.47 (registration). Listing particulars must be independently
registered. See *Publication of listing particulars, infra.* Reg. 12(3) also states that s.45
(power of Stock Exchange to dispense with or abridge Sched. 3 content of prospectus)
shall not apply to the document. The Directive, as implemented by the 1984 Regulations, in fact gives the Stock Exchange power to abridge the listing particulars in
specified circumstances, as to which see n. 21g, *infra.*

[21e] Stock Exchange, *Admission of Securities to Listing*, Appendix, Sched. II: Contents
of Prospectus.

[21f] 1984 Regulations, reg. 3(2), Admissions Directive (79/29/EEC), Arts., 9.3, 10,
13.

[22] Some of these exceptions are designed to avoid duplication, *e.g.* the case of
securities which have been publicly issued before listing, and in respect of which
within the previous 12 months before their admission to listing a document (*e.g.*, a
prospectus) regarded by the Stock Exchange as satisfying the Listing Particulars
Directive has been published: Listing Particulars Directive, Art. 6.1(a); others reflect
the circumstances of the issue, *e.g.* the curtailed disclosures required on a rights issue
in respect of listed securities: *Ibid.*, Art. 8; and others relieve the issuer from disclosing
matters unnecessary for the protection of the public, *e.g.* "information of minor
importance only and . . . not such as will influence assessment of the assets and liabilities, financial position, profits and losses and prospects of the issuer": *Ibid.* Art. 7.

abridged prospectus must be invoked to avoid the application of Schedule 3.[23] If application has been made to the Stock Exchange for a quotation in respect of the shares or debentures to be offered to the public by prospectus, the Stock Exchange may pursuant to section 45 certify that the prospectus should be exempt from the requirements of Schedule 3 if:

> "having regard to . . . the size and other circumstances of the issue . . . and . . . any limitations on the number and class of persons to whom the offer is to be made, compliance with the requirements of the Third Schedule would be unduly burdensome."

We now turn briefly to review the prospectus requirements in relation to some of the commoner methods of flotation employed by public companies. Naturally, in the case of a *direct invitation* by the company to the public a prospectus will have to be issued. Section 51 extends the prospectus requirements to a common type of *offer for sale*, a mechanism by which the company allots the shares to be floated to a single allottee, acting as an issuing house, which then proceeds to market them to the public, renouncing its allotment *pro rata* in favour of the applicants. In effect, this procedure involves the allottee in underwriting the issue to the public, the underwriter's reward being the difference between the issue price and the offer price.[24] In so far as the public issue fails, the allottee will have to get rid of the unsold shares by *placing* them, a method by no means confined to a failed issue. Placing commonly involves a firm of stockbrokers privately inviting selected clients, institutional investors, for example, to take up blocks of shares or debentures. If they do so, the shares or debentures are said to have been "placed." A prospectus will be required if the brokers circularise sufficient of their clientele to render the invitation no longer "a domestic concern of the persons making and receiving it."[25] Clients of a particular firm are, as we have seen,[26] capable of constituting "the public." *Offers by tender* have the purpose of confounding the "stags," speculators who apply for new issues with a view to selling them at a premium over the offer

---

[23] Contrast the manner in which the U.K. implemented these three Directives: The Stock Exchange (Listing) Regulations 1984 (S.I. 1984 No. 716) [*U.K.*]. These regulations repeal the British equivalent of s.45.

[24] This must be disclosed: s.51(3).

[25] s.61(2) (p. 391, *supra*); the word "otherwise" in "otherwise a domestic concern seems to qualify the whole sub-section.

[26] s.61(1), (p. 391, *supra*).

price before calls become due.[27] The offer fixes a minimum price, and provides that the securities will be allotted at the highest tendered price above this at which all shares will be allotted, thereby, it is hoped, channelling the best part of what would otherwise be a market premium into the pockets of the company. A prospectus is necessary. Prospectuses issued with a *rights issue* need not, as we have seen,[28] comply with Schedule 3, and forms of application for them need not be accompanied by a prospectus. A *bonus issue*, since it does not involve "subscription or purchase," needs no prospectus.

The content of a prospectus

We delve into the detail of Schedule 3 only to illustrate its philosophy. Its object is disclosure so that potential investors may make fully informed judgments for themselves on the merits of the issue, including particularly disclosure of matters which the unscrupulous promoter of yesteryear might have found it inconvenient to mention. Taking examples, the full story must be told of property to be paid for out of the proceeds of the issue: from whom is it being bought? for how much? if bought recently, how much did the vendor then pay? Has any promoter or director recently acquired any direct or indirect interest in it? The information demanded by paragraph 9[29] is designed to elicit answers to these and similar questions. Paragraph 8 puts a finger on a tender spot by requiring disclosure of the non-cash consideration for shares. Paragraphs 13 and 16 ask in effect: what is in it for them? Here will be disclosed *inter alia* inducements offered to the directors to act as such,[30] and benefits given or to be given to promoters. Options to subscribe for the company's shares must be disclosed, and the option price so that potential investors may know whether their equity will be diluted: paragraph 8. Paragraph 14 requires disclosure of a residual category of "material contracts." These are contracts out of the ordinary course of a company's business, disclosure of which would according to *Jury* v. *Stoker*[31] "assist a person in determining whether he would become a shareholder of the company."

---

[27] Thus, if shares issued at £1, payable as to 25 per cent. only on application, are perceived by the market as worth a 10 per cent. premium, the "stag" is set to make 40 per cent. on his outlay.

[28] s.44(7), (p. 392, *supra*).

[29] As amplified by paras. 23 and 24.

[30] *e.g.* the "buying" of a director in *Jury* v. *Stoker* (1881) 9 L.R., Ir. 358, a fact which ought, as legislation then stood, to have been disclosed as a "material contract." Material contracts now fall within para. 14 as a residual category of disclosure, *infra*.

[31] (1881) 9 L.R., Ir. 358, 402, following *Sullivan* v. *Metcalfe* (1880) 5 C.P.D. 455, 55.

Schedule 3 does not concern itself only with thwarting the suppression of embarrassing facts, and therefore their very existence in the first place. It also aims towards providing the potential subscriber with objective financial information. The company's auditors must report in the prospectus on its dividend record and the profits and losses of it and its subsidiaries during the preceding five years, and on the assets and liabilities of it and its subsidiaries.[32] If any part of the proceeds of the issue is to go towards the acquisition of a business, the prospectus must contain a report by a named accountant on its profits and losses during the preceding five years, and its assets and liabilities[33]; there must be a similar report on any company and its subsidiaries control of which is to be acquired through the proceeds of the issue, distinguishing the participation rights of any minority interest which will be left outstanding after the acquisition.[34]

The listing particulars

The Schedules to the Listing Particulars Directive[35] require information to be provided in specific and copious detail by a company whose securities are the subject of any application for official listing on the Stock Exchange.[35a] Their flavour may be imparted by a brief summary of what is required of a company applying to have its shares listed. The topics covered include the identification of the individuals responsible for furnishing the information and the company's auditors,[35b] a description of the shares to be listed and the rights attached to them,[35c] the costs of the issue and the purposes to which the net proceeds will be devoted,[35d] information (so far as is known) about the company's controllers,[35e] the extent to which persons have preferential rights to subscribe for its capital,[35f] information about its activities, number of employees and investment policy,[35g] its financial affairs including its accounts for the preceding three years,[35h] information about the persons comprising its admin-

---

[32] Para. 19.

[33] Para. 20.

[34] Para. 21.

[35] 80/390/EEC, carried into law by the European Communities (Stock Exchange) Regulations 1984, reg. 3(1).

[35a] Art. 2(*c*) of the Directive.

[35b] Sched. A, Chap. 1.

[35c] Sched. A, Chap. 2.

[35d] Sched. A, Chap. 2.

[35e] Sched. A, Chap. 3.

[35f] Sched. A, Chaps. 3 and 7.

[35g] Sched. A, Chap. 4.

[35h] Sched. A, Chaps. 1 and 5.

istration and management, their interests in the company activities outside it, their remuneration and benefits in kind, loans to them by the company, and any dealings between them and the company not in the usual course of business.[35i] Different specifics are required where debentures are the subject of the application.[35j] But specifics apart, there is an overriding standard imposed on those responsible for preparing the listing particulars. It is contained in the key Article 4 of the Listing Particulars Directive:

> "The listing particulars shall contain the information which, according to the particular nature of the issuer and of the securities for the admission of which application is being made, is necessary to enable investors and their investment advisers to make an informed assessment of the assets and liabilities, financial position, profits and losses, and prospects of the issuer and of the rights attaching to such securities."

Rescission

A contract induced by misrepresentation of material fact may be rescinded by the party misled. Contracts of allotment are no exception. As Sir Peter O'Brien L.C.J. said in *Components Tube Co. Ltd.* v. *Naylor*[36]:

> "No doubt a contract to take shares may be rescinded if it has been induced by a material allegation which is not true. . . . "

But there are some features peculiar to company law. The general bar that *restitutio in integrum* is impossible may be raised against a subscriber if rescission would prejudice creditors of the company, there being a conflict here between fairness to the subscriber and the principle that the creditors may look to and rely upon the subscribed capital as their safeguard.[37]

Secondly, it has long been established that "the public, when invited to subscribe to an undertaking, are entitled to be clearly and truthfully informed of the purpose to which their money is intended to be applied."[38] They are entitled to have stated, therefore, "every

---

[35i] Sched. A, Chap. 6.

[35j] Sched. B.

[36] [1900] 2 I.R. 1, 26.

[37] *Tennent* v. *City of Glasgow Bank* (1879) 4 App. Cas. 615. One must doubt whether a subsequent winding-up should really be a bar to rescission (*Oakes* v. *Turquand* (1867) L.R. 2 H.L. 325) if the company would, even after rescission be able to satisfy its creditors.

[38] *Per* Madden, J. in *Components Tube Co. Ltd.* v. *Naylor* [1900] 2 I.R. 1, 75.

known fact which, if disclosed, would prevent a prudent man from taking shares at all, and also every known fact which materially qualifies or alters the effect of the previous representations made to induce persons to subscribe,"[39] and "to have the same opportunity of judging everything . . . as the promoters themselves possess."[40] Thus, a high extra-statutory duty of disclosure is added to the duty to be truthful. A breach of either duty in a prospectus which induces a contract of allotment may lead to that contract being rescinded at the instance of the allottee.

Compliance with Schedule 3 does not of itself discharge this general duty of disclosure. This emerges from *Aaron's Reefs* v. *Twiss*[41] which went from Ireland to be affirmed by the House of Lords, and constitutes the only known contribution to jurisprudence of Captain Twiss of Birdhill, Co. Limerick who was being sued for the £24 4s 6d which he had agreed to subscribe on the basis of a very persuasive prospectus which managed to give the impression, without actually saying so, that money subscribed was to be used to buy machinery to work a gold mine in Venezuela. In truth, the money was to go by "an open drain" into the pockets of the promoters themselves to pay them for the mine itself, and nothing was to be left over to start the mining and produce those 100 per cent. dividends so alluringly described as the probable returns in the prospectus. The existence of the contracts which set the funds flowing in the direction of the promoters was in fact disclosed in the prospectus. Disclosure of the existence of such contracts was all that *statute* required at that time. Suppression of their highly material content, however, resulted in the contract of allotment being voidable on the broad principles abovementioned, and a remedy of rescission for Captain Twiss. Schedule 3 would now, incidentally, require disclosure of the content of such a contract.[42]

---

[39] *Per* Fitzgibbon L.J. in *Aaron's Reefs* v. *Twiss* [1895] 2 I.R. 207, 273; affirmed by the House of Lords, [1896] A.C. 273, and followed in *Components Tube Co. Ltd.* v. *Naylor* [1900] 2 I.R. 1.

[40] *Per* Lord Chelmsford in *Central Railway of Venezuela* v. *Kisch* (1867) L.R., 2 H.L. 99, 113, following Kindersley V.-C. in *New Brunswick, etc., Co.* v. *Muggeridge* (1860) Dr. & Sm. 363, 383, and cited with approval in the two Irish cases abovementioned.

[41] [1895] 2 I.R. 207, affirmed [1896] A.C. 273 where three of the court of si adopted the reasoning of Fitzgibbon L.J.

[42] See *The content of a prospectus, supra*; likewise the suppression in *Components Tube Co.* v. *Naylor* [1900] 2 I.R. 1 described by Palles C.B. at p. 60: " . . . their invitation to the public suppresses the two material facts: 1, that the real vendors are the promoters themselves; and 2, that their sale to the company is part of one entire transaction, b the other part of which they acquire the undertaking at £60,000 less than the price a which they offer it to the public."

Compensation

Rights to rescind may be lost under the general principles of the law of contract.[42a] The allottee may, for example, have affirmed the contract, or *restitutio in integrum* may no longer be possible, perhaps through the inability of the company to return his money. Therefore, or perhaps in any event, the allottee may wish to pursue compensation for his loss.

It is in theory open to an allottee to bring an action in tort against the company and all persons responsible for issuing the false prospectus on its behalf, but in practice this will not happen because section 49 of the Companies Act 1963 provides a statutory right of compensation "to all persons who subscribe for any shares or debentures on the faith of" a false prospectus against a wide range of defendants, and imposes on a claimant a lighter burden of proof than those in deceit[43] and negligence.[43a]

The statutory remedy lies in respect of "loss or damage . . . sustained by reason of any *untrue* statement included" in a prospectus.[44] "Untrue" is given a meaning akin to that which it bears in an action for damages for deceit. For the purposes of the statutory remedy, a statement is untrue "if it is misleading in the form and context in which it is included."[45] As in an action for deceit, but unlike a claim for rescission, mere concealment of facts does not suffice.[46] The concealment must be such as to make some material statement in the prospectus untrue, such as, for example, a misleading half-truth which states "all the properties have excellent tenants" whilst suppressing that they have all given notice and are leaving in the morning.

[42a] Perhaps under the shaky rule in *Seddon* v. *North Eastern Salt Co. Ltd.* [1905] 1 Ch. 326 which states that a contract induced by an *innocent* misrepresentation may not be rescinded on that ground after it has been executed by the transfer of property under it, in our case the actual allotment of the shares. s.44 of the Sale of Goods and Supply of Services Act 1980 abrogated this rule for some contracts, but not for contracts of allotment: *ibid.* s.43. For the rule, and doubts about it, see Pollock, *Principles of Contract,* 13th ed., Winfield, London, 1950, pp. 444–445, and Anson, *Law of Contract,* 26th suped., A.G. Guest, Oxford, 1984, p. 228.

[43] See *Jury* v. *Stoker* (1881) 9 L.R., Ir. 358 for probative difficulties in deceit.

[43a] Damages in lieu of rescission for innocent misrepresentation are not available in espect of a contract of allotment: s.43 of the Sale of Goods and Supply of Services Act 1980. See Companies Act 1983, ss. 14, 17 for aspects of the same reasoning.

[44] s.49(1) including any prospective to which Sched. 3 does not apply. Italics supplied.

[45] s.52(*a*).

[46] See *Components Tube Co.* v. *Naylor* [1900] 2 I.R. 1; in particular, Palles C.B. at p. 9.

All the claimant under section 49 need prove is his loss or damage, and a causal link between it and the "untrue" statement. He need not prove that any of the wide range of defendants afforded by the section had complicity in the making of it, or any degree of culpability, thus distinguishing the statutory claim from one founded in tort. The section casts the burden of exonerating themselves on the defendants.

The defendants provided by the section comprise:

> "every person who is a director of the company at the time of the issue of the prospectus; . . . every person who has authorised himself to be named and is named in the prospectus as a director or as having agreed to become a director either immediately or after an interval of time; every person being a promoter of the company; . . . [and] every person who has authorised the issue of the prospectus."[47]

A "promoter" for the purposes of section 49 is:

> "a promoter who was a party to the preparation of the prospectus, or of the portion thereof containing the untrue statement, but does not include any person by reason of his acting in a professional capacity for persons engaged in procuring the formation of the company"[48]

a definition which narrows for this purpose the field of promoters in the extra-statutory context described in *Promoters, supra*.

The "issue" of a prospectus is a key expression in the above extract from section 49. By definition,[49] a document does not become a prospectus until it actually offers a company's securities to the public, and, assumedly, it is not to be considered as "issued" until that event occurs. The registration of a prospectus with the Registrar of Companies, required by section 47, *infra*, cannot be an "issue" of it, since this formality is to be complied with before it is issued. If a prospectus is actually issued, and if it contains a report by an "expert," he will inevitably, if proper procedures have been followed become potentially a defendant as a "person who has authorised the issue of the prospectus," *supra*, because, by section 46, an expert's written consent to the inclusion of his report "in the form and context in which it is included" is a necessary preliminary to the issue of any prospectus. But his potential liability is limited to "an

---

[47] s.49(1), (*a*)–(*d*).
[48] s.49(8)(*a*).
[49] s.2, set out at p. 391, *supra*.

untrue statement purporting to be made by him as expert."[50] As a corollary, other defendants may, as we shall see, more easily disclaim liability for the statements of "experts" than for other untruths.[51] An expert includes an "engineer, valuer, accountant and any other person whose profession gives authority to a statement made by him."[52] Each prospectus complying with Schedule 3 will inevitably contain a statement by an expert because Schedule 3 compels the inclusion of a report on the company by its auditors[53]; other possibilities include the accountants' reports on businesses or companies to be acquired, likewise required by Schedule 3, or a geologist's report in a prospectus issued by a minerals exploration company.

How do defendants exonerate themselves? They may do so either by proving that they disassociated themselves from the prospectus, or that in relation to the falsehood they were in a state of objectively justifiable innocence. The measures necessary to accomplish disassociation are each statutorily defined[54]; for example, a person who has become a director exonerates himself if he proves that "he withdrew his consent before the issue of the prospectus, and that it was issued without his authority or consent."[55] Objectively justifiable innocence is established by a defendant who proves, *inter alia*, that "he had reasonable ground to believe and did . . . believe" that the statement was true, or that an expert making it was competent to do so.[56]

Some only of the defendants who have successfully disassociated themselves from the issue of a prospectus are given a right of indemnity in respect of the cost of exonerating themselves against "directors of the company, except any without whose knowledge or consent the prospectus was issued, and any other person who authorised the issue thereof."[57] The indemnity extends only to directors who have not consented to act as such, or who have withdrawn their consent before the issue of the prospectus, and to experts who have not consented to its issue or withdrawn consent before issue. Perhaps the indemnity should be extended to other defendants who have successfully exonerated themselves by disassociation.[58]

---

[50] s.49(2).
[51] s.49(3)(*d*)(ii).
[52] s.46(3).
[53] See *The content of a prospectus, supra.*
[54] s.49(3)(*a*), (*b*), (*c*); s.49(5)(*a*), (*b*).
[55] s.49(3)(*a*).
[56] s.49(3)(*d*)(i), (ii); s.49(5)(*c*).
[57] s.49(6).
[58] See n. 54, *supra.*

Compensation: false listing particulars

Listing particulars are deemed to be a prospectus for the purposes of section 49, *supra,* when a document setting them out or saying where they can be inspected has accompanied a form of application offering shares or debentures for subscription or purchase.[58a] Thus, persons subscribing on the faith of the listing particulars may invoke the statutory compensation remedy.

The 1984 Regulations appear to contemplate an independent action for damages against those responsible for the preparation of the listing particulars for failures by them to comply with the overriding duty in Article 4.1, the duty to enable investors to make an informed assessment.[58b] Regulation 4(1) states that "obligation referred to in Article 4.1 of the Listing Particulars Directive shall be incumbent on the persons" responsible for preparation. That is the imposition of a statutory duty. Breaches of statutory duty sound in damages if that is construed as being the intention of the statute. The remainder of regulation 4 tends towards that intention. Regulation 4(4) states that "an issuer," *i.e.* the company whose securities are being issued,[58c] and being in fact only one of the persons who might be responsible for the listing particulars,

"shall not be liable in damages by reason only of non-compliance with, or contravention of, the provisions of these Regulations (*other than paragraph (1) of this Regulation*)[58d]: Provided that any such non-compliance or contravention does not give rise to any liability under any provision of the Companies Act, 1963."

Regulation 4(2) states that a person responsible for the listing particulars "shall not incur any liability" by reason of non-compliance with or contravention of the central obligation imposed by Article 4.1 of the Directive if

"in relation to any matter not disclosed, he proves he did not know it; or . . . he proves that the non-compliance or contravention arose from an honest mistake of fact on his part, or . . . the non-compliance or contravention was in respect of matters which in the opinion of the court dealing with the case were immaterial or was otherwise such as ought, in the opinion of the

---

[58a] Such at any rate appears to be the intent of the 1984 Regulations, reg. 12 which is unhappily drafted.

[58b] The full text of Article 4.1 of the Listing Particulars Directive is set out on p 397, *supra.*

[58c] 1984 Regulations, reg. 2(3); Listing Particulars Directive, Art. 2(c).

[58d] Italics supplied.

court, having regard to all the circumstances of the case, reasonably to be excused."

No qualifications for plaintiffs are stipulated. Assumedly, anyone suffering loss through such a failure, whether original subscriber or subsequent investor or otherwise, is qualified.

Registration of prospectus

Prospectuses are required by section 47 to be registered with the Registrar of Companies before issue, and "on or before the date of its publication." The date of publication is prima facie the date required by section 43 to be stated in it, the date from which it speaks. Some documents must be attached to it or endorsed on it. They are the consents of experts to its issue, copies of material contracts,[59] and, if the financial reports required to be set out in the prospectus contain adjusted figures, a statement by the experts concerned justifying them.[60]

Publicity in respect of listed securities

One of the primary purposes of the Stock Exchange is the maintenance of a fair and orderly market in securities. To that end, every company whose securities are listed enters into an agreement, called the Listing Agreement, with the Stock Exchange. A major object of the Listing Agreement is that of ensuring prompt disclosure of pertinent information to the market, particularly price-sensitive information. The Listing Agreement is of contractual force between the Stock Exchange and the company. Its content has now been overlaid, but not superseded,[60a] by the disclosure requirements imposed as public duties by the European Communities (Stock Exchange) Regulations 1984 applicable to companies whose securities are listed on the Stock Exchange. These regulations, administered for the most part by the Committee of the Irish Unit of the Stock Exchange, in some respects echo the Listing Agreement, and in others impose less rigorous requirements. The content of the Listing Agreement, as such, is not the subject of this book. The 1984 Regulations must be, since they impose public duties. In view of the Listing Agreement, the reader should not regard the duties now to be described as a pic-

---

[59] See *The content of a prospectus, supra.*

[60] Or if the necessary adjustments have been indicated in the reports without giving the reasons for them. For the financial reports, see *The content of a prospectus, supra.*

[60a] 1984 regulations, reg. 3(2).

ture of the disclosures actually met in practice; they should be regarded more as a description of the standards below which listed companies may not by law be permitted by the Stock Exchange to fall.

We have seen that the listing particulars prepared pursuant to these Regulations need not be registered as a prospectus.[60b] Regulation 13, however, requires the delivery of the listing particulars to the registrar of companies, and any document in which the listing particulars are published to state in a clear and conspicuous manner that this duty has been fulfilled. Publication of listing particulars before a copy has been delivered to the registrar may be an offence.[60c]

The Directives[60d] as implemented by the 1984 Regulations impose further publicity requirements arising out of the process of listing, and afterwards.

The Admissions Directive[60e] obliges a company whose shares are admitted to official listing on the Stock Exchange to make available to the public as soon as possible its latest annual accounts and annual report, "to inform the public as soon as possible of any major new developments in its sphere of activity which are not public knowledge . . . and which may lead to substantial movements in the prices of its shares," and to inform the public without delay of any changes in the rights attaching to its various classes of shares, and of changes in its major shareholders and their holdings from the information, if any, on this topic, "previously published."[60f] All such information must be immediately communicated to the Stock Exchange; also, it must be brought to the attention of the public through publication in a newspaper having a national circulation: either the information itself or an announcement indicating where it may be obtained must be so published; and the Stock Exchange may stipulate alternative equivalent methods of publication.[60g] In addition, the Interim Reports Directive obliges companies whose shares are listed on the Stock Exchange to publish interim reports by similar means.[60h] By interim report is meant a half-yearly report on the company's activities (including turnover) and profits and losses

---

[60b] See pp. 392–393, *supra*.

[60c] 1984 Regulations, reg. 13(3).

[60d] The Admissions Directive (79/279/EEC); the Listing Particulars Directive (80/390/EEC); and the Interim Reports Directive (82/121/EEC).

[60e] See note 60d, *supra*.

[60f] Admissions Directive, Sched. C, paras. 4 and 5. Sched. D imposes similar obligations on a company whose debentures are listed.

[60g] Admissions Directive, Art. 17.

[60h] Interim Reports Directive, Art. 7.

during the first six months of each financial year; the report must include "any significant information enabling investors to make an informed assessment of the trend of the company's activities and profits or losses together with an indication of any special factor which has influenced those activities and those profits and losses during the period in question . . . and must so far as possible refer to the company's likely future development in the current financial year."[60i]

The listing particulars[60j] approved by the Stock Exchange in respect of securities admitted to listing must, as we have seen, be registered with the registrar of companies.[60k] They must also be published either in a newspaper with a national circulation, or in the form of a brochure to be made available free of charge at the Stock Exchange and at the company's registered office[60l]; also, the complete particulars, or a notice stating where they may be obtained must be published in the Stock Exchange Official List—Irish.[60m] If any "significant new factor capable of affecting assessment of the securities" occurs between the adoption of the listing particulars and the commencement of Stock Exchange dealings, a supplement must be prepared, approved and published.[60n]

Criminal sanctions

The criminal consequences of failing to issue a prospectus when one ought to be issued, or issuing one not complying with the statutory disclosure requirements are really quite light, a fine not exceeding £500,[61] and honest mistakes of fact, and ignorance of matters not disclosed will negative liability.[62] Issuing a prospectus without an expert's consent,[63] or failing to register a prospectus,[64] are treated as being of similar gravity.

The heavier criminal penalties are reserved for false statements in a prospectus. Any person authorising the issue of a prospectus containing any untrue statement is rendered liable by section 50 to

---

[60i] *Ibid.* Arts. 5 and 2.
[60j] For an indication of the contents of this Directive, see pp. 396–397, *supra.*
[60k] 1984 Regulations, reg. 13.
[60l] And at the offices, if any, of the company's "paying agents": Listing Particulars Directive, Art. 20.1.
[60m] *Ibid.* Art. 20.2; 1984 Regulations, Sched. 2, para. 8.
[60n] Listing Particulars Directive, Art. 23.
[61] s.44(8); fine raised by 1982 Act, Sched. 1.
[62] There is also a power to excuse: s.44(5)(*c*).
[63] Contrary to s.46.
[64] Contrary to s.47.

imprisonment for a term of up to two years, or to a fine not exceeding £2500, or both, if convicted on indictment, or if summarily convicted, to a term of up to six months, or a fine of £500, or both.[65] The defence is proof by the accused either that the statement was immaterial, or that he was in relation to it in a state of objectively justifiable innocence, namely "that he had reasonable ground to believe and did, up to the time of the issue of the prospectus, believe that the statement was true." An "untrue statement" in this context has the same meaning as in the context of the statutory civil liability for misstatements in a prospectus[66]; namely, a statement misleading in the form and context in which it is included. Thus, ignorance of the inclusion of a particular statement, or of the suppressed facts which render it untrue will not relieve an accused from liability.

A director, manager or officer of a company *knowingly* issuing a false prospectus with intent to induce anyone to become a member of the company may be guilty of the far more serious offence created by section 84 of the Larceny Act 1861, carrying a term of imprisonment of up to seven years. Here, in contrast to the Companies Act liability, the burden remains on the prosecution to prove all ingredients of the offence, including knowledge.[67]

Listing particulars are deemed to be a prospectus within the meaning of the Companies Act 1963 when an application form for the subscription or purchase of securities is issued with a document setting out the listing particulars, or saying where they may be obtained or inspected.[68] Accordingly, the criminal sanctions applicable to such a prospectus apply in that event to the listing particulars.

Also, the company and any person knowingly a party to the publication of listing particulars before a copy has been delivered to the registrar of companies is guilty of a summary offence carrying a fine of up to £IR1000.[69]

Any person who knowingly publishes any information required to be published by any of the three EEC Directives affecting listed securities[70] which is false or misleading in any material respect is likewise guilty of a similar summary offence; so is any employee or

---

[65] Fines raised by the 1982 Act, Sched. 1. An expert giving his consent pursuant to s.46 to the issue of a prospectus is not for that reason alone to be deemed to have authorised its issue for the purposes of s.50: s.50(2).

[66] s.52(*a*): see p. 399, *supra*.

[67] For this offence which is much paraphrased in the text, see generally *R.* v. *Kylsant* [1932] 1 K.B. 442, and s.84 itself.

[68] 1984 Regulations, reg. 12(3).

[69] *Ibid.* reg. 13(3).

[70] Described in n. 21b, *supra*.

former employee of the Stock Exchange—Irish who breaks the duty of confidentiality imposed by the Directives.[71]

Foreign corporations

Part XII of the Companies Act 1963 governs the circulation within the State of prospectuses offering for subscription shares or debentures of a company incorporated outside the State. It requires similar safeguards to those required of domestic companies, and offers similar exemptions.[72] One point of difference is that the foreign corporations code requires the inclusion in the prospectus of particulars of the foreign laws and instruments under which the corporation is established, and its place of business in the State, if any.[73]

[71] 1984 Regulations, reg. 6; Admissions Directive, Art. 19, and Listing Particulars Directive, Art. 25.

[72] *e.g.*, s.362, equivalent to s.45; and see the European Communities (Stock Exchange) Regulations 1984, reg. 12 for exemptions in cases where listing particulars have been approved.

[73] s.361.

Chapter 13: Investigations

Introduction

The Minister for Industry, Trade, Commerce and Tourism has power to bring a derivative action[1] on behalf of a company for the recovery by it:

> "of damages in respect of any fraud, misfeasance or other misconduct in connection with the promotion or formation of that body corporate or the management of its affairs, or for the recovery of any property of the body corporate which has been misapplied or wrongfully retained."[2]

He may also present a petition for the winding up of a company on the just and equitable ground,[3] or for oppression or disregard of the interests of the members[4]; or a petition for any of the variety of orders available under section 205.[5]

The Minister has never, so far as can be gleaned from the published evidence,[6] pursued any of these remedies, of which the derivative action would in practice be the most important. Suppose that a company, apparently insolvent, has gone into liquidation, leaving a host of unpaid, unsecured creditors; there is a suspicion that the company's controllers may in some manner have siphoned off its assets, but for lack of evidence these creditors are not inclined to throw good money after bad by pursuing the matter themselves. This is a structural problem arising out of the very nature of limited liability, and the Minister, having overall superintendence of the system, might legitimately be called upon in the public interest to undertake the pursuit himself.

The Minister may act only on the report of an inspector appointed

---

[1] For derivative actions, see Chap. 8, *supra*.
[2] s.170(4).
[3] s.170(3), 213(*f*). See pp. 268–274, *ante*; p. 479, *post*.
[4] s.170(3), 213(*g*). See p. 479, *post*.
[5] s.170(3); see pp. 256, *et seq.*
[6] *Annual Reports*, Department of Industry and Commerce, and its successors.

408

by him to investigate the affairs of the company.[7] This report does not actually decide any question of liability; that is the function of the subsequent proceedings. Inevitably therefore, the investigation before the inspector is to an extent duplicated by the substantive hearing,[8] and the question is raised whether the preliminary inquisition involves a waste of resources. To answer that it does is to mistake its function. In part, it has the function of carrying out the task which falls to any prospective litigant, private or public, of gathering the facts and evaluating possible causes of action before commencing proceedings, and, in part, it serves to allay public concern that the law may have been flouted to the detriment of others by the controllers of a particular company, and that nothing is being done about it. In this latter respect, a report produced and published swiftly after the events in question is of value, whether it exonerates or inculpates those under suspicion, since its very appearance assures the public that the applicability of law to recurring company crises is actively being monitored. However, such reports are not in practice published in Ireland,[8a] unlike England, though a statutory mandate to do so exists in section 169. There are only two companies currently under investigation; one investigation began in 1978, and the other in 1979; one concerns a company connected with a retailing group which collapsed to the accompaniment of much publicity and perturbed comment in 1976,[9] and, neither was at the time of writing complete.[10] Disquiet is periodically expressed in the Press and by some politicians about the present system of company law; essentially, the cause of this disquiet is the inadequate enforcement of adequate laws, but its manifestation commonly consists of appeals, often underinformed, for the "reform" of the laws themselves, particularly those relating to limited liability. The sparse use by the Minister of his investigatory powers has contributed to the present climate of opinion. Unfortunately, the present system of investigation attracts constitutional difficulties. See pp. 415–417, where some suggestions for resolving them are made. The Minister is also unduly restricted in the circumstances in which he may appoint an inspector. A broadening of these is suggested at p. 413, *infra*.

---

[7] s.170, *passim*. The inspectors are appointed under s.165 or s.166. See *The appointment of inspectors, infra.*

[8] For doubts about the probative value of the report in subsequent proceedings, see p. 417, *infra*.

[8a] For an exception, see *Enquiry into Irish Estates Ltd—Inspectors' Report*, October 23, 1963.   [9] *e.g. The Irish Times*, November 22, 1976.

[10] This sentence records information supplied to the author on 23rd March 1984 by the Department of Trade, Commerce and Tourism. On the importance of speed in reporting, see Sachs L.J. in *Re Pergamon Press Ltd.* [1971] Ch. 388, 403, a case arising under the equivalent British legislation.

The actual mechanism of conducting preliminary investigations through the medium of inspectors appointed ad hoc by the Minister is a Victorian legacy.[11] Public needs might be better met by the Minister having a full-time team of investigators within his Department. There would have to be amending legislation, giving the Minister inquisitorial powers at least equal to those currently possessed by inspectors appointed by him, and a power to commence proceedings in respect of a company whenever he thinks fit.

The consequences of an inspector's report may not be only civil; the Minister *must* if the report discloses what appears to him to be a criminal offence committed by any person in relation to the company investigated refer the matter to the Director of Public Prosecutions.[12]

The appointment of inspectors

The Minister may, and sometimes *must*, appoint inspectors to investigate the affairs of a company. Mandatory appointments occur in theory, but not in practice, under section 166(*a*) of the Companies Act 1963 by which the Minister is bound to start an investigation if the company itself by special resolution, or the court by order, declares that there should be one. Those in control of a company are unlikely positively to request that they be subject to the embarrassment of an investigation; accordingly, such special resolutions will be passed, if at all, when those with voting strength in general meeting are out of office. Thus in *R.* v. *Board of Trade, ex p. St. Martin Preserving Co. Ltd.*,[13] directors who had been ousted by a receiver and were displeased with his management, were able to compel the appointment of inspectors under the equivalent British legislation by the use of their votes in general meeting. The rôle of the Court in ordering an investigation, assumedly at the request of any interested party,[14] is problematical. What must the applicant establish? If he proves a prima facie case of remediable wrongdoing within the company, his application is self-defeating since substantive proceedings will be indicated as the appropriate course of action. He scarcely needs an investigation to confirm his own researches. If he shows less than a prima facie case, he will be asking the court to act only on suspicion, and that the court may be reluctant to do; yet, the very

---

[11] See the Companies Act 1862, s.56 [1908 Act, s.109]. These origins account for the archaic language of some of the present day provisions.

[12] s.170(1), (2); Prosecution of Offences Act 1974, s.3.

[13] [1965] 1 Q.B. 603.

[14] See *Re Miles Aircraft* (*No. 2*) [1948] W.N. 178.

nature of the remedy sought dictates that suspicion alone should be a sufficient criterion upon which to grant it. The Act, unfortunately, is silent on the relevant criteria. If an applicant persuades the court to order an investigation, the costs of it will not be recoverable from him personally; other personal applicants for an investigation are, in this respect, at risk, as we shall see.[15] An appreciation of this fact may lead to applications for investigations being made by way of the court; there is no evidence that they are at present. The court's power to order an investigation under section 166(*a*) includes also, one assumes, the freedom to act on its own motion whenever a matter meriting investigation comes to its attention in the course of proceedings before it. If, however, that matter appears to be criminal, the court will be more likely to refer it and the papers in the case directly to the Director of Public Prosecutions as Costello J. did in exercise of his inherent jurisdiction in *Re Kelly's Carpetdrome Ltd.*[16-17] Or, if the company is being wound up, and it appears to the court that any past or present officer, or any member, of the company has been guilty of a criminal offence in relation to it, then the court may on its own motion, or on the application of any interested party, refer the matter to the Director of Public Prosecutions pursuant to section 299 of the Companies Act 1963.[18]

Discretionary appointments by the Minister are founded either on section 165, or on section 166(*b*). Section 165 is not in fact fruitful. It gives a fairly small proportion of the members of the company[19] the opportunity of asking the Minister to appoint an inspector, and the Minister the opportunity of graciously refusing. Most years bring in their small crop of a handful of applications under section 165[20]; all are refused. Again, as in the case of the court's discretion, the Act gives no guidance on what the Minister should take into account in exercising his section 165 power. It is understood that in practice "substantial grounds" must be shown. Yet the applicant already in possession of substantial grounds probably has no need of an investigation; he is already sufficiently armed with facts to commence substantive civil proceedings should he so wish, or to bring the alleged

---

[15] See *Costs, infra.*

[16-17] High Court, unreported, July 1, 1983.

[18] As amended by Prosecution of Offences Act 1974, s.3.

[19] *e.g.* in the case of a company having a share capital "on the application either of not less than one hundred members or of a member or members holding not less than one-tenth of the paid up share capital of the company": s.165(1)(*a*).

[20] See *Annual Reports*, Department of Industry, Trade, Commerce and Tourism and its predecessors. The statement in the text adverts to practice in recent years up to and including the latest available evidence at the time of writing, the *Annual Report* for 1983.

criminality to the attention of the Director of Public Prosecutions. This prerequisite stifles the purpose of the section; it is precisely in those cases where those who have abused the privileges of incorporation have effectively covered their tracks against private investigation that the resources of the State should be brought up in aid of those who feel they may have suffered.

The Minister may on his own motion appoint inspectors under section 166(*b*). This is the provision under which investigations are in practice begun, albeit rarely. Section 166(*b*), empowers the Minister to act if it appears to him:

"that there are circumstances suggesting—

(i) that the company's business is being conducted with intent to defraud its creditors or the creditors of any other person or otherwise for fraudulent or unlawful purposes or that the affairs of the company are being conducted or the powers of the directors are being exercised in a manner oppressive to any of its members or in disregard of their interests as members of the company or that it was formed for any fraudulent or unlawful purpose; or

(ii) that persons connected with its formation or the management of its affairs have in connection therewith been guilty of fraud, misfeasance or other misconduct towards it or towards its members; or

(iii) that its members have not been given all the information relating to its affairs which they might reasonably expect."

So far as disappointed creditors are concerned there is in paragraph (i) a displeasing persistence of the present tense, and in paragraph (ii) an alarming omission to mention them at all. Creditors of a company which has already collapsed and gone into liquidation are therefore only to be beneficiaries of this limb of the investigation procedure at one remove. Only if they have suffered indirectly through wrongs done to the company itself are they to be within the ambit of the Minister's section 166(*b*) power. Creditors of such a company who suspect that they have suffered directly through straightforward fraudulent trading (of such a kind as not to involve breaches of duty to the company itself) have no *locus standi* to ask for an investigation, otherwise than through an order of the court pursuant to its untested jurisdiction under section 166(*a*). The Companies Acts regard the pursuit of malefactors within a collapsed company as being primarily the task of the liquidator. He may, for example, bring section 297 proceedings with a view to fixing those responsible with personal liability for the company's debts, but all too often the liquidator has no funds with which to carry out his investigation. Some suggestions

to alleviate this situation will be made in Chapter 16,[21] but of themselves they are unlikely to reverse the present malaise in the operation of Irish company law, of which the crux is the lack of effective
post-collapse investigation, private or public. It is all too easy to
avoid breaking the Eleventh Commandment: "Thou shalt not be
found out," and it is trite to say, but worth saying, that this encour-
ages an atmosphere of commercial immorality. Revision of the law is
necessary here. The precise lines it should take is a matter for public
discussion, but it is suggested for consideration that it be mandatory
upon the Minister to order an investigation where the court on the *ex
parte* application of the liquidator, or a substantial body in number
or value of the creditors of a company in liquidation, is satisfied that
there is a reasonable suspicion that its creditors have been prejudiced by the acts or omissions of its controllers or managers, and
that it is reasonable whether through lack of funds or otherwise not
to expect the liquidator to pursue the matter himself. Also, the
Minister's section 166(*b*) power to act on his own motion should be
augmented to include the presence of circumstances suggesting that
creditors of a company have *in the past* suffered prejudice direct or
indirect from the wrongful conduct of the company's business or
affairs.

The emphasis in this chapter has been on creditors, and rightly.
They may legitimately be viewed as a section of the public for whom
the Minister as a guardian of the public interest, and as overseer of
the system of limited liability, has a responsibility.

Members of a company, on the other hand, are expressly the
objects of the Minister's discretion in section 166(*b*), expressly the
applicants in section 165, and impliedly possessing *locus standi* for an
application to the court under section 166(*a*). Does the Minister's
guardianship of the public interest require him to be much concerned with the complaints of members of *private* companies? One
would think not. Private companies are closed societies; their members are not as such part of the investing public. Yet, despite this
intimacy, they are clearly encompassed by the Minister's powers.
This may be explained, in part, by the fact that the investigation
provisions of the Companies Act 1963 antedate the invention of the
private company. Echoes of this are found in section 165 which
speaks of applications to the Minister, by *inter alios*, "not less than
one hundred members," whereas the membership of private companies is limited to 50. At present, a participant in a private company, pursuing what is essentially a private quarrel, is tempted to
ask for, or to threaten to ask for, an investigation which he is suf-

---

[21] At pp. 526, *et seq.*

ficiently close to the facts not to need. Such requests are an abuse of the process, and a waste of public time. Perhaps the Act should be amended to exclude members as such of private companies from the class of applicants.

The criteria, set out above, to which the Minister should have regard in the exercise of his section 166(*b*) power are, save one, tolerably comprehensible, being either self-explanatory or illuminated where necessary by other sections of the Act.[22] The exception is contained in paragraph (iii), and relates to a company whose "members have not been given all the information relating to its affairs which they might reasonably expect." The reasonable expectation of members of public companies is that they should receive the annual accounts, and the directors' and auditors' reports, in respect of which they have enforceable statutory rights.[23] There is no general duty to provide them with more information,[24] though a duty of disclosure may arise in particular fiduciary and like circumstances.[25] In private companies there may, in addition, be a quasi-duty arising under section 205 to consult members occasionally.[26] The most frequently occurring breaches of these duties manifest themselves in so undisguised a fashion as not to justify an investigation of them: one does not, for example, need an inspector to tell one whether or not the accounts of a company have been circulated to the members. The paragraph must be concerned with more subtle derelictions, such as, one must suppose, circumstances suggesting that published accounts are false, by reason of the auditors having been deceived, or by reason of their collusion or negligence.

The investigation

The investigation is to be into "the affairs of the company." Phillimore J., in interpreting this expression in the equivalent British legislation in *R.* v. *Board of Trade, ex p. St. Martin Preserving Co. Ltd.*,[27] was prepared to say that it was so wide as to include the company's:

> "goodwill, its profits or losses, its contracts and assets including

---

[22] *e.g.* ss.205, 297.

[23] A right precipitated by an a.g.m.: s.159. Failure to hold an a.g.m. is independently remediable by the Minister: s.131(3).

[24] *P.M.P.A. Insurance Co. Ltd.* v. *New Ireland Assurance Co. Ltd.*, [1975] *Irish Times*, October 23. No official record of this judgment survives.

[25] See Chap. 7 at pp. 204 *et seq.*

[26] *Re Clubman Shirts Ltd.*, O'Hanlon J., High Court, unrep. November 19, 1982, discussed at p. 89, *et seq.*

[27] [1965] 1 Q.B. 603, 613.

its shareholding in and ability to control the affairs of a subsidiary, and perhaps in the latter regard a sub-subsidiary. . . . "

Statute, furthermore, gives an inspector an express power with the consent of the Minister to extend the investigation to include certain associated bodies corporate in so far as they are relevant to the investigation of the affairs of the company.[28] The use here by the Act of the expression "body corporate" makes it clear that foreign registered companies may be brought within the ambit of an investigation of an Irish registered company.[29]

The Act gives teeth to the inspector's inquisition by requiring past and present officers and agents (including bankers, solicitors and auditors) of the company, or other body corporate being investigated as abovementioned, to assist in the investigation, to produce books[30] and documents in their custody or power, and to submit themselves to examination by the inspector under oath.[31] Failure by such officers and agents to co-operate with an inspector in the foregoing manner has now been made a specific criminal offence carrying heavy penalties by section 7 of the Companies (Amendment) Act 1982.[32] An inspector may apply for other persons than those abovementioned to be examined on oath before the Court.[33]

What standards of conduct need the inspector observe in the conduct of his investigation? An inspector's report is not of itself determinative of rights, and no administrative decision will be taken on it, other than one to bring matters arising before the courts where every issue remains fully justiciable. Prima facie therefore it might seem that the inspector is not obliged in his investigation to observe the rules of fair procedure derived from principles of natural and constitutional justice, just as the Director of Public Prosecutions in deciding whether or not to prosecute, or a private litigant in deciding whether or not to sue, are not before the commencement of the sub-

---

[28] They are "any . . . body corporate which is or has at any relevant time been the company's subsidiary or holding company or a subsidiary of its holding company or a holding company of its subsidiary": s.167.

[29] "Body corporate" is defined in s.2(3) "as including a company incorporated outside the State," and "company" in s.2(1) is defined as being Irish registered. Only the latter fall within the primary power of investigation.

[30] Assumedly also print-outs of computerised records: s.4(3) of the 1977 Act, in which the draftsmanship might be improved by adding "or any other person" after "company."

[31] Fuller details are in s.168(1)(c); some evidence may be withheld by solicitors and bankers: s.173.

[32] Repealing s.168(3) which gave rise to one of the constitutional difficulties revealed by *Re Haughey* [1971] I.R. 217.

[33] Fuller details in s.168(4).

stantive proceedings obliged to invite comments on their findings from the potential defendants.[34] But, an inspector's report, if published (as it may be[35]), may be highly prejudicial to the reputations of interested parties; furthermore, such publication will by statute be absolutely privileged so that persons wrongly defamed therein are debarred from seeking redress.[36] These circumstances have led the English Court of Appeal in *Re Pergamon Press Ltd.*[37] to import some of the requirements of fair procedures into inspectors' investigations. In that country, inspectors, if they find themselves disposed to criticise someone in their report, must first allow that person the opportunity to correct or contradict allegations made against him. A summary of the allegation will usually suffice; the identity of the witnesses upon whose evidence the allegations are founded may be kept secret, and there is no right to cross examine them. In Ireland, the position of persons investigated is arguably stronger, so much so that the Companies Act 1963 may have to be amended if the investigation provisions are not to be stultified. The key to the difficulty is found in the fact that inspectors' reports, if published, are absolutely privileged. Accordingly, a person wrongfully defamed therein will have been deprived of his constitutional right to his "good name" conferred by Article 40, section 3 of the Constitution. If the possibility of publishing an absolutely privileged inspector's report is to be maintained, a person thus "accused" should, it seems, on the authority of *Re Haughey*[38] be allowed to cross examine his accusers, to introduce rebutting evidence, and to address the inspectors in his own defence, doing these things through counsel should he so wish. This is scarcely the kind of investigation envisaged by the Act, or, indeed, a practicable use of public resources. The difficulty might be circumvented by amending the Act to remove privilege from a publication by the Minister of an inspector's report. In practice, non-defamatory reports could still be published, thereby performing the useful function, already mentioned, of clearing the air in cases of public disquiet. The circulation of defamatory reports would remain qualifiedly but adequately privileged, if confined to those whose duty it is to consider commencing proceedings on the basis of them,

---

[34] *Wiseman* v. *Borneman* [1971] A.C. 297, 308; cited in *Re Pergamon Press* [1971] Ch. 388, 403.

[35] s.169(2), (3).

[36] The privilege is expressly conferred by s.169(3). In England, inspector's reports are absolutely privileged at common law: *per* Lord Denning M.R. in *Re Pergamon Press Ltd.*, *supra*, at p. 400.

[37] [1971] Ch. 388.

[38] [1971] I.R. 217. This litigation concerned public sessions of the Committee of Public Accounts of Dáil Eireann.

namely the Minister himself, the Director of Public Prosecutions, and their respective officers.[39]

The report as evidence

As stated, the inspector's report is determinative of nothing. Section 172 of the Companies Act 1963 does however say that a

> "copy of any report of any inspectors appointed under the foregoing provisions of this Act, shall be admissible in any legal proceedings as evidence of the *opinion* of the inspectors in relation to any matter contained in the report."[40]

It is difficult to see what probative value the *opinion* of inspectors may have in respect of *facts* to be proved in subsequent proceedings. English decisions on like statutory provisions have raised the inspector's report from the status of opinion to prima facie evidence of the facts stated therein,[41] chiefly because the inspector will have acted in a statutory fact-finding capacity. Such a reason would be unacceptable to Irish constitutional jurisprudence because the persons affected would not have been accorded the procedural safeguards in the fact-finding process.[42] Doubtless, opinion may in Ireland be raised to the status of fact, if there is an express statutory warrant for taking such a course, but even then the resultant "evidence" must remain fully challengeable in the proceedings,[43] including the cross examination of those whose assertions are relied on.[44] In so far as the English cases[45] suggest, as they appear to, that such challenges must be confined to the introduction of rebutting evidence, they are likewise unacceptable in Ireland.

Costs

The costs of an investigation (including those of a consequent derivative action) are primarily to be borne by the Minister, but anyone convicted on a prosecution instituted as a result of the investigation,

---

[39] The Minister's duty under s.169(2) to supply copies would have to be curtailed.
[40] Italics supplied; modelled on the Companies Act 1948 [U.K.], s.171.
[41] *Re Travel & Holiday Clubs Ltd.* [1967] 1 W.L.R. 711; *Re S.B.A. Properties Ltd.* [1967] 1 W.L.R. 799; *Re Armvent Ltd.* [1975] 1 W.L.R. 1679; *Re St. Piran Ltd.* [1981] 1 W.L.R. 1300.
[42] See text at n. 38, *supra.*
[43] *Maher* v. *Att. Gen.* [1973] I.R. 140.
[44] *Re Haughey* [1971] I.R. 217.
[45] See n. 41, *supra.*

or unsuccessful in a consequent derivative action may be liable to reimburse the Minister, as may be the company itself to the extent of spoils recovered in such an action.[46] Furthermore, where the investigation is brought about otherwise than by the Minister himself under section 166(*b*) and no prosecution results, any body corporate dealt with by the report, and the applicants for the investigation in the case of an inspector appointed under section 165, may be liable too,[47] a deterrent against frivolous applications. Persons liable for costs may be indemnified by those found to be wrongdoers.[48]

[46] Fuller details in s.171(1)(*a*), (*b*).
[47] s.171(1)(*c*).
[48] The rights of indemnity are more fully described in s.171(4).

Chapter 14: Floating Charges and Receivers

FLOATING CHARGES

Introduction

Were a debtor not able to create an immediate charge capable of binding property to be subsequently acquired by him, a floating charge could not exist. The recognition of this essential preliminary, the ability of a debtor to charge after-acquired property, has been depicted[1] as a development made in English courts of equity, culminating in *Holroyd* v. *Marshall*.[2] In fact, Irish equity had earlier more solidly come to the same conclusion,[3] not that the English developments were in any way influenced by unremarked events across the water.

The modern floating charge, now an everyday corporate security, was first recognised as an equitable charge in 1870 in England in *Re Panama, New Zealand, etc. Co.*,[4] and by the time an occasion for judicial approval in Ireland arose in 1884 in *Re Dublin Drapery Co. Ltd.*,[5] it was well established.

Fixed or floating?

It is often important, as we shall see, to distinguish a fixed from a floating charge. General descriptions of a floating charge are not

---

[1] *e.g.* L.C.B. Gower and Others, *Principles of Modern Company Law*, (4th ed., 1979), p. 272; R.R. Pennington, "The Genesis of the Floating Charge" (1960) M.L.R. 630; J.H. Farrar, "Floating Charges and Priorities" (1974) 38 Conv. N.S. 315.

[2] (1862) 10 H.L.C. 191. See also *Tailby* v. *The Official Receiver* (1888) 13 App.Cas. 523.

[3] *Lyster* v. *Burroughs* (1837) 1 Dr. & Wal. 149, 176 (Plunket L.C.); *White* v. *Anderson* (1850) 1 Ir. Ch. R. 419 (Maziere Brady L.C.); *Creed* v. *Carey* (1857) 7 Ir. Ch. R. 295 (Maziere Brady L.C., Blackburne L.J.); *Stack* v. *Royse* (1861) 12 Ir. Ch. R. 246 (Cusack Smith M.R.); *Galavan* v. *Dunne* (1881–2) 7 L.R. Ir. 144 (Sullivan, M.R.); and *Re Dublin Drapery Co. Ltd.* (1884–85) 13 L.R., Ir. 174, 193 (Porter M.R.).

[4] (1870) L.R. 5 Ch. 318.

[5] (1884–85) 13 L.R. Ir. 174. Citations included, *inter alia*, *Re Panama, New Zealand, etc. Co.*, n. 4 *supra*, and *Re Florence Land Co.* (1878) 10 Ch.D. 530.

always helpful, however often adopted. Take that of Lord Macnaghten in *Illingworth* v. *Houldsworth*,[6] one of the more popular:

> "I should have thought that there was not much difficulty in
> defining what a floating charge is in contrast to what is called a
> specific charge. A specific charge, I think, is one that without
> more fastens on ascertained and definite property or property
> capable of being ascertained and defined; a floating charge, on
> the other hand, is ambulatory and shifting in its nature, hover-
> ing over and so to speak floating with the property which it is
> intended to affect until some event occurs or some act is done
> which causes it to settle and fasten on the subject of the charge
> within its reach and grasp."

This description misses the essence of the security. Essentially, a
floating charge permits a company to deal in the ordinary course of
its business with the assets for the time being comprised in the
charge. At its simplest, this will involve assets departing out of the
ambit of the charge, to be replaced by others. This process may continue until, if ever, the charges become fixed, or specific, by an event
called *crystallisation*, of which more below. Fitzgibbon L.J. in *Re Old
Bushmills Distillery, ex p. Brett*[7] took a tidal analogy to describe the
company's dealings with goods subject to a floating charge:

> "The debentures are a floating security, always subject to the
> continual ebbing and flowing under them of the working capital
> of the undertaking—the conversion of money into goods, and
> back again."

Adverting the company's authority to deal with the assets subject to
the charge, he said:

> "It is involved in such a charge that the company shall continue
> as a going concern and the debenture holder has no power to
> interfere until his charge becomes payable. He can claim no
> account of mesne profits or challenge any authorised dealing by
> the company with its property or business. The directors, as
> masters, carry on the business for which the company was
> incorporated according to its constitution, and remain clothed
> with the power of doing all things necessary for carrying on that

---

[6] [1904] A.C. 355, 358, often cited, including by Kenny J. in his dissenting judgment in the Supreme Court in *Welch* v. *Bowmaker (Ireland) Ltd.* [1980] I.R. 251. He
refers, *obiter*, to Lord Macnaghten, Ulster born and Trinity educated, as "that great
Irish judge."

[7] [1897] 1 I.R. 488, 504.

business, including the meeting of special emergencies. Assets may be withdrawn by sale, and the proceeds then takes their place, or other assets may be substituted or additional assets added by trading; but the floating security follows the concern, reduced or added to, through every form of its trading existence, which existence continues as if the debentures were not there till the floating charge becomes a fixed one. Till then, to use the words of one learned judge, 'the charge is dormant.' "[8]

Costello J. took up the same theme in *Re Lakeglen Construction Co. Ltd.*,[9] finding that the "true element"[9a] distinguishing a floating from a fixed charge was this ability to deal. The case concerned a charge on book debts, and clearly determinative of the finding that it was floating was the fact that "the parties intended that the company should carry on its business in the ordinary way and that for this purpose it was licensed (until some future contingency arose which would justify the intervention by the debenture holders) to receive payment from its debtors from time to time without regard to the charge created by the debenture over the book debts."[10]

Costello J. was invited, as courts considering such questions usually are, to apply a test suggested by Romer L.J. in *Re Yorkshire Woolcombers' Association Ltd.*,[11] which he did, finding it satisfied too. That Romer L.J. did not intend his test to be an exclusive definition is made clear by his prefatory remarks. He said:

"I certainly do not intend to attempt to give an exact definition of the term 'floating charge,' nor am I prepared to say that there will not be a floating charge within the meaning of the Act, which does not contain all the three characteristics that I am about to mention, but I certainly think that if a charge has the three characteristics I am about to mention it is a floating charge. (1) If it is a charge on a class of assets of a company present and future; (2) if that class is one, which in the ordinary course of the business of the company, would be changing from time to time; and (3) if you find that by the charge it is contemplated that, until some future step is taken by or on behalf of

---

[8] Fitzgibbon L.J. was here referring assumedly to a passage, also often cited (*Ex p. Brett* being no exception), from the judgment of Lord Macnaghten in *Government Stock Co.* v. *Manila Railway* [1897] A.C. 81, 86.

[9] [1980] I.R. 347 (reported *sub nom. Kelly* v. *McMahon Ltd.*) following *Re Yorkshire Woolcombers' Association Ltd.* [1903] 2 Ch. 284, 288, 298; *Illingworth* v. *Houldsworth* [1904] A.C. 355, 357.

[9a] At p. 353.

[10] At p. 356.

[11] [1903] 2 Ch. 284, 295.

> those interested in the charge, the company may carry on its
> business in the ordinary way so far as concerns the particular
> class of assets I am dealing with."

This is certainly a picture of a typical floating charge. As a definition
however, it fails in respect of (1) because one may create a fixed
charge on future assets,[12] and, indeed, a floating charge on exclusively present assets, albeit an odd security; characteristic (2) was
relied upon by Kenny J. in his dissenting judgment in the Supreme
Court in *Welch* v. *Bowmaker (Ireland) Ltd.*[13] as excluding a particular
piece of land owned by the company from a floating charge created
by it because "it certainly [was] not a class of asset which would be
changing from time to time,"[14] but his brethren, in coming to the
contrary conclusion, preferred simply to construe the debenture
deed as it stood. Characteristic (3) alone is thus left in possession of
the field.

In practice, the precise definition of a floating charge, and its distinction from a fixed charge is important in three contexts. Floating,
but not fixed, charges created within twelve months before the commencement of the winding up of a company are singled out for complete or partial avoidance by the Companies Act 1963, ss.288 and
289 unless, with some qualifications, it is proved "that the company
immediately after the creation of the charge was solvent."[15]
Secondly, a floating charge, but not a fixed charge, may under sections 98 and 285(7)(*b*) give way in a receivership or on liquidation to
the claims of preferential creditors[16] insofar as the uncharged assets
of the company are insufficient to meet them. Faced with such infir-
mities, lending institutions have sought to create fixed charges over
assets which more naturally would be the subject of a floating
charge, in particular fixed charges over a debtor company's present
and future book debts, *i.e.* debts arising out of a company's trade or
buiness, whilst at the same time seeking to ensure that the company
is not deprived of the cash flow derived from those debts. Technically, a fixed charge over present and future book debts is possible,
as we have seen,[16a] but the measures employed to ensure that the
company nonetheless has whilst it remains a going concern the benefit of the receipts generated by its trading may lead the courts to

---

[12] See n. 3, *supra.*
[13] [1980] I.R. 251.
[14] *Ibid.* p. 258.
[15] This topic is discussed in Chap. 16, *Liquidations,* at pp. 511, *et seq.*
[16] For preferential creditors, see Chap. 16, *Liquidations* at pp. 501–503.
[16a] See p. 419, *supra,* and also *Evans (Coleman) & Evans Ltd.* v. *R.A. Nelson Construc
tion Ltd.* (1958) 16 D.L.R. (2d) 123.

find that the charge is in substance floating, whatever label the parties have chosen to apply to their transaction. Such a case was *Re Keenan Brothers Ltd.*[16b] Here the parties professed to create a fixed charge over present and future book debts; notice of it to the debtors was not contemplated; the company itself was to collect the debts in the normal course, and pay them into a designated bank account upon which the company could draw by permission of the chargee, but not as a matter of right. The decision that the charge was floating turned on the fact that the company had in effect been given a licence to deal with the proceeds of the book debts, a fundamental characteristic of a floating charge, though there were other subsidiary grounds for Keane J.'s decision.[16c]

The third context arises out of the company's power to deal with the assets comprised in the floating charge, and is the next topic for discussion.

Negative pledge clauses

A floating charge assumes by its very nature that the company has power before it crystallises to deal with the assets for the time being comprised in it in the ordinary course of business. Since the decision in England in 1885 in *Wheatley* v. *Silkstone and Highmoor Coal Co.*[17] it has been recognised that the power to deal includes the power to create specific, or fixed, charges, such as legal mortgages of land, equitable mortgages of land by deposit of title deeds, and pledges of goods, taking in each case priority over the security given by the

---

[16b] High Court, Keane J., October 5, 1984, unreported. An appeal to the Supreme Court has been heard in this case, but the reserved judgment had not yet been handed down when this Chapter went finally to press in August 1985. For a discussion of Keane J.'s decision, see Byrne and Tomkin, "Charges on book debts—Siebe Gorman in Ireland," (1985) 135 *New L.J.* 443.

[16c] Among them (at pp. 12 and 21 of the transcript) the fact that the debtors could continue to operate a set-off (as to which see pp. 432, 434, *infra*) against book debts comprised in the charge, but this does not necessarily indicate a floating charge. It is an infirmity possessed also by a *fixed* equitable charge of which the debtors do not have notice. Also (at pp. 11–12 of the transcript), the learned judge found as indicative the fact that the company collected the debts itself, but might it not have done so as fiduciary for the chargee? Even if the charge were fixed, the company would, in the absence of notice to the debtors, have retained the legal title to the debts. In coming to his decision, Keane J. differed from the English High Court decision of Slade J. in *Siebe Gorman & Co. Ltd.* v. *Barclays Bank Ltd.* [1979] 2 Lloyd's Rep. 142, and derived support, *inter alia*, from *Re Armagh Shoes Ltd.* [1982] N.I. 59. He did not, unfortunately, advert to *Re Lakeglen Construction Ltd.* [1980] I.R. 347 (reported *sub nom. Kelly* v. *McMahon Ltd.*, and cited at p. 421, *supra*) which contains a useful discussion of principle.

[17] (1885) 29 Ch.D. 715. See Parke J. in the Supreme Court in *Welch* v. *Bowmaker (Ireland) Ltd.* [1980] I.R. 251, 260. Also Henchy J. at p. 253.

floating charge.[18] Accordingly, lenders began to take the precaution of inserting in debentures creating a floating charge a restrictive or "negative pledge" clause with the object of curtailing what would otherwise be the company's authority to create prior charges. Recognising the efficacy of such a clause as between chargor and chargee, Chatterton V.-C. said in 1896, in *Re Old Bushmills Distillery, ex p. Brydon*[19] that:

" . . . without it a company could specifically mortgage or pledge any amount of their assets to subsequent lenders without notice, and thus all, or at least a large portion, of their assets might be withdrawn from the security of the debentures . . . there is nothing to prevent or render illegal such an express contract being made between persons advancing money on debentures and the Company with which they contract."

And the next year, Walker L.J. in *Re Old Bushmills Distillery, ex p. Brett*[20] remarked that such clauses "are of a class which have become not unusual since the decision in 1885 of *Wheatley v. Silkstone and Highmoor Coal Co.*" By 1979, Henchy J. in *Welch v. Bowmaker (Ireland) Ltd.*[21] was able to say that such clauses are "more or less common form in modern debentures."

A typical negative pledge clause will state that "the company is not to be at liberty to create any mortgage or charge on its property for the time being in priority to or *pari passu* with this debenture."

Problems arise when the company despite the negative pledge clause and in breach of it creates a fixed charge on property otherwise within the floating charge. Has the new charge priority?

The answer turns on whether the new chargee has notice of the prior restriction. The degree of notice depends upon how the courts categorise that restriction. They have a choice, though not one overtly stated in the cases, between classifying it as a matter affecting the quality of the floating chargee's equitable interest[22] in the assets charged, or as being exclusively a matter of contract between

---

[18] Interests taking priority may also be created by operation of law, such as a purchaser's equitable lien: *Re Barrett Apartments Ltd.* High Court, Keane J. July 15, 1983 (unreported) (subsequently reversed by the Supreme Court on the ground that no such lien was created (*Irish Times*, March 23, 1985).

[19] [1896] 1 I.R. 301, 315, following *English and Scottish Mercantile Investment Co.* v. *Brunton* [1892] 2 Q.B. 700.

[20] [1897] 1 I.R. 488, 506.

[21] [1980] I.R. 251, 256.

[22] For the equitable interest conferred by a floating charge, see *Merchant Banking Co of London* v. *Spotten* (1887–88) I.R., 11 Eq. 586, 596; *Dublin Distillery Ltd.* v. *Doherty* [1914] A.C. 823, 859; *Lynch* v. *Ardmore Studios (Ireland) Ltd.* [1966] I.R. 133; *Landall Holdings Ltd.* v. *Caratti* [1979] W.A.R. 97 (Supreme Court of Western Australia).

floating chargor and chargee, not giving rise to proprietary consequences. Implicitly, the courts have taken the latter course. The former supposes that a charge containing such a restriction creates in
effect a *fixed* equitable security in the assets charged, which the chargor is licensed to disregard, or let float, in all business transactions
concerning them, *except* in the creation of further security interests in
them. If assets consist of land, and conflicts of priorities in this context usually concern charges on land, then under this formulation
the application of familiar rules would result in the later chargee as
purchaser being fixed with notice of, and therefore bound by, a prior
equitable interest of which he knew, or ought to have known had he
followed usual conveyancing procedures. In falling short of these
standards, he is deemed particularly to know the *content* of documents of which he was aware, or the existence of which he ought to
have discovered, *e.g.* he would be deemed to know of the existence of
the floating charge because of the fact of its having been registered in
the Companies Registry,[23] and would be deemed also to have followed up its content, and learned of the restriction and of the prior,
fixed charge thereby created. The shorthand for such deemed
knowledge is "constructive notice." The courts have not, however,
adopted this categorisation. It would seem that a floating interest,
whilst it remains floating, floats for all purposes; it cannot at the
same time be partly fixed and floating. In other words, the quality of
the equitable interest created by the floating charge is untrammelled
by the restriction, and being in all respects floating is susceptible to
defeat by all subsequent dealings done in the ordinary course of
business, including the creation of later fixed charges. A subsequent
purchaser or fixed chargee is not therefore not obliged to enquire
into a floating equitable interest *as such* since its very nature assumes
an authority to deal. Into what then must a subsequent fixed chargee enquire, and why? Under this second categorisation, he is in a
position akin to someone negotiating with an agent. The agent's
actual authority from his principal may be limited, as is the company's licence to deal by reason of the negative pledge clause, but
the outsider may rely upon the ostensible authority of the agent to
do what usually would be within his authority, unless the illusion of
authority as communicated to the outsider is in some manner destroyed.[24] In agency, ostensible authority is destroyed by express
notice, *i.e.* actual knowledge on the part of the outsider that it is lacking, or by circumstances being brought home to him which actually

---

[23] s.99 *et seq.*, fully discussed in Chap. 15: *The Charges Register and Other Disclosures.*
[24] See Chap. 5, *Contract and Tort.*

"put him on enquiry" about the existence of the authority, a subjective test, conceptually different from constructive notice.[25] In the context of floating charges, there is a slight, statutory intrusion into this formulation since particulars of a floating charge (but not the presence or absence of a negative pledge clause contained therein[26]) are required by the Companies Act 1963, s.99(2)(*f*) to be registered in the Companies Registry, thereby making them one of the company's public documents of which the world, including an outsider dealing with the company, has constructive notice.[27] The intrusion does not go far, since it has been established for a long time, and recently affirmed,[28] that constructive notice of the registered particulars is confined to them, and does not include those contents of the charge of which particulars are not registered, such as a negative pledge clause.

Let us see how subsequent chargees are in practice fixed with express notice, of which the burden of proof lies on the floating chargee.[29]

There have been several cases in the Irish courts in which subsequent chargees have been shown to have had actual knowledge of a negative pledge clause[30]; in some of them this knowledge caused the outsider to alter his dealings with the company so as to take an outright sale of assets instead of an intended security interest in them.

There have not as yet been cases where the subsequent chargee has been fixed with express notice through ignoring circumstances which have "put him on enquiry"[31] as to the existence of a negative pledge clause. The reason is that the most obvious circumstances, namely knowledge of a prior floating charge, coupled with knowledge that negative pledge clauses are "more or less common form"[31a] in a modern floating charge, have been held of themselves not to give rise to a duty to enquire. Such was the conclusion of the Supreme Court in *Welch* v. *Bowmaker (Ireland) Ltd.*,[32] despite Henchy

---

[25] *e.g. English and Scottish Mercantile Bank* v. *Brunton* [1892] 2 Q.B. 700, 707–78.

[26] For the particulars to be registered, see s.105.

[27] See Chap. 5, *Contract and Tort*, at pp. 148–151.

[28] *Welch* v. *Bowmaker (Ireland) Ltd.* [1980] I.R. 251, following *Wilson* v. *Kellana* [1910] 2 Ch. 306.

[29] *Coveney* v. *Persse* [1910] 1 I.R. 194, 213 *per* Palles C.B.; *Cox* v. *Dublin City Distiller* [1906] 1 I.R. 446, 462 *per* Fitzgibbon L.J.; Holmes L.J. *dubitante* at p. 465.

[30] *Re Old Bushmills Distillery, ex p. Brydon, ex p. Bank of Ireland* [1896] 1 I.R. 301; *ex p Brett* [1897] 1 I.R. 488; *Cox* v. *Dublin City Distillery* [1906] 1 I.R. 446.

[31] See text at n. 25, *supra*.

[31a] *per* Henchy J. in *Welch* v. *Bowmaker (Ireland) Ltd.* [1980] I.R. 251, 256.

[32] [1980] I.R. 256, discussed (1982) S.J. 74.

J. having seen "attractions"[32a] in the contrary proposition. This contrary view, it was said, would upset commercial practice built on a long settled rule, for which only English authorities were cited in the judgments.[33] In fact, in the earlier Irish case of *Coveney* v. *Persse*[34] Holmes L.J. had come to the same conclusion, remarking that: "it would be somewhat startling for a Court to hold that such knowledge [*i.e.* of the existence of a prior floating charge] would amount to constructive notice of provisions calculated to prejudice the customers of a commercial or manufacturing Company in their dealings with it in the ordinary course of business." Earlier, in *Re Old Bushmills Distillery, ex p. Brydon*,[35] Chatterton V.-C. had however entertained, *obiter*, the idea that a duty to enquire might arise merely from knowledge of the existence of the prior floating charge. He said:

> "Cases were referred to where a person has notice of a deed which from its nature must affect the property in question, and others, where from its nature, it may or may not affect it. In the former the person is held to be affected with notice whether he inquires or not; and in the other he is bound to inquire, but if informed that it does not deal with the property, he is not affected with notice although the answer to his inquiry was false."[36]

Although the most obvious circumstance founding a duty to enquire has been outlawed, one does not rule out the existence of the duty. More esoteric circumstances must be found for the breach of it.

The Supreme Court in *Welch* v. *Bowmaker (Ireland) Ltd.* in rejecting a duty to inquire founded only on knowledge of the prior floating charge spoke, as did Holmes L.J. in *Coveney* v. *Persse*, in terms of a rejection of "constructive notice." One may sympathise with the wish of the Supreme Court, shown in this case and in *Bank of Ireland Finance Ltd.* v. *Rockfield Ltd.*,[37] and by Gavan Duffy P. in *Sean O'Neill Ltd.* v. *McKenna*[37a] to outlaw constructive notice from commercial

---

[32a] *Ibid.* at p. 256.

[33] *Re Standard Rotary Machine Co. Ltd.* (1906) 95 L.T. 829; *Wilson* v. *Kelland* [1910] 2 Ch. 306; *G & T Earle Ltd.* v. *Hemsworth R.D.C.* (1928) 44 T.L.R. 605 are cited by Henchy J. Parke J. refers to the "long line of authorities already decided both in this country and in England" without specifying the former.

[34] [1910] 1 I.R. 194, 218.

[35] [1896] 1 I.R. 301, a case in which the subsequent chargee had actual knowledge.

[36] At p. 317.

[37] [1979] I.R. 21. But in that case, and in *Welch* v. *Bowmaker (Ireland) Ltd.* one must question the categorisation "commercial," since in each a public registry was involved.

[37a] High Court, January 12, 1951, unreported.

transactions, Parke J. saying that "the doctrine of constructive or implied notice, like that of public policy, may be an unruly horse, and should be ridden with a firm hand."[38] But there is a difference upon which it is not pedantic to insist between the standards enforced by a duty to inquire and those imposed by constructive notice. Constructive notice deems a person to know what he ought to have known but did not, by reference to an objective standard, usually that of the reasonably competent conveyancer. A duty to inquire is founded on considerations of honesty, a requirement which no court could wish to remove from the commercial law. The imposition of a duty to inquire guards against wilful blindness, a deliberate shutting of the eyes against facts which a person, viewed subjectively, might not wish to discover on the grounds that they would impede the proposed transaction, a species of dishonesty or lack of good faith.[39] The actual state of mind of the subsequent chargee was not however examined in the judgments.[40]

Whilst on the subject of good faith, it is surprising that the Supreme Court did not canvass the applicability of regulation 6 of the European Communities (Companies) Regulations 1973 to the situation before it. This states so far as material:

> "(1) In favour of a person dealing with a company *in good faith*, any transaction entered into by any organ of the company, being its board of directors or any person registered under these regulations as a person authorised to bind the company, shall be deemed to be within the capacity of the company and *any limitation* of the powers of that board or person, whether imposed by the memorandum or articles of association *or otherwise*, may not be relied upon as against any person so dealing with the company.
> (2) Any such person shall be presumed to have acted in good faith unless the contrary is proved."[41]

The question is whether a negative pledge clause constitutes "a limitation of the powers of the board." It is arguable that it does, in that a company's agents in acting on its behalf are subjected to the same restrictions as their principal. The majority judgments suggested

---

[38] [1980] I.R. 251, at p. 262.
[39] See n. 25, *supra*, and Chap. 4: *Objects* where good faith is discussed at p. 135 *et seq.*
[40] It is not intended to suggest that this, or any, party acted in any way in bad faith.
[41] Italics supplied. S.I. 1973 No. 163 is primarily discussed at pp. 134 *et seq.*, and pp. 153 *et seq.*, *supra*; also in Ussher, "Questions of Capacity" (1975) *Irish Jurist* 38. For the significance in the context of negative pledge clauses of the materially differentl worded s.9 of the European Communities Act 1972 [*U.K.*], see J.H. Farrar, "Floating Charges and Priorities" (1974) 38 Conv. N.S. 315, 326 *et seq.*

that any change in this area of the law should be brought about, if at all, by statute. It would appear[42] that the Supreme Court was not given the opportunity to consider whether this existing statutory intervention had any bearing on the problem before it. Regulation 6, if applicable, focuses the investigation onto the state of mind of the subsequent chargee, which, it is submitted, should in any event have been the main subject of investigation.

A more positive reform would involve including negative pledge clauses among the prescribed particulars to be filed in the Companies Registry.[43]

Crystallisation

First we deal with crystallising events, and next with the consequences of crystallisation. A floating charge will necessarily crystallise, and thereby become a fixed equitable interest on the assets then comprised in it, when the company goes into liquidation or when a receiver is appointed.[44]

There is some doubt in other jurisdictions whether the company's ceasing to carry on business, or ceasing to be a going concern, also necessarily results in crystallisation.[45] In Ireland, however, *Halpin* v. *Cremin*[46] is a strong authority to the contrary. The case concerned adverse possession, and was held to turn upon whether a floating charge over a railway company's undertaking, including some land, had already crystallised in 1925 when a squatter took possession of that land. Lavery J. held that crystallisation had not yet occurred in 1925, despite the fact that the company had gone out of business in 1924, and by 1925, though not actually in liquidation, was as defunct as it possibly could be; it had "vanished" as one witness expressively put it.

The extent to which the parties to a floating charge are free to stipulate events upon which crystallisation will occur in addition to the two upon which it necessarily occurs, the appointment of a receiver or going into liquidation, remains an open question. Such further agreed events (called by some, "automatic crystallisation") might

---

[42] The arguments of counsel are not reproduced in the Report.
[43] s.103 contains the prescribed particulars.
[44] *Halpin* v. *Cremin* [1954] I.R. 19, 24, relying heavily on *Evans* v. *Rival Granite Quarries Ltd.* [1910] 2 K.B. 979; see also *Re Panama, etc. Royal Mail Co.* (1870) 5 Ch. pp. 318, 322–323, and *Re Florence Land Co.* (1878) 10 Ch.D. 530, 541.
[45] See Farrar, (1976) 40 Conv. N.S. 397, 399.
[46] [1954] I.R. 19.

include default by the company in payments due under the floating charge followed by notice from the charge holder calling in the principal money, the levying of an unsatisfied execution against the property of the company, the company's ceasing or threatening to cease to carry on its business, the swearing of an affidavit preliminary to the creation of a judgment mortgage over any of the property comprised in the floating charge, and dealings or attempted dealings contrary to a negative pledge clause. There are dicta suggesting that the parties to a floating charge have full freedom to define crystallising events, among them Lord Macnaghten in *Illingworth* v. *Houldsworth*,[47] and also, more strongly, Buckley L.J. in *Evans* v. *Rival Granite Quarries Ltd*,[48] a judgment heavily relied upon in *Halpin* v. *Cremin, supra.* Buckley L.J. said:

> "This crystallisation may be brought about in various ways. A receiver may be appointed, or the company may go into liquidation and a liquidator be appointed *or any event may happen which is defined as bringing to an end the licence to the company to carry on business.*" [49]

Against this freedom it may be argued that crystallisation should be a public event. Statute strives to ensure that the two events upon which crystallisation necessarily occurs, the appointment of a receiver or the entry into liquidation, are publicised,[50] and, in practice, the occurrence of either of these events in relation to a company of any significance will very soon become known to its creditors, in contrast to the happening of some of the other crystallising events which the parties may have stipulated in the charge. Such secret crystallisations could involve subsequent execution creditors in wasted expenditure, and might deprive holders of subsequently

---

[47] The quotation is set out at p. 420, *supra.* It was approved by Kenny J. in *Re Interview Ltd.* [1975] I.R. 382, 395. He said: "The charge floats over the assets of the company until some act is done which causes it to fasten on to the property and goods of the company. The appointment of a receiver has this effect."

[48] [1910] 2 K.B. 979.

[49] At p. 1000. Italics supplied.

[50] See s.107 (publication in newspaper and *Iris Oifigiúil* and notice to Registrar of appointment of receiver), s.143(4)(*e*) (voluntary winding up resolution to be forwarded to Registrar), s.278 (liquidator in voluntary winding up to notify Registrar), reg. 4(3) of S.I. 1973 No. 163 (liquidator in voluntary winding up to publish notice of appointment in (*Iris Oifigiúil*), s.227 (liquidator appointed by court to publish that fact in *Iris Oifigiúil* and notify Registrar), and s.221 (copy of winding up order to be forwarded to the Registrar), s.317 (all invoices, orders, business letters after receiver appointed to state that fact).

created equitable interests of their priority over an apparently floating but secretly fixed charge.[51]

Consequences of crystallisation

Crystallisation, the event upon which the previously inchoate
equitable rights of the holder of a debenture secured by a floating
charge become fixed equitable rights, is usually described as an
equitable assignment to the debenture holder of all the property
comprised in it.[52] Future assets falling within the ambit of the crystallised charge are likewise automatically assigned in equity to the
debenture holder as they arise, *i.e.* rights inchoate at crystallisation
which subsequently become substantive such as a tax repayment
claim in respect of a terminal loss[53] or an order for costs in favour of
the company which becomes a due debt on taxation,[54] and rights
generated by the receiver's own activities.

Being an equitable assignment, it is in theory vulnerable to the
claims of subsequent purchasers of legal rights in relation to the
property comprised in it, who have not had notice of the crystallising
event. But in practice where crystallisation has occurred on the
appointment of a receiver, the most common crystallising event,
such conflicts do not occur. So far as dealings *inter partes* are concerned, the receiver is in control of the assets, and therefore a third
party will not be in a position to acquire subsequent claims in
respect of them without his concurrence. Opportunities for independent action by third parties are also thwarted. Thus, a judgment
creditor for a pre-crystallisation debt seeking to impose a judgment
mortgage on lands comprised in a crystallised floating charge acts in
vain since, as an execution creditor, he is not a "purchaser."[55]

---

[51] This last point is arguable. The general observations in *Kelly* v. *Munster & Leinster Bank* (1892–93) 29 L.R., Ir. 19, 43 might provide a starting point for that argument. Generally on the merits of allowing secret crystallisation, contrast *The Queen* (*in
right of British Columbia*) v. *Consolidated Churchill Copper Corp. Ltd.* [1978] 5 W.W.R. 652
with *Re Manurewa Transport Ltd.* [1971] N.Z.L.R. 909, both discussed in Farrar, (1980)
1 Co. Law 83. The Cork Committee Report on the insolvency law and practice in
England and Wales, 1982 Cmnd. 8558, para. 1580, would outlaw secret crystallisations.

[52] *Lynch* v. *Ardmore Studios (Ireland) Ltd.* [1966] I.R. 133, 149 ("tantamount to an
equitable assignment," *per* Budd J.); *Re Interview Ltd.* [1975] I.R. 383, 395; *Murphy* v.
Revenue Commrs. [1976] 15, 17; *Tempany* v.*Hynes* [1976] I.R. 101, 116; *Kilgobbin Mink &
Stud Farms Ltd.* v. *National Credit Co. Ltd.* [1980] I.R. 175, 180; *Hoban* v. *Bute Investments
Ltd.* (High Court, Hamilton J., February 14, 1980, unreported).

[53] *Murphy* v. *Revenue Commissioners* [1976] I.R. 15.

[54] *Lynch* v. *Ardmore Studios (Ireland) Ltd.* [1966] I.R. 133, 152.

[55] *Eyre* v. *McDowell* (1861) 9 H.L. Cas. 619; *Tempany* v. *Hynes* [1976] I.R. 101 which
held that a crystallised floating charge is an "unregistered right" under the Registration of Title Act 1964, s.71(4)(*c*), to which the judgment mortgagee takes subject.

Secondly, a debtor (D) of the company (C) who after crystallisation acquires by assignment from a third party (X) a pre-crystallisation debt owed by C to X cannot, if he had notice of the crystallisation at the time of the assignment, set off the acquired debt against what he, D, owes to C. If this ploy worked, it would be to the advantage of both X and D, since X could demand as the price of his assignment something more than he would get as an unsecured creditor of an insolvent company, the balance going to D.

Its failure is explained in accordance with the following reasoning. "Mutual" debts between a plaintiff and defendant may be set off against each other.[56] Ordinarily, the debtor D may set off against his creditor C the debt owed by C to X which D has acquired by assignment from X.[57] Where however another party, Y, has before that assignment acquired rights in the debt owed by D to C, "mutuality" between C and D is said to be lacking, and a set off impermissible.[58] Y, in our case, is the debenture holder who on crystallisation acquired fixed equitable rights in the debt owed by D. Since Y's rights are equitable, D, in order to be bound by them, should have had notice of them before taking the assignment from X,[59] inevitable in the circumstances.

A corporate security

A floating charge is exclusively a corporate security. Conceptually, individuals, trading solely or in partnership, are capable of creating them but are practically debarred from doing so by aspects of the bills of sale and bankruptcy legislation not applicable to companies. The Bills of Sale (Ireland) Acts 1879 and 1883 require such a charge to specify the goods comprised within it,[60] impossible in the case of after-acquired property. On a trader's bankruptcy, goods "in his possession, order or disposition . . . whereof he was reputed owner,"[61] may be applied for the benefit of his general creditors. Goods comprised in a floating charge would be within the reputed ownership of the chargor, thereby rendering it a useless security. Nevertheless, circumstances could be artificially contrived under

---

[56] s.27(3), Supreme Court of Judicature (Ireland) Act 1877.

[57] *Bennett* v. *White* [1910] 2 K.B. 643.

[58] *Lynch* v. *Ardmore Studios (Ireland) Ltd.* [1966] I.R. 133, following *N.W. Robbie & Co. Ltd.* v. *Witney Warehouse Co. Ltd.* [1963] 1 W.L.R. 1324.

[59] Had *Y* been the *legal* assignee of *D*s debt to *C*, no question of set-off in respect of *C*s unconnected debt to *X* could have arisen after the notice to the debtor completing the assignment: *Roxburghe* v. *Cox* (1881) 17 Ch.D. 520, 526.

[60] 1879 Act, s.4. *Re Royal Marine Hotel, Kingstown Ltd.* [1895] 1 I.R. 368 affirms that securities given by a limited company are not within these Acts.

[61] Irish Bankrupt and Insolvent Act 1857, s.313.

which an individual could create an effective floating charge,[62] but nothing upon which to build a regular lending practice.

RECEIVERS

Every well-drawn debenture gives the debenture holder power to appoint a receiver and manager of the property comprised in it, and confers on him specific further powers beyond those of receiving and applying the income which a receiver as such would ordinarily have.[63] The debenture will usually give him express powers to take possession or otherwise assume control of the property comprised in the charge, to sell that property, to carry on the business of the company, and to compromise claims. Usually, the debenture holder may appoint a receiver only after the principal moneys have become payable under the debenture, something which depends upon its terms. For example, they may be repayable on demand in the case of a debenture granted to secure an overdraft, or on the expiry of a fixed term, or, in the case of a "perpetual" debenture, upon the company giving notice of an intention to redeem, *and*, whatever the period of repayment chosen, it is usual to stipulate that the principal moneys may be called in if the company defaults on interest payments, and also shall be immediately payable on such events as an order being made or a resolution passed for the winding up of the company, or the company ceasing or threatening to cease carrying on business.

The court under its equitable jurisdiction may also appoint a receiver. It is unlikely to be called upon to do so by a debenture holder possessing an express power, but some unforeseen event, not anticipated by the debenture, and placing the security in jeopardy may occasion an application.[63a] Where, exceptionally, a debenture

---

[62] See *Merchant Banking Co. of London* v. *Spotten* (1877–78) I.R., 11 Eq. 586, 596.

[63] For such powers, see J.C.W. Wylie, *Irish Land Law*, 1975, 3–166 *et seq.*, 13–052 *et seq.*; Snell, *Principles of Equity*, (28th ed., 1982), pp. 663 *et seq.* The powers possessed by a receiver in the absence of express provisions are found in the Conveyancing Act 1881. s.19(2) thereof gives a mortgagee *by deed* of *any* property power to appoint a receiver upon whom s.24 confers power to demand and recover income, and to retain his remuneration out of receipts. s.24 also directs the disposal of receipts. It is customary in drafting a debenture to give to a receiver, in addition to the express powers outlined *infra*, the mortgagee's and receiver's powers as conferred by the Conveyancing Act 1881, as amended by the Conveyancing Act 1911.

[63a] However, see Kenny J. in *Angelis* v. *Algemene Bank Nederland* (*Ireland*) *Ltd.* (High Court, July 4, 1974; unreported) where at p. 2 of the transcript he says "it is not necessary to cite authority for the proposition that when assets charged by a debenture are in danger of seizure, a debenture holder may immediately appoint a receiver." Here assets comprised in a floating charge had become vulnerable to execution by a judgment creditor, and the debenture holder had responded by appointing a receiver.

creating a security does not reserve a power to appoint a receiver, and none is implied,[64] recourse must be had to the court. Thus in *Alexander Hull & Co. Ltd.* v. *O'Carroll Kent & Co. Ltd.*[65] the court appointed a receiver at the suit of a lender which had advanced money to a company which agreed to execute a charge, but never did.

Bodies corporate and undischarged bankrupts are disqualified from acting as receivers of the property of a company.[66]

The appointment of a receiver under a floating charge is, as we have seen,[67] a crystallising event. A receiver appointed in pursuance of a floating charge must immediately notify the company of his appointment,[68] and thereupon, as an aid to the discharge of his functions, becomes entitled to receive a statement of the company's affairs showing its assets, debts and liabilities, creditors and their securities.[69] This statement must be submitted by one or more of the directors and the secretary, or, at the option of the receiver, one or more of a wider class of persons likely to have knowledge of the company's affairs, such as any present or past officer, including assumedly an auditor,[70] and employees.[71]

A receiver, howsoever appointed, in asserting the claims of the company is generally[72] not in a better position than the company would be. Thus, in *Murphy* v. *The Revenue Commissioners*[73] a claim for tax repayment in respect of a terminal loss asserted by the receiver on behalf of the company against the Revenue Commissioners was subject to a set-off by them in respect of a debt due from the company to them. In *Kilgobbin Mink and Stud Farms Ltd.* v. *National Credit Co. Ltd.*[74] an estoppel binding on a company in respect of a claim by it against a third party bound also the subsequently appointed receiver, Hamilton J. saying, "In effect, the receiver steps into the

---

[64] As where the debenture is not created by deed, thereby ruling out the implication of the power given by the Conveyancing Act 1881 s.19(2).

[65] (1955) 89 I.L.T.R. 70.

[66] s.314 and s.315.

[67] At p. 429, *supra*.

[68] s.319(1)(*a*). It applies to the "receiver of the whole or substantially the whole of the property of a company . . . appointed on behalf of the holders of any debenture of the company secured by a floating charge."

[69] s.319(1)(*b*); s.320(1).

[70] For an auditor's liability as an "officer" for the purpose of misfeasance proceedings, see pp. 369, 382, *ante*.

[71] Fuller details in s.320(2).

[72] For the inhibition of the right of set-off of a post-crystallisation assignee of debt see p. 432, *ante*.

[73] [1976] I.R. 15, following *Rother Iron Works Ltd.* v. *Canterbury Precision Engineers Ltd* [1974] 1 Q.B. 1.

[74] [1980] I.R. 175.

shoes of the company and does not acquire any rights which the company does not itself possess."[75]

A receiver appointed under a debenture drafted in common form[76] is the agent of the company, and not of the debenture holders who, in appointing him, are construed as doing so as agents of the company.[77] He is constituted agent of the company in order to avoid the debenture holders being subjected to the onerous regime of a mortgagee in possession.[78] Taking control through a receiver of a debtor's business does not *per se* result in such a community of interest between creditor and debtor as to render them partners in that business, or otherwise the latter the principal of the former in its conduct.[79] There is not therefore a liability on the debenture holders for dealings between the receiver and third parties, a conclusion which the express declaration in common form debentures that a

---

[75] *Ibid.* at p. 180. Contrast *Ardmore Studios (Ireland) Ltd.* v. *Lynch* [1965] I.R. 1 in which a trade dispute within the meaning of the Trade Disputes Act 1906 was held not to exist between a receiver and a trade union. The dispute concerned a restraint on the company's trade which it had before crystallisation agreed with the union to impose. The receiver in conducting a fresh, post-crystallisation trade on the company's behalf refused to abide by this agreement. Picketing ensued which the receiver sued in the company's name to restrain. The case appeared to turn on the fact that the receiver would incur personal liability under s.316(2), discussed at p. 436, *infra*, for this trading, and that he was primarily concerned on behalf of the debenture holders ([1965] I.R. 1, 30, 40). "As agent for the Company, the Company is made responsible for his acts but it is not a corollary to this that he is bound by all Company contracts entered into by the Company before the date of his appointment," (*per* McLoughlin J. at p. 40). This decision would be more readily digestible if the receiver had been appointed by the court, since in those circumstances he does not trade on behalf of the company (see n. 83, *infra*), but as a trustee of the assets committed to him, the debenture holders and the company (to the extent that there is a surplus) having beneficial interests in those assets. In any event insofar as a business is transferred to a receiver, the European Communities (Safeguarding of Employees' Rights on Transfer of Undertakings) Regulations 1980, see nowadays S.I. 1980 No. 306, on the continuity of collective agreements.

[76] For the dangers of departing from the common form, see *Deyes* v. *Wood* [1911] 1 K.B. 806.

[77] *Gosling* v. *Gaskell* [1896] 1 Q.B. 669, 692–93 (dissenting judgment of Rigby L.J. adopted by the House of Lords, [1897] A.C. 575); followed in *Lynch* v. *Ardmore Studios (Ireland) Ltd.* [1966] I.R. 133. The Conveyancing Act 1881, s.24 deems a receiver appointed under that Act, in the absence of provisions to the contrary, to be the agent of the mortgagor appointing him, "a statutory recognition and approval of . . . practice" (*per* Rigby L.J. [1896] 1 Q.B. 693).

[78] J.C.W. Wylie, *Irish Land Law* (1975), 13–041 *et seq.*; *W. and L. Crowe Ltd.* v. *Electricity Supply Board* (High Court, Costello J., May 9, 1984; unreported) at p. 16 of the transcript; and *Irish Oil and Cake Mills Ltd.* v. *Donnelly* (High Court, Costello J., March 7, 1983; unreported) at p. 6 of the transcript.

[79] See Rigby L.J. in *Gosling* v. *Gaskell* [1896] 1 Q.B. 669, 688–91.

receiver appointed by debenture holders is the agent of the company serves to reinforce. Though a receiver is not the agent of the debenture holders, he nonetheless owes them fiduciary obligations since he is concerned primarily on their behalf.[80-81] He also owes duties to the company, and others, as we shall see.

By the Companies Act 1963, s.316(2), a receiver of the property of the company, however appointed,[82] incurs a personal liability on any contract entered into by him in the performance of his functions, "unless the contract provides that he is not to be personally liable." If personal liability is excluded, whether expressly or through the receiver's subsequent bankruptcy, claimants in respect of obligations entered into by him will look to the assets subject to the charge for payment, in priority to the debenture holders.[83] Section 316(2) gives the receiver an indemnity out of those assets in respect of his personal liability on such contracts.

A receiver appointed under an ineffective charge may be relieved by the court from any personal liability arising from his purported receivership, and upon that relief being granted, the liability is automatically transferred to those who appointed him.[84]

Several classes of persons have an interest in the manner in which a receiver discharges his functions, and their interests are to some extent competing. The debenture holders are concerned that their security should be sufficient; likewise, the guarantors of the company's indebtedness to the debenture holders; the company, and through it its general creditors, and, after them, its members, are all concerned that the realisation of assets should yield a surplus in which they might participate; and the employees will wish the business to continue.

Of these, the law is least concerned with the employees for the car-

---

[80-81] *Re B. Johnson & Co. (Builders) Ltd.* [1955] Ch. 634, 645. *per* Evershed, M.R.

[82] Before the enactment of s.316(2), only a receiver appointed by the court incurred personal liability on contracts. The receiver appointed out of court acted simply on behalf of the company. Contrast s.369(2) of the Companies Act 1948 [*U.K.*], with s.316(2).

[83] *Re British Power Traction and Lighting Co.* [1906] 1 Ch. 497 (creditors indemnified to the extent of receiver's indemnity out of assets); also *Healy* v. *Oliver* [1918] 1 I.R. 366. A receiver appointed by the court is not an agent of the company in carrying on its business (*Moss Steamship Co. Ltd.* v. *Whinney* [1912] A.C. 254, 259, 271), and *semble* the liability of such a receiver is absent or worthless, his creditor cannot look further than the assets subject to the charge for payment. A receiver appointed out of court technically acts on behalf of the company as well, and therefore his unpaid creditor may also rank as general creditors of the company.

[84] s.316(3), partly following Jenkins Committee, para. 299. The charge could, *e.* be ineffective through non-registration. See Chap. 15: *The Charges Register and Other Disclosures*, at pp. 451, *et seq.*

dinal reason that the receiver under usual terms of appointment is not *bound* to carry on the company's business,[85] even if it remains possible to do so. He merely has *power* to do so, and whether he exercises that power is a matter for his discretion. The appointment of a receiver out of court by the debenture holders does not as such terminate contracts of employment,[86] except where the continuance of the employment of a particular employee is inconsistent with the role to be assumed by the receiver. Thus, the appointment of a receiver to run a company's business full-time will terminate the contract of a managing director.[87] The appointment of a receiver *by* the court transfers the business to him, and was held at common law to terminate all contracts of employment.[88] Now however there has been statutory intervention in the form of the European Communities (Safeguarding of Employees' Rights on Transfer of Undertakings) Regulations 1980[89] which impose on the transferee of a business the contracts of employment of the employees in that business. A receiver appointed by the court is, it would seem, a transferee of a business within the meaning of these Regulations. If a receiver, however appointed, is proposing to sell the company's business or any part of it, he is obliged by these regulations to consult and inform the employees' representatives.[90] A receiver, however appointed, is bound to observe the consultation and notification procedures laid down in the Protection of Employment Act 1977. If, as is supposed above, a receiver appointed by the court is substituted as employer, he becomes personally responsible for all the usual consequences[91] of the dismissal of an employee dismissed by him. A receiver appointed out of court does not incur these personal consequences since, in dismissing, he acts as agent for the company, except to the extent that he has renewed[92] a contract of employment

---

[85] *Kernohan Estates Ltd.* v. *Boyd* [1967] N.I. 27; *Re B. Johnson & Co. (Builders) Ltd.*, *supra.*

[86] That much at least can be extracted from the English authorities which are not wholly consistent: *Re Foster Clark Ltd's Indenture Trusts* [1966] 1 W.L.R. 125; *Re Mack Trucks (Britain) Ltd.* [1967] 1 W.L.R. 780; *Griffiths* v. *Secretary of State for Social Services* [1974] Q.B. 468; *Deaway Trading Ltd.* v. *Calverley* [1973] I.C.R. 546. For a fuller discussion, see *Rideout's Principles of Labour Law,* (London, 1983).

[87] *Griffiths* v. *Secretary of State for Social Services* [1974] Q.B. 468, 486.

[88] *Reid* v. *Explosives Co. Ltd.* (1887) 19 Q.B.D. 264.

[89] S.I. 1980 No. 306, implementing Council Directive 77/187/EEC of February 14, 1977 (O.J., L61 of March 5, 1977).

[90] *Ibid.* reg. 7.

[91] These are beyond the scope of this work. See Redmond, *Dismissal Law in the Republic of Ireland,* (Dublin, 1982).

[92] *e.g. Re Mack Trucks (Britain) Ltd.* [1967] 1 W.L.R. 780.

or made a fresh one, and has not disclaimed personal responsibility under the Companies Act 1963, s.316(2).

The Companies Act 1963 provides some, but not much, assistance to those interested parties who wish to monitor the progress of a receivership. A receiver[93] must circulate the statement of the company's affairs which he has obtained[94] together with his comments upon it to the registrar of companies (who will place it on public file) and others[95]; the receiver must periodically render abstracts to the registrar of companies of assets coming into his hands, their estimated value, proceeds of sale, and his receipts and payments.[96] These duties of disclosure may be enforced by members and creditors, as well as by the registrar of companies.[97] A liquidator, if one is appointed, may insist that the receiver account to him for all receipts and payments, and that he pay over the balance, if any, due.[98] There is also a statutory safeguard against the receiver taking excessive remuneration. The court has power, on the application of any creditor or member of the company or of its liquidator, to fix the remuneration of the receiver, even retrospectively, and at a rate different from that agreed in his terms of appointment.[99]

But the interested parties may want more than is provided by this statutory skeleton of remedies, a demand to which the courts are in the process of responding. A receiver appointed out of court is, as we

---

[93] Whether appointed in or out of court, provided that he is a receiver "of the whole or substantially the whole of the property of a company," and the debentures are secured by a floating charge: s.319(1).

[94] See p. 434, *supra*.

[95] s.319(1)(*c*), (3).

[96] s.319(2), and 321(1) which applies to receiverships other than those covered by s.319(1): see n. 93, *supra*. The abstracts must be filed six-monthly during the receivership, and within one month of its termination. After the receivership has come to an end, and if he was appointed out of Court under a debenture in common form (see pp. 433, 435–436, *supra*), the abstracts may be supplemented at the instance of the company by virtue of the equitable duty to account subsisting between principal and agent: *Smiths Ltd.* v. *Middleton* [1979] 3 All E.R. 842 (a case in which the company survived the receivership) as explained by Costello J. in *Irish Oil and Cake Mills Ltd.* v. *Donnelly*, n. 2, *infra*. If liquidation supervenes, the liquidator is entitled to "proper accounts" pursuant to s.322(1)(*b*).

[97] s.322.

[98] s.322(1)(*b*). A receiver appointed by the court accounts to it.

[99] s.318. A receiver appointed under the statutory power contained in the Conveyancing Act 1881 is not permitted, whatever the terms of his appointment to charge more than 5 per cent. of the gross amount of all money received: the Conveyancing Act 1881, s.24(6). But note that Gavan Duffy J. remarked in *Clery & Co. Ltd.* v. *Shaw* (High Court, May 8, 1941; unreported) that a receiver appointed under a debenture in common form "is not the kind of receiver with which [the Conveyancing Act 1881] is concerned, a mere collector of income" (at p. 16 of the transcript).

have seen,[1] usually constituted the agent of the company. In *McGowan* v. *Gannon*[2] there was treated as flowing from this agency a duty on the part of the receiver to furnish to the company information on his negotiations for the sale of the company's principal asset. The company's guarantors and creditors were held not to be entitled to such information, because they were not parties to the agency contract. Since however a guarantor is certainly, and a creditor is possibly, within the ambit of a receiver's duty of care, *infra*, they may if they bring proceedings to restrain an apprehended breach of that duty, apply to obtain such information by way of discovery.

Further, it has long been recognised that a receiver, however appointed, is a fiduciary,[3] and would seem to bear that character in relation to all persons possessing *proprietary* interests in the property under his control.[4] That property has subsisting in it not only the equitable rights of the debenture holders and those if any, with later security interests, but also an equitable interest owned by the company itself, insofar as there may be a surplus after the satisfaction of these secured creditors.[5] That the receiver's prior concern lies with the debenture holders is well established.[6] But what of the others, first the company? In managing the company's business, it is unlikely that he would as fiduciary be subjected to a greater degree of liability than directors doing so would be, and, in applying the standards applicable to directors, it may be argued that he should as a professional (which he usually will be) be expected to exert his professed skills.[7] In realising the assets, the closest analogy is with the standards required of a mortgagee exercising a power of sale. Formerly, the duty of a mortgagee in such circumstances could accurately be stated in classical, predominantly subjective, fiduciary terms. He must not abuse or exceed his powers, and he must act in

---

[1] See pp. 435–436, *supra*.

[2] [1983] I.L.R.M. 516. However, in the later case of *Irish Oil and Cake Mills Ltd.* v. *Donnelly* (High Court, Costello J., March 27, 1983; unreported) Costello J. declined to imply into this contract a term under which the receiver would have been obliged to furnish accounts and very detailed information on all aspects of the company's business only four months into the receivership.

[3] *e.g. Alven* v. *Bond* (1841) Fl. & K. 196, 211 (Rolls Court, Ireland: Sir Michael O'-Loghlen M.R.); *Eyre* v. *M'Donnell* (1864) 15 I.Ch.R. 534, 548, 551 (Sir Maziere Brady L.C.); *Re Magadi Soda Co.* (1925) 41 T.L.R. 297.

[4] Such would seem to be the principled conclusion, and see *Re Ronayne's Estate* (1863) 13 I. Ch. R. 444, 450.

[5] *Gosling* v. *Gaskell* [1896] 1 Q.B. 669, 699.

[6] *Lynch* v. *Ardmore Studios (Ireland) Ltd.* [1966] I.R. 133, 147, following *Re B. Johnson (Builders) Ltd.* [1955] Ch. 634.

[7] For director's duties, see Chap. 7, *supra*.

good faith: a reckless disposal of the mortgaged property indicates bad faith.[8] In 1966, however, the Supreme Court in *Holohan* v. *Friends Provident and Century Life Office*[9] substituted for the fiduciary regime applicable to mortgagees exercising a power of sale the objective, but in this context less certain, standards of the reasonable man, a shift explicable by the apparently inescapable magnetism of *Donoghue* v. *Stevenson*.[10] "The reasonable man," according to 0 Daláigh C.J. delivering the unanimous judgment of the Supreme Court, "sets himself a higher standard than to act in good faith. There is no room for doubting the *bona fides* of a reasonable man. He will, while rightly looking to his own interest,[11] also bear in mind the interest of the mortgagor. Whether or not the property to be sold is value for the amount of the mortgagee's debt the mortgagor has very real interest in the best price being obtained. If there should be a surplus it is for his benefit; equally he benefits by the best price being obtained: his indebtedness is thereby reduced as much as possible. Mortgagor and mortgagee are not in like case in this respect. A mortgagee who is not fully paid off because the best price is not obtained still has the right to sue the mortgagor for the balance, while the mortgagor must abide the disadvantage of a poor price being realised. Moreover, there is the interest of second and other mortgagees to be safeguarded."[12] Lord Denning M.R. in *Standard Chartered Bank Ltd.* v. *Walker*[13] described the similar but later development in England[14] as being "only a particular application of the general duty of care to your neighbour which was stated by Lord Atkin in *Donoghue* v. *Stevenson* . . . and applied in many cases since," and held, further, that a *receiver* owes a similar duty, not only to the company, but also to the company's guarantor, to exercise the reasonable care of the reasonable man in the disposal of the assets. and in obtaining the best possible price which the circumstances of the case permit. This formulation of a receiver's duty has been

---

[8] This formulation is drawn from the judgments in the House of Lords in *Kennedy* v. *De Trafford* [1897] A.C. 180, followed by Budd J. at first instance in *Holohan* v. *Friends Provident and Century Life Office* [1966] I.R. 1, 9 *et seq.*, and rejected by the Supreme Court.

[9] [1966] I.R. 1.

[10] [1932] A.C. 562, though express reference to it is not made. Overt influence were *Downes* v. *Grazebrook* (1817) 2 Mer. 200, 223; *Robertson* v. *Norris* (1858) 1 Giff. 421 *Jenkins* v. *Jones* (1860) 2 Giff. 99, 108; *McHugh* v. *Union Bank of Canada* [1913] A.C. 299 311 (P.C.). For a later Privy Council excursion into this field, see *Tse Kwong Lam* v. *Won Chit Sen* [1983] 1 W.L.R. 1394.

[11] As transposed to a receiver, this refers to the interests of the debenture holders.

[12] [1966] I.R. 1, 21.

[13] [1982] 3 All E.R. 938, 942–43.

[14] *Cuckmere Brick Co. Ltd.* v. *Mutual Finance Ltd.* [1971] Ch. 949.

accepted in Ireland in *Lambert Jones Estates Ltd.* v. *Donnelly*,[15] and in *McGowan* v. *Gannon*[16] and in *Irish Oil and Cake Mills Ltd.* v. *Donnelly*.[16a]

The practical consequence of this change in the nature of a receiver's duty is that he may no longer say to a complainant (and hence to a court): "The discretion on how to act was mine, not yours. In the exercise of my independent judgment, I honestly decided what to do for the best. Therefore, you cannot touch me." He is now subject to the court's sense of what is appropriate. That, essentially, is what the standard of "the reasonable man" means. Consequently, one cannot be certain in advance on all aspects of the content of the duty. The reasonable man, one must suppose, takes professional advice, and acts on it. Following his own judgment, if at variance, is risky, and must be justified. The vendor in *Holohan* v. *Friends Provident and Century Life Office*[17] who sold a tenanted property without fully exploring the alternative of selling it with vacant possession which professional advice indicated would yield an enhanced price, was restrained from completing the sale as being in breach of duty. Consideration of this case raises one of the unanswered questions on the role of the reasonable man as receiver: how hard is the reasonable man? Though the tenants in that case would have been compensated for their departure, must a receiver who has been advised that a higher price will be obtained if he clears the property of those tenants who do not happen to have security of tenure always follow that advice? Under the old formulation he was allowed, according to Sir Michael O'Loghlen M.R. in *Alven* v. *Bond*,[18] to decide not to follow a course of conduct "in which avarice prevails over the dictates of humanity," and to leave the tenants undisturbed. The importance of relying nowadays on professional advice is illustrated by *Lambert Jones Estates Ltd.* v. *Donnelly*.[19] A receiver was held justified in rejecting on expert advice a method of disposal of the property, supported by other expert opinion. The rejected method would have involved him in the expense and delay of planning applications, but would have resulted in a higher price. Pending realisation, interest was running against the company at £3206 a day. During the unsuccessful proceedings for an interlocutory injunction to restrain him from acting as he wished, the receiver let

---

[15] High Court, O'Hanlon J., November 5, 1982, (unreported).
[16] [1983] I.L.R.M. 516.
[16a] High Court, Costello J., March 27, 1983, unreported.
[17] [1966] I.R. 1.
[18] (1841) Fl. & K. 196, 223 (Rolls Court, Ireland).
[19] High Court, O'Hanlon J., November 5, 1982, (unreported).

it be known that he would in any event be seeking the approval of the court for a sale at the price he was ultimately offered, a wise course for any receiver faced with difficult choices and the reconciliation of conflicting interests. Since much of his former discretion is in effect surrendered to the court in proceedings seeking to impugn his actions or proposed actions, he should be able to protect himself by seeking its *imprimatur*.[20]

It would seem that a vendor selling as mortgagee or as receiver is not obliged in times of depression to wait for a rising market, the advent of which is scarcely predictable with reasonable certainty, even by the reasonable man *Clery & Co. Ltd.* v. *Shott*[20a] establishes that a sale by a receiver at a very improvident time, 1941, at the best price then available is not of itself a breach of duty. For some properties a rising market never comes, but if it does, its arrival does not render an earlier sale at the best price then obtainable a breach of duty: *Casey* v. *Intercontinental Bank Ltd.*[21]

Finally, on the content of the receiver's duty of care, one should note that in *Irish Oil and Cake Mills Ltd.* v. *Donnelly*[21a] Costello J. emphatically rejected the assertion that it included a general duty "to keep the company appraised of how the business of the company is going."[21b] Further, the receiver was not obliged in the performance of his duty of care to the company to make information available to it calculated to assist it in formulating an advantageous scheme of arrangement,[21c] if that scheme remained only hypothetical. The inference is that he *would* be obliged to assist concrete proposals calculated to lead to an enhanced price. Also, the company was not entitled to demand on behalf of its directors interested in purchasing the assets any more information than would be available to another prospective purchaser.

We have seen the persons to whom the receiver's duty of care is owed include with certainty the company, a guarantor of the company's debts, second and other chargees, and, of course, the debenture holders at whose instance he is acting. What of the company's unsecured creditors? Or members of the company? Each of these groups, if there is a surplus and depending on its size, have an interest in the property within the security being disposed of to best

---

[20] This course does not reflect past practice. Even a receiver appointed by the court was discouraged from coming to it with difficulties: *Windschuegl* v. *Irish Polishes Ltd.* [1914] 1 I.R. 33.

[20a] High Court, Gavan Duffy J., May 8, 1941; unreported.

[21] [1979] I.R. 364.

[21a] High Court, March 27, 1983; unreported.

[21b] *Ibid.* at p. 12 of the transcript.

[21c] For schemes of arrangement, see Chap. 9 at pp. 289, *et seq.*

advantage, and are therefore, it might be argued, within the receiver's duty of care, insofar as there is a reasonable prospect of a surplus to benefit them. A recognition of this argument would constitute merely yet another particular application of the proximity test in *Donoghue* v. *Stevenson*, and results in a potentially wider class of plaintiffs than those encompassed within the older fiduciary duty. But it gives rise to difficulties if used to support a claim for damages for breach of duty, since it duplicates a claim by the company itself.[22] The unsecured creditors' and members' complaint is that the company has suffered, and through it indirectly themselves. There is only one set of damages, and it would seem that the company is the proper plaintiff to claim them, through its liquidator or board of directors if winding up has not supervened. It is to be noted that Lord Denning M.R. in *Standard Chartered Bank Ltd.* v. *Walker*[23] left open the position of the general creditors. This constraint does not necessarily apply where there is an attempt only to restrain by injunction an apprehended breach of duty by a receiver. In *Lambert Jones Estates Ltd.* v. *Donnelly*[24] the plaintiffs seeking to restrain the receiver from acting as he wished included not only the company itself, but also a minority shareholder in it, chargees of the majority shareholding in the company, some unsecured creditors of the company, and its directors.

Avoidance of floating charges

The avoidance of floating charges under sections 288 and 289 of the Companies Act 1963 is dealt with in Chapter 16, *Liquidations* at pp. 511 *et seq.*

---

[22] This topic is discussed in Chap. 2 at pp. 55 *et seq*, and in Chap. 7 at pp. 202–204 *et seq., supra.*
[23] [1982] 1 W.L.R. 1410.
[24] See n. 19, *supra.*

Chapter 15: The Charges Register and Other Disclosures

Throughout this book[1] and the companies legislation there will be found occasions when some document or information has to be filed in the Companies Registry. One of the most prominent is the duty to file annual accounts and related statements, which, as we saw in Chapter 11, is soon to be extended to private limited companies. The efficacy of that disclosure was questioned in that Chapter. In this Chapter we concentrate on other prominent disclosures, through the Companies Registry and otherwise, not dealt with elsewhere in this book.

The annual return

We take first annual returns, considered by officialdom to be so important that a power summarily to strike off a company failing to make them for three consecutive years was granted to the Registrar of Companies by the Companies (Amendment) Act 1982.[2] Some of the information designed to be elicited by this annual chore is irrelevant; some is misleading; and some is duplicated by other enactments.

Once upon a time it was vital that a creditor should be able to find out who a company's members were, but the identity of members and their creditworthiness became insignificant, save in respect of partly paid shares, after the advent of limited liability in 1855.[3] Yet we still find that the annual return of every company must give the

---

[1] *e.g.* the discussion of constructive notice at pp. 148 *et seq.*, the description of a company secretary's duties at pp. 106 *et seq.*, returns in connection with the allotment of share capital (at pp. 312 *et seq.*), and receiverships (at pp. 430n, 438). For a trenchant reappraisal of the disclosure idea and the way it works, see Sealy, "The 'Disclosure Philosophy and Company Law Reform," (1981) 2 Co. Law 51, and Sealy, *Company Law and Commercial Reality*, London, 1984, at pp. 21 *et seq.*

[2] 1982 Act, s.12. See also s.311, as amended by 1982 Act, s.11.

[3] This story is told in Chap. 2: *Incorporation and its Consequences* at pp. 18 *et seq.*

names and addresses of all members of the company, and of all those who have ceased to be members since the last return.[4] Before the 1982 Act[5] it was necessary to give these persons occupations too, an aid to the mid-19th century creditor in deciding whom to sue. The changed world is further recognised by exonerating public companies from specifying and distinguishing between shares transferred by persons who are still members and by those who have ceased to be members, as private companies must.[6] These criticisms of the public register are not addressed to the company's own register of members[7] which it is obliged to keep at its registered office, and to allow members to inspect.[8] In larger companies, this right may be important to a member wishing to muster votes in general meeting,[9] and in all companies this internal register determines membership itself, as we have seen.[10]

Another main concern of the annual return is the company's share capital.[11] We have seen how unimportant in practice share capital as a source of finance is for most companies, and how for them concentration by the Companies Acts upon it is a false premise.[12] Worse, the layout[13] of the return as it will appear on file highlights the company's *authorised* capital, a purely potential item.[14] The uninitiated, not realising that they must pursue the matter down the columns to issued capital, may be deceived as to the company's worth. And, in any event, even issued share capital is far from being an indication of worth, or creditworthiness. The separate disclosure of the current state of a company's share capital by means of an annual return will become otiose once all limited companies become obliged to place their accounts on public file.[15]

Next,[16] the annual return requires to be disclosed "the total amount of the indebtedness of the company," but only in respect of "all mortgages and charges which are required to be registered with

---

[4] s.125; Sched. 5, para. 5.

[5] 1982 Act, s.20.

[6] s.125(1)(*d*). Also, companies which have given full particulars as required by Sched. 5, para. 5 for five years need not thereafter distinguish transfers by persons remaining members as a separate item: s.125(1)(*c*).

[7] s.116, *et seq.*

[8] s.119. The public too may inspect it.

[9] See pp. 105–6, *supra.*

[10] See pp. 185 *et seq., supra.*

[11] s.125; Sched. 5, para. 3.

[12] See pp. 303 *et seq., supra.*

[13] See Sched. 5, Part II.

[14] See p. 303, *supra.*

[15] See pp. 356 *et seq., supra.*

[16] s.125; Sched. 5, para. 4.

the registrar of companies," *i.e.* most debts owing to its secured creditors. These depend for their validity upon being recorded on public file in the Companies Registry, a topic discussed in full below under the heading *Registration of charges*. That the total currently owing should be disclosed may be useful to persons proposing to deal with the company, but it is no longer the case that secured debts can be categorised as the sole major threat to potential unsecured creditors about to deal with a company. State claims in respect of unpaid taxes and social insurance contributions, some of which rank as preferential debts[17] in a liquidation, have the potential to bring down many an enterprise. If secured debts should be disclosed, so should these. When publication of accounts becomes compulsory for limited companies, total indebtedness will truly be disclosed.

The annual return duplicates other obligations. Companies legislation already has a system whereby particulars of a company's first directors and secretary, and subsequent changes, must be notified to the registrar.[18] Yet the annual return requires this information too.[19] Similarly, every company must have a registered office, and notify changes in its situation to the registrar.[20] Yet the annual return requires the same information to be repeated.[21]

A conclusion which might be drawn from this discussion is that the annual return might usefully be scrapped for limited companies obliged to file their accounts, *i.e.* most companies after the coming into force of the 1985 Bill, and that it be remodelled for others to seek more pertinent information.[22]

A company's annual return, signed by a director and the secretary must be sent to the registrar of companies within 60 days after its *a.g.m.*[23] The accounts and financial statements of companies obliged to file them must be annexed to it.[24] A private company must send with its annual return a certificate[25] signed by a director and the secretary certifying that it has not since the last return (or since incorporation, if it be the first return) issued any invitation to the public to subscribe for any shares or debentures of the company; also, if the return discloses that the members of the company exceed the limit of

[17] For a general description of preferential claims, see p. 502, *infra*.
[18] s.195; 1982 Act, s.3 and s.8.
[19] s.125; Sched. 5, para. 6.
[20] s.113, as amended by 1982 Act, s.4; 1982 Act, s.3(1)(*c*).
[21] s.125; Sched. 5, para. 1.
[22] s.126 deals with annual returns of companies not having a share capital.
[23] s.127.
[24] s.128. See Chap. 11: *Accounts and Auditors* at p. 356.
[25] s.129.

50, the certificate must state that the excess is composed of employees and certain former employees allowed to be excluded from the total.[26]

Registered office

Every company must at all times have a registered office, and notify changes to the registrar of companies.[27] The registered office is a place for the receipt of communications and notices; in particular, any document required to be served on a company, such as the process of a court, may be served by being left at the registered office (as recorded on its file in the companies registry) or by being sent by post to it.[28] The registered office is not necessarily a company's place of business; indeed, many companies choose the offices of their solicitor or accountant as their registered office.

Register of directors and secretaries

A company is obliged[29] to keep a register of its directors and secretaries, containing certain particulars about them including former names and, in the case of a director, his residential address, other directorships,[30] business occupation (if any) and nationality, if not Irish. This last requirement must in the case of EEC nationals have succumbed to the Treaty of Rome which does not permit discrimination on the grounds of nationality againt nationals of fellow member States.[31]

These names and particulars should be available on the company's file at the Companies Registry; any changes must be sent within 14 days to the registrar of companies.[32] The register is also to be open to the inspection of the public for at least two hours in each day at the company's registered office.[33]

Register of directors' and secretaries' shareholdings

By section 190 of the Companies Act 1963 every company, other than a private company of which all the members are directors,

---

[26] See s.33(1)(*b*).

[27] s.113, as amended by 1982 Act, s.4; see also 1982 Act, s.3(1)(*c*).

[28] s.2(1); s.379 and R.S.C., Ord. 9, r. 7.

[29] s.195, as amended by 1982 Act, s.8.

[30] Unless a directorship of a wholly-owned subsidiary, or of a wholly-owning holding company or of a wholly-owned fellow subsidiary: s.195(3).

[31] Treaty of Rome, Art. 7.

[32] s.195(6), as amended by the 1982 Act, s.8. First directors will have been notified to him in the formation process: 1982 Act, s.3. For a possible consequence of these disclosures of officers, see p. 150, *supra*.

[33] s.195(9).

must keep a register showing in relation to each of its directors (including a person in accordance with whose directions or instructions the directors of a company are accustomed to act) and secretaries the shares and debentures in it and other related companies held by, or beneficially for, him or any spouse or child of his. The related companies are the company's subsidiary, holding company or fellow subsidiary company. The interests to be declared are comprehensively defined. A person's beneficial interest includes not only securities held through a nominee but also a limited, reversionary or contingent interest, or an interest as the object of a discretionary trust, or an interest held by him through any body corporate accustomed to act in accordance with his directions or instructions, or in respect of which he controls one-third or more of the voting power in general meeting. The register is not public; it is open to the inspection only of members and debenture holders of the company, being designed for their protection.

Were it not for this register, directors and secretaries could hide their holdings from fellow members by means of nominee[34] and other indirect holdings. Thus disguised they could, inspired by inside information, deal in their securities to the disadvantage of those with whom they are dealing. That the purpose of this register is the discouragement through disclosure of such dealings appears from section 190(2) by which a transaction in shares and debentures on the register must likewise be recorded, including its date and the consideration for it; this purpose appears also from the pre-legislative history of the section.[35] The register may also serve as an aid to the enforcement of fiduciary duties.[36]

The system set up by section 190 has serious defects. Those suffering from insider dealings are not necessarily coterminous with those entitled to inspect the register; if insider dealing has involved a breach of fiduciary duty, the company not the sufferer is the proper plaintiff; insider dealing is by no means confined to directors and secretaries; and the criminal sanctions are slight.[37-38]

There is not yet in Ireland a system of disclosure of all substantial beneficial interests in shares,[39] nor a code specifically having the

---

[34] For nominee holdings, see pp. 102–104, *supra*.

[35] *e.g.* the Cohen Committee (Cmd. 6659 of 1945, paras. 77 *et seq.*), and the Jenkins Committee (Cmd. 1749 of 1962, paras. 141 *et seq.*).

[36] For fiduciary duties and their enforcement, see Chapters 7 and 8.

[37-38] A fine not exceeding £500: s.190(5), as raised by 1982 Act, Sched. 1.

[39] Such as that imposed by the Companies Act 1967 [*U.K.*], s,33.

purpose of outlawing, punishing and providing compensation for loss suffered through all insider dealings.[40]

Business letters and place of business

A company's business letters must contain a nucleus of information about it. Its name must appear[41]; also the names of its directors, their former names and nationality (if not Irish)[42]; its place of registration and the number with which it is registered, the address of its registered office, the fact, if it has been exempted from the obligation to use "limited" or "teoranta" as part of its name,[43] that it is in reality a limited company and the fact that it is being wound up, if that be the case, must also be stated; likewise, if it is in receivership.[44a]

A company must conspicuously display its name on the outside of every office or place in which its business is carried on,[45] and have its name "engraven in legible characters on its seal."[46]

Iris Oifigiúil

The fact that certain documents have been delivered to the registrar of companies and that certain documents have been issued by him must be published in Iris Oifigiúil, the efficacy of which as a means of communication we have already noted.[47] Regulation 9 of the European Communities (Companies) Regulations 1973 lists such documents, and so does section 55 of the Companies (Amendment) Act 1983, the latter applying only to public limited companies. It is understood that the companies registry, without being obliged to do so, itself undertakes the publication of these notices.

Resolutions

Section 143 of the Companies Act 1963, as expanded in 1982 and 1983[48] requires certain resolutions to be filed with the registrar of

---

[40] For attempts towards such a code, see the measures introduced by the Companies Act 1967 [*U.K.*], s.25, and the Companies Act 1980 [*U.K.*], Pt. V.

[41] s.114(1)(*c*). This obligation applies also to such commercial documents as invoices, bills of exchange, orders for goods *etc.*

[42] s.196. For an objection to the requirement that nationality be stated, see p. 447, *supra*.

[43] s.24, as amended by 1983 Act, s.58.

[44] European Communities (Companies) Regulations [S.I. No. 163 of 1973], reg. 9. These obligations also apply to "order forms."

[44a] s. 317.

[45] s.114(1)(*a*).

[46] s.114(1)(*b*).

[47] See p. 154, *supra*.

[48] 1982 Act, s.5; 1983 Act, s.20(6) and Sched. 1, para. 15.

companies. We have seen how the fulfilment of this requirement may affect the ostensible authority of a company's agents.[49] Here we briefly note the ambit of the disclosure of resolutions. Almost all board resolutions fall outside it. The exceptions are board resolutions changing the status of the company, and some board resolutions affecting its share capital. Those changing the status are resolutions passed by a public company already in existence, or in the process of formation when the 1983 Act came into force, opting to apply for the new plc status,[50] and, rarer, board resolutions changing a plc to some other form in the event of its allotted share capital having fallen below the authorised minimum upon its having been obliged to cancel share capital in which it had a beneficial interest.[51] The board resolutions affecting share capital which must be filed are those by which the board defines the terms of issue of its unissued share capital, a function which articles sometimes delegate to the board. In that event, such resolutions may rank as resolutions attaching rights or restrictions to any share, or resolutions varying such rights or restrictions, or resolutions classifying any unclassified share, or resolutions converting shares of one class into shares of another class, each of which were added to section 143[52] as resolutions to be filed by section 5 of the 1982 Act. Usually, however, articles leave these functions in relation to unissued share capital to the general meeting.[53]

Only four types of ordinary resolution in general meeting must be filed. They are resolutions in general meeting affecting the directors' authority to allot shares,[54] resolutions that a company go into creditors' voluntary liquidation,[55] resolutions affecting unissued share capital required to be filed by section 5 of the 1982 Act, and described above, and resolutions increasing a company's share capital.[56] This last category duplicates information which a company is in any event bound to provide to the registrar under section 70 of the Companies Act 1963.[57]

Most resolutions to be filed are those needing a special majority in

---

[49] See p. 150, *supra.*
[50] 1983 Act, s.12(3) and Sched. 1, para. 15.
[51] *Ibid.* s.43 and Sched. 1, para. 15.
[52] As s.143(4)(*f*) to (*i*).
[53] *e.g.* Table A, art. 2.
[54] 1983 Act, s.20(6).
[55] s.143(4)(*e*); s.251(1)(*c*). For creditors' voluntary liquidations, see pp. 472 *et seq. infra.* The rare resolution under s.251(1)(*a*) terminating the life of a company of fixed duration, or whose existence is to be terminable on a stipulated event, also qualifies.
[56] s.143(4)(*d*).
[57] See also s.69 which requires information about such topics as the consolidation sub-division, cancellation, *etc.* of shares to be communicated to the registrar.

general meeting or in a class meeting, or agreements in lieu ranking as such resolutions.[58] Prominent examples are special resolutions in general meeting,[59] special resolutions passed at meeting of shareholders of a particular class sanctioning a variation in their class rights or the written consents of a like number,[60] and resolutions passed by members of a company, or any class of them, agreeing to a compromise or arrangement pursuant to section 201 of the Companies Act 1963.[61]

Statements in lieu of prospectus

A statement in lieu of prospectus must be filed with the registrar of companies either when a private company is in the process of transforming itself into an *unlimited* public company,[62] or when a company has been formed as an *unlimited* public company with a share capital and has not issued a prospectus on formation, or, if it has, has not proceeded with allotment on the basis of it.[63] The filing of a statement in lieu of prospectus is thus a rare event. The content of a statement in lieu of prospectus is similar to the compulsory contents of a prospectus, and is designed to elicit answers to similar questions.[64] It acts as a safeguard to the public at times when the company is free to allot shares to anyone, but would not, if it were to do so, be acting on the basis of a current published prospectus.

REGISTRATION OF CHARGES

The compulsory publication by a company of security interests created by it over its assets is one of the few disclosures which may be valuable to persons dealing with the company. We have such a system of registration in sections 99 *et seq.* of the Companies Act 1963. Section 99 contains a list of charges in respect of which it declares:

" . . . every charge created . . . by a company, and being a

---

[58] s.143(4)(*a*), (*b*), (*c*).

[59] See p. 63, *supra.*

[60] *e.g.*, in accordance with 1983 Act, s.38.

[61] See pp. 289 *et seq., supra.*

[62] s.35, as amended by 1983 Act, Sched. 1, para. 6.

[63] s.54, as curtailed by 1983 Act, s.7, and as amended by 1983 Act, Sched. 1, para. and see the restrictions on the commencement of business and the exercise of borrowing powers in s.115, as amended by 1982 Act, Sched. 1, para. 14.

[64] For a discussion of the contents of a prospectus and the obligation to issue one, see Chap. 12. For the specific content of a statement in lieu of prospectus, see Sched. 2 nd Sched. 4.

charge to which this section applies, shall, so far as any security on the company's property or undertaking is conferred thereby, be void against the liquidator and any creditor of the company, unless the prescribed particulars of the charge verified in the prescribed manner, are delivered to or received by the registrar of companies for registration in manner required by this Act within 21 days after the date of its creation, but without prejudice to any contract or obligation for repayment of the money thereby secured, and when a charge becomes void under this section, the money secured thereby shall immediately become payable."

The duty to register section 99 charges is placed by section 100 on the company itself, failure being visitable by a fine not exceeding £500[1] on it and every officer in default, but since the major sanction against failure to register a section 99 charge is the avoidance of any security afforded by it section 100 allows any person interested in it to effect the registration.

Sections 101 and 102 extend the duty to register to certain charges *not* created by the company, namely existing charges on property acquired by the company and judgment mortgages affecting any property of the company. Here, by contrast, the only sanctions for failure to effect registration with the registrar of companies is a fine not exceeding £500.[2] The security is not avoided by non-registration, as it is in section 99. Section 99 applies only to the following charges:

"(*a*) a charge for the purpose of securing any issue of debentures; (*b*) a charge on uncalled share capital of the company; (*c*) a charge created or evidenced by an instrument which, if executed by an individual, would require registration as a bill of sale; (*d*) a charge on land, wherever situate, or any interest therein, but not including a charge for any rent or other periodical sum issuing out of land; (*e*) a charge on book debts of the company; (*f*) a floating charge on the undertaking or property of the company; (*g*) a charge on calls made but not paid; (*h*) a charge on a ship or any share in a ship; (*i*) a charge on goodwill on a patent or a licence under a patent, on a trade mark or on a copyright or a licence under a copyright."

We turn to consider the section 99 system in greater detail. If full disclosure is the ideal behind section 99, the present system falls short of it. Such an ideal system would allow the person who is about

---

[1] Penalty increased by Sched. 1, 1982 Act.
[2] Penalty increased by Sched. 1, 1982 Act.

to become a creditor, whether secured or unsecured, of the company to know the extent to which there are already in existence secured claims which will take priority over him if a liquidation were then to supervene. Such a system would thus be obliged to cover *all* security interests affecting all the property of the company, and would assure potential creditors that they would be deferred only to what was revealed to them on the register before perfecting their securities, or giving credit, as the case may be.[3] The present system does not fully attain these ideals, as we shall see, but is not necessarily to be criticised for failing to do so in all respects. The price of idealism is sometimes impracticability.

Not all security interests

The first objection was that not all security interests created by a company are covered by section 99. The chief among these is that section 99(2)(*d*) has been interpreted as not requiring the registration of equitable liens over land.[4] *Lien* is merely a generic term employed loosely, covering a variety of legal creatures. Some of them could not be described as "charges" at all, being only personal and passive rights to retain possession of chattels until certain money due to the person exercising the lien has been paid.[5] But those under discussion here, the non-possessory equitable liens over land, chiefly the purchasers' lien and the unpaid vendor's lien, are in essence equitable charges[6] with similar remedies.[7] In their juridical justification they do not differ perceptibly from equitable mortgages by deposit. They and equitable mortgages by deposit each are created by an act to which the company is party; each results in a charge; in neither is the charge expressly created by the parties: yet in one, the mortgage by deposit, the charge is registrable, but in the others not. On what grounds then do they escape? They are said to fall outside section 99 as not being "*created . . . by a company,*" in words of that

---

[3] An ideal system would also disclose to the world the limits (if any) on a floating chargor's ability to create subsequent interests having priority over the floating charge. This topic is discussed, and suggestions made, under the heading *Negative pledge clauses*, in Chap. 14.

[4] *i.e.* they are held to fall outside s.99(2)(*d*).

[5] Crossley Vaines, *Personal Property*, (3rd ed., 1962), p. 361. The solicitors' general lien is an example: *Brunton* v. *Electrical Engineering Corp.* [1892] 1 Ch. 434; so is the bankers' general lien: *Re Farm Fresh Frozen Foods Ltd.* (High Court, Keane, J., June 23, 1980, unrep.), discussed *infra* at pp. 465–466, 470–471.

[6] *Tempany* v. *Hynes* [1976] I.R. 110, 114 (Supreme Court), following Lord Cranworth in *Rose* v. *Watson* (1864) 10 H.L. Cas. 672, 683–684.

[7] *Rose* v. *Watson*, n. 6 *supra*; *Re Stucley* [1906] 1 Ch. 67.

section. Instead, as in the case of all liens, they are said to arise "by operation of law," an anomalous fiction, since liens arise from acts *inter partes* and are far removed from the main area in which the law imposes proprietary rights by operation of law, namely occasions when the law finds itself obliged to define the proprietary conse-quences of a change, usually involuntary, in the quality of a prop-erty-owning legal personality, such as its disappearance through death or diminution through bankruptcy. How very far removed are liens from that type of situation, particularly those under discussion here. Of them, the purchaser's lien arises as an equitable charge over the property of a vendor for the amount of any deposit (with interest) which the purchaser has paid towards the acquisition of that property; an unpaid vendor's lien creates an equitable charge in his favour over property which he has contracted to sell to the extent of the purchase price still outstanding, and persons who have contri-buted to the discharge of this purchase price may correspondingly be subrogated to the benefit of his lien. The proposition that security interests over the property of the company created by such liens are not registrable by reason of their not being "created . . . by a com-pany" was established on tenuous grounds in English law,[8] and was thence accepted unquestioningly in Ireland: *Bank of Ireland Finance Ltd.* v. *D.J. Daly Ltd.*[9]; *Re Barrett Apartments Ltd.*[10]

In *Re Barrett Apartments Ltd.* members of the public had paid "booking deposits" for apartments which the company was to build for them on a site owned by it, but never did. Instead, it went into liquidation in such circumstances that unless the depositors were to rank as secured creditors, they would get nothing. In fact, they would be in the same plight as the company's general creditors. As the law stands, the depositors would by establishing a lien have been raised above the general creditors by a security interest of which the law requires no warning to be given to the general creditors. In the policy of the law, the price of a valid security is the giving of a warn-ing through the registration system to those who might suffer from the security's existence. It is anomalous that in the absence of such a

---

[8] *London and Cheshire Insurance Co. Ltd.* v. *Laplagrene Property Co. Ltd.* [1971] Ch. 499, purporting to follow *Brunton* v. *Electrical Engineering Corp.* n. 5 *supra*, which concerned a possessory lien outside the scheme of the Act (and impractical to include within it), and following some *obiter dicta* in *Capital Finance Co. Ltd.* v. *Stokes* [1969] 1 Ch. 261. See the contrary argument of counsel (Mr. Gavin Lightman) at [1971] Ch. 499 at pp 513–514.

[9] [1978] I.R. 79, discussed at pp. 455, 470, *infra*.

[10] High Court, Keane J., July 15, 1983, unrep.; later reversed by the Supreme Court (*Irish Times*, March 23, 1985) on the ground that no lien in fact existed in that case.

warning, the depositors should defeat those of a class whose moral claims were in no way inferior to their own, such as, say, an unpaid supplier of goods or services. Certainly, requiring the lien holder to register his security would cause him inconvenience. As McMahon J., referring to a vendor's lien, remarked in *Bank of Ireland Finance Ltd.* v. *D.J. Daly Ltd.*[11]

> "If registration were necessary, every vendor selling to a com-pany would be put to the inconvenience of having to register the unpaid vendor's lien as a matter of course on the off chance that circumstances might arise which would render it necessary for the vendor to rely on the unpaid vendor's lien."

The answer to that is: so be it, if the result produces fairness. After all, land registration systems allow for registration of contracts affecting land to protect the proposed grantee pending performance and against the rare eventuality of non-performance. Most securities too are taken on the "off chance" that they might be necessary. Only a few prove to be so. As it happened in *Re Barrett Apartments Ltd.*, the depositors failed in the Supreme Court to establish a lien on the ground that an essential prerequisite to a lien, a valid contract to purchase, was lacking. The deposits had been paid informally, not on the footing of a contract to acquire any interest in the site. But for this circumstance their claim to priority would have prevailed.[12]

Another gap in the requirement contained in section 99(2)(d) that charges on land or any interest therein be registered is the prob-ability that charges on the present or future proceeds of sale of land are outside this provision. In *Re Kum Tong Restaurant Dublin Ltd.*; *Byrne* v. *Allied Irish Banks Ltd.*,[13] a company had sold some land, its principal asset, and had been advanced bridging finance by a bank on the undertaking that the documents of title would be held for the bank pending completion and that there would be handed over to the bank "sufficient monies out of the proceeds of the sale to redeem

---

[11] [1978] I.R. 79, 84, echoing Brightman J. in the *London and Cheshire Insurance Co. Ltd.* case, n. 8, *supra*.

[12] Keane J. at first instance (see n. 10, *supra*.) had in an innovative judgment held that the depositors' quasi-contractual *in personam* claims to recover their deposits created corresponding liens over the site. It was innovative in that the passage the learned judge cited from the judgment of Vaughan Williams L.J. in *Whitbread and Co. Ltd.* v. *Watt* [1902] 1 Ch. 835, 838 as authority for the proposition that a proprietary lien can arise on a quasi-contractual claim in fact said that there was no need for there to be contract *that* there should be a lien before one could arise, *i.e.* there was no need for a contract of lien before the remedy of a lien was granted. Vaughan Williams L.J. did not say that there was no necessity for an initial contract of purchase (in respect of which the lien would be remedial).

[13] [1978] I.R. 446.

this bridging finance as soon as the sale [was] closed." The argument revolved mainly around the question whether the equitable charge thus created was exclusively a charge over the proceeds of sale as opposed to over the land itself, and whether if the charge was confined to the proceeds, as was found in favour of the bank, those proceeds might constitute a "book debt" owed to the company, thereby bringing about a charge over them within section 99(2)(e). Since book debts are those arising in the course of a business and, as a matter of practice are of a kind which would in the ordinary course of the business, be entered as such in well-kept books relating to the business,[14] the bank succeeded on this ground as well, and its charge was valid despite non-registration. Assumedly, if the company had been a land dealing company, the money due to it under the sale might have been a book debt. The point which was not argued in this case was that the proceeds of sale of the land might themselves for the purposes of section 99(2)(d) have been considered an interest in land. Certainly, there are authorities from different contexts suggesting this conclusion, though they are not clear cut. For example, the Irish courts have interpreted their right to assume jurisdiction over trusts "affecting land" within the jurisdiction as including trusts affecting the proceeds of sale of such land,[15] and, in an English case, *Cooper* v. *Critchley*,[16] a contract for the sale of a beneficial interest in the future proceeds of sale arising under a trust for sale of land was held to be a contract for the sale of an "interest in land" for the purposes of the English equivalent of the Statute of Frauds. Such authorities would tend to suggest that a company intending to create a fixed charge over its land will not obviate the requirements of section 99 by first ensuring that the land be vested in trustees for sale for itself, and then charging the resultant present beneficial interest in the notional future proceeds of sale. *Re Kum Tong Restaurant (Dublin) Ltd., Byrne* v. *Allied Irish Banks Ltd.*,[17] though not specifically dealing with the point, suggests the contrary, and the question therefore remains open.

Next we consider the fact that the only fixed charges on choses in action requiring registration are those falling within section 99(2)(a), (b), (e), (g), (h), (i). What of fixed charges on choses in action falling outside these categories? One prominent gap in these

---

[14] *Paul & Frank Ltd.* v. *Discount Bank (Overseas) Ltd.* [1967] Ch. 348, apparently adopted in *Re Kum Tong Restaurant (Dublin) Ltd.*, n. 13, *supra*. See generally also *Re Kent and Sussex Sawmills Ltd.* [1947] Ch. 177.

[15] *Att-Gen* v. *The Drapers' Company* [1894] 1 I.R. 185, discussing R.S.C., Ord. 11, r. 1(b). There was also land within the jurisdiction in that case.

[16] [1955] Ch. 431 but *cf. Cedar Holdings Ltd.* v. *Green* [1981] Ch. 129.

[17] [1978] I.R. 446.

requirements has often invited comment[18]: a holding company by creating a fixed charge over its shares in its subsidiary company, and by making a judicious transfer of assets to that subsidiary, may in effect create a secret charge over those assets, whatever their nature and even if such a charge would have been registrable if it had been effected directly over the assets by the company itself. This anomaly would appear to invite statutory reform, and should not be left as a temptation to the judiciary to find, contrary to the scheme of the Act, that the two companies concerned are but one.[19] There is a second prominent gap which does not, it is submitted, warrant legislative attention. Any fixed charge created over a chose in action of a type other than those described in paragraphs (*b*), (*e*), (*g*), (*h*), and (*i*) of section 99(2) escapes the registration requirements *unless* there was more than one secured creditor created by the transaction. This happens because it is generally considered, following the New Zealand Court of Appeal in *Automobile Association (Canterbury) Inc.* v. *Australasian Secured Deposits Ltd.,*[20] that the words "any issue of debentures" in section 99(*a*) are used in a collective sense and are not construed as including the singular. In view of the potentially very wide meaning of "debenture,"[21] any other interpretation would put an intolerable burden upon commerce. Take one example by way of illustration. A bank advances money to a company against a facility letter (perhaps, temporary) signed by the company and backed by a deposit of negotiable instruments or other choses in action, with a provision for the withdrawal and substitution of securities from time to time. Under the alternative interpretation, every withdrawal and substitution would demand a trip to the registry. The particulars of the property charged[22] would when

---

[18] *e.g.* Fitzgerald, (1968) *The Irish Jurist* 258; McCormack, (1984) I.L.T. 67 (an article which contains a useful summary of most of the Irish cases on registration of charges); Jenkins Committee, para. 301.

[19] For such exercises in lifting the veil of incorporation, see Chap. 2.

[20] [1973] N.Z.L.R. 417. This interpretation is also implicit in s.99(6) which proceeds upon the premise that the deposit of a negotiable instrument as security, plus an nowledgement of indebtedness, is not of itself registrable. *Aliter* if such a transaction were considered to be an "issue of debentures."

[21] "Debenture" is unhelpfully defined for the purposes of the Companies Acts by s.2 as *including* "debenture stock, bonds and any other securities of a company whether constituting a charge on the assets of the company or not." So general is the term that judicial definitions go no further than saying that it comprises any acknolwedgement of indebtedness: *British India Steam Navigation Co.* v. *I.R.C.* (1881) 7 Q.B.D. 165; *Edmonds* v. *Blaina Furnaces Co.* (1887) 36 Ch.D. 215; *Levy* v. *Abercorris Slate & Slab Co.* (1888) 37 Ch.D. 260. There may be but one obligation and one original holder, secured or unsecured: *Robson* v. *Smith* [1895] 2 Ch. 118; *Knightsbridge Estates Trust Ltd.*v. *Byrne* [1940] A.C. 613. Debenture "stock" enables public participation; the actual debt will usualy be owed to trustees for the debenture stockholders.

[22] s.103(1)(*b*).

registered in many cases be already out of date, and therefore mislead; likewise in the case of a temporary facility which has been discharged. Those dealing with the company must remain consoled by the fact that choses in action in so far as included in the all important charges on cash flow, *i.e.* floating charges generally and fixed charges on book debts, are in any event covered: section 99(2)(*e*) and (*f*).

We turn to consider chattels. Security interests over chattels are exempt from registration unless the chattel happens to be a ship[22a] (section 99(2)(*h*)), or unless the chattel is charged "for the purpose of securing any issue of debentures"[22b] (section 99(2)(*a*)), or unless they are floating charges (section 99(2)(*f*)), discussed in Chapter 14, *Floating Charges and Receivers*, or unless they are "created or evidenced by an instrument which, if executed by an individual, would require registration as a bill of sale" (section 99(2)(*c*)) under the Bills of Sale (Ireland) Acts 1879–1883. This last category requires some explanation. As the words of section 99(2)(*c*) imply, such charges, if created by companies are not independently registrable under the bills of sale legislation.[23] This legislation is designed primarily to counteract the false impression of creditworthiness given by *A* to the world through his possession of goods whilst in fact *B* has rights in relation to them. Unlike the bills of sale legislation, registrability under section 99 is confined to transactions which have given *B* rights by way of security, *i.e.* a charge. Furthermore, as with the bills of sale legislation, the rights must have depended for their creation, perfection or enforcement on some instrument, *i.e.* a document. Thus, a common law pledge brought about by simple delivery of goods falls outside the legislation, whereas a constructive delivery brought about by use of a document does.[24] Section 4 of Bills of Sale (Ireland) Act 1879 spreads its net widely in describing the documents to which the

---

[22a] *Re South Coast Boatyard Ltd., Barbour* v. *Burke,* Supreme Ct., July 31, 1980, unrep. decides that a 3-ton yacht is not a "ship." It is however a vessel and is therefore expressly excluded from the bills of sale legislation, *infra.*

[22b] For the meaning of an "issue of debentures," see text at n. 21, *supra.*

[23] The bills of sale legislation is construed as not applying to charges registrable under the Companies Acts: *Re Royal Marine Hotel, Kingstown, Ltd.* [1895] 1 I.R. 368. Debentures issued by a registered company are expressly excluded from the operation of the Bills of Sale (Ireland) Act (1879) Amendment Act 1883, the second of the two Acts comprising the legislation.

[24] *Dublin City Distillery Ltd.* v. *Doherty* [1914] A.C. 823. Likewise, a contract transferring title to goods by way of security constituted a bill of sale as an "assurance of personal chattels," (Bills of Sale (Ireland) Act 1879, s.4) despite the fact that they had been independently delivered to the chargee: *Union Paper Co. Ltd. and Another* v. *Sandyford Printers Ltd. and Others* (High Court, Barron J., April 27, 1983, unrep.). The contract, though construed as being in substance a security transaction, took the form of a sale with provisions for repayment of the purchase price.

legislation applies. In the present context, we should note that it includes assignments, transfers, declarations of trust without transfer, inventories of goods with receipts attached, receipts for purchase monies of goods, any other assurances of personal chattels, powers of attorney, authorities, or licences to take possession of personal chattels as security for any debt, and any agreement, whether intended or not to be followed by the execution of any other instrument, by which a right in equity to any personal chattels, or to any charge or security thereon, is conferred.

The most topical context in which the registrability of security interests over chattels arises is that of "retention of title" clauses. In recent years, vendors parting with the possession of goods on credit to purchasers have insisted on the inclusion of a clause in the contract of sale retaining, or granting, proprietary interests in the goods until payment for them has been received. Such clauses are called loosely "retention of title" clauses.[25] The object, of course, is an attempt to ensure that if the purchaser company gets into financial difficulties, the vendor will come out of them ahead of unsecured and preferential creditors and the holders of floating charges. We discuss here the extent to which where the purchaser is a company the interests of a vendor under a retention of title clause must be registered under section 99 to ensure their validity.

Retention of title clauses in common use differ in form, substance and complexity. As far as their registrability is concerned, one may distil two major axioms from the decided cases. First, in so far as a vendor in his claim against the company is relying upon having retained actual legal ownership of goods, he will not be defeated by non-registration. Secondly, in so far as he seeks to rely upon any other proprietary interest, registration will have been necessary. In the first case, the retention escapes section 99 because there has been no *charge*; and, in the second whatever interest is taken is invariably by way of security, and is therefore a charge. The first axiom depends upon the freedom which vendor and purchaser have under section 17 of the Sale of Goods Act 1893 to stipulate that the general property in goods sold "is transferred to the buyer at such time as the parties to the contract intended it to be transferred." Thus, in several Irish cases a simple clause retaining the general property in

---

[25] See generally Phillips and Schuster, "Reservation of Title in the Commercial Laws of England and Ireland," (1979–1980) D.U.L.J. 1 in which they brought to light *Bateman* v. *Green and King* (1868) I.R., 2 C.L. 166, 607 by which a retention of title clause was given effect by the Irish courts over a century before the *Romalpa* decision (*Aluminium Industrie Vaassen BV.* v. *Romalpa Aluminium Ltd.* [1976] I.W.L.R. 676) began the present cycle of litigation on the topic in Ireland, England and elsewhere.

the goods has been held effective without registration,[26] as has like-wise been the simple retention element in more complex clauses.[27] Let us now consider some of the limits on the efficacy of a simple retention of title clause. It only has effect as long as the goods remain identifiable: thus, title may be extinguished by their use in a manufacturing process, but remains alive until that occurs even if such a use was contemplated by the contract of sale.[28] Furthermore, if the purchaser sells the goods to a sub-purchaser, the vendor's title to them will be lost under section 25(2) of the Sale of Goods Act 1893, provided, in the terms of section 25(2), the sub-purchaser "acts in good faith" and does not have notice that the sale to him was unauthorised.[29] In fact, unless the goods sold are to be employed as fixed assets in the purchaser's business,[30] sub-sales will be contemplated and, indeed, expressly authorised. In such cases, a well-drafted clause will define the limits of the purchaser's authority to deal. It will say that the authority ceases upon notice from the vendor (without the necessity for assigning a reason), upon the appointment of a receiver over any assets of the purchaser, upon the purchaser passing a winding-up resolution or an order for winding up being made against it, upon the cessation or substantial cessation of the purchaser's business, or upon the purchaser becoming insolvent. The imposition of such limits will not prevent an appropriately qualified sub-purchaser from obtaining a clear title under section 25(2) of the Sale of Goods Act 1893, but will render it more likely that the vendor will be able to proceed in conversion against whomsoever within the purchaser company was responsible for causing it to sell the goods unauthorisedly, particularly a liquidator.[31] Also, such an unauthorised sub-sale could arguably render the original purchaser a constructive trustee of the proceeds of sale for the original vendor, thereby giving him a proprietary interest in them which does not, not being a security interest, require registration under section 99 of

---

[26] *Re Stokes & McKiernan Ltd.* (High Court, McWilliam J., December 12, 1978); *Frigoscandia (Contracting) Ltd.* v. *Continental Irish Meat Ltd.* [1982] I.L.R.M. 396; *Re Charles Dougherty & Co. Ltd.*, rep. sub nom. *Somers* v. *James Allen (Ireland) Ltd.* [1984] I.L.R.M. 437.

[27] *Re Interview Ltd.* [1975] I.R. 382; *Kruppstahl AG.* v. *Quitmann Products Ltd.* [1982] I.L.R.M. 551.

[28] *Re Charles Dougherty & Co. Ltd* n. 26, *supra.*, following *Borden (U.K.) Ltd.* v. *Scottish Timber Products Ltd.* [1981] Ch. 25 on extinguishment by manufacture. See also *South Australian Insurance Co.* v. *Randell* (1869) L.R., 3 P.C. 101.

[29] *Re Interview Ltd.* [1975] I.R. 382, 394; *Union Paper Co. Ltd. and another* v. *Sandyford Printers Ltd. and Others*, n. 24 *supra.*

[30] *Frigoscandia (Contracting) Ltd.* v. *Continental Irish Meat Ltd.* [1982] I.L.R.M. 396.

[31] A *receiver* on the other hand would have no authority to sell the goods in any event, since the equitable charge which he is realising would never have attached to them: *Re Interview Ltd.* [1975] I.R. 382.

the Companies Act 1963. The same cannot be said of attempts by a vendor to carve out proprietary interests in the proceeds of *authorised* sales, since they fall foul of the second axiom discussed below. Most retention of title clauses provide that authorised sub–sales are effected by the purchaser as a principal.[32] The possibility of an agency relationship between vendor and purchaser is expressly negatived in this way in order to avoid bringing the vendor into direct contractual relations with the sub-purchaser which would give the latter Sale of Goods Act rights against the former, particularly in respect of the quality of the goods. In *Re Stokes & McKiernan Ltd.*[33] in which there was no such express provision, McWilliam J. held that a purchaser in making an authorised sub-sale "was selling on behalf of the vendor *to the extent which money was still owing to the vendor in respect of the goods,*"[34] so that the vendor was enabled to claim title to the proceeds of sale as a consequence of the original retention of title in the goods themselves, but only to the extent that money was still owing. There is a confusion here between property and debt. If, as was the case, the sole ground of the original vendor's proprietary claim was the ownership of the goods themselves, the corresponding proprietary claim to the proceeds should have extended, if at all, to the whole of them, as it does in the case of unauthorised sub-sales. But it is unlikely that such a result was intended by the parties in the absence either of an express declaration of agency, or of trust over the proceeds, of which more below. In an express agency one would expect to find a definition of the profit element on a sub-sale attributable to the original purchaser, *i.e.* a commission.[35] Without such a definition, the more natural inference is that the purchaser is trading on his own account in entering into authorised sub-sales.[36]

To summarise the argument so far, we have seen that retaining legal title to the goods themselves does not of itself (1) bestow any

---

[32] And contain a consequential statement that title to the goods shall pass to the purchaser immediately before the acquisition of title by the sub-purchaser.

[33] See n. 26, *supra.*

[34] At p. 8 of the transcript. Italics supplied.

[35] Also one would expect to find an indemnity by the purchaser against liabilities which the agency would impose on the original vendor such as those in respect of misrepresentations made by the purchaser to the sub-purchaser.

[36] The *Romalpa* case (n. 25, *supra*) contained clauses indicative of the express agency found in that case. McWilliam J.'s judgment in *Re Stokes & McKiernan Ltd.* is overshadowed by his own doubts about it prompted by the later decision in *Re Bond Worth Ltd.* [1980] Ch. 228 and expressed by him in the *Frigoscandia* case, n. 30, *supra.* Though his doubts did not concern the implication of agency on authorised sub-sales (that point not arising in *Frigoscandia*), *Re Bond Worth Ltd.* does in fact take an attitude towards the implication of agency helpful to the view expressed in the text, *e.g.* at p. 247(B).

proprietary interest in articles which have been manufactured from those goods in such a way as to deprive the former of their separate identity; nor does it of itself (2) bestow any proprietary interest in the future proceeds of authorised sub-sales of the goods. Although an unpaid vendor may by appropriate draftsmanship in a retention of title clause obtain the proprietary interests itemised in (1) and (2), he will in doing so cross over into the territory of the second axiom (stated on p. 459, *supra*), and registration under section 99 will be necessary to ensure their validity. In fact, most vendors find it impracticable to do so. These proprietary interests may be conferred in a variety of ways. For example, the contract of sale may contain an express declaration of trust in favour of the vendor over articles ultimately to be manufactured from the goods: *Kruppstahl AG* v. *Quitmann Products Ltd.*[37]; or there may be an express assignment of rights to arise out of anticipated sub-sales: *Re Interview Ltd.*[38]; or there may be the retention of equitable ownership in the future proceeds of sub-sales or manufactured goods: *Re Bond Worth Ltd.*[39] Whatever the form adopted however, if, as will almost invariably be the case, "the accountability is limited to the extent only of the indebtedness . . . [it will as such be] . . . in the nature of a charge upon the property as a means of security . . ." *per* Gannon J. in *Kruppstahl AG* v. *Quitmann Products Ltd.*[40] Accordingly, it will require registration under section 99 of the Companies Act 1963. Charges over articles manufactured from the goods are registrable under section 99(2)(*c*) as instruments which, if executed by an individual, would require registration as a bill of sale: *Kruppstahl AG* v. *Quitmann Products Ltd.*; *Re Charles Dougherty and Co. Ltd., Somers* v. *James Allen (Ireland) Ltd.*[41]

---

[37] [1982] I.L.R.M. 551.

[38] [1975] I.R. 382.

[39] [1980] Ch. 228, in which the clause in question also reserved only an equitable interest in the goods themselves, an undesirable form upon which see below, as well as an equitable interest in the proceeds.

[40] [1982] I.L.R.M. 551, 560. See also Kenny J. in *Re Interview Ltd.* [1975] I.R. 382, 396; and the reasoning in *Re Bond Worth Ltd.*, n. 39 *supra*.

[41] [1982] I.L.R.M. 551, and [1984] I.L.R.M. 437, respectively. In neither judgment was the possibility canvassed that the charges created consisted of "transfers of goods in the ordinary course of business of any trade or calling" so as to take them altogether out of the ambit of the bills of sale legislation: s.4 of the Bills of Sale (Ireland) Act 1879. *Cf. Re Slee* (1872) L.R. 15 Eq. 69 and *Re Love* (1877) 5 Ch.D. 35. The fact that the widespread use of such clauses is a comparatively new mercantile practice does not prevent it from falling within the exception. Lord Sumner in *Dublin City Distillery Ltd.* v. *Doherty* [1914] A.C. 823, 867 said that "it is plain that the Legislature intended to save certain documents, already well known in commerce, and other which, by the usage of business, might come into existence notoriously and for the same or similar purposes." Such a mercantile practice must be proved: *ibid.* pp. 856, 857, 867; which should not be too difficult.

Charges over the future proceeds of authorised sub-sales are registrable as charges on book debts: *Re Interview Ltd.*[42]

The arrangements so far described for acquiring an interest in the proceeds of sale of the goods, or articles manufactured from them, assume that the legal title to the goods was retained until the sub-sale, or loss of identity, as the case may be. If legal title to the goods is relinquished *ab initio*, and only an equitable title to them is retained, that retention will be construed as an equitable charge: *Re Bond Worth Ltd.*[43] Furthermore, it is likely to be an equitable charge of the *floating* variety, since it leaves the original purchaser free to deal with the goods in the ordinary course of business, and is therefore registrable under section 99(2)(*f*).[44] This is an undesirable form from the point of view of the original vendor because even his interest in the goods themselves is dependent on registration; and even if his charge is registered, it runs the risk of being deferred to another floating charge which has crystallised first, and deferment to preferential creditors.[45]

Inconclusiveness of register

The Companies Act 1963 neither regulates nor creates priorities between charges registered under it. This it leaves to the ordinary principles of common law and equity, and in the case of land, to other statutes as well.[46] The Act simply imposes a consequence for non-registration, the avoidance of the security given by the charge. This abdication renders the register inconclusive. For example, a fixed legal charge of personalty created on day one and registered on day 20 will take priority over a like charge over the same subject matter created on day two and registered on day three, despite the blank searches of the second chargee. Since the function of the register is to protect those who trouble to search in it, the legislature

---

[42] [1975] I.R. 382, 396.
[43] [1980] Ch. 228, considered without disapproval in *Kruppstahl AG.* v. *Quitmann Products Ltd.* [1982] I.L.R.M. 551, 560, but it should be noted that in the latter case it was the assignment to the vendor by the purchaser of its future claims under German law over goods to be manufactured by it, which was found to create a floating charge. The other security interests created by the purchaser were found to be registrable as bills of sale, as mentioned above.
[44] *Re Bond Worth Ltd.,supra.*
[45] For floating charges and deferment to preferential creditors, see Chapter 14, *Floating Charges and Receivers.*
[46] See generally J.C.W. Wylie, *Irish Land Law,* (London, 1975), 13.127 *et seq.*

ought to make that protection effective. There are models in other jurisdictions and in land law which may serve as starting points for reform.[47]

Consequences of non-registration

Section 99 of the Companies Act 1963 results in any security conferred by an unregistered charge being void[47a] as "against the liquidator and any creditor of the company," and renders the erstwhile chargee an unsecured creditor, having a debt immediately due.

The unregistered charge void for non-registration is void even against the holder of a subsequently created registered charge who, when the latter was created, had notice of the existence of the former.[48]

Late registration

Section 106 of the Companies Act 1963 gives the court, on the application of the company or any interested person, the discretionary power to extend the time[49] for the registration of charges if it is satisfied that the omission to do so was:

> "accidental, or due to inadvertence or to some other sufficient cause, or *is not of a nature to prejudice the position of creditors* or shareholders *of the company*, or that on other grounds it is just and equitable to grant relief."[50]

It is strange that section 106 is drafted disjunctively. In view of the fact that the policy behind the requirement that charges be registered is that of warning prospective creditors, one would have thought that the avoidance of prejudice to them should in the drafting have been made paramount. Though in practice the courts in their exercise of this discretion go some way towards making good this deficiency, they do so chiefly for the benefit of secured creditors

---

[47] For comments on the Canadian and Australian reforms in this area, see L.S Sealy, *Company Law and Commercial Reality*, (London, 1984), pp. 31 *et seq.* Likewise land law models should not be confined to Ireland. See as an example the Land Charges Act 1972 [*U.K.*].

[47a] Charges registrable under ss. 101 and 102 are not void for non-registration. See p. 452, *ante*.

[48] *Re Monolithic Building Co.* [1915] 1 Ch. 643 which *per* Kenny J. "is a decision of the Court of Appeal in England that is cited with approval in all the text books of company law," and was therefore followed by him in *Re Interview Ltd.* [1975] I.R. 38 396. But contrast the Irish cases dealing with priorities in the Registry of Deeds Wylie, *op. cit.*, 3.088 *et seq.*, and the distinguishable situation in *Re Clarets Ltd., Spain v McGann*, n. 57, *infra*.

[49] The jurisdiction also extends to allowing rectification of mis-statements or omissions in the filed particulars, or in memoranda of satisfaction.

[50] Italics supplied.

and it is arguable that they should go further in the interests of unsecured creditors.

An applicant for an extension under section 106 must expect the court to insert in its order a proviso to the effect that it is to be "without prejudice to the rights of parties acquired before the actual time of registration."[51] It is accepted beyond dispute that this usual proviso extends only to rights acquired against the property of the company, *i.e.* only to security interests, and the rights of a liquidator if and after liquidation has commenced.[52] In *Re Farm Fresh Frozen Foods Ltd.*,[53] an unregistered chargee unsuccessfully sought to have this usual proviso omitted. The company had already gone into liquidation, and therefore an order containing the proviso would have been useless to the chargee since the liquidator had proprietary rights in the sense described above. Keane J. rejected this attempt at omission chiefly on the ground that the applicant's predicament was entirely his own fault, adding a comment that in any event "to register the charge at this stage without preserving the rights of intervening creditors would be entirely unjustified, having regard to the mischief which the registration sections of the Act are designed to avoid." The chargee had in fact received the company's documents of title (so as to create an equitable mortgage by deposit) on the very day that the winding up petition was presented, but in respect of an advance made to the company some 18 months before on an undertaking that the documents would forthwith be forwarded. The learned judge found that the chargee could have avoided his difficulties by entering into arrangements by which the money would have been advanced to the company only against the receipt of the documents of title, or it could have refused to make the advance until the company's agreement to deposit the documents of title had itself been registered.[54] Be all this as it may, the curious point about this case is that the application for an extension was substantively enter-

---

[51] This form is taken from *Re Clarets Ltd., Spain* v. *McGann* (High Court, Costello J., November 22, 1978, unrep.), a form habitual, with minor variations in syntax, since *Re Joplin Brewery Co. Ltd.* [1902] 1 Ch. 79. It is generally considered wiser to adopt the slightly amended form of proviso used in *Watson* v. *Duff, Morgan and Vermont (Holdings) Ltd.* [1974] 1 W.L.R. 450 in order to protect subsequent chargees whose charges were created within 21 days after the creation of the charge for which the extension is to be granted. The "actual time of registration" is not to be equated with the time at which the particulars of the charge are lodged with the registrar for registration: *Re Telford Motors Ltd.* (High Court, Hamilton J. January 27, 1978, unrep.).

[52] *Re Spiral Globe Co. Ltd.* [1902] 1 Ch. 396 and *Re Ehrmann Bros. Ltd.* [1906] 2 Ch. 97, each followed in *Re Telford Motors Ltd.*, n. 51 *supra*.

[53] High Court, Keane J., June 23, 1980, unrep.

[54] *Alexander Hull & Co. Ltd.* v. *O'Carroll Kent & Co. Ltd* (1955) 89 I.L.T.R. 70; *Re O'Carroll Kent & Co. Ltd.* (1955) 89 I.L.T.R. 72.

tained at all. Some English authority goes so far as to suggest that the applicant will be non-suited if liquidation has supervened.[55] The case also implies that the usual proviso might in some exceptional circumstances be omitted, at any rate if the delay has not been the applicant's fault.

The usual proviso is intended to defer the late registered charge to any creditors whose charges over the company's property have been registered before it, even if they were created subsequently. It is immaterial that the subsequent chargee might have known of the prior unregistered charge.[56] But where the subsequent charge is expressly by its terms made subject to the rights given by a prior charge, earlier registration of the later charge will not diminish those rights provided that the earlier charge eventually becomes registered: *Re Clarets Ltd., Spain* v. *McGann*.[57] The usual proviso in such a case does not serve to promote the rights of such a second chargee.

What safeguards are accorded to the *unsecured* creditor in an application under section 106? In *Re International Retail Ltd.*,[58] Kenny J. stated that it was the invariable practice of the courts in Ireland and England on a section 106 application:

> "to require evidence that no winding up of the company is pending or contemplated and that no judgments have been recovered against it which are unpaid before extending the time for registration."[59]

Further, Kenny J. pointed out that if a winding up is in contemplation an order for extension, if granted, should reserve liberty to the liquidator to apply to have the extension order discharged.[60] A similar line was taken by Dixon J. in *Re O'Carroll Kent Ltd.*,[61] and by Hamilton J. in *Re Telford Motors Ltd.*[62]

Should the courts go further than this in an attempt to protect the interests of unsecured creditors? In England, the courts do not investigate the solvency as such of the company, and in *Re International Retail Ltd.*, Kenny J. expressly stated that the solvency or otherwise

---

[55] *Re Resinoid and Mica Products Ltd.* (1967) 111 S.J. 654 (English Court of Appeal *per* Lord Denning M.R.); others, *e.g. Re S. Abrahams & Sons Ltd.* [1902] 1 Ch. 695 and *Re Mechanisations (Eaglescliffe) Ltd.* [1966] Ch. 20, 36, admit the possibility of there being "very exceptional cases."

[56] See n. 48, *supra.*

[57] High Court, Costello J., November 22, 1978, unrep.

[58] High Court, July 26, 1974, unrep.

[59] At p. 3 of the transcript, following *Re Bootle Cold Storage Co.* (1901) W.N.39.

[60] Following *Re L.H. Charles & Co.* (1935) W.N. 15.

[61] (1955) 89 I.L.T.R. 72.

[62] High Court, January 27, 1978, unrep; at pp. 4–5 of the transcript.

of the company was not a ground of his decision. In Australasia there is a different approach. As Street J. said in *Re Dudley Engineering Pty. Ltd.*,[63] "it is relevant to take into account in the exercise of a wide discretion such as is conferred by [s.106] the solvency or insolvency of the company and the possible or probable effect of the grant of an extension upon the interests of unsecured creditors . . . ," but solvency or the lack of it was not to be the "governing consideration"; it was "but one of the overall complex of facts upon which the court must exercise its discretion . . . ." In fact, one may endorse this latter view by reflecting that there are circumstances where even if the company is insolvent, registration should not thereby necessarily be refused. Fresh money may have been put up by the applicant on condition of receiving a corresponding charge. Or, an unsecured creditor who did not actually make use of the system by making a search in the Registry before giving credit might find it difficult to show that he had suffered sufficient prejudice to warrant his special protection.

The measures taken to protect unsecured creditors in Australasia depend upon the circumstances. In *Re Flinders Trading Co. Pty. Ltd.*,[64] for example, an extension order was after investigation made without prejudice to the rights of particular unsecured creditors only. But whatever the ultimate outcome it is generally accepted that unsecured creditors have a right to be heard,[65] and advertisements are ordered to bring the proceedings to their attention.[66] Such a right to be heard is in accordance with the spirit of Irish constitutional jurisprudence.

As an alternative to applying for an extension of time for registration, a chargee whose charge is void for non-registration may instead take and duly register a fresh charge, if liquidation has not supervened and if the borrower is co-operative. Such a fresh charge would not, of itself, be a fraudulent preference.[67] It would, of course, be deferred to superior charges created before it, and after the void charge, and duly registered.

What the unregistered chargee should *not* do, unless he is happy about the prospect of being indicted on a charge of forgery, is falsely

---

[63] [1968] 1 N.S.W.R. 483. The Australian decisions mentioned in the text are, with others and decisions from New Zealand, discussed in Paterson, Ednie and Ford, *Australian Company Law* (3rd ed.).

[64] (1978) 3 A.C.L.R. 218 (Supreme Court of South Australia).

[65] *Commercial Banking Co. of Sydney Ltd.* v. *George Hudson (Pty.) Ltd.* (1973) 47 A.J.L.R. 732; 2 A.L.R. 1 (High Court of Australia).

[66] *Re Flinders Trading Co. (Pty.) Ltd.*, n. 64, *supra*.

[67] *Re Tweedale* [1892] 2 Q.B. 367, followed in Ireland in *Re Oliver* [1914] 2 I.R. 356. For fraudulent preferences, see Chap. 16, *Liquidations* at pp. 504 *et seq*.

to date the unregistered charge with a date which makes the date of lodgment appear to fall within 21 days of its creation, with the object of misleading the Registrar, and so obtaining a certificate of registration which section 104 of the Companies Act 1963 declares to be "*conclusive evidence* that the requirements of this Part[68] as to registration have been complied with." That the courts will not go behind that certificate is illustrated by *Lombard and Ulster Banking (Ireland) Ltd.* v. *Amurec Ltd.*[69] There was no suggestion of fraud, forgery, or deliberate wrongdoing in that case, nor is there here. In *Amurec*, a liquidator was prevented by the conclusiveness of the registrar's certificate from questioning the registration of a charge in respect of which 17 months had elapsed between its execution and its lodgment for registration. The charge had been left undated at its creation, and a much later date inserted shortly before its lodgment.[70] In coming to his decision, Hamilton J. relied on English cases[71] which, on identical statutory provisions, emphasised the importance commercially of the register being truly conclusive, as the policy of the Act intended. But these English cases have recently been by-passed at first instance in England by *R.* v. *Registrar of Companies, ex p. Esal (Commodities) Ltd.*[72] which for the first time[73] allowed judicial review of the registrar's certificate, despite its statutory conclusiveness. The registrar had erroneously accepted a form out of time in substitution for a defective form delivered within the time limit, and certiorari lay to correct him. Would the registrar's certificate in *Amurec* have yielded to judicial review? Certainly, the armoury of arguments in support of the susceptibility of administrative decisions to review is nowadays well-stocked to the point of overflow. For example, one might say that the registrar in purporting to register the charge acted beyond his jurisdiction because there was no charge to register, it having been avoided 21 days after its creation,[74] or that its registration was reviewable as a decision taken on

---

[68] Pt. IV of the Companies Act 1963; italics supplied.

[69] High Court, Hamilton J., December 10, 1976, unrep.

[70] Even if the charge had been executed in escrow, the insertion of the later date would have been impermissible: *Alan Estates Ltd.* v. *W.G. Stores Ltd.* [1981] 3 W.L.R. 892.

[71] Chiefly *National Provincial and Union Bank of England* v. *Charnley* [1924] 1 K.B. 431; *Re Eric Holmes (Property) Ltd.* [1965] Ch. 1052; and *Re C.L. Nye Ltd.* [1971] 1 Ch. 442.

[72] *The Times*, November 26, 1984.

[73] Emboldened by *Anisminic Ltd.* v. *Foreign Compensation Commission* [1969] 2 A.C. 147 and *O'Reilly* v. *Mackman* [1983] 2 A.C. 237.

[74] A similar argument was taken by counsel (Mr. H. Barron) in *Amurec*, but *inter partes*, and not in support of judicial review which was not invoked. For jurisdictional errors, see H.W.R. Wade, *Administrative Law* (5th ed., Oxford, 1982), Chap. 9.

the basis of inadequate facts, albeit inadvertently.[75] But the facility with which such arguments may be paraded overlooks the consequence that review will thereby follow on *any* slip from the statutory norms in the registration process, rendering the registrar's certificate uncertain and depriving section 104 of meaning. It would be better to interpret the statute as making section 104 dominant over the other registration provisions, so that in effect a registered charge is defined as one which the registrar has certified as having been registered, effectively enabling his certificate to override errors.

Where would this suggested interpretation leave persons injured by wrongful registration? Two courses of action are possible, one against the registrar, and the other against the actual applicants for wrongful registration and their agents, *e.g.* their solicitors. Each depends upon proof that the injury was a consequence of the misfeasance, an element which will usually be lacking. In particular, a plaintiff who did not search the register before advancing credit to a company could scarcely claim to have been prejudiced by the omission of a charge later wrongly registered. The cause of action against the registrar would be founded on breach of statutory duty.[76] Whether that duty is absolute or not has yet to be decided.[77] The cause of action against the applicants and their agents depends upon the ordinary principles of tort, *i.e.* actions based on deceit or negligence may be appropriate, depending on the circumstances.[78]

It is sometimes suggested that the acceptance by the court of the registration in the *Amurec* case was unconstitutional because the unsecured creditors were thereby prevented from vindicating their rights,[79] a question not canvassed by the court. This charge cannot be answered by asserting that the registrar in giving his certificate was exercising "limited functions and powers of a judicial nature" permitted by Article 37 of the Constitution, since that answer would itself suppose that the liquidator and unsecured creditors should have been entitled to address representations to him.[80] Perhaps the

---

[75] Wade, *op. cit.*, p. 295.

[76] Examples in Wade, *op. cit.*, pp. 666 *et seq.*

[77] In *Ministry of Housing and Local Government* v. *Sharp* [1970] 2 Q.B. 223, the duty of a registrar of local land charges was found on the interpretation of the relevant statutes not to be absolute but to be one of exercising due diligence. However, the judgment of Lord Denning M.R. is a good starting point for the construction of an absolute duty on the registrar of companies. In addition to the duties imposed on the registrar by ss.103 *et seq.*, see the rights and duties conferred and imposed by Pt. XIII.

[78] The possibility of an action for deceit was mentioned by Russell L.J. in *Re C.L. Dye Ltd.*, n. 71, *supra*.

[79] Art. 40, s.3. *Maher* v. *Att.-Gen.* [1973] I.R. 140 concerned Art. 38 (criminal charges) and is not material here.

[80] *e.g. Re Haughey* [1971] I.R. 217.

short answer is that the registrar did nothing to affect the rights as such of these persons: the registration merely made those rights worth less, a traditional answer in company law.[81]

Another line of approach adopted by unregistered chargees is to attempt to find that there has arisen within the failed transaction some other security interest which remains alive because it was not susceptible of registration. We have seen that security interests arising by operation of law, chiefly liens, do not require registration. Accordingly, much legal ingenuity is employed to establish that a lien has arisen in favour of a lender whose *inter partes* security has not been properly taken, and thus to defeat the scheme of the Act. In *Bank of Ireland Finance Ltd.* v. *D.J. Daly Ltd.*,[82] the lender had advanced money to the company for the purpose of enabling it to buy certain land, it being agreed that the documents of title of the land would be deposited with the lender by way of equitable mortgage. Such a deposit was never made. If it had been, and if the security thereby created had remained unregistered, the lender would not have succeeded in its argument that it was entitled to be subrogated to the vendor's lien over the land acquired because the lender would have obtained everything which the contract of loan stated that it should obtain by way of security, thereby negativing the creation or continuance of any other security interest.[83] But in this case the lending contract had not been fulfilled. In fact, two other security interests in favour of the lender were extracted from the transaction. First, it was held, as is well established, that the *agreement* to deposit itself created an equitable charge in favour of the lender.[84] Such a charge would itself require registration, and therefore provided no assistance to the lender.[85] Secondly, the lender having supplied the purchase money to discharge the vendor's right, was subrogated to the unpaid vendor's lien, and this security interest, giving marginally less than the security contemplated by the contract of loan, and not being registrable, survived.

An attempt to salvage a lien from the wreckage of an unregistered

---

[81] See Chap. 9 at pp. 282–283.

[82] [1978] I.R. 79.

[83] *Ibid.* following *Burston Finance Ltd.* v. *Speirway Ltd.* [1974] 1 W.L.R. 1648 and *Orakpo* v. *Manson Investments Ltd.* [1977] 3 W.L.R. 229. And see also *Re South Coast Boatyard Ltd., Barbour* v. *Burke* at first instance (McWilliam J., November 20, 1979 unreported) at pp. 8–9 of the transcript.

[84] Following *Ex p. Crossfield* (1840) 3 Ir. Eq. R. 67 and *Simmons* v. *Montague* [1909] I.R. 87. *Alexander Hull & Co. Ltd.* v. *O'Carroll Kent & Co. Ltd.* (1955) 89 I.L.T.R. 70 to similar effect was apparently not cited.

[85] This point is implicit in the judgment. On it see *Re O'Carroll Kent & Co. Ltd.* (1955) I.L.T.R. 72 and *Re Farm Fresh Frozen Foods Ltd.*, n. 86 *infra*.

charge failed in *Re Farm Fresh Frozen Foods Ltd.*[86] In that case, documents of title had been deposited with the bank by way of equitable mortgage, but the charge thereby created failed through non-registration. The bank's contention that the general bankers' lien over securities deposited with them by customers extended also to these documents of title failed, primarily because a deposit specifically by way of security, albeit a security deemed void *ab initio* through non-registration, constituted in effect an agreement between the parties ousting the bankers' lien. A further potential lien also failed in that case. A creditor who has taken a deposit of the company's documents of title by way of an equitable mortgage which has become void for non-registration cannot assert that the lien over the documents implicit in such an arrangement survives independently of the failed charge.[87]

---

[86] High Court, Keane J., June 23, 1980, unrep.
[87] Following *Re Molton Finance Ltd.* [1968] Ch. 325.

Chapter 16. Liquidations

The process leading towards a company's dissolution and legal death is called *winding up* or *liquidation*. It is conducted by a liquidator whose method of appointment differs with the mode of liquidation adopted. These modes are either voluntary, or by order of the court[1] (known also as compulsory winding up).

VOLUNTARY LIQUIDATION

All voluntary liquidations are begun by a resolution in general meeting.[2] The type of resolution depends upon the circumstances. An ordinary resolution suffices if a simple majority resolves that the company "cannot by reason of its liabilities continue its business,"[3] or, more rarely, if the articles have stipulated that the company is to be dissolved on the expiry of a certain period or on the occurrence of a certain event, and the period has expired or the event happened, as the case may be.[4] In all other cases there must be a special resolution.[5]

A voluntary liquidation may be either a members' voluntary winding-up[6] or a creditors' voluntary winding-up.[7] It will of necessity be of the latter type if the directors have not before the passing of the winding-up resolution made a declaration of the company's solvency.[8] Even if such a declaration has been made, it may be chal

---

[1] s.206.
[2] s.253.
[3] s.251(1)(c).
[4] s.251(1)(c), (a).
[5] s.251(1)(b). For ordinary and special resolutions, see Chap. 3, at p. 63, *supra*.
[6] ss.257–264 are of particular application.
[7] ss.265–273 are of particular application.
[8] For the contents, see s.256. s.256 has been amended by s.9 of the 1982 Act.

lenged in court by the creditors, and the winding up converted to a creditors' voluntary winding-up.[9] Furthermore, if during the currency of a members' voluntary winding-up it appears to the liquidator that the company will not be able to pay its debts in full as predicted in the declaration of solvency, he will be obliged to summon a meeting of the creditors,[10] and will thereafter report to them as well as the members on his conduct of the liquidation.[11]

In a member's voluntary winding up the liquidation is predominantly a domestic matter between the liquidator and the members. The company in general meeting appoints the liquidator,[12] fixes his remuneration and fills vacancies in his office[13]; and he reports to them through the medium of prescribed meetings.[14]

In a creditors' voluntary winding up, by contrast, the members share their role with the company's creditors, with dominance to the latter. In a creditor's winding up, the company must cause a meeting of its creditors, presided over by a director, to be held on the same day as, or the day after, the day on which the company in general meeting considers the proposal for voluntary liquidation.[15] This creditors' meeting considers statements[16] prepared by the directors of the company, covering its financial position, the identity of its creditors and the amount of their claims; it may appoint its own nominee as liquidator so as to override the appointment by the members[17]; it may fix the remuneration to be paid to the liquidator[18]; subsequent creditors' meetings may be summoned from time to time by the liquidator "for the purpose of ascertaining their

---

[9] s.256(3). The time limit is 28 days from the advertisement, pursuant to s.252, of the passing of the resolution, and the application must be supported by at least one-fifth in number or value of the creditors.

[10] s.261.

[11] s.264: through the means of the meetings he is obliged to summon under ss.272 and 273.

[12] Or liquidators, though joint liquidatorships are rare.

[13] ss.258 and 259.

[14] ss.262 and 263.

[15] s.266.

[16] s.266(3).

[17] s.267(1). If no one is nominated by the creditors, the person, if any, nominated by the members will be the liquidator. If there is a clash between the members' and the creditors' nominations, any director, member or creditor may apply to the court for an order that the members' nominee or some other person be appointed liquidator.

[18] s.269(1): if there is no committee of inspection (*infra*). Any creditor or contributory who alleges that the remuneration is excessive may apply to the court for the remuneration to be fixed: s.269(2).

wishes in all matters relating to the winding up"[19]; a meeting convened by any creditor may fill vacancies in the office of liquidator[20];
creditors' meetings will also receive the liquidator's interim account
(if any) and final account,[21] as will the members at separate meetings.[21] Any creditors' meeting may also appoint a committee of
inspection to which the Act delegates certain of what would otherwise be the creditors' functions.[22] The company in a general meeting
may nominate members of this committee, but again their nominations may be overridden by the creditors.[23]

The company's corporate status and powers survive the commencement of a voluntary winding-up, but the company must cease to
carry on its business, "except so far as may be required for the beneficial winding up thereof."[24] Thus, any authority given by the company to any person to act on its behalf in the ordinary course of its
business ceases at the resolution: *Re Tailteann Freight Services Ltd.*[25]
Included under this head is the agency of a receiver[25a] appointed out
of court by a secured creditor. But as Goulding J. said in *Sowman* v.
David Samuel Trust Ltd.[25b]:

> "Winding up deprives the receiver . . . of power to bind the
> company personally by acting as its agent. It does not in the
> least affect his powers to hold and dispose of the company's

[19] R.S.C., Ord. 74, r. 55(2). Rules 59 to 84 inclusive govern these meetings. Creditors' meetings may be asked to back the liquidation financially if the company lacks
the immediate assets to continue it, but there is the prospect of recovering more, *e.g.*
Re Custom Line Ltd., High Court, Murphy J., February 27, 1984; reported in *The Irish
Times*, February 28, 1984. For the deleterious effect on the administration of justice
arising through the lack of a "pursuit fund" for the liquidator, see the discussion on
Fraudulent trading, at pp. 527–529, *infra*.

[20] s.270: other than a liquidator appointed by, or by the direction of the court.

[21] Pursuant to ss.272 and 273 respectively.

[22] s.268. These functions given by the Act in a voluntary liquidation are (i) to fix
the remuneration of the liquidator: s.269(1); (ii) to sanction the continuance of the
directors' powers despite the appointment of a liquidator: s.269(3) (and see p. 475,
infra); (iii) to give the liquidator leave to exercise the powers contained in s.231(1)(*d*)
(*e*), (*f*); s.276(1)(*a*) (see *Duties and powers of Official liquidators, infra*); (iv) to decide the
destination of the books and papers of the company: s.305; (v) to sanction a s.260
reconstruction in a creditors' voluntary liquidation. This last function is the only one
for which a committee of inspection is necessary: the others may be exercised by the
creditors' meeting. For s.260 reconstructions in a members' voluntary liquidation, see
Chap. 9, pp. 288–289 *et seq.*

[23] s.268(2).

[24] s.254. Also by s.255 share transfers are void unless to or with the sanction of the
liquidator: this provision is designed to counter the avoidance of liability for calls.

[25] [1975] I.R. 376, 379. [25a] See Chap. 14 at pp. 435–436.

[25b] [1978] 1 W.L.R. 22, 30. The termination of the agency was established by
Gosling v. *Gaskell* [1897] A.C. 575, and the continuance of the powers *qua* security
holder by *Gough's Garages Ltd.* v. *Pugsley* [1930] 1 K.B. 615, 621.

property comprised in the [charge], including his power to use the company's name for that purpose, for such powers are given by the disposition of the company's property which it made (in equity) by the [charge] itself."

On the appointment of a liquidator in a voluntary winding up, the liquidator represents the company as its agent,[26] and all powers of the directors cease, except to the extent that in a members' winding-up the liquidator or the company in general meeting shall have sanctioned their continuance, or in a creditors' winding-up such a sanction shall have been obtained from the committee of inspection, or, if none, from the creditors' meeting.[27]

The liquidator's primary duty is briefly encapsulated in section 276(2) which states that the liquidator "shall pay the debts of the company and shall adjust the rights of the contributories[28] among themselves." He must also notify the registrar of companies of his appointment,[29] and publish the fact of it in *Iris Oifigiúil*.[29a]

The powers given by statute to a liquidator in a voluntary liquidation are similar to but less trammelled by restrictions than those given to the official liquidator in a winding up by the court. In brief summary, he may[30] for the exercise of his functions, without obtaining the sanction of anyone, bring or defend any action or legal proceeding, carry on the business of the company so far as may be necessary for the beneficial winding up thereof,[31] appoint a solicitor, sell the company's property (including by means of the creation of fee farm and leasehold interests), do everything necessary to obtain payment in respect of deceased or bankrupt contributories, appoint agents to do business which he is unable to do himself, enter into negotiable instruments, raise money on the security of the assets of the company, give security for costs in proceedings, and do all these things (and anything else which may be necessary for winding up the affairs of the company and distributing its assets) in the name and on behalf of the company, using its seal when necessary. If the

---

[26] *Re Tailteann Freight Services Ltd.* [1975] I.R. 376, 380.

[27] ss.258(2) and 269(3) respectively.

[28] "Contributories" are defined by s.208 as meaning "every person liable to contribute to the assets of a company in the event of its being wound up," and pending the final determination of contributories includes "any person alleged to be a contributory. The persons bound to contribute as aforesaid, members, past members and the rare category of directors with unlimited liability (s.197) are described in s.207. Ancillary powers in relation to contributories are contained in s.276(1)(c), (d).

[29] s.278.

[29a] European Communities (Companies) Regulations 1973, reg. 4(3).

[30] s.276(1)(b); s.231(1)(a), (b), (c) and s.231(2).

[31] *Re Great Eastern Electric Co. Ltd.* [1941] Ch. 241; *Willis* v. *Association of Commonwealth Universities* [1965] 1 Q.B. 140.

liquidator wishes to pay any classes of creditors in full, or to compromise the claims of creditors or debtors (including contributories) he will need to obtain prior sanction. In a members' voluntary liquidation that sanction is obtained by a special resolution of the company in general meeting, and he may summon the meeting; in a creditors' voluntary liquidation he will need the sanction of the court, or of the committee of inspection or, if none, of a meeting of creditors.[32] In a members' voluntary liquidation he has power to attempt to effect an amalgamation pursuant to section 260; in a creditors' voluntary liquidation he will need the sanction of a committee of inspection.[32a] He may in all voluntary liquidations initiate schemes of arrangement under sections 201–203.[32b]

Wide though these powers are, the liquidator may be in some doubt about their ambit in the particular circumstances of his task, or he may need further powers. In either case, he should apply to the court for its sanction before proceeding. He does this pursuant to section 280 which allows him (or any contributory or creditor):

> "to apply to the court to determine any question arising in the winding up of a company, or to exercise . . . all or any of the powers which the court might exercise if the company were being wound up by the court. . . . "

Thus in *Re Slaney Valley Co-operative Creameries Ltd.*[33] the court approved, as the only course open in the circumstances, a temporary lease by the liquidator of property which he had failed to sell, and which, as the law then stood, he had no express power to grant. A liquidator who would like to sell the business of the company as a going concern, but who doubts whether his proposed decision to continue the business of the company pending that event, is indeed "necessary" for its beneficial winding up would be well advised to apply for sanction. What if he is faced with a decision which it is clearly within his powers to take? Even in those circumstances the courts will accept the surrender of his discretion, and sanction or refuse the transaction. This element of the jurisdiction is vital to the liquidator in view of the ready and widening grasp of the modern tort of negligence. A fiduciary in the position of a liquidator is nowadays no more than the receiver[34] to be exonerated from breach of duty through having acted honestly, and the conduct of the reasonable liquidator (whose standard he must emulate) in a difficult property market is not readily predictable. In *Re Hibernian Transpor*

---

[32] s.231(1)(*d*), (*e*), (*f*); s.276(1)(*a*), (*e*).
[32a] s. 271: see n. 22, *supra*. For this type of reconstruction see Chap. 9 at p. 288.
[32b] See Chap. 9 at pp. 289 *et seq.*
[33] (1935) 70 I.L.T.R. 134.   [34] See Chap. 14 at pp. 439 *et seq.*

Companies Ltd.,[35] a case in which the price being offered to the liquidator was lower than the reserve at a previous unsuccessful auction, the Supreme Court said that it understood why the liquidator should "wish to be reassured beforehand by the approval of the court."[36]

Certain of the consequences of the commencement of a compulsory winding up, discussed more particularly in that context, *infra*, also occur on the passing of a resolution for voluntary winding up. Briefly for present purposes, they are that judgment mortgages registered against the land of the company within three months before the resolution confer no priority if the company proves insolvent: section 284(2); and that, where an execution has been issued against a company before it has passed a resolution for voluntary liquidation, benefits of that execution obtained after the passing of the resolution (or after the execution creditor has had notice of the meeting at which that resolution is to be proposed) may, if the liquidator objects, only be retained with the leave of the court: section 291. Also, since by section 280 the court may in a voluntary liquidation, as we have seen, "exercise all or any of the powers which the court might exercise if the company were being wound up by the court," certain automatic and other consequences of a compulsory liquidation may be imported into a voluntary winding up, if a case is made. This importation has the object of preventing interference with the guiding principle of all liquidations, stated for voluntary liquidations by section 275, that the company's liabilities should be satisfied *pari passu, i.e.* fairly and rateably among creditors entitled in equal degree. Thus, actions and proceedings against the company may be restrained: sections 217 and 222; and executions launched after the commencement avoided: section 219.

When the affairs of the company have been fully wound up, the liquidator must present his final account to the company in a general meeting, and in a creditors' winding up to a meeting of them as well.[37] Afterwards, the liquidator must send to the registrar of companies a copy of his final account, and a return specifying these meetings, or the lack of a quorum at them, if that be the case.[38] The registrar on receiving the requisite returns and the final account

---

[35] [1972] I.R. 190.

[36] *Per* Walsh J., *nem. con.*, at p. 200. This case concerned a compulsory winding up by the court, but that does not affect the point under discussion. An official liquidator in a winding up by the court who has, pursuant to s.231(2), a power to sell without obtaining the court's approval may be equated to a liquidator in a voluntary winding up who likewise has that power, and who may pursuant to s.280 likewise invoke the control of the court under s.231(3).

[37] ss.263 and 273.   [38] ss.263(3) and 273(3).

must register them. Three months after that registration, the company is dissolved and ceases to exist.[39]

If the liquidator in the course of the voluntary winding up has come across circumstances from which it appears to him that "any past or present officer, or any member, of the company has been guilty of any offence in relation to the company for which he is criminally liable," he must forthwith report the matter to the Director of Public Prosecutions, and assist him with such information and access to documents as he may require.[39a] This duty may be enforced by the court on the application of any person interested.[39b]

Later in this Chapter we consider in depth fraudulent trading, and in brief, criminal offences connected with a company which has gone into liquidation. Both topics may be relevant to voluntary liquidations. We pass on now to compulsory liquidations. Several topics, material to voluntary liquidations, are dealt with there to avoid undue duplication. Readers are referred in particular to the lines of enquiry to be pursued by any liquidator (pp. 490–491, *infra*), the possibility that he might initiate misfeasance proceedings (pp. 239 *et seq.*, *supra* and p. 491, *infra*), the power to disclaim onerous property (pp. 496–498, *infra*), the order of administration of assets (pp. 498 *et seq.*, *infra*), fraudulent preferences (pp. 504 *et seq.*, *infra*), the avoidance of floating charges (pp. 511 *et seq.*, *infra*), the effect of the commencement of liquidation on the continuance of employment (pp. 514–515, *infra*), and the fiduciary status of all liquidators (pp. 515–516, *infra*).

WINDING UP BY THE COURT

Grounds

The only grounds upon which a company may be wound up by the court are stated in section 213 of the Companies Act 1963, as amended. No other grounds will do.[40] The grounds are:

> "(*a*) the company has by special resolution resolved that the company be wound up by the court;
>
> (*c*) the company does not commence its business within a year from its incorporation or suspends its business for a whole year;
>
> (*d*) the number of members is reduced, in the case of a private company, below two, or, in the case of any other company below seven;

---

[39] ss.263(4) and 273(4).
[39a] s.299, as amended by Prosecution of Offences Act 1974, s.3.
[39b] s.299(3). The court may also act on its own motion.
[40] *Re Cork Shipping and Mercantile Co. Ltd.* (1881–82) 7 L.R. Ir. 148.

(*e*) the company is unable to pay its debts;

(*f*) the court is of the opinion that it is just and equitable that the company should be wound up;

(*g*) the court is satisfied that the company's affairs are being conducted, or the powers of the directors are being exercised, in a manner oppressive to any member or in disregard of his interests as a member and that, despite the existence of an alternative remedy, winding up would be justified in the general circumstances of the case so, however, that the court may dismiss a petition to wind up under this paragraph if it is of opinion that proceedings under section 205 would, in all the circumstances, be more appropriate;

(*h*) after the end of the general transitional period, within the meaning of the Companies (Amendment) Act 1983, the company is an old public limited company within the meaning of that Act;

(*i*) after the end of the transitional period for share capital, within the meaning of the Companies (Amendment) Act 1983, the company has not complied with the conditions specified in section 12(9) of that Act."[41]

Only the registrar may petition under grounds (*h*) and (*i*).[42] The Minister may petition under grounds (*f*) and (*g*).[43] Members, called somewhat inexactly "contributories"[44] in this portion of the Act, may petition on any grounds save (*h*) and (*i*),[45] but there are limitations on petitions by members who have held their shares for only a short time.[46] We have already explored in some depth the extent to which *members* of a company can force it into liquidation by recourse to the "just and equitable" ground of compulsory winding up given by section 213(*f*) of the Companies Act 1963,[47] their ground of first and last resort if they have anything substantive about which to complain, and for which winding up would be an appropriate remedy. The company itself may petition[47a] but it has recently been affirmed that the board of directors may not cause it to do so without

---

[41] A former ground (*b*) was deleted by the 1983 Act, and grounds (*h*) and (*i*) added. For these transitional periods, see Chap. 1.

[42] s.215, as amended by para. 18, Sched. 1, 1983 Act.

[43] s.170(3); s.215(*d*).

[44] "Contributory" in this context means *any* present or past member, whether his shares are fully paid or not: ss.207, 208; *Re Anglesea Colliery Co.* (1868) 1 Ch. App. 555.

[45] We have already seen that the "tangible interest" bar of English law to a contributory's petition does not appear to exist in Irish law. See p. 000, *supra*.

[46] s.215(*a*).

[47] Chiefly discussed in Chap. 9 at pp. 268 *et seq.* See also pp. 139 *et seq.*, and pp. 95 *et seq.*

[47a] s.215.

the benefit of an authorising or ratifying resolution in general meeting, or specific authority in the articles.[47b]

In this chapter we are concerned mainly with *creditors*. Though all grounds save (*g*), (*h*) and (*i*) are open to them,[48] their primary means of forcing the company to be wound up is section 213(*e*) which states that a company may be wound up by the court "if it is unable to pay its debts." To avoid the difficulties of proof involved in such an assertion, section 214 usefully *deems* a company unable to pay its debts if an execution issued against a company on a judgment debt has not been satisfied, or if the company has not satisfied within three weeks a statutory demand[49] in respect of an indebtedness exceeding £50.

An individual petitioning creditor who brings himself within section 213(*e*) is entitled *ex debito justitiae*[50] as between himself and the company to a winding-up order. The court has no discretion to defeat his right by entertaining excuses by the company or offers by it to pay within a reasonable time.[51] The only way the company may defeat such a petition is by establishing that the debt founding it is disputed in good faith and on substantial grounds: *Re Pageboy Couriers Ltd.*,[52] a particularly strong example. In that case, the petitioner had begun parallel proceedings for the alleged debt, which the company was vigorously defending. Such a petitioner is not regarded as a creditor entitled to present a petition at all[53]; his petition is, in other words, demurrable, and will be dismissed without the court going into the merits of the dispute over the debt.[54]

Although as between himself and the company, a petitioner

[47b] *Re Cannock Ltd.* (High Court, Murphy J., September 8, 1984; unreported, but see McHugh (1985) 3 I.L.T. (N.S.) 93, following *Re Galway and Salthill Tramway Co.* [1918] 1 I.R. 62, 65, and *Re Emmadart Ltd.* [1979] Ch. 540.

[48] Assuming that s.215(*e*) and (*f*) (as added by para. 18, Sched. 1, 1983 Act) though both drafted facultatively are intended to exclude other petitioners; similarly in respect of members' petitions under grounds (*h*) and (*i*).

[49] *i.e.* a demand framed and served in accordance with s.214(*a*). See Form 4, Appendix M, R.S.C., Ord. 74, r. 8.

[50] *i.e.* as a matter of right. See *Re Belfast Tailors' Co-partnership Ltd.*, nn. 55 and 56 *infra*. A voluntary winding up is not, as between a qualified creditor and the company, a bar to a compulsory order: s.282.

[51] *e.g.*, *Re International Contract Co.* (1866) 1 Ch. App. 523; *Re Home Assurance Assn.* L.R. 12 Eq. 112.

[52] [1982] I.L.R.M. 510, following *Stonegate Securities Ltd.* v. *Gregory* [1980] 3 W.L.R. 168, and *Mann* v. *Goldstein* [1968] 1 W.L.R. 1091.

[53] Within the meaning of s.215 which defines the persons entitled to present a petition.

[54] Prospective or contingent, but *undisputed* creditors are, on the other hand entitled to petition but must, if the petition is to be heard, first give such security for costs as the court thinks reasonable and establish a prima facie case for winding up: s.215(*c*).

within section 213(*e*) is entitled to an order, he may as between himself and other creditors be constrained to submit to their wishes for the continuance of a voluntary winding up. He is, as regards them, merely one representative member of a class, and the court may give effect to the wishes of the other members of that class, regard being had to the amount of each creditor's debt, and may direct meetings of creditors to be held to ascertain those wishes.[55] Thus, in *Re Belfast Tailors' Co-partnership Ltd.*[56] a majority of the creditors opposed the winding-up petition, favouring the continuation of a creditors' voluntary liquidation. In view of the smallness of the assets, the integrity and independence of the liquidator, and the absence of any apprehended difficulty in the winding up and of any special circumstances justifying an order, the petition was dismissed. But if the court is of the opinion that the rights of any creditor may be prejudiced by the continuance of a voluntary winding up, a compulsory order will be made, notwithstanding the wishes of the majority of creditors to the contrary: *Re George Downs & Co. Ltd.*[57] In that case the prejudice was established by showing that there were many matters requiring investigation by a court, but other circumstances which might justify a petitioning creditor's plea of prejudice were alluded to, including delay in the conduct of the voluntary liquidation.

The official liquidator

The court after making a winding-up order will appoint a liquidator, styled "the official liquidator" of the company.[58] Though the petitioner nominates a prospective appointee, the court has regard to nominations made by other interested parties; and indeed may appoint someone other than a specific nominee.[59] Once appointed, the official liquidator is subject in carrying out his functions to the control of the court, and that control may be invoked at the instance of any creditor or contributory of the company.[60] In exercising that control, the court has regard, as in all matters relating to the winding-up of a company, to the wishes of the majority in value of its

---

[55] s.309(1), (2). *Re Belfast Tailors' Co-partnership Ltd.* [1909] 1 I.R. 49, 55 *et seq.*
[56] Following *Re Langley Steel Mill Co.* (1871) L.R. 12 Eq. 26, *Re Uruguay Central, etc., RIY.* (1879) 11 Ch. D. 372, *Re Chapel House Colliery Co.* (1883) 24 Ch. D. 259.
[57] [1943] I.R. 420. See also *Re Wicklow Textile Industries Ltd.* (1952) 87 I.L.T.R. 72.
[58] ss.225, 228(*b*).
[59] R.S.C., Ord. 74, r. 30.
[60] s.231(3). "Contributory" in this context means *any* present or past member, whether his shares are fully paid or not: ss.207, 208; *Re Anglesea Colliery Co.* (1868) 1 Ch. App. 555.

creditors or contributories, as the case may be, as expressed through creditors' and contributories' meetings, should they wish to attend.[61] As a further means of consultation, the court may, should it be desired by creditors or contributories, appoint a committee of inspection from among them to act with the official liquidator.[62] The sanction of this committee, or of the court, is a necessary prerequisite to the exercise by the official liquidator of certain of his powers.[63] The remuneration of the official liquidator, payable out of the company's assets, is fixed by the court[64]; he is dismissable by the court; vacancies caused by death, dismissal or resignation are filled by the court; the court fixes the security (if any), usually by way of insurance bond, to be given by the official liquidator against the proper performance of his duties[65]; and it is to the court that he presents and vouches his interim and final accounts.[66]

The company is dissolved by order of the court on the completion of the winding up.[67]

Relation back

A winding up by the court is deemed to commence at the time of the presentation of the petition, unless a resolution for voluntary winding up has been passed earlier, in which case the time of its passing marks the commencement.[68] Thus, a winding-up order, if made, relates back to these commencing events. The chief consequences of this relation back are now described. Some, as we have noted above, apply also to the commencement of a purely voluntary winding up.

[61] s.309. See R.S.C., Ord. 74, Pt. X.

[62] ss.232 and 233.

[63] Those listed in s.231(1). See *The duties and powers of official liquidators, infra.*

[64] s.228(*d*), R.S.C. Ord. 74, rr. 47, 48 and 129. The liquidation will be placed in jeopardy if the assets are insufficient to support the liquidator and his disbursements In that event, he must summon a meeting of creditors to solicit their financial support: *Re Custom Line Ltd.* (High Court, Murphy J. February 27, 1984, reported in *The Irish Times*, February 28, 1984). Failing that support, he will find it in his interests to lodge his accounts and resign: *Re Northern Waterproofs Ltd.* [1967] N.I. 17. His remuneration and costs are dischargeable out of the assets ahead of the claims of any unsecured pre-liquidation creditor: R.S.C., Ord. 74, r. 129, as previously determined in *Re Redbreast Preserving Co. (Ireland) Ltd.* [1958] I.R. 234; but are deferred to other items listed in r. 129. Interim payments of remuneration are permissible: Ord. 74 r. 47.

[65] s.228(*a*): R.S.C., Ord. 74, rr. 32–35; s.228(*c*): R.S.C., Ord. 74, r. 37; s.228(*e*).

[66] R.S.C., Ord. 74, rr. 33, 49.

[67] s.249. R.S.C., Ord. 74, Pts. XXIII and XXIX.

[68] s.220: all proceedings in the superseded voluntary winding up are deemed to have been validly taken "unless the court, on proof of fraud or mistake, thinks fit to direct otherwise."

First, by section 218 of the Companies Act 1963, any disposition of the property of the company made after the commencement is void, unless the court orders otherwise. This provision has the object of ensuring that all pre-liquidation creditors of like degree are treated alike in the winding up.[69] How does it work in practice? Obviously, a company cannot be expected to suspend its business simply because a winding-up petition has been presented against it. After all, there may be grounds for believing that the petition may not succeed. Unfortunately, persons dealing with such a company are not in a position to be so sanguine. Their transactions with it are at the mercy of the discretion of the court, if winding up does in fact supervene. In the exercise of this discretion there is a broad divide between those who knew that a winding up had commenced, and those who did not. Dispositions of the company's property to the latter "if carried out in good faith in the ordinary course of business . . . will normally be validated, unless there is ground for thinking that the transaction may involve an attempt to prefer a disponee."[70] Recently, it has been held rather extraordinarily in *Re Pat Ruth Ltd.*[71] that a lodgment by a company into an overdrawn current account, whilst certainly a "disposition" of its property, is not one made in the ordinary course of business. In that case there was a distinction, drawn on grounds which are unapparent, between the discharge of pre-liquidation debts to a bank unaware of the presentation of the petition, which the court disallowed, and the discharge of debts of other unaware pre-liquidation creditors, which the court validated. What if the disponee knew of the petition? Here the court is most disinclined to validate the payment of *pre*-liquidation debts, unless special circumstances exist. Such special circumstances may be found in the payment of a pre-liquidation debt as a necessary part of a post-liquidation transaction which is beneficial to the general body of unsecured creditors. Thus in *Re A.I. Levy (Holdings) Ltd.*[72] the court validated prospectively the sale of a lease held by the company, which was liable to forfeiture if a winding up order were to be made against the company, and authorised the payment to its landlord of pre-liquidation arrears of rent, since the landlord was justifiably refusing his licence to assign until the arrears were met. The validation would also have been made retro-

---

[69] *Re Pat Ruth Ltd.* [1981] I.L.R.M. 51, 53; *Re Gray's Inn Construction Ltd.* [1980] 1 W.L.R. 711, 717.

[70] *Ibid.* at p. 820, followed in *Re Pat Ruth Ltd.* [1981] I.L.R.M. 51, 52. For voidable attempts to "prefer" a creditor, see pp. 504–511, *infra.*

[71] [1981] I.L.R.M.; differing therefore in this respect from *Re Gray's Inn Construction Ltd.*, n. 69, *supra.*

[72] [1964] Ch. 19, adopted in *Re Pat Ruth Ltd.*, n. 70, *supra.*

spectively had that been necessary. Entirely post-liquidation debts are subject to different considerations, since the criterion of fairness as between pre-liquidation creditors does not apply to them. They will be validated if they were calculated to be for the benefit of the general body of creditors, for example, the sale by the company of an asset at full market value, or the continuance of the company's business when the advantage of ultimately being able to sell it as a going concern outweighs the prospect of incurring fresh losses. Prospective post-liquidation creditors should however be warned that the court's cool *ex post facto* appreciation of relevant facts and opinion of appropriate precautions to be taken in the interests of the general body of creditors may prove different from their own, arrived at in the heat of the events.[73] In most cases, it will therefore be advisable to seek a validating order under section 218 before entering into the transaction.

A second consequence of the relation back of a compulsory winding up to its commencement is that no judgment mortgage registered against the land of an insolvent company within three months before the commencement shall confer "any priority or preference over simple contract creditors": section 331 of the Irish Bankrupt and Insolvent Act 1857, introduced into company liquidations by section 284(2) of the 1963 Act.[74] These words may seem to imply, but should not be taken as implying, that a judgment creditor whose judgment mortgage is impugned only because of infringing this time limit will nonetheless still achieve priority over unsecured creditors not of the "simple contract" variety, chiefly claimants in tort, and also State-preferential creditors under section 285. By developments in bankruptcy law after 1857, but applicable to insolvent company liquidations,[75] all unsecured creditors rank *pari passu*, and therefore equally benefit from section 331. That some unsecured creditors may be elevated to preferential treatment is irrelevant to this conclusion.[75a]

Thirdly, "any attachment, sequestration, distress or execution put in force against the property or effects of the company" after the commencement is by section 219 declared to be "void to all intents."

---

[73] For a general discussion of the jurisdiction and the authorities, see Buckley L.J in *Re Gray's Inn Construction Ltd.*, n. 69, *supra*.

[74] Thereby reversing *Re Irish Attested Sales Ltd.* [1962] I.R. 70. Astoundingly, the *Bankruptcy Law Committee Report*, 1972, Prl. 2714, says at p. 110: "The Companies Act 1963 does not contain restrictions on judgment mortgages similar to those in section 331 of the 1857 Act."

[75] Civil Liability Act 1961, s.61; s.284(1); also s.275 in respect of voluntary liquidations, and s.223 in respect of winding up by the court.

[75a] For preferential creditors, see pp. 501 *et seq.*, *infra*.

If an execution creditor has actually received proceeds of his execution before the commencement, they have *pro tanto* discharged his debt and he may retain them, even if the execution is not complete.[76] It has been long established that an execution creditor does not rank as a secured creditor to the extent that his pre-liquidation execution remains unsatisfied.[77] This principle has now been encapsulated in section 291, with some modifications. By section 291, he may retain as against the liquidator the post-liquidation fruits of executions begun, but not completed, before commencement only to the extent and on such terms as the court thinks fit: section 291. There is little positive guidance about how this puzzling discretion should be exercised, save that "weighty reasons" should be produced to justify upsetting the normal *pari passu* distribution among all unsecured creditors.[78] Section 291(5) provides that for the purposes of section 291:

> "an execution against goods shall be taken to be completed by seizure and sale, and an attachment of a debt shall be deemed to be completed by receipt of the debt, and an execution against land shall be deemed to be completed by seizure and, in the case of an equitable interest by the appointment of a receiver."

Executions and attachments over assets within section 291(5) are to be deemed complete only in the circumstances it describes.[79] A judgment mortgage is a process of execution. Assume that a judgment mortgage against a company's land has not been avoided by section 331 of the 1857 Act (*supra*) through having been registered more than three months before the presentation of the petition, but that actual possession of the land had not yet been taken at date of the petition. That judgment creditor falls within the court's discretion under section 291. Thus, *Re Irish Attested Sales Ltd.*[80] which decided before the enactment of section 291 that a judgment creditor who had registered a judgment mortgage against the land of a com-

---

[76] *Re Andrew, ex. p. Official Receiver* [1937] Ch. 122, 134.

[77] *Re Lough Neagh Ship Co. Ltd., ex. p. Thompson* [1896] 1 I.R. 29 (in so far as this case says at pp.39–40 that a judgment creditor will obtain priority over unsecured creditors if he has before the commencement of the liquidation obtained an unrealised charge (*e.g.* if he has registered a judgment mortgage) against the assets of the company, it must be regarded as having been superseded by ss.284(2) and 291); *Re Leinster Contract Corporation Ltd.* [1903] 1 I.R. 517 (which was mainly concerned with deciding that a judgment creditor did not achieve priority over other unsecured creditors, merely through having obtained a judgment).

[78] *Per* Salmon L.J. in *Re Caribbean Products (Yam Importers) Ltd.* [1966] Ch. 331, 353, a decision which contains a useful, if somewhat despairing, account of the authorities.

[79] *Re Andrew, ex. p. Official Receiver*, n. 76, *supra*.

[80] [1962] I.R. 70.

pany shortly before the commencement of its winding up, but had not entered into possession, gained priority over general creditors has been superseded not only by the introduction of section 331 to company liquidations, but also by section 291.[81]

A purchaser in good faith of goods actually sold in execution will acquire a good title to them as against the liquidator.[82]

In addition to these instances of relation back, the presentation of a winding-up petition has the fourth consequence that any "action or proceeding" against the company in any court may be stayed or restrained at any time after presentation but before a winding-up order has been made, on the application of the company, or any creditor or contributory.[83] The grant of the application is discretionary, and the applicant will usually be required to give an undertaking as to damages, and to pay the plaintiff's costs of appearing on the application to stay.[84] Processes of execution come within the description of a "proceeding."[85]

Provisional liquidators

At any time after the presentation of a winding-up petition, but before the appointment of an official liquidator, the court acting *ex parte* may appoint a provisional liquidator[86] upon the application of a creditor, or of a contributory, or of the company, but usually at the request of the petitioner, and will generally do so unless the petition seems to be opposed on grounds which will prove effective. Such an appointment does not signify that a winding-up order will eventually be made, but it usually will be, and in that event the provisional liquidator will usually be appointed as the official liquidator.

On the appointment of a provisional liquidator, no action may be commenced or proceeded with against the company, except with the leave of the court.[87]

---

[81] This case also decided as a secondary point that a judgment creditor who registered a judgment mortgage *after* the commencement of the liquidation in respect of a pre-commencement judgment also thereby achieved priority over unsecured creditors. Unfortunately, the then equivalent of s.219, *supra*, s.211 of the 1908 Act, was not considered in the judgment which must in this respect therefore be regarded as having been delivered *per incuriam*.

[82] For the sheriff's duties *vis-à-vis* the liquidator see s.292, the provisions of which relating to the costs of executions supersede *Re Whiterock Quarries Ltd* [1933] I.R. 363.

[83] s.217: applications are to the Supreme Court in the case of appeals pending before it; otherwise the High Court is the appropriate forum.

[84] *Pierce* v. *Wexford Picture House Co.* [1915] 2 I.R. 310.

[85] *Re Artistic Colour Printing Co.* (1880) 14 Ch. D. 502.

[86] s.226; R.S.C., Ord. 74, r. 15.

[87] s.222. The section covers a "proceeding," and therefore processes of execution.

Section 229 imposes a duty on the provisional liquidator "to take into his custody or under his control all the property and things in action to which the company is or appears to be entitled." Indeed, the preservation of the company's property and the *status quo* are often the primary motives for the appointment of a provisional liquidator.[88] In fact the order appointing him is required to describe the property of which he is to take possession, as well as his particular duties.[89] As aids to the execution of his duties, he should have the benefit of the statement of the company's affairs prepared by persons connected with it pursuant to section 224[90]; he may apply to the court under section 245 for an order summoning for examination anyone "known or suspected to have in his possession any property of the company or supposed to be indebted to the company, or any person whom the court deems capable of giving information relating to the promotion, formation, trade, dealings, affairs or property of the company"[91-92] and he may also invoke the court's power to order the arrest of absconding contributories given by section 247, *infra.*

In addition, he has such powers as he may specifically be conferred on him by the court. These are granted according to the needs and circumstances of the company in question. Often the provisional liquidator will be given power to carry on the company's business only "so far as may be necessary for the beneficial winding up thereof,"[93] as in *Donnelly* v. *Gleeson*.[94] But in *Re Gourmet Restaurants Ltd.*[95] the company's most valuable asset was the goodwill of a celebrated restaurant business, which would have to be preserved so that it could ultimately be sold as a going concern, and accordingly the provisional liquidator was given power to continue the restaurant business.[96] The more limited form would probably have confined the liquidator to such business activities as disposing of the

---

[88] *Levy* v. *Napier* (1962) S.L.T. 261.

[89] R.S.C., Ord. 74, r. 15(2).

[90] R.S.C., Ord. 74, r. 20.

[91-92] See McBryde, "The powers of provisional liquidators," (1977) S.L.T. (News) 145, an article on Scots law to which in this respect Irish company law bears a greater resemblance than to English law.

[93] *i.e.* the beneficial winding up of the business (not of the company), echoing the official liquidator's power, given by s.231(*b*), and exercisable with the consent of the court or of the committee of inspection, if any.

[94] High Court, Hamilton J. unrep. July 11, 1978.

[95] High Court, Egan J. August 3, 1984, reported in *The Irish Times*, August 4, 1984.

[96] The petition for winding up was the company's own. (See s.215). The appointment of a provisional liquidator can therefore provide a means whereby the company may itself initiate moves to continue trading where for it to continue trading through its directors might expose them to liability for fraudulent trading under s.297. For this liability see pp. 516 *et seq.*

company's perishable stocks of food. Other powers commonly conferred on provisional liquidators include the power to appoint a solicitor to assist him in the performance of his duties, and powers to
negotiate the sale of assets. Since the appointment of a provisional
liquidator, unlike the making of a winding-up order,[97] does not constitute notice of dismissal of employees,[98] a provisional liquidator
will usually wish to have power to dismiss employees, as was
obtained in *Re Gourmet Restaurants Ltd.*[99] The appointment of a provisional liquidator does not result in the board of directors being
entirely superseded. They retain for example, power to cause the
company to resist the winding up petition.[99a]

The provisional liquidator may have recourse to the assets of the
company to satisfy his costs, charges, expenses and such sum as the
court shall have allowed him by way of remuneration, even if the company does not eventually go into liquidation.[1]

Consequences of winding-up order

We have already looked at those consequences which flow from
the fact that a compulsory winding up is deemed to commence at the
presentation of the petition.[2] The other immediate consequences of a
winding-up order are that the company must forthwith deliver to the
registrar of companies an office copy of the order[3]; no action or proceeding (including processes of execution) may be continued or
commenced, except by leave of the court[4]; and a statement of the
company's affairs must be filed in court, unless it orders otherwise.[5]
This statement describes the company's assets, liabilities, creditors
and their securities. It is to be made by one or more of the company's directors at the date of the winding up order, and by the company's secretary at that date, but the court may order others,
including past officers and certain employees, to make the statement.[6]

---

[97] See generally *Termination of employment, infra.*
[98] *Donnelly* v. *Gleeson*, n. 94, *supra.*
[99] n. 95, *supra.*
[99a] *Re Union Accident Insurance Co. Ltd.* [1972] 1 All E.R. 1105, 1113.
[1] Ord. 74, r. 15(3). If winding up supervenes, he will claim in priority under r. 129
in respect of "fees and expenses properly incurred in preserving, realising or getting in
the assets." For the order of application of assets, see pp. 498 *et seq., infra.*
[2] See pp. 482 *et seq.*
[3] s.221.
[4] s.222. For "proceeding" as including processes of execution, see p. 486, *supra.*
[5] s.224.
[6] The full list is in s.224(2).

The official liquidator supersedes the board of directors[6a] (who are thereafter *functus officio*), and all other agents, including a receiver.[6b]

Qualifications of official liquidators

There are no qualifications for the post of liquidator, whether official or otherwise, save that a body corporate is incapable of being appointed.[7] An accountant in private practice is usually appointed.

Duties and powers of official liquidators

An official liquidator is, *per* Johnston J. in *Re Whiterock Quarries Ltd.*,[7a] "the executive officer appointed by the court" for the purpose of the winding up proceedings. He is potentially subject to the control of the court in all aspects of the winding up, even where statute gives him powers which he may exercise independently. Section 231(3) declares that his exercise of them is nonetheless "subject to the control of the court, and any creditor or contributory may apply to the court in relation to any exercise or proposed exercise of any of those powers." He may also, as we shall see, surrender any such independent discretion to the court, and be ruled by its decision.[8]

He may apply for directions on any issue arising in the liquidation, and persons necessary to the determination of the issue will be joined as parties.[8a] He is appointed "for the purpose of conducting the proceedings in winding up a company and performing such duties in reference thereto as the court may impose."[9] More specifically, statute imposes duties to publish the fact of his appointment in *Iris Oifigiúil*, and to deliver an office copy of the order appointing him to the registrar of companies,[10] to take "into his custody or under his control all the property and things in action to which the company is

---

[6a] *Fowler* v. *Broad's Patent Night Light Co.* [1893] 1 Ch. 724; *Re Union Accident Insurance Co. Ltd.* [1972] 1 All E.R. 1105, 1113.

[6b] For the termination of a receiver's agency, see pp. 474–475, *supra*. For other agents see p. 474, *supra* and *Re Tailteann Freight Services Ltd.* [1975] I.R. 376.

[7] s.300.

[7a] [1933] I.R. 363, 366.

[8] *Re Hibernian Transport Companies Ltd.* [1972] I.R. 190 and p. 495, *infra*.

[8a] *e.g. Re Galway Concrete Ltd.* (High Court, Keane J., December 10, 1982; unreported) in which the rights of interested parties in machinery and plant were determined.

[9] s.225.

[10] s.227.

or appears entitled"[11]; to proceed "with all convenient speed after he is appointed . . . to make up, continue, complete, check and rectify the books of account of the company"[12]; generally to take upon himself and discharge the duty imposed by section 235 of causing "the assets of the company to be collected and applied in discharge of its liabilities"[13]; to set in motion the process of ascertaining the debts and claims due from the company[14]; should the court so direct, to ascertain whether the creditors and contributories wish to have a committee of inspection appointed[15]; to send to creditors and contributories a summary of the statement of affairs[16] compiled in relation to the company, together with any comments he may wish to add, including the causes of its failure[17]; and to settle a list of contributories,[18] unless the court dispenses with this requirement, as it should in the case of a company limited by shares of which all are fully paid and were regularly issued.

If, as is usually the case with a creditor's petition, the company is unable to pay its debts in full, the court may as part of its process of control, order the official liquidator on his appointment to prepare and submit to it a report on the company on the lines indicated by Murphy J. in *Re Custom Line Ltd.*[19] He said that this report should deal with

> (1) an estimate of the assets and liabilities of the company; (2) the cause of the failure of the company; (3) whether, in the opinion of the official liquidator, further enquiry was desirable as to any matter relating to the promotion, formation or failure of the company or conduct of its business; (4) whether, in the opinion of the official liquidator, any fraud was committed by any person in the promotion or formation of the company or since the formation of the company; (5) an estimate of the time required to complete the liquidation; and (6) any other matter which, in the opinion of the official liquidator, was of interest to the liquidation and should be shown to the court.

[11] s.229. R.S.C., Ord. 74, r. 92 imposes corresponding duties on listed contributories and "any trustee, receiver, banker or agent or officer of a company" to part with property in his hands to which the company is prima facie entitled. This rule reflects the terms of s.236. Furthermore, by s.230 the court may vest any of the company's property in the liquidator in his official capacity.

[12] R.S.C., Ord. 74, r. 38.

[13] *Ibid.* r. 91.

[14] *Ibid.* Pt. XV.

[15] s.232. For the functions of this committee, see n. 22, *supra.*

[16] For the "statement of affairs," see below.

[17] R.S.C., Ord. 74, r. 29.

[18] *Ibid.* Pt. XII. Calls are governed by Pt. XIV.

[19] High Court, February 27; reported in *The Irish Times*, February 28, 1984.

These are lines of enquiry which, as the learned judge indicated, should be pursued by *any* liquidator of any company. But as appears from the later authority of *Re Merchant Banking Ltd.*[20] an official liquidator should not expend time in preparing an elaborate and full *report* to the court, if one has not actually been ordered. In those circumstances, he runs the risk of having his costs of preparing the report disallowed, though not his reasonable costs of investigating the facts which led to it. In the absence of such an order, his duty to report, according to Costello J. in *Re Merchant Banking Ltd.*, is confined to submitting "a simple statement of the facts (with copies of supporting documents, if necessary)"[20a] tending to show, if such be the case, that in the words of section 299 "any past or present officer, or any member, of the company has been guilty of any offence in relation to the company for which he is criminally liable." This report has the purpose of enabling the court to decide whether to exercise its power under section 299(1) to have the alleged offence referred to the Director of Public Prosecutions. In fact, for some time an official liquidator has been obliged by a practice direction to inform the Examiner at an early stage if he has detected signs of fraud or other criminality.[20b]

Murphy J.'s list in *Re Custom Line Ltd.*, *supra* of the lines of enquiry to be pursued by any liquidator includes, of course, civil as well as criminal matters, and, in particular, items 3 and 4 refer to the need to investigate the possibility that there might be a civil liability for fraudulent trading under section 297, a topic discussed at the conclusion of this Chapter at pp. 516 *et seq.* The list should not be taken as exhaustive of lines of enquiry. For example, a liquidator should be mindful that a director or others may be obliged to recompense the company for breaches of duty, whether or not involving fraud, and may therefore have to consider whether to apply for the leave[20c] of the court or of the committee of inspection (if any) to take out a misfeasance summons under section 298[20d]; or the liquidator might have to consider whether to apply for like leave to take proceedings to set aside a payment to a creditor as a fraudulent preference,[20e] or a floating charge as voidable.[20f]

Often the item of which the liquidator of an insolvent company is most short, apart from funds, is information. Statute attempts to

[20] High Court, Costello J., April 29, 1985; unrep.
[20a] At p. 4 of the transcript.
[20b] For some relevant criminal offences, see pp. 368–369, *supra*, and p. 517, n. 3, *infra*.
[20c] See p. 494, *infra*.
[20d] See pp. 239–242, 369, 382, *supra*.
[20e] See pp. 504–511, *infra*.
[20f] See pp. 511–514, *infra*.

meet this need in several ways. Persons[21] who have been connected with any company ordered to be wound up must make and file in court a statement of its affairs, showing its assets, debts and liabilities, and identifying its creditors and their securities, if any: section 224. The court may also require any of these persons to attend before the court "to give such information in relation to the company as the Court may think fit."[22] Stronger powers to extract information are given by section 245 under which the court may summon before it and examine on oath:

> "any officer of the company or person known or suspected to
> have in his possession any property of the company or supposed
> to be indebted to the company, or any person whom the court
> deems capable of giving information, relating to the promotion,
> formation, trade, dealings, affairs or property of the company,"

and require him to produce any books or papers in his custody or power relating to the company. Section 245 is backed by a power of arrest: section 245(5). The examination may take place in private.[23] The court may require the witness to sign the transcript. It is declared by section 245(4) that his answers are not to be admissible in evidence against him in any *other* proceedings civil or criminal (save proceedings for perjury in respect of his answers), and that any such witness "shall not be entitled to refuse to answer any question put to him on the ground that his answer might incriminate him." O'Hanlon J. has held in *Re Aluminium Fabricators and section 247 of the Companies Act 1963*[24] that the inadmissibility in *other* proceedings does not prevent the transcript being admissible for the purpose of any application to the court in the course of the winding up proceedings, including, as was the issue in that case, section 297 proceedings against the witnesses to impose personal liability for fraudulent trading. If, as may be the case,[25] such section 297 proceedings must constitutionally be classified as criminal, the witness should be

---

[21] They are the secretary and one or more of the directors at the date of the order but the court may require members of a wider class to make the statement, including promoters, officers and former officers, and employees and certain former employees s.224.

[22] R.S.C., Ord. 74, r. 25. For statements of affairs generally, see Ord. 74, Pt. VII Officers may also be made to attend the committee of inspection and meetings of creditors and contributories to give information: s.246.

[23] *Re Redbreast Preserving Co. (Ireland) Ltd.* and s.174 of the Companies Act 1908 (1956) 91 I.L.T.R. 12.

[24] [1984] I.L.R.M. 399.

[25] See the discussion at pp. 525–526, *supra*.

privileged against answering self-incriminatory questions relating to them in the section 245 proceedings. Either that, or O'Hanlon J.'s interpretation must fall in so far as it related to admissibility in the subsequent section 297 proceedings. His interpretation seems acceptable in relation to subsequent unequivocally civil proceedings in the winding up such as those under section 298 brought on behalf of the company to recover its property or obtain damages for breach of duty.[26]

The liquidator must, as we have seen, get in the company's property. But people are often the key to property, and those people may prefer to take up residence abroad than to provide explanations at home. They may have spirited away the company's assets, or otherwise be liable for breaches of duty to the company; or they may potentially be personally liable for all the company's debts as fraudulent traders under section 297. Of course, the liquidator may obtain leave to freeze their assets by means of *Mareva* proceedings in Ireland and abroad, but in view of their opportunities for concealment of assets, their personal presence will usually be required. There is a power of arrest given by section 247 which, though useful, would be still more helpful if it were more widely drawn. It says that the court may:

> "at any time either before or after making a winding up order, on proof of probable cause for believing that a *contributory* is about to quit the State or otherwise to abscond or to remove or conceal any of his property for the purpose of evading payment of calls or of avoiding examination about the affairs of the company, . . . cause the *contributory* to be arrested, and his books and papers and movable personal property to be seized and him and them to be detained until such time as the court may order."[27]

The use of the term *contributory* means that only members[28] of the company come within the ambit of section 247, not debtors generally, nor officers *per se*. Usually, those wanted for questioning will happen to be members, but not always. For example the company may have been owned through nominees. There is therefore a slight

---

[26] For s.298, see pp. 239–242, 369, 382, 491, *supra*.

[27] Emphasis supplied.

[28] The fact that a member is exonerated from contribution through holding fully paid shares in a company limited by shares does not make him any the less a "contributory" as that term is used in various sections of the Act, including this. See n. 60, *supra*. A director with unlimited liability pursuant to s.197 would also be a direct object of s.247, but they are rare.

flaw in the draftsmanship which should be corrected. It does not matter that those sought have no liability *qua* member. Indeed in most companies there will be no such liability since share capital is usually fully paid and of minimal amounts. An arrest order has been made against the director of a deposit-taking company the liquidator of which had been unable to trace the whereabouts of its depositors money, and most of the financial records of which were alleged to be kept in the boot of the director's car.[29] An order has also been made for the arrest of the managing director of a company which, according to its liquidator, had debts exceeding £9 million and had been trading in such a way as to cause him very considerable suspicion; the liquidator further deposed that the managing director had sold his house in Ireland, had residences abroad, and that he believed that the managing director had been deliberately evading him.[30] After arrest, the arrest order may be lifted upon its object surrendering his passport to the court, and undertaking not to leave the country, undertaking to attend court for examination, to notify the liquidator of any proposed change of address, and to attend at his office to give all relevant information about the company's affairs.[31]

Technically, the official liquidator has less opportunity for independent action than a liquidator in a voluntary winding up. The general administrative powers which they are both given by section 231[32] are circumscribed not only by the necessity for getting the consent of others, as must the liquidator in a voluntary winding up, to make compromises and to pay any class of creditors in full,[33] but the official liquidator must also obtain consents before participating in litigation on behalf of the company, carrying on its business so far as may be necessary for its beneficial winding up, or appointing a solicitor to assist him.[34] In his case, the requisite consents are those of the court or of the committee of inspection, if any. It should be emphasised that this difference may in liquidations of any complexity be only a technical distinction, since a liquidator in a voluntary winding up in order to cover himself may, as we have seen

---

[29] *Re Central Trust Investment Society*, High Court, Murphy J. August 1982, reporte in *The Irish Times*, August 31, 1982.

[30] *Re O'Shea's (Dublin) Ltd.*, High Court, Keane J, July 5, 1984, reported in *The Iri Times*, July 6, 1984.

[31] *Re Central Investment Trust Society*, n. 29, *supra*.

[32] Summarised at pp. 475–476, *supra*, save that an official liquidator does not ha an independent power to settle the list of contributories or make calls, rarities now days in any event.

[33] s.231(1)(*d*), (*e*), (*f*).

[34] s.231(*a*), (*b*), (*c*), though the court may if there is no committee of inspection d pense in advance with the necessity for its consent under s.231(1)(*a*), (*b*): s.231(4).

obtain the court's aid in taking difficult decisions, and though by section 231(3):

> "the exercise by the liquidator in a winding up by the court of the powers conferred by [section 231 are] subject to the control of the court, and any creditor or contributory may apply to the court in relation to any exercise or proposed exercise of any of those powers,"

we have seen that that control may also be invoked in a voluntary liquidation.[35]

Nonetheless, in view of the expense of applications to the court, it becomes desirable in the interests of all who hope to benefit from the liquidation that there should be a committee of inspection and its sanction invoked in uncontroversial matters.

The official liquidator may likewise invoke the aid of the court even where he is capable of independent action. As was pointed out by O'Higgins C.J. in *Van Hool McArdle Ltd.* v. *Rohan Industrial Estates Ltd.*[36] an official liquidator in a winding up by the court is empowered by section 231(2) to sell the company's property "by public auction or by private treaty without seeking the approach or consent of the High Court." However, the official liquidator in that case exercised his liberty not to act independently, and chose to enter into a contract of sale containing the express condition that "the sale to the purchaser shall be subject to and conditional upon the consent of the High Court thereto being obtained." The court in granting or withholding consent to such a contract is not reviewing the quality of the liquidator's decision. In other words, its approval is not dependent upon it being satisfied that *he* has in entering into the contract exercised his discretion bona fide and for its proper purpose. *His* discretion has been surrendered to the court. The court must consequently exercise its own independent judgment on the merits of the contract. Therefore it must have regard to a better offer received before it has consented, and refuse to approve the contract.[37]

Once the court has approved such a contract on its merits, no subsequent offer will be considered: *Re Hibernian Transport Companies Ltd.*[38]

---

[35] See p. 476, *supra*.

[36] [1980] I.R. 237, 240.

[37] These statements summarise the judgments in the Supreme Court in *Van Hool McArdle Ltd.* v. *Rohan Industrial Estates Ltd.*, fn. 36, *supra*.

[38] [1972] I.R. 190. See also *Munster and Leinster Bank* v. *Munster Motor Co. Ltd.* [1922] I.R. 15.

The official liquidator may initiate schemes and arrangements under sections 201–203, as to which see Chapter 9 at pp. 289 *et seq.*

Disclaimer

Section 290,[39] a provision borrowed from English bankruptcy legislation,[40] allows the liquidator of any company being wound up to disclaim with the leave of the court:

> "land of any tenure burdened with onerous covenants, . . . shares or stock in companies, . . . unprofitable contracts, or . . . any other property *which is unsaleable or not readily saleable by reason of its binding the possessor thereof to the performance of any onerous act or to the payment of any sum of money* . . . "[41]

The object of the provision is the speedy and efficient administration of the assets. Its consequence is sometimes the reverse because of a failure in it to provide clearly for the consequences of disclaimer, as we shall see. New thinking is required here.

Disclaimer will take effect from a liquidator's written notice of intent[42] to disclaim which must be made within certain time limits, usually a year from the commencement of the winding up.[43] His right to disclaim may be barred by persons interested in the property giving him 28 days to make up his mind.[44] Section 290(3) provides that the disclaimer:

> "shall operate to determine, as from the date of disclaimer, the rights, interests and liabilities of the company, and the property of the company, in or in respect of the property disclaimed, but shall not, except so far as is necessary for the purpose of releasing the company and the property of the company from liability, affect the rights and liabilities of any other person."

From this opaque wording arose the conundrum resolved by Keane J. in *Tempany* v. *Royal Liver Trustees Ltd.*[45] English cases have held that the surety or guarantor of a disclaiming lessee's obligation under the lease would themselves be released for the future by the disclaimer since theirs was a dependent obligation which vanished

---

[39] Supplemented by R.S.C., Ord. 74, Pt. XI.

[40] s.54 of the Bankruptcy Act 1914 [*U.K.*], carried also into s.323 of the Companies Act 1948 [*U.K.*].

[41] Emphasis supplied. These are the words which govern the exercise of the power.

[42] *Tempany* v. *Royal Liver Trustees Ltd.* [1984] I.L.R.M. 273, following *Re H.H. Realisations Ltd.* (1975) 31 P. & C.R. 249, and adverting to *Grant* v. *Aston Ltd.* 103 I.L.T.R. 30.

[43] s.290(2) contains the limits.

[44] s.290(5).

[45] See n. 42, *supra.*

with the disappearance of the primary obligation.[46] Accordingly, in England leave to disclaim is refused where it would involve this consequence.[47] Keane J. found the proposition false. The release of the surety was not, in the words of section 290(3), "necessary for the purpose of releasing the company and the property of the company from liability"; nor was the release of an original lessee. These were not therefore matters which should affect the court's discretion in giving leave to disclaim. Keane J. affirmed that "the exclusive concern of the Court in an application for leave to disclaim must be the interests of all persons interested in the liquidation,"[48] and remarked that the insolvency of a lessee was the very circumstance in which the continuing liabilities of surety, and original lessee (if the disclaiming lessee is an assignee) were designed to protect the lessor.[49]

The only practical consequence of a disclaimer allowed in such circumstances is that the company's proprietary right, an untidy item of undisposable property, disappears. The company's *in personam* liabilities in respect of the lease simply reappear in other guises as provable debts in the liquidation, *e.g.* the lessor insofar as not reimbursed by others claims for his accrued rights up to the date of disclaimer, and in respect of his lost rights thenceforward, under section 290(9) as a "person damaged by the operation of a disclaimer"; the surety, if any, claims in the liquidation under the right of indemnity possessed by all sureties against their principals,[50] and, where the disclaiming lessee took by assignment, the original lessee to whom the landlord may now be looking for payment under the original covenant for rent[51] (insofar as not released *inter partes* on the assignment) likewise proves in respect of his covenant of indemnity.

The court may make a vesting order in respect of the disclaimed property.[52] A disclaimed lease continues in a suspended existence without an owner "like a dormant volcano" as one judge described it,[53] a pretty analogy but not a consequence which a legal system

---

[46] *Stacey* v. *Hill* [1901] 1 K.B. 660; *D. Morris & Sons Ltd.* v. *Jeffreys* (1932) 148 L.T. 6; accepted also in *Warnford Investments Ltd.* v. *Duckworth* [1979] Ch. 127.

[47] *Re Katharine et Cie Ltd.* [1932] 1 Ch. 70.

[48] [1984] I.L.R.M. 273, 289, following Lord Selborne, L.C. in *Ex p. East and West India Dock Co. Re Clarke* (1881) 17 Ch. D. 759, 764–765.

[49] [1984] I.L.R.M. 273, 288.

[50] *Ibid.* at pp. 278, 289.

[51] See *Warnford Investments Ltd.* v. *Duckworth*, n. 46, *supra*.

[52] s.290(7), (8). See *East and West India Dock Co.* v. *Hill* (1882) 22 Ch. D. 14.

[53] *Re Thompson and Cottrell's Contract* [1943] Ch. 97, 100, save that in England, unlike the Irish position as described by Keane J. in *Tempany* v. *Royal Liver Trustees Ltd.*, n. 45 *supra*, and reflected in the text, the lease if disclaimed on behalf of an *original lessee* ceases to exist: *Warnford Investments Ltd.* v. *Duckworth*, n. 49, *supra*.

with claims to precision can tolerate. It so continues until a vesting order is made in respect of it, if at all, or until dissolution of the company when the lease vests in the Minister for Finance pursuant to the State Property Act 1954. He *may* disclaim it, in which case it will vest in the person entitled to the reversion, and the resultant merger will extinguish the obligations flowing from it. Also, if the landlord re-enters, often the practical solution, then by section 7 of Deasy's Act,[53a] it and all obligations flowing from it will cease to exist.[54]

The administration of assets

Before one can arrive at the assets distributable among the creditors, there are certain deductions to be made. In the case of a winding up by the court, they are listed for the most part by R.S.C., Order 74, r. 129. It provides:

> "The assets of a company in a winding up by the Court remaining after payment of the fees and expenses properly incurred in preserving, realising or getting in the assets, including where the company has previously commenced to be wound up voluntarily such remuneration costs and expenses as the Court may allow to a Liquidator appointed in such voluntary winding up shall, subject to any order of the Court,[54a] be liable to the following payments which shall be made in the following order of priority, namely:
> *First*—The costs of the petition, including the costs of any person appearing on the petition whose costs are allowed by the Court.
> *Next*—The costs and expenses of any person who makes or concurs in making the company's statement of affairs.
> *Next*—The necessary disbursements of the Official Liquidator other than expenses properly incurred in preserving, realising or getting in the assets hereinbefore provided for.
> *Next*—The costs payable to the solicitor for the Official Liquidator.
> *Next*—The remuneration of the Official Liquidator.
> *Next*—The out-of-pocket expenses necessarily incurred by the committee of inspection (if any)."

It was held by Carroll J. in *Re Van Hool McArdle Ltd.*[55] that corpo

---

[53a] The Landlord and Tenant Law Amendment, Ireland, Act 1860.
[54] These propositions are taken from the judgment of Keane J.
[54a] The court has power by s.244 to vary the order.
[55] [1982] I.L.R.M. 340, following in this respect *Re Mesco Properties Ltd.* [19?] W.L.R. 558.

ation tax on a capital gain incurred as a result of the realisation by
the liquidator of an asset is not an "expense" incurred in realising it
within the meaning of rule 129, being merely a possible consequence
of a sale at a profit; nor, as was confirmed on appeal to the Supreme
Court,[56] is it a "necessary disbursement" of the official liquidator.
Necessary disbursements, it was said, covered such items as expenditure on the "necessary maintenance of buildings, or wages for car-
etaking,"[57] things of the nature of "costs or expenses incurred by
persons involved in the liquidation," and not a post-liquidation liability for corporation tax. In the High Court, in an argument which
the Supreme Court thought "might well be correct," Carroll J.
rejected the payment of post-liquidation tax as a "disbursement"
under rule 129 on the ground that pre-liquidation taxes are already
given a degree of priority by the Act. Pre-liquidation taxes qualify to
an extent as preferential debts, *infra*, which rank after the items
under discussion, and before other unsecured creditors, and that
being the extent of the statutory priority, it was held that a mere
Rule of Court could not be construed as taking it further. This argument ignores the cast-iron distinction in liquidations described by
Chatterton V.-C. in *Re National Building and Land Co.*,[58] and by many
other judges before and since:

> "the distinction to be observed is one between debts and liab-
> ilities of the company existing at the commencement of the
> winding up which must be proved for and paid *pari passu*,[59] and
> must abate rateably in case the assets of the company prove
> insufficient, and debts and liabilities which arise only in the
> course of the liquidation and as incidental to it, which must be
> paid before any distribution of the assets."

Ignored in *Re Van Hool McArdle Ltd.* was a decision of the Supreme
Court in 1924, *Irish Provident Assurance Co. Ltd.* v. *Kavanagh*.[59a] In that
case, the Supreme Court decided that a company's income generated by a liquidator's activities was liable to income tax. In the
course of delivering the judgment of the Court, O'Connor J. said:

> " . . . all engagements entered into by a Liquidator in his

---

[56] Rep. *sub. nom. Revenue Commissioners* v. *Donnelly* [1983] I.L.R.M. 329, *not* following
in this respect *Re Mesco Properties Ltd.*, n. 55, *supra*.
[57] *Per* O'Higgins C.J. at p. 331.
[58] (1885–86) 15 L.R. Ir. 47, 49. See also *Re Gray's Inn Construction Ltd.* [1980] 1
W.L.R. 711, mentioned at p. 483, *supra*.
[59] Subject now to preferential claims, *infra*.
[59a] [1930] I.R. 231.

official capacity, and all liabilities incurred by him as such, assuming that they are proper, are paramount to the claims of all the creditors and shareholders of the company. They are really in the nature of salvage, because everything done by him, again assuming that it is properly done, is done in their interest."[59b]

Admittedly, it is not clear from the report whether the company was solvent,[59c] but this dictum, had it been cited, might have influenced the courts' interpretation in *Re Van Hool McArdle Ltd.* of the words "expenses" and "disbursements."

The originality of the decision in *Re Van Hool McArdle* led to speculation whether income arising from profitable trading by a liquidator of an insolvent company, or from other sources, might escape tax. The answer was not long in coming. In *Re Hibernian Transport Companies Ltd.* v. *Palgrave Murphy Ltd. and Palgrave Murphy (Carriers) Ltd.*,[60] the liquidator of three insolvent companies which had been in liquidation for 13 years successfully established that the tax payable[60a] by the company in respect of post-liquidation deposit interest could not, rank as a "disbursement" under rule 129; nor could the tax be paid as a debt, whether preferential or otherwise, of the company in the liquidation because the net assets remaining after rule 129 deductions are distributable among pre-liquidation creditors only. The tax could not therefore be paid at all. The latter part of this decision thus faithfully observed the cast-iron distinction between pre- and post-liquidation debts, whilst the former part scrupulously followed the Supreme Court in *Re Van Hool McArdle* which had obscured that same distinction.

The Revenue Commissioners have obtained a corrective enactment, not of retroactive effect, in the form of the complex section 56 of the Finance Act 1983 which expressly renders corporation tax in respect of capital gains by a liquidator a "necessary disbursement." But no corrective action has been taken in respect of other taxes.

One might add under the heading of necessary disbursements post-liquidation rent accrued due in respect of the company's rented property if the liquidator

"has retained possession for the purposes of the winding up, or

---

[59b] At p. 234.

[59c] Authorities affirming taxability of solvent companies in liquidation are *City of Dublin Steam Packet Co.* v. *Revenue Commissioners (No. 2)* [1930] I.R. 217 and *Spa Estates Ltd.* v. *O hArgain (Inspector of Taxes)* (High Court, Kenny J. June 30, 1975, unrep.).

[60] [1984] I.L.R.M. 583.

[60a] Earlier litigation in the same liquidation is reported at [1972] I.R. 190, and discussed at pp. 474, 481–481, 489, *supra*.

if he has used the property for carrying on the company's business, or has kept the property to sell it or to do the best he can with it"

per Lindley L.J. in *Re Oak Pits Colliery Co.*[61] The proper costs properly incurred by the liquidator in litigation on behalf of the company likewise come within the above categories: *Re National Building and Land Co.*[62] The case concerned the costs due to a successful plaintiff in a post-liquidation action,[63] but most such applications of funds will, in the nature of things, be in respect of proceedings brought or continued by the liquidator. Into which category of rule 129 such costs fall would seem to depend on the circumstances. Often they will be of the highest category if they were incurred "in preserving, realising or getting in the assets"; otherwise, they would seem to be in the category of "necessary disbursements." Ripples from *Re Van Hool McArdle Ltd.*[63a] persist even here. Uncertainties engendered by that decision led to Carroll J.'s being asked to rule in *Irish Commercial Society Ltd. and others* v. *Plunkett and others*[63b] whether if a company in liquidation were called upon to honour the usual undertaking as to damages given on its behalf by its liquidator on its obtaining an interlocutory injunction, the resultant damages payable by it would obtain priority under r. 129. This she refused to do, since the question remained hypothetical and because all interested parties had not had the opportunity of being represented, but she did indicate, in continuing the injunction, that she considered it arguable that damages paid by the company in those circumstances would be "expenses properly incurred in preserving, realising or getting in the assets," *i.e.* the top level of priority under rule 129.

The foregoing order of application, though framed for a compulsory winding up, applies also with the deletion of inapplicable items to a voluntary liquidation: *Re Redbreast Preserving Co. (Ireland) Ltd.*[64]

The court may in respect of any liquidation, voluntary or compulsory, alter the order as it thinks just.[65]

Preferential creditors must be paid first out of the distributable assets arrived at by deducting the foregoing items. If the distributable assets are insufficient to satisfy all preferential creditors, they

---

[61] (1882) 21 Ch. D. 322, 330, in which the authorities are reviewed. See also *Re B.C. Coupler and Engineering Co. Ltd. (No. 3)* [1970] 1 W.L.R. 702; *Grant* v. *Aston Ltd.* 93 I.L.T.R. 39; and R.S.C., Ord. 74, r. 107.

[62] See n. 58, *supra.*

[63] For the staying of post-liquidation actions and leave to proceed, see ss.217, 222.

[63a] See n. 55, *supra.*

[63b] High Court, Carroll J., Junr 6, 1984; unreported.

[64] [1958] I.R. 234, 239; and s.281.

[65] ss.244, 280(1).

may be augmented by the property comprised in any floating charge created by the company.[66] In no other respect may a validly secured creditor be forced to give way to unsecured creditors. For the possible grounds of invalidity of floating charges, see pp. 511 et seq. below, and pp. 452 *et seq.*, above.

Preferential creditors are defined by section 285 of the Companies Act 1963 as amended by section 10 of the Companies (Amendment) Act 1982, *and* by a collection of statutes relating to employees, the Minimum Notice and Terms of Employment Act 1973, the Redundancy Payments Acts 1967–79, the Unfair Dismissals Act 1977 and the Protection of Employees (Employers' Insolvency) Act 1984, *and* by statutes imposing taxes, the Capital Gains Tax Act 1975, the Corporation Tax Act 1976, and the Value-added Tax Acts 1972–82, *and* by social welfare legislation, the Social Welfare (Consolidation) Act 1981. In fact, it is not too difficult to surmise from the foregoing list that preferential debts consist of certain employees' claims, certain unpaid social insurance contributions, certain subrogated claims by the Minister for Labour in respect of payments by him to employees of the company out of the public funds (the Redundancy and Employers' Insolvency Fund), and certain back taxes. It is not intended to enter into the detail of them in this work.[67] Reference must be made to the particular legislation. Cahill in his essay *Company Failure in Ireland* [68] has shown from a statistical sample of 20 of the Irish companies which went into liquidation in 1977 that preferential creditors ranged between 22 per cent. and 48 per cent. of the

---

[66] s.285(7)(*b*).

[67] Though perhaps *Re Dairy Lee Ltd.* [1976] I.R. 314 should be mentioned. In that case, whilst acknowledging that a director is not as such an employee of the company (citing *inter alia Hutton* v. *West Cork Railway Co.* (1883) 23 Ch. D. 654: see generally pp 83–85 *supra*), Kenny J. held that a director without an express service contract but who nonetheless worked full-time for the company and drew a "salary" was by implication an employee in addition to being a director (following *Re Beeton & Co. Lt* [1913] 2 Ch. 279). He was therefore a "servant" entitled to preferential payment in respect of accrued holiday remuneration under s.285(2)(*d*). Also to be noted is *Re Pal grave Murphy Ltd.* (High Court, Hamilton J. February 20, 1979, unrep.) in which was held that under the insurance card system the payment of the social insurance contribution was made by affixing the insurance stamp to the card, and not by the purchase of the stamps from the Post Office. Accordingly, a claim in respect of a dishonoured cheque used to pay for insurance stamps was not a claim in respect of a unpaid social insurance contribution so as to gain preference under s. 285. Note also that a person who advanced money before the commencement of the winding up for the payment of the wage bill of a company's employees may be subrogated to the preferential claims: s.285(*b*). For how this subrogation works, see *Re Station Mote Ltd.* (High Court, Carroll J., November 22, 1984; unreported).

[68] Edward Cahill, (1980) April *Accountancy Ireland*, 17.

unsecured creditors as a whole, and that the main preferential items were arrears of Value-Added Tax, wages in lieu of notice,[69] and P.A.Y.E. In five of the 20 companies the preferential creditors were paid nothing, and in three they were paid in part only; whereas the general body of unsecured creditors were paid nothing in 10 out of the 20 cases, and in one they were paid in part only.

The moral justification for the priority of employees' claims must have its origins in a condition of supposed dependance, once true. No moral justification consonant with a work ethic can be found for giving State claims preference over the general body of unsecured creditors who have, after all, supplied goods or services.

All preferential creditors rank equally among themselves, and abate rateably in the event of a deficiency.[70]

We turn now to the general body of unsecured creditors. All money claims are admissible in proof against a solvent company, uncertainties and contingencies being resolved by valuation.[71] In the case of an insolvent company, section 284(1) declares that:

> "the same rules shall prevail and be observed relating to the respective rights of secured and unsecured creditors and to debts provable and to the valuation of annuities and future and contingent liabilities as are in force for the time being under the law of bankruptcy relating to the estates of persons adjudged bankrupt"

and that claimants may prove and be paid correspondingly. This section need not, fortunately, be treated as an invitation to embark upon a journey through the whole maze of the archaic laws of bankruptcy. Section 284 introduces them only in the respects it mentions. Thus, the bankruptcy provisions designed to augment the distribuable estate of the bankrupt, such as the "reputed ownership" clause, do not as such apply to company liquidations.[72] Section 284 does not import bankruptcy law on matters already specifically regulated by the Companies Acts, such as the effect of the levying of executions.[73] Nor, obviously, does it import bankruptcy laws specifically imported by other sections. The bankruptcy law of fraudulent preference is the case in point. It is specifically imported and

---

[69] See *Termination of employment, infra.*

[70] s.285(7).

[71] s.283.

[72] *Re Irish Attested Sales Ltd.* [1962] I.R. 70 (though the provision under discussion here, s.331 of the Irish Bankrupt and Insolvent Act 1857, was subsequently specifically introduced to company liquidations by s.284(2).

[73] *Re Whiterock Quarries Ltd.* [1933] I.R. 363; the specific bankruptcy provision ejected from company liquidations in that case was subsequently brought in by 291.

adapted to company liquidations by section 286. We treat this topic in depth in the next section, *Fraudulent preference*.

First we look in brief at some of the bankruptcy rules imported by section 284.[74] A secured creditor may value his security and prove for the balance, or give up his security and prove for the whole; if he has realised his security, he may prove for the balance.[75] By section 61 of the Civil Liability Act 1961 claims, whether liquidated or unliquidated, for damages for contribution in respect of *any* wrong are admissible to proof, provided the wrong was committed before the commencement of the winding up. Section 61(2) contains provision for the assessment of unliquidated damages. In England, it should be noted, there has recently been a conflict of authority over the admission to proof of unliquidated damages in tort.[75a] In Ireland, with its different statutory background, this controversy is not material. Set-offs of mutual debts and credits are allowed.[76] Annuities and contingent liabilities are valued[77]; and future debts are discounted at the rate 6 per cent. *p.a.*[78]

The rights of members to participate in whatever assets remain is examined in Chapter 6, *Shares and Membership* at pp. 174 *et seq.*

Fraudulent preference

Company law, in dealing with insolvent companies, has, as we have seen, borrowed some of the principles of the law of bankruptcy affecting individuals. Of these, the principle of the "fraudulent preference" is most prominent. Its policy, according to Porter M.R. in *Re Boyd*,[79] is "to secure an equitable distribution of the property of a bankrupt," an object which, as we shall see, is but patchily attained.

---

[74] See generally *Bankruptcy Law Committee Report*, 1972, Prl. 2714, in which the ensuing and other material provisions are discussed.

[75] Bankruptcy (Ireland) Amendment Act 1872, s.4. As to voting by secured creditors in creditors' meetings, see R.S.C., Ord. 74, rr. 69 *et seq*. And see *Re Ligoniel Spinning Co., ex p. Bank of Ireland* [1900] I.R. 324.

[75a] Contrast *Re Berkeley Securities (Property) Ltd.* [1980] 1 W.L.R. 1589 (Vinelott J with *Re Islington Metal and Plating Works Ltd.* [1983] 3 All E.R. 218 (Harman J.), which the latter, ruling against admissibility, seems to have been correct in English law.

[76] Irish Insolvent and Bankrupt Act 1857, s.251; *Re Tailteann Freight Services Ltd* [1975] I.R. 376; *Gresham Industries Ltd.* v. *Cannon* (High Court, Finlay P., July 2, 198 unrep.) at p. 25 of the transcript apply *Ex. P. Waite* [1956] 3 All E.R. 225, and *Re Fe tion* [1931] 1 Ch. 85.

[77] *Ibid.* ss.255–258.

[78] *Ibid.* s.252.

[79] (1885–86) 15 L.R., Ir. 521, 545.

Section 286 of the Companies Act 1963 introduces the principle only referentially. It says:

> "(1) . . . any conveyance, mortgage, delivery of goods, payment, execution or other act relating to property made or done by or against a company within 6 months before the commencement of its winding up which, had it been made or done by or against an individual within 6 months before the presentation of a bankruptcy petition on which he is adjudged a bankrupt, would be deemed in his bankruptcy a fraudulent preference, shall in the event of the company being wound up be deemed a fraudulent preference of its creditors and be invalid accordingly"[80]

We turn to section 53 of the Bankruptcy (Ireland) Amendment Act 1872 (as amended by the Companies Act 1963 Sched. 11) to find that the impugned act must have been done at a time when the individual was "unable to pay his debts as they became due from his own moneys," and that the act must be "in favour of any creditor with a view to giving such creditor, or any surety or guarantor for the debt due to such creditor, a preference over the other creditors." The act is by section 53 "deemed fraudulent and void" as against the bankrupt's assignees in bankruptcy. In the context of company law, that means void as against the liquidator who is concerned on behalf of the general body of creditors; an act by which only secured creditors suffer cannot be a fraudulent preference.[81] The imprecise "invalid" of the Companies Act must be treated as synonymous with the "void" of the bankruptcy legislation. As we have seen,[82] no rights or duties can arise out of a void transaction; in particular, no property can pass in goods delivered or money paid, these being recoverable by a proprietary claim and their transfer giving rise to potential claims in quasi-contract and in tort, and no security interest can arise in the preferred creditor, however it was purported to be effected, whether by a document, delivery of possession, or otherwise. There is one exception to the total avoidance of the transaction. Section 53 provides that the rights of a person who has acquired property "in good faith and for valuable consideration" from a fraudulently preferred creditor shall not be adversely affected. For the meaning of "good faith," see pp. 135–137, *supra*. The preferred

---

[80] Winding up commences on the presentation of a winding up petition to the court, or, on the passing of the appropriate resolution: s.220.

[81] *Willmott* v. *London Cellulloid Co.* (1886) 34 Ch.D. 147; *ex p. Cooper* (1875) 10 Ch.App. 510.

[82] Chap. 4 at p. 123.

creditor, subject to disgorgement of benefits received, ranks *pari passu* with other unsecured creditors in the distribution of assets in the winding up.[83]

There are many cases on what constitutes a fraudulent preference, "the decisions in which," as Holmes L.J. said in *Re Oliver*,[84] "are far from uniform. It would be a labour—not of love—to criticize them, and impossible to harmonize them." Nonetheless, the central principle may be stated clearly, and, indeed, criticised. The key is the statutory expression "with a view to giving . . . a preference," and, accordingly, one searches for the debtor's dominant intention in entering into the impugned transaction, or, as Porter M.R. put it in *Re Boyd*,[85] one conducts "a metaphysical inquiry as to the view or motive influencing" the debtor. In the case of corporations, the principles, discussed in Chapter 2 at pp. 33 *et seq.*, governing the imputation of a mental element to a corporation should apply. One seeks the intention of a person or body of persons within the company to whom responsibility for the transaction has been lawfully delegated. Often this will be the board of directors, but sometimes it may be a lesser agent. In *Kelleher* v. *Continental Irish Meat Ltd.*,[86] for example, it was recognised that the company's intention to prefer a creditor could have been found in the intention of an employee, if he had in fact possessed its authority to enter into transactions of the type in issue. In *Corran Construction Co. Ltd.* v. *Bank of Ireland Finance Ltd.*,[87] one of the company's two directors was *de facto* in charge of its affairs. The absence of an intention on his part to prefer one of the company's creditors was imputed to it.

The burden of proving the dominant intention of the company in entering into the transaction lies on the liquidator.[88] He will not be

---

[83] *Re Cawley* [1959] I.R. 330. Additionally, s.287 is concerned with fairness between those affected by a transaction void as a fraudulent preference under s.286. By s.287(1) if the company discharges its debt to A with a view to preferring B who has charged his property as security for that debt, A who has been bound to reimburse the company may sue B for the amount of the debt to the extent that it was covered by the charge, or the value of B's interest in the property charged, whichever is the less. By s.287(3), B may be joined as a party to the s.286 proceedings against A so that s.287 relief may be given against B for the benefit of A.

[84] [1914] 2 I.R. 356, 370. He was referring in the main to the English authorities.

[85] (1885) 15 L.R. 521, 546.

[86] H.C., Costello J., May 9, 1978, (unreported), (purported sale of company's goods to creditor with a view assumedly to his operating a set-off in respect of the unpaid purchase price).

[87] H.C. McWilliam J., September 8, 1976, (unreported).

[88] *Ibid.* at p. 6 of the transcript, *Peat* v. *Gresham Trust Ltd.* [1934] A.C. 252 and *R F.L.E. Holdings Ltd.* [1967] 1 W.L.R. 1409 being cited.

proving fraud as such, since, as Porter M.R. pointed out in *Re Boyd* [89]:

> " . . . there are often cases where a man, having committed no act of bankruptcy, yet knowing he cannot continue his trading, tries to place some of his creditors in a better position than the rest, by payment in full, or better treatment in some way. This, it may be, is not otherwise, or morally a fraud; because he really owes the money. . . . But it was felt that such a transaction is in its nature a fraud upon the bankrupt laws and therefore an exceptional right grew up in his assignees . . . to rip up the transaction."

Giving a creditor a preference involves placing him "in a position of relative advantage"[90] over the other creditors. Without the benefit of the case law, one might be tempted to think that one factor surely indicative of a debtor's intention to place a creditor in a position of relative advantage over the others would be overt pressure exerted by the creditor on the debtor with that end in view. However, the clear intention to prefer in such cases is allowed to be outweighed by the pressure, the courts adopting the artificial rationalisation that the pressure robs the debtor of the ability to form an intention. Take Porter M.R. in *Re Daly & Co. Ltd.*[91]:

> "Where pressure exists so as to overbear the volition of the debtor a payment is not made with a view to prefer the creditor exerting it, but because the debtor cannot help it. The view to prefer is absent; or at least is not the real view, or motive or reason, actuating the debtor . . . "

Other frailties do not have the same status, for, later in the same case, he says[92]:

> " . . . neither natural love and affection, gratitude, expectation of benefit, sympathy, vindictiveness, or any other mental condition can in such cases eliminate the view to prefer . . . , however strongly the debtor may be convinced that he is doing what is right and fair."

So to distinguish motives reflects the attitudes of an age in which the stigma of bankruptcy exceeded even that of divorce. Though

---

[89] (1885–86) 15 L.R. Ir. 521, 545. See also *Re Patrick and Lyon Ltd.* [1933] Ch. 786, 790, and *Re Station Motors Ltd.* (High Court, Carroll J., November 22, 1984) at p. 8 of the transcript.

[90] *Ibid.* p. 546.

[91] (1887–88) 19 L.R. Ir. 83, 93.

[92] At p. 97.

absurdly at odds with the aim of achieving an "equitable distribution"[93] of the assets of an insolvent, it seems that a creditor doubtful about his debtor's solvency, or even knowing that he is insolvent, is free, so far as the law of fraudulent preference is concerned, to be as unpleasant as lawfully possible with a view to effectively salvaging something from the wreck before it is too late, *i.e.* in the case of a debtor company, before winding up supervenes, or a floating charge crystallizes. The only criterion is that his unpleasantness should have exerted sufficient pressure on the volition of the debtor. Whether he has depends on the state of mind of the debtor: in *Re Boyd* it sufficed that the debtor succumbed to a threat of a criminal prosecution, though his fears were groundless; in *Taylor (Assignees of)* v. *Thompson*[94] the debtor feared he might be accused of embezzlement unless he made the payment; and, in *Taylor (Assignees of)* v. *Killileagh Flax Spinning Co.*[95] he feared he might not in future be employed by particular clients, unless he preferred them. But in *Re Daly & Co. Ltd.*[96] an unfortunate auditor whom the officers of the debtor company were under a strong moral obligation to prefer failed to establish that he had exerted sufficient pressure on them. He had as a personal favour lent money to the ailing company to tide it over for a short period whilst it tried to raise fresh loan capital, which, in the event, was not forthcoming. The liquidator failed to establish an intention to prefer in *Corran Construction Co. Ltd.* v. *Bank of Ireland Finance Ltd.*[97] in which there appear to have been suggestions that the creditor exerted pressure, though the extent to which this was seriously argued is not clear from the transcript.[98] A bank had taken an equitable mortgage by deposit of the company's title deeds, which was void for non-registration. Later, after the bank had been advised that the company was insolvent and had threatened winding-up proceedings in an effort to obtain payment, a fresh deposit of title deeds was made on behalf of the company with the bank. This was the transaction which the liquidator sought to have set aside as a fraudulent preference. The bank's representatives had been pressing for repayment, and it was McWilliam J.s "impression from the evidence"[99] that the director whose intention was material[1]

---

[93] See text at n. 39, *supra*.
[94] (1869–70) I.R.C.L. 129.
[95] (1869–70) I.R.C.L. 120.
[96] (1887–88) 19 L.R. Ir. 83.
[97] See n. 87, *supra*.
[98] McWilliam J. adverted to pressure, *infra*, and an English case involving allegations of pressure, *Re F.L.E. Holdings Ltd.* n. 54 *supra*, was cited.
[99] All quotations are from p. 7 of the transcript.
[1] See p. 506, *supra*.

had been avoiding them for this reason; "when they finally caught up with him when he was ill in bed, it was something of a relief to find that they would be satisfied if he would remedy some defect in the mortgage." At that time, he thought the company could be kept going, despite professional advice to the contrary. In these circumstances, the liquidator's burden of proving an intention to prefer was held not to have been discharged. The persistence of the bank did not, according to McWilliam J. constitute "pressure in the ordinary sense," but this remark does not seem to be material to the decision.[2]

We have seen *what* must be proved. *How* to prove it is often in practice more pertinent. There follow some propositions most of which are condensed from the recent judgment of Carroll J. in *Re Station Motors Ltd.*[3] As ever when a mental element is sought to be proved, a court, in absence of direct evidence, is bound to draw inferences from other proved facts. If the facts proved are equally consistent with the presence of that mental element as with its absence, the burden of proof is not discharged. This amounts to more than saying that the matter has not been proved on the balance of probabilities, the usual standard in civil litigation. On other hand, a court may infer an intention to prefer, even where other less cogent explanations have been proved. Where the persons responsible for causing the company to enter into the impugned transaction themselves stand to benefit from it, the inference in favour of an intent to prefer is very strong. Thus, in *Re Station Motors Ltd.* itself, the payment made to a bank *pro tanto* relieved the persons causing the company to pay from personal liability under a guarantee. If, despite such personal advantage, the alleged preference does

---

[2] This decision should be contrasted with *Re F.P. & C.H. Matthews Ltd.* [1982] 2 W.L.R. 495 (a genuine belief of ability to pay debts at some future time does not of itself negative an intention to prefer), and with *Re Tweedale* (1892) 2 Q.B. 367 (later assignment made in substitution for earlier void under the Bills of Sale Acts not a fraudulent preference), followed in Ireland in *Re Oliver* [1914] 2 I.R. 356 (later cheque issued in substitution for earlier not a fraudulent preference). Neither this, nor any other Irish case was cited in the judgment of McWilliam J. The misapprehension which seems to have governed the bank's conduct in *Corran Construction* (*i.e.* that a freshly executed charge would be a fraudulent preference) seems to have governed the parties' conduct in *Re Welding Plant Ltd.* (High Court, McWilliam J., June 27 and July 25, 1984; unreported) in which a bank, being entitled to have executed in its favour a valid charge over the company's land, nonetheless became party to a transaction by which it funded the purchase of that land by two of the company's directors (also the guarantors of its debts). The sale was avoided as a fraudulent preference.

[3] High Court, November 22, 1984; unreported. The learned judge drew upon observations in *Re Kushler (M) Ltd.* [1943] Ch. 248, and *Peat* v. *Gresham Trust Ltd.* [1934] A.C. 252.

not depart from the normal pattern of payments[4] by the company, the balance will swing back the other way. Finally, facts must be proved from which it can be inferred that those responsible for the company entering the transaction knew, or thought, that the company was, or might be, insolvent, or approaching insolvency. This last is an essential pre-requisite to the claim.

Securing fairness in the distribution of the assets of an insolvent, whether corporate or otherwise, is not necessarily to be achieved by looking into the mind of the debtor. It does seem curious, as Holmes L.J. remarked in *Re Oliver*,[5] "that persons receiving *in good faith* payment of their just demands should be obliged to repay the sum received on account of the mental attitude of the person paying." Conversely, what if the recipients are not in good faith, as that term is ordinarily understood? Take, as an example, the cases involving pressure exerted by the creditor. He will, with few exceptions, have known, or have had a strong opinion, that his debtor was insolvent. He therefore will have been actively involved in a conscious attempt to steal a march on the other creditors, and have complicity in what Porter M.R. in *Re Boyd*[6] called "a fraud upon the bankrupt laws," saved only by the fact that the debtor by reason of the pressure did not have the requisite intention to prefer. And there are other cases not involving pressure where the recipient of the preference believes full well that his debtor is insolvent, yet retains his preference through a lack by the debtor of an intention to prefer. The recipient in such circumstances is not, it is said, dishonest in the eye of the law. In particular, he will not, so it has been held in England in *Re Sarflax Ltd.*,[7] be a party to fraudulent trading by the company within section 297, in all jurisdictions a much later invention than fraudulent preference, which, it is not impossible to suppose, may have been designed to remedy some of the deficiencies of the latter. Knowingly being a party to the incurring by an insolvent company of unrepayable credit is fraudulent trading within section 297.[8] Knowingly depriving fellow creditors of the benefit of the rights

---

[4] For an analysis of lodgments to and withdrawals from a bank account to establish such a pattern, see *Re Industrial Design and Manufacture Ltd.* (High Court [Northern Ireland], Chancery Division, Carswell J., June 25, 1984; unreported).

[5] [1914] 2 I.R. 356, 370. Italics supplied.

[6] See the quotation in the text at n. 89, *supra*.

[7] [1979] Ch. 592. Oliver J. in this erudite judgment decided that a fraudulent preference does not *per se* involve fraudulent trading. He acknowledged, however, "the possibility of circumstances of a very peculiar nature" from which fraud proper could be inferred in a fraudulent preference case.

[8] *Re Gerald Cooper Chemicals Ltd.* [1978] Ch. 262 (creditor party to his debt being repaid out of sum advanced by another creditor).

which will accrue to them in an insolvent liquidation seems equally fraudulent, the only difference in principle being that in this latter instance the creditors are being cheated of the benefit of their rights under a statutory scheme of distribution rather than, as in the former, of the benefit of their rights arising at common law.[9] The Irish courts have yet to decide this point.

More fundamental reforms require the intervention of statute. It may be that fairness as between creditors of an insolvent should be decided by reference to the conduct of the creditors. Thus, it may be argued, a creditor who knowing or believing that his debtor company is, or may be, insolvent, receives payment from it of his debt, ought if liquidation supervenes to reimburse the liquidator the amount thereof in order to place himself in a position of parity with his fellow creditors.[10] Also, in the interests of parity should there not be a duty on a debtor company to suspend all payments if its directors believe it to be irretrievably insolvent? Amending legislation could declare such payments to be *ultra vires*, and recoverable from the directors themselves, insofar as not recovered from the recipients.

Invalidity of floating charges

The security given by way of floating charge[11] by an insolvent company may be invalidated by two independent provisions of the Companies Act 1963, s.288 and s.289. The debt itself survives the invalidity, but in an unsecured form. Each provision places a burden on those who would save the charge of proving that immediately after its creation the company was solvent.[12] The Supreme Court has established in *Re Creation Printing Co. Ltd.* that solvency in this context is to be determined by asking:

> "whether immediately after the debenture was given, the company was able to pay its debts as they became due. The question is not whether its assets exceed the estimated value of its liabilities, or whether a businessman would have regarded it as solvent."[13]

In answering that question, the Supreme Court decided that the

---

[9] See the distinction made by Porter M.R. in the quotation from *Re Boyd* in the text at n. 89, *supra*.

[10] Such fairness is not unknown in equity.

[11] For floating charges, see Chap. 14.

[12] *Re Creation Printing Co. Ltd.* [1981] I.R. 353, 358.

[13] [1981] I.R. 353, 358–59, *per* Kenny J. *nem. diss.*

fixed assets, *i.e.* those held for the purpose of generating income and not for resale, of a company which intends to stay in business will be disregarded, since they will not generally be realised whilst the company remains a going concern.[14] Thus, Creation Printing Co. Ltd. whose assets well exceeded its debts was nonetheless insolvent since the former were predominantly fixed, consisting mainly of machinery and plant.[15] Assumedly, if the company had shown an intention to increase liquidity by realising some of its fixed assets, whether as part of a slimming down of its existing business or as part of a complete change of direction, the released assets would have counted in reckoning solvency.[16] What effect the company's ability, if any, to raise money by a fixed charge on its fixed assets would have had on the computation of its solvency was not canvassed in the judgments.

Section 288 says:

> . . . where a company is being wound up, a floating charge on the undertaking or property of the company created within 12 months before the commencement of the winding up shall, unless it is proved that the company immediately after the creation of the charge was solvent, be invalid, except to the amount of any cash paid to the company at the time of or subsequently to the creation of, and in consideration for, the charge, together with interest on that amount at the rate of 5 per cent. per annum."

The security is thus preserved only to the extent that fresh money has been put up for it. In *Re Lakeglen Construction Ltd*,[17] for example, a floating charge given by a company shortly before the commencement of its winding up to a group of unsecured creditors in consideration of their forbearing to enforce the immediate payment of their debts was invalid. The fresh credit is not however confined to money advanced after the date upon which the charge was actually

---

[14] Following *ex p. Russell* (1882) 19 Ch.D. 588 (which concerned the voidability of dispositions of an individual bankrupt) and a dictum in *Re Patrick and Lyon Ltd.* [1933] Ch. 786 (fraudulent trading). Kenny J.s reference to "fixed assets and moveable assets" may be regarded as a slip. Contrast McWilliam J. in the court below at p. 357. For "fixed assets," see Chap. 10 at p. 330.

[15] Kenny J. at p. 363, in considering what assets *were* available, appears to have confused assets with the source of finance from which they were derived.

[16] McWilliam J. at p. 357 seems to support this assumption. It appears also to be material to Kenny J.s judgment: at p. 363 he says "On 4th June 1975 [the date of the creation of the floating charge], Creation Printing *intended to carry on its trade*. Therefore, the value of the fixed assets must be excluded in deciding whether it was solvent."

[17] Rep. *sub nom Kelly* v. *McMahon Ltd.* [1980] I.R. 347.

executed. It was affirmed in *Re Daniel Murphy Ltd.*[18] that "cash paid . . . at the time of . . . the creation of . . . the charge" includes money paid between the agreement to create a charge and its creation, provided that the delay was not intended to deceive creditors, was not unreasonable or culpable, and the chargee neither suggested it nor acquiesced in it. In this case the delay found acceptable, 55 days, was due to the parties' professional advisors having proceeded at a normal pace. Neither need the debt to the chargee be incurred contemporaneously with the creation of the charge. Thus, money drawn in pursuance of an overdraft facility secured by a floating charge nevertheless qualifies as being "paid . . . in consideration for" the charge.[19] In determining what sums within a continuous overdrawn account fall within the ambit of fresh money advanced in consideration for a charge the usual rules of appropriation apply.[20]

Section 289, by contrast, contains no allowance for fresh money advanced by the creditor. It provides:

"where—(*a*) a company is being wound up; and (*b*) the company was within 12 months before the commencement of the winding up indebted to any officer of the company; and (*c*) such indebtedness was discharged whether wholly or partly by the company or by any other person; and (*d*) the company created a floating charge on any of its assets or property within 12 months of the commencement of the winding up in favour of the officer to whom such company was indebted; then (without prejudice to any rights or liabilities arising apart from this section) such charge shall be invalid to the extent of the repayment referred to in paragraph (*c*) unless it is proved that the company immediately after the creation of the charge was solvent. . . . In this section, "officer" includes the spouse, child or nominee of an officer."[20]

The rationale behind section 289 seems to be that directors of a company running into trouble should not abuse their control of it and inside information to elevate themselves above the other unsecured creditors. The fact that they may be putting up fresh money would not provide a moral justification, since while the company continues to trade it will be incurring fresh credit likewise from the general creditors.

---

[18] [1964] I.R. 1, following *Re Colombian Fireproofing Ltd.* [1910] 1 Ch. 758 and *Re Alderfleet Shipbuilding and Engineering Co. Ltd.* [1922] 1 I.R. 22.

[19] *Re Daniel Murphy Ltd., supra.*

[20] *i.e.* in the absence of express appropriation, the rule in *Clayton's Case* (1817) 1 Mer. 572 applies: *Re Daniel Murphy Ltd.* [1964] I.R. 1, 11–14.

Section 289 leaves open the question whether the granting of the floating charge to the officer in question constitutes also a fraudulent preference of him.[21]

Termination of employment

In *Re Forster & Co. Ltd., ex p. Schumann*,[22] Chatterton V.-C. stated the general principle that a

> "resolution or order for winding up operates in law as *notice* of discharge to the company's servants. The liquidator is in the same position as any other employer of labour, who is bound to give notice of dismissal or compensation in lieu of such notice. The resolution operates as notice, and takes effect from the expiration of the period corresponding with the length of notice to which the person is entitled."[23]

In that case, Mr. Schumann was entitled by his contract of employment with the company to three month's notice of termination. The business of the company had been continued by the liquidator after the commencement of the winding up, since he was trying to sell it as a going concern, and Mr. Schumann had carried on working as usual. It was held that he was not entitled to fresh notice (or compensation in lieu) at the expiration of the three months from the commencement of the winding up. He had merely been working out his notice. No new service agreement with resultant new notice requirements could therefore be implied:

> " . . . the liquidator was entitled to Mr. Schumann's services in the same manner that an ordinary employer is entitled to the services of his servant during the currency of a notice of discharge."

Of course, in any liquidation circumstances may occur which amount to a waiver of the automatic notice of discharge.[24] Such a waiver might be implied from employees being retained beyond

---

[21] *Cf. Re Daly & Co.* (1887–88) 19 L.R. Ir. 83.

[22] (1887–78) 19 L.R. Ir. 240. Unfortunately this leading Irish authority was no adverted to in *Donnelly* v. *Gleeson*, n. 28, *infra*. *Re Forster & Co., ex p. Schumann* concerned a voluntary liquidation under the supervision of the court, a discontinued form. There are English authorities indicating that in that jurisdiction a resolution for voluntary winding up is not to be taken as a notice of dismissal of employees: *Midland Counties District Bank Ltd.* v. *Attwood* [1905] 1 Ch. 357. For the English law generally see Graham, "The effect of liquidation on contracts of service" (1952), 15 M.L.R. 48.

[23] Emphasis supplied; following *Chapman's Case* (1866) L.R. 1 Eq. 346.

[24] *Re English Joint Stock Bank, ex p. Harding* (1867) L.R. 3 Eq. 341, approved in *Re Forster & Co., ex p. Schumann*, n. 22, *supra*, and in *Donnelly* v. *Gleeson*, n. 28, *infra*.

their notice entitlement,[25] or might be express. Or the circumstances might be such as to indicate a fresh contract, but on the old terms.[26]

None of these variants arise where no part of the company's business is continued in the liquidation. In those circumstances, the entry by the company into liquidation stands as a wrongful dismissal of employees,[27] and they may claim as preferential creditors in the winding up the compensation in lieu of the notice to which they were entitled by common law or statute.

In *Donnelly* v. *Gleeson*,[28] it was held that the appointment of a provisional liquidator did not of itself constitute notice of discharge of employees, with the consequence that for the purpose of their statutory entitlements under the Minimum Notice and Terms of Employment Act 1973 and the Redundancy Payments Act 1967 the continuity of their employment by the company had not been interrupted by the assumption by the provisional liquidator of control of its business.

The liquidator as fiduciary

As Budd J. remarked in *Re Redbreast Preserving Co. (Ireland) Ltd.*[29] a "the official liquidator works for the benefit of all concerned, including the creditors, in the winding up of the company." In other words, he (and a liquidator in a voluntary winding up, for there can on this point be no distinction in principle between them) occupies a fiduciary position in relation to the company and parties claiming under a winding up. The Rules of Court for the winding up of companies[30] trouble to spell out in relation to an official liquidator some of the fiduciary consequences of his position. He must not accept any reward from any solicitor, auctioneer or other person connected with the company; he must not directly or indirectly buy any of the com-

---

[25] For notice entitlements, see Redmond, *Dismissal Law in the Republic of Ireland* 1982, Dublin.

[26] *Re English Joint Stock Bank, ex p. Harding*, n. 24, *supra*. Hamilton J. indicated in *Donnelly* v. *Gleeson*, n. 85 *infra*, that a specific request by the liquidator was necessary to found such a contract. He said at p. 7 of the transcript, summarising the result of the authorities: "A servant can however be kept on in the same terms as his original contract by being specifically requested to do so."

[27] *MacDowall's Case* (1886) 32 Ch.D. 366, accepted as authority in *Re Forster & Co., ex p. Schumann*, n. 22, *supra*, and in *Donnelly* v. *Gleeson*, n. 28, *infra*.

[28] High Court, Hamilton J. July 11, 1978, unrep. It is curious though that one of the "relevant dates" for determining an employee's preferential entitlement to arrears of wages in a winding up should be the appointment of a provisional liquidator: .285(1)(i). This statutory provision seems not to be consistent with the decision. It is not mentioned in the judgment.

[29] [1958] I.R. 234, 237.

[30] R.S.C., Ord. 74.

pany's assets; and he must not, if carrying on the business of the company, buy goods for that purpose so as to give a profit to himself.[1]

For a general description of the fiduciary relationship and its consequences, see Chapter 7.

FRAUDULENT TRADING

Three ideas for the reform of civil liability for fraudulent trading are currently afloat, two of them on a sea of rumour. One was launched on June 9, 1982 by the Cork Committee which reviewed the insolvency law and practice of England and Wales.[2] The Cork Committee would substitute the notion of *wrongful trading*. The others come from the reputed heads of a Bill, called the "domestic" Companies Bill, as yet unpublished[2a] and drafted by the Department of Industry, Trade, Commerce and Tourism. One of these proposals would add *reckless trading* as a head of civil liability, an idea first floated by the Jenkins Committee[3] in 1962, and thought to be long since sunk; the other would impose liability for incurring debts without an honest belief on reasonable grounds that they would be met when falling due; and the existing formulation of liability would be retained as a third head.

These ideas will be criticised below, insofar as they seek to introduce objective standards as a substitute for the honesty which has always exonerated as a matter of right, not discretion.[4] But first we will examine the law as it stands, and look at alternative ideas for reform.

The present law

Section 297(1) of the Companies Act 1963, the "fraudulent trading" section, affords a means by which the cloak of limited liability may be stripped away. It says:

> "(1) If in the course of the winding up of a company it appears
> that any business of the company has been carried on with
> intent to defraud creditors of the company or creditors of any

---

[1] *Ibid.* rr. 39–41. Other persons are also covered by these rules. See also s.301 which renders corrupt inducements in connection with the appointment of a liquidator an offence.

[2] (1982) Cmnd. 8558, para. 92, paras. 1758 *et seq.*, 1775 *et seq.*

[2a] This Chap. went finally to press in September 1985.

[3] (1962), Cmnd. 1749, para. 503.

[4] The "domestic" Bill is reputed to give the court a *discretion* to relieve from liability a respondent who proves that he acted honestly *and* responsibly.

other person or for any fraudulent purpose, the court on the application of the liquidator or any creditor or contributory of the company, may, if it thinks proper so to do, declare that any persons who were knowingly parties to the carrying on of the business in manner aforesaid shall be personally responsible, without any limitation of liability, for all or any of the debts or other liabilities of the company as the court may direct."

In addition, section 297(3) creates an expressly criminal offence of fraudulent trading where any business of the company has been carried on with the intent or for the purpose described in Section 297(1),[5] an offence which upon conviction on indictment carries a penalty of up to two years imprisonment, or a fine or both.

Section 297 has its origins in England in the Report[6] of the Greene Committee in 1926, and in the consequent legislation, the Companies Act 1928 [*U.K.*]. The Greene Committee proposed the remedy as a measure specifically designed to combat a blatant form of misconduct, known as "filling up the floating charge." Directors, having a valid but not very valuable floating charge over the assets of an insolvent company with few assets, would remedy the deficiency by causing the company to order and take delivery of goods for which they had no intention it should pay; they would then cause the company to go into voluntary liquidation, with themselves comfortably secured on the goods, and their supplier out in the cold as an unsecured creditor. This purpose explains the ancillary section 297(2) by which the court may, *inter alia*, cause the personal liability of an unsuccessful defendant to be charged upon any secured debt owed by the company to him. When, three decades later, the Cox Committee came to consider whether Ireland ought to adopt a simi-

---

[5] There are related criminal offences created by ss.293–296 which are seldom, if ever, invoked. Indeed, it may be argued that a chief defect in Irish company law administration is not lack of laws but lack of enforcement of existing laws. One assumes that lack of resources is the reason. Why enact laws if the means to implement them will be lacking? In such circumstances, the cry for "reform" is misplaced, a response of the so very common "words not deeds" variety. A wide variety of offences is created by ss.293–296, some very serious. They concern such things as the disposal or concealment of the company's property, failing to produce or to keep, or tampering with, its books, obtaining credit by fraud, transferring assets of the company whether lawfully or otherwise with intent to defraud creditors, *etc.* We have seen (at pp. 78, 491, *supra*) how s.299 allows the possibility of referral of suspected criminality to the D.P.P. Perhaps the statute should be strengthened to oblige each liquidator in every winding up to file as a matter of course with the D.P.P. an affidavit verifying either that no circumstances which *might* indicate the commission of an offence have come to his attention in the course of the winding up, or indicating those circumstances. In the latter event, the amendment could oblige the D.P.P. to investigate.

[6] (1926) Cmnd. 2657.

lar remedy, they gave a similarly blatant example of what they hoped to thwart by its introduction, the case of a company ordering goods, selling them for the purpose of satisfying a debenture to one of their own number, and leaving the supplier unpaid. They declared it "imperative that the Courts should have the widest powers to deal with this type of dishonesty."[7] The section is thus designed to combat deliberate cheating. The leading case in the hierarchy of the Common Law world, *Hardie* v. *Hanson*,[8] a decision of the High Court of Australia, indorses this view. "Intent to defraud creditors" means what it says; the respondent must "be actuated by a conscious fraudulent purpose"[9] to deprive creditors of the benefit of their rights. In that case, the respondent had caused the company to go on incurring debts to suppliers when the chance of their being paid in full was "so remote that it belonged to the realms of hope rather than belief"[10]; yet, since his intent was "to try, however despairingly, to carry the business through its difficulties to a success, which if it had been reached, would have benefited the creditors as well as himself,"[11] it was not an intent to defraud them, however commercially immoral his conduct was recognised as being. The much cited *dictum* of Maugham, J. in the English case of *Re William C. Leitch Bros. Ltd.*[12] that "if a company continues to carry on business and to incur debts at a time when there is to the knowledge of the directors no reasonable prospect of the creditors ever receiving payment of their debts, it is in general a proper inference that the company is carrying on business with intent to defraud" was interpreted, doubtless correctly, as being an evidential aid, "a proposition of evidence or proof," not to be taken as a derogation from the fundamental fact that "the intent to defraud creditors must be express or actual and real: nothing constructive, imputed or implied will do."[13] In fact, *Re William C. Leitch Ltd.* concerned the rather

---

[7] Para. 201. Floating charges created within 12 months of the commencement of the winding up may in any event be invalid. See pp. 511 *et seq., supra.*

[8] (1960) 105 C.L.R. 451, on appeal from the Supreme Court of New South Wales.

[9] *Per* Dixon C.J. at p. 458.

[10] *Per* Menzies J. at pp. 466–467.

[11] *Per* Kitto J. at p. 464. It is interesting to note that in a pre-fraudulent trading case, *Re Belfast Tailors' Co-partnership Ltd.* [1909] 1 I.R. 49, 56, Porter M.R. found nothing wrong in a person connected with a company "carrying on the business at a loss in the *bona fide* hope of a revival of trade." A trader was not to be prevented "from holding on through a time of temporary depression in expectation of better times."

[12] [1932] Ch. 71.

[13] *Per* Dixon C.J. at p. 460. See also Maugham J.'s more stringent view in *Re Patrick and Lyon Ltd.* [1933] Ch. 786; *Re White and Osmond (Parkstone) Ltd.* (High Court, England, June 30, 1960, unrep., but *Palmer's Company Law*, (23rd ed., 1982), carries an account of it at p. 1192; *Re Sarflax Ltd.* [1979] Ch. 592.

obvious fraud of "filling up the floating charge," mentioned above. For present purposes we may christen the successful respondent in *Hardie* v. *Hanson* the honest super-optimist to distinguish him from those who honestly believe that their company will in due course meet the debts it is incurring. The latter we will dub simply optimists. The super-optimist has hopes which are insufficiently concrete to form a belief. He would, as outlined above, be curbed by one of the reforms[14] in the "domestic" bill; the mere optimist less so: hence the distinction. As will appear, one must doubt whether the distinction is valid in trading practice.

No such fine distinctions were needed in the three Irish cases in which section 297(1) was successfully invoked. Each concerned unequivocally fraudulent conduct, motivated mainly by a desire to cheat the Revenue Commissioners. In the first of these cases, *Re Kelly's Carpetdrome Ltd*,[15] proper books of account were not kept, financial records were deliberately destroyed, assets were siphoned off to a friendly holder, and, when the Revenue was closing in, the company's remaining stocks were transferred to an associated company which paid the company's creditors, other than the Revenue. In *Re Aluminium Fabricators Ltd*,[16] the company had adopted the not unknown expedient of keeping two separate sets of books, one for the auditors and the Revenue Commissioners, and the other for the private perusal of its controllers who, thus prepared, operated "a constant drain on its liquid resources"[17] for their own benefit, and to the detriment of the Revenue and other creditors. In *Re Hunting Lodges Ltd*.[18] a company vastly indebted to the Revenue Commissioners sold its principal asset, a public house, on terms that a substantial part of the true purchase price was concealed, and paid "under the table" to one of the directors.

Fraudulent trading commonly involves a systematic course of conduct in fraud of creditors. A single act may however suffice, as may a single creditor. The Cox Committee clearly thought so, an opinion now affirmed in Ireland by *Re Hunting Lodges Ltd.*, *supra*, following *Re Gerald Cooper Chemicals Ltd.*[19] in which a company was alleged to have channelled a deposit for goods which it had no inten-

---

[14] He seems to be the specific target of the new limb which would create a liability or incurring debts without an honest belief on reasonable grounds that they would be met when falling due. He could also be, one assumes, a "reckless" trader or a "wrongful" trader.

[15] High Court, Costello J., July 1, 1983, unrep.

[16] High Court, O'Hanlon J., May 13, 1983, unrep.

[17] *Per* O'Hanlon J. at p. 9 of the transcript.

[18] [1985] I.L.R.M. 75.

[19] [1978] Ch. 262.

tion of delivering into the pockets of a creditor who was pressing for the repayment of a debt. By a single act is not necessarily meant a completed transaction. Carroll J. in *Re Hunting Lodges Ltd.* was prepared to parse the single transaction of "the payment on the side" into three separate elements (*i.e.* the negotiations culminating in the signing of the contract, the closing of the sale and the disposition of the purchase money), complicity in any one of which would suffice as "carrying on any business of the company" in the words of section 297.

Who may be made liable under section 297? Liability extends to anyone who knew of the fraudulent intent or purpose[20] or part of it,[21] and was party to the acts impugned, or any of them. These will commonly be the active directors of the company, but no formal connection with it is in fact necessary. In *Re Gerald Cooper Chemicals Ltd.*[22] it was held that a creditor of a company who accepted money obtained in fraud of another creditor would be personally liable under the section to the extent of the receipt. Someone "who warmed himself at the fire of fraud could not complain if he was singed," said Templeman J.[23] In *Re Kelly's Carpetdrome Ltd.*,[24] an order under section 297 was made against a respondent who was neither a director, nor a member of the company, and who, in fact occupied no overt position in relation to it. Of him Costello, J. said:

> "The courts are of course used to the strange phenomenon of young typists owning the shares, the issued shares in a company with a very large turnover, and with puppet directors controlled by outside masters. The court gives effect to the reality of these situations, and it looks to see who was the beneficial owner of the shares. Of the two issued in Kelly's Carpetdrome Ltd. I am satisfied [the respondent in question] was the beneficial owner of them, and that he ran the company, and that [the directors] did his bidding at every opportunity that he required them to do so."[25]

The emphasis on the beneficial ownership of the shares is unnecessary; it is not a criterion of liability, but an explanation of how it happened that the directors did the respondent's bidding, thereby rendering him one of the "parties" to the fraud, in the words of the

---

[20] *Hardie* v. *Hanson* (1960) 105 C.L.R. 451, 457.
[21] *Re Hunting Lodges Ltd.*, n. 18, *supra.*
[22] [1978] Ch. 262.
[23] *Ibid.* at p. 268.
[24] See n. 15, *supra.*
[25] Extract from an unofficial transcript in the possession of the author.

section. In *Re Hunting Lodges Ltd.*[26] the purchaser from the company, and the nominee company in whose name he took the conveyance were each held liable.

It is not necessary that each participant be party to a common agreed fraudulent intent; it suffices that a participant acts for a fraudulent purpose though he may be ignorant of some of the aspects of the fraud being perpetrated. Thus, in *Re Hunting Lodges Ltd.* a director who helped conceal money knowing that it belonged in equity to the company but was ignorant of the fraudulent means by which it had been obtained, was held liable.

Mere knowledge without active participation in the acts complained of will not attract liability under section 297. In *Re Maidstone Building Provisions Ltd.*,[27] a company secretary who was also its financial adviser escaped liability on this ground despite the fact that in the latter capacity he had a duty to the company to advise it that it was trading while insolvent. In *Re Kelly's Carpetdrome (No. 2)*[28] the fact that a company's auditors knew that there were irregularities in its internal accounting systems did not render them accomplices in fraudulent practices of which they did not actually know.

What is the extent of the liability which may be imposed on a respondent? Section 297(1) gives a discretion to impose personal liability on participants "for all or any of the debts or other liabilities of the company as the court may direct." There is not yet a uniform approach to the exercise of this discretion. Viewing the matter *a priori*, one might think that the court would wish to be satisfied that there is a causal relationship between the acts of fraudulent trading proved and the personal liability subsequently imposed. Thus, if the acts proved have actually deprived the company of the ability to pay debts, it might seem proper that a personal liability to the extent of that deprivation should be imposed on the miscreants. Personal liability might in a suitable case extend to all the debts of the company without violating this proposition. But do the courts have regard to it? It seems not. Both in *Re Kelly's Carpetdrome Ltd.*[29] and in *Re Aluminium Fabricators Ltd.*[30] personal liability for all debts was imposed on the respondents. Whilst it was possible, even likely, that but for the acts complained of the companies concerned could have paid all their debts, actual causation was not fully explored in the

---

[26] See n. 18, *supra*.
[27] [1971] 1 W.L.R. 1085.
[28] High Court, O'Hanlon J., July 13, 1984, unrep. There is an edited version of the judgment in *The Irish Times*, July 14, 1984.
[29] See n. 15, *supra*.
[30] See n. 16, *supra*.

judgments, O'Hanlon J. saying in the latter case that "it is a moot point whether it would ever have been necessary to wind up the Company had this constant drain on its liquid resources not taken place at the hands of the Directors," and Costello J. in the former case remaining silent on the matter. In *Re Hunting Lodges Ltd.*[31] however, Carroll J. made orders which indicate that she, for one, certainly does not subscribe to the proposition. In only one of the differing orders made against several respondents was there a direct relationship between the order made and the loss their participation in the fraud had caused.[32] She limited the personal liability of the purchaser of the company's assets (and his nominee company) to £12,000, a sum equal to that part of the secret consideration which had not been recovered by the company. But her orders against the other two respondents must be explicable on other grounds. She ordered one director (whose husband, the only other director, in practice ran the company's business and was the instigator of the plot to deprive it of the full proceeds of sale of its public house) to be personally liable for the debts of the company to the extent that she had received any "advancements" from her husband since a date some six years before the commission of the only act of fraudulent trading proved, namely the execution of this plot. This date happened to mark the beginning of a four year period in respect of which the trading records of the company had been destroyed by fire. The implication is, one must suppose, that the learned judge considered that the husband might since that date have been unlawfully channelling the assets of the company to his wife with her connivance, allegations which were neither made nor proved. If such activities were going on, she would in any event have been bound to reimburse the company on the footing of a constructive trusteeship. Therefore the order shows a willingness on the part of the judge to subject this lady in effect to a double indemnity, a criticism which applies to all those fraudulent trading cases in which the essential cause of complaint is that the assets of the company have been wrongfully siphoned off. Is not fraudulent trading action directed against such circumstances in fact misconceived? Section 297 should not be used in effect to duplicate liability. Let us be clear. One does not duplicate liability by imposing a liability for fraudulent trading in respect of an act which was lawful *vis-à-vis* the company but none-

---

[31] See n. 18, *supra*.

[32] Invoking a liability to account on a footing of constructive trusteeship would in any event seem to have been a more appropriate remedy against this respondent (and his nominee company), than bringing fraudulent trading proceedings. See the discussion, *infra*, on the next respondent.

theless fraudulent with regard to its creditors, such as, for example, the taking by a director of authorised remuneration whilst he knows that the company cannot meet its debts as they fall due.[32a]

To return to the theme, whatever the learned judge wished to imply by her order against the wife, the fact remains that the company had suffered no loss through the only act of fraudulent trading proved against her, her help in salting away part of the concealed proceeds of sale of the public house, since all that she had helped conceal had been recovered. Her husband, the other director, fared even worse. The company's money he had attempted to spirit away in the only act of fraudulent trading proved against him amounted to £160,000; all but £12,000 of this had been recovered; nonetheless, he was declared personally liable for *all* the company's debts of which the unsatisfied claims of the Revenue alone exceeded £750,000. Carroll J. expressed herself led to make this order by her disapproval of his behaviour in relation to the company after he had discovered it was insolvent, disapproval so strong that she felt:

> "it is entirely proper that [he] should be personally responsible without any limitation of liability for all the debts of the company. The benefit of limited liability should, in my opinion, be totally withdrawn and he should be put in the same position as if he were a trader carrying on business personally."[33]

Let us look at the acts which excited the learned judge's displeasure. Obviously there was the one proved act of fraudulent trading, but no one had suffered much by that. Then there were other acts which he had caused the company to do after he had discovered its insolvency, which were capable of themselves of constituting fraudulent trading but which were not specifically found to be such or relied upon as such by the learned judge. They were that he had caused the company to continue to pay himself and his wife handsomely as its directors, and to guarantee and then pay off his personal overdraft. Finally, he had, she found, behaved evasively and deceptively towards the company's principal creditor, the Revenue Commissioners. This particular conduct was not in fact as heinous as it sounds: it consisted of failing to keep an appointment and of not being totally frank about his whereabouts, neither of which sins are yet in our law civil or criminal wrongs. One hopes that thus causing annoyance to civil servants did not weigh too heavily with the learned judge.

What, if any, principles governing the exercise of the discretion to

---

[32a] *c.f. Re Hall Garage Ltd.* [1982] 3 All E.R. 1016.
[33] [1984] I.L.R.M. 75, 85.

impose varying degrees of personal liability can be extracted from these three cases? To extract some at least is juridically desirable since the discretion is judicial, and therefore its exercise is not be be considered as being totally at large. In both *Re Kelly's Carpetdrome Ltd.* and in *Re Aluminium Fabricators Ltd.* it seems likely that all creditors would have been discharged in full had no improprieties occurred. If this aspect had been fully explored in the judgments, one might have extracted a principle that the personal liability of respondents should match the detriment to creditors they have caused. But a full exploration of this nature did not take place, and there was certainly no such causal link in *Re Hunting Lodges Ltd.* What then is one left with by way of principle? The message of these cases, inspired chiefly by *Re Hunting Lodges Ltd.*, would seem to be at the very least that proof of one act of fraudulent trading together with proof that its perpetrator had in other respects caused the company to act for his personal advantage to the detriment of its creditors may lead to full liability for its debts being imposed on him. Or perhaps one may extract this stronger, and preferable, message that any person who in effect *controls* (whether with others or not) the affairs of the company and who commits any act of fraudulent trading is likely to suffer the penalty of being made responsible for all the debts of the company contracted or incurred during his period of control.[34] Such an approach is philosophically justifiable by viewing incorporation as a privilege given on condition that it is not abused by its recipients. In practice, a corporation's controllers are the recipients of this privilege. The approach is socially justifiable by the practical consideration that if one act of fraudulent trading has been established, it is often part only of a general pattern of fraudulent trading by the company, proof of which is bound to be frustrated by the opportunities for obfuscation open to controllers, particularly by the "accidental" destruction or loss of records. The approach implicitly recognises that if section 297(1) is to survive as an effective remedy, the proposition which opened this discussion, namely a requirement that there be a proved consequential link between all loss to creditors and specific acts of fraudulent trading by a company's controllers, should not be imported into it.[35] These justifications apply to fraudulent trading by controllers. They do not apply where fraudulent trading has been proved against a non-controller.

---

[34] *Quaere* whether the liability should extend to claims arising otherwise than directly from trading? *e.g.* what of claims against a company in tort for an accident for which it is vicariously liable?

[35] We return to the topic of lack or loss of accounting records below. See *Reform: the author's proposals.*

In assessing the personal liability to be imposed on him, it is submitted that the court should exercise its discretion to ensure that there is some relationship between the personal liability imposed and the acts of fraudulent trading proved. Liability for all the debts of the company could be imposed even on such a person in appropriate circumstances. Such circumstances might be found, for example, where he had participated in a system of false accounting designed to damage all creditors.

Constitutional difficulties

The following discussion raises more questions than it answers, a characteristic of the 1937 Constitution.

We know that section 297(3) specifically creates the criminal offence of fraudulent trading, punishable by fines and imprisonment. But what of section 297(1)? It is in form civil, and proceedings taken under it are not in practice treated as being criminal. Nonetheless, orders made under section 297(1) create fresh liabilities as opposed to enforcing existing liabilities; they do not enforce private rights, being neither restitutionary, compensatory, nor made in aid of the rights of any person. They do not therefore bear the hall-mark of civil proceedings.[36] They are in essence punitive. If, following this argument, section 297(1) proceedings are to be classified as being in substance criminal, certain constitutional consequences should flow. The section 297(1) action should not depart from the due course of law required of criminal proceedings by Article 38, s.1 of the Constitution. At the very least this presently somewhat nebulous requirement should import the criminal standard of proof, *i.e.* proof beyond reasonable doubt of the ingredients of the offence. This constitutional argument has yet to be raised in any judgment. The cases despatch the standard of proof to a limbo of indecision. In *Re Kelly's Carpetdrome Ltd.*[37] Costello J. found some facts proved "on the balance of probability," the civil standard of proof, whilst being satisfied that the charges against the defendants had been established "beyond any doubt." Later, in *Re Kelly's Carpetdrome Ltd. (No. 2)*,[38] in which the liquidator sought impose personal liability for all the company's debts upon its auditors, O'Hanlon J. whilst acknowledging that the standard of proof in such a claim must be heavy took care to exonerate the auditors by reference both to this heavy stan-

---

[36] For attempts towards a definition of civil proceedings, see *Melling* v. *O Mathhamha* [1962] I.R.1; *The State (Browne)* v. *Feran*, [1967] I.R. 147, *Keegan* v. *De Burca* 1973] I.R. 223 and *The State (Murray)* v. *McRann* [1979] I.R. 133.

[37] See n. 15 *supra.*

[38] See n. 28 *supra.*

dard and the lighter standard applicable to civil proceedings.[39] In other cases, the standard of proof passes without remark.

If section 297(1) proceedings are indeed criminal in nature, there might be the further constitutional consequence that respondents to them will possess the right given by Article 38, s.2 to trial by jury in non-minor offences. Would section 297(1), if indeed criminal, create a minor offence? One would think not[40]: the pecuniary sanctions exigible under it are potentially both punitive and grievous, though, unlike a fine, bankruptcy rather than imprisonment would follow an inability to pay.

That section 297 engenders constitutional uncertainties may be explained by the fact that it is a blind copy of section 332 of the Companies Act 1948 [*U.K.*], the product of a sovereign parliament.

Reform: the author's proposals

Before the recent rash of cases, section 297 was seldom, if ever, used. Why not? Lack of fraud in commercial life is certainly not the reason. Liquidators offer the explanation that fraud is difficult to prove. Certainly, it can be, but not where the schemes are as naive as those perpetrated in the three Irish cases in which the liquidator

---

[39] The possibility that constitutionally s.297(1) proceedings must rank as being criminal was not discussed in the judgment. Instead, English authorities were cited for the propositions (1) that since s.297(3) is clearly criminal, s.297(1) which requires proof of the same ingredients ought to bear the criminal standard of proof: *Thurtell* v. *Beaumont* (1823) 1 Bing. 339; *Chalmers* v. *Shackell* (1834) 6 C. & P. 475; *Willmett* v. *Harmer* (1839) 8 C. & P. 695; *Statham* v. *Statham* [1929] p. 131; and (2) that in any event the weight of the civil standard varies with the gravity of the allegations: *Hornal* v. *Neuberger Products Ltd* [1956] 1 Q.B. 247 following *Bater* v. *Bater* [1951] P. 35. But no conclusion was drawn from either of these propositions, and the matter was by-passed in the manner stated in the text. But it should be noted that in *Att.-Gen.* v. *Paperlin Ltd.* [1984] I.L.R.M. 373 Costello J. held that the courts had jurisdiction to grant an injunction on the application of the Attorney-General to restrain a continued breach of the criminal law. The courts were not thereby "trying a criminal charge within the meaning of Article 38," but were "merely exercising a distinct and different jurisdiction in civil proceedings" in which the civil standard of proof was applicable. Costello J. also indicated, albeit *obiter*, that proceedings seeking the recovery of a statutory fine or forfeiture were civil, and not criminal, in nature.

[40] In *Cullen* v. *Att.-Gen.* [1979] I.R. 394, Hamilton J. held that s.57 of the Road Traffic Act 1961 to be unconstitutional, as it authorised the summary trial of a non-minor offence. Section 57 empowered the District Court, in the case of injury to person or property resulting from negligent driving, to fine the defendant the probable amount of a civil award of damages (the section specifying no upper financial limit) and to pay the fine to the injured person. Hamilton J. was of opinion that such penalty could not be properly regarded as a "minor" offence for the purposes of Art. 38.2. See further on this question *Conroy* v. *Att.-Gen.* [1965] I.R. 411; *Kostan* v. *Att. Gen.* High Court McWilliam J. unrep., February 10, 1978; Casey, (1978) *D.U.L.* (N.S.) 50; and *The State (Rollinson)* v. *Kelly* [1984] I.L.R.M. 625.

was successful. Proving fraud, even in blatant cases, is however time consuming and therefore costly. Costs are the nub of the difficulty, and explain why liquidators are not often inclined to take section 297 proceedings, or, indeed, any other proceedings, such as a derivative action, against wrongdoers. Even preliminary proceedings to freeze the assets of respondents by means of a *Mareva* injunction are, of course, expensive.[41] How is a liquidator to be sure of recovering his costs? Of course, he may in theory recover them from unsuccessful respondents, and from the assets of the company, but the former may have made arrangements against that contingency, and the latter may be inadequate. In most cases, a liquidator[42] would be ill-advised to sue unless at the behest and with the indemnity of a creditor with a long pocket, such as the Revenue Commissioners. The recent cases are probably explained by the presence of such an indemnity. But its presence cannot be guaranteed in all cases.

We must see how to make liquidators less inhibited in pursuing remedies available to them, lack of enforcement of this and other kinds being perhaps the factor which more than any other has brought company law into disrepute and contributed to the atmosphere that it is possible "to get away with it." The stock, almost stale, response at present is to suggest that the criterion of dishonesty be dropped from section 297, and that alternatives, or substitutes, supposedly easier to prove, such as "reckless trading," "wrongful trading," and the like, all involving some degree of objective assessment of business conduct, be introduced. We consider these proposals later under the heading *Reform: other proposals*, but for the moment let us suppose that it is desirable that the *honest* director should escape personal liability for his company's debts, and concentrate on specifics for the mischief so far identified, the problem of costs.

This book's first proposal is designed to meet that problem. It is radical, but simple. The liquidator must be given a fighting fund with which generally to pursue malefactors, and to unravel suspect transactions such as fraudulent preferences. Where is the money to come from? A right to call upon a legal aid fund established through sharply increased fees at the Company's Registry (including perhaps the introduction of an annual renewal fee) is one possibility. By this means corporate business would in effect be contributing to an insurance fund for the benefit of the public, rather in the way, to take an Irish precedent, local rates used to serve as a means of spreading

---

[41] Such an injunction was obtained in the *Kelly's Carpetdrome* litigation.

[42] However, creditors and contributories technically also have *locus standi* under 297. A creditor sued in *Re Gerald Cooper Chemicals Ltd.* [1978] Ch. 262.

the burden of malicious damage claims throughout the local community. Or, extra-statutorily, as happens in other jurisdictions, the business community itself could subscribe to an insurance fund, a creditors protection fund, on which liquidators could draw. Another answer, perhaps more palatable (save to the banks), would be to require all secured creditors of the company in liquidation to devote a proportion, say 20 per cent., of their secured claims to the liquidator's fighting fund. The law by recognising the ability to make bargains which may skim off all the assets of an insolvent company unduly privileges a secured creditor. A system which gives such weight to security as to deny other claimants any chance of having their rights vindicated needs some adjustment.[43] In effect, it is proposed that 100 per cent. securities would no longer be possible in law. Entering now the detail of the proposal, the secured creditors' contribution would be reckoned by reference not only to secured claims still outstanding but also by reference to such claims as may already have been discharged, say, within a year before the commencement of the winding up or thereafter. One must ensure that a liquidator actually canvasses the possibility of bringing appropriate proceedings. It is suggested therefore that he should be obliged after a reasonable period for investigation to certify whether there are claims to be pursued.[44] This certificate could be filed as a public document, and interested parties could be given a reasonable period after filing to challenge the certificate in court, and, if necessary, to appoint a new liquidator by way of remedy. One would envisage that no distribution of any kind (save in respect of employees' preferential claims) be made out of the assets of the company (whether security interests exist in them or not) pending the issue of this certificate. Interested parties could apply for an order that he issue the certificate, or show cause why not. The fighting fund should not be jeopardised by a prior receivership. There would have to be an obligation on the receiver to account for 20 per cent. of net realisations to a liquidator whose liquidation supervened within the period of a year suggested above. The receiver's obligation under section 98 of the Company's Act 1963 to pay preferential debts in priority to claims arising under floating charge should likewise yield to the new scheme. It is suggested that such payments by a receiver be confined

---

[43] The Cork Committee propose in Chap. 36 of their Report, (1982) Cmnd. 8558 that 10 per cent. of the net realisations of assets subject to a floating charge should be made available for distribution among unsecured creditors. This proposal is narrower than that proposed in this book, since the former is designed more to achieve equity between different classes of creditors than to provide the liquidator with a "pursuit" fund.

[44] For the present position, see pp. 478, 491, *supra*.

to employees' preferential claims. Why should the State and other public claimants be deferred in this way? To do so recognises that the due administration of justice has a higher social value than the collection of revenue. It also reflects a widespread opposition to giving State claimants any preference at all in the collapse of a private enterprise. This is not the place to elaborate that view, but one might remark in passing that to the extent that State claimants have failed to exact their due from an insolvent company whilst it remained a going conern they have by their inaction allowed that debtor to give a false impression of solvency which may have been adversely relied upon by the commercial world, predominantly the private sector.

To allow State and similar claimants then to step in in advance of the private sector whose liquidity is strained, and very viability battered by State demands, seems not only shortsighted but also immoral.

The suggested scheme does not seek to rob secured creditors of their status as creditor in respect of their contributions to the fighting fund. They would in that respect continue to rank as unsecured creditors of the company, and would have secured interests in accordance with their priorities over any surplus of the fighting fund remaining with the liquidator, including, of course, the net fruits of any action taken by him.

We pass now to this book's second proposal for reform. This second proposal is intended to meet the frequently occurring case of a company in liquidation whose transactions have been obscured, sometimes deliberately. Here it is proposed that the burden of costs be transferred to those responsible for the obscurity. Specifically, it is proposed that where proper books of account kept by the company[45] have not been made available to the liquidator, the costs of any proceedings against any person brought by a liquidator, whether under section 297 or otherwise, in respect of any transaction occurring in the period for which proper books are not so available and to which those books would have been material, should be borne (to an extent to be determined by the court in its discretion) by those who were directors for that period, unless the director can *prove* that such books were properly kept but were lost or destroyed in circumstances for which he bears no responsibility, or, in the case of books improperly kept, that he took all steps reasonably expected of him to secure that they were, and acted honestly in relation to the keeping of them. This suggestion is not wholly unprecedented in Ireland. In

---

[45] On what constitutes "proper books of account" and the existing sanctions for failure to keep them, see ss.147 and 296.

Re David Ireland & Co. Ltd.,[46] a director who had by the commission
of irregularities invited misfeasance proceedings against him under
what is now section 298 of the Company's Act 1963 was adjudged
responsible for the costs of them, even though they established that
nothing in fact was recoverable from him. Likewise, companies
which do not keep proper books invite suspicion, and no tears need
be shed for those responsible for the omission.

For the third proposal for reform we turn to the complaint that
fraud may be difficult to prove, and that consequently, so it is said,
misconduct within the ambit of section 297 escapes action. We will
hold hard to the premise that section 297 with its potentially huge
sanctions should be confined to respondents against whom *dishonesty*
has actually been proved. Accordingly, it is proposed that we should
explore instead the possibility of introducing a new statutory remedy
with a lighter evidential burden on the liquidator and correspondingly lighter sanctions, to exist alongside section 297. For example,
the new remedy might provide that in the case of any transaction (*i*)
entered into by a company which subsequently goes into liquidation
insolvent, and (*ii*) proved by the liquidator to be prejudicial to any
creditor or creditors generally, each participant in the transaction
shall be liable to contribute to the assets of the company for the benefit of the creditors concerned and to the extent of the prejudice,
unless he proves that he in all respects acted honestly in the transaction.

These three proposals for reform are not put forward dogmati-
cally, but rather as a starting point for discussion. Cumulatively
they should do much to allay the widely felt anxiety that limited
liability is often abused, and that much fraud practised on the creditors of limited liability companies goes unredressed.

Reform: other proposals

The proposals for reform outlined in the preceding section did not
fall into the trap of seeking to judge entrepreneurial activity by
objective standards. The means of commercial success and the
possibilities of new products are often beyond the imagination of the
reasonable man, and, above all, he does not take risks if harm is
reasonably foreseeable as flowing from them. All business involves
taking risks. That it does is recognised by the law. Lord Hatherley
L.C. in *Overend & Gurney Co.* v. *Gibb*[47] said:

---

[46] [1905] 1 I.R. 133.
[47] (1872) 5 L.R., H.L. 480, 495. And see L.S. Sealy, *Company Law and Commercial
Reality* 1984, Sweet & Maxwell, pp. 39, 86–87.

" . . . There is a great deal more trust, a great deal more speculation, and a great deal more readiness to confide in the probabilities of things, with regard to success in mercantile
transactions, than there is on the part of those whose habits of
life are of an entirely different character. . . . "

And hear Sterling J. in *Leeds Estates Building and Investment Co.* v.
Shepherd[48]:

"Funds embarked in a trading company . . . are placed under
the control of the directors in order that they may be employed
for the acquisition of gain, and risk (greater or less, according to
the circumstances) is of the very essence of such employment."

The irrelevance of the reasonable foreseeability of harm as a test
for attributing blame and founding liability for commercial activities
may be further illustrated by the following soliloquy, penned for this
occasion:

"It is reasonably foreseeable that there may be bad weather in
Brazil. It does happen. It is reasonably foreseeable therefore
that the coffee crop may fail; that my principal debtor, a com-
modity dealer, will go down as the coffee futures market goes
up; and that he will not be able to pay me; and that therefore I
may not be able to pay others. Let's hope it stays fine in
Brazil."

With this introduction in mind let us consider the possibility of
introducing sanctions for carrying on the business of a company or
trading in a *reckless* manner, an idea which surfaced from the Jenkins
Committee in 1962,[49] was thought to be since drowned, but is now
possibly to be resuscitated in Ireland in the "domestic" Bill. Why is
this proposal so misconceived? All trade involves taking risks. Recklessness also involves taking risks. The latter must therefore refer to
a forbidden ground of risk. But forbidden risks apparent to whom?
They may be risks which appear undue or illegitimate to the actor.
Or they may be unreasonable or unjustifiable risks. This latter
category takes us beyond the individual risk-taker to the reasonable
man. Or the criterion might be neither wholly subjective nor wholly
objective. It might take the form of a conditional subjectivism, *i.e.*
the risk is one *which would have been apparent* to the actor had he
stopped to think about it. This requires not present awareness of the
risk, but general knowledge in relation to it, given the will and
ability on the actor's part to recall that knowledge. The court would

---

[48] (1887) 36 Ch. D. 787, 798.
[49] (1962), Cmnd. 1749, para. 503.

ask: "Is the individual's knowledge of the risk at the forefront or at the back of his mind?" Whatever the reaction of philosophers or psychologists to such a test, it is one which lawyers have employed. If liability for trading in a reckless manner ever sees the light of day in Ireland, it will be imperative to know what form of recklessness is involved. Moreover, even "risk" itself is not free from doubt. Is the risk as to consequences occurring or as to circumstances existing, or both?

The concept of recklessness involves two areas of inquiry. The first has been outlined above: it is necessary to know by what standard the existence of the risk is to be established. If the test is to be an objective one, the concept of reckless trading will extend to business life the standards of a bureaucrat, and expose the failed business person to a judgment coloured with all the benefits of hindsight. If, on the other hand, the test is to be subjective we will find on foot an investigative process which seeks to appraise the quality of the respondent's *prediction*, which is in a business context unreal. Even the most careful market research gives no guarantee of success in business, and, conversely, a "hunch" or intuitive decision is easy to justify only if it has led to success. What level of foresight is therefore required? Will it be necessary for the adverse consequences to have been forseen as possible, or likely, or probable, or highly probable before culpability may be established?

The second area of inquiry concerns the trader's perception of the risk. If the risk has been established on an objective test, should the respondent in order to be liable actually have adverted to that risk in his mind and then have acted in disregard of it, or would it be sufficient to found liability that he gave no thought at all to the possibility of there being any such risk? In the latter event, "reckless trading" would amount to a species of negligence, and if that is what the legislature intends, it would be better to say so at the outset. In the former case, what is to happen to the business person who is fully aware that most others may say that the risk he is about to take is unjustifiable (the objective assessment of risk), but who nonetheless weighs up the situation carefully and cautiously, comes to the opposite conclusion, acts accordingly, and thereby causes loss and damage to the creditors of his company? If this person is to be punished, essentially his only wrong will have been a failure to follow the herd. Is that the kind of irresponsibility which ought to be punished by a society which still purports to believe in the freedom to trade?

Criminal lawyers will find some of the above issues horribly familiar; they know that recklessness is an uncertain concept of chequered provenance.

Does it mean, as Professor Kenny suggested in 1902,[50] cases where the accused actually had in mind the particular kind of harm which might be done, yet had carried on regardless? Or does it mean "gross negligence,"[51] not that anyone could accuse that particular concept of possessing certainty? Or does it mean what the House of Lords said it meant in 1981 when on the same day they handed down *R.* v. *Caldwell* and *R.* v. *Lawrence*[52] which have since reverberated round the Common Law world, and engendered academic discussion of a volume sufficient to tempt students to quit the law and take up another occupation?[53] Briefly, as is well known, these two decisions held that "reckless" conduct in a statute creating a crime encompassed both a decision to ignore an objectively assessed risk of harmful consequences flowing from an act, which risk the accused had recognised as existing, and *also* a failure to give any thought to whether there was any such risk in circumstances where, if any thought were given to the matter, it would be obvious that there was. Much of the dissent from these decisions stems from the fact that they break a broad and well understood thread of distinction between recklessness and negligence, the first, with an element of subjectivity which approaches deliberate wrongdoing, being more worthy in certain contexts as being treated as criminal in the policy of the law, than the second where the actual mind of the perpetrator is less, if at all, involved in the consequences of his acts.

The message is clear. "Recklessness" is conceptually uncertain. Even if all the other objections to the introduction of liability for reckless trading are ignored, at the very least this word, in its present state of odium, should not be used in a statute without a careful redefinition of it.

We turn next to the recommendation of the Cork Committee

---

[50] Kenny, *Outlines of Criminal Law* (1st ed., 1902); approved in *R.* v. *Cunningham* [1957] 2 All E.R. 412, 414.

[51] *Andrews* v. *D.P.P.* [1937] A.C. 576.

[52] [1982] A.C. 341 and [1982] A.C. 570, respectively.

[53] For a specifically Irish comment, see McAleese, "Just what is Recklessness?" 1981) D.U.L.J. (N.S.) 29 which treats also of *D.P.P.* v. *Murray* [1977] I.R. 360. Further afield, see Buxton, "The New Murder" (1980) Crim L.R. 521; Williams, "Recklessness Redefined" (1981) *C.L.J.* 252; Williams, "Divergent Interpretations of Recklessness" (1982) *New L.J.* 289, 313, 336; Williams, "Intention and Recklessness again" (1982) *Legal Studies* 189; McEwan and Robilliard, "Recklessness: the House of Lords and the criminal law," (1981) *Legal Studies* 267; McEwan and Robilliard, Intention and Recklessness again—a response" (1982) *Legal Studies* 198; Syrota, "A Radical Change in the Law of Recklessness," (1982) Crim. L.R. 97; Ashall, "Manslaughter—The Impact of Caldwell?," (1984) Crim. L.R. 467. The more recent English decisions include *R.* v. *Breckenridge* (1984) Crim. L.R. 1874 and *R.* v. *Griffiths* (1984) Crim. L.R. 629.

which reviewed the insolvency law and practice of England and Wales, and whose final Report was published on 9th June 1982.[54] they suggest that personal liability for the company's debts be incurred for participation in *wrongful* trading. A company would be trading wrongfully if, being insolvent or unable to pay its debts as they fell due, it incurred liabilities without a reasonable prospect of meeting them in full. Officers of the company participating in the wrongful trading would be liable if they knew, or ought to have known, that it was wrongful; for other parties, the test would be that of knowledge alone. The reasonable prospect of payment would be judged by the standards of the ordinary, reasonable man, as would the question whether an officer ought to have known that there was no such reasonable prospect. The court would be empowered in its discretion to exonerate an officer who had acted honestly, and in the circumstances ought to be excused.

One does not know what the ordinary, reasonable man is supposed to know about trade and trading conditions. Honesty is at least a certain concept. Probably, imposing the standard of the ordinary, reasonable man does no more than substitute the court's opinion of the prospect the company had of meeting its liabilities for the opinion actually held by the company's directors, save that the court has the advantage of knowing that the company did not in fact manage to do so. At present, company directors know where they stand: they must act honestly for what in their opinion is for the benefit of the company, and not act dishonestly in relation to creditors; under the proposal, they must predict where an observer *ex post facto* will tell them they were in fact standing.

Those are the theoretical difficulties with the Cork proposal. What practical difference will such a change make in the operation of section 297? It will curb the honest optimist, the company director who is attempting to trade his way out of trouble, honestly believing or more likely hoping (the super-optimist) that things will come right.[55] Such activity is by no means uncommon in Ireland at the moment, but it is not the social evil that deliberate fraud is; indeed, there are arguments that it is socially better that these beliefs or hopes of success should be tried instead of requiring a business to close down at the first firm hint of insolvency. Such an abstract ideal, if implemented, will lead to a chain of insolvencies, and resulting unemployment, in an already endangered private sector. Examples could be given, particularly from other jurisdictions, of directors causing their company to close down for fear of being

---

[54] (1982) Cmnd. 8558, para. 92, paras. 1758 *et seq.* and 1775 *et seq.*

[55] See *Hardie* v. *Hanson*, discussed at pp. 518–519, *supra.*

accused of fraudulent trading, and yet all of the creditors being paid in full in the subsequent liquidation with, furthermore, a surplus for distribution among the members. With penalties as cataclysmic as those offered by section 297, an honest director who knows of their existence will obviously err on the side of caution, a tendency which will be exaggerated if they were to know that someone else's judgment will, in the event of their honest endeavour failing, be substituted for their own, that substituted judgment being likely, moreover, when faced with the fact of failure to be scornful of there ever having been prospects of success. Proponents of reforms involving this consequence would do well to reflect upon the suffering, particularly through unemployment (not only in the company itself, but if it is a large enterprise, among suppliers and even customers), that erring on the side of caution may bring about. These responsible directors are not a problem. The rogue is the problem. This book's proposals are aimed directly at the rogue. The other reformers seem intent on eradicating the patient as well as the disease, an overkill which if attempted in Ireland would be based on the misdiagnosis that honesty is, shall we say, sufficiently the norm.

It is submitted, furthermore, that the present law already achieves a satisfactory balance in relation to honest optimists of all sorts. He already runs a severe risk of being found guilty of fraudulent trading because, as we have seen,[56] once it has been established that he knew there was no *reasonable* prospect of creditors being paid in full, an evidential inference arises that his conduct was fraudulent, and thenceforward the burden is on him to exonerate himself by proving bona fides.

Finally, we turn to the reputed proposal in the "domestic" Bill which would impose liability for incurring debts without an honest *belief* on reasonable grounds that they would be met when falling due. Enough has been said here on the dangers of importing the objective standards implicit in a requirement that there be reasonable grounds. The use of the word "belief" must however be despatched. No sensible person in trade has an actual *belief* in the quality of his prediction. In trade, only a fool believes. Wise traders *hope* on grounds that seem reasonable to them. If by rejecting the use of the word "belief" one fails to curb the super-optimist in the sense described above,[57] that is but a small price to pay for not introducing the attributes of the fool as a condition of exoneration from liability.

---

[56] At pp. 518–519, *supra*.
[57] At p. 519, *supra*.

Index